THE CHURCH IN ASIA

THE CHURCH IN ASIA

Edited by

DONALD E. HOKE

MOODY PRESS
CHICAGO

Main entry under title:
The Church in Asia.
Includes bibliographies and index.
1. Christianity–Asia. 2. Asia–History
3. Asia–Religion. I. Hoke, Donald E.
ISBN: 0-8024-1543-1
BR1065.C45 209'.5 75-11879

Printed in the United States of America

To

Martha,

a true partner, expert at many things:

evangelism, homemaking, teaching, entertaining,

and—most of all—loving people,

especially me!

CONTENTS

CHAPTER PAGE

Foreword—*Billy Graham* 9

Preface—*Donald McGavran* 11

Editor's Preface—*Donald E. Hoke* 13

1. Asia's Opening Doors—*Donald E. Hoke* 17
2. Afghanistan—*Anonymous* 57
3. Bangladesh—*Warren Webster* 67
4. Bhutan—*Billy Bray* 85
5. Brunei—*Peter Hsieh and Russell Self* 97
6. Burma—*William D. Hackett* 103
7. China—*Arthur F. Glasser* 131
8. Christianity Comes to Asia—*Gordon H. Chapman* 181
9. Hong Kong—*David Woodward* 205
10. India, a Seething Subcontinent—*Theodore Williams* . . . 217
11. Indonesia—*Frank Snow* 261
12. Japan: A Brief Christian History—*Gordon H. Chapman* . . 303
13. Japan's Postwar Renaissance—*Alvin H. Hammond* . . . 329
14. The Khmer Republic (Cambodia)—*Edward A. Cline and Billy Bray* 349
15. Korea—*Samuel Hugh Moffett* 369
16. Laos—*G. Edward Roffe* 391
17. Malaysia—Singapore—*W. O. Phoon* 411
18. The Republic of Maldives—*Lennie de Silva* 435

19. The Mongolian People's Republic—*Stuart Gunzel and Donald E. Hoke* 441

20. Nepal—*Samuel R. Burgoyne and Jonathan Lindell* . . . 451

21. Overseas Chinese—*David Woodward* 469

22. Pakistan—*Warren Webster* 475

23. Papua New Guinea—*Geoffrey Smith and John Hitchen* . . 501

24. The Philippines—*Ralph Tolliver* 525

25. Sikkim—*Billy Bray* 555

26. South Vietnam—*Reginald Reimer* 565

27. Sri Lanka (Ceylon)—*B. E. Fernando* 593

28. Taiwan—*David Woodward* 609

29. Thailand—*Leon B. Gold* 625

30. Tibet—*G. Tharchin and David Woodward* 643

31. Important Religions of Asia—*Gordon H. Chapman* . . . 659

Introduction to Appendixes 682

Appendix A: Christian Population by Percentage of Total Population 684

Appendix B: Christian Population by Percentage of Major Ethnic Groups 693

Appendix C: General and Christian Populations of Asian Nations 698

Index 699

FOREWORD

by Billy Graham

RECENTLY Asia has become the focal point of world interest. That is probably inevitable, with two-thirds of the world's population within its borders.

But Asia presents a confusing picture of divided allegiance and growing tensions, which keeps its people in constant ferment. Yet there has has been one development that brightens the heart of every Christian: doors of evangelism have been opening ever wider. More people are turning to Christianity in Asia today than at any previous time in history.

In the face of all the strong currents of opinion which clamor for human dignity, national recognition, and the alleviation of poverty, the voice of Christ calling Asia to salvation has reverberated clearly through this colorful continent.

Asians are hard at work building their international image. As one Indonesian put it, "The job of building our own house for the first time generates a sense of exhilaration, perhaps long-forgotten by older nations which have become settled in their ways."

But in their haste to formulate this diet of newfound freedoms, they have produced what Don Hoke calls a "seething caldron" which sports the "three witches of political, economic, and social change."

Dr. Hoke has lived most of his adult life in Asia and speaks Japanese fluently. He has the knowledge and expertise to assess the best ways to penetrate Asia for the gospel.

Don and I have been close friends since college days. As a former *Chicago Tribune* reporter, founder of Japan Christian College, president in the Japan Evangelical Missionary Association, founder and president of the Japan Evangelical Theological School Association, and chairman of the board of Word of Life Press (Japan's largest religious publishing house, producing the *New Japanese Bible*), Dr. Hoke is well qualified to speak on Asia.

Don Hoke was selected to be the director of the International Congress on World Evangelization at Lausanne in 1974. He gave invaluable leadership and insight to that historic Congress.

He writes with a balanced perspective on world issues, including the ecumenical movement. All may not agree with him, and some of his conclusions will be controversial. But his comments, like those asserting the present importance of the Asian laity and the great needs of Asian theological education today, reflect close association with Asian affairs. He says very properly of the Asian church that it "needs to find its own soul."

Don knows well the repressive power of totalitarian governments. You can't read *The Church in Asia* without being impressed with the fact that the continent of Asia is in painful ideological conflict. Don realistically points out that this is a land which has become a prime seedplot for totalitarian expansion. Yet he is soberly optimistic about the future of the gospel and the church in Asia, and he is hopeful that the continent can be biblically evangelized in the next twenty-five years.

The book has its necessary share of reports, statistics, and analyses, yet the words of all the authors whom Don has compiled are lucid and provocative, reflecting much insight and prayerful consideration.

Don Hoke has performed a great service in compiling the articles in this book. If, as many suspect, the gravitational center of Christianity is shifting from the West to the East, then this volume is both timely and critically important. Reading it will be very worthwhile, for it will maximize your understanding of the evangelization of Asia and minimize your time spent on extraneous material unrelated to the advancing kingdom of God.

The Church in Asia is a benchmark production in Christian scholarship. It comes, appropriately, at a time when the "greening of Asia" signals a fresh burst of Holy Spirit power in evangelizing the world before our Lord's return.

PREFACE

by Donald McGavran

THIS MAGNIFICENT DESCRIPTION of the modern church in Asia is a notable contribution to world evangelization. Every church with missionaries in Asia should own a copy. Every school of missions and every Bible school or seminary should add this book to its library.

Courses on the contemporary church will use *The Church in Asia* as a text. After reading this work, no one can remain parochial, limiting his interests to his own nation. The risen and reigning Lord commanded His followers to disciple *ta ethne*—the castes, tribes, classes, and kindreds of men. This striking volume illumines what that command means in the nations of Asia today.

The book is comprehensive. Churches in all the countries of Asia east of Persia are described. Huge nations like China, India, Japan, Indonesia, and Bangladesh are covered. Medium-sized nations like Burma, the Philippines, Korea, and Pakistan have a chapter apiece. Even little nations like Sikkim, Nepal, Cambodia, and Tibet are carefully viewed in the light of their eventual evangelization.

The book is contemporary. It tells how Asia appears at the beginning of the last quarter of the twentieth century. When statistics are shown for 1960 or 1970 (as occasionally they had to be), the percentage of increase necessary to arrive at more recent figures is also given. Comment on Christian events covers what has been happening in the early seventies or the late sixties. One has the impression of hearing a current broadcast.

The book is broad-based. While from beginning to end it is concerned with world evangelization, it is correctly entitled *The Church in Asia.* It deals with world evangelization as the classical missionary enterprise has always dealt with it—a wide-ranging, broad-based enterprise which heals the sick, spreads the light of learning, and develops and betters human relationships even as it preaches the gospel and multiplies congregations. The many contributors to *The Church in Asia* believe that, in this business of making a more humane world, the longest step forward which anyone can take is to lead unbelievers to become disciples of Christ and responsible members of His church. The most potent ingredient in the betterment of conditions under which men live today is the multiplication of vibrant Christian cells—churches. So contributors to this volume describe educational enterprises, medical missions, agricultural development, and modernization—conscious that when all these are carried forward under the Great Commission, they achieve their maximum effectiveness.

The book is courageous. Editor Hoke advocates neither cowardly retreat nor timorous substitution of other, safer activities. He and the authors he has assembled believe that the church in Asia stands at the beginning of a century of great advance. They know this will be costly and involve blood, sweat, toil, and tears; but they are confident it is God's will, and they are obedient Christians. World mission is emerging from the slump which it experienced after World War II and the collapse of European empires, and this book is welcome evidence of a bold strategy which includes the churches of Asia as well as those of Europe and North America.

Read it. Own it. Send it to friends in this or other countries to help them see God's will in the last quarter of the twentieth century.

Pasadena, California, USA
February 1975

EDITOR'S PREFACE

by Donald E. Hoke

AFTER MY FIRST fifteen years in Asia I came to realize during brief forays back into North America that the entire Asian continent was relatively unknown to most Westerners. Travel agents seeking to promote tours of Christians to the Far East almost universally failed until the last year or two, I discovered. Christians, I felt, need an insightful glimpse of the great continent of Asia in order to understand its magnitude, its problems, its rich history, and its populous religions. Above all, Christians must realize and respond to the great spiritual needs and challenging opportunities of the continent where more than half the world's people live.

Stimulated by the splendid volume *Let Europe Hear,* which was authored by an outstanding missionary leader and an old friend of college days, Dr. Robert Evans, I approached Moody Press with the ambitious hope of producing a sister volume in two years. Now almost six have passed, and even now I present this volume with hesitancy. Much research and analysis still remains to be done in order to provide a truly in-depth picture of the state of the church in Asia today. The complexity and fluidity of affairs in southeast Asia during the last five years have rendered it impossible to keep up-to-date on the rapid and numerous changes. No sooner was one chapter finished than new material surfaced or the contemporary political picture changed. And since the editorial struggle of producing these chapters over a period of six years has resulted in some being written as early as 1968 and some as late as 1974, updating has always been difficult and in a few cases impossible. Still, I present *The Church in Asia* as a contemporary analysis of the church and mission in Asia today, hopefully in greater depth than most survey books are able to provide. I have endeavored, particularly with regard to the statistical charts, to emphasize the church-growth viewpoint, seeking to discover if the churches in the various nations have grown appreciably, and why.

Originally intending to cover Asia as it is traditionally defined—from the Middle Eastern lands of the Mediterranean to the Pacific—I later limited the volume to central, southeastern, and eastern Asia. My major reasons for eliminating southwestern Asian nations are their somewhat greater familiarity, their frequent grouping as Middle Eastern nations (because they bridge Africa and Europe), and my own unfamiliarity with that area of the world. I have also eliminated what is commonly called Australasia, with the exception of the newly independent nation of Papua New Guinea, because the Australian scene is distinctively more Western than Asian.*

In the introductory chapter I have endeavored to collate and summarize the great spiritual facts of Asia today—its thrilling record of evangelistic fruitfulness in many nations, its challenging opportunities, its staggering needs, and its hopeful future. Subsequently, each chapter deals with a different nation of Asia. The material in each of the chapters (with a few exceptions) has been organized to conform to the following outline:

A. *The Church Today*—A summary of the present state of the church, of evangelism, and of missions, with a particular reference to growth, needs, problems, and opportunities.

B. *Nation and People*—A brief review of the geography, population, government, economy, and society of the nation.

C. *National History*—A background of the nation's history.

D. *National Religions*—A summary of the non-Christian religions, including a description of their size and influence.

E. *Christian History*—A brief survey of the history of Protestant and Catholic evangelism and church growth from earliest beginnings to the point which is emphasized in the section on The Church Today.

F. *The Future*—Some chapters include a statement of opportunity and expectation for evangelism in the days ahead.

For the sake of immediacy and firsthand information, I have selected for nearly every chapter knowledgeable authors who have lived and worked extensively in their respective countries. Their very deep involvement in the lives of their countries has in part contributed to the delay in publication. In most cases I have selected missionaries rather than nationals. There are several reasons for this: first, adequately informed nationals, those capable of writing a manuscript in English, are usually overloaded with significant responsibilities for the kingdom of God. Secondly, in a volume like this, which has required literally hundreds of letters, communication is easier with missionary contacts. Finally, standards of style and documentation are different in many nations, and it was easier to secure from Western lands men who would accept the editorial

*The term *Asia* is used in this book and in all statistics to exclude Southwest Asia (Iran, Iraq, etc.) but to include Papua New Guinea.

requirements of this volume. To all of these authors and to the many other consultants who have given sacrificially and capably of their time, effort, and attention to this project over the last five years I am deeply grateful. Their cooperation has been splendid despite their busy lives.

In my instructions to the authors of each chapter, I designated the book as a reference work, suggesting footnotes and bibliographies for each chapter in order to make study simpler for persons more deeply interested in a particular nation. Some of the bibliographies are more complete than others. Too, there are differences in the content and editorial approach to the various chapters, due to the different authorship of each. The chapters on some nations, like India (which is actually more a subcontinent), have of necessity been greatly condensed. Certain smaller nations, like Cambodia, have received lengthier treatment because of the dramatic events which are still taking place there. Thus, though there will be disappointing factors caused by these editorial conditions, I trust that the total content will contribute to variety and interest. At the end of the volume is a series of charts. In these the emphasis is on church-growth trends. The charts are of uneven value, since for some nations accurate information and statistics have been almost impossible to obtain, even by authors locally present (see introductory note to the charts).

In addition to communicating with the authors of each chapter, I have corresponded frequently with and relied heavily upon the counsel of a number of men experienced in Asia. I would like to mention particularly the assistance of Rev. Leslie Lyall of England, Dr. Frank Cooley and Dr. Ebbie Smith of Indonesia, Mr. T. N. Kurien and Mr. Bruce Nichols of India, Rev. Merle Graven of Cambodia, Rev. Don Rubesh of Sri Lanka, Rev. Robin East of Laos, Rev. A. G. Lindholm and Rev. Ed Torjeson, formerly of Mongolia, Rev. Tom Stebbins and Rev. Gordon Cathey of Vietnam, Dr. Norman Nyun-Han of Westmont College, Dr. Ralph Winter of Fuller Theological seminary, and Dr. Herman Tegenfeldt of Bethel Theological Seminary.

Rev. Don Goss of Japan and Mr. Richard Whiteman of England have both supplied excellent pictures, as have many authors. Faithful and helpful friends on three continents have typed parts of the manuscript. I would like to extend my appreciation especially to these ladies: Mrs. Judy Seen, Mrs. Betty Dew, Miss Dorothy Stermer, Mrs. Edith Lautz, Mrs. Claudette Willems, Mrs. Frances Parker, Miss S. Ishitani, Mrs. Bessie Simonsen, Miss Grace Tweten, Miss Pat Newth, and Miss Mary Steele. Credit should also be given to the authors and publishers of the large number of volumes quoted. I would like to make particular reference, however, to the excellent, continually updated population statistics supplied by the Population Reference Bureau of Washington, D.C.

This volume is presented with the prayerful hope that it will contribute not only to an understanding of the growing church and mission in Asia, but also to the advancement of its evangelism and great churches and to the hastening of the second advent of our Lord and Saviour Jesus Christ (Matthew 24:14; 2 Peter 3:12).

Lausanne, Switzerland
August 1974

1

ASIA'S OPENING DOORS

by Donald E. Hoke

INTRODUCTION

THE EXISTENTIAL NEEDS of greater Asia can be described only by superlatives. Here are concentrated the greatest population, the most extensive physical, economic, and social needs, some of the greatest emotional suffering, and supremely, the quantitatively greatest spiritual need and opportunity of our generation.

With one-third of the world's land, greater Asia houses almost two-thirds of the world's population. Central and east Asia cradle six of the world's eight most populous nations; India and China alone comprise one-third of the world's peoples. Throughout most of the continent, population is growing exponentially. Eighty percent of Asia's people live in villages, yet Asia houses the world's largest city, Tokyo, which by the end of the century is estimated to become a megalopolis of 50 million people. India alone will have twenty cities of more than 12 million each by that time. And China will probably equal or surpass Japan and India.

DONALD E. HOKE served as a pastor in Illinois for six years and later taught at the Columbia Bible College, Columbia, South Carolina. He worked with The Evangelical Alliance Mission in Japan for more than twenty years. He was founder and first president of the Tokyo Christian College and was a cofounder of the Japan Bible Seminary. He was also founder and first president of the Japan Association of Theological Schools. He served as director of the International Congress on World Evangelization, held in Lausanne, Switzerland in 1974, and is presently director of the Billy Graham Center at Wheaton College.

The material in this chapter is presented under the following subheadings: Introduction, Great Spiritual Facts of Asia, The Future of Asian Evangelism, Asia in Retrospect, Asian Christian History, Conclusion.

These factors make Asia a prime seedplot for subversion, overt communist expansion, and political revolution. Here, apart from Israel, have been fought the major wars of the last twenty-five years, wars which have brought death, dislocation, economic destruction, and social tragedy to tens of millions of people.

This seething cauldron of Asian humanity is in constant foment today, stirred by the three witches of political, economic, and social change. Since World War II many new nations have emerged, and several governments have shifted their policies radically. Communism has seized Asia's most populous nation and overflowed into North Korea and the Indochina subcontinental area. Indonesia and the Philippines are struggling to modernize and industrialize, while constantly being undermined by leftist elements. Japan's potential for peaceful leadership is great, but it is hindered by growing Asian fears of economic neocolonialism. And in most nations of Asia may be heard the despairing cries of the hungry, the dispossessed, and the homeless—the burgeoning millions for whom there is little food, few homes, fewer jobs, and no future. These problems may—and undoubtedly will—erupt like festering cancers into a myriad of ugly forms. Politically and economically there is little realistic hope for the future of much of Asia.

But more significant than these factors is that greater Asia, birthplace of the world's five greatest religions (Judaism, Christianity, Buddhism, Hinduism, and Islam) embraces the globe's greatest quantitative spiritual need. Here live almost 2 billion people who know nothing of Christ's redemptive power. Missiologist Ralph Winter's startling statistical analysis reveals that in Asia there are more than 1½ billion fast-growing Chinese (800 million), Hindu (600 million), and Muslim (200 million plus) populations "that are mainly beyond the reach of the ordinary evangelism of Christians . . ." and even missionaries.[1] In India alone are half a million towns and villages with no witness at all for Christ. Developed Japan has over sixteen hundred spiritually needy small cities and towns without a church. The Indonesian and Philippines archipelagos still have numberless island communities to be evangelized. And mainland China's millions reside in tens of thousands more of such cities and towns yet to be opened to the gospel, hopefully in our generation.

Despite recent communist victories in Asia, tens of millions of people, who were unreachable a few years ago, have become receptive to the Gospel. Political changes in Asia have broken open many new national doors for the Gospel. All the nations of Asia, except Japan and Thailand, have experienced bitter colonial rule. Now, all except Hong Kong, Brunei, and Sikkim (recently annexed by India with little international outcry!) are independent. Reliable reports indicate that the underground church in China is vigorous and growing. Martyred churches in Vietnam and Cambodia may continue to witness and grow.

The thesis of this volume is that Asia is not only the world's greatest evangelistic need, but it is also the church's most challenging opportunity in this last quarter of the twentieth century.

Great Spiritual Facts of Asia

Have the crises of the postwar generation done anything to bring Asia closer to Christ? How far has the gospel penetrated the hundreds of diverse cultures there? Is it the sunrise or sunset for cross-cultural evangelism (foreign missions) in Asia today? This volume explores these questions. It seeks to give contemporary, analytical answers, nation by nation. My conclusions are hopeful.

Asia is the world's greatest evangelistic opportunity in this last quarter of the twentieth century. It is the last great frontier of gospel advance. The overwhelming majority of the "three billion unreached" are in Asia. And the sovereign God has been significantly at work in the post-World War II generation, opening and shutting doors (Rev 3:7) to advance his gracious cosmic purpose. The Great Commission is being fulfilled. The church of Jesus Christ on the multicontinent of Asia is vitally alive and growing. It is the only international body which is bridging the political and cultural chasms betwen the many great, diverse nations there. Though the church's presence is still only token in many areas, there are thrilling indications that it is beginning to grow and fulfill its evangelistic mission in many nations. Many of the last great unreached areas and tribes are hearing the gospel.

The continent of Asia can be biblically evangelized in the next twenty-five years. Strong national churches are being and will be planted where they are not now, and many older churches can be renewed in presence and witness. The gospel to every creature (Mk 16:15) and churches of disciples in every ethnic unit (Mt 28:18—*ta ethne*) are reasonable probabilities within this century, I believe. Though Asia's size and needs stagger one's imagination, it must stir our faith to claim from God great new evangelistic thrusts, an abundant spiritual harvest, greatly increased church growth, and the entire continent evangelized. For more likely than not it will be in Asia that the last witness is given, the last word preached, the last disciple made, and God's cosmic plan of redemption completed, thereby triggering the trumpets of his glorious second advent.

Here are great spiritual facts of Asia today:

1. My computations from the statistics compiled by these authors and other researchers indicate that, in the year 1972, the total number of Christians in Asia probably equalled 81 million plus. Of these, 24 million plus

were Protestants; and 57 million plus, Roman Catholic. These figures do not include the Chinese mainland. Excluding Southeast Asia, this means the total Christian population of Asia equalled approximately 0.37-.04 percent of Asia's 2,170 millions! Thus, the number of Christians in Asia today is thirteen times larger now than it was in 1900, and the percentage of Christians is larger now also despite the fact that the population has more than doubled. This percentage is increasing in many areas, so that by the year 2000 the percentage of Christians may be 50 percent greater and the number thirty-four times as large!*

Probably the greatest evangelistic miracle of the twentieth or any century is Papua New Guinea. Only exploration and a few gospel beachheads were made into her interior stone-age civilization before World War II. In the postwar period many new missionary thrusts were begun. Difficult forays were made into the interior, discovering scores of tribes. Today the national is nominally 92 percent Christian; the parliament is opened with the Lord's prayer. Great peoples' movements have swept significant sections of the total population into the church, though obviously many are still only nominal Christians and the task of discipling is great.

2. Evangelical Protestant Christianity is the fastest-growing religion in northeast India, Indonesia, Korea, Taiwan, Hong Kong, Cambodia (possibly also Pakistan, small though the growth is), and in many great tribal areas, church growth is outstripping the rate of population growth in these and other countries. Dramatic illustrations cheer the heart of the Christian seeking first the kingdom of God in today's world:

The Church in Taiwan (Formosa) has grown twentyfold in twenty-seven years, from thirty thousand believers before World War II to an estimated six hundred thousand today. Of these probably no more than fifty thousand are mainland refugee Christians, but from among them came spiritual leaders who have figured in this growth. An almost exactly similar percentage of growth has taken place among the remote, primitive mountain tribesmen, who have grown from four thousand to over seventy thousand Christians, whole villages often having turned to Christ. Today over 4 percent of Taiwan's population is Christian. Probably the key has

*"The number of Asian Christians between the years 1900-1975 grew at the rate of 2.8 per year per hundred Christians, while the non-Christians grew only by 1.0 per hundred. Between the years 1975-2000 Christians will grow 50% faster than non-Christians. Thus in 1900 non-Christians outnumbered Christians 75 to 1; today the ratio is 22 to 1. If the present rate continues the ratio will be only 17 to 1 by the year 2000" (Ralph Winter, "Seeing the Task Graphically," *Evangelical Missions Quarterly*, Jan. 1974, pp. 13, 14). These calculations are impressive but, it must be warned, they are based on simple projections of present growth rates, ignoring many other possible factors, such as adverse political conditions, etc., in the future. On the other hand, a great spiritual awakening and extensive evangelism may exceed these estimates many times.

been aggressive evangelism by laymen as well as clergy, especially among indigenous evangelical groups.

Korea is now over 10 percent Christian, proportionately the largest Protestant Christian community in Asia, and it is overwhelmingly evangelical. Christianity is the largest organized religion in the island. Why?

> . . . the Good News, according to the Scriptures, the power of the Spirit, the enthusiasm of the witness, faithfulness in adversity, rootage in the national soil, and the providence of God in history,

says veteran missionary Samuel Moffett.[2]

A remarkable revival also has been going on in the Korean conscripted army. It was 12 percent Christian in 1970, and two years later, over 35 percent. Over 140,000 were baptized in two years; 16 percent of the professional military academy cadets profess faith in Christ.

Indonesia, with one of the oldest Protestant churches, has seen at least 300 percent growth in church membership in the last ten years. A charismatic revival has swept a number of areas, primarily that of Timor. Youth evangelistic teams spearhead bold advance. Most significant has been the conversion of thousands of Muslims. A group of converted Indonesian Muslims in 1971 held meetings in Muslim Pakistan with dramatic results.

In the Philippine archipelago the "Christ the Only Way" nationwide effort in total mobilization evangelism now has over ten thousand Laymen's Evangelistic Studies meeting weekly. A spiritual awakening in Protestant churches, accompanied by conversions from Catholic and heterodox churches and pagan groups, has marked the nationwide effort.

A small microcosm of phenomenal growth has been that of the Cambodian evangelical churches, which increased over a thousand fold in the area around Phnom Penh since the change of government in 1970. Whereas there was only one church with seventy members then, now there are nineteen churches and more than a thousand enthusiastic, baptized church members, with possibly five thousand communicants, including many high government officials. Outstanding in the movement has been the bold witness of laymen and leading converts. Though this movement has not yet spread nationwide, it has encouraging characteristics which presage continual growth.

3. In the last twenty-five years entire nations which were formerly closed to Christ for a millennium have been opened for evangelism, limited though it still is in some of these nations. Notable among these are the Himalayan kingdoms of Bhutan, Sikkim, Nepal, and the Tibetan refugee kingdom on the Indian border. The stone-age cultures of the interior of New Guinea (both Indonesian and Papuan) have not only opened to Christ but responded to him in great people's movements. The anti-

communist military coup in Indonesia threw the third-largest nation in Asia wide open to gospel witness. Japan's defeat after World War II has given complete religious liberty to evangelize there, and the Protestant church has more than doubled, though results are still relatively slow and small. Bangladesh has experienced new openness since the tragic civil war which separated it from Pakistan. Awakening is reported in some tribal areas; there have been several thousand conversions, and broadened spiritual awakening seems imminent. Thus, despite the almost complete cessation of gospel witness in China and restricted foreign missionary witness in India, throughout Asia God has opened these other new doors with dramatic results in the last two decades.

4. Revival with resultant remarkable growth has taken place among a number of tribal peoples in Asia. The Sindhis in Muslim Pakistan show considerable openness to Christ, with many conversions. The Nagas in north India are more than 50 percent Christian and are aggressively evangelizing neighboring tribes. The Karens, Chins, and Kachins in Burma have maintained solid growth and are now beginning to evangelize their neighbor tribes. The Montagnards of South Vietnam have experienced continuing revival and growth in the last few years, culminating with over fifty thousand people coming to Christ at the end of 1973. Almost 2,000 percent growth has taken place among Taiwanese mountain tribesmen. The animistic peoples of Asia are apparently spiritually prepared for great people's movements to Christ in these opportune days.

5. National and local churches are maturing rapidly. It is probably safe to say that the majority of churches in Asia have become independent of the West (self-governing, self-propagating, and self-supporting) since World War II. A wholesome spirit of self-confidence and conscious identity has replaced dependence on foreign mission organizations. Among growing evangelical churches all unreal aspects of expectant Christianization have gone. Indigenous principles have been largely accepted and adopted. This is not to say that there are not weak, struggling churches without clear aims or evangelistic programs, but as a whole the churches in Asia have risen from adolescent dependency into vigorous young adulthood. Asian churches today are entering a new international phase in their development.

6. Related to this has been the rise of intelligent evangelicalism. The minimal (if any) growth of ecumenical churchianity is increasingly evident, and nowhere more dramatically than in Japan, where the war-born United church has been evangelistically stagnant and torn by internal strife from 1968 onward. It is increasingly evident in Asia that evangelical churches with clear convictions of doctrine and mission are the growing churches. Witness the evangelical Presbyterians in Korea, the Taiwanese

tribal churches, the Nagaland Baptists, the South Vietnamese Evangelical church, and others. Many national evangelical fellowships and biblically-ecumenical, cooperative efforts have made encouraging starts in several nations, though at present they are often clouds no more than the size of a man's hand on the spiritual horizon.

7. Asian foreign mission societies are being organized and missionaries are multiplying. "There are now far more Asian missionaries today (1972) than there were missionaries from Europe and the whole world in 1810."[3] The first annual congress of Asian missionary societies, representing twelve nations and twenty churches, met in Seoul, Korea, in August, 1973. They pledged themselves to two hundred new foreign missionaries from their lands within one year. They concluded with a strong appeal "to the Christian churches in Asia to be involved in the preaching of the gospel, especially through sending and receiving Asian missionaries to strengthen the witness to the saving power of Christ. . . . These missionaries will also be sent to plant evangelistic churches where they do not already exist."

At their second conference, in August 1974, this All Asia Missions Consultation proposed that Asians try to send out ten thousand new missionaries by A.D. 2000. They further proposed an East-West Center for Missionary Research and Development and an All-Asia Missionary Training Center for Asian missionaries, calling for East-West missionary cooperative efforts to meet Asia's vast needs in the future.

8. Across Asia the laity is awakening from its clergy-induced slumber. The spectacular evangelistic growth in Taiwan, Indonesia, Cambodia, and other areas has been sparked by laymen. There is factually encouraged hope that the traditionally clerical churches of Asia are recognizing the biblical ministry and the incalculable power of an awakened, scriptually taught laity.

9. For the first time in Asian history converts from Islam are being counted in hundreds rather than in twos and threes. Most notable have been the results in Indonesia. (There one observer assesses that this is due in part to disillusionment in the face of Israel's rise over her Arab adversaries, and to the Christians being first to reach the moon!)

10. Factors encouraging evangelism and church growth are present and evident in Asia today. Current spiritual events indicate that this is the hour when in his sovereign grace God has sent his Spirit to move over this vast area of the world in special power. Though there are incidental variations, the following factors and conditions are evident in awakening areas with growing churches:

a. Political strife and/or economic and social conditions which produce suffering, unrest, and rapid cultural changes.

> The great advances in missionary expansion have been in periods when the church was in contact with cultures that were in the process of disintegration. Never before has the church lived in the midst of so many disintegrating cultures—and such an intensive period of cultural transition.†

b. Cultures in which traditional animistic religions are declining in influence.
c. Clear vision and enthusiasm on the part of one or more leaders or churches to reach a target area.
d. Bold preaching of evangelical truth in the power of the Holy Spirit.
e. Enthusiastic encouragement of people's movements to maximize evangelistic opportunities. "At least two-thirds of all converts in Asia, Africa, and Oceania have come to Christ through people's movements."[4]
f. Widespread involvement of laymen in witness. This is evident particularly in indigenous Christian groups and in the growing non-Christian new religions of Japan, as well as in historical and resurgent Islam.

Though in individual instances many specialized strategies and methods have been used, these factors have been present among the successful, growing churches in the last twenty-five years and should be recognized in the churches' planning and development of resources in the next twenty-five years, I believe.

Numerous other factors point encouragingly to continually bright hopes for Asian evangelism and church growth in the days ahead:

a. Church-growth emphasis and research, emanating from Dr. Donald McGavran and the Fuller Seminary Institute of Church Growth, has inspired great new interest and refocused activity in evangelism in many nations. This study and activity is steadily spreading throughout Asia.
b. The Asia-South Pacific Congress on Evangelism in Singapore in 1968 sparked a series of national congresses on evangelism, which in turn have initiated chain reactions of gospel witness in India, Taiwan, Japan, the Philippines, and elsewhere. The International Congress on World Evangelization held in Lausanne in 1974 has already begun to accelerate existing and faster new evangelistic vision and programs.
c. Nationwide, total mobilization programs of evangelism are in progress

†Russel A. Cervin, "Focus on Asia," p. 4. Bradshaw, living and working in Asia, states this: "Growth of movements comes when the Sovereign God has prepared the way by making a culture ready for a change. Church growth theory is saying that the church must be ready to move in on the situation which God has prepared" (*Church Growth Through Evangelism in Depth,* p. 109).

or are being planned in several nations, notably the populous ones of Japan and the Philippines.

d. Theological education by extension is beginning to cause trained laymen to seize the evangelistic opportunities of such populous nations as India; interest is beginning in other nations also.

e. Three new graduate schools of theology designed to serve evangelical churches on both interdenominational and international bases were begun in 1974: one serving the Chinese-Asian community in Hong Kong, one serving the northern Asia area from Seoul, Korea, and one serving central Asia from Yeotmal, India.

f. Evangelical theological societies are being organized in many countries, mobilizing evangelical theologians of many churches to write indigenous texts, defend the biblical faith articulately, and undergird the doctrinal foundations of the local churches. An all-Asia consultation of evangelical theologians met and organized in December, 1973.

g. Bible distribution throughout Asia is mushrooming. The United Bible Society reports that distribution has grown from only 13.5 million Scripture portions in 1960 to well over 50 million in 1970. By 1980 they estimate that 500 million Scripture portions will be distributed yearly, all through local church channels. Other Bible translations are multiplying: more than a score of *Living Bible* paraphrases are planned for Asia, primarily where there are no modern translations. Versions similar to the *New American Standard Bible* have been completed in Japanese and are underway in Chinese. At least two other Bible translations in the popular script of the mainland have already been prepared in Hong Kong for mass distribution on the mainland in the future.

God is at work in Asia, and future opportunities are almost limitless.

11. But almost as superlative as Asia's needs and concomitant opportunities today are the many problems which the tiny church of Jesus Christ faces.

a. Foremost among these are the incalculably large masses of people. For the gospel of the Lord Jesus Christ to reach Asia's 2 billion plus, what is required?‡ If evangelists and missionaries were to do it, it

‡The Population Reference Bureau has tellingly visualized the immensity of the task in its reference sheet, "What Is a Billion?" An ordinary halftone printer's engraving has 2,500 dots to every square inch. The printed area of a single page of the New York metropolitan telephone book is 8 by 10 inches, or 80 square inches. If such a page were covered with halftone engraving dots at the rate of 2,500 to the square inch, there would be a million dots on five such telephone book pages. A billion dots would cover 5,000 such pages. The Manhattan telephone directory in 1967 had 1,800 pages. Thus, at one dot per person the population of Asia would fill more than six Manhattan telephone books. By the end of the century it would fill more than ten books!

would require a minimum of 10,000, each with a parish of over 250,000 persons, increasing over 5,000 a year. (The ratio in Switzerland, by comparison, is four pastors for every 12-15,000 persons.) If 20 million Christians were to be mobilized for this evangelism in Asia today, it would require each one to witness effectively to 10 persons per year for the next twelve years, and then to continue for at least eight more years in order to cover simply the growth in general population that would have taken place during that time. To adequately present Christ to the mushrooming urban jungles of Asia, to the tens of thousands of as-yet-unevangelized villages, and to the thousands of islands in the Philippine and Indonesian archipelagos, and to communicate in the hundreds of languages dividing these peoples is a gargantuan task.

b. It is clear that the single greatest opposition to the growth of the gospel in Asia in the past twenty-five years has been communism. It now controls Asia's largest nation and has conquered or divided the Korean peninsula and the Indochina subcontinent, isolating over 800 million persons from gospel witness. Communism remains a persistent threat to political security and spiritual opportunity in many nations. But Western Christians and missionaries must understand that for most developing Asian nations the alternative to this threat is not Western-style democracy and capitalism. These are an impossibility in many Asian nations today. The largely uneducated and often illiterate peoples are incapable of creating and operating truly democratic institutions. The people own no capital with which to build an industrial economy. And widespread poverty and a multitude of problems demand rapid and radical solutions.

Fifteen years ago Tibor Mende, eminent French economist, sociologist, and journalist, opened my eyes to the fact that socialism is an economic and political inevitability in most developing nations today. There must be government investment, initial government ownership, and massive, coordinated effort in order to build a nation. Economic socialism for these nations is a necessity. The tragedy lies in the fact that such socialist economies often move increasingly to the left politically, soon passing a point of no return, whereby they begin to lose rather than gain freedoms. Often the first of these freedoms to be lost is religion. Prior to the democratic revolt in Indonesia the church was under severe oppression there. Burma today has little religious liberty outside the remote tribal areas. Full religious liberty—especially for missionary evangelism—is being increasingly limited in India.

Thus the often tiny minority churches in many Asian countries live in tense political situations over which they have no control. Already suspect for its international ties and its refusal to put loyalty to the state above loyalty to God, the Christian church frequently becomes a whipping dog of the government and is often blamed for its political failures, just as Nero blamed first-century Roman Christians for his problems. It is in such contexts that many Asian churches are called upon to witness to truth and to evangelize. Therefore Western Christians and churches need to show great understanding, sympathy, and prayer toward these minority churches trying to survive and witness under communist and restrictive socialist governments. And for a missionary-evangelist allowed to enter a socialist state there is need for a deep understanding of the situation (including abandonment of any Western political attitude of superiority) and keen sensitivity to his role as a supranational, nonpolitical ambassador of the kingdom of God.

c. Non-Christian religious opposition to Christianity virtually isolates over a third of Asia from effective evangelistic mission still today. The majority of India's 600 million population is Hindu, hostile to the gospel. Islam bitterly opposes the gospel in Afghanistan, western Malaysia, Pakistan, much of Indonesia and Bangladesh, other large communities in other Asian countries. Ralph Winters has graphically pointed out that these mammoth, rapidly growing population blocs of Hindus, Muslims, and Chinese will number well over 2 billion by the year 2000. And they are currently resistant to the gospel, mainly beyond the reach of the ordinary evangelism of Christians and missionaries.[5] Common to all of these non-Christian religious and political blocs is the false conception that Christianity is a Western religion to which Eastern and more indigenous religions are superior.

d. Catholics are competing with Protestant evangelicals in doing Christian evangelism in Asia. Catholic efforts have often matched or surpassed Protestant efforts, even in the postwar period, notably among Tibetan refugees, in many areas of Indonesia, in Taiwan, and elsewhere. Do they preach a counterfeit gospel? Have their converts really entered the kingdom of God? Who can accurately answer these questions? Probably the evangelical revival in some Catholic circles in North America and Europe has not reached most of these countries as yet. Yet among them undoubtedly are biblically aware evangelists. Thus the churches they have planted or are developing are of varying spiritual value and pose serious questions for evangelical Protestant evangelism.

e. Religious syncretism is a way of life in Asia: a good Thai can be 100 percent Buddhist, 100 percent Hindu, and 100 percent animist. A good Japanese can be both Buddhist and Shinto—the combined memberships of both religions still exceeds the national population—and he believes that he can also bring Jesus into his pantheon as well. Catholics in Vietnam are Confucian in their attitudes. The rapid growth of the church in Papua has carried with it many animistic beliefs and customs. To build strong, biblically taught churches in these contexts is in itself a staggering challenge. Christian believers need strong indoctrination with biblical truth against syncretism and relativism in its local forms in each nation and/or culture.

Related to this problem of syncretism is the demand of some younger, liberal theologians for an Asian theology. Their voices were loud at Bangkok (a meeting of the Commission on World Mission and Evangelism of the World Council of Churches in 1972). Their basic principle seems to be that theology should spring from the cultural milieu, experiences, and felt needs of the people, rather than from the revealed Scriptures. They therefore wish to discard the traditional creeds and doctrinal formulations as being Western, and to develop instead an indigenous theology. In practice this means the compromise of Christian truth with indigenous non-Christian religious ideals and customs and with current political and social aspirations. Theology must be made to serve the desires and demands of religio-political leaders economically, politically, and socially. Their voices are loud and strong in many of the larger churches of Asia.

The related problem of universalism has also widely infiltrated the older churches of Asia. To the tiny minority of Christians in Asia (many of which have ancestor worship as a facet of their religions) the question of the eternal destiny of departed ancestors has troubled many. The doctrine of universalism, largely propagated by such influential theologians as the late D. T. Niles of India (a former president of the World Council of Churches), has lately found relatively popular acceptance. In the Asian religious context this concept is appealing even to biblically grounded evangelicals, and the troubling question of ancestors plagues both seekers without and believers within the church.

f. "Mission," "evangelism," and "salvation" are being redefined by the ecumenical movement, and the new concepts are being urged upon Asian churches. A historical watershed for the future of evangelism and missions (primarily within the ecumenical movement) took place in Asia at the conference of the Commission of World Missions and Evangelism of the World Council of Churches at Bangkok, Thailand, in December 1972. Over three hundred churchmen from every continent met to redefine terms, set goals, and chart the future course of evangelism and missions for most of the World Council of Church's member denominations. The message of Bangkok has since been aggressively promoted around the world.[6]

Under the new ecumenical missionary mandate *salvation* is "the peace of the people in Vietnam, independence in Angola, justice and reconciliation in Northern Ireland, and release from the captivity of power in the North Atlantic community." (No mention of the eastern European community!) Evangelism is now something which happens cooperatively *with* non-Christians and not *for* them. Christians should simply face the world hopefully and work out life-styles which produce creative change. The method of evangelism is to be dialogue which is ". . . depaganization: it is finding what we have in common with people of other religions; the purpose of dialogue is to find the spiritual resources which will contribute to the salvation of common problems in society and also to express our content of the Christian faith." Thus evangelism by proclamation of the gospel is denigrated or denied.

Finally, *mission* is now anything which God wants done through the church. Dr. Emilio Castro, new director of the CWME, has stated:

> We are at the end of the missionary era. We are at the beginning of world mission. It is the affirmation of African culture, the conveying of Indian spirituality, the challenge of social revolution, the cry for help of brothers in Europe, the expression of concern for the world mission of delegates of the socialist countries.

The final report of the Bangkok assembly called for a moratorium on foreign missions—in a world with almost 3 billion people who have not yet been evangelized! A Catholic observer commented on Bangkok,

> In the debate the mission provided by Christ to all of His disciples was not considered: the world, with its expectations and needs was overlooked: the biblical message was not invoked: the intentions, devotion, and love of the missionaries with their mistakes and methods were not taken note of. . . .[7]

As an intent observer of the proceedings of that conference, as well as a student of its subsequent literature, I must conclude that the thrust of the ecumenical movement (and in particular the CWME) with regard to Asian evangelism for the future is ominous. The message has become sociopolitical even to the extent of fomenting revolution where necessary. The method has been to fund political, economic, and social reform and revolution movements, and to dialogue with non-Christian religions in an attempt to gain mutual understanding and cooperative effort—not to convert people who are outside of Christ. The historic biblical concepts of salvation, evangelism, and missions have been all but totally abandoned. Apparently the goal of the WCC, working through the CWME, is to integrate all missionary and evangelistic activities under their leadership, control them according to their definitions, and become a center of integration for all religions and idealogies, as Dr. Peter Beyerhaus has pointed out in a widely delivered address following Bangkok.§

g. Conservative (nonconciliar) evangelical missions do not guarantee effective evangelism and continuing church growth. In some Asian countries the greatest church growth has been among prewar, old-line Protestant groups associated with local National Christian Councils (though it is true that in other areas evangelicals affiliated with mission churches and bodies outside the conciliar movement are most effective in evangelism and church planting). It must be honestly admitted that many evangelical organizations are quantitatively large and extensive in missionary effort, but often qualitatively ineffective. Inadequately trained missionaries, nonstrategic approaches (such as the historic concentration of prewar Protestants on the upper classes in Pakistan when the outcaste groups have subsequently proved to be most responsive), shallow mass evangelism, and inadequate discipling of converts—all are glaring needs among evangelicals in many Asian countries and call for a reassessment of their goals and methods.

These problems of evangelism in Asia today are great but not insuperable, and evangelicals are facing them with increasing faith and strategic thinking.

The Future of Asian Evangelism

The Chinese (and Japanese) ideograph for the word "crisis" is made up of two characters, one meaning "danger" and the other "opportunity." What are the "dangerous opportunities" with which Asia challenges the church in these crisis days?|| Though once-in-a-millennium opportunities

§See Peter Beyerhaus, "The Challenge of Bangkok." In June 1974 the powerful All Africa Conference of Churches, following the lead of Bangkok, called for a moratorium on both foreign missionary personnel and funds. "Should the moratorium cause missionary sending agencies to crumble," the assembly said, "the African church would have performed a service in redeeming God's peoples in the Northern Hemisphere from a distorted view of the mission of the church in the world!" (from a Religious News Service release dated June 14, 1974).

||"Until recently monumental myopia has caused Americans to see Asia by looking not westward, but eastward, as though it lay across the Atlantic, filling the vast

ASIA'S PRESENT PROBLEMS

The early postwar "revolution of rising expectations" in the third world (Asia, Africa, and Latin America) has in most of Asia given way to a new revolution of rising frustrations. While political subversion and conflict outwardly occupy center stage, Asia's greatest single problem is probably uncontrolled population growth with its resultant endemic hunger, poverty, and excessive urban migration. These obviously spawn the unrest in which subversion and revolution flourish.

Asia's population at the end of 1974 was conservatively estimated at 2,170 million.[8] The United Nations median estimate for the year 2000 is 3,462 million.[9] In the light of the preeminent fact that over half of Asia's population today is under twenty years of age and therefore just entering the productive years, this estimate is conservative. Radically lowered and still lowering death rates may accelerate even further this considered estimate. These statistics are not cold evaluations, but tragic indices of throbbing human need.

These numbers first of all portend widespread hunger and famine. In 1967 biological scientist Paul Ehrlich of Stanford University wrote:

> Sometime between 1970 and 1985 the world will undergo vast famines—hundreds of millions of people are going to starve to death unless plague, thermonuclear war, or some other agent kills them. Many will starve to death in spite of any crash programs we might embark upon now. And we are not embarking upon any crash programs. These are the harsh realities we face.#

Has this prophecy come true? The conference of the Food and Agricultural Organization of the United Nations released a preliminary report entitled *The State of Food and Agriculture, 1973* in September of that year. Their conclusion:

> The world food situation in 1973 is more difficult than at any time since the years immediately following the devastation of the Second World War. . . . World food production in 1972 was slightly smaller than in 1971, when there were about 75,000,000 fewer people to feed. . . . [There was] a substantial drop in the Far East (estimated at present of

dimness of the world beyond Europe. In recent years events have rearranged our understanding of geography, and new media of communication have given us front-row seats for the performance of high drama . . . but we are no longer spectators; we have become participants" (Peter Beyerhaus, "The Challenge of Bangkok," p. 4).
are before us, the problems are staggering in size and complexity.

#*New Scientist*, Dec. 14, 1967, quoted in the *Population Bulletin* of the Population Reference Bureau, Dec. 1968. In the March 1974 issue of *Church Growth Bulletin*, McGavran reasons that famines or fear of them will force worldwide population stabilization at 6 billion by A.D. 2000. I know of no secular demographers who agree. Most talk of 7 billion, almost half of whom will be Asians!

> about 4%), causing a decline of about 1% of the total food production of the developing countries. . . . In the face of a constantly growing population these events are extremely disquieting. Per capita food production in the Far East is 8% below the peak level of 1970.[10]

The prophecy of Rev. Thomas Malthus in 1798 is upon us: "I say that the power of population is infinitely greater than the power of the earth to produce subsistence for man."[11] Especially is this true in the Far East, as the FAO report indicated. The widely publicized "green revolution" of miracle grains has been only a partial help. It has led in turn to another crisis, a nutritional one, as lands given over to vitally necessary protein-rich beans have been replaced with starchy rice.[12]

Crash food programs are proving inadequate in much of Asia, particularly in India. Experts point out that the reasons are numerous: land is lacking for increased production in most places; the will to improve food productivity or reduce population is absent; expertise is lacking (to exploit agricultural production in the United States there are forty-five thousand agricultural experts for 3 million farmers; in India there are only fifteen hundred experts for 50 million); fertilizers are inadequate; favorable temperate-zone conditions are not present; etc. In addition to these conditions, political instability, poor health, inadequate mobility, and absentee-ownership of land are aggravating the situation. Startlingly enough for the socialist and communist critics to ponder, in many sections where large estates have been broken up and distributed to peasants, this has often decreased rather than increased food production.[13] The conclusion of the Food and Agricultural Organization report is that agricultural resources are simply not adequate to feed Asia's burgeoning population. Endemic hunger and widespread famine are an almost inevitable result. R. B. Sen, former director general of the FAO said in 1968:

> The vicious circle continues with virtually incurable poverty as a result of the inadequate resources mentioned above. The average GNP for Asia, (omitting only Japan and Hong Kong but including rapidly industrializing nations like Korea and Taiwan) is only $140. The average income is much less.[14]

Only a massive, continent-wide concern can solve the problem.[15] The impossible requirement is a massive *Christian* concern on the part of 2 billion *non-Christian* peoples. In 1960 demographic expert Philip Hauser of the University of Chicago glumly prophesied that the inevitable collision between population growth and inadequate food production in this century would doom nations to fighting themselves to death like scorpions in a bottle, simply for the food to live.

The problem of urbanization compounds this situation. Most of the major nations of Asia have more than 10 percent of their population in their capital cities, (e.g., Tokyo, Manila, Bangkok, Taipei, and Seoul). Huge metropolitan areas are beginning to spring up in all of the developing nations. Hungry rural youths are moving to the cities by the hundreds of thousands yearly. With inadequate housing and job opportunities they become vulnerable to crime, escapism through drugs, and political exploitation by subversive elements. All the problems the West has been ineffectually attacking in the last decade will strike the urban centers of Asia with hurricane force and extent in the next few years. And in the underdeveloped nations there is little hope for solution. They do not yet have the money, jobs, or expertise to grapple with problems of this magnitude. Revolution is the all-too-likely result, and massive famines in many nations are only a few years off.

Kipling's "East is East and West is West, and never the twain shall meet" is simply not true. "The world is Westernizing at a rapid rate," declared historian Arnold Toynbee. After twenty-one years in Asia, I feel that particularly in the growing urban centers we are witnessing the spread of a great, gray, materialistic, secular uniculture across the entire continent. Jet down into any city of Asia and the sights are the same: glaring neon advertisements (usually of Japanese products!); movies from every country of the world (many of them pornographic); standard-looking taxis, clothing, recreation, and central shops. If it be complained that these are superficial similarities, I answer that under the surface lies the same existential meaninglessness, the same search for pleasure, the same indifference to old religions (except for marriage and death ceremonies), the same practical agnosticism, and the same openness toward Western "improvements." This is the real Asia of today. Only the quaint tourist sights, a few traditional religious ceremonies, physical racial characteristics, and superficial psychological differences distinguish the various Asians of today.

The entire continent is in painful ideological and political ferment. Asia's problems in number and magnitude are increasing almost exponentially. The seemingly insoluble social and economic needs are multiplying. Asian youth, painfully involved and increasingly knowledgeable, are wishfully idealistic and are thus exploited by subversive elements, notably Communism. Cervin has well said:

> Asians want meaning and integrity. Incredible as it may seem, the crisis of integrity is often greater than the crisis of hunger. The right for self-determination and a sense of personal and national worth is the right Asians demand of the world.[16]

But such times of radical social and political change and economic insecurity have always been great hours for evangelism!

PRIORITIES FOR EVANGELISM AND MISSION

In this context of crisis in Asia certain evangelistic priorities are clear, I believe. Let me list those of greatest importance in my opinion:

1. The *receptive peoples* in Asia today should certainly be given primary consideration, as Professor Donald McGavran has so frequently emphasized. Primary among these are the animistic tribal peoples in many of the great nations. To mention a few, the recently responsive Sindhis in Pakistan, the Montagnards in Vietnam, the tribal groups in Laos, Cambodia, Burma, and the Indonesian islands (only approximately 50 percent of Indonesia's people are Muslim), the Taiwanese highlanders, the non-Malay Filipinos, the "scheduled castes" (former outcastes) of India and Pakistan, etc.

2. Great in importance are those *cultures in radical change or disintegration* of which Cervin speaks.[17] Japan, Korea, Bangladesh, and Taiwan are outstanding examples. Korea and even Japan—free, totally literate, and not unresponsive—have great possible potentials in Asia for future evangelistic leadership. After the death of chairman Mao, China may suffer radical disruption and may suddenly open to evangelism, though probably not to Western emissaries. As the China chapter reports, there was a strong reaction among youth to the brutal radicalism of the Red Guard revolution at the end of the sixty's. As a result, according to reliable sources, hundreds—maybe thousands—of young people came to Christ through the quiet evangelism of underground churches. If even limited religious freedom is permitted in the future, there is hope that this response could be multiplied many times over, sparked by the witness of a liberated church.

3. *Increasingly receptive urban areas,* such as Singapore, Hong Kong, etc., warrant concentrated evangelism. One experienced Asian observer expects that "the region in which we may see the next large-scale eruption of dissatisfied humanity will be India. Here as dislocated rural peoples move to new urban centers, opportunities will be great."

4. *Responding Islamic areas,* should be wisely and prayerfully, yet quickly and energetically, evangelized. The initial response in Indonesia has been heartening in recent years, though the total Christian population of the Javanese (who make up 50 percent of the nation's population) is still only 1 percent. Robert Bowman, president of the Far East Broadcasting Company, observes, "Islam cannot stand Westernization. The result may be that the archaic orthodoxy of the Moslems will yield to Christ's life-giving evangel."[18] Pakistan also should be closely observed as a possible open door in this regard in the months to come. It would be naive to think that Muslim youth are unaffected by the modernization and

secularization of the world. They could soon be open to the gospel as never before.

5. *Specific national opportunities.* The thousands of villages and the numerous mushrooming urban centers of India must somehow be evangelized, though this may be done through many of the newly growing Asian missionary societies, since Western missionaries are slowly being excluded. Certainly the open doors of Taiwan, Indonesia, the Indochina peninsular nations, Bangladesh, and the Philippines should be considered as strategic opportunities for the concentration of evangelistic and missionary forces and funds.

The world church of Jesus Christ must prepare for the *possible opening of China* to the gospel. Mr. Bowman wisely observes:

> China may open again. It is doubtful if it will open to the old concept of missionary activity within our lifetime. It is possible that we shall see a great revival and a large harvest of souls in China in the future. Mao's Communism has roughly handled the old China and radically changed her life. When the iron hand of Communism is removed, we shall see a purified Church prepared of the Lord to evangelize the 800,000,000 souls in that land. It will be the business of the western Church to aid the Chinese Church as she takes the initiative in her land.[**]

Though some initial studies are being carried out by China-watching organizations in Hong Kong and Singapore, accelerated preparation of materials and strategic thinking needs to be done if this incomprehensibly great opportunity is to be utilized to its maximum when God finally brings a change in the government attitude toward religion there.

SOME GUIDELINES FOR EVANGELISTIC AND MISSIONARY STRATEGY IN ASIA TODAY

Based on the contribution of the twenty-three authors of this volume and on my own observations and insights as an Asian missionary for twenty-one years, I now want to suggest several principles for evangelism and church-building strategy in the dangerously opportune generation ahead in Asia. The church must maximize the effective use of its limited resources if the tremendous opportunities and needs of evangelizing Asia are to be met.

A. Of primary importance is a *realistic appraisal of the situation.* Facts are needed. James Wong of Singapore, an aggressive young Anglican, has pioneered research in his populous city-state, and he is concerned for all of Asia. He concludes:

**In the same vein Dr. Philip Teng, chairman of the Alliance churches and senior evangelical leader in Hong Kong, told the editor in May 1972 that he doubted if "outsiders"—all non-mainlanders—would be allowed to preach the gospel in China in this generation, no matter how much the government liberalized or changed.

> . . . as a step toward achieving church growth throughout southeast Asia, we must undertake comprehensive investigations of the present situation of the churches in these countries. A start has been made in Singapore, South Vietnam, Indonesia, and the Philippines. But further research and study projects are needed. We must seek to encourage others to participate in a coordinated program that embraces all the churches of southeast Asia. . . . The overall aim is to help the churches of southeast Asia to make use of the opportunities God is giving in these days so that many may hear the gospel and become disciples of Jesus Christ. Evangelism and church growth are to be linked together. The facts which are gathered should be transformed into hard, bold plans for the growth of the churches. Targets must be set up so that we will expect God to give the increase. We must act and plan now so that all responsive peoples shall be brought to a saving knowledge of Christ and incorporated into the churches to be planted in all the receptive segments of these countries.[19]

Without further study, computation, and evaluation of facts and statistics concerning church and mission in Asia, missionary resources—whether Western and Asian—may be dissipated rather than concentrated toward the goal of evangelizing Asia. Church growth research is needed in every nation.

B. Based on the above, the thoughtful *development of new, comprehensive strategies* is essential. During World War II Winston Churchill's insistence for victory in Europe was upon an "overall strategic concept." In the middle of the Vietnam War, Dr. Edwin Reischauer, then U.S. ambassador to Japan, wrote in *Beyond Vietnam* that the United States had suffered and paid for the lack of a clear Asian foreign policy. The same can be said of the church of Jesus Christ with regard to Asia, I believe. There is an immediate and imperative need for churches and missions to hammer out realistic strategies with clearly enunciated long- and short-range objectives. An overall strategic concept for Asian evangelism and church growth should include the following elements:

1. *Strengthening existing churches.* Dr. Akira Hatori, a leading Japanese evangelical, says the primary spiritual needs of Asia are spiritual renewal and enlarged vision. Dr. Stanley Mooneyham, widely traveled president of World Vision, believes:

> The most pressing spiritual needs are *in* the churches of Asia. . . . I believe the churches of Asia need renewing. . . . The church needs an inner spiritual life that will make it dynamically evangelistic and aggressive in outreach. "The minority religion complex" needs to be cast off, and a New Testament aggressiveness needs to be cultivated. The church in Asia needs to find its own soul and its own dynamic life apart from the umbrella of Western missions and churches. This would give it confidence to stand in the power of the Holy Spirit rather than in

> the strength of Western relationship and would help release the church from its defeatist syndrome.[20]

My own experience confirms this judgment. Dr. Michael Griffiths, general director of the Overseas Missionary Fellowship, continues:

> With the increased number of independent, indigenous churches throughout the area, I think we are going to need a fresh emphasis upon a goal for the church . . . upon quality in terms of holiness of life, not only with individuals but in a total Christian community. In the divine goal of a "beautiful church without spot or wrinkle" we shall find a continuing need for Bible teaching of a high quality, showing the relevance of the Christian gospel not only to life after death but to colonies of heaven existing on earth until death.[21]

Quiet, prayerful assistance to the churches in nurturing their spiritual lives must be a prime priority of both mission and church leaders.

2. *Careful long- and short-range planning* for effective, goal-oriented evangelism on the part of both missions and churches. The recent success of the so-called "Venezuela experiment" and the use of the excellent manual on church planning and growth by Dr. Virgil Gerber is a dramatic illustration of amazing results from the use of simple planning tools.[22] In my experience with denominations and missions in Asia, I found that few of them have clearly defined goals with step-by-step plans for meeting them. Strategic planning is long overdue. Certainly nothing is more important than this if the more than 2 billion people of Asia are to be evangelized by the small Christian community. Excellent guidelines have been coming from the School of World Missions and Church Growth at Fuller Seminary, Evangelism-In-Depth and other saturation evangelism experiments, and other groups. It is up to church and mission in Asia to study, adapt, and innovate in the face of the church's greatest missionary challenge.

   I would like to see planning conferences projected in every nation in Asia within the next two years. Using the "Gerber" plan or a similar one (it is the exercise of growth analysis, goal setting, and planning that is important—there is no magic in Gerber's or any other method), goals and plans to reach the unevangelized peoples need to be made by every mission and church in every nation. Annual review and up-dating is essential. On a continent-wide plane, I would like to suggest three regional strategy conferences for Asia, each conference to meet three times in a period of fifteen to twenty-four months. They could best be convened one each for Chinese Asia, central Asia, and east Asia. To them would be invited leaders of the churches and missions working in each area, possibly on a numerically proportionate basis.

Speakers and group leaders in the first session would outline the major problems, buttressed with all available statistics. The conference would then break down into small study groups to outline the further needs for research for the next conference, including analyses of political and religious conditions, church growth statistics, etc. At the second conference reports would be brought, further in-depth analyses made, and evangelism plans formulated. At the third conference, possibly as long as a year later, a review of the initial plans could be made, necessary revisions could be suggested, and new, more ambitious plans could be projected. Subsequent annual or biannual review conferences could do much to stimulate strategic thinking, cause self-reflection, and continually refocus the churches and Christians on the goal of evangelizing all of Asia.

3. *Evangelical cooperation—biblical ecumenicity.* Reacting against modern ecumenism and politicized evangelism, many evangelicals have fragmented themselves into unduly independent operators. This is true of individuals, missions, and churches. (Although missions are frequently criticized for importing Western denominational divisions—and they have often unwisely done so—many evangelical denominations within a given nation are even less inclined to cooperation than missions from many different lands.) If the vast populations of Asia are to be reached, it will not be done by any one denomination or mission, but only by all evangelicals working constantly at evangelism both individually and together. Total mobilization evangelism plans need to be carefully reviewed and adapted to local situations. The time for some evangelicals to repent of prideful denominationalism, personal ambitions, and undue emphasis on doctrinal nonessentials that divide is long past. Neither Asia nor any great nation in it will be evangelized apart from a new spirit of cooperation and courage to confront the formidable anti-Christian adversaries.
4. *Recruitment of many new men* for evangelism in the coming generation. Speaking at the International Congress on World Evangelization in July 1974, McGavran warned:

> This Congress must beware of pessimistic generalizations to the effect that evangelism is passé, missionaries are not wanted, modern man demands bread, not God, and a pluralistic world simply cannot conceive of one way to God and one revelation of His will. Some of these gloomy generalizations are the fruit of the Eurican guilt complex. Some Europeans' good news consists of beating their breasts and proclaiming their guilt! Other pessimism is caused by decades of defeat in resistant populations and is set forth as universal truth concerning world evangelism. Much negativism is the outcome of eroded faith, nonbiblical

> presuppositions, and heretical opinions phrased in seemingly objective judgments about "the modern mind" and "current trends." This Congress must reject sub-Christian philosophies and theologies masquerading as scientific assessments of the situation.
>
> The facts support a far different assessment—unprecedented receptivity! Facts call for evangelism on a greater scale. Churches from more nations than ever before must thrust out more ambassadors of Christ. Latfricasian churches are beginning to send significant numbers. They must be helped to send still more and guided so that their missionaries and evangelists take advantage of two hundred years' experience when Euricans had to initiate world evangelization alone. Eurica also must increase the quantity and improve the quality of her sendings. The church in all six continents must surge forward in evangelism.[23]

What kind of workers are needed for the dangerous opportunities of the next few decades? A greatly increased number of non-Western missionaries are especially needed in order to liberate spiritually the nations and areas where nationalism has made white faces unwelcome. "Cross-cultural evangelists who are not necessarily Western may replace the traditional concept of missionaries," Mooneyham believes. The whole Asian church must become increasingly involved in missions. The upsurge of interest in Asian-to-Asian missionary groups must be encouraged and assisted. Missionaries from all six continents in large numbers are needed and wanted in Asia today. Yet it must be realistically faced that the number of missionaries who are able to be recruited and supported by the national churches in Asia will be relatively few compared to the need in the next decade. Winters points out that if the closed or resistant communities in China, plus the Hindus and the Muslims, were to have missionaries in the same proportion as the rest of the more nonresistant areas of the world, Asia would immediately have 180,000 more missionaries—more than a hundred times as many as are now laboring in those resistant areas![24] Thus Western foreign missionaries are still a high priority in many nations of Asia. Hatori speaks strongly for many Asian church leaders when he says, "We want more Western missionaries!" He points out that three types are needed: pioneering, evangelistic church builders, Bible teachers, and specialists. (His priority is significant here; care must be exercised not to overemphasize the role of the narrow specialist.) The plain fact is that thousands of Western missionaries are still needed and wanted in Asia today, despite widely publicized individual statements to the contrary!

A higher quality of worker is increasingly needed. Mooneyham observes that "If the church is serious about winning 90% of Asians to

Christ who do not know him, we will have to stop investing large sums sending ordinary people abroad to do ordinary jobs . . ." Cross-cultural evangelists with some understanding of cultural anthropology and most certainly with wide reading of the increasingly available literature on innovative evangelism and church growth principles are imperative if strategic planning and effective ministry is to be done in the days ahead. Shortsighted, inflexible workers—whether from Western or Asian churches—will hinder rather than help the total cause of Asian evangelization in the days to come. Above all, deep spiritual life, tested in the crucible of experience before involvement in Asian mission, is the sine qua non of the missionary needed for Asia today.

5. *Many multinational, parachurch, evangelistic, and missionary organizations* must be organized or expanded if the vast challenge of Asia is to be met today. Such multinational organizations may take two forms: the first is the organizing of multiracial teams of witnesses—professional and lay, specialists and general, short- and long-term workers. This means the inclusion of Asian missionaries in Western mission organizations, and possibly even some Western missionaries in Asian organizations where expedient. The Overseas Missionary Fellowship has pioneered in this since the war, but the numbers of Asians in the organization has probably been too small for us to draw any conclusions from the effectiveness of such organization. McGavran believes, however, that a second type of multinational mission organization is more effective:

> A band of missionaries from one country working together on one salary scale, one income, under one board, one church behind them, one heart language (whether English, Korean, or Japanese) makes a better missionary team than the multiracial teams which may spend most of their time demonstrating that they can work together and get precious little church planting or evangelism done. If you have 50 Americans and 50 Englishmen as missionaries, you will get far more work and far less talk and friction if the Americans work in this country and the English in that. The same is true of all mixtures. Needless to say, the various teams should work in cooperation and harmony with the blessing and cooperation of the local church.

Again the Overseas Missionary Fellowship (then the China Inland Mission) wisely exploited this method of multinational mission with excellent results for fifty years in China before World War II.

Whichever method is followed, new ways of financing must be developed. This is a sensitive and difficult problem. Church and missionary leaders in every country have witnessed foreign money corrupting many heretofore useful national Christian workers. On the other hand, if the challenge and opportunity are to be met in many countries presently closed to Western missionaries, Asian missionary societies will probably need extensive financial help in sending workers into these opening areas. From wide observation and experience in postwar Asia I believe that the dangers of Western subsidization to Asian societies can be avoided, and that effective means can be found of channeling funds into Asian missionary projects and organizations.††

a. There must be clear safeguards and guarantees that the donated funds will be used for the designated purposes. Old-line denominations in particular have seen hundreds of thousands of dollars diverted from evangelism into pension funds, pastors' salary increases, and other nonevangelistic activities in nearly every nation. It is simply good ethics and good stewardship that guarantees be written into grants given for mission and evangelism.
b. Funds should be administered through reputable national organizations with established bylaws and principles administered by men of unquestioned integrity. It is wise to insist that these organizations have clear, detailed accounting and reporting procedures, if not to the donating or Western organization, at least to themselves. It must be remembered that many newer Asian mission and evangelistic organizations have not as yet had the long, often-painful experiences that their Western brothers have. Nonpaternalistic counseling may assist them to avoid these expensive pitfalls.
c. Donors should insist that funds be invested only in experienced workers who are thoroughly screened, are firmly related to their own local churches and denominations, and enjoy the full confidence of their own national peers. Many gullible Western individuals and Christian organizations have been deceived and defrauded of huge amounts of money by personable, English-speaking foreign nationals who, upon investigation, are found to have no status or confidence among their fellow national Christians.
d. Prayer and care are needed, primarily on the part of the Asian mission leaders, that local workers and churches are not denied the blessing of sacrificial giving by the availability of foreign funds.

Multinational investment in the evangelism of Asia is an imperative in our generation. India, Nepal, Pakistan, Indonesia, and other lands may best be evangelized by Asian missionaries. The oneness of the body of Christ may be beautifully evidenced by financial cooperation of Western churches with our Asian brothers, and a few simple principles like the ones previously mentioned will guard misuse of funds and corruption of the workers.

††I would suggest the following simple principles to guide Western funding of Asian missions for the future:

6. *A new sensitivity* to the altered cultural and political situation of Asia is needed by both mission organizations and individuals. More extensive training for cross-cultural evangelism is urgent for all missionaries, whether from the U.S., Sweden, or Japan. The errors of so-called Western missionary colonialism (however great they may or may not have been) will be repeated by Asian missionaries unless they are carefully taught the lessons of the past. The extensive problems of mission-church relationships will be faced all over again by newer Asian missionary societies unless their leaders seriously study the wealth of Western literature and experience on this subject. True cooperation in evangelism and church nurture, as well as in mission- and church-building, must be prayerfully and pragmatically practiced by all partners in the twentieth-century mission to Asia. Even greater sensitivity to and identity with the suffering millions of Asia in their problems must be sought.

> The millions we seek to reach with the gospel of new life exist in perpetual struggle with chronic starvation, backwardness, and political insecurity. The question faced by Christians and misisonaries in Asia today is: can we evangelize in the safety and security of isolation from the struggles of society? Or must the Word be carried into the midst of the struggle if men are really going to be reached for Christ? If we effectively speak a word for Christ, it will be in solidarity with the people in their struggle, their sinfulness, and their need of total salvation. There is a hunger for an inclusive meaning of life which offers unfragmented hope—for now and always.[25]

7. *Upgrading every phase of theological education.* After twenty-one years of involvement in theological education in the Orient, I find little theological education on any level in any country that is creative, innovative, and aggressively evangelistic. In most of the churches in Asian nations (with but few exceptions) clericalism has cut the nerve of lay witness. The church must revive the ministry of the laity (Eph 4:11-12) and promote a twentieth-century reformation in that area. Reviewing theological education in Asia as I understand it, I believe the following suggestions would contribute to its greater effectiveness:

   a. All curricula, whether in lower-level Bible schools or higher-level seminaries and graduate schools, need reorientation to the end that every worker who graduates be inner-directed toward aggressive evangelism, church planting and growth, and cross-cultural missions.

   b. Theological-education-by-extension programs must be vastly multiplied, not only to train potential lay pastors for rural areas, but also to encourage laymen and to upgrade their status and recognition in the local churches. A small start has been made through the Union Biblical Seminary in India, where the need is probably the greatest.

c. Asian theological schools generally need academic upgrading and increased support. As a rule libraries are pitifully small, qualified teachers limited, curricula unbalanced. Theological education consultants from other lands and substantial foreign funds can make a major contribution here to evangelism and church growth in the years ahead.

d. Advanced theological education should be encouraged within Asia. The three schools started in Hong Kong, Seoul, and Yeotmal in 1974 are an encouraging answer to this problem. These schools deserve the support of every evangelical church and mission, for to them promising young Christian leaders can go with much less fear of becoming deculturalized or corrupted by Western schools and standards of living.

e. Wisely administered scholarship programs for key pastoral and lay leaders to obtain specialized training abroad are needed. If only mature, proven men are sent, and if they are sent by and responsible to national churches or schools, the dangers of nonreturn are minimized. It must be recognized that certain types of broad theological training and balanced perspectives on world issues (such as on the ecumenical movement) can usually be gained only when a local leader is exposed to new experiences and broader insights than are usually available in his own country. Scholarships for this kind of advanced, controlled study are imperative.

The key to the future church's vision and program lies in the adequate theological training of its future leaders, both lay and professional. Evangelicals have been slow to grasp this, and the church in Asia has suffered.

8. *Full utilization of modern mass communication media.*

> The key opportunity presenting itself to the church now and for the years ahead is multimedia. Radio, television, and literature are tools which can make possible the saturation evangelism of the great mass of the people of the Orient. I don't think the job can be done apart from the total use of these tools. The immediate task is to enlighten Christians in Asia, as well as in the West, to the importance of these tools so that the whole church will see the wisdom of investing large sums of money in great reservoirs of Christian lives and talent in multimedia evangelism in the Orient,

says FEBC's Robert Bowman.[26] I second his views heartily. Christian broadcasting stations, the availability of purchasable commercial time, and the cheap, almost universal Japanese transistor radio are present realities and opportunities in Asia. TV is coming but is still expensive. Well over half of Asia is already literate, and most of the rest will be literate by the end of this generation. All communications media must be fully utilized and developed with funds and personnel. A new mass communication consortium, "Encouraging Contemporary Communication Enterprises," has been established, with branches in India and Thailand and another branch soon to be established in Hong Kong for all of Chinese-speaking southeast Asia. With supporting cooperation it can be a seminal group to foster the development of mass communication efforts in all of the main ethnic and linguistic areas in Asia. In this strategic development Western funds and technical specialists can play an important part in many Asian countries where expertise in media use is lacking.

Sold as I am on the essentiality of widespread use of mass communication media, I close with the precaution that these are merely gospel seed-sowing. The church-planting evangelist-husbandmen must follow up if the Great Commission is to be fully completed in the nations of Asia. There must be developed more effective combinations of media and men to baptize, disciple, and build churches.

The above strategic considerations are meant only to be suggestive. When bathed in prayer, creative and innovative thinking will open many new effective avenues of evangelism in the next two decades. Viewing evangelism and mission as a ministry of all the people of God in every country, the perceptive Westerner needs to face these opportunities thoughtfully and to humbly and sensitively seek to maximize his contributions in those areas where they are most needed.

REALIZABLE BIBLICAL OBJECTIVES IN ASIA TOMORROW

As a postscript to this summary estimation of the future of Asian evangelism, let me suggest briefly the biblical objectives of the evangelist and the church in Asia at this hour. A clear view of these is essential, for some well-intentioned evangelicals (as well as liberals) would involve the church deeply in nation-building, commit it to international reconciliation efforts, and expend excessive time and massive resources in the alleviation of physical needs. This they would call a contemporary extrapolation of the cultural mandate (Gen 1:28). Though individual Christians should be involved in these activities as part of their ethical responsibilities as citizens, these activities are not, I believe, the direct mission of the church.

Almost inevitably these activities confuse the church's goal, siphon off its strength, and compromise its eternal message with programs which substitute Christianization for evangelization.

What, then, are the biblical goals and expectations for evangelism today? I believe they are clear and attainable:

1. That all men have at least one opportunity to hear, understand clearly, and respond to the essential content of the gospel of Jesus Christ (Mk 16:15; Ac 1:8; 1 Co 15:3; etc.);

2. That God's righteousness and honor be thereby vindicated before the world of men and the universe of principalities and powers (Ro 3:26; Eph 3:10; et al);

3. That disciples of Jesus Christ be made and his church be firmly planted in every tribe (*ta ethne*), which I understand to mean in every truly ethnic group (Mt 28:18-20);

4. That as a result of this our expectation is not that the world will be converted or Christianized, but that even in the fulfillment of the above, true Christians and true churches in Asia (and throughout the world) will be a minority (Mt 7:14; Lk 18:8; and the whole tenor of eschatological passages in the epistles and the Revelation).‡‡

Keeping these biblically inescapable principles in mind, the Christian looks basically with optimism on the Asian scene. As J. Robertson McQuilkin points out, for the church to total only 10 percent of Japan's population, there is room for more than 1,000 percent growth. What God has done in people's movements in Indonesia, Taiwan, and elsewhere in Asia

‡‡While agreeing with my principle here, Professor Donald McGavran makes three comments regarding this important point:

1. "Biological growth . . . sends non-Christian populations soaring and is sending Christian populations soaring even more, so that the percentage of Christians in Asia is actually slightly increasing by biological processes alone."
2. "I scarcely think that the Bible will allow us to believe that it is God's will for 700 out of every thousand persons in North America to be baptized or members of a baptized family . . . while in North India less than one out of every thousand has Christ's power flowing in him. Granted that a minority will be Christian—a minority of the population of India in the year 2,000 would be 400 million souls!"
3. Speaking of point 3 above, that disciples of Christ be made in every *ethne,* McGavran states, "We must put churches in every piece of the human mosaic, in all dialects, in all groups, in all close-knit units, such as fishing villages and factories. Only then, *when each individual in the ethnos* (whether that is a community of 500 or of 100), can hear the gospel from his own kith and kin, in his own dialect, without any barrier of foreignness, the only scandal being that of the cross, then the Lord will (I am convinced) rule that all have had a real chance to hear, His righteousness will have been satisfied. He will return" (from a personal letter to the editor dated Feb. 1974).

With McGavran's description of the *ethne* in point three I cannot agree. Judging by the experience of almost two thousand years of evangelism, if this be the condition of fulfilling the Great Commission, then I do not think it is ever humanly possible of fulfillment.

he may continue to do in other nations, bringing tens of millions into Christ's church. Yet evangelicals must be realistic, avoiding both false triumphalism and postmillennial optimism. The evangelical evangelist's hope is clear and finely balanced. He believes and works for tens of millions to be won to Christ and discipled into churches in Asia in this generation. Yet he knows that the total will be only a remnant, not a reformed continent. He prays and works for the church to be spiritually pure and evangelistic, salt and light—not a power structure or a socio-economic pressure group. He believes supremely that Jesus Christ is church-building, not nation-building (Mt 16:18) in Asia today. And he constantly looks ahead to glorious days of evangelistic fruitfulness in the next two decades or until Christ comes.

Obviously many readers will still want to redefine my statement of these goals, but for most evangelicals the meaning is clear. If these goals be accepted, as I believe they must, then the church of Jesus Christ must concentrate her resources and efforts on the pursuit of them, and not on other humanly desirable but not divinely commanded objectives. With the *dunamis* of the Spirit the church today has the three resources necessary to achieve God's mandates as never before in Christian history: global transportation and communication technology, potential manpower within the church (as a result of the thousands of youth who have come to Christ with deep commitment in the last decade), and money—vast treasures of as-yet-unconsecrated funds are in the hands of evangelical Christians, particularly in the West. It is more a matter of vision, commitment, and deployment of these resources than of availability. In the above meaning the Great Commission of our Lord is fully possible of completion in Asia within this century.

Asia in Retrospect

To understand the complex continent of Asia, a brief look at her origins is helpful. Greater Asia stretches from the Red Sea to the Pacific, from the Arctic Ocean to the islands of the South Pacific, embracing almost 17 million square miles, one-third of the world's land area.

> The American geographer Carl Sauer believes the great cradle of civilization or heart was in southeast Asia. From there he traced the extension of agriculture westward through India into Europe and Africa, northeast into China and Japan, and southeast into Malaya and Indonesia.[27]

The geographical heart of Asia is the great Himalayan mountain triangle, which tapers down into great mountain spurs and plateau masses. To the southeast these run through eastern Burma and ultimately into the Malay peninsula, Thailand, and Vietnam. This rugged terrain has produced a geographical isolation which may explain why southeast Asia's populations have a history very different from those of China and India. South of the mountain heart lies the subcontinent of India and Pakistan. Westward the Himalayas merge with other great mountain chains and then diverge again, enclosing between them the lofty plateaus of Afghanistan, Iran, and Asia Minor. The fabled mountains of the Hindu Kush on the north pass through Iran down to Turkey.

Ethnologists point out that these great mountain ranges are not simply geographical boundaries; they constitute a transitional zone of cultural influence, bounded by deserts in the southwest and some of the world's wettest jungles on the south. Mongolian peoples dominate the center of the continent, including the mountain tribes of the Himalayas, the Burmans, Thais, Laotians, Malays, and the hundred other peoples of southeast Asia. The southern area seems originally to have been populated by darker skinned, kinky-haired peoples still found among jungle tribes in Sri Lanka, Malaya, and Indonesia. These were probably related to the Australian aborigines and the pre-Dravidians of southern India, but they have long been racially mixed with the Aryan and Indo-European peoples who overcame southwestern Asia and the Indian sub-continent millennia ago. Thus today no clear racial strains are evident in such areas as China. Asia as a whole is an ethnic polyglot with vast extremes of cultures, social patterns, and educational and economic rates of progress.[28]

The cultures and civilizations of Asia were early and great. Men of Mongoloid strain overflowed into southeast Asia, where they came into contact with the Australo-negroids who had migrated from the south via the Indonesian island chain. These "southern Mongoloids" created Indochina's first great civilization. Although art, languages, pottery, bronze crafts, and urban societies are well known to have flourished in China during the age of the patriarchs, long before this a Hoabinhian culture existed in Vietnam, which may have been the first in the world to make pottery and do bronze casting. These people ground and polished stones and planted rice possibly as early as 20,000 B.C., as revealed by recent excavations in the war-shattered city of Hoa Binh on the northern Vietnamese border.[29] However, the bronze culture came to flower much later, from the fourth century B.C., in the great kingdom of Funan, which reached its zenith in the first century A.D. and stretched from South Vietnam's Mekong delta to Bangkok and possibly even to the Malay peninsula. Funan was succeeded by the great Khmer civilization from the eighth to the fifteenth century. Later, when European conquerors invaded much of Asia in the early eighteenth century, only Thailand and Japan escaped colonization. As a result of these conflicting historical influences, Asia today (particularly southeast Asia) embraces numerous and varied ethnic enclaves, each with its own religious heritage and distinctive responses to the gospel.

Religion has always played a major role in the life of Asia. The Aryan invaders are believed to have brought Brahmanism to India three thousand years before the Christian era. This evolved into the present pantheistic Hinduism, which still dominates and blights the cultural and social life of India. It was in northern India also that the young Indian prince Gautama received enlightenment, became the Buddha, and founded a new world religion five centuries before Christ. Buddhism took deep root in and then was uprooted from India, but it flowered in Tibet to the north, Ceylon to the south, and Burma, Thailand, Japan, and Indonesia to the east. In China Buddhism encountered and often syncretized with the indigenous Confucianism, founded by the ethicopolitical philosopher Confucius, who was a virtual contemporary of the Buddha. In Japan both Buddhism and Confucianism synthesized with the indigenous nature religion of Shinto. In the seventh and eighth centuries Islam spread rapidly from the Middle East to central Asia and eventually dominated much of Indonesia, Malaya, and northern India, leading eventually to the creation of the basically religious state of Pakistan.[30]

Thus central and eastern Asia gave birth to Hinduism, Buddhism, Confucianism, and Japanese Shinto.§§ (Chapter 31, "Important Religions of Asia," helpfully summarizes more of the nature of these religions on the continent.)

Throughout Asia, but especially in the central and southeastern areas, these religions faced deeply rooted primitive animism among all of the tribal peoples. In nearly every case an indigenous syncretism of animism resulted: with Buddhism in Thailand, with Islam in Indonesia, with Hinduism in India, with Confucianism in rural China, etc. Unfortunately, this was often also the case with Christianity in areas where teaching was inadequate, notably in Indonesia and recently in New Guinea. Thus throughout Asia there are many strange religious amalgams and syncretisms.

If anything, the postwar period has accelerated religious syncretizing. "There is a religious resurgence among the living religions in Asia, often in close alliance with nationalism," Dr. Bong Ro observes from Singapore.[31] Japan affords many interesting examples. In the postwar period the nation has spawned more than a hundred so-called "new religions," most of which are offshoots of centuries-old Buddhist schools of thought (though some have Shinto origins). The largest of these is the well-known Sokka

§§The *Japan Christian Yearbook* for 1970 gives the general breakdown of religions in Asia as follows: Hinduism, 22.8%; various sects (Animism), 21.6%; Shinto, 3.6%; Islam, 19.2%; Christianity, 4.0%; Buddhism, 9.3%; Confucianism, 19.3%.

Gakkai, an interesting microcosm of how religion can be made to serve the nationalistic spirit, infusing thinly disguised nationalism with religious sanctions. Sokka Gakkai is probably representative also of a trend in these postwar syncretized religions to fuse cleverly religious ideas with completely this-worldly materialistic and hedonistic goals. In Sokka Gakkai, for example, there is no hamartiology, soteriology, or eschatology—no pie in the sky by and by. The Buddha for this age is a thirteenth-century Buddhist priest, Saint Nichiren, whose teachings are destined to rule the world (peacefully!) in this century. Simple, frequent repetition of the virtually untranslatable prayer, best rendered "Adoration to the lotus sutra," will bring wealth, happiness, marital harmony, and all desired blessings in this life. The superb organization of Sokka Gakkai ties all worship into religion in three ways: by neighborhood study groups, by age clubs, and by hobby interests. The underlying nationalistic motif became apparent ten years ago, when they began organizing a political assault against the nation and became its influential fourth party in the elections of 1970.

Some of Asia's revived older religions, as well as newer religions, are also a reaction against colonialism, again invoking religious sanctions for nationalistic purposes. Where Christianity has been strong (or become strong in the postwar years) these same patterns usually follow. Animism has syncretized with Catholicism in the Philippines, liberal Protestantism with leftist political groups in Japan and elsewhere, and nominal evangelical Protestantism with animism in Papua New Guinea, resulting in the unique "cargo cults."

That Communism itself is a de facto religion must be underlined from the postwar experience of Asia. First through compromise and then through outright murder, the church in China was weakened and totally suppressed. In recent years, however, there seems to be an underground resurgence which is being accelerated by revulsion against the Red Guard revolution of the late sixty's. Apparently Communism's obdurate rejection of religion has been aimed not only against the Christian church but also against other established religions, with only residual Confucianism having been sublimated into communist teachings, and that not without strong criticism. Though various unverifiable reports have filtered through from North Korea, the latest word (1974) from authoritative sources in this peninsula is that the encouraging political detente on the horizon of early 1973 has now evaporated. The church situation has been bad since the civil war. No pastors are known to be active, and what churches exist are probably underground. In North Vietnam the situation is reported to be somewhat better. Some Catholic churches are meeting regularly, and probably a few Protestant ones as well. But as a whole, Communism with its love for the common land, with its exaggerated hopes for the future, with its "worship of collective human power" (Toynbee) has become the religion of the expectant masses of much of Asia.|| ||

Asian Christian History

Central Asia was the scene of one of the first great missionary movements of Christian history. The ancient church of the East, or Syrian church (called mistakenly the Nestorians), may well have come to India at the latter part of the first century. At first I was skeptical of this tradition, rooted as it is in the Mar Thoma church of India, which claims its origin in the evangelistic work of the apostle Thomas himself. But a careful review of the historical evidence now inclines me to believe that it is at least 50 percent likely that the church of Christ was initially planted in India, Turkestan, Afghanistan, Mongolia, and probably Tibet within the first two centuries of the Christian era. There is good probability that the Mar Thoma church is the world's oldest living church. The Changan stone stele, which is clearly dated A.D. 781, evidences that the church was in China in the eighth century, though it was never influential there and probably was forced into extinction by the tenth century. Interestingly enough, possibly the oldest church in southeast and eastern Asia was not a Catholic one, but a tiny Protestant church established by Dutch missionaries in Molucca in the early sixteenth century. The incredible missionary endeavors of Saint Frances Xavier in the mid-sixteenth century resulted in the planting of the Catholic church by his hand in India, China, Japan, and Indonesia. His followers made the spread of Catholic Christianity more widespread than Protestantism in the early eras.

The great Protestant missionary invasion of Asia began around the beginning of the nineteenth century, with men like William Carey and Henry Martyn going to India and Robert Morrison to China. These men followed the great trade routes opened by the European colonial powers. Thus the church was first planted and growth seen in those major nations which attracted the colonial powers: India, China, Formosa, Indonesia, Singapore, Burma, etc. Many smaller Asian nations had little or no witness till the end of the nineteenth and beginning of the twentieth centuries. While it is common to curse European colonialism, the facts are that the church in Asia has been most firmly planted where the European nations ruled. A case in point: the Dutch gained a foothold in Taiwan in 1624 and sent their first missionary in May 1627. Within thirty-five years more than

|| ||Dr. Bong Ro comments that Asia today "can be divided into two sections: east of the Mekong River comprises those under Chinese influence and culture, the more intense people, those more likely to take to communism because it is a demanding taskmaster. West of the Mekong River are those influenced by the Hindu civilization" (*Theological News*, Oct. 1973).

a score of missionaries from the Reformed churches of Holland baptized more than fifty-nine hundred people and planted over seventy congregations. Many Christians were horribly slaughtered when the Chinese regained control of Taiwan in 1662.[32]

With the hindsight of currently popular (often exaggerated) nationalism, colonialism is condemned for much. A more cautious, objective reading of history is painfully needed. Colonialism contributed incalculably to the educational, economic, and medical development of many of the Asian countries. It is incontrovertible that colonialism, however it might be politically assessed, was an instrument in the hands of the sovereign God to open doors for the penetration of the gospel into these lands. Though more research is undoubtedly needed to assess the degree of interaction between colonial governments and foreign mission agencies, a study of the writings of William Carey, who inaugurated the "great century of missions," reveals his penetrating, objectively critical attitude toward colonial relations. And some of his writings on the importance of proper methods for establishing indigenous churches were radical for his day and relevant to ours. It is interesting that in Thailand and Japan, two great Asian nations which were not colonized, the church has had its smallest and weakest footholds until recent days.

Though he speaks primarily of China, Dr. Raymond Fung (a Chinese scholar) speaks cogently for all of Asia and its need for a balance on this subject:

> The missionary thrust of the West has long been under serious challenge, and for a whole variety of reasons. One of the most disturbing charges (for everyone concerned) is cultural imperialism—that Christianity has been introduced by Western missionaries at the inevitable expense of the indigenous cultures. . . . Throughout the twentieth century whatever the meaning of the missionary thrust in China, it was not cultural imperialism. . . . On the other hand, Western missionaries, whatever their racial outlook, often came to China with respect, if not deference. . . . [there is] the absence of cultural imperialism from the West. . . .[33]

Then, speaking of a possible future for missions in China, Fung enunciates some excellent principles which also have application to other lands:

> . . . The church in the West must not deny its missionary past in China. . . . The movement as such must be affirmed. . . . There is no demand from the Chinese that the West repudiate the missionary enterprise in China. . . . Among equals there is no place for bitterness. The missionary enterprise, with all its glory and stupidity, was a manifestation of belief in the oneness of God's people. So today we must affirm that particular manifestation in order to affirm that despite racial and ideological differences, Chinese Christians and Western Christians are one in Christ, in

order that a different form or manifestation for the future can be worked out.[34]

Recognizing this, veteran missionary Gordon Chapman, author of chapter 12 (on Japan) and chapter 31 (on Asia) contributes a significant observation on the passing of colonialism and the future ideological milieu in which evangelism must be done:

> . . . The most important development of modern times is the end of Western colonialism. This fact has profound significance for the missionary movement which penetrated Asia along with, and in some senses as a part of, the political, economic, and cultural impact of the Western nations on the Asian nations. Coincident with the resurgence of Asian nationalism is the emergence of what may be regarded as a common world culture, the mastery of which is identified with modernization. This single world culture, to which all Asian nations aspire, has its basis in science and technology as developed in the West, and facilitates the rapid urbanization of society, which is primarily dependent upon the modern means of communication and transport. This culture holds forth the hope that through rational planning, based on science and technology, adequate provision can be made for total human welfare. If it has a faith, it is that of humanistic scientism, with little or no regard for the great verities of the Christian faith, which furnished the milieu in which Western science developed. Japan (for example), though retaining much of her traditional cultural heritage, was the first Asian nation to master the emergent world culture and thereby achieve modernization and has become one of the three great industrial powers of the world. In fact, she may be regarded as the microcosmic model for the undeveloped nations of Asia to follow.[35]

Another erroneous judgment about the weaknesses or failures of early Asian missions should be avoided, I believe. There are those theorists with differing views of the evangelistic and so-called cultural mandates who assert that the course of Christian history and missionary penetration would have been greatly advanced by a broader view of the missionary mandate in earlier generations. These men allege that those visionary pioneers who laid the foundations of the church in Asia had a truncated, shortsighted ministry. Had they sought greater social and political involvement, the argument runs, the church would have been stronger and more indigenous today. History does not bear this out. By and large, the indigenous churches in Asia today with the greatest impact and success in evangelism, church-planting, and growth, as well as the strongest resistance to persecution, are those who have shunned overt political involvement and devoted their efforts to the spiritual nurture and extension of the body of Christ. They have rendered unto Caesar only that which was

Caesar's and rendered supremely unto God that worship and service that is his. In particular, Christian syncretists and men with a low view of Scripture are neither planting new churches nor nurturing growing churches in Asia today.

Returning briefly to the history of the Christian mission and church in Asia, it is well to note that the outwardly largest numerical growth during the nineteenth and early twentieth centuries was in the Catholic church. And this growth again was largely in the major nations of India, China, and the Philippines. Though seedplots were established, little growth was experienced in nations like Japan, Korea, present-day Pakistan, and other nations until the twentieth century's increased knowledge of the area and improved travel possibilities made Asia more readily accessible.## But the ancient mountain heart of the continent in the Himalayas remained firmly closed despite bold and sacrificial pioneering attempts by such intrepid evangelists as Sadhu Sundar Singh until recent postwar years. Little effective witness resulted from ventures like this in most cases, as the histories in the succeeding chapters will elucidate.

Conclusion

If the twentieth century can be called the "Christian century," it is because a mounting tide of interest vastly increased the breadth and depth of missionary and evangelistic work throughout the Asian continent, particularly in the post-World War II era. Organized churches of Jesus Christ have now been planted in all Asian nations except Mongolia and Afghanistan, as far as is humanly known. Tender young shoots of witness are spreading out from even the newest churches. With a few notable exceptions the church of Jesus Christ is growing throughout the continent and islands of Asia. People's movements in several nations have seen the churches there more than double in the last decade. Centuries-closed nations are now opening to the gospel. There is a new openness and response in Bangladesh and Cambodia since 1973, in Indonesia since 1968, in Korea since 1950, and in Japan since 1945. Even China may provide limited opportunities for evangelism soon.

The greatest days for Asian evangelism are still ahead, in the last quarter of this century. Asia may well be on the verge of a great spiritual awakening. "We are entering the greatest period of [Asian] evangelistic outreach in history. God is at work in an unprecedented manner," declares Philip Armstrong, general director of the Far Eastern Gospel Crusade. Though

##Following Frances Xavier's amazing two years of aggressive evangelism beginning in 1549, the Catholic church there burgeoned until membership may have reached two hundred thousand within 150 years. But vicious persecution exterminated the visible church for almost two hundred years, until the nation was opened to the West by Admiral Peary in 1859.

the huge, seething conglomerate of Asian subcontinents has until now never been adequately evangelized, for four hundred years missionaries have planted gospel seed and fertilized it with their blood and tears. Now the Holy Spirit is giving the firstfruits of harvest in many places. Japan's Akira Hatori declares, "Some of us have expectation and vision to see a third Pentecost, the Holy Spirit's explosion in Asia in a few years." The time of widespread reaping is just ahead. Favorable winds of opportunity are ripening some fields, while frosty winds of suffering are preparing still others to respond to God's love in Christ.

The greatest chapters of the Acts of the Holy Spirit for Asia will be written within the last twenty-five years of this century, I believe. Let national churches and foreign missions continue to believe, pray, and evangelize together, so that Asia will speak the praises of Christ from millions of throats when our Lord returns.

NOTES

1. Ralph Winter, "Seeing the Task Graphically," pp. 15-16.
2. "What Makes the Korean Church Grow?," *Christianity Today,* Nov. 23, 1973.
3. James Wong et al, *Missions from the Third World.*
4. Donald McGavran, *Understanding Church Growth,* p. 298. See also Samuel Moffett, "What Makes the Korean Church Grow?", p. 12.
5. Winter, "Seeing the Task," p. 15.
6. Peter Beyerhaus, "The Challenge of Bangkok," and Ralph Winter, *The Evangelical Response to Bangkok.*
7. "The United States Catholic Mission Council."
8. *World Population Sheet 1975.*
9. Ibid.
10. *Preliminary Report on the State of Food and Agriculture,* p. iii.
11. *Population Bulletin,* vol. 24, Dec. 1968, p. 83.
12. See the chilling report on "Malnutrition and Human Development," *Population Bulletin,* vol. 29, no. 1 (Washington: Pop. Ref. Bureau, 1973).
13. *Population Bulletin,* vol. 24, Dec. 1968, p. 95.
14. Ibid.
15. See article by Allan Berg in *Population Bulletin,* vol. 29, no. 1, 1973, p. 36.
16. Russel A. Cervin, "Focus on Asia," p. 3.
17. Ibid., p. 5.
18. Letter to the editor dated Nov. 1973.
19. James Wong, *Should We Plan for Church Growth Throughout Southeast Asia?"*
20. From letters to the editor received Oct.-Nov. 1973.
21. Ibid.
22. Virgil Gerber, *A Manual for Evangelism/Church Growth.*
23. Donald McGavran, "Address to the International Congress on World Evangelization."
24. Winter, "Seeing the Task," p. 17.
25. Cervin, p. 5.
26. Letter to the editor dated Nov. 1973.
27. "Asia," *Encyclopaedia International,* vol. 2, p. 93.
28. Ibid., pp. 89-99.
29. W. C. Solherm, "New Light on a Forgotten Past," pp. 330-339.
30. "Asia," *Encyclopaedia International,* vol. 2, p. 93.
31. *Theological News* (World Evangelical Fellowship, Oct. 1973).
32. William Campbell, *An Account of Missionary Success in the Island of Formosa,* pp. 3-203.
33. Raymond Fung, "Why Christian Mission Today," p. 17.
34. Ibid., p. 18.
35. See chapter 12, "Japan, A Brief Christian History."

BIBLIOGRAPHY

"Asia." In *Encyclopaedia International,* vol. 2.

Berg, Allan. Article in *Population Bulletin,* vol. 29, no. 1. Washington: Population Reference Bureau, 1973.

Beyerhaus, Peter. "The Challenge of Bangkok." Address following conference of Commission of World Missions and Evangelism of the World Council of Churches. Thailand, Jan. 1973.

Bowman, Robert. Letter to the editor, Nov. 1973.

Bradshaw, Malcolm. *Church Growth Through Evangelism in Depth.* Pasadena, 1969.

Campbell, William. *An Account of Missionary Success in the Island of Formosa.* London: Trüber & Co., 1889.

Cervin, Russel A. "Focus on Asia." In *The Covenant Companion,* Mar. 15, 1969.

Erlich, Paul. Article in *New Scientist,* Dec. 14, 1967.

Fung, Raymond. "Why Christian Mission Today." In *New World Outlook.* New York: United Methodist Church, June 1973.

Gerber, Virgil. *A Manual for Evangelism/Church Growth.* Pasadena: Wm. Carey Library, 1973.

Griffiths, Dr. Michael. Letter to the editor, Oct.-Nov. 1973.

Hatori, Dr. Akira. Letter to the editor, Oct.-Nov. 1973.

Japanese Christian Yearbook, 1970.

McGavran, Donald. "Address to the International Congress on World Evangelization." Lausanne, Switzerland, July 1974.

———. *Church Growth Bulletin,* Mar. 1974.

———. Personal letter to the editor, Feb. 1974.

———. *Understanding Church Growth.* Grand Rapids: Eerdmans, 1970.

Moffett, Samuel. "What Makes the Korean Church Grow?" In *Christianity Today,* Nov. 23, 1973.

Mooneyham, Dr. Stanley. Letters to the editor, Oct.-Nov. 1973.

Preliminary Report on the State of Food and Agriculture. Food and Agriculture Organization of the United Nations, Sept. 1973.

Ro, Dr. Bong. *Theological News.* World Evangelical Fellowship, Oct. 1973.

Solherm, W. C. "New Light on a Forgotten Past." In *National Geographic,* vol. 139, no. 3, Mar. 1971.

Teng, Philip. Letter to the editor, May 1972.

'The United States Catholic Mission Council." In *Mission Intra,* vol. 26, June-July 1973.

Winter, Ralph. *The Evangelical Response to Bangkok.* Pasadena: Wm. Carey Library, 1973.

———. "Seeing the Task Graphically." In *Evangelical Missions Quarterly,* Jan. 1974.

Wong, James et al. *Missions from the Third World.* Singapore: Church Growth Study Centre, 1973.

Wong, James. *Should We Plan for Church Growth Throughout Southeast Asia?* Pasadena: Fuller School of World Mission, 1971.

World Population Sheet 1973. Washington: Population Reference Bureau.

Kabul has been rapidly modernized since World War II.

The Community Christian Church was bulldozed to the ground by the government in 1973 but was being reconstructed in 1975.

In the country millennia-old lifestyles continue.

Photos by Saltan Hamid

2

AFGHANISTAN

Anonymous

The Church Today

Afghanistan, a little-known Moslem mountain kingdom beyond the Khyber Pass in the Himalayas, was just opening to the hearing of the gospel in the early 1970's when tragedy struck. After more than a millennium of obdurate resistance to Christianity, the first Protestant church ever to be constructed in the country was dedicated in 1970. But on June 13, 1973, government authorities took possession of the beautiful building, which had been erected with gifts from Christians around the world. On July 16 government workmen finished bulldozing it to the ground.

Almost simultaneously over a dozen missionaries working with the International Afghan Mission were ordered to leave the country. The only two institutes for the blind in the country, both operated by the International Afghan Mission, were closed. More than forty doctors and nurses working with the National Organization of Ophthalmic Rehabilitation, both in the capital city of Kabul and in the regional clinics, were given 120 days to get out by October 21.

But God's providences may be at work. The night after the church's demolition a coup deposed King Mohammed Zahir Shah. A republic was proclaimed, a dramatic change from the 226 years of monarchy. Though it is too early to predict the ultimate attitude of the new government, it is reported that it has expressed sorrow and sympathy concerning the action of the former regime in destroying the church. The government attitude has been more sympathetic to the Christian workers and has overruled the order for the doctors and nurses working with the eye program to leave the country.

This new and more favorable attitude may have been prompted in part by a widely publicized statement sent to the previous king by several prominent Christian leaders (headed by Dr. Billy Graham) which protested the destruction of the church. In addition, thousands of letters decrying this action poured into the capital and the Afghan Embassy in the U. S. Since the course of the new republican government is still uncertain, its ultimate attitude toward the Christian church and workers is still problematical. Because Afghanistan is a Muslim nation, great liberty is not expected. Yet the seeming tragedy of the church's demolition may well force a greater openness as world public opinion has been brought to bear on the nation's bigotry. Christians within and without the country prayerfully wait to see. But meanwhile medical and social work is quietly, if limitedly, continuing.

No indigenous Christian church has existed in Afghanistan in this century, and its eighteen million people may therefore constitute the largest unevangelized nation in the world. (Remember that China was extensively evangelized until 1949). Until World War II, a sign on the borders of the country warned, "No one is allowed to go past this point without special permission of the Amir (king) of the country." Only a few Christians were allowed to visit and then only for short periods as travelers, diplomats, doctors, and businessmen. But with the partition of India and Pakistan in 1947, the country was freed to develop independently. No longer was there a need for a buffer between the British Empire and Russia. To hasten progress, the government invited teachers into the country, and Dr. Frank Laubach was asked to bring a team for an adult literacy project in March 1951. At that time UNESCO estimated that 97 per cent of Afghanistan's people were illiterate.

Soon Christian "tentmakers" entered the country to fill regular positions as teachers, workers with the United Nations projects, representatives of various diplomatic missions, and engineers. These were first allowed to establish a simple Christian fellowship, and services were at first held in private homes and in various embassies under the leadership of Dr. J. Christy Wilson, Jr., chaplain to the international community and son of Persian Presbyterian missionaries. As the international community grew, there was a need for Sunday school classes and vacation Bible schools for the children from several countries. Thus the Community Christian Church was established in December 1952 to meet this need of instruction and worship. Today small foreign congregations also meet in various parts of the country where people from other nations are serving.

Not only did these Christians feel it necessary to worship regularly, but they also wanted to help the people in practical ways. Under the direction of a Chinese Christian agriculturalist, rainbow trout eggs were flown into the country from the United States and Japan, and were cultivated and introduced as fingerlings into various lakes, rivers, and streams. The king was out fishing with one of his sons one day when the prince hooked one of these trout. It fought so hard and tasted so good that His majesty ordered the ministry of agriculture to expand the project to include fish hatcheries, which are now stocking the streams and lakes of all the country.

Since Afghanistan is mainly an agricultural land, the king requested that Long Island ducks also be imported. Four dozen fertile eggs were ordered by Christians in the summer of 1957. Since it took eighteen days to fly them from the United States to Afghanistan, it was feared that none would survive. But Christians prayed that God would enable one pair at least to live, and three ducks hatched, one female and two drakes. Taken to the king's farm, the lone female laid over eighty eggs the first season. Now these ducks are raised all over the country (largely in irrigation ditches) and provide not only food but feathers for warm clothing and quilts. But the greatest benefit from the ducks has come to Afghanistan's major industry—sheep raising for wool, carpets, karakul lamb skins, meat, and casings. Many of the sheep had long been infected with a liver fluke disease transmitted through snails. But the ducks are eating the snails, cutting the life cycle of the parasites, and thereby helping to limit this disease among the sheep.

In 1966 the International Afghan Mission was officially established. (The name of this fellowship was chosen for its abbreviation, IAM, after our Lord's title of the great "I Am.") Its purpose is to "minister to the people of Afghanistan mainly through medical and educational projects." The mission formally organized and expanded several desperately needed medical and social ministries. It quietly attracted talented workers from many nationalities and individuals long burdened for the distant mountain kingdom. The IAM was established simply, along the lines of a similar organization for united evangelical work in Nepal. At present many organizations send assistance and personnel for cooperative work with the IAM: the Afghan Border Crusade; the Assemblies of God in Britain, Ireland, and the U.S.A.; the Bible and Medical Missionary Fellowship (Australia, Canada, India, New Zealand, U.K., and U.S.A.); the Brethren (Germany and New Zealand); the Central Asian Mission (U.K.); the Christoffel-Blinden Mission in Orient (Germany); the Church Missionary Society (Australia and U.K.); the Danish Pathan Mission (Denmark); Dienste in Ubersee (Germany); the Finnish Lutheran Mission (Finland); the Indian Evangelical Mission (India); the Kabul Community Christian Church, Inc. (U.S.A.); Laubach Literacy, Inc. (U.S.A.); the Medical Assistance Programs, Inc. (U.S.A.); the Mennonite Brethren churches (U.S.A.); the Missionary Aviation Fellowship (U.S.A.); the Presbyterian Church of Canada; the Evangelical Alliance Mission (U.S.A.); the United Methodist Church (U.S.A.); the United Presbyterian Church in the USA; and the World Mission Prayer League (U.S.A.). The number of full-time

Christian workers in the country has increased to more than a hundred, from eleven different countries; eight years ago there was only one worker.

After work for the handicapped had been initiated, the new mission enabled it to expand. A Christian visitor found a small blind boy on the street, and with him blind work began in the country. Before the government closed the school in 1973, there were sixty-five blind students in the institute in Kabul, and a similar work had been started in Herat in the western part of the country with twenty more. It was reported that after the institutes were closed some of the blind students were back in the street begging. Besides rehabilitation of the blind, medical care for eye diseases was inaugurated. These two ministries were formally recognized by the government in 1966 under a protocol agreement with the National Organization for Ophthalmic Rehabilitation (NOOR) of the International Afghan Mission. (The Afghan word *noor* means "light.") Christian eye doctors and nurses from many lands have come to assist this greatly needed ministry; in 1973 an eye hospital was opened in the capital, and teams now travel around the country doing operations in various areas. Thousands of cataracts have been removed, and corneal transplants are performed with eyes that have been donated and flown to Afghanistan from England. These works are now continuing with permission from the new government.

Another related medical ministry has opened up through the medical assistance program of the International Afghan Mission, working in outlying areas of the country. Starting with a mobile unit which traveled to various parts of the nation, treating patients and surveying the prevalent diseases, doctors found a high incidence of untreated leprosy in the central part of the country. The Afghan government therefore asked the medical program to staff, equip, and run a small hospital in Nyak in the central mountainous Hazarajat region. Satellite clinics are also being established in points around this area, and at present hundreds of patients with leprosy are being treated on a clinical basis. Already twenty thousand clinic visits have been recorded and two thousand operations performed. Since the region is isolated by snows in the high passes during the winter, contact with the clinics and workers is kept up by radio, and a Missionary Aviation Fellowship pilot and plane, equipped with skis to land on the snow, is greatly expanding the medical ministry in these isolated areas.

For children of the international community in Afghanistan, a Christian school, Ahlman Academy, was established in 1957. Now to a great extent self-supporting and staffed by dedicated teachers, the academy enrolls over twenty nationalities, including children from Communist countries. The Bible is taught in every grade, and classes are opened with prayer.

Like Switzerland, Afghanistan uses the languages of the surrounding areas, and thus the Scriptures are already available in the two main tongues of Pushto and Persian. But these need revision to adapt them to the local dialects. In addition the Uzbeks, Turkomans, Kazakis, and Kirghizis in the northern part of the country speak dialects of Turkish, and there are many other languages spoken by smaller groups which have not as yet been reduced to writing. So far gospel recordings have been made in fifty-one languages spoken in the country, twenty-six of which are spoken in the valleys of Nooristan in the eastern section of the land.

Challenges and Opportunities

An illiteracy rate of 95 percent is still a great problem in Afghanistan. Personnel are needed to teach teachers and prepare reading materials as well as to propagate widespread medical programs and schools for the blind.

Another opportunity for Christian service has been the provision of gifts of clothing for the poor. Beggars in Kabul are taken by the municipality to a poor farm to work. The church has purchased and collected clothing from the international community and distributed it to these and other indigent groups. In a recent famine caused by a two-year drought in the central highlands, World Vision assisted through the local church in feeding and clothing hungry children and mothers. The Red Crescent Society (the Muslim counterpart of the Red Cross) has also assisted in relief operations.

Afghanistan first opened to tourism in 1959, and there were only 453 visitors that year. However, since then the number has increased to over a hundred thousand annually. Because such drugs as hashish and opium derivatives are readily available, a large influx of hippies has entered in recent years. In 1970 "Youth with a Mission" started a ministry to these needy young people which has resulted in wonderful conversions. A hostel for these youth, Dilaram (meaning "heart peace"), was begun. Hundreds of hippies from all over the world, mostly drug addicts, have passed through there. Scores have come to Christ. Beginning in the summer of 1970, Christian young people from the West have come to Afghanistan to assist in this ministry to international wandering youth. From this work similar centers have now been started along the "hippie trail" from Amsterdam to Kathmandu.

More and more, Afghans traveling abroad as students, businessmen, diplomats, and tourists afford a great opportunity for evangelism outside the limiting context of their own country. But the law of apostasy in Islam is still the law in Afghanistan: if a Muslim changes his faith, he could be killed. Even when an Afghan receives Christ while abroad he faces persecution upon his return. Several Afghans who have received Jesus Christ as their Saviour have already given their lives for their faith.

Though long isolated from the rest of the world, Afghanistan is finally opening up more and more to the outside world. The recent political upheaval may hasten this and relax pressure against the Christian faith. There are already opportunities for Christian service and witness among various assistance programs run by the United Nations, the British Council, the Peace Corps, USAID, and Voluntary Service Overseas. There are also openings in various embassies and international businesses. Furthermore, Christian students can enroll in the University of Kabul or engage in research programs in the country, while offering a witness to their faith. Afghanistan doors may yet swing wide open, and the IAM and its associates seek others to be ready to enter with them.

Nation and People

Long shrouded in mystery because of its inaccessible location beyond the Khyber Pass in the heart of central Asia, Afghanistan has had a violent, colorful history. Little is known of the tribes that roamed the high mountains and valleys there until the Persian empire annexed the area in the sixth century B.C. But then it began to change under the hands of successive conquerors, beginning with Alexander the Great in 330 B.C. Central Asian tribes overran the kingdom four hundred years later; then Persia, India, and Parthia vied over parts of it for seven hundred years, until the Arabs conquered the northern and western areas early in the seventh century A.D. Persians, Hindu Indians, and Turks successively battled over the country till the Mongol hordes of Genghis Khan swept Afghanistan into his empire about A.D. 1220, where it remain until the 1700's.

The Persians retook the nation in 1729, until the Afghan tribes revolted twenty years later and briefly established local rule. Then, when Britain and Russia began expansion in Asia, Afghanistan became a "no-man's-land" between the expanding Russian domains to the north and the British Indian empire to the south. Missionaries and others were not permitted to enter, nor were settled Afghans allowed out of the country; the only ones who could come and go were the nomads on their annual migrations with flocks and camels. As a buffer state, Afghanistan was given the long Wakhan corridor, the ancient caravan route to China which Marco Polo used as a silk route in the thirteenth century. Along this mountain route roam the prized, rare Marco Polo sheep (*Ovis Poli*), whose horns sometimes measure over six feet around the curve on each side. (The area has only recently been opened to hunters, who pay up to six thousand dollars to shoot one of these prized big-game animals.)

Early in the 1920's Britain relinquished the vestiges of its colonial rule, and Afghanistan became a full constitutional monarchy in 1923. Neutral during World War II, and holding to a precarious neutrality between the U.S. and Russia even now, Afghanistan became a UN member in 1946 and has struggled to modernize with liberal grants and loans from both Russia and the U.S. The compulsory military service involves many of the soldiers in development projects, such as road building, agriculture, and reforestation.

In recent years the government has become more largely representative under a new constitution. Women were allowed to remove their veils in 1959, and many of them are taking positions in government offices, educational institutions, and businesses.

However, this government was overthrown suddenly on July 16, 1973, and the church was destroyed on this night. Prince Daoud, a cousin of the king and a former prime minister (1953-63), seized control of the government in a midnight coup, deposed the king, and declared the nation a republic. What this means for the Christians and their work is still uncertain.

Neither rich nor poor in resources, Afghanistan is about the size of France or Texas, but only a small part of the land is being farmed because of the low rainfall. The high Hindu Kush range covers three-fourths of the country and tapers down into two deserts in the southwest. The vast majority of Afghanistan's eighteen million people are farmers and nomadic herdsmen, compounding the education and literacy problems.

National Religions

The prophet Zoroaster was born in Balkh, in the northern part of Afghanistan, in the sixth century B.C., and his dualistic religion of "light and darkness" spread throughout Persia from this area in the pre-Christian era. (For a more complete description of religions in Afghanistan, see chapter 28, "Important Religions of Asia.") The local name for the sunflower reflects the Zoroastrian heritage in that it is called the *aftau parast* or "sun-worshipper." But this religion never fully captured the loyalty of the Afghan people, and today only about a hundred thousand Zoroastrians remain in all of Asia, centered mainly in Iran around Teheran and in India around Bombay.

Buddhism soon supplanted Zoroastrianism and became the dominant religion, being memorialized by the giant statues of Buddha in the cliffs of the Bamian valley of central Afghanistan. The largest of these statues is 170 feet high, taller than Niagara Falls. Thousands of Buddhist caves are nearby, and remains of ancient *stupas* still dot many parts of the country.

Buddhism in turn gave way to the Muslim conquest of the country, which was accomplished in stages during the seventh and eighth centuries A.D. Most of the population became followers of the Sunni or orthodox branch of Islam, though there has always been a large minority of the Shiah sect. There are also quite a few Ismailis or followers of the Agha Khan in the country, along with small minority groups of the Hindus, Sikhs, and Jews. Thus the reign of Islamic religion and culture has continued virtually unchallenged to the present. Even now Islamic law forms the basis of the civil laws of the state.

Christian History

Remote Afghanistan has not always been without an indigenous Christian presence and witness. Though few details are known, during the expansion of so-called "Nestorian Christianity" to this part of central Asia in the fifth century A.D., churches were founded in Afghanistan and a bishop was located in Herat in the northwest (see chapter 7, "Christianity Comes to Asia"). One suburb of Herat is still called *Ingil* or "Gospel." These ministers and missionaries of the Church of the East were required to memorize the whole New Testament and Psalms as part of their training, resulting in a zeal and evangelistic passion which carried them far across Asia.

But the Syriac Bible text became a dead language and was not retranslated into the vernacular of the people. The churches became liturgical, lost their spiritual fervor, and were soon wiped out by the advancing Muslims. Yet even today Nestorian crosses are reproduced in Afghan carpets as a silent witness to the former Christian presence in this area, even though the craftsmen who weave them are unaware of their significance and merely copy them as designs which have been handed down over the centuries.

A small church reappeared in the capital of Kabul in the nineteenth century and ministered to a refugee Armenian community. But, tragically, British military forces destroyed this group in 1896, and its adherents were exiled shortly thereafter. Then for a time there were no known Christians in Afghanistan.

Yet Christian missions have been working on the borders for over a hundred years, and much prayer has been offered for the land. With the urge to modernize, the government has allowed many young people to study overseas, where some have come in contact with the gospel. The Christian presence is quietly serving as salt and light as it awaits a divine opportunity to extend its service. God's hour for Afghanistan may soon strike.

BIBLIOGRAPHY

Clifford, Mary Louise. *The Land and People of Afghanistan.* Philadelphia: Lippincott, 1962.

Fletcher, Arnold. *Afghanistan: Highway of Conquest.* Cornell, 1965.

Jones, Paul F. *Afghanistan Venture.* San Antonio: Baylor Co., 1956.

Thomas, Lowell. *Beyond Khyber Pass.* New York: Century, 1925.

Toynbee, Arnold J. *Between Oxus and Jumma.* London: Oxford University Press, 1961.

Wilber, Donald Newton. *Afghanistan: Its People, Its Society, Its Culture.* New Haven: HRAF Press, 1962.

Open market in Dacca, East Pakistan.

Photos courtesy Medical Assistance Program

Houseboats used for fishing and living.

3

BANGLADESH

by Warren Webster

Introduction

While Bangladesh ranks eighth in world population (75 million), the nation has far fewer Christians than any of the world's other ten most populous countries. The total Christianity community is estimated at 245,000, which is only *one-third of one percent* of the total population. Roman Catholics account for approximately 135,000, with the Protestant Christian community comprising the other 110,000.

Several reasons may be adduced for the very slow growth of Christianity in the area that is now Bangladesh. First is the resistance to the gospel of Asia's ethnic religions. Islam and Hinduism are deeply rooted in the history and soil of Bangladesh and claims at least nominal loyalty of 99 percent of the people. While it is not impossible to communicate the gospel to the followers of these faiths, they have historically been among the least responsive, especially when they have identified Christianity with Western ideologies or cultural imperialism. Secondly, the very resistance and apparent indifference of Muslims and Hindus to the Christian message led early missionaries in India to concentrate on education at the expense of evangelism. In time education frequently became a substitute for evangelism. The degree to which education was emphasized by early missionaries in Bengal is indicated by the report that 80 percent of the Christians in Bangladesh are literate, compared to the national average of about 23 percent. But however desirable the benefits of education may be, education as an evangelistic tool has not proved particularly effective there. Absent in Bangladesh has been the emergence of any "people's movement" to Christianity of the size and scope found in parts of India and Pakistan. Where such movements have begun, they have primarily

For information on author, see chapter 22, "Pakistan."

been among the tribal peoples, leaving the Bengali majority largely uninfluenced. (There was a small Christian movement among Bengalis in the nineteenth century.)

A third factor impeding the growth of Christianity in what is now Bangladesh has been that of neglect. The problems of resistance and unresponsiveness, coupled with an enervating and debilitating climate, have discouraged many missionaries from continuing—or even beginning—persistent efforts for the evangelization of the Bengali people. When Pakistan was formed in 1947, several hundred additional missionaries began to serve in that new Muslim country, but the eastern wing (now Bangladesh), with more than half the country's population, received only about one-third as many missionaries as the western province. Today in Bangladesh the established churches are assisted and augmented by the labors of only 260 Roman Catholic and 190 Protestant missionaries—less than half the numbers working in Pakistan. The ratio of Protestant missionaries to the population—approximately 1 to 375,000—is the lowest in any major country open to Christian missions.

The Church Today

EVANGELISM

Many established churches and missions in recent years have been concentrating more resources on the welfare of the Christian and non-Christian communities than on any direct evangelistic mission to the large Muslim and Hindu blocs. It is not perhaps surprising, then, that in one ten-year period during which only fifty converts from Islam to Christianity were reported, at least twice that many nominal Christians embraced Islam for marriage or other reasons. The climate for evangelism has recently improved, however. One factor is the new secular constitution of the government, which guarantees religious freedom to all faiths without supposedly favoring any. The turmoil of the conflict with Pakistan (when Muslim attacked Muslim) and the resulting independence, coupled with recent events in the Middle East, have produced a greater interest and openness in wanting to know what Christianity and the Bible have to say about times like these. While overt Muslim conversions are still not frequent, the demand for Bengali Bibles and Scripture portions has skyrocketed since 1971, so that now the Bible Society has trouble keeping them in stock.

Far more Christians have come from the sizable Hindu minority than from Islam, but the rate and number of Hindu conversions had dwindled to very few prior to the recent civil disturbances. The testimony of Christian concern and sharing which was witnessed at the time of the civil war, with its bitter hatred and communal killings, is moving a growing number of Hindus to consider the Christian faith and to request Christian teaching once again.

Though the non-Bengali tribal peoples with animistic backgrounds—Garos, Santalis, Khasis, Lushais, Tipperas, Bawns, and others—comprise only about 1 percent of the country's total population, they have in the past been relatively more responsive to the Christian faith than the Bengali-speaking majority and so constitute a large and growing segment of the Christian community. Many of them living in border areas frequently migrate back and forth to India or Burma. During the months of internal struggle in 1971 approximately half of the Christian community fled to India, especially from among the Garos living on the far northern border. When they returned, they found many of their homes and churches destroyed. Considerable assistance has been provided for the relief and rehabilitation of these segments of the Christian community, among whom the faith continues to grow.

Christians have not been particularly active in evangelizing the Buddhist minority (less than 1 percent), but some conversions have been recently reported both in urban centers and among tribal peoples near the Burma border. The six hundred thousand or more Urdu-speaking Biharis have likewise remained largely unevangelized.

In seeking to evangelize the large Bengali-speaking Muslim and Hindu populations, one of the methods most used in recent years has been Bible correspondence ministries. The Seventh-Day Adventists pioneered this field with their "Voice of Prophecy" courses, but a broad-based evangelical correspondence school ministry commenced in 1960, when the International Christian Fellowship established the East Pakistan (now Bangladesh) Bible Correspondence School as a service to all interested churches and missions. As the work has grown it has decentralized out of Dacca; it now has five branch centers maintained by missionaries and nationals working in those areas. Since 1960 more than fifty thousand students have enrolled, approximately half Muslims and half Hindus. Since independence in 1971, average enrollments have doubled, reflecting new freedom and a new spirit of inquiry.

In addition to BBCS there is a series of Emmaus Bible School correspondence courses operated by the Brethren and the recently inaugurated International Correspondence Institute of the Assemblies of God. By means of student camps and follow-up meetings, efforts are being made to lead inquiring students to decisions for Christ and into the fellowship of new or established churches. While Bible correspondence schools are generally regarded as the prime evangelistic tool in Bangladesh, such courses are limited in effectiveness to the one-fourth or less of the people who are literate, and other means need to be found to make disciples and establish growing churches among the 75 to 80 percent who cannot read.

CHRISTIAN LITERATURE

An unprecedented interest in reading among the literate masses is reflected in the growing demand for Bibles and Christian books. In 1973 the Christian Literature Center, specializing in quality literature for both Christian and non-Christian readers, published a record million pieces of literature and then doubled that in 1974. Their book club, tract club, and periodicals are all increasing in circulation. Many other groups are also involved in the production of evangelistic tracts, Sunday school materials, and Christian books. An equally active, highly productive Christian Literature Center has been established more recently by A.B.W.E. workers in Chittagong.

The Bangladesh Bible Society reports a nearly tenfold increase in annual Scripture distribution—from less than a hundred thousand copies in 1971 to nearly a million by 1974. This phenomenal growth parallels the progress of the Bible correspondence school movement and has been further stimulated by aggressive distribution spear-headed by literature teams from Operation Mobilization. When the OM ship "Logos" made port visits, large book exhibitions were held, and national teams were mobilized and trained for mass literature distribution campaigns throughout the country. This ministry is being continued by teams of young Bengali Christian workers. To communicate Christian truth even more effectively, several Bible translations and revision projects are underway. Since the vocabulary of the standard Bengali Bible is somewhat archaic and difficult for the common reader, two modern language Bengali translations are being prepared by the Association of Baptists for Word Evangelism to be distributed by the Bangladesh Bible Society. The first translation, especially suited to the minority groups (Christians, Hindus, Buddhists) is in the common language standard Bengali. The common language Muslim Bengali translation is in the heart language of the nation's 85 percent Muslim majority. The translators produced the first Muslim Bengali pocket dictionary as a necessary precursor to the translation.

Additional Scripture translations are in process in the languages of several tribal groups, where considerable numbers have become Christians (for example, the Bawm people).

CHRISTIAN EDUCATION

Church and mission societies have been engaged for more than 150 years in educational programs, which have helped to spearhead government movements toward public education. Today, of some 32,000 elementary and high schools in Bangladesh, fewer than 500 are church or mission sponsored. In the past, Christian schools have contributed significantly to the training of Christian leaders while also educating Muslim and Hindu students for their roles in community development. Apart from Roman Catholics, Christians in Bangladesh have not played a very significant part in the development of higher education. Among 170 colleges and technical schools scattered throughout the country there is no Protestant Christian college and only one small technical school.

Of even greater significance is the fact that after 175 years of missionary activity there is not a single Protestant seminary or major Bible training institute in this country of 75 million people. Among tribal churches the Garo Baptist Union maintains a small Bible school, and for Santali and Tippera believers short-term Bible institutes are held. But those desiring formal training for leadership in Bengali-speaking churches have had to go to England, India, Pakistan, or other centers in Asia for further preparation. Is this a cause or a result of the church's slow growth in Bangladesh? There appears to be some question. Sensing the need for more and better-trained Christian leaders, ten mission bodies in 1968 began to coöperate in setting up a type of theological education by extension. Because of a lack of adequate textbooks in Bengali and a shortage of both writers and funds, the resulting non-residential College of Christian Theology of Bangladesh has not been as effective as had been hoped. Other attempts are being made to advance the cause of biblical and theological education, which is a high-priority need for the future growth of churches in Bangladesh.

CHRISTIAN SOCIAL ACTION

Early in the history of missions to India the quality of Christian caring and sharing was demonstrated in ministries of healing and many other ways. The missionary doctors and nurses who pioneered in setting up hospitals, maternity clinics, orphanages, trade schools, and model villages only began to scratch the surface of the total human needs around them. But they pointed the way in the right direction. Now as government after government has risen to the challenge of providing general medical attention and basic human welfare, Christians have been progressively freed to focus their resources on other means of communicating the truth in Christ. Nevertheless, they continue to minister in his name when catastrophes, poverty, and endemic disease overload the facilities which the government is able to provide. In Bangladesh Protestant and Catholic organizations maintain a score of hospitals and dispensaries, most of which are of long-standing operation. Several of the hospitals contribute to national development through nurses' training programs. Most have been actively involved in setting up relief and rehabilitation programs for the recurrent disasters which have struck the country.

The massive cyclone which struck the southern coastal regions of Bangladesh in November 1970, claiming more than 250,000 lives in one fateful night, has been called the worst natural catastrophe of the twentieth century. Before the country had a chance to fully recover from the cyclone, the civil strife and fighting between East and West Pakistan, which continued from March to December 1971, resulted in an even greater loss of life and property than from the preceding natural disaster. In both of these situations Christians were quick to respond with sympathy and assistance. Missions, voluntary agencies, and Christian governments supplied millions of dollars of relief goods and personnel to assist with rehabilitation. Christian students from America went in groups to rebuild homes that had been destroyed. These acts of mercy did not go unnoticed by the government of Bangladesh or unappreciated by the people who saw Christian concern at work.

Across the border, in India, some 10 million East Pakistani (Bangladesh) refugees (three-fourths of them Hindus) fled during the civil disturbances of 1971. They, too, saw faith at work as Christians stood neutrally between Muslims and Hindus, selflessly and heroically administering food, medicine, inoculations, and other forms of assistance without partiality. After Bangladesh won its independence, most of these refugees returned home, where they were again aided in getting settled. They did not soon forget either the assistance which was given or the spirit with which it was done. While in most cases there was no particular spiritual or evangelistic ministry connected with these expressions of Christian compassion, within months reports came from districts in Bangladesh in which Bengali Hindus and Santali tribesmen who had returned from India were requesting Christian teaching and Christian baptism by the thousands. Nor was the impact of recent events totally lost upon Bengali Muslims. In one district of Bangladesh, leaders of twenty-five Muslim families came in an almost unprecedented move to request Christian teaching. One of the leaders told the missionary, "All the people in Bangladesh are going to become Christian, so it is wise for us to be among the first."

While one might not subscribe to the easy optimism of that leader, there are reasons to believe that the best days for the expansion of biblical Christianity in Bangladesh lie in the future. Because Bangladesh is located next to Assam, which has the highest concentration of Christians in Asia, and because Bangladesh bears similarities to the Muslim-majority nation of Indonesia, where God has been pleased in recent years to bring Christian triumph out of national crises, the day for Christ to be more widely known, loved, and obeyed across Bangladesh may be just ahead. There is a new spirit of evangelism and of evangelical cooperation, which bodes well for the future. Much will depend on what Christians do with today's opportunities. More career missionaries are urgently needed. Short-term missionaries and teams can have a fruitful ministry of social action combined with evangelism. Suffering Bangladesh is one of Asia's greatest present-day opportunities. But it may be short-lived unless the present open doors and interest are developed.

Nation and People

Bangladesh is the youngest politically independent nation in Asia. What was known until 1947 as eastern Bengal in British India became East Pakistan for nearly twenty-five years, until its independence in 1971, when the present name was adopted, which means "the Bengal nation." The country faces the Bay of Bengal and is almost entirely surrounded on the other three sides by 1;500 miles of common borders with India. On the southeast it shares 120 miles of frontiers with Burma. Small in area—about the size of the American state of Wisconsin, which has 5 million people—Bangladesh has 75 million citizens and an annual growth rate of 3 percent. It ranks as the world's eighth most populous nation (just after Brazil) and is situated in one of the most densely inhabited spots on the globe (its population density is 1360 per square mile—almost double that of Japan).

The major areas of the country are alluvial plains formed by numerous branches and tributaries of five river systems, including the Ganges, Brahmaputra, and Meghna rivers; most of the land is less than fifty feet above sea level. Situated in a cyclone belt, Bangladesh is ravaged by tropical hurricanes from the Bay of Bengal with devastating regularity. In November, 1970, for example, a typhoon and accompanying tidal wave killed over 250,000 persons. Bangladesh also has one of the highest annual rainfalls in the world, averaging 85 inches nationwide. As much as 250 inches of rain per year may fall in the northeastern regions. Two-thirds of the rain comes in the tropical monsoon season, from June to September. The combination of heavy rainfall on low-lying plains makes devastating floods a frequent occurrence. In August 1974 some four hundred thousand homes were destroyed and 30 million people dislocated in one of the most serious floods of the century.

Since the country is largely a deltaic plain without mountains, there is a shortage of indigenous stone and cement for road building. The vast networks of rivers and rivulets necessitates scores of expensive culverts and bridges for every mile of road, so transportation by riverboat is both cheaper and easier. A great many people are employed in making, repairing, and operating boats of every type, from dugouts to river steamers.

Bangladesh has some 5000 miles of waterways, compared with only 3600 miles of paved roads and 1800 miles of railroad track.

In this tropical climate heavy monsoon rains, high humidity, and fertile soil combine to cover the country with lush, green vegetation. Mango, banana, coconut, date, betelnut, and various palm trees, as well as bamboo, grow in great profusion. The forests contain an abundance of wildlife, including big game. Hunters track the Bengal tiger, swamp crocodiles, leopards, deer, monkeys, and pythons and also find elephant herds roaming the hill tracts. Rice and fish are the staple foods. Nearly every village has a number of ponds in which fish are bred, and river and deep-sea fishing provide a livelihood for many other people.

Of Bangladesh's 75 million people, 98 percent are ethnically Bengalis and speak Bengali, the official language. About 1 percent are Urdu-speaking Muslim immigrants from India, known generally as Biharis. The remainder include about a million tribal peoples of Tibeto-Burman extraction. The literacy rate of 23 percent in Bangladesh is somewhat higher than in Pakistan (17 percent), suggesting a slight advantage for literacy education in a country where people speak one language and live close together. The per capita income of under $80 a year is somewhat less than for either India or Pakistan ($100-110). In an era of growing urbanization it is surprising to note that only 5 percent of the people in Bangladesh are urban dwellers (compared with 20 to 25 percent in India and Pakistan). While the trek from the villages to the cities is just beginning, the contact with the cities has already begun to transform the villages. The cities, in turn, are becoming a melting pot for influences from the countryside and abroad.

Religiously, about 85 percent of the people are Muslims, making Bangladesh the world's most populous Muslim country (after Indonesia). About 14 percent (10 million) are Hindus. The remainder are Buddhists (370,000), Christians (245,000), and animists. But Bangladesh is experiencing an explosion of expectations, spiritually as well as materially. People are not content with the traditional life of the past. They want to share in the good things which they hear about or see other people possess.

National History

The early history of what is now Bangladesh is shrouded in the legends of Hindu and Buddhist epic literature. The story begins to unfold more clearly with the entrance of Islam into India in the eighth century. Muslim sailors and traders from Arabia early found their way along the coast of India as far east as Bengal. Islam was spread initially by the personal example and missionary spirit of these trades, but eventually all of northern India became a Muslim majority area by conquest. By 1245 Muslim rule encompassed all of the Ganges valley, including Bengal, where a sizable Muslim population emerged from the conversion of Hindus and Buddhists. Dacca became an important center for local Muslim rulers, who owed allegiance to the emperor in Delhi. Muslim culture and learning flourished across the subcontinent for several centuries under the Mogul empire, until the rise of European power in the Indian Ocean. The Portuguese who followed Vasco da Gama in 1498 dominated trade with India for a hundred years and broke the Arab maritime power. The Dutch, British, and French arrived in the seventeenth century to establish trading centers, but by the end of the eighteenth century the British had the upper hand. Bengal was the first part of India to be conquered by the British, and by the 1850's most of the subcontinent was under their control. The suppression of the Sepoy mutiny in 1857 dealt a final blow to Muslim rule.

On the Bengal side of India the Hindus generally gained more from the rise of British power than did the Muslims. This was partly because the British wanted to make sure the Muslims from whom they had wrested power did not regain it, and partly because Hindus were more open to Western education and ideas. Bengal was first divided along Hindu/Muslim lines in 1905 in an attempt to improve administrative efficiency and to concentrate on the relatively backward and neglected region of eastern Bengal. Predominantly Hindu West Bengal, including Calcutta, was administered separately from the largely rural and predominantly Muslim areas of East Bengal. This was opposed by Hindu politicians, however, who persuaded the British to reunite Bengal in 1911, causing the Muslims to further distrust both the British and the Hindus.

In 1906 the Muslim League, which eventually espoused the concept of Pakistan, was organized in Dacca to champion Muslim interests. In several provinces attempts had been made to forcibly convert Muslims back to Hinduism, leading to communal riots in many places. Oppressed by the Hindus and thwarted by the British, Muslims began to demand safeguards for their religion, culture, and way of life. By 1930 some Muslim leaders, led by the philosopher-poet Muhammed Iqbal, began to feel that the best safeguard for Muslim interests lay either in some type of separate provincial autonomy within India or in complete political independence in a sovereign state of their own. The historic meeting of the All-India Muslim league at Lahore in 1940 passed a famous resolution declaring that

> . . . no constitutional plan would be workable in this country or acceptable to the Muslims unless . . . the areas in which the Muslims are numerically in a majority, as in the northwestern and eastern zones of India, should

be grouped to constitute independent states in which the constituent units shall be autonomous and sovereign.*

This action, popularly known as the Pakistan Resolution, electrified Muslims all over the subcontinent and progressively fostered demands for a separate Muslim homeland. Hindus opposed the demands, and the British were less than enthusiastic about partitioning the country, but there seemed to be no good alternative.

When India was given independence and partitioned into the two successor states of Pakistan and India on August 14-15, 1947, the Bengal area was again divided along religious lines: the predominantly Hindu West Bengal remained part of India while Muslim-majority East Bengal plus one district of Assam became East Pakistan—the eastern wing of a new nation whose two disparate provinces were separated by a thousand miles of India. The communal disorders and dislocations which followed this partition saw as many as 12 million people uprooted from their homes in perhaps the greatest mass migration of history, during which one million people died or were killed attempting to move from one country to the other. Though a much larger Hindu minority remained in East Pakistan than in West, still the Muslim percentage there increased through the influx of Bengalis from the Calcutta side and nearly a million non-Bengali, Urdu-speaking Muslims from the Indian states of Bihar and West Bengal.

From the beginning the inequalities of this division bred trouble. Though East Pakistan contained only one-sixth of the land area of West Pakistan, it had more than half the population, giving the Bengalis a 55 percent majority among various ethnic groups. These Bengalis resented the fact that they were not proportionally represented in either the government, the military, or the economic development which centered in the western side. Also, East Pakistan, with more than the total population and earning 60 percent of the country's foreign exchange by the export of jute, received less than 40 percent of national earnings and income for development. Even though the Bengali language was given equal status with Urdu as an official language and a second capital was built in Dacca, where the national assembly convened every other session, still disparities and dissatisfaction remained in the eastern section. The problems of distance, compounded by cultural religions and linguistic differences, progressively gave impetus to a movement for provincial autonomy as a solution to the gross inequalities between the two wings. One of the chief leaders of the Bengali cause was Sheikh Mujibar Rahman, president of the East Pakistan Awami ("People's") League.

The agitation for Bengali autonomy within Pakistan continued through

*Rafique Akhtar, ed. *Pakistan 1973 Year Book* (Karachi: East and West Publishing Co.), p. 34.

the rule of several elected and military governments. By 1970 it seemed about to reach a successful solution, but then East Pakistan's majority Awami party in free elections gained an absolute majority of 167 seats in the proposed 313-seat national assembly and proposed to establish truly democratic rule. When the military-political combine in West Pakistan saw that the balance of power was about to pass to East Pakistan, they postponed the seating of the new national assembly, thus precipitating further unrest and a civil disobedience movement throughout East Pakistan. When negotiations between East and West Pakistan leaders broke down, the Pakistan army, made up largely of soldiers from the west, was secretly ordered to repress violently all Bengali opposition. On the night of March 25-26, 1971, they launched a bitter campaign of burning, looting, and killing in which Sheikh Mujibur Rahman was arrested and jailed in West Pakistan, causing many of his followers to flee to India. There they set up a provisional government and declared an independent People's Republic of Bangladesh.

In the following months of internecine strife the Mukti Bahini ("Liberation Army," made up of Bengali insurgents) waged fierce guerrilla warfare with the Pakistan army. In the resulting carnage hundreds of thousands of people lost their lives, and as many as 10 million people (mostly Hindus) fled to refugee camps in India. While Indian sympathies had been with the people of East Pakistan from the beginning, it was late November before the Indian army openly joined the struggle on behalf of the Bengali people. Within a few short weeks the Pakistani forces, badly outnumbered and cut off from their supply lines a thousand miles to the west, surrendered on December 16, 1971, marking the bloody birth of the new but seriously scarred nation of Bangladesh.†

The government of the People's Republic of Bangladesh was installed at once in Dacca. Sheikh Mujibar Rahman, who had been imprisoned for treason in Pakistan, was released in early January and returned to a hero's welcome in Dacca, where he became prime minister of Asia's newest country. Known affectionately by his nickname "Mujib" or even more endearingly as "Bangabandhu" ("Friend of Bengal"), he used his tremendous popular appeal with the Bengali masses to focus Bengali nationalism on the staggering problems confronting the new nation. The most immediate concerns following the war were relief, the rehabilitation of refugees, and the reconstruction of the war-torn economy. Problems of food shortages, labor unrest, and high unemployment had to be resolved simultaneously

†For further details concerning the historical, religious, and cultural background of Bangladesh during the nearly twenty-five years it existed as East Pakistan and for a more complete analysis of the factors leading to the eventual dissolution of Pakistan as originally constituted, see chapter 22, "Pakistan."

with constitution-making, establishing law and order, and dealing with collaborators and war criminals.

Unlike Pakistan in the west, which remains an Islamic republic, Bangladesh declared itself a secular state like India. One early evidence of this new neutrality in cultural and religious matters was heard on Radio Bangladesh shortly after independence, when the day was begun with readings from Hindu, Buddhist, and Christian Scriptures in addition to the regular readings from the Holy Koran. The domestic policy of the new government is predicated on the four principles of parliamentary democracy, secularism, socialism, and nationalism. The prime minister is generally described as a moderate socialist. The new secular constitution of Bangladesh, promulgated in 1972, assures the religious minorities full citizenship and the right to both practice and propagate their faith.

The new nation's foreign policy is based upon the premises of neutrality and nonalignment. She seeks good relations with all nations, including Pakistan. Of the three great powers, the USSR consistently supported India and Bangladesh in the conflict with Pakistan, while the People's Republic of China sided with Pakistan and has refused to recognize Bangladesh, even vetoing her application for membership in the United Nations. Unlike Pakistan, where Communist parties are not permitted to function, the pro-Soviet Bangladesh Communist party and the Peking-oriented National Awami party are officially recognized and operate openly. Friendly U.S. relations with West Pakistan initially clouded American understanding of the developing unrest that led to the secession of Bangladesh, but American efforts at mediation followed by generous U.S. humanitarian relief efforts during and after the months of civil strife served as tangible evidence of genuine American concern. During the troubled months from March to December of 1971, 75 percent of the total relief aid for the people of Bangladesh was provided by the U.S. government and numerous American voluntary agencies, including church and mission bodies. These activities have helped restore the American image.

Christian History

Christians in Bangladesh are relatively few in number, though not because Christianity was late in coming. As early as 1576 Jesuit missionaries entered the Indian region of Bengal in the wake of Portuguese explorations. In the decades that followed, Augustinians and Dominicans also opened work there. By 1666 it was estimated that there were thirty-three thousand Roman Catholics in Bengal, most of them centered around Portuguese trading establishments.

Protestant missions in what is now Bangladesh followed the Catholics by more than two hundred years, when William Carey was sent to India in 1793 by the Baptist Missionary Society. (It had been founded the preceding year as the first foreign mission sending agency in England.) Carey began his work in Bengal, and the first BMS mission station was founded in 1795 at Dinajpur in what is now Bangladesh, though Serampore in India's state of West Bengal later became the center of Carey's varied activities (which later branched out all over the region as far as Burma and Assam). Dacca, the capital of Bangladesh, was opened as a BMS center in 1816. Perhaps Carey's greatest and most lasting contribution to church history was the translation of the Bible into Bengali, a strategic accomplishment which the earlier Catholic missionaries had not undertaken. For over 180 years the work of the Baptist Missionary Society has continued among Bengali Muslims and Hindus in this part of the world. The present Baptist Union of Bangladesh is an outgrowth of the pioneer efforts of William Carey and the BMS. This group now comprises the largest Protestant church body in the country, having a total community of nearly twenty thousand.

Since the time of Carey various other Baptist groups have also had a significant role in Protestant missionary efforts in East Bengal. In addition to British Baptists, the Australian Baptist Missionary Society began work in 1882 and found particular responsiveness among the animistic Garo hill peoples along the Assam border, where the resulting churches have formed the Garo Baptist Union. The New Zealand Baptists arrived in 1886 and currently operate a large Christian literature agency in Bangladesh, serving many churches and missions. The Bengali-speaking congregations resulting from the Australian and New Zealand Baptist work are associated in the Bangladesh Baptist Union (which is distinct from the Baptist Union of Bangladesh).

Baptists from the United States added their contribution following World War II, when American missionaries under the Association of Baptists for World Evangelism arrived in Chittagong in 1956 to begin an evangelistic, church-planting ministry. The need for medical ministries in the neglected area south to the Burma border soon became evident. Memorial Christian Hospital now stands in the center of that previously unevangelized area. The mission further extended its ministry to the tribal peoples of the nearby Chittagong Hill Tracts. ABWE now has the largest group of Protestant missionaries serving in Bangladesh. In 1957 Southern Baptist missionaries came in response to an invitation to take over some of the work begun by Australian Baptists and have since opened several centers, working in fellowship with the Bangladesh Baptist Union. More recently, following independence, Swedish Baptist missionaries have also begun working in Bangladesh.

Other Protestant communions were early represented in eastern Bengal while it was still part of India. Members of the Church Missionary Society (Anglican) began work in 1805, not long after Carey. English Presbyterians came in 1862 and the Oxford mission (Anglican) in 1895. The Anglicans and Presbyterians early engaged in medical and educational ministries, which continue to the present. When church union came to Pakistan in 1970, the work of these three historic missions was carried on under the diocese of Dacca until independence, in December, 1971, when the diocese became the Church of Bangladesh, having a constituency of approximately twelve thousand adherents.

Lutheran work in what is now Bangladesh also began in the late nineteenth century, predominantly among the Santali tribal peoples of the western border regions, who have been particularly responsive to the Christian faith. Various Lutheran church and mission bodies from Norway, Denmark, and the U.S.A. have cooperated in the mission to the Santals. Believers among them number some nineteen thousand on the Bangladesh side of the border, with many more in India. Lutheran churches are also growing among Garo, Lushai, and Khasi people in the border areas of northeastern Bangladesh, where Lutherans are continuing work begun by Welsh Presbyterians. In the early twentieth century American missionaries from the non-Pentecostal Churches of God as well as the Pentecostal Church of God began ministries which continue in separate church bodies. The Assemblies of God from the U.S. started work in 1945, just prior to the formation of Pakistan. These groups for the most part have worked among relatively unresponsive Hindu and Muslim groups, and their work has remained small.

Two of the larger church bodies in Bangladesh are presently unrelated to any overseas mission or denomination. The Evangelical Christian church in the Chittagong Hills Tracts, where travel is restricted, reportedly numbers some twelve thousand adherents. The churches there are the outgrowth of missionary work conducted by the North East India General Mission, which dates back to 1918, when a response was found among a tribal group known as the Bawms. The churches are now independent of any mission and function with their own presbytery and church council. A second indigenous group of more recent origin is the All One in Christ Fellowship. This Bengali-speaking movement spread from Calcutta and has grown fairly rapidly in the south, where is now claims some fifteen thousand followers. Interdenominational missions have been slow in coming to Bangladesh. The first to arrive was the International Christian Fellowship (formerly Ceylon and India General Mission), which came in 1958 from West Pakistan and subsequently began a cooperative outreach now known as the Bangladesh Bible Correspondence School.

Since 1970-71, when world attention was focused on Bangladesh following the double tragedy of a devastating cyclone followed by civil war, many groups not previously working in the country have sent medical and relief teams. These groups include the Evangelical Fellowship of India, the Mennonites, the Salvation Army, World Vision, World Relief Commission of NAE, Medical Assistance Program, Bible and Medical Missionary Fellowship, and the German Liebenzeller Mission—all in a continuing expression of Christian compassion and concern.

Doors to aggressive evangelism are open to Muslims and Hindus in Bangladesh today as never before. The destitution in the wake of the civil war, the natural tragedies of flood and cyclone, and the goodwill earned by Christian missions following these disturbances have created new opportunities in this large and long-neglected nation. The opportunities must be seized before it is too late.

APPENDIX 1

Religions of Bangladesh

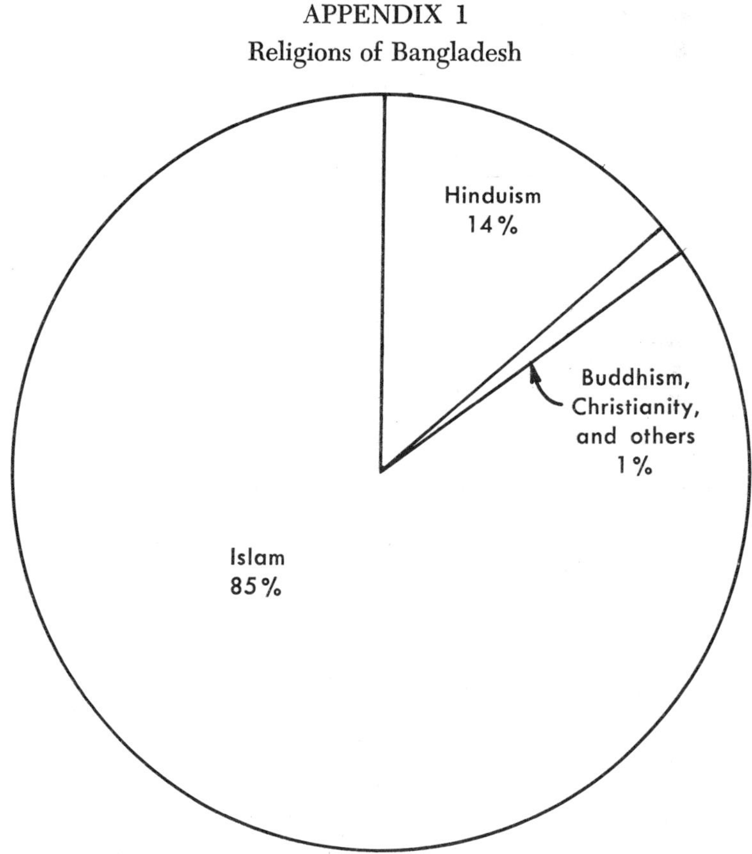

APPENDIX 2

Adherents of Major Christian Traditions

Roman Catholic
Protestant
20 40 60 80 100 120 140
Thousands of community

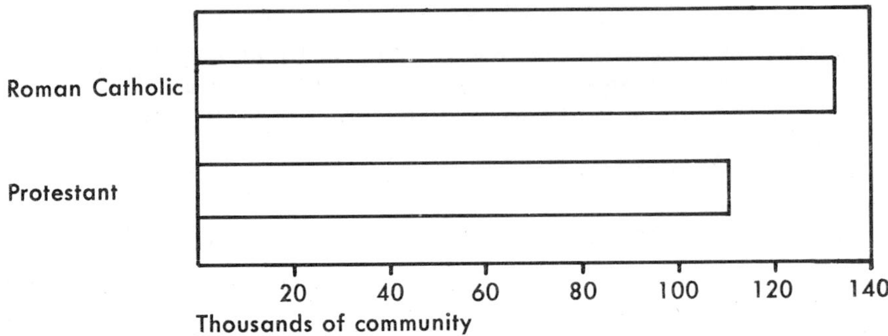

Community Statistics of Major Protestant Churches

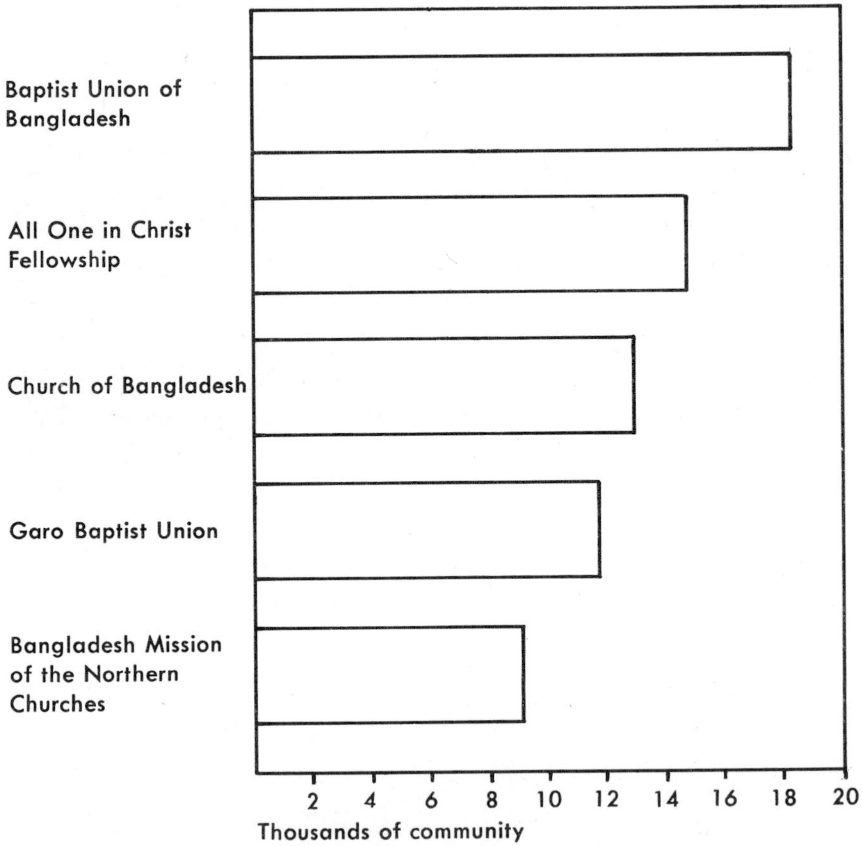

Baptist Union of Bangladesh
All One in Christ Fellowship
Church of Bangladesh
Garo Baptist Union
Bangladesh Mission of the Northern Churches
2 4 6 8 10 12 14 16 18 20
Thousands of community

BIBLIOGRAPHY

Background Notes on Bangladesh. Washington: U.S. Department of State, Feb. 1973.

Goddard, Burton L., ed. *The Encyclopedia of Modern Christian Missions.* Camden: Thomas Nelson and Sons, 1967.

Hefley, James. *Christ in Bangladesh.* New York: Harper and Row, 1972.

India, Pakistan and Bangladesh. Issues in U.S. Foreign Policy, no. 7. East Asian and Pacific Series 154 (publication 8673). Washington: Department of State, Oct. 1972.

Kane, J. Herbert. *A Global View of Christian Missions.* Grand Rapids: Baker, 1971.

Lockerbie, Jeannie. *On Duty in Bangladesh.* Grand Rapids: Zondervan, 1972.

Neill, Stephen. *The Story of the Christian Church in India and Pakistan.* Grand Rapids: Eerdmans, 1970.

Olsen, Viggo. *Daktar: Diplomat in Bangladesh.* Chicago: Moody Press, 1973.

Parshall, Phil. *Profile on Bangladesh.* Published privately. Dacca, May 1974.

4

BHUTAN

by Billy Bray

THE CHURCH TODAY

HIGH IN THE HIMALAYAS lies the virtually unknown "Kingdom of the Thunder Dragon," tiny Bhutan. Accessible only by treacherous mule trails until ten years ago, its xenophobic tribesmen were open mainly to Tibet alone, and were bound by primitive religious Lamaism and animism.

No Christian witness ever effectively penetrated to the remote mountaineers; only along the borders was limited contact made. But in this last decade the Christian missionaries have been able to begin stable institutional work. One gospel has been printed in the major language. One tiny church has been planted, and recently it has seen a work of the Holy Spirit which trebled its membership. In Bhutan the door to Christ has been opened for the first time in history!

The thrilling story of the recent moving of God which resulted in the founding of the first church within Bhutan was told in December 1971 by its first pastor, P. S. Tingbo. (This church is apparently made up entirely of Nepali, whose ancestors immigrated to Bhutan.)

> God's time for Bhutan has come, and its first church has been formed.
> On the day, November 22, 1970, that the small Christian community at

---

BILLY BRAY is a free-lance journalist-photographer serving primarily Christian organizations in Southeast Asia. After serving with the American military forces in the area, he stayed on as a reporter for a Bangkok newspaper and as a stringer for *Newsweek* magazine and the American Broadcasting company. In 1970 he formed *Newsasia,* a feature news service. He has contributed numerous articles and pictures to Christian publications, especially those which promote Christian relief work in the war areas.

Chengmari was declared a congregation by the Church of North India, I was consecrated as its first pastor-in-charge.

To me the start of this deeply moving and absorbing relationship began almost one year before, when I was ordained at Kalimpong's McFarlane Memorial Church as a mobile pastor for Bhutan. Since then I have been visiting various parts of Bhutan, seeking out Nepali Christians that have come from Darjeeling to work under the Bhutan government, and other Christians from South India.

My greatest encouragement came in Chengmari, southwest Bhutan, on my first visit there on Christmas Eve of 1969. I found only one Christian family, with ten members, the family of D. D. Lama, a commissioner of South Bhutan who is a bulwark of the faith. God has placed this one choice family there to build His church. By their strong witness, many of their neighbors were in constant touch with the gospel. Mr. Lama's mother spends most of her time in prayer and witnessing.

We planned evangelistic meetings for Easter week, 1970. Meetings were held two and sometimes three times a day, and the response to the Word of God was far greater than our expectation. On Easter Day the service lasted four hours and twenty minutes. Forty-eight people took water baptism as evidence of their faith in Christ as their new Lord and Master! The Word of God is not fettered!

The church is now growing rapidly, under the guidance of the Holy Spirit. A beautiful feature is the church's unifying influence. The members are drawn from eleven different caste backgrounds.

Recently more and more people have been inquiring about this Way. Non-Christian neighbors in large numbers attend the evening gospel meetings and Sunday services. The Holy Spirit is giving them listening ears and receptive hearts. Scores of new individuals are being recognized as enquirers and are receiving regular Christian teaching. This led to 111 more being joyfully received into the church through water baptism, on October 3, 1971. Pastors J. Tuli and B. K. Lakra from Jalpaiguri [India] came to assist in that blessed occasion.

In southwest Bhutan witch doctors and sorcerers have been brought to the Lord. With their own hands they are burning the books and strange objects pertaining to their witchcraft. The ever-living Son of God is liberating people who were oppressed by the devil and is destroying the works of the wicked one even today.

The new believers are very fond of singing. They are not concerned about whether they carry the right tune—it is enough for them that they are singing the victorious songs of the Lamb. They sing with their whole hearts, and to their heart's content. Services are held on the verandah of the house of a Christian family. The morning service begins at 9:15, but people start gathering an hour ahead of time. Services are packed to capacity. Now we are planning to build a house of worship, and we firmly believe that God in His own time will guide us to accomplish this, for His honor and glory.

The witness is going on also among the Nepali Bhutanese with Pastor Pema Paul in the south and Pastor Norbu Dukpa in the southeast. Pastors N. T. Malomum and M. S. Tingbo have worked here before us, preparing the way.

The prayers of God's people throughout the world have been going up for this land. The heavenly leaven has begun to work, but the laborers are few. Frequently strange situations develop to obstruct the progress of the gospel. But God is greater than all this, and we believe that in answer to prayer His Spirit will continue to win men and women in this enchanting mountain kingdom. When God acts, who can hinder? Isaiah 43:130.[1]

History of Protestant Missions

Apart from the recent dramatic birth of this Chengmari church, no other organized indigenous witness for Christ is known to exist in Bhutan. And established missionary work inland is also a providential development of the last decade. Missionaries of the Church of Scotland, aided by the presence of Scotch tea-planters in the area, first attempted to evangelize Bhutan in the late nineteenth century, and they were ceded the rugged Himalayan foothills by comity agreement when Britain ruled India in the nineteenth century. But these pioneers were unable to plant any permanent work until Dr. Albert Craig of the Scottish Mission (Church of Scotland Missionary Society, Presbyterian) opened the first leprosy hospital in 1965.

The door to the first inland missionary work was providentially opened through Dr. Craig's treating of the king and queen of Bhutan when they visited the Indian border city of Kalimpong after World War II. He later delivered some of the royal children. Then high government officials occasionally called him in Bhutan to give treatment.

In 1965 Craig was permitted to open the first hospital in the remote, backward kingdom, but health prevented him from staying. Today his hospital is operated by the Mission to Lepers near the capital of Thimbu and is staffed with a British doctor and his wife and an experienced British nurse from India. Darjeeling area Christians work on the staff, and the nurse, Miss Clark, is planning to open another clinic.

Near the border of Assam, the Danish Mission to Lepers now operates a small hospital in the eastern part of the country under Miss Asbjorg Fiske, who is assisted by a young Norwegian doctor. Their future plans are for outstation public health work rather than an enlargement of the present clinic. At points other than Kalimpong (along Bhutan's border) some Indian efforts are still being made to influence the Bhutanese for Christ; Indian believers have invaded border areas with literature and Bible colporteurs.

Though he is presently engaged in relief work in Bangladesh, a Swedish

Lutheran missionary, Rev. Olav Hodne in Cooch Bihar, hopes to begin a Christian university in Bhutan; his wife has been trained for blind school education.

A Pentecostal Bhutanese pastor of a small expatriate congregation in India near the Buxa Duars area has been working for some time translating the Bible into the Bhutanese Jhonka dialect. So far the four gospels have been completed. The Bible Society has so far published only Mark in the Jhonka dialect. Another translation work by others is reported to be underway.

Most Christian leaders feel that the brightest hopes for the growth of evangelical Protestantism in Bhutan today (apart from the Chengmari church) lies in the Indian Christians, a number of whom are stationed in Bhutan officially. Some of these are active in evangelizing and organizing little church groups. The possibility of more foreigners entering Bhutan may come as the country gains greater independence from India and opens negotiations directly with foreign mission societies. Yet even then, few believe that foreign missionaries will be allowed to do direct evangelism. The leper hospital near Thimbu was forced to sign a nonproselyting agreement with the government in order to carry on its hospital work.

Other foreign Christians who will meet some of the scores of pressing physical and other needs among the people may find open doors, subject to various restrictions. One dedicated Western Christian is working in a high and influential post, hopefully with future results for the gospel.

History of Catholic Missions

Catholic work in Bhutan, also newly begun, is limited to a rapidly growing Roman Catholic boy's school, St. Xaviers, in Thimbu. It is run along Cambridge lines by a group of Canadian Jesuits. But they too have had to enter into a nonproselyting agreement, and one of the priests told me in an interview, "We wouldn't even think of baptizing a boy, even if he insisted, while he was still in school."

Although the school has a chapel "for the use of missionary priests only," there is no Catholic church. The school is principally helping to prepare an elite potential leadership for future Bhutanese government training. In the past many Bhutanese royalty, however, have attended the St. Joseph's School in Darjeeling, India, where there is a large Catholic church. Some Catholic efforts to penetrate Bhutan have come from this base.

Nation and People

The mystery surrounding this "hermit kingdom" in the clouds is explained both by its geographical isolation and the fiercely independent spirit of its Mongolian and Tibetan mountaineer farmers. Until Red China conquered Tibet in 1959, this equally remote kingdom was Bhutan's main trading partner and source of news and cultural interchange. Historically, Bhutan has been even more exclusive than Tibet. Her only other intercourse with the world was along narrow mule trails of trade with northern India.

But the conquest and harsh subjugation of Tibet by Red China dragged reluctant Bhutan into the realities of the modern world. Then then reigning maharajah, Jigme Dorji Wangchuk, was young, having taken the throne in 1952, when he was only twenty-five years old. He has brought his people into the wonders of the twentieth century as fast as the almost universally illiterate population has been able to adjust. Yet most Bhutanese are preparing to enter the twentieth century reluctantly and with mixed emotions. "The younger generation desires outside contact," explained one Bhutanese official, "but at the same time, His Majesty realizes we need to preserve our traditions and culture—keeping our character as Bhutanese. We are seeking the coexistence of tradition and progress."

While younger Bhutanese remain impatient, King Wangchuk has sought considerable social reform and achieved certain successes in improving transportation, communication, and defense. Early in his reign, for example, he boldly moved to free the nation's slave population. Since 1960 four roads from the Indian border now penetrate the mountains where only mule and foot paths did before. Other achievements Bhutanese officials proudly point to as signs of progress include the formation of a National Assembly (1953), Land Reform (1956), appointment of a Royal Advisory Council (1965) and Council of Ministers (1968), codification of laws (1968), and a new capital at Thimbu (1968). Increasingly anxious to exhibit national sovereignty, the king sought and gained Colombo Plan membership in 1962 and Universal Postal Union membership in 1969, both with the help of India.

Bhutan joined the United Nations in the 1971 General Assembly. In just over a decade the country has come from almost total isolation, signalling its desire to join the community of nations and has even gone so far as to put out feelers for foreign aid, a move vigorously scotched by India. (Like its neighbor Sikkim, Bhutan has turned over its foreign relations to India. All contacts with the outside world are screened by India's enormous bureaucracy, and visitors are almost never permitted into Bhutan.)

Until 1907 a loose feudal "theocracy," the country appears to be moving toward a constitutional monarchy. With the help of Indian technocrats the administration in Thimbu is now concentrating on constructing a basic governmental infrastructure. But on a visit to Kenya in July 1972, King

Wangchuk died suddenly, and his seventeen-year-old son, Crown Prince Jigme Singhi Wangchuk, was enthroned in Thimbu a few weeks later. Effects of this sudden leadership change could be serious for the tiny, emerging nation.

About as big as Vermont and New Hampshire combined or half the size of Indiana, the "forbidden kingdom" actually embraces only nineteen thousand square miles. The northern border with its three hundred miles of icy peaks and the thickly jungled Duar Plain border in the south are both almost uinhabited. With mountains plunging from a snowy twenty-four thousand to a warm five thousand feet, the land is well watered and most of the people practice terrace agriculture in the planting of rice, wheat, and barley. Eleven demonstration farms have been constructed by Indian agriculturists, who are attempting to introduce new crops and products like cheese, fruit trees, and poultry. The Bhutanese already herd yak for milk and butter.

The Bhutanese are round-faced Orientals of Mongolian origin. The population was estimated at about nine hundred thousand in 1971,[2] and the people are concentrated mostly in the rich central valleys. They cluster around monasteries called "dzongs" very much like European peasants used to live in the shadow of medieval castles. Tibetan-style Lamaism has played a powerful role in traditional Bhutan. As the focus of religion, government, and defense, many of the dzongs were built to command strategic mountain passes. Tattered prayer flags whip and snap in the wind as one approaches the dzongs, which are the center of many colorful festivals that provide relief from the obviously grim struggle against the ferocious Himalayan elements. Built of heavy timber and stone, the many-tiered temples give the unmistakable impression of structures seen in China or Japan.

Not as monolithic as they like to appear to outsiders, the Bhutanese are actually composed of several ethnic and language groups. Dominating the population are the Sharchops or Bhote tribes of the north. Apparently coming originally from Tibet, they are now considered to be the indigenous people and are the main strength of Lamaistic Buddhism. The largest minority group, the Nepalese of southern Bhutan, make up about 25 percent of the population. Smaller minority groups include Tibetans from Kham in western Tibet, Lepchas from Sikkim, and Santal descendants of Indian Bihari migrants.

Historically an isolated but martial people, the Bhutanese tribes were united by a militant Buddhist priest in the mid-sixteenth century. They frequently swept down from their mountain redoubts to make predatory raids on India through the eighteen strategic Duar passes into India and Assam. Tibet and Sikkim border towns were also frequent victims of the

Bhutanese sword. A treaty in 1730 with Tibet recognized Bhutan's independence.

This penchant for fighting led to a long series of battles in the early nineteenth century between the British forces in India and Bhutan's semi-religious god-kings. Finally defeated in the nineteenth century at the Duars, Bhutan signed the Sinchula Treaty with the United Kingdom in 1865, and the present hereditary dynasty began when Britain recognized Uggyen Wangchuk as king in 1907. Finding Bhutan worth less than the effort to police it, the British allowed the fiercely independent mountain people a free reign in their murky internal affairs. During this whole period, Bhutan's royalty looked northward to Tibet for trade, cultural intercourse, and religious inspiration.

"With the fall of Tibet in 1959," said an official at the Bhutan mission in New Delhi, "the question of security arose, and people started to realize we needed to be in contact with the outside world for development." Even unofficial trade with Tibet ended as the Bhutanese, who still have a largely barter economy, found the new Communist paper currency worthless. Fearful of further territorial expansion on the part of the Communists, Bhutan turned to India for what they carefully emphasized were to be "advisors." The Indians (some of them Christians) in the last decade have helped the Bhutanese carve out 1,040 kilometers of roads, build eight telephone exchanges with 320 miles of line, construct thirty-five post offices and seven hospitals, and open one hundred schools for fifteen thousand students. Under government scholarships, 450 students are now studying abroad, mostly in India.

Economically, the future of the country, like that of nearby Sikkim and Nepal, could be very bright. Over 70 percent of the land area is forested. Abundant rivers promise almost unlimited electrical power, much of which can eventually be fed into Indian grids as a tangible export. Coal, dolomite, gypsum, and graphite have been discovered, though lack of capital and transportation have hindered full development of mining operations.

India is now cooperating with Bhutan in establishing modern industries in the country. A fruit-preserving plant and a distillery are working at Samchi, near the border in southwestern Bhutan. Bhutan's small-scale cottage industries, which produce textiles, wooden articles, paper craft, leather goods and metalware, are being modernized. Factories to manufacture fertilizer, cement, paper, matchwood, and plywood are now being constructed. India has also extended her cooperation to the Bhutanese people in the fields of education and technology. To exploit Bhutan's forests, a forestry department has been established. A number of Bhutanese have been trained at the Indian Forest Research Institute and are now serving in the Bhutan Forest Service. Similarly, a number of Bhutanese were trained in India as veterinary doctors and in animal and dairy farming, and they are now serving their country at a number of centers. Bhutanese have also been trained in agriculture, orchard, and horticultural sciences. There are at present also a number of Indian teachers in Bhutan, educating children at the primary and secondary levels.

Thus the present economic and cultural development of Bhutan rests on the stability of the Indo-Bhutanese friendship. If this relationship continues to grow, Bhutan will surely continue to prosper more and more.

National Religions

The all-powerful role which religion has traditionally played in the life of the Bhutanese people is in evidence everywhere. The national flag of Bhutan, "the land of the dragon," displays a snarling thunder dragon appliqued over a diagonally divided field, half a brilliant yellow (representing the secular authority of the king) and the other half a fiery orange (representing the Buddhist religion). This balance is also seen on the national seal, where the Buddhist jewel with "eight points for the eightfold path" crowns the whole design. The emphasis on religion is not surprising.

The country was first united by Sheptoon La-Pha, a traveling Lama from Tibet who skillfully wielded both temporal and spiritual power. For three hundred years the country was ruled as a Buddhist "theocracy," and Bhutanese tend to associate their religion with their national identity so strongly that western missionaries were hardly ever permitted even to visit the country, let alone proclaim the message of Christ. Buddhism is still the state religion, and today a quarter of the state revenue is said to go for the support of four thousand orange-robed lamas attached to eight monasteries.

But as in all the other Himalayan kingdoms, Buddhism in Bhutan only thinly veils the all-prevailing animism that rules the lives of the common people. In their family prayer rooms, most Bhutanese worship relics of a devil worship cult called "bon." Belief in ghosts, witches, and what have been described as "clawing spirits" shadows everyday life. For the Bhutanese spirits are everywhere: in trees, rocks, hilltops, and the skies. Witch doctors are called upon in illness, and prayer scrolls or amulets are essential parts of every family medical insurance plan. Their "bonism" is essentially a religion based on expelling demons and propitiating spirits through the sacrifice of animals or even human beings. Thus Bon, coupled with Mahayana Buddhism and Hindu Tantric meditation, recitation, and incantation, forms the core of Bhutanese religion today.

Outlook for Christian Missions

The Indian border city of Kalimpong was long the traditional focus of attempts to reach Bhutan (as well as Nepal and Sikkim) with the gospel. In 1891 the Scottish Mission at Kalimpong began a mission to Bhutan and in one of their prayer letters described the people there as the "most immoral of the immoral races of the world." A Scottish missionary, A. K. Graham, who later did a great deal to influence many border Bhutanese for Christ, wrote in 1895 that they were then "on the threshold of these closed lands."

But while the optimistic missionaries were able to make some progress in contacting Bhutanese who ventured outside their homeland, they were unable to plant churches inside Bhutan. One missionary, a Mr. Sutherland, did start some primary schools in Bhutan. But when he died, his obituary in a 1924 edition of the *Mission News* sadly reported that he was able only to "teach some 45 lads from Bhutan, the first to gain an education under Western influence." Thus, until the last few years, schools for Bhutanese children in Kalimpong have been virtually the only means of communicating any Christian teaching to the nation. The Church of Scotland still supports a school there called the Scottish University Missionary Institution, which has had many Bhutanese students for years. There are no longer missionaries there now, and it is run by Nepali and Lepcha Christians from Sikkim.

The pioneer Scottish missionaries were never able to see the land penetrated in their lifetime. Decades later Dr. Albert Craig's leprosy hospital was the first successful beachhead for internal Christian witness.

Most heartening of all developments in Bhutan's history has been the organization of Bhutan's first Christian church in 1971 at Chengmari. At present nearly all its members are Nepalese, the second largest minority group in Bhutan.

Bhutan desperately wants to open its windows to the fresh breezes of modernization. One official told me, "We are afraid we'll be left behind as far as development is concerned." Yet many still fear progressing too fast. This fear, coupled with widespread anti-Christian religious prejudice, will probably continue to delay the evangelization of Bhutan, barring further miracles of divine intervention. But the recent miraculous growth of the small Nepali Christian church within that country is a harbinger to stir prayer and faith for the tiny nation at this opportune time.

NOTES

1. P. S. Tingbo, *Light of Life*.
2. *World Population Data Sheet* (Washington: Pop. Ref. Bureau), June 1971.

BIBLIOGRAPHY

Appasamy, A. J. *Sundar Singh: A Biography.* London: Lutterworth Press, 1968.

Dash, Arthur Jules. *Darjeeling.* Alipore and Bengal: Bengal Government Press, 1947.

Hooper, J. S. M., and Culshaw, W. J. *Bible Translation in India, Pakistan, and Ceylon.* Mysore: Oxford University Press, 1963.

Hunter, W. W. *Imperial Gazetteer of India.* Vol. 4, "Cochin-Ganguria." London: Trubner & Co., 1885.

Karen, Pradyumna P., and Jenkins, William M. *The Himalayan Kingdoms: Bhutan, Sikkim, and Nepal.* Princeton, N.J.: D. Van Nostrand Co., 1963.

Rustomji, Nari. *Enchanted Frontiers: Sikkim, Bhutan, and India's Northeastern Borderlands.* Bombay: Oxford University Press, 1971.

Stewart, William. *The Church Is There in North India.* Edinburgh: Church of Scotland Overseas Council, 1966.

Tingbo, P. S. *Light of Life.* New Delhi, 1971.

Weir, Robert W. *A History of the Foreign Missions of the Church of Scotland.* Edinburgh: R. & R. Clark, 1900.

Churches—old and new. The traditional Anglican Church

A Brunei "high rise" which houses the Bethel Chapel

5

BRUNEI

by Peter Hsieh and Russell Self

Introduction

LIKE TWO INDENTED TEETH sunk midway into the northern shore of Indonesian Borneo lies the small country of Brunei. On either side are the two East Malaysian states of Sarawak and Sabah. The seventy-five mile coast, rich in oil deposits, faces the South China Sea. The country stretches back for fifty miles into the jungles and hills, which are inhabited by 15,000 multitribal people, the major groups being Dusan, Kedayan, and Iban. More than half of the 145,000 population are Malay people, which gives the religious stance of Islam to the nation. The remainder are Borneo tribal people, formerly considered untouchable, and Chinese immigrants, who over the years have contributed about 25 percent to the population and are the local businessmen and traders.

The Church Today

Brunei Christians are mostly Chinese and migrant workers in the growing oil industry and number about 4,300, or a little more than 3 percent of the total population, of whom 80 percent are Catholic. The dominant and oldest Protestant group is Anglican because of Brunei's historical link with the British. Saint Andrew's Church has a weekly service in English for about two hundred worshippers, and the same Chinese priest conducts a

---

PETER HSIEH is now general secretary of the Bible Society of Singapore. A graduate of Fukien University and Western and Union Theological seminaries (U.S.), he has been a Presbyterian pastor in Malaysia and dean of Trinity Theological College, Singapore.

RUSSELL SELF, a former Presbyterian missionary to Thailand, is now Asian distribution consultant for the United Bible Societies, based in Singapore.

Chinese service for about twenty-five. There is one other small Anglican community at Seria with a Christian worker in charge, supervised by the bishop of Kuching, Sarawak, who is an Iban tribesman. Traditionally the emphasis has been on ritual and education, with little evangelistic concern.

In the last decade two independent and dynamic evangelically-oriented Christian groups were established in the capital city of Bandar Seri Begawan. Starting with a small group meeting in a house in 1964, Bethel Chapel has expanded into a rented flat with an average weekly attendance of 75. This congregation is related to a very excellent biblical testimony in the heart of the oil fields at Seria. There about 150 people gather in a church for services in Chinese, English, and Indian languages.

The other independent Christian group, meeting in a second-floor flat in the heart of the capital, is known as the Brunei Christian Fellowship. A Chinese graduate from the Singapore Bible College is pastoring a very vigorous youth group of about sixty. They have another full-time Chinese worker in the coastal oil town of Kuala Belait, which has a dozen or so Chinese believers. With the support of Grace Chapel in Manila, the Brunei Christian Fellowship is doing some very effective work among the tribal people.

Since 1971 some forty Korean Christians, migrant workers in the oil fields, met with their own pastor at Sungai Liang. Other Protestant groups include the Chinese indigenous Little Flock, with about twenty members, and the True Jesus churches. The Jehovah's Witnesses and Seventh-Day Adventists are evangelizing in Brunei by mail.

Accurate statistics are difficult to obtain, but in 1971 out of the total population of 135,000 about 3,500 Catholics were reported and 800 Protestants. These were reported as 550 Anglican and 250 other, most of whom would be small evangelical congregations. The Anglicans reported three Christian workers, and there were four others as well.

The only non-Catholic missionaries in the country are two workers of the Anglican SPG mission, who devote most of their energy to education. No other missions are permitted, for the government policy has been to allow the status quo of the existing Christian groups but to refuse applications from mission boards.

Thus the few evangelical Christian groups in Brunei are all small and lacking in strong leadership. There is not one full-time native Christian worker in Brunei. The lay participation is good, running the Sunday schools and opening their homes for meetings. Since overt evangelism is not permitted and since most Christians are immigrants, they are reluctant to be aggressive in Christian witness in this Muslim state. Evangelism has been largely limited to tract distribution and a few public meetings conducted by outside evangelists. However, Christian literature and Scriptures in the major languages are readily available. Greater cooperation, if not actual union, between the few Christians in Brunei would seem to be desirable but is apparently impossible at present.

Nation and People

While there is unequal distribution of wealth and goods in Brunei, there is no economic privation. For most people life is very simple, although automobiles per capita of population are considered very high for such a small nation. The comparatively high standard of living enjoyed in Brunei is based largely on its oil fields. In 1929 the first oil field was opened in Seria, and since then offshore discoveries have been very successful. Crude oil experts exceed 100 million U.S. dollars annually, and with the current world energy crisis a steady and substantial income is assured for future development of the country. There is no personal income tax, for oil revenues cover all national expenses and development projects. The per capita income of Brunei is 1000 U.S. dollars, based on a 97 percent oil economy. The country is modernizing steadily, and a recently completed international airport will open it to the world.

Many of the older generation still cannot read and write, but the government is doing everything possible to increase literacy; from a low of 26 percent in 1947 literacy has jumped to 47 percent in 1960 and continues to rise steadily. Most children receive a primary school education; secondary schooling is available; and there is one teachers' training college. Many young people are sent overseas for college education, and the flow of graduates back to Brunei is now noticeable in a number of government departments. The establishment of a university in Brunei is under discussion. The big problem will be the meaningful utilization of future graduates through the development of new economic structures.

Malay is the national language and English is the most important second language. Other schools use Chinese. In 1971 government subsidies were stopped to all private schools, but there is minimal interference in their programs because of their high standards.

National History

Brunei was an old established state in the Malay world as early as A.D. 600. Chinese history relates visits of envoys from a country of forty-five sailing days from China. Historian Moor claims that the name "Brunei" is of Sanskrit origin, indicating Hindu influence. It was only at the comng of Islam that Brunei started to record its history. The first sultan was Sultan Muhammad, who embraced Islam upon his marriage to a princess of Johore. During the reign of a Sultan Bolkiah, the rule of Brunei was said to have stretched as far as the Philippines.

Throughout the sixteenth century the Spaniards and the Portuguese occupied Brunei but failed to secure a permanent footing. When the mainland of Borneo became the center of a power struggle during the eighteenth century among the British, Dutch, Portuguese, and Americans, James Brooke, a British explorer and son of a civilian in the East Indian Company's service, in 1871 named himself "Raja of Sarawak," which embraced the whole of North Borneo. In 1888 Brunei became a British protectorate. Following World War II and Japanese occupation the last white raja, Sir Charles Vyner Brooke, grand nephew of the founder of the Brooke dynasty, ceded the country to the British Crown in 1946. In 1963 Brunei became part of the independent Federation of Malaysia but, along with Singapore, withdrew to establish the separate state of Brunei in 1965.

The ruling sultan is the head of state and chooses his own legislative council. The British government through the resident high commissioner offers advice on foreign affairs and defense. In October 1967 the sultan abdicated the throne in favor of his son, who became Sultan Hassanal Bolkiah.

While Brunei's state religion is Islam, the sultan is tolerant of other religions. In 1973 he reaffirmed the policy of his father, that existing church groups would be respected and that no new mission groups would be allowed to enter. Visiting Asian evangelists have no difficulty in working through the existing churches.

Christian History and the Future

Apart from the tiny Anglican mission, which was an outgrowth of the British settlement in the nineteenth century, the Christian communities of Brunei are almost exclusively immigrants from Hong Kong and the Chinese province of Tukien. A few Christians on trips abroad encouraged workers to visit Brunei and to help in the witness there also. Some of these immigrated before World War II, though most have come since.

The sprawling one million Ibans throughout the large island of Borneo, which surrounds Brunei, have shown a remarkable Christian growth—from 3.6 percent in 1947 to 20 percent in 1972. This could be God's way of reaching the almost-untouched tribal people of Brunei. A common-language Iban New Testament promised by the Bible Society in 1975, along with other up-to-date tribal translations, continue as important media for evangelism.

If the church is to grow, the local laity will have to be trained to assume responsibility for evangelism. Christian young people will have to be sent abroad for training. New forms of witness, such as camps and campus clubs, will have to be developed. With no new missionaries allowed, the native church must somehow be renewed to evangelize this tiny state.

Evangelist visits a Padaung village. He must speak several languages to reach the tribes in any given area.

Photo by William Hackett

6

BURMA

by William D. Hackett

Introduction

Famous in missionary lore as the Asian beachhead of the heroic Judson, North America's first foreign missionary, Burma has been in a state of turmoil since the Japanese occupation in 1942. Though the end of the Pacific war brought independence from both Japanese occupation and British colonialism, it threw the nation into a bitter power struggle between factions of inexperienced national leaders.

This conflict was forcibly terminated by the military coup of 1965 and the establishment of the "Burmese way to socialism." This led in 1966 to the expulsion not only of nearly all foreign missionaries, but also of all foreigners as well, thereby drawing a bamboo curtain of ignorance around the nation and its church.

How has the church fared under left-wing socialism in a Buddhist country? Are Christians free or persecuted? Little news has leaked from Burma since 1966, and there was an initial fear of reporting church activity abroad lest there be reprisals against the church. But finally in June 1970 I was

---

William D. Hackett is a second-generation missionary to Burma under the American Baptist Foreign Mission society. After receiving his B.A. from Drury College (Springfield, Mo.), his M.A. from Kennedy School of Missions, and his Ph.D. from Cornell University, Dr. Hackett began his career among the Shans in northeast Burma as an evangelist and rural church developer in 1937. He has served on numerous denominational boards and commissions and has traveled extensively throughout the country, teaching and helping to establish demonstration farms. His wife, Marion Shaw Hackett, has translated the major part of the New Testament into Pa-o, a Karen language. After expulsion from Burma in 1966, Dr. Hackett served at Chung Chi College in Hongkong, making four visits to Burma in as many years.

able to visit Christian leaders in Burma and conduct an in-depth investigation of the work of God during the four years of silence.

The Church Today

All church leaders except the Roman Catholic bishops stated that since independence there has been a slow but steady growth of church membership. What few figures they could supply seemed to indicate an increase of 2 to 2½ percent per year over the last five years. In 1972 the increase in baptized church members was 3 percent, with a new church being organized every week. In 1974, Baptists registered 10,450 new members.

Many reported an encouraging response to preaching among both Buddhists and animists and substantial numbers of conversions in many places. The leaders gave the impression that, in the light of the adjustments which every denomination has been forced to make after all foreign personnel left, the growth rate has been good.

Christians are exerting an influence upon the total society far beyond their numerical strength. Because they had often been identified with the British colonial rulers, there was a time after independence when they were suspect as not being nationalistic enough in spirit. For a time nationalism and Buddhism were bracketed together; i.e., a good Burman is a good Buddhist. But since many Christians have been serving loyally in the army, the civil service, the school system, and the medical profession, there has been a more tolerant attitude in recent years.

Many leaders, especially at local levels in the frontier areas, are Christians and have great influence in local affairs. Although there is no Christian in the revolutionary council, there are many serving in high administrative posts in government departments throughout the land.

This not to say that all of society and its institutions have not suffered from the turmoil in Burma, including all religions. But the Ne Win government has declared itself for freedom of religion. It set aside the Nu-inspired bill establishing Buddhism as the state religion. Although some observers have interpreted as anti-Christian the expulsion of foreign missionaries in 1966, this may be viewed as the culmination of a program of strict neutralization and the elimination of all foreign influences, aimed alike at business, voluntary aid programs, and foreign government cultural agencies, as well as at international church organizations.

But what of the health of the church itself in Burma today, almost a decade after the revolution? What are the character and scope of the Protestant church and its activities? How has the expulsion of missionaries affected the work?

Almost all the denominations of the church in Burma today would be classified as theologically conservative, if not fundamentalist. They use Bible translations prepared by conservatively trained scholars of the Bible Society. Such doctrines as the virgin birth, the verbal inspiration of the Scriptures, the creation, the trinity, and salvation through atonement are held by the vast majority of Christians. Liberal theology is now being discussed in theological training institutions, but the faith of the people is based confidently upon a strict interpretation of the Scriptures.

All branches of the church are strongly evangelistic. Pastors and evangelists travel to non-Christian villages to preach. Gospel teams from seminaries and Bible schools spend weekends and a large part of the summer visiting villages in frontier areas, witnessing in song and word. No project brings forth more money than a plan to send the gospel into a new area. Many churches support an additional evangelist beside the pastor, often placing him in a village to serve for many years. Associations of churches plan to support numerous trained men and women workers in mission stations, either among people of their own ethnic strain or among those of other ethnic minorities. Youth groups, women's societies, and other church organizations fully or partially support evangelistic workers among peoples too poor to support their own pastors. In my opinion the Burma churches are second to none in their devotion to their evangelistic mission.

However, the picture is not universally good. Recent reports[1] detail severe persecution of certain Christian Kachin tribes in the north, who must fight for freedom and survival in primitive jungle conditions. Possibly rebels against the central government, they are caught between army troops and the Chinese Communists on the nearby border. They report that Bibles have been forbidden them, that Buddhism was being taught in the schools, and that Christian witness was restricted.

For those who have fled across the Chinese border, pastors are called on to denounce Christ, and Mao's little red book is taught in the churches. These isolated tribes are now suffering from disease, poverty, and persecution. How widespread this persecution is no one can clearly ascertain. But prayer and relief are urgently needed.

Evangelistic work among tribal groups in other frontier areas has also been ordered closed by army authorities; travel to and from these areas is strictly limited and travel permits are required. However, in most areas evangelism still goes forward, though army commanders often use large church conferences for consultation with leaders of the Christian community. Church organizations are carrying on their work much as before, and new converts are being added in impressive numbers in some communities. Many Christians fear, however, that the government disapproves of their contracts and correspondence with foreigners and of their receiving foreign parcels and books. Perhaps this is an understandable fear for the more timid living under military dictatorships.

Leadership training for full-time Christian service has been and continues to be a prime concern of the churches. Burma is one of the few countries of the world where there are more trained pastors and evangelists than there are organized churches, with the result that literally hundreds of young people are placed in non-Christian villages to win men and women to Christ and to eventually organize new churches. It may take twelve to fifteen years, but they have the financial and prayer support of some group until the task is accomplished. The Burma Baptist convention alone recognizes twelve seminaries and Bible schools, and in June 1970 there were almost a thousand students in these schools.* Similar training institutions of other denominations, including the Catholics (who were very late in entering this field), now enroll more students than ever. Those who apply to the seminaries are now more highly qualified academically than ever before, with many holding baccalaureates in arts, law, or education.

Though the possibility of an order requiring all foreign missionaries to leave was not unforeseen, when the order came in March 1966 the Christians were stunned. However, most of the major denominations had been preparing the leaders for that day, and much of the work of the church was already in the hands of the nationals, with missionaries acting only as advisors. For instance, on the 150th anniversary of Judson's arrival in Rangoon, celebrated in October 1963, American Baptists handed over complete responsibility to the Burma Baptist convention. Though Anglican and Methodist bishops were still westerners in 1966, there were auxiliary bishops trained and ready to take over within a few years. Accordingly, after the first shock the Christians began to make the necessary adjustments to carry on, including doing the many tasks that the missionaries had done. Herman Tegenfeldt, veteran Baptist missionary to Burma, comments cogently on the lessons learned from missionary expulsion.

*Ed. note. After a visit to Burma in early 1973, Bishop Chandu Ray reported the following in the *COFAE NEWS* of June 1973.

> Nearly 300 pastors and church leaders gathered on the Seminary Hill in Insein, Burma, for a conference under the auspices of World Vision. It was a time of real sharing and caring; study and training; encouragement and excitement. There was no dearth of either pastors or seminary students, nor was there any attitude of defeatism. One heard of many conversions in tribal areas on the borders of China and India; among headhunters and among more settled people; among the educated and illiterates. Evangelistic teams of preaching and singing groups have opened new areas and the joy of the Lord has done the rest. In the light of the rigid socialistic pattern imposed by the government, the churches are adopting non-stipendiary ministries for men and women who will earn their living by secular work, but will be ordained to supplementary ministries in the church.

1. Responsible national churches must be established *from the beginning.*
2. Cultural differences must be recognized and efforts made to bridge them. Though Judson labored exclusively among the Burmese, later missionaries found Karen and Kachin tribespeople more responsive, and concentrated on them. The result has been large minority group churches often separated from the great cultural and national majority.
3. Doors open and close; missionaries must enter when they can!

(Herman Tegenfeldt, *Burma Speaks to Us All,* pp. 209-220)

In June 1970 one prominent Baptist leader, while viewing the many problems during a private conversation, felt that it might take as many as ten years to deal with them all, but was confident that they would be solved and that the Christian community would grow stronger and continue the work of church and mission with greater success than ever before. This was the consensus of more than a score of leaders from major denominations with whom I talked in 1970. The only exception was in the Roman Catholic Church, whose leaders seemed to reflect a fear of the future based on the fact that most of the bishops and priests are foreigners. A crash program of seminary training will rectify this shortage, but it will take years.

Since foreign personnel have left, the Burmese church leadership has gained in confidence and stature in the eyes of both the revolutionary government and their own people. Some expected that the Christian churches would weaken without foreign support; instead, the Christian witness, after a period of adjustment, is as strong and active as ever, and the Buddhist majority holds a higher opinion of Christianity. The churches are proving their independence and are gaining confidence steadily.

A brief summary of the Christian community will provide perspective. The total Christian church numbered approximately 923,000 in 1970, the last date for which figures are available. Of these the Baptist Convention totaled 520,000, or 56 percent of all Christians.† Catholics were second with 252,000. All other Protestant groups numbered 30,000 each or less. It is estimated that 95 percent of these Christians were from the tribal (animistic) groups, among whom small "peoples movements," both past and present, have swelled the churches spectacularly from time to time.

Thus from the beginning it has been the tribespeople more than the Burman Buddhists who have been open to Christian evangelism. And the history of missions in Burma records largely the labors and successes of those who have labored among these spirit-fearing tribal minorities, the Karens, Kachins, and Chins. Many of them are as open today as they ever were. But now the evangelists are from among their own or neighboring

†Ed. note. After a visit to Burma, Bishop Chondu Ray reported in the *COFAE News* of April 1973 that Baptist growth continued strong, with a total of 540,000 adherents at the end of 1972.

tribespeople, and their message is thus easier to understand and accept than when the white missionaries first reached them. In many local areas, it is reported, the churches receive requests from nearby heathen villages for evangelists and Bible women in such numbers that they cannot meet them.

But this very success of continuing evangelism among the minority peoples has led to some conflicts with the Buddhist-dominated government. Mutual distrust has often placed the ethnic minorities on one side and the Burman majority on the other side of such political questions as Buddhism as a state religion, loyalty to Britain and her army during World War II, or loyalty to U Nu's government in 1948 as opposed to seeking an autonomous Karen state. Because Christians in the minority groups have received more education and have arisen as new leaders, they have often appeared to be anti-Burman and anti-nationalistic.

Since Christians comprise only 3 percent of the population and Buddhists comprise more than 75 percent, Christians tend to interpret any overt action which is detrimental to them as being a form of discrimination or persecution. For instance, in its program to develop national unity and to create a prosperous socialist state, the army regime was sometimes ruthless in dealing with any organization which would delay a quick realization of this goal. The churches, with their loyalties to international church denominations and a higher loyalty to God, sometimes felt that the government dealt more harshly with them than with others. Recent conversations with church leaders reveal that retrospectively they view their government's treatment of the Christian community as fair.‡ But there is still a lurking fear that they may yet be the object of persecution by the Buddhist majority.

‡Ed. note. However, one expatriate Burmese college professor feels strongly that this view is too charitable, and cites the following facts.

1) Ne Win and his government are xenophobic and, like all Burmese politicians, regard Christianity as an alien religion. 2) Scientific Marxism, the socialism which the revolutionary government has espoused, is antagonistic toward Christianity and other religions. Religion is still considered an opiate of the masses. The expression of traditional Buddhist beliefs on the part of the revolutionary leaders of contemporary Burma is only for political purposes, and the Buddhist public knows this. 3) The addition of new converts to the church in Burma is made possible through the providence and grace of God alone. Evangelism is restricted by the government by requiring travel permits and by the presence of military intelligence officials in church conferences and even in church services. The military government, knowing the explosive nature of the religious sentiment of the people, is tolerating their religious practices. But all religious activities, as well as other activities of the population, are under surveillance. One has to be prepared for the fact that such tolerance on the part of the military government will eventually come to an end, since the goal of the very secular and materialistic "Burmese way to socialism" has to be reached. Christians are reluctant to express their feelings in their correspondence with the outside world. This is not entirely founded on their timidity, but on the actual danger with which they are confronted in their daily dealings with the government. Such fear is something the outside world of free countries cannot sense or visualize. (From a letter to the editor).

Opportunities and Needs in Evangelism Today

Burma has been in the crucible now for almost three decades. None of the young people and few of their elders have ever known a life without uncertainty. Most of the Christians are members of rural churches, and for decades the rural areas have been outside effective government control. Yet through the years of the Japanese occupation and the subsequent rebellions since independence the church has continued to grow at a steady 2.7 to 3.0 percent annual rate, largely among the tribal groups.

Seminary students spend many weeks each summer in non-Christian villages at the invitation of the villagers, conducting evangelistic campaigns and giving moral support to evangelists sent to these areas. Karen Baptist associations support new churches and workers in new areas, often among Nagas, Was, Lisus, and smaller Karen tribes, and have seen new churches organized every year. In Kayah State the local Baptist association has opened work in eleven non-Christian villages in the four years since 1966. They report that other villages are asking for workers, but they have neither the personnel nor the finances to meet all the calls. There are fifty-one Baptist churches in Kayah State, with an average of about sixty members each; these churches, with some help from Lower Burma, have thirty-three home mission projects. This story could be repeated concerning several other areas where animism is the major faith.

Reports of response to evangelistic work among Burmans are scarcer; there is still resistance to conversion among the majority Buddhist population. Some Karen leaders feel that they should make a major effort to reach the Burmans, but deep-seated fears between ethnic groups inhibit such preaching. However, a Christian center program, begun in spite of great opposition in a suburb of Rangoon a few years ago, has won 120 converts from among Buddhist Burmans, some of whom have high status in the community.

The latest available report of the Bible Society identifies 1969 as the most successful year in its history, in spite of "exhaustion of stocks of New Testaments and Bibles in many languages." Local contributions to the society increased by almost 30 percent over the previous year. In spite of lack of stock, distribution was the second highest on record, just over 7,800 short of the highest mark of 264,627 copies. Portions of Scripture and tracts are still used extensively in evangelistic work.

Modern media is not being ignored in evangelism. Though it is difficult to secure time on government-controlled radio, programs are being broadcast from Manila over Far East Broadcast station and Southeast Asia Radio voice, and letters from listeners request much Christian literature and Scripture. This work is under the direction of the Burma Christian Council, as is also an audio-visual department which supplies films and travels from place to place to show Christian and educational films.

Most of the churches in both towns and villages are filled with young people. Members of church youth groups and students from seminaries and Bible schools conduct many of the evangelistic services, youth speaking to youth. Laymen participate in many meetings, singing in choirs and giving personal witness. Annual meetings of associations of the churches and the Burma Baptist convention are open to all comers, and evangelistic preaching is emphasized. Often as many as 60 percent of those attending are non-Christian, and large numbers of attendees are under thirty years of age.

In spite of some few difficulties, religious freedom is still a fundamental human right and is guarded by the state. Almost all forms of evangelism are possible in most parts of Burma. Because of nationalization of all industry, evangelism in the industrial sector is not permitted, though outdoor meetings in open spaces are allowed with community approval. Whole communities, and especially community leaders, are invited to the special meetings, most often at Christmas and Easter. In rural districts special temporary tabernacles roofed with grasses and branches are built for meetings, which may last several days. Often the headman's house, with its large room for village meetings, is offered for four or five hours of preaching and discussions. At many of these meetings tracts, pamphlets, and Scripture portions are given to any who show an interest.

There has always been an emphasis upon lay evangelism; many laymen have preached and witnessed as ably as many pastors. New emphasis is now being placed on person-to-person witnessing, and many churches are conducting classes in methods.

In summary, there are no problems posed to Christian evangelism in Burma which cannot be met by careful planning and courageous presentation of the gospel. The declaration of freedom of religion by the revolutionary council gives freedom to preach, to distribute books and pamphlets, to proselytize, and to carry on evangelistic activities, limited only by the unsettled conditions in the country and the restriction of travel to frontier areas where rebel forces are in control. There seems to be a genuine religious tolerance among the larger segment of the Buddhist community, allowing Christians to witness as long as they do not offend the religious sensibilities of Buddhists.

However, an expatriate Burmese intellectual disputes this rosy view of liberty to evangelize in Burma today (1971).

> It is no doubt true that Christians can preach and worship within the confines of their churches and their homes. But freedom to worship and to practice Christianity often does not include freedom to propagate

Christianity. Christian books and pamphlets cannot be printed and published freely without being officially censored. In fact the government controls the paper supply for printing purposes. It is only with the government's permission that Christian tracts and pamphlets can be published. In 1965 Burmese Bibles shipped by the Gideons International from Great Britain were detained in the government customs shed for several years. Gideons in Burma could not place Bibles in hotels or public places, since Bibles were regarded by the government military personnel as subversive literature, antagonistic to their socialist cause. The situation has not changed much, if at all.

Evangelistic activities now carried on by the native Christians themselves are limited in scope or prohibited altogether on grounds of security. Even if they are permitted they are under strict surveillance of the military intelligence. Christians there have to be as wise as serpents and as harmless as doves.

The socialist revolution in Burma has affected not only the economic, social, and cultural realms but also the place and life of the churches. The reconstruction of society was based on clear pre-suppositions of an ideology claiming to be the sole authority in all the essential public spheres. This is the ideology of the "Burmese way to socialism," which is in essence Marxism-Leninism in a Burmese garb, an ideology programmatically materialistic and atheistic. Sharp criticism of the churches and religion is a fundamental, persistent Marxist tradition. Thus the concept of a cultural revolution entailed the task of overcoming the hold of religion over the people. For a socialist man, religious practice is a sign of imperfection. Allegiance to a church is understood as a lack of socialist consciousness.§

The history of the growth of the church in Burma is replete with stories of first-generation Christians who have organized missionary projects to the farthest borders of the land. Ko Tha Byu, a bandit-turned-Christian, became a great Karen evangelist, and the Karens have followed his example by reaching other ethnic groups with the gospel message. So the church in Burma has a history of missionary enterprise that sets goals for today.

Many who have visited Burma in the past few years have come away thrilled by the continuing vision of new Burmese church leaders and the vigor of the Christian community. Plans for extending home mission work to all major, and some minor, ethnic groups have been worked out. National conventions and conferences, district associations, individual churches, Christian Endeavor societies, women's societies, and even individual church members support hundreds of workers in the field.

The *Ecumenical Press Service*, November 1969, reported the following

§Ed. note. The pessimistic observations of this Christian professor-in-exile are at variance with some of Dr. Hackett's observations at present. Yet they may realistically presage the future attitude of the government once it is further confirmed in power.

under the heading "World Council of Churches Executive Sees Vital Church in Burma":

> On returning to Geneva, Gill reported the immense vitality of the church in Burma and said, "These days we're rather critical about some of the things missionaries have done; but after seeing the vigor of the Christian community, I can only conclude they must have done something right!"

The evangelistic zeal of many hundreds of workers, both western missionaries and national pastors and evangelists, has carried the good news to the far corners of Burma. This same zeal is still present in much of the church in Burma today, which looks ahead with faith, confidence, and consecration and says in the words of Adoniram Judson, "The future is as bright as the promises of God."

The following overview of the country of Burma will help explain the contemporary milieu in which the courageous Burmese church is evangelizing.

Nation and People

The Union of Burma, with an area of 262,000 square miles, is the largest country on the Southeast Asian mainland. It shares long borders on the east with Thailand, on the northeast with China, and on the northwest with India as well as shorter borders with Laos and Bangladesh on the east and west. On the south and southwest Burma has thousands of miles of coastline on the Bay of Bengal and the Gulf of Martaban. Burma is also rimmed on the north by mountain ranges up to 12,000 feet and on the east and west by ranges of 8,000 feet. Burma's high mountains and deep river valleys have discouraged east-west movements and contributed to her historical isolation from her neighbors. Within the horseshoe-shaped curve of rugged mountains lie a central plain and river deltas of great fertility. Combined with a low population density and a tropical, monsoon climate, these geographic features have made Burma a food-surplus area for most of her modern history. The annual rainfall varies between 200 inches in coastal areas and 40 inches in the central "dry zone," and annual temperatures range from about 80 degrees (Fahrenheit) in the south to the low 70's in the northern lowlands.

No census has been taken for many years, but the 1971 estimate was 28,400,000.[2] Population density is about 103 per square mile, and the growth rate is estimated at 2.3 percent annually.

The predominantly rural population is concentrated in the lower reaches and deltas of the Chindwin, Irrawaddy, Sittang, and Salween rivers. On the mountains and plateaus some of the ethnic minorities practice shifting hillside cultivation and live in small, widely scattered communities, but the majority of the people farm wet rice paddies.

Approximately 19,500,000 Burmans comprise the dominant ethnic group. Depending upon how they are classified and grouped together, the other large ethnic groups include approximately 3,000,000 Karens, 1,500,000 Shans, 500,000 Chins, 500,000 Kachins, 500,000 Chinese, 500,000 Indians and Pakistanis, and numerous small ethnic groups who are probably all related distantly to the original Tibet-Burmans.

Burmese, related to Tibetan and Chinese, is the official national language and is fast becoming the lingua franca in most of the country, though there are still about 128 other languages and dialects spoken. This linguistic confusion, plus divisive colonial tactics used to suppress rebellion, has caused ethnic groups to maintain their cultural identity in the face of government programs to establish a national identity and has contributed to the inter-ethnic conflict which has plagued Burma since its independence in January 1948.

In 1866, when the British invaded upper Burma, the Burmans in Lower Burma seized the opportunity to rebel. Until then, the inhabitants of Lower Burma—Burmans, Mons, and Karens—had been coming closer together. But the missionaries, who had made considerable progress among the Karens, induced the government to arm the latter against their Burman neighbors. This led to continued government recruitment of Karens, as well as Chins and Kachins in smaller numbers, for the army of occupation, which was mainly composed of Indians. Thus one effect of British rule on the character of society in Burma was to foster division among the indigenous peoples.[3]

The ethnic origins of Burma are most complicated. Melanesold, Negrito, and Veddoid peoples—nomadic, hillside cultivators speaking scores of distinct dialects, including various types of Karens, Lahus, Was, and Kachins—occupied the country before Christ. The historically important Mons entered Lower Burma via the Sittang and Salween River corridors about the time of Christ. The Pyus migrated south from eastern Tibet in the early centuries of the Christian era into the Irrawadj basin. The Shan, or Thai, peoples long occupied the area now known as Yunnan, and under the Nan Chao (Lao) kingdom they dominated the area from about A.D. 750 until the Mongol armies crushed them in 1253. The second wave of Tibeto-Burmans took over the central plain of Burma after the Nan Chao and liquidated the Pyu state. The Burmans had had little contact with China; they learned the arts of war, horsemanship, rice cultivation, and slope terracing from the Thai-Shans.

Toward the end of the ninth century the Burmans founded a capital at Pagan and either conquered the alien peoples or absorbed them. What is now Burma was first united under King Anawrahta in 1044. During the next eight centuries the fortunes of the Burman kingdom ebbed and flowed.

Because of her contacts and conflicts with many neighbors Burma absorbed new ideas and forms of culture. Not the least of these were Theravada Buddhism and the symbols of kingly power taken from Hindu cults.

Later in her contacts with Western powers Burma was unfortunate to have to deal with empire-building governor-generals of India, and in a series of three wars over sixty years Burma was conquered by the British and finally brought under colonial domination in 1885. It was sixty-three years before Burma again became independent, and during that period of colonial domination the country suffered severe social disintegration and cultural decline. The elimination of the traditional Burman elite from the king down to the *Myothugji* (literally "town headman") deprived the society of leaders possessing symbols of power and led to the erosion of manners, cultural life, literature, the arts, the use of the Burman language, and monastic discipline. Eventually a semi-westernized elite developed apart from the villagers, a self-seeking people who were qualified only for Class II civil service. In this capacity they were responsible for executing the orders of the British officials, and they frequently lost contact with the ordinary people.

The early onset of World War II in the Pacific soon converted Burma into a bloody buffer state, famed as the locus of the romantic Burma Road into West China. When Chiang Kai-shek was hard pressed by the Japanese in the late 1930's, the original Burma Road was planned and built by Chinese labor over some of the most rugged terrain in the world. Rangoon was to be the port at which supplies would land, and some of the was material was to go by rail to Lashio, about 110 miles from the Yunanese border, and then by truck over the road almost 1,000 miles to Kunming and thence on to the wartime capital in Chungking.

But before this road was carrying much traffic the Japanese captured Burma, and other means for supplying the Chinese nationalists had to be developed. For approximately two years all supplies went in by air, the famous C-47s shuttling back and forth from northeast India to Kunming. But as American military forces pushed into Northern Burma, the engineers laid a new road through some of the most primitive country in the world. This road was variously known as the Ledo Road (since its terminus was in India), the Stilwell Road (after "Vinegar Joe" Stilwell, U.S. commanding general), or the Burma Road. The new section crossed Burma in the far north and joined the original Burma Road at the China border.

Areas which had formerly been inaccessible except by pack-ox or mule-train were now on a broad, gravel-surfaced, all-weather road. Scores of exceedingly primitive tribes in the area were plunged into modern warfare and disintegrating cultural situations. But the road also became a pathway for communication of the gospel, and many of the churches and conferences of churches in north Burma sent missionaries to this area. In some cases whole Christian villages moved into good land along the Burma Road and preached Christ to animistic tribes that had never before been reached. Quite a few of these tribes were headhunters, placing their enemies' heads on poles in front of their tribal houses in the belief that by so doing they enlisted the help of the spirits of the beheaded to protect the village.

Thus war opened up the country for the gospel, and Christian Kachins, Nagas, Chins, and Karens have been establishing churches and schools there ever since and sending out promising young people for training in Bible Schools and seminaries. The first of these trained leaders are now back among their people.

Back in Rangoon after independence from the British in 1948, the prime minister, U Nu, tried to establish parliamentary democracy in a devastated nation which had suffered materially more than any other in World War II. His constitution took some of its ideas from that of the United States, but the forms were predominantly British. Political leadership fell into the hands of often meagerly trained and inexperienced young men drawn from the ranks of the Anti-Fascist Peoples Freedom League. Only a few experienced members of the colonial civil service remained. Government functions of tax-collecting, policing, and dispensing justice collapsed because of rebellion and violence in the first four years of the new government. Representative government was emasculated by feuding based on personal, ethnic, and ideological rivalries.

Beset with these many problems, U Nu tried to win his way by advocating a combination of democracy, socialist welfare state, and personal and public dedication to traditionalist religious revival. But a growing number of undisciplined Buddhist monks took advantage of his deference toward members of the strict Buddhist monastic orders by pressuring voters and members of parliament and threatening the religious freedom of minority groups in defiance of the constitution. U Nu, though he qualified as ruler-patron of Buddhism, was inefficient and indulgent. Thus General Ne Win's second military coup of March 2, 1962, overthrew the government with a claimed need to stop the disintegration of the Burma Union politically and territorially.

The new military government brushed aside the pattern of constitutional government. "The Burmese way to socialism," an ideology of socialist revolution, was instituted and ruthlessly enforced by naked military force. Private businesses—lands, factories, stores, and theaters—were confiscated. All medical and educational institutions were nationalized; the government took over all assets but left the liabilities in the hands of the former owners. It imprisoned political opponents without trial for as long as six years and rudely silenced its critics in business and press, often by putting them in custody. It made the civilian court system serve the aim of the revolution.

Early in his rule General Ne Win saw Burma as becoming an ideological battleground between China and the West; the country was being subjected to propaganda from both sides, and this was causing serious political upheavals and making the nation almost ungovernable. So Ne Win forced out literally hundreds of thousands of foreigners who were representatives of one or the other ideology, and in effect said, "Leave us alone to work out our own socialism—the Burmese way." Under this order foreign missionary personnel were ordered to leave in 1966.

The immediate provocation, we think, was the going underground of three American missionary families who worked on the border area between Burma and China. They went underground (and are still in the area) in December 1965, and the order requesting all to leave was issued in March 1966. For administrative purposes the approximately six hundred foreign missionaries, including a few Hindus, were divided into three groups. Almost all Americans were in group one, to be out by the end of May 1966. A second group was given until August 31 and a third group until December 1.

The first and second groups were actually required to leave, but the third group, including most of the foreign bishops and many of the older priests of the Roman Catholic Church (mostly Italian and French, with a few Americans and Irish), did not leave; many are still there.

There are no exact figures published as to how many missionaries had to leave. The figure of 600 is a very rough estimate of the number who were listed, but since the third group never left, it is likely that between 350 and 400 were actually expelled. Of these, not more than 70 were Protestants, all of whom left before May 31, 1966.

Burmese nationals were forbidden to leave the country except as official government representatives, thus cutting off international contacts. Until 1970 no tourist visas were issued. No books printed in the languages of Burma could be imported or sold, and niggardly granting of import licenses for books in other languages effectively cut off reading materials.

The principal emphasis in economic development under Ne Win has been on the agricultural sector. Burma's economy depends almost entirely upon exploitation of natural resources, primarily through farm production, with rice leading all other commodities. Teak and hardwoods, minerals, oil, fisheries, and jade and precious stones all contribute a small percentage to national income. Most of the recent industrial development has been for facilities needed to process agricultural output. However, other economic emphases have included electrical energy, oil extraction and refining, increased mineral and timber output, and fishing. But painfully slow economic progress, with inexperienced army men making decisions, has undermined the prestige of the army regime.

"The Burmese way to socialism" as devised by Ne Win's "revolutionary council" emphasizes the peasants' position in society but has not moved in the direction of land communalization.

General Ne Win's efforts to establish a one-party system of government with the Burma Socialist Program Party (Lanlin) replacing all others has failed, and many major groups of Burma's elite have been alienated. Although popular resistance has been uncoordinated, it is a major force in holding back progress. Even the peasants for whom the program has been planned have often refused to cultivate more than enough to meet their own needs. Some people, especially in frontier areas, prefer to smuggle goods across the border rather than cultivate crops.

The general economic level and condition is very poor. Farm production is low, partly because the peasants lack faith in the socialist system. Money supply is at an unprecedented high level, and prices have soared from 300 to 500 percent above normal. Industrial production has declined, due to lack of raw materials and machinery parts and to an undisciplined labor force.

Statistics are distrusted. The *Working Peoples Daily*, a government-controlled newspaper, reported on January 16, 1969: "There seems to be an unhealthy tendency to hide reality. . . . Many are afraid they will come to harm if the truth is revealed. . . . The result is hypocrisy and deceit."

Despite the fact that the entire economy depends on rice output and export, export figures have been declining sharply since 1959. The budget report for 1968-69 gave these figures: prewar average (1937-40), 2.68 million tons; 1959, 1.77 million tons; 1968, 0.34 million tons. In the 1968 Peasants' Seminar the reason for this condition was revealed as the need for more agricultural implements, good seeds, water for fields, fodder for cattle, marketing facilities, security, and honest land committees.

Per capita income for 1968-69 was estimated as approximately $80 (U.S.) per year, a slight improvement over the previous year, yet one of the lowest in Asia. People on fixed incomes (about $21-24 on the average) are struggling to make ends meet. Since essential goods are in short supply from legal sources (the "people's shops"), many persons are forced to buy on the black market or go without. Black market prices range from three to five times normal, controlled prices. In the 1972-73 period the economy deteriorated still further because of rice shortages.

In some ways current political conditions seem to be more relaxed. Recently Ne Win has been talking more with the peasants and workers and listening to them. He repeatedly emphasizes collective leadership, and his government is urging that the army must participate in social affairs and engender political consciousness. Some government participation by new segments of society has been encouraged. Many political detainees have been released, and some have been called upon for token advice to the military government. Some criticism of government policies has been permitted in newspapers, and Ne Win has admitted that the army may have erred in certain fields. But basically the party's course follows the direction of its leftist leaders.

At the same time, observers in Thailand believe that rebel activities extend over 40 percent of the country. James Dalton, writing in the *Far Eastern Economic Review,* states:

> Most former political leaders of the states are either in exile, associated with armed rebel groups, jailed, or confined to residence within the Rangoon area. The government relies upon its radical ideology to remould all the people of Burma into Burmese socialists and nationalists. In sum, the ethnic minorities confront a situation in which the national government at Rangoon appears to be the least sympathetic of any that has held power since independence in 1948. And as a consequence one of Burma's unique claims to fame continues and grows. Today it is a country harboring more civil wars of long duration than any other nation in the world. There are at least four going on aside from two Communist-inspired rebellions. The physical destruction, loss of life, and retardation of national development caused by these conflicts defy exact calculation.[4]

News media in Thailand and Hong Kong reported extensively the activities of Red Chinese forces in northeast Burma in early 1970. Nine major battles were admitted by the Burma army, and other sources in Burma report many more. Non-communist civil wars by ethnic groups against the revolutionary government have split the country into segments, thus making it more vulnerable to Red Chinese pressure. Because of Burma's peculiar problems since independence and her deliberate isolation in recent years, the outcome of these developments is unpredictable.

Like most Southeast Asian countries, Burma has been influenced by Marxist ideology. Before World War II, the Rangoon university students' union was the center for communist ideas, but it is hard to assess their influence because the RUSU was also the hotbed of nationalism and the movement for independence. The first premier of Burma, Dr. Ba Maw, was leftist in ideology and an unspoken advocate of socialistic proposals to help the poor. After independence U Nu, then premier, declared that Burma would follow Marxist ideology, and he tried to get the Communists to join in a coalition government. However, the Communists chose rebellion against the fledgling government, hoping to receive aid from China, but it was not forthcoming. In 1952 the Communists took a beating, and in 1953 the Communist party was declared illegal. It has continued to harass the government but has never secured a large popular following. Periodically there have been alliances of convenience between Communists and ethnic minority rebel groups, some of whose leaders seem to have accepted Communism, but the true strength of this ideology is questionable.

Despite Marxist talk the Burma Socialist party, which provided the political theory of the present government, resembles the British Labor party. Nationalization was the foundation of party doctrine, and social welfare was the goal; destruction of the capitalistic system was not envisaged. Such organizations as the Trades Union Congress, though affiliated with communist World Federation of Trade unions, were primarily political bodies designed to mobilize the masses in order to give support to the party leaders, who were businessmen and capitalists.

For many years Burma has looked to China as the arena of a great new experiment in social change and has patterned many of her programs on what her leaders saw on numerous visits to China. With a long, undefended border she chose a posture of neutrality, hoping to avoid becoming the battleground between western and communist ideologies. China exerted great pressure at times, with Chou En-lai a frequent and often uninvited guest in Rangoon. Often Burma has been accused of being neutral with a tinge of red influence. In recent years, however, Burma seems to be disenchanted with her neighbor to the north. Serious anti-Chinese riots in Rangoon in mid-1967 seem to indicate a shift toward the true neutral position. The Communists are an underground opposition to the present military government. Some observers interpret the recent direct attack of Red Chinese forces in northeast Burma as an admission by Peking that communist infiltration has not been successful. This failure may be attributed in part to the facts that 1) the Buddhist monastic order does not support the Communists; 2) U Nu, speaking to more than a hundred thousand people in an AFPFL Congress in 1958, declared, "The AFPFL rejects Marxism as a guiding philosophy or as the ideology of the AFPFL;" 3) Communism cannot be harmonized with Buddhist beliefs; and 4) the village people have been revulsed by the communist atrocities.

National Religions

Religion is inextricably woven into the fabric of Burmese society; religious beliefs and practices are integrated into the life of the family, the community, the tribe, and the nation. This is true of both of the traditional faiths, Buddhism and animism. As a matter of fact Buddhism still retains belief in the *nats* (spirits) which were traditional before Buddhism was introduced to the Burmans in the eleventh century by the founder of the Pagan empire, Anawrahta. Primitive animistic beliefs include two categories of spirits: those associated with natural objects, such as sky, earth, lakes, trees, rocks, etc., and those associated with people of former days, some ancestral and some vagrant. At the time of Anawrahta, the Burmans had developed a nat pantheon of thirty-six identifiable vagrant spirits, all of whom had died a violent death. Sometime later a thirty-seventh nat was added for Buddha.

Spiritism is combined with magic, omens, and astrological signs. A protective spirit was attached to a strategic place, i.e., a guard tower or gateway, by burying some unfortunate victim alive in the foundations. Appropriate spirits were propitiated before any important action was undertaken. Invulnerability could be achieved by tattooing certain patterns on the arms or back, and magical potions were used for protective purposes.

Thus it is almost impossible to draw a sharp line between Buddhism and spirit-worship. It is more nearly correct to express the religious adherence of most Burmese peoples as a continuum, with a very few at one end adhering to philosophical Buddhism, and a goodly number at the other end following strictly animistic practices.

It is estimated that more than 22 million people follow to some extent the tenets of Theravada Buddhism, a very old and simple form of Buddhism predominating in Southeast Asia. Primitive animism claims perhaps as many as 2 million followers. A 1970 church census by the Burma Christian Council places the number in the Christian community at 923,000. The important minority religions in Burma include Islam, Hinduism, and Chinese folk religion.

Theravada Buddhism emphasizes the original teachings of Buddha, with fewer accretions than other forms. It is based on the Hindu premises of *maya* and *karma* but emphasizes moral principles of conduct as opening a way of escape from the otherwise endless wheel of existence. The sufferings of life, according to Gautama Buddha, issue from desire, which can be overcome by following the "noble eightfold path" of right belief, right aspiration, right speech, right action, honest livelihood, sustained mental exertion, alertness, and serenity. Everyone is on his own, with little possibility of borrowed merit. There is no savior, no God of grace and mercy. The five precepts to be followed by all laymen are the prohibitions against stealing, deceit, murder, adultery, and intoxication. All life is considered sacred, and all killing, whether of men, animals, fish, or insects, must consequently be avoided. *Nirvana* is attained when all desires are conquered and the soul-substance of man is merged with the absolute essence. Theoretically, all men can attain Nirvana without priestly magic or aid of the gods.

Most Buddhist religious practices are done on an individual basis, but they are given some social recognition and are often combined with social events. Each individual makes an offering or completes a worship pilgrimage on his own and for his own merit, though other individuals performing similar religious acts may be present. In every household there is a *paya-sin* (god-shelf or altar) at which a daily offering is made, usually of the first rice cooked before dawn by the woman of the house. An attitude of respect in bodily mien toward the paya-sin is always maintained, and in many households each member spends some time in respect and meditation before the shrine. This shelf usually holds an image of Buddha, a religious-astrological calendar, sacred objects and pictures brought back from pilgrimages, and fresh flowers. This worship center, which is often in the front room, is a constant reminder to the household that Buddhism is the path to Nirvana.

Many people go to the pagodas or monastery shrines on sabbath days, which occur four times per lunar month. Special worship days fall on full moons, when throngs of people visit worship places; many even go for an all-night vigil on the preceding night in order to prepare themselves. In connection with full-moon days, except during Buddhist Lent (which coincides with the monsoon rain season) there are great festivals which might be compared with the country fairs or festivals held in the cathedral squares in Europe in the nineteenth century. These are great social occasions, drawing people from a wide area and affording a chance to see friends and exchange news. Free entertainment is provided as an act of merit of some *Daga* (see below).

Some older people whose children have grown up and can give them a certain degree of security and care devote their time to religious duties. Their purpose is to build up a store of merit which will assure progress into a higher realm in the transmigration process, which will finally culminate in Nirvana. Every male of whatever station in life can aspire to be a patron or trustee of a pagoda, a shrine or an outbuilding in the monastery grounds, or else he can aspire to support a monk. Such a person is given social recognition with the title *Daga.* Thus all meritorious gifts and deeds are socially recognized, and every good Buddhist strives for such recognition.

Under U Nu, Burma became in many ways the acknowledged center of the Buddhist world. He encouraged religion in personal attitudes and in the political life of the country. His own driving force was a religious belief that permeated every thought and action. In the midst of rebellions, civil war, and economic chaos, U Nu arranged to bring Buddhist relics from Ceylon and India in 1950. He instituted the study of Pali scriptures, examinations for monastic candidates, and conferring of honored titles. He encouraged development of new missionary efforts, both to the hill peoples of Burma and to the wider world. A great movement to rebuild and refurbish famous pagodas steadily gained momentum under U Nu's leadership. The Sixth Buddhist Council was held under his aegis, ending on the 2500th anniversary of Buddha's attainment of Nirvana. This activity undoubtedly influenced a Buddhist revival, the effect of which is hard to measure.

Public opinion still regards religious observance as an essential duty. The highest government official or his lowliest clerk would not pass a pagoda without stopping to make obeisance. The most serious accusation against the Communists is their contempt of religious beliefs. Some Marxists in the government are careful to state their belief that dialectical materialism and Nirvana can be harmonized.

Ne Win's government, though it declared that it does not emphasize one religion at the expense of another, "has committed itself to the need for religion as a key element in its ideology, the Burmese way to socialism.[5] Ne Win himself has visited famous Buddhist holy places on his trips to India. A high proportion of his revolutionary council as well as most army officers participate in religious ceremonies and worship in all parts of the country to which they are posted. Often they are the main support of the mission efforts in those hill areas where monks are building monasteries and schools to reach animists. Yet many observers feel that these moves are only expedient political ploys.

The other traditional faith, animism (spirit worship), has very little official standing in the country today, though parts of its beliefs survive as folk religion within the Buddhist community.|| Spirits may be classed in two broad categories, those associated with natural objects and localities and those once associated with people now dead. These people-spirits may be ancestors, or else they may be "free" or vagrant because they have died by accident, were executed as criminals, or committed suicide; they are vengeful because proper funeral and burial procedures have not been followed. Since most spirits are mischievous, vengeful, and truculent, life is an unending struggle to avoid, propitiate, or repel the attacks of these beings. In fact, worship is not a truly descriptive word for various rites and ceremonies which the animist performs to placate and avoid the spirits in his world.

Attitudes of Burmese Buddhists toward Christianity are many and varied. Buddhism is not dogmatic; it does not presume to set forth a final or exclusive statement of truth, but represents itself as a way. Therefore,

||Animism may be defined as "the belief that everything within the experience of man, both animate and inanimate, is possessed of an individual spirit which, most of the time during the life of such animate or inanimate object, is connected with the life and activities of that object" (W. D. Hackett, "Christian Approach to Animistic Peoples," *Southeast Asia Journal of Theology*, Apr. 1969, p. 4).

missionaries find it relatively easy to discuss Christian theology with many of its adherents, comparing and contrasting elements of both faiths; even monks will listen and discuss such matters in their monasteries. When representatives of the two faiths come together, the dialogue is often open and frank. Purely on the basis of religion, there has been little persecution of the Christian minority by the Buddhist majority. However, in the stress of struggle for independence, when other factors entered in, there has been some open opposition and hatred of Christians. One must bear in mind that under the British colonial rule there was a high degree of cultural disintegration, and Buddhism itself suffered a sharp decline. Now in the process of rebuilding, Burmans have blamed the "Christian" British for the low prestige of their own faith. Militant monks have encouraged such thinking.

Christian History

The first "Christians" in Burma of whom we have any record were captive Portuguese soldiers and a few traders and adventurers. In 1554 the first Catholic priests, two Dominican friars, came to serve them as chaplains, but after three years they left, for they were not well received by the Portuguese free-booters; the priests declared they would rather preach to pigs! Later, captive soldiers were taken to central Burma, where they married Burmese women and served as musketeers and gunners in the royal guard. In the early sixteen hundred's two Jesuits served them as chaplains. Some hundreds of descendants of this community still live in Burma.

The missionary efforts of early Roman Catholic priests were completely rejected by the Buddhist population. Fear and distrust of foreigners were so prevalent that any subject of the Burmese king who consorted with them was likely to be threatened. Anyone who listened to a new religious doctrine was considered a traitor to the king, who was regarded as the supreme protector of all things Buddhist. Among the few early missionaries it is recorded that two members of the *Mission Estrangeres* "were mistreated and drowned" in 1693; that the first bishop of Burma, Father Gallizia, and two Barnabite priests were murdered in 1746; and that a Bishop Nerini was executed in 1756. The hostility of Buddhist monks and the xenophobia of the Burmese court meant that there were no recorded conversions to Christianity before American Protestant missionaries arrived in Burma in 1813.

Ann and Adoniram Judson left the United States as missionaries of the Congregational Churches, but after careful study of the Scriptures during their four-month journey to India Judson decided that the Baptist doctrine on immersion was the correct one, and they were subsequently baptized by immersion. The East India Company ordered them to leave within a month, and rather than go back to America on the same ship they went first to Mauritius and finally to Rangoon. When they arrived there they were taken to the home of Felix Carey, who had tried to set up an English Baptist mission but had so far failed because the Burmese people were not permitted to accept the new religion.

Judson was a rare combination of meticulous scholar and utterly realistic evangelist. Within a few days of his arrival he began to study the Burmese language. Finding that much of Buddhist religious thought was expressed in Pali terms, he soon compiled a Pali-Burmese dictionary. By 1817 Judson was publishing tracts and Matthew's gospel; by 1823 he completed the New Testament and by 1834 the complete Bible. Considering that there were no grammars, dictionaries, or other teaching helps; that his teachers knew no English; and that he had to instruct them how to teach him, this was a truly prodigious accomplishment!

Judson decided early that he would preach the gospel rather than anti-Buddhism, and he opened a small roadside *zayat* (rest-house) where he spent many hours talking with anyone who would stop for a few minutes. It was just over six years before his first convert, U Naw, was baptized. Shortly after this, Judson went to Ava to try to secure the king's approval for his preaching, but he was scornfully rejected. Nevertheless, the work continued with the opening of the first school by Mrs. Judson in 1821 and the arrival of the first medical missionary during the same year.

In 1823 the king invited the missionaries to settle in Ava. Soon after their arrival, however, the first Anglo-Burmese war broke out, and Judson and Dr. Brice were imprisoned. A year-and-a-half later Judson was released by the king to act as translator at the peace talks.

After peace was restored the missionaries decided to begin work in Tenasserim, which had been ceded to the British. First at Amherst and later in Moulmein a strong educational and evangelistic program was developed. A number of new missionaries were assigned to the Karens, who welcomed the gospel and thus influenced the tribal direction of mission work for decades to come. Although some of this work was done under the protection of the British, much of the work in the delta was within the Burmese kingdom and, after the Second Anglo-Burmese war, in the hills east of the Sittang River. Within a very few years during the 1860's associations of churches were established, and plans for support of Karen evangelists in work among other Karen tribes, non-Karen ethnic minorities, and even in Thailand were quickly brought into effect.

The phenomenal development of self-support among the Karens has been commented on by many students of mission method. This self-support was immediately extended to evangelistic mission work throughout all parts of Burma. Karen evangelists often accompanied pioneer missionaries as they went farther and farther inland, but in many parts of Burma, especially to the tribes in border areas, the Karens themselves were the first bearers of the gospel message.

Josiah Nelson Cushing was the first great missionary to the Shan, beginning his many travels in the Shan States in 1868. William Henry Roberts, who arrived in Bhamo in 1879, is remembered by the Kachins as the man who brought them the knowledge of Christ. Arthur Carson first went into the Chin Hills in 1899, but he lived only a few years; it was J. Herbert Cope who spent thirty years in that rugged country and gave impetus to a rapid growth among the people, now the second-largest language group in the Christian church in Burma.

From the earliest days, Baptist missionaries in Burma planned for development of the church under indigenous leadership. The pattern was set in the 1840's among the Karens, and methods and goals were then extended to every new district. Thus among the larger ethnic minority groups, methods used and developed in Karen fields became the model for missions. These included the organization of associations of churches with annual meetings for planning evangelistic outreach; persuading the nomadic villagers to settle in permanent villages, where they could support the churches, schools, medical facilities, cottage industries, and permanent agriculture; training large numbers of young people in schools, Bible schools, and theological seminaries; placing and supporting pastors and evangelists in non-Christian villages to build congregations through conversion of whole villages; a plan of in-service training for all Christian workers, with pastors' classes and laymen's institutes once or twice a year, often lasting for ten days; and the constant emphasis on limited economic development as an essential element in self-support. Many pastors and evangelists made regular evangelistic tours, often of many weeks' duration, spending a few days in each village and following a regular circuit periodically until such time as a resident evangelist could be assigned.

Although the response to the gospel among the Burmans has always been very small, among the Karens, Kachins, and China it has been great; more than 80 percent of the Christians today are from these three families of tribes. One can only speculate as to why the Burmans rejected the gospel; contributing factors undoubtedly include the facts that they are the majority, that they have an ethical humanitarian code for living supported by strong social approval, and that they have an ethnocentrism which has always viewed foreign or non-Burman ways as less good than Burman Buddhist ones.

On the other hand, the three ethnic groups who have accepted the Christian faith were animists, to whom the gospel appeared as a new and more positive and rewarding system of beliefs. Too, the Karens, Kachins, and Chins were all minorities, despised by the majority and devoid of social standing among Burmans; thus they were more willing to listen to the gospel. The Christian message that was preached and demonstrated by the missionaries and early Karen converts dealt with the whole of man—his spirit, mind, and body—and created a sense of personal worth among the "worthless." The missionaries and Karen evangelists were the instruments by which these peoples came to know the pride of being sons of God.

Mission and church institutions have been an integral part of the proclamation of the gospel in Burma. Christian village primary schools, secondary schools in town centers supported by associations of churches, Bible Schools, seminaries, and colleges—all have been an important part of the life of the church. Always they have been open to any who applied for admission, and they have been looked upon as another tool for evangelism as well as a necessity for leadership training for the Christian community. The support has come from church members, most of whom view life and the Christian vocation as their service to God and the church.

Hospitals and dispensaries, a large press for printing Bibles, hymnbooks and tracts in twenty different languages, and agricultural schools all served the communities and raised living standards, so that Christian people could support their churches and pastors. Dr. A. C. Henderson, forty-four years a medical missionary to the Shans, was also a very effective evangelist, enthralling the Shan princes and their lowest subjects with his excellent Shan preaching. Brayton Case was head of the agricultural school in Pyinmina, but he could preach as no Burman had ever preached in Burmese. And his "Christian" pigs and chickens witnessed in small villages from one end of the land to the other. The first leper colonies, orphanages, and institutions for the physically handicapped were all in the hands of church and mission organizations, witnessing to the love of God as expressed through His church.

The preceding reports are based largely upon records of the Burma Baptist Convention, whose constituency is about 56 percent of the Christian community. Much of what has been said applies to other Protestant denominations, with a few exceptions. Though the Roman Catholics have had chaplains in Burma since the sixteenth century, they have usually served foreigners and enjoyed only limited success in missionary work until recently. In Rangoon and other cities they built big churches and schools, but these served mostly foreigners and therefore contributed little to missionary success. In Rangoon and other cities the Catholic mission successes have been greater in the twentieth century, mostly among animists (Karens, Kachins, and small ethnic groups). The Catholics have neglected the training of national priests; Italian, French, Irish, and American mission fathers have held the reins fairly tightly, and six of the eight bishops in Burma are foreigners today. They are now hurriedly trying to rectify the shortage of trained leaders. For some reason, when foreign missionaries were expelled from Burma in 1966, although all Protestant foreigners left, about 175 Roman Catholic bishops and priests were permitted to remain and are still there today.

The first Anglican clergy to reach Burma were chaplains to British civil servants and army personnel. The first bishop was appointed in 1877, and many church members have come from the civil service and from the Anglo-Burman and Anglo-Indian communities, the vast majority of whom have now left Burma. There are many Karen members of the Church of Burma, as it is now known, and the present Archbishop, Francis Ah Mya, is a Karen.

The Methodists of Upper Burma have in recent years increased their membership rapidly, partly because they absorbed Lushai Christians who migrated into Burma after being evangelized by the Welsh Methodist Church in Assam. The Presbyterian Church is also largely made up of Lushais who migrated into Burma en masse. The Assemblies of God and the Church of Christ, both located in the far north, are also made up largely of ethnic groups who have moved into Burma after Communism took over the government of Yunnan Province in China; many of these people were converted by the work of the China Inland Mission in their homeland.

Thus evangelism among the tribal groups by all denominations seems to be spiritually prospering in Burma today. The Holy Spirit is at work in Christ's church in continuing power without foreign missionary assistance. At this time prayer is the primary ministry of the world's churches to their courageous sister church in Burma.

APPENDIX

Number of Christians in Burma[a]

Denomination	*Adherents*
The Church of Burma (Anglican)[b]	27,000
Burma Baptist Convention[c]	520,000
Lutheran	300
The Methodist Church, Burma[d]	18,770
Methodist (Lower Burma)[e]	2,819
Presbyterian Church of Burma[f]	9,600
The Salvation Army	300
Self-Supporting Karen Baptists	5,000
St. Gabriel's Church of India, Burma, and Ceylon	200
Lisu Christian Church	8,000

Assemblies of God	30,000
The Church of Christ	20,000
The Independent Church of Burma	8,500
Seventh Day Adventists	14,734
The Roman Catholic Church	252,000
Other Small Churches and Denominations	5,700
Total	922,923

a) Statistics supplied in June 1970 by Rev. John Thet Gyi, General Secretary of the Burma Christian Council.

b) The Church of Burma (Anglican) is the result of the work of the Church of England.

c) The Burma Baptist Convention grew out of more than 150 years of work of the American Baptist Foreign Mission society.

d) The Methodist Church, Burma, is related to the English Wesleyan Church in Burma.

e) Methodist (Lower Burma) is in the outgrowth of the American Methodist Mission.

f) Presbyterian Church of Burma is the result of migration into northwest Burma of a large group of Lushais, formerly connected with the Welsh Presbyterians of Assam.

NOTES

1. Stanley Mooneyham, *World Vision International Letter.*
2. *World Population Data Sheet* (Washington: Pop. Ref. Bureau), June 1971.
3. John S. Furnivall, "General Character of the Society," ed. Frank N. Tager, *Burma Human Relations Files,* pp. 35-64.
4. James Dalton, "Babes in the Woods," pp. 27-32.
5. S. J. Banerji, "Burma Awakes," p. 15.

BIBLIOGRAPHY

Banerji, S. J. "Burma Awakes." *Far Eastern Economic Review,* Aug. 27, 1970.

Bible Society of Burma. *Report for the Year 1968.* Rangoon, 1969.

"Burma Yearbook, 1969." *Far Eastern Economic Review,* 1969, pp. 113-120.

Cady, John F. *Southeast Asia: Its Historical Development.* New York: McGraw-Hill, 1964.

———. *Thailand, Burma, Laos, and Cambodia.* Englewood Cliffs, N.J.: Prentice Hall, 1966.

Dalton, James. "Babes in the Woods." *Far Eastern Economic Review,* Aug. 20, 1970, pp. 27-32.

Furnivall, John B. "General Character of the Society." Edited by F. N. Trager. *Burma Human Relations Area Files.* New York: University Press, 1956.

Hackett, William D. "Christian Approach to Animistic Peoples." *Southeast Asia Journal of Theology,* vol. 10, no. 4 (1969), pp. 48-83.

Hall, D. G. E. *Burma.* 3rd ed. London: Hutchinson University Library, 1960.

Htin Aung. *A History of Burma.* New York: Columbia University Press, 1967.

Maung Maung. *Burma and General Ne Win.* London: Asia Publishing House, 1969.

Maung Shwe Wa. *Burma Baptist Chronicle.* Rangoon: Burma Baptist Convention, 1963.

Mooneyham, Stanley. *World Vision International Letter.* Monrovia, Calif., Jan. 1, 1972.

Tegenfeldt, Herman G. *Through Deep Waters.* 2nd ed. Valley Forge: American Baptist Foreign Mission Society, 1968.

———. "Burma Speaks to Us All." *Evangelical Missions Quarterly,* Summer 1970.

Tinker, Hugh. *The Union of Burma.* 4th ed. London: Oxford University Press, 1967.

Trager, Frank N. *Burma: From Kingdom to Republic.* New York: Frederick A. Praeger, 1966.

Win Lin Yaung. "Burma: The Forgotten Domino." *Bangkok Magazine,* July 26, 1970, pp. 10-23.

Much information and background material for this chapter was taken from typewritten and mimeographed reports and letters from the officers of the Burma Christian Council and the Burma Baptist Convention in 1969 and 1970.

Evangelism in China before the communist take-over. A Christian student conference

A country baptism

Hospital evangelist

IVF student leaders

Photos by Overseas Missionary Fellowship

7

CHINA

(THE PEOPLE'S REPUBLIC OF CHINA)

by Arthur F. Glasser

FOR TWENTY-FIVE YEARS relative mystery has shrouded the true condition of the church of Jesus Christ in Red China. Information received has been fragmentary and sometimes even contradictory. Political attitudes and movements have frequently changed radically. How fares the church today?

Those who have visited China in the early seventies uniformly speak of a nation "intensely alive, determined, cracking with kinetic energy, collectively engaged in the sweaty tasks of nation-building, yet characteristically gracious, cordial, and open to visitors from abroad." There appears to be neither starvation nor poverty. Admittedly, life is spartan and society is highly regimented. Some would even characterize China today as "a puritanical society" possessed by an ideology of service rather than of profit. Its capacity for sacrifice for that ideology has led some observers to con-

---

ARTHUR GLASSER is dean of the School of World Missions and Church Growth at the Fuller Theological Seminary, Pasadena, California. After graduating from Cornell University, Moody Bible Institute, and Faith Theological Seminary, he served as a U.S. Navy chaplain in World War II. In 1946 he went to Southwest China under the China Inland Mission, returning home in 1951. After a period of teaching at Columbia Bible College, Dr. Glasser served first as assistant and then as home director of the CIM-Overseas Missionary Fellowship from 1955 through 1969. He is presently dean of the School of World Mission and Church Growth at Fuller Theological Seminary, Pasadena, California. He is the author of numerous articles on missions, communism, race, and biblical studies printed in many periodicals, as well as author of a book, *And Some Believed,* and co-author of another, *Missions in Crisis.*

Dr. Glasser writes lucidly of Chinese history; and his views, particularly of the failures of the missionary movement, are his own and are not shared by all historians of the missionary movement there (ed.).

clude that it embodies aspects of the ethical norms of the Judeo-Christian world view. Whether this will continue remains to be seen. If one were to judge from the experience of other communist countries, notably the Soviet Union, he would be pressed to affirm that communist idealism, with its professed desire to change human nature and produce a "new man" who will serve his fellows selflessly and sacrificially, eventually flounders on the predictable frailty of human nature. The Scriptures are adamant on this point. Unregenerate man is incapable of perfecting human society.

A spiritual vacuum of enormous proportions has been created in the hearts of hundreds of millions of people created in the image and likeness of God. And this vacuum will eventually prove the undoing of all that the Maoists have sought to do to remake man. For man will continue to feel the world to be haunted (the Numinous) and will grope outward and upward in his search for the Ultimate. Man will continue to sense the ethical structure of his nature and will strive to cope with rightness and wrongness, conscience and oughtness. He will never rest until he meets in Jesus Christ, the Haunter of the universe and its moral Governor.

Apparently some people in China are meeting Him. Persistent reports keep coming out of China of the activities of an informal, underground, cell-type Christian movement. Occasionally one hears of revivals. In mid-December, 1974, *Time* magazine reported on "China's Secret Christians." After reviewing the manner in which Premier Chou En-lai promised religious freedom in 1950, and guaranteed it in the 1954 constitution, the article described the devastating effects of Mao's efforts to suppress the church, but climaxed with the affirmation that "The Christian faith can still spark enthusiasm in a land where Mao's Revolution has tried to snuff it out."[1] Some see significance in the fact that the new constitution, adopted late in January, 1975, guaranteed freedom for religious worship, with this ominous rider: "freedom not to believe in religion and freedom to propagate atheism."[2]

These hopeful signs are a call to Christians outside China to pray. Will God liberate His people in China? In our day Christians all over the world are increasingly praying to this end. The Exodus motif comes to mind, for it is relevant. God knows the sorrow of His people and he will come down to deliver them in his time (Exodus 3:7, 8).

The Chinese Encounter With Christianity

Before Moses met God at the burning bush, the Chinese had already begun to emerge as one of mankind's major races. The dynamic complex of their culture—life-style, world view, religious customs, and social institutions—all had been formulated and gained wide acceptance in remote antiquity. By the time of Christ the Chinese had been forged into a political whole. They would not know a major cultural revolution until the advent of the People's Republic in 1949. Indeed, during the chaotic period from A.D. 500 to 950, when western Europe was facing total castastrophe (being assaulted by Muslims from the South and East and by Vikings from the North), T'ang China was serene, easily the "mightiest realm on the planet" (Latourette).

In our day China is reaching for her rightful place of greatness in the midst of the nations. Mao Tse-tung and his compatriots have taken a war-weary, poverty-stricken, largely illiterate, and foreign-dominated people—"The Sick Man of Asia"—and have forged a nation that is both politically stable and economically self-sufficient. Within two decades its people have been transformed in spirit and now take great national pride in their achievements.[3] This being so, no greater task faces the worldwide Christian church than to discover what the new China means in Chinese terms, and what this should mean in terms of Christ's universal concern for all men. But before the church reflects on her missionary responsibility touching this people, she should review the record of the past, both remote and recent.

China's encounter with Christianity covers almost fifteen hundred years. However, long before the first missionaries came from the West, the Chinese people were confronted by people who worshipped the God of Abraham, Isaac, and Jacob. China's first missionaries were silk-trading Israelites who wandered far from their ancestral land in search of this highly prized cloth. Apparently, in the ancient world silk came only from China, or Sinim, as it was known in Isaiah's day (49:12). It is interesting that Ezekiel mentions silk (16:10, 13). Actually, Jewish colonies existed in China from very early times (c. 700 B.C.), hundreds of years before the development of rabbinic Judaism.[4] Perhaps it was from these ancient Israelites that the Chinese developed some of their distinctive ideographs that have Old Testament significance (e.g., the character for "boat" intimates Noah's ark; the character for "righteousness" portrays the rebel "I" seeking shelter under a lamb). Perhaps the Jewish celebration of an annual Day of Atonement prompted the emperor to seek once a year to make atonement for the sins of his people.

Some of the early Western missionaries were understandably surprised to discover these ancient Jewish communities in inland China. However, little resulted from these contacts. Although both Jew and Christian worshipped the same God, the gulf between the ethnic religion of the Hebrews and the universal Christian faith inhibited further interaction.

When we turn to the long record of the Chinese encounter with Christianity, our task is vast. How to extract its gold! Throughout almost the whole Christian era, China was the object of successive waves of missionary effort. Thousands of devout men and women went to China. They represented scores of nationalities and all types of religious traditions. Merchants, friars, nuns, clergymen, wives, laymen and laywomen, teachers, medical workers—all played their part. They served during the most glorious, most tragic, and most tumultuous periods of China's history. Although they encountered enormous difficulties and considerable opposition, their faith was rewarded, and many of the proud, self-reliant, and able people of China responded to the Christian message. We must trace the highlights of this heroic story.

SYRIAN CHRISTIANITY (SEVENTH TO TENTH CENTURIES)

Christianity was first introduced into China during the T'ang dynasty (A.D. 618-905). It came through representatives of the church of the East, popularly known as the Nestorians. They initially entered China more as traders than as professional missionaries. The Nestorians were largely of Hebrew extraction, tracing their lineage to those who did not return to Palestine following the Assyrian and Babylonian captivities. During the early centuries of Christian expansion, their Jewish faith found fulfillment in Jesus Christ. Eventually the Nestorians intermarried with other Syriac-speaking peoples east of the Euphrates and spread their faith throughout Turkestan, Mongolia, China, and Japan. Some records indicate that Jacobite Christians also visited China during this period, but their impact was minimal. A stone stele erected in the T'ang capital of Chang-an in 781 and rediscovered in the seventeenth century describes flourishing communities of Christians throughout China, but beyond this and a few other fragmentary records relatively little is known of their history.

What is known, however, is significant. The Nestorians faced the world's vastest empire at the zenith of its cultural, intellectual, and administrative attainment. T'ang China possessed a most sophisticated religious and ethical system; its people had long lived in an environment of religious syncretism. When T'ang forces conquered Turkestan (630) and reopened the ancient trade route to the West, Alopen, the Persian bishop, felt the time had come to evangelize this mighty empire. Indeed, he was welcomed by the authorities in line with their broad policy of toleration and interest in fostering foreign religions. When Alopen arrived at Chang-an (635) he was almost immediately commissioned to translate the Nestorian sutras into Chinese. Scholars were assigned to assist him. In 638 the first Christian book was published, *The Sutra of Jesus the Messiah.* It sought to introduce the Chinese to the Christian faith and specifically pointed out that the gospel contained nothing subversive to China's ancient traditions, loyalty to the state and filial piety being of the essence of the law of Christ. This pleased the emperor, and by decree he proclaimed the virtue of the Nestorian religion, gave Alopen the title of "Great Spiritual Lord, Protector of the Empire" (i.e., metropolitan Chang-an), and opened China's doors to the gospel: "Let it be preached freely in our empire."

Unawed by the challenge, the Nestorians proceeded to build and staff monasteries in China's key cities. They were also quite aggressive in their proclamation of the Christian faith. They persevered in their efforts to phrase the Christian message in the philosophical language of the Confucian court in order to make it intellectually acceptable to the literati. Although the ancient stele says, "The religion spread throughout the ten provinces. . . . Monasteries abound in a hundred cities," the Nestorians experienced a series of setbacks as a result of court intrigues, the jealousy of Taoist and Buddhist leaders, and the upheavals of civil war. By their medical knowledge and surgical skill the Nestorians gave a good name to the religion of Jesus, but by their top-heavy, non-Chinese leadership they tended to be classed with Buddhism and Zoroastrianism as another "foreign religion". Although their monasteries were self-supporting, self-governing, self-propagating entities, Chinese clergy were only permitted to fill the lowest ranks. From this we gather that the Nestorians gave an inordinately high priority to serving the foreign trading community. At any event, they depended largely upon its representatives for initiative and leadership.

The vitality of this church diminished with the passage of time. The massive contributing factor to this diminution was the frequent disruption of its linkage with home centers in Mesopotamia. In its isolation the Nestorian church fell prey to syncretistic tendencies. However, in its best periods it represented historic, biblical Christianity. At those times it was accurately portrayed as follows:

> Their simplicity of faith and worship, their reverence for Scripture, their abhorrence of image and picture worship, of the confessional and of the doctrine of purgatory, and their not adoring the Host in the Communion Supper constitute them the Protestants of Asia.[5]

But by the middle of the ninth century, due to government hostility toward Buddhism, the emperor decreed that Christianity also be proscribed:

> As for the Ta Ch'in (Nestorian) and Muhu (Zoroastrian) temples, these heretical religions must not alone be left when the Buddhists have been suppressed; they must all be compelled to return to lay life and resume their original callings and pay taxes, or if they are foreign they shall be sent back to their native places.[6]

This particular decree forced several thousand Chinese Nestorian clergy to return to secular life. After a succession of such decrees and the fall of the T'ang Dynasty, Nestorianism went into rapid decline. In 986 a monk reported to the Patriarch:

> Christianity is extinct in China; the native Christians have perished in one way or another; the church has been destroyed and there is only one Christian left in the land.[7]

Obviously, this was an overstatement, for the Nestorian church continued to flourish throughout central Asia well into the fourteenth century among the northern tribes: the Uigurs, Turks, and Mongols. However, the record of the closing years of the Nestorians in China is replete with references to necrology—prayers for the dead. This evidence of theological corruption raises questions. Had the Nestorians' policy of deliberate cultural adaptation resulted in their being captured by Confucian ancestor worship? Had their isolation from the theological schools of Mesopotamia rendered them incapable of maintaining their doctrinal integrity? We do not know. What is known is that a movement that went to China to proclaim life in Christ ended up in the service of the dead. Indeed, this became the only element of Nestorian Christianity to survive the centuries. To this day both Chinese and Japanese Buddhists offer prayers for the dead, although this was not originally part of Buddhist practice.

The Nestorian presence in China was contingent upon retaining the favor of the T'ang court. This made the Nestorians vulnerable when the rising power of Confucian scholars influenced the court to eliminate all foreign religions. Also, their accumulation of land for monasteries and for the support of agricultural operations made them appear to the authorities as a state within a state, diverting people from their economic and political responsibilities to the T'ang authorities. Naturally, this was resented. In the late spring of 1951 the author heard a communist official in southwest China (Kun-ming) berate Catholic missions for their extensive land holdings and sharecropping activities in that part of China. Indeed, part of the tragedy of Western missions in China is that they tended to overlook the hard lessons of those who had gone before them.

CATHOLIC CHRISTIANITY—THE FRANCISCANS (THIRTEENTH AND FOURTEENTH CENTURIES)

During the thirteenth century the Mongols, under the leadership of Genghis Khan, began reaching outward from central Asia, invading neighboring countries and incorporating them into an empire that at its height included all China (the Yuan Dynasty—1260-1368) and extended westward to Persia, Mesopotamia, and parts of Europe. A political bridge was thereby provided that surmounted the vast wasteland of Asia and eventually brought China into direct contact with Western Christianity. Because the Mongols were known for their toleration, political hegemony, and outright religious patronage, the Nestorians flourished throughout central Asia. Those who were living on the frontiers of China were emboldened to return. Unfortunately, their subservience to the hated Mongols meant that they tended to serve Mongol rather than Chinese interests. They located in the key cities along major trade routes in relative isolation from the Chinese people.

When the Mongol threat to Europe was at its height, reports came to Rome of Asian Christians living freely within what was regarded as a sea of pagan violence. Particularly astonishing and exciting was a vague reference to "a certain Presbyter Johannes—a king and a priest and a Christian." The pope became interested and decided to investigate. No missionary impulse moved him; he merely acted in self-interest, hoping that by diplomacy the Mongols might be diverted from sacking Europe. Communication was begun, and delegates were sent to the court of the great Khan. This eventually brought European Catholicism into contact with Asian Nestorianism. One of the tragedies of church history is that this encounter was never friendly. In 1271 the Marco Polo brothers brought an invitation from Kublai Khan to the pope imploring him that a hundred teachers of science and religion be sent to reinforce the Nestorian Christianity already present in his vast empire. The great Mongol leader concluded:

> So shall I be baptized, and when I am baptized all my barons and lords will be baptized, and their subjects will receive baptism, and so there will be more Christians here than in your own countries.[8]

This came to nought due to the hostility of influential Nestorians within the largely Mongol court. When in 1253 the Franciscan William of Rubruck arrived at Karakorum, the western Mongol capital, and sought permission to serve its people in the name of Christ, he was forbidden to engage in missionary work or remain in the country, and he had to return home.[9] Fortunately, the Eastern court under the more immediate rule of Kublai Khan was eager to secure Western assistance in its rule over the Chinese. In 1289 Pope Nicholas IV sent the Franciscan John of Monte Corvino to China by way of India, thereby bypassing Karakorum. Although the great Khan had already died by the time John arrived (1294), the court at Cambaluc (Peking) received him graciously and encouraged him to settle there.

John was China's first Roman Catholic missionary, and he was significantly successful. He labored largely in the Mongol tongue, translated the New Testament and Psalms, built a central church, and within a few years (by 1305) could report 6000 baptized converts. He also established a lay training school of 150 students. But the work was not easy. Although often opposed by the Nestorians who had over the years increasingly filtered back into China's cities, the Franciscan mission continued to grow. Other priests joined him and centers were established in the coastal provinces of Kiangsu (Yangchow), Chekiang (Hangchow) and Fukien (Zaitun). One of John's most vigorous younger missionaries was Blessed Odoric, who arrived in Cambaluc in 1326 and whose subsequent sixteen years of unremitting journeys throughout China, preaching the gospel in the vernacular, resulted in over twenty thousand converts.[10] Some scholars report that by 1381 the total number of communicants exceeded a hundred thousand.[11]

But the mission was of relatively short duration. In the latter half of the fourteenth century the Black Death in Europe so depleted Franciscan houses that they were unable to sustain the mission to China with a steady stream of younger friars. Two massive political catastrophes also hastened the extinction of this second wave of missionaries to China. First, the Chinese rose up and drove out the Mongols, thereby launching the Ming Dynasty (1368). Then a new Mongol uprising erupted in the broad reaches of central Asia under Tamerlane (1387) and menaced both East and West. Tamerlane was a Muslim convert, and he turned with fury on Roman Christians and Nestorians alike. Few survived. When the Mongols in turn were defeated by the Osman Turks, the whole of central Asia became a vast Muslim sea. Only here and there did remnants of the Golden Horde manage to survive as encapsulated enclaves of Lamaistic Buddhism.

It is tragic that from the very beginning of their mission to China, the Franciscan friars were suspicious of the Nestorians and critical of everything they said and did. They refused to cooperate and would not give ground on such peripheral matters as their use of Latin in worship and their particular method of catechetical training. Most disastrous was their public denunciations of the Nestorians as heretics. Scholars are agreed that the hatred that eventually characterized relations between these two groups largely nullified the gospel of love and forgiveness which both preached. Obviously, such a Christianity made no lasting contribution to the life and institutions of the Chinese people. In fact, with the collapse of the Mongol Dynasty the Chinese were quick to expel them. This brought about the early collapse of their churches, since the Franciscans had trained no Chinese clergy. All traces of Franciscan Christianity were suppressed by force. In Chinese eyes, the religion of barbarians was unworthy of a civilized people. When the Jesuits came to China in the sixteenth century, they found no trace of either Franciscan or Nestorian Christianity.

CATHOLIC CHRISTIANITY—THE JESUITS (SIXTEENTH AND SEVENTEENTH CENTURIES)

By the fifteenth century a new type of Europeanism emerged that did not augur well for the Christian world mission. This was the Europeanism of the Age of Discovery, which legitimized the fusion of missionary outreach to colonial expansion. Kings conceived it their God-given duty to seize control of the empires of the heathen and spread the faith by whatever means lay at hand. Behind this was a burgeoning nationalism that not only provoked intense competition between the European powers but also made them incapable of appreciating the cultures of those whom they sought to subjugate and convert.

It was inevitable, then, that the sixteenth century would become the great century of Roman Catholic missions. By 1517 the Portuguese reached Canton, lured by the prospect of being the first Western power to establish a lucrative trade agreement with its commercial leaders. They were also prodded by the church to make spiritual conquest of China's idolatrous people. The missionaries of this period were religious imperialists of the first order, whether Dominicans, Franciscans, or Augustinians. Fearing their cultural arrogance and imperialistic designs, the Chinese emperor denied them access to his country. For almost fifty years these missionary priests were cooped up in Macao, a short distance from present-day Hong Kong on the south China coast.

Then came the Jesuits (1574), and a new day dawned with "the generation of the giants." The Jesuits were men whose vision went far beyond the Macao status quo, priests serving churches on the fringes of a pagan society. They were possessed by a dream—the creation of a Sino-Christian civilization that would match the Roman-Christian civilization of the West. Although lacking a fully developed plan of action, their objective was

> . . . that Christianity enter as deeply as possible into the streams of Chinese life; that through a gradual diffusion of Christian ideals and ideas, minds [would] be acclimated to the Christian message.[12]

This unique approach was largely the outworking of two Italian Jesuits, Michele Ruggieri (1543-1607) and Matteo Ricci (1552-1610). Both were determined to adapt to the religious qualities of the Chinese: Ruggieri to the common people, in whom Buddhist and Taoist elements predominated, and Ricci to the educated classes, where Confucianism prevailed.

This policy was largely devised by the scholarly Ricci. Earlier, he had discovered through his studies of Confucius that the Chinese originally had a monotheistic concept of a Supreme Being. He reasoned, Why not use this as the basis for presenting the Christian gospel to them? Ricci sought out friends among Chinese scholars and shared his enthusiasm for Confucius. The more he conversed with them, however, the more aware he became of the need for a special type of missionary to implement his methodology. Furthermore, he saw that this new type of approach would require a special dispensation from the pope. This was granted. Ricci then wrote to the Jesuit houses in Europe and called for priests—men who would not only be "good," but also "men of talent, since we are dealing here with a people both intelligent and learned."[13] A few responded, and Ricci began to train them so that they might approach the Chinese authorities, offering the court scholarly and scientific assistance with the deliberate intention of making a Confucian adaptation of their style of life, patterns of thought, preaching, and religious worship. They were determined to completely dewesternize themselves.

Both Ricci and Ruggieri felt that it would be possible to "prove that the Christian doctrines were already laid down in the classical works of the Chinese people, albeit in disguise." Indeed, they and their followers were convinced that "the day would come when with one accord all missionaries in China would look in the ancient texts for traces of primal revelation.[14]

Unfortunately, tension developed between Ricci and his followers and those of Ruggieri. This was inevitable, since both were exploring different segments of the Chinese intellectual tradition. Ricci's thoroughgoing adaptation to Confucianism and his radical rejection of Taoism could not but conflict with Ruggieri's thesis that there was a closer affinity between the Tao of Chinese thought and the incarnate *Logos* of the New Testament. Actually, in their deliberate and arduous efforts to restate the Christian gospel in Chinese thought-forms, they were not innovators. They were merely adopting the same approach toward Chinese thought that the early church fathers had adopted toward Greek philosophy. Their objective was to identify all the elements of truth which the Chinese literary heritage contained, to supplement them with the insights of the Western understanding of the natural order, and then to introduce the wholly distinctive truths of the Christian gospel.

In 1584 Ricci published his first Chinese book: *Tien Chu Shih-lu* (The True Account of God). In it he discussed the existence and attributes of God, as well as his providence. He explained how a man might know God through the natural law, the Mosaic law, and the Christian law. He wrote of the incarnation of Christ the Word and discussed the sacraments. We mention this because in our day there are those who charge that Ricci was so intent on achieving a complete synthesis of Eastern and Western thought that he failed to be a faithful witness to Christ and the gospel. His diary speaks otherwise: "From morning to night, I am kept busy discussing the doctrines of our faith. Many desire to forsake their idols and become Christians."[15] His missionary directives were explicit:

> The work of evangelization, of making Christians, should be carried on both in Peking and in the provinces . . . following the methods of pacific penetration and cultural adaptation. Europeanism is to be shunned. Contact with Europeans, specifically with the Portuguese in Macao, should be reduced to a minimum. Strive to make good Christians rather than multitudes of indifferent Christians. . . . Eventually, when we have a goodly number of Christians, then perhaps it will not be impossible to present some memorial to the Emperor asking that the right of Christians to practice their religion be accorded, inasmuch as it is not contrary to the laws of China. Our Lord will make known and discover to us little by little the appropriate means for bringing about in this matter His holy will.[16]

When Ricci died (1624) more than two thousand Chinese from all levels of society had confessed their faith in Jesus Christ. Unfortunately, however, Ricci's fellow Jesuits were largely men of their times, firmly convinced they should also promote Western objectives while planting the Roman Catholic church in China. As a result, they became involved with the colonial and imperialistic designs of Portugal. In time, Spanish power also came to the Far East, likewise drawn by dreams of conquest. Their missionaries (Franciscans, Dominicans, and Augustinians) used traditional methods, with limited results. They envied the growing success of the Jesuits, while lacking their capacity for appreciating Chinese culture.

This tension led to what became known as the "Rites Controversy," a bitter struggle that broke out after Ricci's death and lasted for over a hundred years. At first the focal point of dissension was Ricci's contention that the ceremonial rites of Confucianism and ancestor worship were primarily social and political in nature and could be practiced by converts. The Dominicans charged that they were essentially idolatrous; all acts of respect to the sage and one's ancestors were nothing less than the worship of demons. European rivalries invaded the debate, even the issue of Portuguese royal patronage. A Dominican carried the case to Rome, where it dragged on and on, largely because no one in the Vatican knew Chinese culture sufficiently to provide the pope with a ruling. Naturally, the Jesuits appealed to the Chinese emperor, who endorsed Ricci's position. Understandably, he was confused: missionaries attacked missionaries in his very capital! Should he expel them all?

The timely discovery of the Nestorian monument in 1623 enabled the Jesuits to strengthen their position with the court by meeting an objection the Chinese often expressed—that Christianity was a new religion. They could now point to concrete evidence that a thousand years earlier the Christian gospel had been proclaimed in China; it was not a new but an old faith. The emperor then decided to expel all missionaries who failed to support Ricci's position.

The Spanish Franciscans, however, did not retreat without further struggle. This was the age of the inquisition, when the charge of heresy meant the dungeon and the sword. Eventually they persuaded Pope Clement XI that the Jesuits were making dangerous accommodations to Chinese sensibilities. In 1704 he proscribed against the use of the ancient Chinese words *Shang Ti* (supreme emperor) and *T'ien* (heaven) for God. Naturally, the Jesuits appealed this decision. The controversy raged on. In 1742 Pope Benedict XIV officially opposed the Jesuits, forbade all worship of ancestors, and terminated further discussion of the issue. This decree was repealed in 1938. But the methodology of Matteo Ricci remained suspect until 1959, when Pope John XXIII, by decree in his encyclical *Princeps Pastorum*, proposed that Ricci become "the model of missionaries."

In the intervening years the Ming dynasty collapsed (1644), to be replaced by the "nonscholarly" and foreign Manchus. The influence of the various Catholic missionary orders began to wane. Pope Clement XIV dissolved the Society of Jesus (Jesuits) in 1733. The withdrawal from China of this dynamic segment of the missionary force exposed the church to successive waves of persecution. Although many Chinese Christians were put to death and the congregation scattered, the church continued to manifest a "tough inward vitality" and kept growing. Clark has well summarized:

> When all is said and done, one must recognize gladly that the Jesuits made a shining contribution to mission outreach and policy in China. They made no fatal compromises, and where they skirted this in their guarded accommodation to the Chinese reverence for ancestors, their major thrust was both Christian and wise. They succeeded in rendering Christianity at least respectable and even credible to the sophisticated Chinese, no mean accomplishment.[17]

One should commend the Jesuits for planting a Chinese church that has stood the test of time. "By 1844 Roman Catholics may have totalled 240,000; in 1901 the figure reached 720,940."[18] However, one should not overlook the fact that the Jesuit financial policy grievously aggravated the difficulties of that church. Their missionaries involved themselves in business ventures of various sorts; they became the landlords of income-producing properties, developed the silk industry for Western trade, and organized money-lending operations on a large scale. All these eventually generated misunderstanding and tension between the foreign community and the Chinese people. The Communists held this against them as late as the mid-twentieth century.

NINETEENTH-CENTURY CHRISTIANITY—THE PROTESTANTS

During the last half of the eighteenth and the opening decades of the nineteenth century little was done to advance the cause of Christ in China. Eventually, however, the release of national dynamism brought about by the Industrial Revolution and the spiritual renewal that came to the churches by the evangelical awakening throughout the English-speaking world combined to usher in the era of Western colonial expansion and "The Great Century" of modern missions.

In 1807 Robert Morrison of the London Missionary Society reached Canton via America despite the opposition of the British East India Company and the ship's captain (or owner) with his famous sally: "And so, Mr. Morrison, you really expect to make an impression on the idolatry of the great Chinese empire?" Morrison's reply is worth noting: "No, sir, I expect God will." After twenty-five years of intense work he translated the whole Bible and baptized ten Chinese. We associate with him such giants as Medhurst and Milne (the printers), Dyer (Hudson Taylor's father-in-law), Gutzlaff (the Prussian linguist), and Parker (China's first medical missionary). For years their only beachheads into China were Canton and Macao. They concentrated on literature distribution among members of the merchant class, gained a few converts, and laid the foundations for educational and medical work.

Then came the opium wars. The East India Company was determined to force China to trade with the West, both legitimately and otherwise. At an early date opium grown in British India began to prove a most profitable export commodity. Although opium was known in China, the emperor had wisely and officially forbidden its importation. Some Chinese traders, however, circumvented the law and prospered. In 1839 the Chinese court ordered confiscation of all opium in Chinese warehouses and on British ships in Canton. They burned twenty thousand cases of opium. British merchants protested this interference with their "legitimate" trade. The First Opium War broke out in 1841, when the British fleet assaulted Canton and demanded reparations (plus Hong Kong!). In 1842 the fleet attacked Nanking and the Chinese were at the mercy of the British. By the Treaty of Nanking (1842) they were forced to grant Western nations five ports for residence and trade plus several other concessions, including Hong Kong to British rule, indemnity for opium destroyed, and British monitoring of tariff rates. The following year (1843) the British infringed further on Chinese sovereignty and forced the emperor to grant extraterritoriality to all British citizens. This meant that Chinese officials were not permitted to have jurisdiction over them. By extraterritoriality, foreigners, "when they were defendants in any criminal action against Chinese, were to be tried under their own laws and by their own authority; in civil cases with Chinese they might invoke the aid of their consuls; and in controversies among themselves they were not to be subject either to Chinese laws or courts."[19] Travel inland was not permitted; missionary activity was confined to Canton, Amoy, Foochow, Ning-po, and Shanghai.

Due to the breakdown of these terms, however, the Second Opium War broke out in 1856. The French joined the British and made the conflict more unequal than before. When peace was declared in 1860, the Chinese were forced to increase their concessions. What was particularly galling to them was the "most-favored nation" clause, under which the Chinese had to grant the same privileges to all foreign nations alike. This was to prevent any one nation from gaining an upper hand in securing concessions from China. From henceforth China would be at the mercy of every nation from the predatory West. Along with extraterritorial status she was forced to enlarge the freedom of missionaries to proclaim their faith. They could now travel inland. Furthermore, the Chinese themselves were guaranteed the right to become Christians.

At this time France publicly championed Catholic missions. Capitalizing on the treaty, she forced China to restore all church properties that had been appropriated by the Chinese during the repression of Catholicism in the seventeenth and eighteenth centuries "regardless of how many Chinese owners had altered or used them for other purposes during the intervening years."[20] In contrast, the more subtle British declined any particular sponsorship of Protestants, although everyone knew that her direct aid would be available to them should any emergency arise. The era of "missionary gunboat policy" had begun. Of course, this was carefully explained in "spiritual" terms to the churches in Britain.

> While it is not right to do evil that good may come, still God often brings good out of evil, as the following will clearly prove. . . . War may compel strong foreign governments to open the door and to give freedom and security to the missionary and his converts. . . . Hear the words of Bishop Moule: "It is probable that in consequence of the exclusive policy of China and her intolerable arrogance nothing but a series of humiliating defeats, such as she experienced in 1841-42 and 1856-60, could have opened her brazen gates and have brought to the more amenable and friendly common people the blessings of honesty and Christian truth."[21]

We can appreciate the depth of China's humiliation at the hands of the British if we keep in mind that within a period of nearly thirty years in the mid-nineteenth century she was also internally torn by at least six major rebellions, the average duration of which was nearly fourteen years. These were widely scattered, erupting in all parts of China except in the northeast. All were put down, but at great cost. The Taiping Rebellion (1848-65) is estimated to have taken at least twenty million lives. This widespread unrest was due to the mounting pressure of population growth coupled with the inability of the government through the inadequacy of its social ideology to provide adequate livelihood for all. China had yet to go through a technological revolution comparable to the West.

The Taiping Rebellion began in the mind and heart of Hung Hsiu-ch'uan, an unsuccessful candidate for the civil examinations, who somehow obtained and read a lengthy Christian treatise (compiled by one Lung Fan, a Mallaccan convert of Milne, Morrison's colleague). In a vision he later felt called of God to cleanse the country of idolatry and corruption. His goal was to establish a heavenly kingdom known as the *Tai P'ing* (Great Peace).

Was this a Christian movement? In recent years the Taiping Rebellion has come under renewed scrutiny by scholars. They underscore the religious context from which it sprang: the decay of the organized religions (Buddhism and Taoism) and the hated foreign Manchu dynasty's dominance of the official Confucian cult. The time was ripe for the emergence of a new religious movement which would replace the older faiths and pave the way for a political renaissance that would be Chinese through and through. The weight of current scholarship is on the side of those who contend that this movement was primarily a religious revival and only secondarily a revolt against the Manchus. It was the most formidable rebellion to confront the Manchu dynasty, "a product of China's new contact with European civilization, and the most positive consequence of Christian missionary enterprise, [yet it was] ignored by the missionaries themselves and was finally destroyed by the armed intervention of the Christian powers." Earlier European histories of China either misrepresent or deride the religious dimensions of the rebellion, yet to the Taiping leaders their faith mattered more than victory over the Manchus. The object of foreign intervention was to preserve the corrupt and defenseless Manchus, because a Taiping victory would have made China strong and independent.

Admittedly, Hung did not have a balanced grasp of the gospel, although he possessed a complete Bible. Following his conversion he served for some years—and rather successfully—as a missionary among his own clan. His converts were taught to oppose all existing religions, and particularly Buddhism because it was idolatrous. This aroused official hostility, and Hung was charged with promoting civil disorder. This led to armed conflict.

During the early years of the Taiping movement, not a few prominent missionaries, such as William C. Burns and W. A. P. Martin, were favorable to its efforts to bring about religious and social reform. How could it have been otherwise? The Taipings forbade foot-binding and opium, elevated the position of women, lowered taxation, and made those who earned more pay more. They were more friendly to foreigners than the Manchus, for they wanted China opened to Western trade and travel. Moreover, they were pro-missionary. Even the Anglican bishop of Hong Kong "frequently asserted his entire conviction that the Taiping movement was a Christian crusade, if perhaps unorthodox and ill-instructed in certain doctrines."[23] However, when the British and French authorities in 1860 exacted their highly favorable concessions from the Manchus, the missionary community was easily persuaded to represent the Taiping creed as gross superstition, replete with blasphemous distortions of Christian truth.

What did the Taipings actually believe? They began as a sect: "The Worshipers of Shang Ti" (a Protestant term for God). Their "Trimetrical Classic" (a long creedal statement, made up of three character sentences for catechetical use) ranged over such themes as creation, the Egyptian oppression, the exodus, Sinai and the Ten Commandments, and the coming of Jesus. Did it contain the gospel? One section read:

The great God
Out of pity to mankind
Sent His firstborn Son
To come down into the world;
His name is Jesus,
The Lord and Saviour of men,
Who redeems them from sin
By the endurance of extreme misery.
Upon the cross
They nailed His body,
Where He shed His precious blood
To save all mankind.[24]

Some missiologists characterize the Taipings as a "people movement" under charismatic leadership. This is not an uncommon phenomenon in the long history of the expansion of Christianity. But some missionaries, both then and now, are somewhat reluctant to grant the possibilitiy of God bypassing their Western missions and reaching large numbers of people through indigenous prophetic leadership.

> In 1850 the Taipings began fighting in earnest to overthrow the corrupt Manchu dynasty. W. A. P. Martin felt the time had come to rally the missionary community to their support. He defended the rebels as "instruments of a superhuman power, destined for the achievement of a glorious revolution." In his judgment it was a case of the "dissolute and atheistic, or idolatrous Imperialists" versus "the abstemious, devout, and image-

> breaking followers of Taiping." His argument was that missionaries should help to mature their understanding of Scripture and quell the fanaticism that was beginning to mar this army of liberation.[25]

By 1852 the Taipings began moving down the Yangtze Valley. A year later they made Nanking their capital and proclaimed a new Tai Ping dynasty. When they threatened Shanghai in 1860, a foreign force was hastily organized to oppose them. By now missionaries almost totally sided with the thoroughly decadent Manchu court. Tragic and ironic indeed that spontaneous Chinese Christianity was defeated with the help of the "Christian" Western powers (1864)! Although corruption and violence invaded and defiled the Taipings during their closing years, the "glimmer of Christian idealism" remained in the movement to the very end. (Admittedly, many conservative missions historians seriously doubt that the Taipings were doctrinally orthodox from the outset.)

How shall we evaluate this unique movement? The words of Fitzgerald bear pondering:

> The failure of the Taiping movement was a turning point in the cultural history of China. The success of a great national and religious revolution would have replaced the effete Manchus by a new dynasty and a new cultural outlook, ready to accept the ideas of the West as a corollary of the new creed. It is very probable that the substitution of Taiping Christianity for Buddhism and Taoism would have given an impulsion to art and literature which the old faiths were no longer capable of performing. Under a political system to which they were accustomed, and to which they were alone suited, the Chinese would have been prepared, in the later nineteenth century, for the great changes which modern industry has forced upon the world. As it was, they remained sunk under a decaying despotism, until at its fall they were involved simultaneously in a political, cultural, and economic revolution complicated by foreign aggression. For this tragic outcome the cynical policy of Western imperialism in 1860 was mainly responsible.[26]

Chinese liken the intervention of foreigners in their affairs from the end of the opium wars to the triumph of Mao in 1949 to the parable of the uninvited guests who ask the host for equal treatment, then help themselves freely from his table and end up taking steps to dispossess him of his home. At first, only Hong Kong was lost to the British. Then the Russians took Amur (1858). In 1895, due to a swift and humiliating defeat by Japan, China lost the Pescadores, Taiwan, and Korea. Then came the French and Germans, looking for concessions. In 1899, when China appeared to be on the chopping block for final dismemberment, the United States came to the rescue with its "Open Door" policy. Although America also had an economic interest in China trade, she nevertheless checked the rapacity of the various powers that were eager to transform their spheres of interest in China into colonial style protectorates. America's "Open Door" policy called for the preservation of China's territorial and administrative integrity and for the maintenance of equality of commercial opportunity for all nations.

We now turn to the missionary movement. In 1860 Protestant missions were confined to five coastal cities. By the end of the century, however, the picture had vastly changed. Scores of new societies had been organized, and several thousand missionaries were working in all parts of inland China. This amazing transformation can be largely traced to the dynamism released by the 1859 awakening in Britain and the genius of J. Hudson Taylor (1832-1905). It is a fascinating story. Hudson Taylor went to China (1853) at the age of twenty-one under the auspices of the Chinese Evangelization Society. His work was largely in Ning-po. By 1860 he was back in England, broken in health and with little prospect of ever returning. His society had already disintegrated through poor management. Taylor's future looked dark had he not been "challenged by the open Bible and the ever-accusing map."[27] Things began to happen, however, when Taylor was asked to write a series of articles on the needs of Ning-po, to be published in a Baptist magazine. He agreed, for he was eager to promote this work and hoped his articles might stimulate prayer and recruit workers for the small clinic he had established there.

The editor liked the articles and, like most editors, asked for more! He told Taylor: "Add to them. . . . Let them cover the whole field . . . as an appeal for inland China." Taylor agreed. When he tackled this assignment, however, a crisis was provoked in his mind and heart. His biographer gives the details:

> Compiling facts as to the size and population of every province in China, and making diagrams to show their neglected condition, stirred him to a desperate sense of the sin and shame of allowing such a state of things to continue. Yet what was to be done? The number of Protestant missionaries, as he had discovered, was diminishing rather than increasing. Despite the fact that half the heathen population of the world was to be found in China, the missionaries engaged in its evangelization had actually been reduced, during the previous winter, from one hundred and fifteen to only ninety-one. This had come to light through his study of the latest statistics and, naturally, added fuel to the fire that was consuming him.[28]

In time these articles were published in a book entitled *China's Spiritual Needs and Claims.* Overnight it became a bestseller among the evangelicals of Victorian England. Taylor began by affirming the biblical truths that all men are lost, that the gospel is for all, and that the Great Commission specifies that the church is to "make disciples" of all peoples.

He then identified those in China who had yet to hear the gospel and believe in Jesus Christ. Indeed, Taylor's research had uncovered

> . . . the startling fact that even in the seven provinces in which such work had begun there were still a hundred and eighty-five millions utterly and hopelessly beyond the reach of the gospel. . . . And beyond these again lay the eleven inland provinces—two hundred millions more without a single witness for Christ.[29]

Taylor emphasized this "by comparisons and diagrams." These statistics were profoundly and unutterably real to him. "A million a month in China are dying without God, and we who have received in trust the Word of Life—we are responsible."[30] This young man was now determined to confront the churches of the West with these terrible realities. In no time at all churches on both sides of the Atlantic were awakened. Many new societies were formed and hundreds of workers were recruited, largely from the thousands of university students influenced by the ministry of D. L. Moody.

In 1865 Taylor founded the China Inland Mission to implement his vision of bringing all China to Christ through the rapid and widespread preaching of the gospel. By 1895 this society counted 641 missionaries, 462 Chinese helpers, 260 stations and outstations, and 5,211 communicants.[31] "In no other land of so large an area and population was there ever a single society which planned so comprehensively to cover the whole and came so near to fulfilling its dream."[32] Nondenominational, evangelical, and international, this society became the model for the worldwide "faith mission" movement of the nineteenth and twentieth centuries.

But what of the nineteenth-century missionaries sent by the churches in the West to evangelize China? Latourette is very generous in his evaluation of them. He writes:

> Those who laid the foundation of the future Protestant churches did so usually with heroism and often at the sacrifice of comfort, health, and even life . . . and . . . in the face of frequent unfriendliness and hostility of the populace and officials.[33]

This is fair. These men and women (who made up two-thirds of the total force!) were devout in their evangelical commitment. But even Latourette grants that they were poorly prepared to tackle the task facing them. "Many of them remained ignorant of the wider reaches of Chinese institutions, literature, and thought, and looked upon the culture around them with critical and unappreciative eyes. . . ."[34] Their ignorance made them vulnerable to the delusion of Western moral superiority. Their insensitivity to local customs and their proneness to pass moral judgments estranged them from the gentry and ruling class. Their readiness to identify

China's endemic dirt, suffering, and disease with moral corruption alienated them from the common people. Their public denunciation of idolatry unwittingly challenged the semi-divinity of the emperors and undermined the Confucian system of public order. This was misinterpreted as political subversion. Their demand that converts not participate in village religious festivals and theatricals was regarded as an attack upon the communal structure of rural China. They aggressively proclaimed the superiority of Western values but were tragically unaware of the deep social and political implications of abruptly substituting them for Chinese standards. Because of their failure to understand the nature and implication of ancestor worship, they unwittingly gave the impression that the West condemned all forms of filial respect.

Since the foreign exchange was in their favor, it was relatively easy for missionaries to acquire land and erect impressive buildings for residences, hospitals, schools, and chapels. By their "foreign rights" they declared these walled-in compounds free from government encroachment. By interceding with local magistrates they secured redress for their converts from lawsuits, and in times of economic crisis, such as famines and floods, they were able to provide them with physical sustenance. Unfortunately, these compounds were often regarded as the beginnings of "foreign enclaves, set up to take over the country."

As the nineteenth century drew to a close, the Protestant missionary enterprise depended heavily upon 2800 foreign workers; 60 percent were women and only half the men were ordained. Whereas the large majority were obscure men and women, there were giants among them. Mention has been made of W. A. P. Martin, the educator who was a Protestant Ricci in his conviction that missionaries must catch the full measure of China's ancient and venerable cultural heritage. His thesis was "Confucius plus Christ," not the antithesis of "Confucius or Christ."[35] Timothy Richard, the English Baptist, is justly remembered as "the founder of famine relief in China" as well as "the promoter of Western civilization through higher education." Griffith John of the London Missionary Society, the leading evangelist of central China, influenced scores of young missionaries with his "techniques of direct evangelism." All these and many more labored with a Christian community of a hundred thousand, over half of whom were in the coastal provinces.

The latter part of the nineteenth century found China caught up in the sequence of reform-reaction-reform. From 1895 to 1910 thousands of students went overseas, chiefly to Japan, to learn the skills of the modern world (science, medicine, engineering, military science, education, and law). Some, such as Dr. Sun Yat-sen, absorbed a "variety of un-Chinese social philosophies: eighteenth-century republicanism and democracy, nineteenth-century social Darwinism, national patriotism, and even such radical doctrines as socialism and anarchism."[36]

Although responsible officials tried to reform and strengthen China, they were opposed by the empress dowager and her reactionary clique. In the end the tension erupted in the antiforeignism of the Boxer uprising of 1900. In one sense, this was a revolt by destitute farmers and disenfranchised handcrafters whose house industries had been undercut by imported machine-made merchandise. But it was also surreptitiously supported by the court in the naive hope of eliminating the problem of the Western powers once and for all by killing off all foreigners. Yu Tung-chen, the Boxer leader, made much of the antiforeign issue in the promotion of his movement. He stridently called out:

> These foreigners, under the pretext of trading and teaching Christianity, are in reality taking away the land, food, and clothing of the people. Besides overturning the teaching of the sages, they are poisoning us with opium and ruining us with debauchery. Since the time of Tao Kuang (emperor during the Opium War), they have seized our territory and cheated us out of our money. They have eaten our children as food and piled up the public debt as high as the hills. They have burnt our palaces and overthrown our tributary states, occupied Shanghai, devastated Formosa, forcibly opened Kiaochow, and now wish to divide up China like a melon.[37]

This type of diatribe attributed China's economic and social distress to her political and national weakness. It awakened the resentment of the depressed classes, whose problems the government could not solve. In their desperation they accepted the imperial court's simplistic solution for their distress: the foreigners must be eliminated!

We need not detail the events of the Boxer rebellion of 1900. The attempt to renew China through slaughtering foreigners (chiefly missionaries and those whom they influenced, the Chinese Christians) led to a damaging war which climaxed with the invasion of Peking by troops of eight nations. It was followed by another futile burst of reform, this time directed by the empress dowager herself. But it only prolonged the life of the tottering dynasty a few more years. Latourette summarizes this period as follows:

> Between 1860 and the close of the nineteenth century the missionary was often the source of great annoyance to the Chinese population and officialdom. His intolerance of the customary honors to ancestors seemed to threaten the Chinese family. Religious practices which formed an integral part of the guild, community, and political life were anathema to him. Christians, therefore, seemed to their neighbors recreant to moral, social, economic, and political obligations and to be attacking the foundations of society and civilization.[38]

Thus Christians bore the brunt of the Boxer uprising. Approximately 180 missionaries and several thousand Chinese Christians known to have been associated with them were ruthlessly slain. Tales of heroism and unflinching witness for Christ were innumerable, and through this baptism of fire the Chinese church was sifted, purified, and renewed. The way was prepared for a revival movement which took place within the next decade.

We conclude this summary of nineteenth-century missions in China by underscoring the political and missionary-related problems which contributed in part to this tragic period in Chinese history. As the dominant power in China, Great Britain had been obliged to pursue two disparate objectives throughout this century. Her primary task was to promote favorable conditions for trade. However, she also had to permit missionaries the freedom they demanded to evangelize inland China. This involved seeking to protect them when the Chinese interfered with their work. Since missionaries tended to scatter rather than concentrate, their calls for consular help tended to come from all parts of the country! Naturally, as the Western powers squeezed more and more political concessions from a weakening China, and simultaneously demanded rights also for missionary activity which no strong, self-respecting China would have granted, they generated a growing Chinese hatred for the West. Whereas Christianity is in essence a universal faith, in the Chinese mind it meant foreigners and exploitation. Those who spoke to the Chinese of Jesus Christ came with the backing of Western powers who seemed determined to exploit China's weakness every chance they got! This did not augur well for the future of Christianity in China should the country ever become strong and free.

REFORM AND REVOLUTION (1900-12)

The Western nations that smothered the Boxer uprising imposed harsh terms on Peking and demanded exorbitant compensation for the loss of life and destruction of property. They pressed missions to follow their lead. Sadly, many responded. But a few, particularly those who had suffered the most, such as the China Inland Mission, decided to ask for nothing and thereby show the Chinese that not all foreigners were alike. Their aim was to reflect the meekness and gentleness of their Lord and Master. They neither filed claims nor accepted compensation when it was offered. The Chinese were amazed. In Shansi province a government proclamation was posted far and wide extolling Jesus Christ and His principles of forbearance and forgiveness. This official endorsement served to diminish the antiforeign spirit of the people and contributed not a little to the growth of the church in China in the years that followed.

Indeed, a new mood was in the air. In revulsion and reaction against their own violence and resistance to change, the Chinese now began to embrace eagerly and all too uncritically what the West had to offer, particularly in the area of scientific and technological skill. A new spirit of religious inquiry also began to manifest itself. When missionaries returned to inland China following the Boxer madness, they were inevitably overwhelmed by the hundreds who desired to hear their message. The following excerpt from a letter from Szechwan is characteristic: "Men crowded into our preaching hall as never before. . . . There is a friendliness toward us such as there never was before."

Politically, this period was characterized by mounting tension between those who sought to reform the Manchu (Ch'ing) government and those who called for its revolutionary overthrow. Ssu-yu Teng summarized the situation as follows:

> The classical metaphor for describing the dilemma of the Ch'ing government in the 1900's is that it was in quicksand. It could only sink deeper the harder it struggled to save itself. Thus the reform program stressed the training of personnel, but this meant a modern type of education to be found only outside the country, and this in turn led to the growth of patriotic anti-Manchu revolutionary sentiment among the student class. By giving modern education to its prospective official class the dynasty reared its own executioners, dug its own grave, and signed its own death warrant. Essentially this was because the dynasty, as an alien monarchy, was itself incapable of becoming moderate.[39]

Among the constructive reforms was the abolishing of the thousand-year-old civil service examination system in 1905. A new educational program was adopted, based on Western and Japanese models. Overnight, mission schools had new status. Instead of drawing students exclusively from the lower economic classes, they now began to attract the children of the elite gentry-official class. Naturally, this led to the beginning of a spirit of inquiry among officials as to the true nature of the Christian faith. Latourette says that "never before in the entire history of the church had so large a body of non-Christians been physically and mentally so accessible to the Gospel."[40]

Behind the facade of frantic attempts at modernization, the old culture remained largely intact. Manchu officials resented the easy dismissal of Confucian values and the peaceful aggressiveness of the Western powers with their railroads, river steamers, factories, schools, and missionaries! The missionaries themselves sensed that troubled times were ahead for China and gave themselves as never before to the widespread proclamation of their message. Their numbers doubled from 1900 to 1913 (to over 5600) and represented all major denominations of the West. Missions increased during this period from 61 to 92, and communicant members of Protestant churches doubled in number, to two hundred thousand.

With the passing of the years it became apparent that the Manchus were incapable of genuine self-renewal and reform. Various revolutionary groups which drew their main support from overseas Chinese appeared to be the only hope for China. One of their leading organizers was Dr. Sun Yat-sen (1866-1925), a sort of half-caste, educated in medicine in Hawaii and Hong Kong and more committed to Christianity than to the Chinese classics. He called for the end of the Manchus, the restoration of China to the Chinese, the country transformed into a republic, and its land redistributed among the peasants.

When the revolution eventually broke out, even its leaders were taken by surprise. An accidental bomb explosion in the city of Hankow led to the discovery of a group of revolutionists. They were summarily executed. In reaction, local imperial troops mutinied. This took place on October 10, 1911, when a soldier shot his commanding officer. The revolt soon spread throughout the Yangtze Valley. When rebel troops captured Nanking, the Manchus saw the handwriting on the wall and pressed for a negotiated peace. Dr. Sun became the president of a provisional government, and on February 12, 1912, the Manchu dynasty ended. Yuan Shih-k'ai, a retired general, more dictator than republican, assumed the presidency of the new republic.

Missionaries welcomed the republic. They had known long decades of hostility at the hands of the Manchus and had grown weary of expecting local officials to act responsibly on behalf of the Chinese people. It is significant that in the years following the Boxer holocaust, missionaries identified increasingly with the Chinese as Chinese. Isaacs described this period (1900-11) as marking the first step in the transition "from the Age of Contempt into the Age of Benevolence."[41]

Actually, missionaries were so busily involved in enlarging their educational and medical programs (in order to capitalize on the post-Boxer euphoria of Chinese friendliness) that events in Nanking and Peking were only of passing interest. Mission school enrollment in the aggregate—elementary, secondary, and collegiate—jumped from 28,000 to 160,000. When the republic began, missions were already operating over 250 hospitals.

But what was accomplished by this rapid expansion of mission and church-related institutions? The missionary community was not agreed. True, they had initiated education for girls and thereby contributed to the abolition of foot-binding, girl slavery, and female infanticide as well as to the general emancipation of womanhood. But many missionaries voiced skepticism over the efficacy of their institutions as evangelizing agencies. They argued that mushrooming institutional growth meant that the majority of students were solely interested in Western learning and were not sympathetic toward mission efforts to maintain a religious atmosphere. This generated no little tension between evangelistic and educational missionaries. In defense of their evangelical concern some schools began to put excessive stress on evangelism to the neglect of academic standards, and students came to despise this type of education, which eroded the good will with which the church had come to be regarded after 1900. The rapid growth of medical institutions likewise led in some places to a lowering of early missionary medical standards.

At the World Missionary Conference in Edinburgh (1910) missionary leaders from China enthusiastically endorsed the pattern of regarding their institutions as evangelistic and church-planting agencies. They were deeply committed to the highly individualistic ethic that reasoned that if people were converted through schools or hospitals, in turn they would eventually improve social conditions. They had no counsel to share with those Chinese who felt they should search for a new type of society for China, having political institutions that would guarantee a just economic order. Missionaries could only naively suggest that China imitate America! Since they were themselves the products of Western societies wealthy in natural resources, led by a powerful middle class, and committed to gradual evolutionary growth, it never seemed to occur to them that China was a collapsing civilization whose basic institutions (family, clan, guild, and decentralized pattern of government) were actually being undermined by the political and economic dynamism of the West.

Missionaries could not understand the growing antiforeign spirit of their students. Had they studied Chinese social structure more closely, they would have uncovered vast differences between it and the West. They might have been able to suggest more realistic approaches to the massive obstacles standing in the way of China's renewal: the disorientation of her political institutions; the vested interests of her landlords; the deep-rooted causes of the terrible poverty of peasants, and the desperate working conditions of her emerging industrial proletariat. The tragedy is that the emerging leadership class came to regard Christianity as possessing no solution to their national problems. To them, this "foreign" religion could only preach individual improvement, chiefly through a subjective religious experience. As a result, some Chinese no longer opposed Christianity on the grounds of its hostility to their ancient religions; they now felt that it denationalized people. In the end they concluded that the West's agnostic materialism was better than its Christianity. So "Science without Christianity" became the new slogan.

It is unfortunate that even during this period a minority of missionaries still continued to appeal to their consuls for aid in settling difficulties over such matters as property rights, the protection of Chinese converts, and their treaty-guaranteed, privileged status. Years later, when the Communists came to power, they dug up these appeals and publicized them widely to discredit the missionary movement.

CONFUSION AND WARLORDISM (1912-26)

Shortly after Yuan Shih-k'ai came to the leadership of the republic, it became apparent that he was a monarchist at heart and desired nothing less than the establishment of a new dynasty with himself as the first emperor! Within little more than a year Dr. Sun led his party, the Kuomintang, in revolt. It failed, and he had to flee the country. From then on Yuan ruled as a dictator. This was tolerated, but when he maneuvered himself into the role of emperor (1915), the Western powers became alarmed, and China broke apart internally. With the ascendance of regional leadership, warlordism came to China. This meant that although a series of governments ruled from Peking, the real power was in the hands of these regional leaders. Some were former imperial officials; others were peasant-bandits. Each one sought to secure supreme power by eliminating his competitors. Rowe describes the effect of this internecine struggle as

> hitting the common man with hard tax levies and conscription for the armies. By and large, however, the struggle between the rivals for supreme power seemed of no direct interest with the people, who only wished it "would go away and leave us alone."[42]

During this period Japan emerged as China's major menace with her "Twenty-One Demands" (1915), designed to make China a Japanese protectorate. The European powers were too involved in World War I to protest. Indeed, they were prepared to sell out China to Japan to secure the latter's naval support against Germany. Fortunately, the United States stepped in and temporarily checked Japan's rising aspirations. China entered the war on the side of the Allies and was granted all the former Austro-Hungarian and German concessions outside Shantung province (which the Japanese took but reluctantly surrendered in 1922). China also joined the League of Nations and canceled the extraterritoriality rights of all defeated and new nations. The new USSR instantly responded with an astute propaganda ploy by voluntarily relinquishing her rights, but Britain and America retained theirs until 1943. All this was not lost on Chinese nationalists.

During the warlord period Dr. Sun and his Kuomintang were largely ineffective due to his inability to cope with the small-minded men who dominated his party. Only in his agitation for "socialism" or "people's livelihood" did he gain followers. When the Western powers refused to help, he turned to the Russians. This brought Communists into the Kuomintang and precipitated the rise of Chiang Kai-shek. By 1926 the stage was set for the rupture of the Kuomintang into two factions: the Communists and the anticommunists. When Chiang Kai-shek began his "northern march" to deal with warlordism once and for all, he began to realize that the Communists might eventually pose a greater obstacle to the unification and renewal of China than Japan.

During this period the old civil service perished, and the scholar class withdrew from active participation in government. With the diminishing of traditional restraints on the people, exploitation of class by class increased. The rich fled to the cities, and the peasants sank deeper into debt. Floods and famines took their toll. All China was exposed to the double menace of soldiers and brigands. One earthquake in the northwest claimed more than a million lives. A "second revolution" seemed impossible to avoid.

But this proved to be a time of gospel advance. Missionary reports from the period 1912-26 are replete with accounts of multiplication of chapels, secondary schools, and Bible training institutes along with orphanages, schools for the blind, theological colleges, hospitals, clinics, opium refuges, and literacy programs, but not without a heavy toll. Typical is the following excerpt from a mission superintendent's quarterly report from one corner of Honan province:

> Seven times have our outstations been plundered; nineteen times have workers been held up and robbed by highwaymen; twice have workers been condemned to be shot; one who was shot still lies in a precarious condition; two of the Christians have been killed; three times have they been seized and held for ransom.[43]

Missionaries were also kidnapped and held for ransom. Captivities varied from a few months to years; some were never released. Bishop W. W. Cassels of the China Inland Mission Anglican diocese in Szechwan province concluded a report of the looting and pillaging in his diocese by an army of 120,000 well-armed brigands in the following fashion:

> Notwithstanding these difficulties—perhaps I might almost say because of them—the doors are wide open, wider than ever before. Classes are largely attended, churches are fuller, and our schools more crowded.[44]

The revolution of 1911-12 greatly accelerated the development of Chinese nationalism. The popular slogan was "China for the Chinese." Chinese Christians found this attractive, too. They asked one another: "Why should we not control our own churches? Why should we continue to depend on the foreign missionaries?" Reacting, the missionaries argued: "The Chinese are not yet sufficiently developed in character, discipleship, and ability to exercise independent leadership among their own people."

Mission periodicals and study books designed for use in the West during this period abound with derogatory generalizations about the Chinese people (opium, footbinding, infanticide, double-mindedness, backward-looking, ancestor worship, idolatry, extreme poverty, immoral monks, etc.). And yet in all fairness we must affirm that these same publications also began to portray the positive dimensions of the Chinese character. W. A. P. Martin, the president of the Imperial University, was among the first to give the West a totally new conception of the Chinese when he wrote:

> Never have a great people been more misunderstood. They are denounced as stolid, because we are not in possession of a medium sufficiently transparent to convey our ideas to them, or transmit theirs to us; and stigmatized as barbarians, because we lack the breadth to comprehend a civilization different from our own. They are represented as servile imitators, though they have borrowed less than any other people; as destitute of the inventive faculty, though the world is indebted to them for a long catalogue of the most useful discoveries; and as clinging with unquestioned tenacity to a heritage of traditions, though they have passed through many profound changes in their history.[45]

American public opinion, while sympathetic to China, was based on the assumption of Western superiority, with the result that American political leadership was never able to regard China as an equal. It was felt that the best that could be done for China was to encourage the missionaries in their philanthropic work. More schools and more hospitals! Presidents McKinley, Roosevelt, Taft, and Wilson all publicly endorsed this type of activity and agreed that it was the best way to minister to China's needs.[46] None lifted an official finger to grapple responsibly with the task of helping China rehabilitate economically. In the end they were as surprised as the missionaries when volatile Chinese nationalists, in their economic desperation and cultural pride, attacked the church's paternalism and cultural imperialism along with the government.

It needs to be emphasized that throughout the republican period the vast majority of missionaries were essentially nonpolitical. They accepted without question the thesis that evangelistic and church-planting work would eventually bring about the social regeneration of China. Although somewhat aware of the economic problems besetting the peasants as well as the members of the new industrial proletariat, they tended to regard China's poverty in moral terms. The Chinese simply wasted their money on gambling. They devoted too much land to opium cultivation! Besides, Chinese worshiped idols! When asked about the rents and taxes paid by his parishioners in a remote area of western China, a member of the China Inland Mission "expressed complete surprise at the question and said he had never inquired into such matters." In all fairness to this missionary it should be pointed out that his reaction to this question was no indication of any lack of concern for the Chinese people. Varg, who expounds his observation at some length, is quick to point out that "members of the China Inland Mission lived in extremely modest circumstances when compared with those who enjoyed a regular salary from a denominational mission board, and consequently they were able to get closer to the people."[47]

On the other hand, there were those missionaries and Chinese leaders, popularly dubbed as "the socializing wing of the church," who felt strongly that their task was to integrate Christianity with the new movements in China working for her economic and social rehabilitation. They were indifferent to theology, being more taken with Christian idealism and the contemporary belief in progress. They struggled to incorporate the socio-ethical teachings of Christianity with the revolutionary aspirations of the people. By 1927 they dominated the faculties of sixteen church-related universities and colleges, ten Christian professional schools of collegiate rank, four schools of theology, and six schools of medicine—enrolling a total of four thousand students. Understandably, they were "profoundly disturbed" over the disinterest of their students in Christian worship. Only later did they become aware of the importance of theology and evangelism. Non-Christian students rarely, if ever, became Christians simply by attending Christian institutions. Christ's personal call in the gospel was rarely sounded by "the socializing wing" of the missionary force in China.

Mention of "the socializing wing" points up a growing polarization within the Protestant movement which emerged toward the end of this period. The sufferings of 1900 had tended to unite the missionaries, but in the years that followed, the rising tide of responsiveness to everything Western on the part of the Chinese demanded the multiplication of cooperative efforts. Some Chinese pastors began to wonder whether the time had come to do away with all mission and denominational labels and unite all Christians in one Chinese church. At the World Missionary Conference of Edinburgh in 1910, Ch'eng Ching-Yi, the pastor of an independent church in Peking and London Missionary Society delegate, declared that "Chinese Christians were looking forward to a united Christian church without any denominational distinctions." He audaciously challenged its Continuation Committee to explore with Chinese pastors the best means for bringing about such a united church.[48] Little wonder that when the history of the church of Christ in China was published in 1974, it was dedicated to this devout and farseeing pastor (*Adventure in Unity,* by Wallace C. Merwin). Cheng's challenge resulted in the visit of John R. Mott to China in 1913 and the formation of a China Continuation Committee to carry out this mandate. In time it brought to birth (1922) the National Christian Council, which in its early years was supported by the

China Inland Mission and the Christian and Missionary Alliance. But their support only lasted for four years; it was withdrawn when they "felt that they could not assent to what they deemed the modernist trends due to its prevailingly liberal membership."[49] Before we review the factors behind this withdrawal and the subsequent polarization of missionaries and Chinese Christians, we must refer to Mott's 1913 visit to China.

Mott was concerned that all mankind hear the gospel "in this generation." Hence, while in China he convened conferences in five major sections of the country to help missionaries become more effective in their work. At each conference he asked, "Have the Christian forces in this area formed a clear and definite plan for its missionary occupation?" The uniform reply was an embarrassed silence. No missionaries could produce either plans or point to measurable goals. They were diligent and sacrificial in their work, but were lacking in any sense of the need to develop an overall church-planting strategy. And this, even though they agreed with Dr. Robert E. Speer that there should be a local church in the midst of every concentration of people, so that its believers might "present Christ to every individual with such clearness and completeness as to place upon him the responsibility of or rejection of the gospel." But still, they had to confess to having no strategy for their work. Even within separate missions the work all too often lacked coordination. For instance, it was the widespread observation that any church near a thriving mission hospital or educational institution was bound to remain small ind ineffective. Evangelistic activities were often not related to local congregations and their growth. Plans were not devised for increasing membership growth within existing congregations and multiplying the number of congregations in populous areas. Again and again congregations were allowed to turn inward and focus their energies on their own spiritual development. Institutions were allowed to become ends in themselves.

As a result of Mott's questions a commission was formed to study the extent of the Christian penetration of China. In 1922 its report was finally published. It is a massive, 579-page affair that describes the complex range of activities and institutions of the Christian movement, province by province. Although it failed to detail the steps which needed to be taken to achieve greater church growth throughout China, it was of considerable value in generating missionary concern in the sending countries and particularly within Chinese congregations. Indeed, this was regarded as its main purpose, as the editor summarized:

> We have made this study to awaken a greater interest and a deeper sense of responsibility among the Chinese Christians for the evangelization of this country; and by presenting the vision of the inadequacy of the foreign missionary force and its ability ever to minister to more than a small frac-

> tion of China's religious needs, to generate in the Chinese Church a missionary dynamic which shall be commensurate with the urgency and greatness of the task.[50]

Sidney J. W. Clark of the World Dominion Movement produced a sixteen-page booklet entitled "The Art of Using the China Mission Survey" to challenge mission administrators to use this massive study in their strategic planning. His concerns have a familiar ring. They resemble those of Dr. Donald A. McGavran and the church growth movement a generation later. Clark based everything on the premise "There is only one argument against using this survey; it is the argument that ignorance is better than knowledge." We have little information as to the outcome of Clark's counsel. All we know is that his plea for strategic planning came at a time when missionaries were being encouraged, for supposedly biblical reasons, to cease listening to one another.

It was during the twenties that the Protestant movement in Britain and North America was experiencing internal tension over the issue of the authority of the Scriptures and the uniqueness of the Christian faith. In 1920 "conservatives" in China organized what they called the Bible Union to "contend for the faith once-for-all delivered to the saints" (Jude 3). By 1926 they had grown to such size and strength that they were able to persuade the China Inland Mission and Christian and Missionary Alliance to withdraw from the National Christian Council. Their thesis was that the unity of the true church was a "given" and that cooperative efforts with those with whom one was not in complete doctrinal agreement were dishonoring to Christ. Whereas there was a measure of truth to this position, its obvious weakness was that it left disunity in triumphant possession of the visible expressions of the church's life, resigned its adherents to a passivity regarding cooperative ventures, and developed a "holier-than-thou" self-righteousness which made many conservative evangelicals indifferent to the demands of Scripture that Christians actively receive and love all whom God has received (John 13:34-35; Luke 9:49-50; etc.). This subbiblical legacy marred the Protestant movement for the remainder of its organized existence in China.

NATIONALISTS AND COMMUNISTS (1926-37)

From 1923 to 1927 the two revolutionary parties, Nationalist (Kuomintang) and Communist (Kungchantang–organized as a party in 1921) cooperated in what came to be called the "National Revolution." Their united aims were to unify China ("Overthrow the Militarists!") and work for a new and better economic order ("Land Reform!"). The Soviet Union helped with money, arms, and advisors; the West was uninterested. For a time all went well. The united front had enormous public appeal. Labor unions, farmers' associations, student organizations, movements for women's rights—all rapidly developed through the dynamism of an intense nationalism. But when a major section of southern China was under their joint control and ultimate victory was in sight (1927), the two parties polarized and the alliance between them came to an end. For the next twenty-two years they competed for the support of the Chinese people and the control of the country. From 1928 to 1937 the Nationalists were dominant. They seized control of the rich Yangtze River area and the financial, industrial, and commercial power of the port cities. By 1936 Chiang had subdued most rival groups and forced the Communists to retreat to the northwest (the celebrated "Long March").

The Nationalists, however, were only partially successful in bringing renewal to China. They modernized the government, improved taxation, stabilized the monetary and banking system, expanded education, developed transportation and communication facilities, and encouraged industry and commerce. Their cities flourished. Unfortunately, however, they did little to modernize agriculture or ameliorate the conditions of the rural poor, who made up more than 80 percent of the total population. It was on these people that the Communists concentrated.

It is difficult for us to imagine what missionary activity was like at the outset of this period, when China was in the midst of unbelievable internal confusion. Two separate governments claimed supreme authority. In every province, in almost every county, their representatives either openly or covertly competed for the taxes and loyalty of the peasants. In early 1927 the political situation rapidly deteriorated. It is a tribute to the missionary obedience of the churches of the West that, despite this political turmoil, by 1926 the total number of Protestant missionaries in China had reached the high point of 8,325.

But the crisis had come. Consular authorities ordered missionaries to evacuate the interior. A short time later Communist-inspired anti-foreign outbreaks erupted simultaneously in all major inland cities. Hundreds fled to the coast, their homes looted behind them, their congregations scattered. For a time it seemed no power could control the communist fury. Christian schools and hospitals were destroyed. Even the graves of missionary dead were desecrated. Although relatively few Chinese Christians and foreign missionaries lost their lives (as in the Boxer madness), it was a time of unprecedented suffering for the Christian movement throughout China.

And yet the uprising of 1927 had a major salutary effect. The missionary evacuation compelled Christians to assume responsibility for the church, with the result that within a matter of months a new vigor began to characterize its life and outreach. Missionaries were filled with amazement! The Chinese were doing a far better job than the most sanguine had expected. Not a few missions translated this into formal decrees to the effect that from henceforth no Western missionaries would be allowed to hold administrative responsibility in the national church.[51] Church leadership must be Chinese! Some missions even began to consider launching "forward movements," since their missionaries were now free to penetrate those areas still without functioning local congregations.

Most of this planning came to nought, however, because of the worldwide Great Depression (1930-35). This not only afflicted the nations of the West; it also compounded China's anguish. In terms of missionary activity it forced drastic retrenchment of the overseas operations of American and British missions. The painful process of slashing budgets precipitated no little debate on mission priorities. Laymen were drawn into the discussions. In the end a Laymen's Foreign Missions Inquiry was launched (1931-32) to make a thorough study of the problem. Its "Commission of Appraisal" spent 2½ months in eastern China. Their report, *Re-Thinking Missions,* provoked intense controversy, since its theological bias was both syncretistic and relativistic. "The missionary will look forward, not to the destruction of these [non-Christian religions], but to their continued coexistence with Christianity, each stimulating the other in growth toward the ultimate goal, unity in the completest religious truth."[52]

Statements like this provoked intense and necessary reaction on the part of missionaries and Chinese leaders committed to historic, biblical Christianity. Unfortunately, their protests were summarily dismissed. Their separatist policy of withdrawal from the National Christian Council meant that they had made themselves irrelevant to the leaders of the new national church that had emerged. During early October, 1927, the church of Christ in China was formed "in our faith in Jesus Christ as our Redeemer and Lord . . . in our acceptance of the Holy Scriptures of the Old and New Testaments as the divinely inspired Word of God and the supreme authority in matters of faith and duty . . . in our acknowledgment of the Apostles' Creed as expressing the fundamental doctrines of our common evangelical faith."[53] Missionaries who were unable to participate in a united church with such an evangelical basis were understandably regarded as peripheral to the Christian movement and their objections not worthy of serious attention.

It was this policy of isolation that made these same missionaries incapable of profiting from the positive aspects of the Laymen's Report. Anderson's summary is very much to the point: "Unfortunately, the controversy surrounding theological aspects of the report diverted attention from the great wealth of information and material presented elsewhere in the report, and also in the supplementary series of seven volumes published in 1933."[54]

It would be faulty in the extreme to conclude that in the depths of the Depression the energies of non-Church of Christ in China missions were largely confined to nonproductive polemics with "liberals" and everything "liberals" endorsed. Some societies, notably the China Inland Mission and its associated missions, issued stirring worldwide appeals for more workers. They sent out two hundred new workers within two years, but not without criticism because of China's chaotic condition during those years. In reply, a China Inland Mission director, Dr. Robert H. Glover, replied:

> Conditions in China for the present seem to grow no better but rather worse. . . . Lawlessness abounds, and bandit raids upon hamlets, towns, and even larger cities are of almost daily occurrence. . . . Missionaries have been robbed in their homes or while journeying. . . . A considerable number have been taken captive and held for ransom . . . and rumors seem to be confirmed that four, one in Kweichow and three in Kiangsi, have been brutally done to death. It not unnaturally raises the question as to whether missionary work should continue under such conditions, and particularly as to whether the mission is justified in undertaking a forward movement and appealing for new workers at such a time as this. We can only reply: Our Lord has commanded. It will be a bad day for the church when it takes for its motto "Safety First."[55]

So then, throughout this period, despite significant enlargement of missionary outreach, an increasing polarization took place within China's missionary community. One party stressed the saving of souls, the other the salvation of the whole man. One party became increasingly more critical of those whose educational and medical institutions failed to "make disciples" and multiply congregations. The other party began to implement a recommendation of the Laymen's Report and selected key rural communities all over China in which they might expand local congregations into training centers for scientific agriculture, credit cooperatives, and health and sanitation programs. Within a few years (1937) the program was sufficiently widespread to warrant an evaluation of results. Two-thirds of the centers surveyed reported the sponsoring of community service projects, such as literacy classes, supplementary industries, farmers' cooperatives, and improved seed programs. But these efforts were too few and too weak in leadership and finance to play a significant role in China's economic and social reconstruction. Most community projects fell victim to the Japanese War from 1937 onward.[56] This failure stems more from lack of missionary vision than from the weakness of rural churches. The stability of China depended on her ability to improve living standards and establish a viable political order. Evangelical missionaries, however, sidestepped political and economic issues and sought to convince the Chinese that their problems were spiritual. Their failure to minister to the total needs of China shunted Christianity into the realm of the esoteric.

It needs to be remembered that during this period missionaries were only beginning to identify with the Chinese people in their total experience. Many sensed little responsibility to bring societal and economic renewal to China. Varg summarized the situation succinctly when he commented:

> Few Americans ever fully grasped the appalling demand for political and economic change in China; and when they did understand to some degree, they could only offer solutions in terms of their own experience with capitalism and democracy. They were the prisoners of their own experience, an experience different from that of China. It is doubtful that they could have offered China a solution to her economic problems. Economic planning and a considerable degree of state enterprise were called for, and few Americans had faith in such an approach.[57]

INTERNAL TRUCE AND JAPANESE INVASION (1937-45)

The more Chiang Kai-Shek and the Kuomintang Nationalists were able to consolidate their unification of China, the more apprehensive Japan became. She feared that China's growing sense of nationhood would eventually result in her being pushed out of Manchuria, a valuable slice of Chinese real estate she had earlier appropriated. To prevent this, Japanese armies began moving southward from Manchuria as early as 1931, slowly extending her imperial power.

The Nationalists tried to build up their army and air force in anticipation of eventual collision with Japan. They were also determined to hold the Communists at bay. By means of negotiation and diplomatic pressure they attempted to secure the assistance of other nations to contain the Japanese threat. By military operations they sought to check the Communists within their borders. Public opinion, however, eventually forced them to terminate the internal struggle and devote all their energies to oppose the Japanese. Because of Soviet fear of the growing might of Germany and Japan, the Chinese Communist party was ordered (1935) to work for a "united front" with the Kuomintang. Chiang was persuaded to drop his civil war with the Communists after what came to be known as the Sian incident, when Chiang's Manchurian officers abducted him and refused to release him until he pledged to lead a united China against Japan. Thus Chinese nationalism and Japanese imperialism finally collided in outright war in July 1937.

Chinese resistance to the Japanese during the first year of the war was stubborn and costly. They sought to protect the coastal cities and railway lines, but were eventually forced to retreat. This brought about the most massive migration of peoples in all human history. Over sixty million Chinese left their homes and trekked westward. Hankow and later on Chungking became the capital of "Free China." The Japanese pursued the Chinese inland chiefly along the rivers and railways, but were never able to break China's will to resist. After two years the war came to a stalemate. From 1939 to 1943 the battle lines changed very little.

But the fortunes of the Nationalists and Communists altered drastically during this period. Social and economic conditions deteriorated. Inflation, factionalism, corruption, and frustration came to the Nationalists. In contrast, the Communists gained in inner cohesion and in effectiveness in winning and mobilizing the countryside. The conviction increasingly possessed them that they alone could solve China's ills.

Prior to the surrender of Japan in 1945 these two factions sparred, clashed, and withdrew but always avoided mortal combat. Each tried to nullify the activities of the other. The tactics were subversion, secret police, totalitarian controls, concentration camps, and executions. While the Communists grew in the struggle, the Nationalists were weakened by it. While Mao built up a monolithic political machine, Chiang encouraged cliques in his party, played one off against another to keep himself in power, and was ultimately weakened in the process. Some argue that, given the circumstances, it was all he could do. In any event, he was not prepared for the final showdown that began in the fall of 1945.

During this decade of the war the sounds of crashing bombs, bursting shells, and marching armies almost drowned out all voices calling for social justice and public order. Missionaries remained in east China until the Japanese attack on Pearl Harbor (December 7, 1941). This suddenly brought World War II to China. Overnight, missionaries fled westward to escape certain internment. Many were unsuccessful and suffered long years of harsh imprisonment. Those who reached "Free China" had the privilege of sharing more intimately than ever before in China's sufferings. They ministered to the hungry and homeless as they were able. When the fighting cut them off from the support of their societies, the economic distance that formerly tended to isolate them from the poor evaporated. Indeed, they became poor themselves. Instances are on record when Chinese Christians came to their rescue with food. Actually, it was their patient participation in China's anguish that gave them new standing among all classes. Even the intelligentsia became curious to hear their gospel. During the war years a vigorous Christian movement emerged among university students. It can be largely traced to the loving example and faithful witness of these dislocated missionaries.

What impressed missionaries during this war period was the phenomenal growth of those segments of the Chinese church that were most independent of the West. Their emergence could be largely attributed to a vigorous Chinese leadership that capitalized on the growing spirit of nationalism and its attendant resentment against missionary paternalism. They wanted Jesus Christ to be "Chinese to the Chinese." The "True Jesus Church," which had been founded in 1917 by Barnabas Tung, rapidly expanded to a membership of a hundred thousand, slightly edging in size the antiwestern "Assembly Hall Church" or "Little Flock," founded in 1921 by Ni To-sheng ("Watchman Nee"). At this time the "Jesus Family" also came into existence. Its founder was Ching Tien-ying, a former Methodist evangelist, and it grew to more than 140 communal groups in eight provinces. These vigorous groups virtually split every mission-planted congregation in China and the process succeeded in drawing away many of their most vigorous laymen. Some great evangelists and Bible teachers emerged, such as John Sung, Andrew Gih, and Wang Ming-tao. Within a short time this widespread disruption just about doubled the number of congregations throughout China. This resulted in a rapid increase in the number of communicant members. This forward surge was a vivid demonstration of a key church growth principle: to increase significantly the number of Christians in a country one must deliberately increase the number of congregations, not work to make existing churches larger.

Naturally, missionaries were profoundly grateful for this new openness of the Chinese to the Christian message. It is virtually impossible for the outsider today to appreciate the depth of Chinese resistance to Christianity (cultural, social, psychological, and at times governmental) that had characterized the preceding 120 years. Throughout this long period, in the public mind it had been widely felt that for a Chinese to become a Christian meant

> . . . withdrawal from the moral duties of family and community, loss of honor and conscience in the standard terms of the culture, and betrayal of the national heritage for some selfish advantages at the hands of eccentric and aggressive aliens. As traditional ties and beliefs irregularly slackened . . . the newer forces of secularizing nationalism, with their indiscriminate attacks on superstition and religion as blocking the science needed desperately for survival, rose in influence.[58]

One must be charitable in his evaluation of the missionary movement during this decade of unprecedented adversity. Under the stress of Japanese, communist, or Kuomintang occupation missionaries rarely saw political issues clearly. They were badly fragmented because of their partisanship. War weariness also took its toll. At no time were they free from theological tension. Fundamentalists strove with liberals. They misunderstood one another and opposed one another. And their numbers steadily decreased. When V-J Day came in 1945 fewer than a thousand missionaries were still in China.

CIVIL WAR AND COMMUNIST VICTORY (1945-49)

When Japan surrendered, many hoped that a new era would dawn for China. The unequal treaties had been abolished; Manchuria and Taiwan had been regained; and China was regarded in the United Nations as one of the five great powers. But could she rehabilitate herself from the ravages of eight years of war and resolve her internal division at the same time? Did the Kuomintang have the concern, the program, and the will to deal with the economic problems facing the peasant in his unending struggle for existence?

During the closing years of the war the Communists had established guerrilla bases behind the Japanese lines throughout north China. They particularly coveted Manchuria and China's key northern cities. Following the Japanese surrender the Soviets equipped the Communists with Japanese weapons. When the civil war began, a militarily weaker communist movement that was united faced a stronger Kuomintang that was faction-ridden. The Communists occupied the countryside, and the Kuomintang most of the cities. This made it possible for the Communists to call for a "people's war" led by the peasants. Their slogan was "land reform." After suffering disastrous defeats in Manchuria (Mukden) and Kiangsu (Su-chou), Chiang suddenly announced his retirement (January 1949) and made it a cover-up for withdrawal to Taiwan. By the end of that year the Communists had complete control of the mainland, the Nationalist army having been "betrayed from within by corruption, maladministration, and dissension in high places."[59]

C. P. Fitzgerald, a diplomat in China for over fifteen years, summarized the reasons for Chiang's downfall:

> The attempt to modernize China without interfering with the land system; the endeavor to fit some rags of Confucian doctrine to a party dictatorship which itself was supposed to be temporary; to deny the practice of democracy and still pretend to be preparing the people for it; to proclaim and teach nationalism and yield to the national enemy—this medley of contradictions could not form a coherent policy which would win mass support.[60]

The Kuomintang failed for lack of vision. It became prey to selfish ambitions, to corruption, and to nepotism.

After V-J Day, when missionaries returned to east China, they were appalled at the physical destruction of the country and war-weariness of its people. Instead of flourishing urban and rural churches they found the wastage of war: ruined buildings, dispirited pastors, and scattered congregations. Fortunately, the missionary force rapidly grew. By the end of 1948 more than three thousand missionaries were involved in a restorative ministry, bringing spiritual renewal to Christians and financial assistance to reconstruct chapels, schools, and hospitals. Unfortunately, resources were too limited to effect the urgently needed integration of rural congregations into the life of peasants beset by rapacious landlords, exorbitant money lenders, runaway inflation, and inadequate stock and seed. Many of these rural congregations had been weakened through the migration into the cities of their more vigorous laymen.

In contrast, mission schools were never so crowded. In 1947 alone school administrators turned down more than 110,000 applicants for entrance into their colleges. Approximately 10 percent of all college students in the entire country were attending such institutions. The tragedy, however, was that these colleges were only nominally Christian. As a result they unwittingly contributed to the debacle soon to take place. They were unwilling to incur the displeasure of the government and embrace the challenge of a bankrupt social order which was disintegrating through poverty and injustice. Their lack of social concern only enlarged the social vacuum. Teaching staffs did not challenge the students to participate with Christ in solving the individual and social problems of China. These "Christian" colleges only managed to turn out urbanites. In contrast, the largely indigenous, theologically conservative Chinese Inter-Varsity Christian Fellowship was instrumental in leading many Chinese students to Christ in the secular universities. But neither this organization nor its converts manifested a biblical sense of social concern. Their gospel was a truncated, individualized version of the good news of the kingdom proclaimed by Jesus and the apostles. Its distinctive was the production of "converted" instead of "secular" urbanites.

In the face of growing communist power some missionaries sought to anticipate and prepare for the ordeal ahead. Regional conferences were convened to unite denominational ranks. Special literature was prepared to achieve better indoctrination of laymen. But no amount of zealous "church" work could offset a corrupt government, ruined economy, raging civil war, and the breakdown of the Confucian family system with its ancient commitment to moral order.

It should be mentioned that the missionary force was deeply divided over the Kuomintang. Some endorsed it totally; others condemned it out of hand. A third group sought to contend for a more neutral position, but with little success. Missionaries in contact with the Communists during the war years came to admire them: "Hardship means nothing to them so long as they are helping their country. Such spirits are not easily conquered." This represented a striking change from the prewar years, when the Communists publicly declared it their intention to eliminate Christianity from China and were described in mission periodicals as "the hand of Satan . . . seeking to overthrow God's cause."[61] Those missionaries who became involved in rural reconstruction believed, among other things, that

> the Communists are only too right when they scorn the Church and insist that it has no more power to attack the fundamental social evils at the heart of China than did the Buddhist monastery situated in calm detachment among the trees on the hillside.[62]

These differences within the missionary community, however, never equaled in intensity their theological disagreements. The liberal wing was taken with the horizontal dimension—the Cultural Mandate—man's obligation to his fellowman and Christianity's relevance to societal questions. They largely concentrated on institutional activity. In contrast, the conservative wing was almost solely concerned with the vertical dimension—the Evangelistic Mandate—man's relation to God. Although they had some schools and hospitals, and engaged in a measure of relief and rehabilitation work, they largely poured their energies into the widespread dissemination of the Scriptures, evangelistic outreach, and the multiplying of new congregations. Inasmuch as both dimensions are biblical, each needed the other. It is a tragedy that leaders on both sides were unable to listen and learn from their opposite numbers. In large measure they were content to reproduce, albeit unconsciously, all the characteristics and weaknesses of the Western churches from which they had come. The conservatives brought to China an introverted religion, weak in theology, and indifferent to the Old Testament with its concern for social righteousness.[63] In contrast, those who were theologically liberal and whose concerns were economic and political tended to have little interest in traditional forms of evangelism, discipleship training, and the organizing of new congregations.

The doctoral dissertation of Jonas Jonson ("Lutheran Missions in a Time of Revolution," 1972, *Studia Missionalia Upsaliensia* XVIII) details the strengths, weaknesses, differences, and unifying factors within the large Lutheran missionary force, American and European, in China from 1944 to 1951. The picture Jonson paints, although somewhat devastating, would be typical of all societies during this period.

In the closing days of the Kuomintang, L. H. Lee, a Chinese Christian, wrote an article entitled "Why the Goodwill Failed." He was temperate and measured in his evaluation of the Protestant missionary movement, stressing both its strengths and its weaknesses. But he concluded with an indictment of missionaries for the incompleteness and the imbalance of their presentation of the Christian message:

> Throughout the missionary movement there has never been a clearly defined theory, practice, or experiment by and for Chinese Christians as to what a better and more abundant life, the brotherhood of man, or the Kingdom of God would mean in China. To, by, and for the Chinese, the Christian message was one of personal salvation. There was no clearly defined sociopersonal preaching that one could be saved only in relation to the society in which he lives. The result has been that the Christian convert in China might become a better parent or child but not a new man of the world as St. Paul exemplified, nor a new citizen of his community. Without new citizens there can be no new China. Accordingly Christianity has so far failed.[64]

It is not enough to call the Chinese through the gospel to repentance toward God and personal faith in Jesus Christ; it is not enough to tell them that they must follow Christ in the inner world of their hearts. "He must be taught," Lee wrote, "how to act upon Christian principles in the problems that confront a Christian every day in this common, mundane world." Good counsel, but it came too late.

Despite all the tensions and divisions within the Christian movement during the decade prior to Mao Tse-tung's 1949 proclamation which constituted China a People's Republic, the church grew rapidly. The widespread labors of independent Chinese evangelists and the popularity of strictly Chinese movements largely account for Protestantism's more rapid growth than Catholicism. It is difficult to compare membership figures of these two churches because of differences in record keeping. While there were 4 Catholics to 1 Protestant in 1900, by 1949 the ratio had narrowed to 2 to 1 overall, 3,266,000 to 1,811,700 baptized members, and 1,502,000 to 823,506 communicant members.[65] The widespread distribution of Christians was also impressive. One could draw a line across China in any direction and on the average of every twenty-five miles come upon a Christian congregation!

THE CHURCH UNDER COMMUNIST PRESSURE (1949-PRESENT)

In May 1950 a group of several Christian leaders began meeting with Chou En-lai, the premier, to discuss the future of the church in China. These men were Mr. Wu Yao-Tsung of the YMCA, Mr. Liu Liang-mo of the YMCA, Rev. Tsui Hsien-hsiang of the Church of Christ in China, and Rev. George Wu of the National Christian Council. They went as representatives of their respective Christian organizations, but they were by no means representative of the whole church in China. The outcome of these conferences was the "Christian Manifesto" (July 1950), which condemned "all imperialism and aggressive design in China," pledged their "patriotic support of the Common Program," and set before themselves "the goal of self-support in the near future."[66]

The manifesto was written and approved by government authorities before the majority of church leaders had had any opportunity to discuss or alter it. Then it was widely publicized and was signed by more than four hundred thousand Protestants. The manifesto was adopted as a matter of course by the National Christian Council in its biennial meeting that October. In the months that followed its publication, foreign missions began reluctantly ordering their missionaries to withdraw from China. Prior to the withdrawal, Protestant missionaries numbered approximately 4500 and Roman Catholics 5500.[67] The government Religious Affairs Bureau demanded the deeds of all mission-owned properties and took over all church institutions. In 1951, the "Year of Fear," the government also carried out its first major attempt at land reform. "Several million people are reported to have been killed in the process of liquidating the landed gentry as a class."[68] Inevitably, not a few Christians lost their lives in this purge.

Then began the era of the "Three-Self Movement." This followed hard on the release of the manifesto and was formally constituted in mid-April, 1951. Wu Yao-Tsung, a relative unknown to the churches, suddenly emerged as its leader. This movement had as its goal the fusion of Catholics and Protestants into a program of total isolation from "the imperialists" (all foreign missionary personnel), total support of the land reform program, and total identification with the "Oppose America–Aid Korea" movement brought about by China's earlier intervention in the Korea War (October 25, 1950). In order to attain its objectives Wu launched a program of enforced "denunciation meetings."

Wu was ruthless in the manner in which he pressed Christians of every tradition and conviction to comply. He demanded that a particular style of accusation and denunciation be convened in every church. Using a variety of subtle pressures his minions produced the nationwide spectacle of Christians denouncing Christians for alleged "imperialist and reactionary acts." Catholic nuns whose orphanages had been heartily supported by the authorities a few months earlier for caring for the foundlings they had picked up on the street were now accused of "criminal negligence resulting in the deaths of thousands of infants."[69] Pastors accused pastors of using Christianity as a tool to promote the interests of American imperialism. Bishops attacked bishops. Churches found that they could not register for tax exemption until they could submit proof of having held "a successful accusation meeting against at least four of their own members."[70] This diabolically organized witch-hunt brought great anguish to large numbers of Christians, particularly the clergy. Many to their subsequent sorrow attacked both the missionaries who had served them and their own laymen. Those who participated rationalized that the church needed a cathartic; it was a "public duty" to serve in this fashion. At this distance we do well to withhold our judgment, since we cannot feel the pressures brought to bear on those who carried out Wu's directives. One who was terribly abused at a public trial, but who refused to deny his Christian faith and later "published several articles attacking American imperialism and defending the new China" was Dr. Chao Tzu-ch'en, dean of the Yenching School of Religion and a president of the World Council of Churches. In retrospect he wrote, "In the Three-Anti (anti-corruption, -waste, and -bureaucracy) Campaign I ate a great deal of bitterness, more than I can say. [It was] the best and most effective education for an old man set in his ways."[71]

Mention should be made of the widely publicized witness of Wang Mingtao, a prominent Peking pastor and an outstanding conservative evangelist. He sought to challenge the leaders of the Three-Self Movement to return to the biblical faith. Eventually, with the help of the government, they were successful in silencing him ("one of the most clearcut cases of religious persecution that has come out of China").[72] He was imprisoned with "two persuasive exponents of Communism" in the same cell with him to break him down. They succeeded. After a year of intense suffering Wang was released, broken in health and in spirit. It was widely publicized that he had confessed to being "a counterrevolutionary offender." Later, Wang repudiated this confession, was rearrested, and eventually died. The government also took severe action against the leaders of all independent church movements. This is significant when it is realized that they had no connections with Western mission societies. Ching Tien-ying, the founder of the "Jesus Family," Watchman Nee, the founder of the "Little Flock," and Isaac Wei, the leader of the "True Jesus Church," were all imprisoned, along with their associates, for opposing the Three-Self Movement.

In 1956 the "Hundred Flowers Campaign" was inaugurated with the call "Let a hundred flowers blossom, a hundred schools of thought contend." For the next year no little freedom was granted the Protestant churches. Pastors spoke out against religious discrimination. Many church activities were re-commenced. This campaign was abruptly terminated in mid-1957. By 1958 China was forced into the "Great Leap Forward," which called for her complete collectivization. A commune system was extended to include all the people. This regimentation snuffed out all the "blooming and contending" of the earlier period. Bush contends that "there are those who think that the Hundred Flowers Campaign was initiated with the precise intent of uncovering those who did not follow the accepted line. . . . Criticism was invited and encouraged in order to flush out hidden opponents."[73]

All we know is that many courageous men who spoke out during this period of freedom were subsequently cut down. From 1958 onward the government sought to root out all "illegal activities," such as faith healing, the exorcism of demons (in the True Jesus Church), inviting free-lance evangelists, emphasizing "negative and pessimistic" themes (such as the universality of sin and the return of Christ), and holding meetings in private homes.[74]

The tragedy of the Three-Self Movement was that in the end, rather than lead the Christian movement in China into a new era of self-government, self-support, and self-propagation, it made her utterly servile to the state. The initial slogan had been "Love your country; love your church; resist imperialism." By 1959, during the commune regimentation, Christians were being urged, "Hand over your hearts to the party." With the passage of time the church was slowly immobilized as an effective institution and finally destroyed. During its closing years, if one may judge from its few publications, it had almost no witness to the gospel of "Jesus Christ and Him crucified."

In 1966, when chairman Mao launched the "Great Proletarian Cultural Revolution," designed to seize power from a rather noncoöperative, bureaucratically oriented Communist party and to inject a fiery revolutionary spirit into China's two hundred million teenagers, he called for the destruction of the "four olds" (old ideology, old culture, old customs, and old habits). In the wake of this, religion generally and the Christian religion in particular were singled out for attack by the youthful Red Guard, which had been mobilized for this purpose. Dr. Masao Takenaka, professor of Christian ethics at Doshisha University, Japan, spent three weeks in China in the spring of 1967. He wrote:

> Certainly in those cities I visited the churches were closed. Except for one in Peking . . . we did not see any crosses on the church buildings of China. It is symbolic to see churches without the cross, a sign of suffering. . . . It is difficult to tell for what purposes the buildings are used, but it is certain at the present time that they are not used for religious activities.[75]

The Future

Not only were all vestiges of organized Christianity destroyed during the Cultural Revolution of 1966-69, but Confucianism, Buddhism, Islam, Taoism, and folk religion—all ancient competitors for the souls of the Chinese—have likewise come under state control and have been reduced to impotence. It is staggering to realize this: all the religious systems that formerly bound the Chinese from birth through life and onto death have been irreparably broken. Ancestor worship is forbidden. Idols have been destroyed. Monasteries, temples, and mosques have been confiscated. The Chinese Communists have been rigidly orthodox in their adherence to the Marxist mandate that religion must be destroyed.

Whereas Marx, Lenin, and Mao have all eagerly desired to transform human society, their materialistic construction of reality has rendered them incapable of answering adequately the ancient question, "What is man?" Is he just animal? Merely matter? A machine? Or something more? If so, what? Is there another dimension to life for which their ideology makes no provision? At any event, the hope of China lies in the grace of God and in the witness of its suffering church—stripped of "imperialist" associations and shorn of all foreign trappings. This church (Christians still doubtless exist in large numbers) has been given the deposit of truth by the churches of the West. It knows that only in Jesus Christ can men be made new. More, it has the Scriptures, which in their fullness call these new men to possess their nation for Him so that with His help a just egalitarian society shall emerge.

But a new Moses, a new deliverer, is needed. He will doubtless arise from the midst of the suffering remnant of God's people. Perhaps he will come from the innermost courts of a Chinese commissar "who knows not the Lord"; perhaps from Peking itself, where in the past such mighty Christians as Wang Ming-tao proclaimed so widely and so powerfully the Lordship of Jesus Christ. May he quickly arise. May the latter glory of the Chinese witness to Christ exceed the former glory. Let us pray to this end.

NOTES

1. *Time,* Dec. 16, 1974, p. 87.
2. *Time,* Feb. 3, 1975, p. 24.
3. Robert C. Larson, *Wansui: Insights on China Today,* p. 123.
4. Richard R. DeRidder, *The Dispersion of the People of God,* pp. 58-63.
5. C. E. Couling, *The Luminous Religion,* p. 41.
6. Keung, *Ching Feng,* p. 120.
7. Ibid., p. 120.
8. Marco Polo, *The Travels of Marco Polo the Venetian,* pp. 111 ff.
9. Joseph Schmidlin, *Catholic Mission History,* p. 233.
10. Ibid., p. 235.
11. Liao, p. 281.
12. George H. Dunne, *Generation of Giants,* p. 28.
13. Leonard M. Outerbridge, *The Lost Churches of China,* p. 85.
14. Johannes Beckmann, "Dialogue with Chinese Religion," pp. 124-30.
15. George H. Dunn, *Generation of Giants,* p. 44.
16. Ibid., pp. 86-88.
17. Clark, p. 32.
18. Kenneth Scott Latourette in *Christian Missions in China,* edited by Jessie G. Lutz, p. 83.
19. Latourette, *A History of the Expansion of Christianity,* p. 363.
20. Outerbridge, p. 111.
21. Laycock in *Missionaries, Chinese and Diplomats,* by Paul A. Varg, p. 35.

22. C. P. Fitzgerald, *Revolution in China,* p. 572.
23. Ibid., p. 577.
24. Ibid., p. 587.
25. Peter Duus in *Science and Salvation in China: The Life and Work of W. A. P. Martin,* edited by Liu Kwang-Ching, pp. 16-17.
26. Fitzgerald, pp. 584-85.
27. Dr. and Mrs. Howard Taylor, *Hudson Taylor and the China Inland Mission: The Growth of a Work of God,* p. 24.
28. Ibid., p. 30.
29. Ibid., p. 39.
30. Ibid.
31. *China's Millions,* p. 124.
32. Latourette, *A History of the Expansion of Christianity,* vol. 6, p. 326.
33. Latourette, *A History of Christian Missions in China,* p. 407.
34. Ibid., p. 409.
35. Duus, p. 33.
36. Wilbur, p. 37.
37. Helmut G. Callis, *China: Confucian and Communist,* p. 217.
38. Latourette, *The Chinese: Their History and Culture,* pp. 298-99.
39. Ssu-yu Teng, pp. 195, 196.
40. Latourette, *A History of Christian Missions in China,* p. 533.
41. Harold R. Isaacs, *Scratches on Our Minds: American Images of China and India,* p. 71.
42. David Nelson Rowe, *Modern China: A Brief History,* p. 41.
43. *East Asia Millions,* vol. 73, no. 6, p. 82.
44. Ibid., vol. 73, no. 7, p. 98.
45. W. A. P. Martin, *The Lure of Cathay,* p. 8.
46. Paul A. Varg, "A Survey of Changing Mission Goals and Methods," p. 133.
47. Ibid., p. 5.
48. William Richey Hogg, *Ecumenical Foundations,* p. 128.
49. Latourette in *A History of the Ecumenical Movement, 1517-1948,* edited by Ruth Rouse and Charles Neill Stephen, p. 382.
50. Milton T. Stauffer, ed., *The Christian Occupation of China,* p. 2.
51. *International Review of Missions,* vol. 17, pp. 306-326.
52. William Ernest Hocking, *Re-Thinking Missions: A Layman's Inquiry After One Hundred Years,* p. 44.
53. Wallace C. Merwin, *Adventure in Unity: The Church of Christ in China,* p. 214.
54. Stephen Charles Neill, Gerald H. Anderson, and John Goodwin, eds., *Concise Dictionary of the Christian World Mission,* p. 340.
55. *East Asia Millions,* vol. 73, no. 8, p. 114.
56. Brown in Liu, pp. 217-48.
57. Varg, *Missionaries, Chinese and Diplomats,* p. 321.
58. Bates in *China and Christian Responsibility,* by William J. Eaton Richardson, p. 58.
59. M. Searle Bates, ed., *China in Change: An Approach to Understanding,* p. 59.
60. Fitzgerald, p. 73.
61. *China's Millions,* vol. 94 (Jan. 1936), p. 4.
62. Butterfield in Liu, pp. 249-301, esp. p. 258.
63. Victor E. W. Hayward, *Ears to Hear: Lessons from the China Missions,* pp. 17-49.
64. L. H. Lee in Varg, p. 307.
65. Swanson, pp. 281-89.
66. Merwin, p. 175.
67. Richard C. Bush, *Religion in Communist China,* pp. 46, 47, 60.
68. O. Edmund Clubb, *Twentieth Century China,* p. 319.
69. Bush, p. 92.
70. Ibid, p. 192.
71. *Tien Feng,* July 8, 1957.
72. Francis Price Jones, *The Church in Communist China,* p. 105.
73. Bush, p. 228.
74. Ibid., pp. 228-29.
75. *Ecumenical Press Service,* No. 23.

BIBLIOGRAPHY

Books

Bates, M. Searle, ed. *China in Change: An Approach to Understanding.* New York: Friendship Press, 1969.

Beckmann, Johannes. "Dialogue with Chinese Religion." In *The Church Crossing Frontiers,* pp. 124-38. Edited by Peter Beyerhaus and Carl F. Hallencrentz. Uppsala: Gleerup Publishers, 1969.

Boardman, Eugene Powers. *Christian Influence Upon the Ideology of the Taiping Rebellion 1851-1864.* Madison: University of Wisconsin Press, 1952.

Bush, Richard C. *Religion in Communist China.* Nashville: Abingdon Press, 1970.

Callis, Helmut G. *China: Confucian and Communist.* New York: Holt, 1959.

Clark, Sidney J. W. *The Art of Using the China Missionary Survey.* Shanghai: China Continuation Committee, 1922.

Clark, William H. *The Church in China.* New York: Council Press, 1970.

Clubb, O. Edmund. *Twentieth Century China.* New York: Columbia University Press, 1964.

Cohen, Paul A. *China and Christianity: The Missionary Movement and the Growth of Chinese Antiforeignism 1860-1870.* Cambridge: Harvard University Press, 1963.

Couling, C. E. *The Luminous Religion.* London: Carey Press, 1925.

DeRidder, Richard R. *The Dispersion of the People of God.* Kampen, Holland: J. H. Kok N.V., 1971.

Dunne, George H. *Generation of Giants.* Notre Dame: University of Notre Dame Press, 1962.

Duus, Peter. "Science and Salvation in China: The Life and Work of W. A. P. Martin 1827-1916. In *American Missionaries in China,* pp. 11-41. Edited by Liu Kwang-Ching. Cambridge: Harvard University Press, 1970.

Fitzgerald, C. P. *Revolution in China.* New York: Frederick A. Praeger, 1952.

Forsythe, Sidney A. *An American Missionary Community in China, 1895-1905.* Cambridge: Harvard University Press, 1971.

Foster, John. "The Christian Origins of the Taiping Rebellion." In *International Review of Missions,* vol. 40. Geneva and New York, 1951.

Hayward, Victor E. W. *Ears to Hear: Lessons from the China Missions.* London: Edinburgh House Press, 1955.

Hocking, William Ernest. *Re-Thinking Missions: A Laymen's Inquiry After One Hundred Years.* New York: Harper and Brothers, 1932.

Hogg, William Richey. *Ecumenical Foundations.* New York: Harper and Brothers, 1952.

Isaacs, Harold R. *Scratches on Our Minds: American Images of China and India.* New York: J. Day Company, 1958.

Jones, Francis Price. *The Church in Communist China.* New York: Friendship Press, 1962.

Larson, Robert C. *Wansui: Insights on China Today.* Waco: Word Books, 1974.

Latourette, Kenneth Scott. *A History of Christian Missions in China.* New York: The Macmillan Company, 1929.

———. *A History of the Expansion of Christianity.* New York: Harper and Brothers, 1944.

———. *The Chinese: Their History and Culture.* New York: The Macmillan Company, 1964.

Lutz, Jessie G., ed. *Christian Missions in China.* Boston: D. C. Heath and Company, 1965.

Lyall, Leslie T. *Red Sky at Night.* Chicago: Moody Press, 1970.

MacInnis, Donald E. *Religions Policy and Practice in Communist China.* London: Hodder and Stoughton, 1972.

Martin, W. A. P. *The Lore of Cathay.* New York: Fleming H. Revell Company, 1901.

Merwin, Wallace C. *Adventure in Unity: The Church of Christ in China.* Grand Rapids: William B. Eerdmans Publishing Company, 1974.

Neill, Stephen Charles; Anderson, Gerald H; and Goodwin, John, eds. *Concise Dictionary of the Christian World Mission.* Nashville: Abingdon Press, 1971.

Outerbridge, Leonard M. *The Lost Churches of China.* Philadelphia: The Westminster Press, 1952.

Paton, David M. *Christian Missions and the Judgment of God.* London: Student Christian Movement Press, 1953.

Patterson, George N. *Christianity in Communist China.* Waco: World Books, 1969.

Polo, Marco. *The Travels of Marco Polo the Venetian.* New York: E. P. Dutton and Company, 1925.

Richardson, William J. Eaton. *China and Christian Responsibility.* New York: Maryknoll Publications and Friendship Press, 1968.

Rouse, Ruth and Charles, Neill Stephen, eds. *A History of the Ecumenical Movement, 1517-1948.* Philadelphia: The Westminster Press, 1967.

Rowe, David Nelson. *Modern China: A Brief History.* Princeton: Van Nostrand Company, 1959.

Saeki, Yoshio P. *The Nestorian Documents and Relics in China.* Tokyo: Maruzen Company, Ltd., 1937.

Schmidlin, Joseph. *Catholic Mission History.* Techny, Illinois: Mission Press, Society of the Divine Word, 1933.

Soothill, W. E. *The Three Religions of China.* Translated and edited by Hans H. Garth. Glencoe, Illinois: Free Press, 1951.

Stauffer, Milton T., ed. *The Christian Occupation of China.* Shanghai: China Continuation Committee, 1922.

Taylor, Dr. and Mrs. Howard. *Hudson Taylor and the China Inland Mission: The Growth of a Work of God.* London: China Inland Mission Press, 1920.

Teng, S. Y., and Fairbank, J. K., eds. *China's Response to the West.* Cambridge: Harvard University Press, 1954.

Torrance, Thomas. *China's First Missionaries: Ancient Israelites.* London: Thynne and Company, Ltd., 1937.

Varg, Paul A. "A Survey of Changing Mission Goals and Methods." In *Christian Missions in China*, pp. 1-10. Edited by Jessie G. Lutz. Boston: D. C. Heath and Company, 1965.

———. Missionaries, Chinese and Diplomats. Princeton: Princeton University Press, 1959.

Periodicals

China Notes. East Asia Office, Division of Overseas Ministries, National Council of Churches, New York.

China's Millions. China Inland Mission, Philadelphia.

Ching Feng. Quarterly Notes on Christianity and Chinese Religion and Culture, Hong Kong.

East Asia Millions. Overseas Missionary Fellowship, Philadelphia.

Information Letter. Lutheran World Federation Marxism and China Study, Geneva.

Tien Feng. Official organ of the Three-Self Movement, Peking.

8

CHRISTIANITY COMES TO ASIA

by Gordon H. Chapman

Introduction

Judging from the New Testament account of the rise and expansion of the early church, who would suppose that during the first few centuries of Christianity the most extensive dissemination of the gospel was not in the West but in the East? In fact, conditions in the Parthian Empire (250 B.C. to A.D. 226), which stretched from the Euphrates to the Indus rivers and the Caspian to the Arabian seas, were in some ways more favorable for the growth of the church than in the Roman world. And though opposition to Christianity increasingly mounted under successive Persian and Islamic rulers, Christian communities were eventually established in the vast territory which stretches from the Near to the Far East possibly as early as the first century of the church.

Gordon H. Chapman has had a distinguished career of more than 45 years as a missionary to Japan sponsored by the United Presbyterian Church. He has done pioneer missionary work in both Hokkaide and the Tokyo area. Mr. Chapman served for thirteen years as professor of Old Testament studies in Central Theological seminary before World War II and taught Bible in two private church colleges in Hokkaido and in Tokyo's Meiji Gakuin university after the war. He is the founder of the Hokkaido Christian Center for student evangelism and lay training and has served on the boards of many Christian organizations. Mr. Chapman was editor of *Japan Christian Yearbook* from 1964-1966 and has contributed widely to periodicals in both Japan and the United States. Following his undergraduate work at the University of California in Berkeley, Mr. Chapman did graduate work at San Francisco Theological seminary, Pacific School of Religion, and Berkeley Baptist Divinity school.

Mr. Chapman also authored chapters 11 and 31 of this volume ("Japan, A Brief Christian History" and "Important Religions of Asia").

Easterners at Pentecost

Luke informs us in Acts 2:5-11 that there were present in Jerusalem on the day of Pentecost "devout men from every nation under heaven." Among these were "Parthians, Medes, Elamites, residents of Mesopotamia . . . and Arabians." Moreover, these pilgrims included "both Jews and proselytes," alike in their familiarity with the culture of their respective countries and the revelation of the Old Testament Scriptures. The most plausible explanation of the early appearance of Christian communities in these lands is that some of these pilgrims were converted and returned to the East as Spirit-filled missionaries. Furthermore, the question immediately arises as to whether any of the apostles had a part in this eastern mission. According to two ancient historians, Eusebius (c. A.D. 260-340) and Socrates (c. 380-450), the twelve apostles parceled among themselves missionary responsibility for the known world. Thomas was assigned to the Parthian empire and India, with Bartholomew sharing in the latter area of mission.[1, 2]

The many Jews who lived in the vast territories of the Middle East were the descendants of those who were exiled at the time of the Assyrian and Babylonian captivities and later deportations. Most settled down in the comparatively stable and tolerant society of the East, and many prospered and became influential. Their biblically-inspired Messianic hope was doubtless a contributing factor to the widespread expectation of the coming King, so vividly portrayed in the visit of the magi (Mt 2:1-12). It is not without significance that this visit is only recorded in Matthew, the gospel which had wide circulation in the East, including India, from the first century.[3] The spoken language of the dispersion was Aramaic, and the Syriac version of the Old Testament was in common use. Syriac or Aramaic was destined to become the religious language of the eastern or Assyrian church, commonly known as Nestorian. Many of the early churches grew out of the Jewish synagogues of the dispersion, with these often serving as a kind of bridge between Israel and the Gentiles.

Though the early establishment of churches in the vast and populous countries of the East cannot be questioned, there is a scarcity of original sources of information. Thus we are often almost completely dependent upon traditional material, which is difficult to verify with absolute certainty. With few exceptions, the Christian community never became a dominant element in the population, nor did Christianity become the state religion. Moreover, the church usually found itself confronted by long-established ethnic religions of eclectic character, which were resistant to the exclusive claims of the gospel. Thus, from the third century there were long periods of persecution which involved the ruthless destruction of churches and monastic institutions and other depositories of invaluable historical documents. Also, in the latter part of the period under review, the Catholic church, long opposed to the church of the East for its refusal to recognize the primacy of Rome, became party to similar destructive measures. Thus it is little wonder that few ancient historical documents have survived.

Strangely, the church which spread throughout most of Asia bears the appelation "Nestorian," after the fifth-century patriarch of Constantinople, Nestorius, who was condemned by Rome as a heretic in A.D. 430. The name is actually a misnomer which became current in the West; the Roman See had sought to discredit this church, which had renounced Rome's primacy for geographical, political, linguistic, and doctrinal reasons. Nestorian was not the name by which the church knew itself, nor was it so commonly designated in Asian lands. It was rather known as the church of the East, or Easterns, to distinguish it from the Greek and Latin churches of the West which were divided by subtle theological controversies little appreciated by the eastern Christians. It also came to be known as the Assyrian church because of the location of its successive headquarters, and also as the Luminous Religion, especially in China. This ancient church claimed a first-century origin and developed almost wholly apart from the Greek and Roman churches. It did not embrace the heresy of which Nestorius was accused, though it endorsed his opposition to the Romish doctrines of purgatory and Mariolatry, especially her title as "Mother of God." For at least twelve hundred years the church of the Easterns was noted for its missionary zeal, its high degree of lay participation, its superior educational standards and cultural contributions in less developed countries, and its fortitude in the face of persecution.

Origin and Expansion of the Church in the East

PARTHIAN AND PERSIAN EMPIRES

The Church of the East had its inception at a very early date in the buffer zone between the Parthian and Roman empires in Upper Mesopotamia. The vicissitudes of its later growth were rooted in its minority status in a situation of international tension. The rulers of the Parthian Empire (250 B.C. to A.D. 226) were on the whole tolerant in spirit, and with the older faiths of Babylonia and Assyria in a state of decay, the time was ripe for the rise of a new and vital faith. The rulers of the second Persian empire (A.D. 226-640) also followed a policy of religious toleration to begin with, though later they gave Christians the same status as a subject race. However, these rulers also encouraged the revival of the ancient Persian dualistic faith of Zoroastrianism and established it as the state religion, with the result that the Christians were increasingly subjected to repressive measures. Nevertheless, it was not until Christianity became the state religion in the West (in A.D. 30) that enmity toward Rome was focused on the eastern Christians. After the Mohammedan conquest in the seventh century, the caliphate tolerated other faiths but forbade proselytism and subjected Christians to heavy taxation.

Edessa (now Urfa) in northwestern Mesopotamia was from apostolic times the principal center of Syriac-speaking Christianity. It was the capital of an independent kingdom from 132 B.C. to A.D. 216, when it became tributary to Rome. Celebrated as an important center of Greco-Syrian culture, Edessa was also noted for its Jewish community, with proselytes in the royal family. Strategically located on the main trade routes of the Fertile Crescent, it was easily accessible from Antioch, where the mission to the Gentiles was inaugurated. When early Christians were scattered abroad because of persecution, some found refuge at Edessa. Thus the Edessan church traced its origin to the apostolic age (which may account for its rapid growth), and Christianity even became the state religion for a time.

An ancient legend recorded by Eusebius (A.D. 260-340) and also found in the *Doctrine of Addai* (c. A.D. 400) (from information in the royal archives of Edessa) describes how King Abgar of Edessa communicated with Jesus, requesting Him to come and heal him, to which appeal he received a reply. After the resurrection, the apostle Thomas sent one of the seventy (Lk 10:1), Addai or Thaddaeus, to preach the gospel and heal the king, with the result that the city was won to the Christian faith. In this mission he was accompanied by a disciple, Mari, and the two are regarded as cofounders of the church, according to the *Liturgy of Addai and Mari* (c. A.D. 200), which is still the normal liturgy of the Assyrian church. The *Doctrine of Addai* further states that Thomas was regarded as the apostle of the church, which long treasured a letter written by him from India.[4, 5]

Thus it was from Edessa that a missionary movement began which gradually spread throughout Mesopotamia, Persia, Central Asia, and China. According to another ancient tradition, Mari was sent as a missionary to Seleucia (on the Tigris River near Baghdad), which, with its twin city of Ctesiphon across the river, became another center of missionary outreach. Mari was also regarded as the pioneer evangelist in the whole region of Adiabene to the north, of which Arbela (now Erbil) was the capital.[6] By the latter half of the second century, Christianity had spread east throughout Media, Persia, Parthia, and Bactria (modern Iraq, Iran, and Afghanistan). The twenty bishops and many presbyters were more of the order of itinerant missionaries, passing from place to place as Paul did and supplying their needs by such occupations as merchant or craftsman. By A.D. 280 the metropolis of Seleucia assumed the title of "Catholicos," and in A.D. 424 a council of the church at Seleucia elected the first patriarch to have jurisdiction over the whole church of the East, including India and Ceylon. The seat of the Patriarchate was fixed at Seleucia-Ctesiphon, since this was an important point on the East-West trade routes which extended both to India and China. Thus the shift of ecclesiastical authority was away from Edessa, which in A.D. 216 had become tributary to Rome. The establishment of an independent patriarchate with nine subordinate metropoli contributed to a more favorable attitude by the Persian government, which no longer had to fear an ecclesiastical alliance with the common enemy, Rome.

CONDITIONING FACTORS OF MISSIONARY EXPANSION

Several important factors help to explain the extensive growth in the church of the East during the first twelve hundred years of the Christian era. Geographically, and possibly even numerically, the expansion of this church outstripped that of the church in the West in the early centuries. The outstanding key to understanding this expansion is the active participation of laymen—the involvement of a large percentage of the church's believers in missionary evangelism.[7] The following significant factors inducing that church growth are all based largely on the fact that it was a lay as well as a clerical movement.

1) The church promoted an effective system of popular education, producing a literate Christian community, knowledgeable in the Scriptures. This training was based on use of the Syriac Old Testament and had available the canonical gospels before the end of the first century, though the *Harmony of the Four,* a life of Christ compiled by Tatian (c. A.D. 160), an Assyrian Christian, was the most popular Scripture portion for several centuries. Traveling Christians carried with them everywhere these portions of the Scripture, usually a gospel or the *Harmony* and parts of the Old Testament.

2) The church backed specialized training programs for youth, monastic Bible schools for laymen, theological schools for clergy, etc. As they traveled, the Christians introduced Syriac learning to the illiterate Turks, Uigurs, Mongols, and Manchus, whose alphabets as a result are largely derived from the Syriac writing system. The first monastic school at Edessa, later moved to Nisibis in 489, had eight hundred students enrolled. The church trained deaconesses, medical students in church hospitals, and musicians in church music schools, which stimulated an indigenous hymnody of the church of the East. Thus from scores of such schools a constant stream of well-trained Christians, clergy and lay, traveled throughout Asia, self-supporting and often enthusiastically witnessing—a strategy of mission which was not achieved in the West for hundreds of years.

3) Persecution strengthened and spread the Christian movement in the East. A great influx of Christian refugees from the Roman persecutions of the first two centuries gave vigor to the Mesopotamian church. And persecution within the Persian empire saw thousands slain for the faith (at least sixteen thousand under the reign of Sapor II, A.D. 309-79) and numberless thousands more reported or fleeing as refugees to witness as far as Arabia, India, and other central Asian countries. Following a period of relative quiet in the empire under Bahram V (420-38), more terrible persecution broke out, culminating in the massacre of ten bishops and 153,000 Christians within a few days.

Early Muslim conquest of these lands in the seventh and eighth centuries did not introduce direct persecution. However, Muslim apostasy was curbed by threat of death, and many nominal Christians began to gradually defect to Islam to avoid discrimination and heavy taxation. This type of subtle oppression stifled Christian growth, backed the church into ghetto communities, and discouraged evangelism. Muslim governments eventually gained control of the great trade routes, and the Islamic world became virtually closed to proclamation of the gospel.

ARABIAN PENINSULA

In our consideration of the penetration of the Arabian peninsula by the gospel, it is necessary to distinguish between the marauding Bedouin nomads of the interior, who were chiefly herdsmen and unreceptive to foreign influence, and the inhabitants of the settled communities of the coastal areas and oases, who were either middleman traders or farmers and were receptive to influences from abroad. Christianity apparently gained its strongest foothold in an ancient center of Semitic civilization in southwest Arabia or Yemen, (sometimes known as Seba or Sheba), whose queen visited Solomon (1 Ki 10:1-10). Because of geographic proximity, acculturation with Ethiopia was always strong, and the royal family traces its ancestry to this queen. In the early years the Sabeans shared a dual monarchy with the Himyarites to the east, with the latter later dominating the south of Arabia. These southern nations engaged in extensive trading operations, especially through Alexandria, but also with Syria, Mesopotamia, and even India, thereby opening themselves to Christian influences from the churches of these areas through missionaries who followed the main trade routes.

The presence of Arabians at Pentecost (Ac 2:11) and Paul's three-year sojourn in Arabia (Gal 1:17, 18) suggest a very early gospel witness. A fourth-century church history, which used excellent sources, states that the apostle Bartholomew preached in Arabia and that Himyarites were among his converts.[8] Arabia's close relations with Ethiopia give significance to the conversion of the treasurer to the queen of Ethiopia (Ac 8:26-39), not to mention the tradition that the apostle Matthew was assigned to this land.[9] Eusebius says that "one Pantaneus (c. A.D. 190) was sent from Alexandria as a missionary to the nations of the East,"[10] including southwest Arabia, on his way to India. The Roman Emperor Constantius II (A.D. 310-61) reportedly sent a well-equipped mission to southwest Arabia headed by Bishop Theophilus, who labored among the Himyarites. The native ruler was converted and churches were established in the metropolis, Aden, and in a famous Persian trading center at the mouth of the Persian Gulf. He also found existing churches with customs different from his own.[11]

Cosmas Indicopleustes, navigator and geographer of the sixth century, wrote about Christians, bishops, monks, and martyrs in Yemen and among the Himyarites.[12] In the fifth century a merchant from Yemen was converted in Hira, in the northeast, and upon his return led many to Christ. Subsequent political controversy in the whole area plus strife between the competing churches of East and West for supremacy there stifled church growth in the succeeding two centuries.

During the early centuries Christianity also penetrated Arabia from numerous points on its periphery. The kingdom of Hira in northeastern Arabia and near the border of Mesopotamia flourished from the end of the third to the end of the sixth century and was apparently evangelized by Christians from the Tigris-Euphrates Valley in the fourth century. The kingdom of Ghassan on the northwest frontier was also a sphere of missionary activity. In fact, by A.D. 500 many churches were also in existence along the Arabian shore of the Persian Gulf and in Oman, with all connected with the church of the East in the Persian Empire. Arabian bishops were found among those in attendance at important church councils in Mesopotamia. In the seventh century, however, the rise of Islam seriously inhibited the growth of the church in Arabia, and existing churches were gradually eliminated by Muslim oppression. In the eighth century, many of the remaining Christians fled the country and found refuge in Mesopotamia. With the quenching of these tiny early lights, spiritual darkness fell again over Arabia, to remain more than a millennium.

INDIA

Are there good reasons for believing the various ancient traditions which often assign the beginnings of Christianity in India to the apostolic age? Viewed by strict canons of historical criticism demanding original documentation, the origin of the church is somewhat shrouded in obscurity. The problem is further complicated by the sometimes doubtful miraculous accounts, which critical scholars will not recognize.

But in addition to the possibility of the witness of converted proselytes from the Parthian empire (including northwest India) at Pentecost, and Eusebius' record that Thomas and Bartholomew were assigned to Parthia and India, the *Didache* (dating from the end of the first century) states, "India and all countries bordering it, even to the farthest seas . . . received the Apostolic ordinances from Judas Thomas, who was guide and ruler in the Church which he built." Moreover, there is a wealth of confirmatory information in the Syriac writings, liturgical books, and calendars of the church of the East, not to mention the writings of the Fathers, the calendars, the sacramentaries, and the martyrologies of the Roman, Greek, and Ethiopian churches.[13] Since trade routes from the East were wide open at the time and were used by early missionaries, there are no circumstantial reasons why Thomas could not have visited India in the first century. And his visit is the most plausible explanation for the early appearance of the church there.

An early third-century Syriac work known as the *Acts of Thomas*[14] connects the apostle's Indian ministry with two kings, one in the north and the other in the south. According to one of the legends in the *Acts*, Thomas was at first reluctant to accept this mission, but the Lord appeared to him in a night vision and said, "Fear not, Thomas. Go away to India and proclaim the Word, for my grace shall be with you." But the Apostle still demurred, so the Lord overruled the stubborn disciple by ordering circumstances so compelling that he was forced to accompany an Indian merchant, Abbanes, to his native place in northwest India, where he found himself in the service of the Indo-Parthian king, Gundaphorus. The apostle's ministry resulted in many conversions throughout the kingdom, including the king and his brother.[15]

Critical historians treated this legend as an idle tale and denied the historicity of King Gundophorus until modern archeology established him as an important figure of North India in the latter half of the first century. Many coins of his reign have turned up in Afghanistan, the Punjab, and the Indus Valley. Remains of some of his buildings, influenced by Greek architecture, indicate that he was a great builder. Interestingly enough, according to the legend, Thomas was a skilled carpenter and was bidden to build a palace for the king. However, the Apostle decided to teach the king a lesson by devoting the royal grant to acts of charity and thereby laying up treasure for the heavenly abode. Although little is known of the immediate growth of the church, Bar-Daisan (A.D. 154-223) reports that in his time there were Christian tribes in North India which claimed to have been converted by Thomas and to have books and relics to prove it.[16] But at least by the time of the establishment of the second Persian Empire (A.D. 226 ff.), there were bishops of the church of the East in northwest India, Afghanistan, and Baluchistan, with laymen and clergy alike engaging in missionary activity.[17]

The *Acts of Thomas* identifies his second mission in India with a kingdom ruled by King Mahadwa, one of the rulers of a first-century dynasty in southern India. It is most significant that, aside from a small remnant of the church of the East in Kurdistan, the only other church to maintain a distinctive identity is the *Mar Thoma* or "Church of Thomas" congregations along the Malabar coast of Kerala State in southwest India. According to the most ancient tradition of this church, Thomas evangelized this area and then crossed to the Coromandel coast of southeast India, where, after carrying out a second mission, he suffered martyrdom near Madras. Throughout the period under review, the church in India was under the jurisdiction of Edessa, which was then under the Mesopotamian patriarchate at Seleucia-Ctesiphon and later at Baghdad and Mosul.

Historian Vincent A. Smith says, "It must be admitted that a personal visit of the Apostle Thomas to South India was easily feasible in the conditions of the time, and that there is nothing incredible in the traditional belief that he came by way of Socotra, where an ancient Christian settlement undoubtedly existed. I am now satisfied that the Christian Church of South India is extremely ancient. . . ."[18]

Although there was a lively trade between the Near East and India via Mesopotamia and the Persian Gulf, the most direct route to India in the first century was via Alexandria and the Red Sea, taking advantage of the monsoon winds, which could carry ships directly to and from the Malabar coast. The discovery of large hoards of Roman coins of first-century Caesars and the remains of Roman trading posts testify to the frequency of that trade. In addition, thriving Jewish colonies were to be found at the various trading centers, thereby furnishing obvious bases for the apostolic witness.

The question immediately arises as to why evangelism on the Indian subcontinent and the development of the church did not progress as rapidly as in other areas of both East and West. For one thing, in contrast to the spiritual vacuum of the Mediterranean and Mesopotamian areas, where the ethnic religions had lost their appeal, Indian religions were still very much alive. Furthermore, the caste system, which undergirds Hinduism and permanently freezes individuals at the various levels of the hierarchical structure, made proselytism more difficult and fraught with dire consequences.

Piecing together the various traditions, one may conclude that Thomas left northwest India when invasion threatened and traveled by vessel to the Malabar coast, possibly visiting southeast Arabia and Socotra enroute and landing at the former flourishing port of Muziris on an island near Cochin (c. A.D. 51-52). From there he is said to have preached the gospel throughout the Malabar coast, though the various churches he founded were located mainly on the Periyar River and its tributaries and along the coast, where there were Jewish colonies. He reputedly preached to all classes of people and had about seventeen thousand converts, including members of the four principal castes. Later, stone crosses were erected at the places where churches were founded, and they became pilgrimage centers. In accordance with apostolic custom Thomas ordained teachers and leaders or elders, who were reported to be the earliest ministry of the Malabar church.*

Thomas next proceeded overland to the Coromondel coast and ministered in what is now the Madras area, where a local king and many people were converted. One tradition related that he went from there to China via Malacca and, after spending some time there, returned to the Madras area (*Breviary of the Mar Thoma Church in Malabar*). Apparently his renewed ministry outraged the Brahmins, who were fearful lest Christianity undermine their social structure, based on the caste system. So according to the Syriac version of the *Acts of Thomas*, Masdai, the local king at Mylapore, after questioning the apostle condemned him to death about the year A.D. 72. Anxious to avoid popular excitement, "for many had believed in our Lord, including some of the nobles," the king ordered Thomas conducted to a nearby mountain, where, after being allowed to pray, he was stoned and then stabbed to death with a lance wielded by an angry Brahmin. Though first buried at Mylapore, his remains were later removed to Edessa and then to Chios, an island in the Aegean Sea, and were finally interred at Ortona in Italy. However, a small portion of the remains and the lancehead are reputedly still preserved in an ancient reliquary in the Cathedral of Saint Thomas, located near the site of the martyrdom. A number of Christians were also persecuted at the same time; when they refused to apostatize, their property was confiscated, so some sixty-four families eventually fled to Malabar and joined that Christian community.[19]

Though we have little in the way of detailed information concerning the development of the South Indian church through the early years, a number of conditioning factors are now quite clear. From the earliest times the language of the Scriptures, liturgies, and theological literature was in Syriac, though it was transliterated into the Malayalam script of the Malabar language. However, although the worship of the church and its theol-

*Though it is impossible to absolutely prove or disprove the apostolic origin of the Indian church because of the paucity of contemporary documentation, a vast amount of literature has been written on the subject. In the bibliography see especially: L. W. Brown, F. C. Burkitt, F. A. D'Cruz, J. N. Farquhar, A. E. Medlycott, A. Mingana, J. Richter, J Stewart, and L. M. Zaleski.

ogy as expressed in the liturgical books remained entirely foreign, the social life and everyday customs of the Christians were completely Indian, thereby indicating the entire assimilation of the community into the local environment. The Christians in southwest India were early given separate, superior caste status by tolerant Indian rulers. While this arrangement doubtless gave them protection and the right to manage their own internal affairs, it increasingly hampered their Christian outreach, for transfer from the caste of one's birth to another caste was well nigh impossible. Also, pride of caste discouraged intercourse with members of lower castes and thereby discouraged evangelism among those who were more open to the gospel then the Brahmin elite. Thus, though the whole system of religious rites and observances of the Mar Thoma church of Malabar was foreign and in the Syriac language, it did serve to maintain the Christian integrity of the community with the parish church at its center. These Christians were noted for their integrity, industry, literacy, natural ability, and skills and also for their respect for parents, elders, clergy, and all those in authority over them. The fact that they were law-abiding, with criminal acts practically unknown among them, doubtless commended them to the rulers and accounts for the special status and privileges accorded them.

The existence of these Christian churches in India from the early centuries is further attested by the reports of occasional visitors from abroad. For example, Eusebius records a visit to India by Pantaenus (A.D. 189-90), who not only found a company of earnest Christians on the Malabar coast but especially noted that they were using a Syriac version of the gospel of Matthew which they said they had received from the Apostle Bartholomew.[20] According to Jerome (c. A.D. 340-420), Pantaenus because of his superior learning was sent to India to preach Christ among the Brahmins and philosophers. Bishop Theophilus, a native of India, in connection with his mission to Arabia also visited various parts of India and Ceylon. He reports that though he was able to improve certain practices of the churches, he found nothing to be corrected so far as doctrine was concerned.[21] However, there is reason to believe that by then the flame of evangelistic zeal had waned in South India.

New enthusiasm and purpose came to the life of the church by way of Christian refugees who fled to the Malabar coast because of persecutions under Sapor II of Persia (A.D. 309-79). According to the tradition of the Mar Thoma church, the most influential of these migrations was one under convoy of a wealthy Christian merchant, Thomas of Cana, which arrived in A.D. 345. This company of believers from Syria and Mesopotamia included a bishop of Edessa, several lesser clergy, and about four hundred men, women, youths, and maidens. This substantial reinforcement was received with great rejoicing and ushered in a flourishing epoch in the life of the Malabar church. Thomas of Cana was a man of business acumen and influence and made a favorable impression on the local king, who granted a charter of special privileges to the Christian community and guaranteed full trading rights. This charter was inscribed on copper plates and treasured as the Magna Charta of the community down through the centuries. Twice married, Thomas of Cana was the progenitor of two large families, which became the nuclei of two important Christian communities.[22] These fourth-century Christians claim to have had the complete Syriac Scriptures prior to the Council of Nicaea (A.D. 325).

Cosmas Indicopleustes, a sixth-century navigator and geographer of about A.D. 530, found Christian communities not only on the southwest coast but in other parts of India as well. He also found Christian churches in Ceylon which were similar to those of Malabar, with a preponderance of Persian colonists. Indicopleustes stated that the doctrine of the churches was in accord with the decrees of Nicaea and that their Scriptures and theological manuscripts were very ancient.[23]

In a work of Bishop Gregory of Tours (A.D. 540-94), *In Gloria Martyrum,* is an account of the visit of a Syrian monk, Theodore, to Mylapore near Madras, where he found a church and the tomb of Thomas, together with a monastery. Both were apparently under the jurisdiction of the patriarch of Seleucia, who about a century later complained in a letter to the metropolitan of Persia and greater India that through his neglect the Christians of India were without properly constituted bishops.[24] Perhaps for this reason India was raised to an independent metropolitanate in A.D. 760 and later became coequal with Persia and China in ecclesiastical jurisdiction. In the ninth century additional groups of Persian Christian colonists arrived on the Malabar coast and reinforced the churches of the area. Three more charter privilege grants, inscribed on copper plates, reveal that at least some of the believers were persons of great wealth and influence and were entrusted with princely authority.[25]

During the ensuing four or five hundred years the South India churches, with their roots chiefly in Mesopotamia and Persia and with so many members belonging to the merchant class, were seriously affected by the Islamic conquests and subsequent Arab domination of the trade routes. The Western Ghats mountain range shielded the Malabar coast from Moslem invasion, but the churches on the Coromondel coast and elsewhere became almost extinct. Spiritual decadence of the churches in some areas was hastened by the restoration of Brahminism after a long and bloody struggle with the Buddhists.

But the conquests of the great Mongols, Genghis Khan and Kubla Khan, in the thirteenth century reopened the lines of communication between East and West. Marco Polo brought encouraging reports concerning

Christianity in India.[26] He regarded the Mar Thoma church in Malabar as by far the most important church in the East and noted that these Christians still retained the Syriac language. While he did not visit the Thomas shrine at Mylapore, he reported much about the martyrdom of the apostle and the large number of Christian pilgrims who resorted there.

During this period Rome, eager to take advantage of the newly opened trade routes, sent the Franciscans and Dominicans on both religious and political missions to the East. The Franciscan John of Monte Corvino (later archbishop of Peking) spent thirteen months in India and baptized a hundred converts there (A.D. 1292-93), chiefly in Madras Province, where the memorial Church of Saint Thomas is located. Early in the fourteenth century a Dominican and four Franciscans visited the Island of Salsette off Bombay and found a number of Christian families, reporting that there were many Christians on the Gulf of Cambay but that their communities in northwest India were being rapidly decimated by the Saracens, who had transformed many churches into mosques. One of them, Jordan, boasted of converting on the Malabar coast ten thousand "Syrian schismatics to the faith . . . and found them ten times better and more loving than European Christians."[27] In the fifteenth century a traveler, Nicolo Conti, reported that Nestorians, (Thomas Christians) were scattered over all India, much as were Jews in Europe.[28] Unfortunately, we have little or no information concerning developments in the Mar Thoma church until the dawn of the sixteenth century.

When the Portuguese under Vasco de Gama arrived on the Malabar coast about 1500, they were welcomed by Christians as deliverers from the oppression of Hindu princes. However, with the arrival of the Jesuit missionaries around the middle of the century it became apparent that the real intention of the Portuguese rulers and missionaries was to make the Malabar Christians pliant tools of Catholic-Portuguese policy by reforming the ancient Mar Thoma church along Roman lines. To accomplish this end they were prepared to use intrigue, deception, mendacity, and even violence and cruel persecution. The priests also sought to block the arrival of bishops and other clergy dispatched by the patriarch in Mesopotamia, plotting their deaths enroute or imprisoning them for life upon arrival. Finally the majority of Malabar Christians submitted to Rome, although about thirty thousand in the hill country refused to abandon their faith. It was not until the defeat of the Portuguese by the Dutch a century later that the way was open for the Thomas Christians to renounce their allegiance to Rome and resume their traditional church life, which the majority soon did. One unfortunate phase of the Roman-Portuguese occupation was the destruction of all the early records of Mar Thoma congregations in Malabar. All Christian literature had to be either submitted to thorough emendation along Romish lines or burned. This vandalism, along with that of the Hindu and Islamic invaders, caused paucity of information concerning the earlier history of the church of the East in India.

THE EXPANSION OF CHRISTIANITY IN CENTRAL ASIA

The agents of missionary expansion in central Asia and the Far East were not only monks and clergy trained in the Mesopotamian monastic schools, but also in many cases Christian merchants and artisans, often with considerable biblical training. They frequently found employment among peoples less advanced in education, serving in government offices and as teachers and secretaries and more advanced medical care. They also helped to solve the problem of illiteracy in backward lands by inventing simplified alphabets based on the Syriac language. Persecution often thrust them forth into new and unevangelized lands to find refuge. The dissemination of the gospel by largely Syriac-using people had its advantages, but it was also a hindrance to indigenizing the church in the new areas. Because Syriac culture never became dominant, competition from ethnic religions was always a serious problem. For these reasons of political vicissitude, in later centuries Christianity suffered an almost total eclipse in Asia until the modern period. The golden age of early missions in central Asia extended from the end of the fourth to the latter part of the ninth century, although in the Far East Christianity again became resurgent in the latter half of the thirteenth century. An important factor which finally inhibited the permanent establishment of the church of the East in central Asia and the Far East was the expansion of Islam and Mahayana Buddhism.

Christianity had an early and extensive dissemination throughout the vast territory north of Persia and west and east of the Oxus River (*Amu Darya*), which flows from the Afghanistan border north into the Aral Sea (present-day Turkmen and Uzbek in the U.S.S.R. and northern Iran). As early as the fourth century cities like Merv (or Mary in modern Turkmen, U.S.S.R.), Herat (northwest Afghanistan), and Samarkand (in Uzbek of U.S.S.R.) had bishops and later became metropolitanates. Christians were found among the Turks and the Ephthalite Huns from the fifth century, and the Mesopotamian patriarch assigned bishops to both peoples, with the result that many were baptized. There was a large ingathering under the metropolitan of Merv in the seventh century.

By the end of the eighth century a king of the Turks was converted, and the patriarch established a new metropolitanate over the bishops south and east of the Caspian Sea. In fact, so successful were the missionary efforts that it appeared that Christianity might become the dominant faith in the whole region between the Caspian Sea and Sinkiang in Northwest

China. The largely animistic and polytheistic religions there offered little or no effective resistance to the higher faith. Moreover, Islam at first made little headway in that area, and the dualistic faith of Manichaeism with headquarters at Samarkand also had scant appeal. Christian Turks visiting Ctesiphon in connection with the election of a new metropolitan about this time were described as people of clean habits and orthodox beliefs and as readers of the Scriptures in both Syriac and their own language. Two ancient cemeteries fifty-five kilometers apart near Lake Issyk-Kul in the Ala-Tau mountains of southern Siberia throw some light on what was a densely populated Christian area prior to the Mongol period. Tombstones, mostly in the shape of crosses, indicate many Christian burials between the ninth and fourteenth centuries and include persons from Persia, India, Turkestan, Mongolia, Siberia, and China. Though there was a mass conversion of Turks to Islam in the eleventh century, the Moslems did not dominate the area until the thirteenth and fourteenth centuries.

Once the Christian faith had been established in the valleys of the Oxus and Jaxartes rivers, it was easily carried further east into the basin of the Tarim River, then into the area north of the Tien Shan Mountains, and finally down into far northwest China, above Tibet. This was the principal caravan route, and with so many Christians engaged in the trade it was natural that the gospel was early planted in the towns and cities which were caravan centers. The Mesopotamian patriarch in the eighth century wrote that he was appointing a metropolitan for Tibet, implying that their churches were numerous enough to require bishops and lesser clergy. Thus Christians were to be found in Sinkiang, and possibly in Tibet, as early as the ninth century. But it was not until the beginning of the eleventh century that the faith spread among the nomadic peoples of this and other central Asian regions. These Christians were chiefly Turco-Tartar peoples, including the Keraits, Onguts, Uighus, Naimans, Merkites, and Mongols.

THE INTRODUCTION OF THE LUMINOUS RELIGION TO CHINA[29]

When Christianity was first introduced to China three major religious systems, Buddhism, Confucianism, and Taoism, were already popular there, woven into the ancient traditions and customs of the people. The average Chinese did not regard himself as an exclusive adherent of any one of the three, but rather as the follower of a general Chinese religion made up of both animistic and polytheistic elements which represented a syncretistic conglomeration of ideas. Thus the church of the East encountered grave difficulties as it sought to introduce the "Luminous Religion" to China. Only in the periods of the *T'ang* (A.D. 618-906) and *Yuan* (A.D. 1206-1368) dynasties did the gospel enterprise have any considerable degree of success.

It is difficult to determine the exact time when the Christian gospel first reached China. The ancient Breviary of the Syrian church of Malabar (India) states that "by the means of St. Thomas the Chinese . . . were converted to the truth. . . . By means of St. Thomas the kingdom of heaven flew and entered into China. . . . The Chinese in commemoration of St. Thomas do offer their adoration unto Thy most Holy Name, O God." Some authors have claimed to have found in a very ancient Taoist writing evidence of a spiritual awakening in China in the latter part of the first century.[30]

Arthur Lloyd relates the story of the Han emperor, Ming-ti, who in A.D. 64 supposedly had a dream on several successive nights of a man in golden raiment who held in his hand a bow and arrows and pointed the emperor to the West. The emperor was much impressed and resolved to send an embassy to the West to seek out "the true man" of his vision. Enroute they met two monks from the West leading a white horse laden with Scriptures. They returned with them to China, where the monks gave their message. They died in A.D. 70 but left some writings, out of which developed the "Sutra of the Forty-Two Sections," a collection of logia containing short, pithy sayings of "the Master" which closely resembled Christian teachings.[31] It has been conjectured that the two monks were actually Christians, disciples of Thomas from India.

Active trade for centuries between China and the West could have brought Christian missionaries at an early date. But aside from one rather obscure reference in the *Adversus Gentes* by Arnobius (A.D. 303) to "the Chinese as among those united in the faith of Christ,"[32] there is little or no evidence of Christians in China before the seventh century. But from then on the evidences of Christianity in China during the T'ang era (A.D. 618-906) are numerous, including references in Chinese writings, imperial edicts, and in particular the famous inscriptions on the so-called "Nestorian monument." During the T'ang period conditions were favorable for the introduction of foreign faiths: the lines of international communication were wide open; foreign trade flourished; the government was tolerant toward all faiths; and foreigners were welcome in various capacities. It was in this T'ang era that the Christianity of the church of the East first came to be known as the "Luminous Religion."

The "Nestorian monument"[33] was erected in A.D. 781 near the capital city of Ch'angan, or Hsianfu (where it was discovered in 1625), to commemorate the charitable acts of a Bactrian Christian who had become noted for his gifts to the poor and his funds for restoring and building churches and monasteries. The top of the monument is adorned not only with a cross but also with the Buddhist emblem of the lotus and the Taoist symbol of the cloud. The writer of the inscription was one Adam, a leader of the "Luminous Religion," and the calligraphist was one Lu Hsiu-yen (two who later collaborated in some Buddhist writing). The earlier part of the inscription is in Chinese, with certain Buddhist terms used to express Christian ideas, probably indicating that a distinctly Christian vocabulary had not yet developed in China. The doctrinal statement mentions the triune God, the Creator of all things, the fall of mankind, the incarnation and virgin birth, the holy life and ascension of Christ, the rite of baptism, and certain Scriptures, but no mention is made of Christ's redemptive death for sin. Following this is an account of how Alopen of Ta Ch'in (the Near East, especially Syria) arrived in Ch'angan in 635 bearing the Scriptures. He was welcomed by the emperor T'ai Tsung, the founder of the T'ang dynasty and one of the most famous of all Chinese rulers. The emperor, having examined the sacred writings, ordered their translation and the preaching of their message. He also directed the building of a Christian monastery in the capital. According to the inscription, his successor, the emperor Kao Tsung, also encouraged Christianity and ordered the building of a monastery in each province of his domain.

The second part of the monument was written in Syriac and listed some sixty-seven names: one bishop, twenty-eight presbyters, and thirty-eight monks. Some of these have been verified from Assyrian church records. The inscription displays considerable grace of literary style, and the allusions and phraseology reveal competence in both Chinese and Syriac and familiarity with both Buddhism and Taoism. Ancient Christian manuscripts were also discovered at Tunhuang from about the same period and are written in the literary style of the Monument. These include a "Hymn to the Trinity" and refer to at least thirty Christian books, indicating that considerable Christian literature was in circulation.[34]

The 250-year span of the Christian movement in the T'ang period was characterized by vicissitudes of imperial favor and prosperity, persecution and decline. Christianity fared badly during the reign of the infamous Empress Dowager Wu (689-99), who was an ardent Buddhist. However, several succeeding emperors were favorable, and the missionary forces were reinforced from time to time. Furthermore, a number of Christians served in high official positions. By this end of the eighth century a metropolitan had been consecrated and assigned by the Mesopotamian patriarch. About the middle of the ninth century the ardent Taoist Emperor Wu Tsung proscribed Buddhism and ordered all monks and nuns to return to private life; he included all the Christians in this interdiction. It was probably in connection with this persecution that the Nestorian Monument was buried or hidden and did not come to light until modern times. The Christian church apparently continued in a feeble state for some time, though isolated Christian remnants survived. The resurgence of the Christian faith had to await the Mongol conquest and the rise of the Yuan dynasty in the thirteenth century.

Why did the Christianity represented by the church of the East fail to secure a permanent foothold in the China of the T'ang era? For one thing, the older Chinese religions had been long entrenched in the life of the people and were meeting their more obvious needs. Furthermore, if the general content of the Monument is any indication, the method of approach to the unbelieving world was that of the soft sell rather than coming to grips with the main need of man for salvation from sin and his reconciliation with God. In trying to clothe Christian teaching in the familiar dress of Buddhist phraseology, Christianity appeared to be just another Buddhist sect, thereby dulling the impact of its outreach. As a result of this and other factors, the faith of the church of the East apparently had little influence on the Chinese masses and remained largely the faith of the Christian foreign community. Though there were said to be about three thousand monks in Christian monasteries in 845,[35] there is little or no evidence that these had any evangelistic fervor. Furthermore, they were geographically so widely separated from the main centers of church life in the Near and Middle East that they were not able to receive help and inspiration from the long-established churches. Also, the closing years of the T'ang dynasty were marked by domestic disorder, followed by fifty years of civil war, which put the lives of alien residents in jeopardy. Thus the life of the Christian groups languished to the point of obliteration.[36]

During the more than three hundred years of the following Sung dynasty (960-1280), the country was subject to attacks from the Khitans and Chin Taters from the north, who wrested part of the provinces from Chinese rule. As earlier indicated, these northern tribes had been subject to the influence of missionaries of the church of the East, and many had become believers. For this reason the Christian religion came to be regarded as the faith of hated Mongol tribesmen, and Christians were practically barred from entering the domain of the Sung emperors.

The dramatic Mongol conquests of the thirteenth century, which established an empire for a brief time that stretched from eastern Europe to the Pacifiic and as far south as northwest India, had a profound effect on the Eastern church, which was still represented by many Christian communities in the Middle East and Central Asia. Genghis Khan (1167-1227), having conquered the peoples in Central Asia (among whom were many Christians—Naimans, Keraits, Uighurs, and Onguts) enlisted many of them in his armies. He married one of his sons to a Christian Kerait princess, who became the mother of Kublai Khan (1216-94), the first Mongol emperor of China and founder of the Yuan dynasty (1213-1368).

She lived and died in the faith, and two of her sons, though not Kublai Khan, became Christians. According to Marco Polo, the great Khan himself was sometimes minded to embrace Christianity but for political reasons refrained. Yet he apparently followed the policy of invoking the help of whatever supernatural powers might exist, and thus he protected Christianity as well as several other religions.[37]

Kublai Khan located his capital at Cambaluc (later Peking), to which came many foreigners from the West to serve as officials, soldiers, merchants, and in other capacities; among these were many Christians, including missionaries. These included not only representatives of the church of the East but also Roman and possibly Greek Catholics. Thus Christians increased and became so important in China that a special government bureau was established to supervise their monasteries and churches. Churches were established in the main cities, though the members seem to have been mainly non-Chinese, who often enjoyed the patronage of highly placed officials. In the city of Chinkiang the Christian governor is said to have built seven monasteries in or near the city.

A fourteenth-century report claims that there were some thirty thousand Christians in China. An Ongut named Mark, born in 1245, was eventually raised to the patriarchate of the Eastern church and had the metropolitanate of Cambaluc (Peking) under his jurisdiction. Though the Franciscan mission in Cambaluc at first met bitter opposition from Assyrian Christians with great influence at court, it prospered under John of Montecorvino, who founded several churches to take care of his six thousand converts. He translated the New Testament and Psalter and was eventually made archbishop of Cambaluc. But the Christians of the Eastern church remained quite largely of foreign birth, apparently owing their presence and well-being to the patronage of the Mongol emperors. They were found chiefly in the cities of the north, especially on the main trade routes. Though it would appear that they carried on some missionary work among the Chinese, arousing the opposition of the Taoist and Buddhist leaders, there is no evidence that many of the nationals became Christians. Thus with the breakup of the Mongol empire and the rise of the Ming dynasty (1368-1644) the church again fell on evil days in China. This coincided with the decline of the church throughout the Middle East and Central Asia, occasioned by the rapid advance of Islam.

The question naturally arises as to whether in either the T'ang era or that of Mongol rule Christians penetrated the cultural satellites of China, Korea, and Japan. Many visitors from these lands came both to Ch'angan, the T'ang capital, and to Cambaluc of the Mongols. Much has been written on the influence of Christian ideas learned by Japanese visitors to China and on the development of the major schools of Buddhism in Japan, especially the Amida sects and the "Pure Land" school. Yoshio Saeki, in his books on the Nestorian movement in China, mentions the visit of a Persian physician to Japan in the eighth century, through whose Christian teaching the Empress Komyu was led to embrace the Christian faith. However, there is little or no evidence that the Christian faith was successfully transmitted to either land in these periods when the church was well represented in the Middle Kingdom.[38]

It was in the middle of the fourteenth century that the Eastern church seems to have had its most extensive expansion and its greatest prosperity. The patriarch based at Baghdad, where Christians were in high favor with the caliphs, is reported to have had a hierarchy of twenty-five metropolitans and more than two hundred bishops. Even after the Mongols supplanted the caliphate rule in the West, conditions continued favorable. However, the disintegration of the Mongol empire in the Far East, Central Asia, and the Middle East as well as the conversion of many in these areas to a more intolerant and ruthless form of Islam marked the virtual extinction of the Eastern church as a missionary force in Asia.

The final cause of the disappearance of Christianity in this great area of the church was the ruthless conquests of Tamerlane (1336-1405), a bigoted Muslim of Mongol extraction who was bitterly opposed to Christianity. His conquests embraced central Asia, Persia, Mesopotamia, and northwest India. All Christians in these areas who refused to become Muslims were slaughtered; churches were destroyed and monasteries sacked. Thus in one generation Christianity was practically blotted out of the greater part of the vast area which had been the field of missionary expansion of the Eastern church. Only small remnants remained in Mesopotamia and the highlands of Kurdistan, as well as the Mar Thoma church in southwest India.

As the late Dr. Samuel Zwemer has said, "The strength of the Nestorian Church was love and loyalty to Christ, emphasis on the Great Commission, and heroism. Its weakness in the later periods was due to compromise in the face of persecution, which led to absorption by other faiths and final extermination in regions once Christian. This holds lessons for the national churches now arising in the Far East and Southern Asia,[39] not to mention all Christians who have a concern for the evangelization of Asian lands."

NOTES

1. Eusebius, *Ecclesiastical History,* bk. 1, ch. 19.
2. Socrates, *Ecclesiastical History,* bk. 3, ch. 1.
3. Eusebius, *History,* bk. 5, ch. 10.
4. Ibid., bk. 1, ch. 13; bk. 2, ch. 1.
5. *The Ante-Nicene Fathers Down to A.D. 325,* rev. by A. C. Coxe, 10 vols. (Buffalo: Christian Literature Publishing Co., 1885-87), 8:558-59, 648-65, 702-07.

6. Mingana, *The Early Spread of Christianity in Central Asia and the Far East,* pp. 300ff.
7. *Didache* 11:3.
8. Philostorgius, *Ecclesiastical History,* 3:1067.
9. Socrates, bk. 1, ch. 19.
10. Eusebius, *History,* bk. 5, ch. 10.
11. Philostorgius, bk. 3, chs. 4, 5.
12. Cosmas Indicopleustes, *Christian Topography,* bk. 3.
13. A. E. Medlycott, *India and the Apostle Thomas,* pp. 18-71.
14. For the text of this work see M. R. James, *Apocryphal New Testament,* pp. 364-436.
15. For an erudite treatment of the legend see Medlycott, pp. 1-17, 213-97.
16. Eusebius, *History,* 4:30.
17. J. N. Farquhar, *The Apostle Thomas in North India.*
18. V. A. Smith, *Early History of India,* p. 235.
19. On the mission in South India see L. W. Brown, *The Indian Christians of St. Thomas,* pp. 49-59 et al.
20. Eusebius, *History,* bk. 5, ch. 10.
21. Philostorgius, bk. 3, chs. 4, 5.
22. Mingana, pp. 45-50.
23. *Christian Topography of Cosmos* (London: Hakluyt Society, 1897), intro., p. 9.
24. Medlycott, pp. 71-80.
25. J. Richter, *A History of Missions in India,* pp. 33-35.
26. H. Yule, *Marco Polo* (Cordiers Revision), 2:353-75.
27. Jordan, *Wonders of the East,* p. 23.
28. Conti, *Travels of Nicolo Conti,* trans. by R. H. Major as *India in the 15th Century* (London: Hakluyt Society, 1857), p. 41.
29. K. S. Latourette, *A History of the Expansion of Christianity,* pp. 18-45.
30. A. C. Moule, *Christians in China Before the Year 1550,* pp. 19-26.
31. Arthur Lloyd, *The Creed of Half Japan,* pp. 76-84.
32. *Catholic Encyclopedia,* 3:667.
33. Moule, pp. 27-52.
34. P. Y. Saeki, *The Nestorian Documents and Relics in China* and *The Nestorian Monument in China;* see also A. C. Moule, *Christians in China,* pp. 52-64.
35. Saeki, *Documents,* pp. 28, 88, 282.
36. Yule, *Cathay and the Way Thither,* 1:104.
37. Moule, pp. 383-410.
38. Lloyd, pp. 218-23.
39. John Stewart, *The Nestorian Missionary Enterprise,* Foreword, pp. 7-8.

BIBLIOGRAPHY

(See also bibliography for chapter 28, "Important Religions of Asia")

General Works

Adeney, W. F. *The Greek and Eastern Churches.* New York: Chas. Scribner's Sons, 1928.

Browne, L. E. *The Eclipse of Christianity in Asia from the Time of Mohammed Till the 14th Century.* Cambridge: University Press, 1933.

Burkitt, F. C. *Early Christianity Outside the Roman Empire.* Cambridge: University Press, 1899.

Cross, F. L., ed. *Oxford Dictionary of the Christian Church.* London: Oxford University Press, 1958.

Eusebius. *Ecclesiastical History.* Bks. 1 and 4. Ante-Nicene Fathers, revised by A. C. Coxe. Buffalo: Christian Literature Publishing Co., 1887.

———. *Early Eastern Christianity.* New York: E. P. Dutton & Co., 1904.

———. *Christian Beginnings.* London: University Press, 1924.

Harnack, Adolf. *The Mission and Expansion of Christianity in the First Three Centuries.* 2 vols. Translated and edited by James Moffatt. New York: G. P. Putnam's Sons, 1908.

Latourette, K. S. *A History of the Expansion of Christianity.* 7 vols. New York: Harper & Bros., 1938-45. See especially vols. 1 and 2.

———. *A History of Christianity.* New York: Harper & Bros., 1953.

Neale, S. *A History of Christian Missions.* Penguin Books, 1964.

Neale, S., *et al. Concise Dictionary of the Christian World Mission.* London: Lutterworth Press, 1970.

Thiessen, J. C. *A Survey of Christian Missions.* Chicago: Moody Press, 1961.

China

Cary-Elwis, C. *China and the Cross: A Survey of Missionary History.* New York, 1957.

Couling, C. E. *The Luminous Religion.* London: Carey Press, 1925.

Foster, J. *The Church of the T'ang Dynasty.* 1939.

Howorth, H. H. *History of the Mongols from the 9th to the 19th Century.* London, 1888.

Latourette, K. S. *A History of Christian Missions in China.* New York: Macmillan Co., 1929.

Legge, J. *Christianity in China.* N.R.C. Prot., 1888.

Moule, A. C. *Christians in China Before the Year 1550.* London: SPCK, 1930.

Saeki, P. Y. *The Nestorian Documents and Relics in China.* 1951.

———. *The Nestorian Monument in China.* 1953.

Soothill, W. E. *The Three Religions of China.* Oxford: University Press, 1925.

Wei, F. C. M. *The Spirit of Chinese Culture.* New York, 1947.

Williams, S. W. *The Middle Kingdom.* New York:, 1888.

Yule, H. *Cathay and the Way Thither: Being a Collection of Medieval Notices of China.* London: The Hakluyt Society, 1925-26.

India and the Thomas Tradition

(Authors which defend the thesis of the ministry of the Apostle Thomas are indicated by an asterisk)

Agur, C. M. *Church History in Travancore.* Madras: SPCK Press.

*Brown, L. W. *The Indian Christians of St. Thomas: An Account of the Ancient Syrian Church of Malabar.* Cambridge: University Press, 1956.

*D'Cruz, F. A. *St. Thomas the Apostle in India.* Madras: Premium Press, 1929.

*Farquhar, J. N. *The Apostle Thomas in North India.* Manchester: University Press, 1926.

*———. *The Apostle Thomas in South India.* Manchester: University Press, 1927.

Firth, C. B. *Introduction to Indian Church History.* Madras, 1961.

*Lloyd, A. *The Creed of Half Japan.* London: Smith, Elder & Co., 1911.

Mackenzie, G. T. *Christianity in Travancore.* Trivandrum: Government Press.

*Medlycott, A. E. *India and the Apostle Thomas.* London: David Nutt, 1905.

Mingana, A. *The Early Spread of Christianity in India.* Manchester: University Press, 1926.

Neill, S. C. *A History of Christianity in India and Pakistan.* Grand Rapids: Eerdmans, 1970.

Rae, G. M. *The Syrian Church in India.* Edinburgh: Wm. Blackwood, 1892.

*Richards, W. J. *The Indian Christians of St. Thomas.* London: Bemrose & Sons, 1908.

Richter, J. *A History of Missions in India.* Edinburgh: Oliphant, Anderson & Ferrier, 1910.

*Smith, V. A. *Early History of India.* London: Oxford University Press, 1919.

*Zaleski, L. M. *The Apostle Thomas in India.* Bangalore: The Cordialbail Press, 1912.

———. *The Saints of India.* Bangalore: The Cordialbail Press, 1915.

The Nestorians or the Assyrian Church (Church of the East)

Buchanan, C. *Christian Researches in Asia.* Cambridge: University Press.

Joseph, J. *The Nestorians and Their Muslim Neighbors.* Princeton: University Press, 1961.

Jordan. *Wonders of the East.* Translated by Yule. London: Hakluyt Society, 1863.

Kidd, B. J. *The Churches of Eastern Christendom from A.D. 451.* 1927.

Mingana, A. *The Early Spread of Christianity in Central Asia and the Far East.* Manchester: University Press, 1925.

Stewart, John. *The Nestorian Missionary Enterprise.* Edinburgh: T. & T. Clark, 1928.

Vine, A. R. *The Nestorian Churches.* London: Independent Press, 1937.

Wigram, W. A. *An Introduction to the History of the Assyrian Church: The Church of the Sassanid Empire, 100-640 A.D.* London: SPCK, 1910.

———. *The Separation of the Monophysites.* London: Faith Press, 1923.

Typical Hong Kong contrasts.

Hillside refugee settlement.

Chung To rooftop chapel.

Worshipers at Hong Kong shrine.

Photos courtesy Conservative Baptist Foreign Missions Society

9

HONG KONG

by David Woodward

The Church Today

The million visitors who pass through Hong Kong each year remember its exotic harbor and peaks, its vast complexes of multi-story buildings and the fantastic bargains of its shopping arcades. Few appreciate Hong Kong as a Mecca for refugees from mainland China and a growing Christian center in the Orient, for neither the refugee population nor the Christian community are very conspicuous.

Yet no other religious groups in this British colony are growing like the Christian churches. Counting both Protestants and Catholics, there were 432,371 Christians in 1972—almost 10 percent of the 4½ million population, with the Catholics numbering 58.47 percent and the Protestants 41.53 percent.[1] Church growth rates were as high as 12 percent annually between 1960 and 1963, though in the seventies the annual increase has fallen to 4 percent annually.[2]

Protestant churches number about six hundred,[3] with many of them being located in flats or converted apartments. Where they have been fortunate enough to enjoy land rights, the churches usually build high-rise structures for both church and school use, with hostels or staff residences on the top floors. Such facilities hum with activity every day of the week. These Chinese churches worship in many languages, reflecting their mainland origin. The major language of churches is Cantonese, but there are other flourishing churches which conduct services in Hakka, Swatow, Shanghai, and Mandarin. Though these differences in language perpetuate some divisions in the Christian community, all read the same Chinese characters and use the same Bible.

For information on author, see chapter 28, "Taiwan."

Churches in Hong Kong are characterized by a high degree of national leadership. Although there is an unusually large force of four hundred missionaries there,[4] these do not generally assume responsibility for church administration, though "missionaries still have wide influence in our church councils because we Chinese are very charitable," one Chinese leader observed. The largest church groups in Hong Kong have their theological roots in the West: Anglicans, Methodists, Lutherans, Baptists. The local "Church of Christ in China" is a union formed from Presbyterian, Congregational, and other denominational strains in past years. Some of the older, pre-World War II churches had difficulty at first adjusting to the influx of new missionary societies and church groups. Only now, for instance, are the prewar English Methodists and the postwar American Methodists seeking to unite their efforts.[5]

The younger churches have been more awake to the opportunities among refugees, rapidly building new congregations from among them.[6] Beside the churches which are identified with the Hong Kong Christian Council, there are a number of strong evangelical church associations, such as the Christian and Missionary Alliance, the Evangelical Free church, the Southern Baptists, the Assemblies of God, the Peniel churches, the Spiritual Food churches, and the Christian Nationals Evangelistic Commission churches. The "Little Flock" and other vital, indigenous Chinese groups of believers are also active, though remaining separate from other Christians.[7]

The Hong Kong Christian Council represents twelve denominations and nine service agencies and touches approximately three-fourths of the registered Protestant Christian community, but its active core membership is only about 40 percent of the total population.[8] Another organization, the Chinese Christian Churches Union, is a federation of 147 local churches.[9] Nevertheless, many denominations and churches go their way without reference to the ecumenical movement. A statement produced in Hong Kong in 1966, *Confessing the Faith in Asia Today*, indicates the gap between it and the churches:

> Traditionally in Asia the emphasis on holy living has often been understood in purely individualistic and pietistic terms . . . some younger churchmen exhibit little or no interest in the ecumenical movement at all.[10]

But ecumenical liberalism is challenging the traditionally conservative churches in Hong Kong now. Philip Teng, President of the Alliance Church Union, observes, "Ten years ago it would have seemed superfluous to try to prove to the Christian churches that evangelism is supported by the teaching of the Bible. But the situation is becoming different even in the younger churches."[11]

Evangelical leadership in Hong Kong tends to be along lines of spiritual influence rather than organizational structure. Teng is one of several key leaders, along with Dr. Samuel Tong of the Southern Baptist Theological Seminary and Dr. John Pao of the Evangelical Free Church Seminary. Dr. Timothy Yü and Mr. Theodore Hsueh are active in the field of evangelical communications and literature, Dr. Yü teaching at the Hong Kong Baptist College and Hsueh as director of Christian Communications, Ltd., an evangelical publishing house resulting from the merger of Christian Witness Press and China Sunday School Association.

Hong Kong Churches are ahead of other Asian churches in the extent of their audio-visual libraries and equipment. The Audio Visual Evangelism committee of HKCC has over 700 film titles and 681 filmstrips.[12] Though local Christian radio programs have been strictly limited by government policy, Chinese programs are beamed to Hong Kong from the Philippines. Chinese Christian literature is extensive, and Hong Kong has been the main publishing center for the overseas Chinese churches. The Chinese Christian Literature council represents the HKCC, while evangelical publishers meet informally from time to time. The leading publishers are the Baptist Press, the Alliance Press, Christian Communications, Bellman House, and the Lutheran Press.

Ever since the detente between the United States and the People's Republic of China the game of China-watching has been extended, permitting Hong Kong-based observers to travel into mainland China. Christian organizations such as World Vision, Christian Communications, and Asian Outreach maintain offices in Hong Kong which collect and evaluate any information bearing on those mainland Christians who remain.

Hong Kong has a smaller student population than most Asian countries because government schools could not keep pace with the demand. Thus two-thirds of all schools are privately operated. This situation has been a golden opportunity for Christian churches, many of whom conduct schools on church premises. In 1973 there were about 325,000 students in Hong Kong secondary schools and colleges.[13] Among these, Scripture Union and the International Fellowship of Evangelical Students have many Bible study groups. IFES publishes evangelistic magazines in both English and Chinese. Three Christian colleges have recently united to form the Chinese University of Hong Kong, with 2,582 students enrolled.[14] There are 4,000 more in other Christian colleges.

Christian welfare agencies proliferated to meet the need of mainland refugees in the late fifties and early sixties. Large food and clothing distributions were done by many Christian agencies, notably the Lutheran Relief Service. On the open roofs of the huge seven-story settlement houses mushrooming throughout Kowloon and the New Territories many churches and missions built schools. Thousands of children have received basic Christian teaching in these, most of which are still operating. But current programs deal less with direct relief and more with rehabilitation and training. Hong Kong Christian Service is the largest cooperative group involved in social welfare. Welfare subsidies from overseas have been on the decrease, and Chinese leaders have been making more direct appeals to the Chinese churches for funds. (The United Christian hospital, which opened in 1973, received donations from 272 local churches and 46 Christian schools.)[15] The Hong Kong government levels land and donates it for philanthropic ventures, and a hospital like this can develop into a self-supporting institution. Yet this Christian institution, like many others in the colony, provides as much free aid as possible for the poor.

Though church growth has slowed in the last few years, probably due to increasing prosperity, Hong Kong is today a vital center of Christian churches. Missionary outreach to other Southeast Asian nations is increasing. A cooperative evangelical graduate school of theology is planned. Despite its dangerous geo-political position, Hong Kong is a brightening spiritual lighthouse in Asia.

Nation and People

As a British crown colony—a tiny island dangling precariously from the mainland of Red China—Hong Kong has survived many political and economic crises with the practical formula of low taxes, few controls, hard work, and quick profits. Its dazzling merchandise and touted bargains owe much to shrewd management but even more to the mass of compliant workers who have fled to Hong Kong and can go no farther.[16] For two out of three adults now in Hong Kong are refugees who have come from all parts of mainland China, though mostly from the adjoining province of Kuangtung. Chinese people comprised 98 percent of the island's population of 4,100,000 in 1972, up from a total of 600,000 in 1945.[17] The colony has a land area of 398 square miles, only a sixth of which could be considered usable. A normal capacity for this space has been estimated at 1,200,000 people, but after the communist revolution on the mainland a host of refugees poured into the city, camping in the streets, on the rooftops, and on the barren hills. Since good building land is scarce, the government has created land by literally moving mountains and casting them into the sea. On this land the government has built over twenty resettlement estates, the largest of which houses 144,000 people. Although economy housing has been provided for 1,600,000 people, in mid-1973 there were still 320,000 squatters living in their own shacks.[18]

The civil service of Hong Kong has over thirty departments, and it is generally administered with an efficiency which keeps the diverse, multilingual public satisfied. However, the hasty departure of the British police chief in 1973 amid rumors of corruption has created an unprecedented outcry from even the most stable elements of the community. Though Chinese business leaders still have but little representation in the highest levels of government, they are nevertheless a potent force in the area of policymaking. When the banks tried to follow Great Britain in devaluating the Hong Kong dollar along with the British pound sterling in December 1967, the business community forced a reversal of this policy. In the final analysis, Chinese interests in Hong Kong are paramount and are not ignored by the British.

There are great wealth and huge business interests on the island: one of the world's largest shipping companies, great textile industries, prosperous motion picture organizations exporting local films to the world—all locally owned—plus multi-million-dollar joint ventures with foreign countries. On the surface it appears to be a stable economy, yet the wealthy who place risk capital in real estate or business expect returns within four or five years. Long-term investment is the exception, for all know that the future is uncertain. In fact, the whole status of Hong Kong will radically change within twenty-five years, for the lease on nine-tenths of the land area expire in 1977, and the so-called "New Territories" must then be handed back to China.

How has this capitalistic society been able to survive next door to the communist People's Republic of China this long? The most commonly accepted view is that China needs Hong Kong as a listening post and as a source of foreign exchange.[19] Certainly life in Hong Kong is in strong contrast to the austere egalitarianism on the mainland, so much so that one committed Christian who came out of China, Mary Wang, said, "My first reactions to Hong Kong were unfavorable. . . . The extreme between the haves and havenots were out of proportion to anything I had seen in China. . . . I reacted against the extravagance and the waste. It seemed unforgivable, as unchristlike as Communism."[20] Hong Kong residents know that they have problems, but they are also aware from frequent visits to mainland China that their standard of living is higher than that of their relatives across the border, and that it is rising steadily. Immigration Department figures show that an average of one in six residents of Hong Kong visited China during the first eleven months of 1972.[21] One of the difficulties that Peking experiences in dealing with Hong Kong is how to convince the people there that they would be better off under Communism. To the mass of Hong Kong's people communist riots and propaganda fail to make sense, for they result in much trouble and no benefits. In spite of six communist newspapers the colony's work force failed to respond to a strike call in 1967; of 1,500,000 people only 60,000 went out on strike! And the women of the colony registered their disapproval by refusing to shop in the communist department stores. The people of Hong Kong then voted for peace and stability under the status quo, and the result was the current economic boom.

Meanwhile, the roar of buses and the tramp of feet tend to blot out everything but today's work. The ferries transport a hundred thousand people daily between Hong Kong island and the Kowloon peninsula on the mainland, while an underwater tunnel opened in 1972 handles an additional thirty thousand vehicles daily. Some twenty-four thousand vessels call at this busy yet beautiful port every year, and it has the reputation of moving freight faster than any other port in the Orient. To maintain this reputation it is opening a new container terminal in the New Territories. Hong Kong's major industry is textiles, which makes up 50 percent of the colony's exports and uses 46 percent of its work force.[22] Electronics is another booming industry. Most labor employed in factories works up to ten hours a day, six days a week. The labor picture is peculiar, with a Communist-controlled Federation of Trade Unions competing with a pro-Nationalist Trade Unions Congress. The latter has the larger number of unions and work force, but the competition benefits the manufacturers, who play one union against the other. Both of these labor unions protect the workers inadequately, and the *Hong Kong Standard* has protested the extent of child labor in the colony.*

Traditional patterns of Chinese society still rule in modern Hong Kong: the elders are still in control; Confucian ethics are both admired and practiced; individualism is frowned on; and most Chinese still operate in the context of family relationships. This keeps the young effectively under their parents and sometimes means that the educated are regulated by the uneducated. As a result chickens are still sacrificed at the site of new buildings and joss sticks burn outside the doors of modern apartments.[23]

National Religions

Any attempt to change the religious beliefs of these hard-driving, clannish, and commercial people must take into account their background of Taoist and Buddhist belief. They come to the gods with much the same businesslike attitude with which they approach secular affairs, far more concerned with immediate help in an emergency than with a world view or a savior. Neither are they looking for a close, personal relationship with

*"The 1961 census showed that working children between the ages of ten and fourteen totalled 24,441. Five years later this statistic had soared to 32,441, and by 1971 it had increased to 36,000. Of these two-thirds are girls; one out of ten is completely illiterate while only four out of five have completed their primary schooling" (*Hong Kong Standard,* Sept. 18, 1973).

the gods. Their own kinship group, both living and dead, seems to suffice for that. Even though they may have household altars in the single room that constitutes "home" for the whole family, they do not feel near the gods except on those specific occasions when engaged in worship. Indeed, there is a problem—how can one feel close to the gods when there are so many of them? The one to be approached in the case of measles is not the same one to help in fertility. Older Chinese in Hong Kong rely on priests or diviners to assist them, and, as a result, fortune-telling is a big business.

Though many are far removed from their ancestral homes on the mainland, they still observe ancestor worship, which secures peace of mind regarding the departed spirits and encourages benevolent actions toward the living. The living and dead of one family are thought of as mutually cooperative in their common interests. By contrast, the gods sometimes seem distant.

Thus in modern, commercial Hong Kong today there are vestiges of all the old mainland religions—Buddhism, Confucianism, Taoism, et al—but the faithful are mostly the older generation. Though some youth observe some of the old superstitions, secularism is the main religion of the colony today.

National History

Hong Kong first appeared on maps 130 years ago when the British wrested the island from the Chinese Empire. One Englishman called it then "a piece of useless granite with no water and nothing to commend it."[24] British trading firms had been engaged in business with China for over 200 years when, wearied by the complications of dealing with the authorities in the port of Canton, they demanded either normal trading rights or the cession of an island. As a result of what has been called the First Opium War the British forced the Chinese to cede Hong Kong to them, occupying it in 1841. It had the natural beauty of a mountainous island just off the China mainland, and it shielded a natural, almost landlocked harbor.[25] The British soon turned its sandy shores and fishing villages into a thriving free market and well-ordered sanctuary, which soon drew waves of immigrants from the central provinces.

They forced the expansion of their territory by taking the tip of the Kowloon peninsula on the mainland during the Second Opium War in 1860. The colony reached its present size in 1898, when the adjacent New Territories were leased for a period of ninety-nine years, an action which was imposed on an unwilling Chinese government. At the time French and Russian warships were docking near Kowloon City, and the British were determined to keep the area clear of other foreign powers.[26]

The British rapidly developed this strategic port into the entrepôt for trade between southern China and the rest of the world. By the turn of the century a wide variety of Chinese business and industrial firms were teamed up with the older British traders in mutually profitable enterprises. The colonial government was a partner by providing enlightened municipal services, including some social welfare; thus during the heyday of the British Empire Hong Kong represented a pocket of security. But this picture was rudely destroyed just one hundred years after the founding of the colony. The Japanese captured Hong Kong in 1941 and held it throughout World War II. When it was finally liberated, the harbor was filled with the hulks of sunken vessels and most of the mansions on the "Peak" were gutted shells.

When the Chinese Communists overran the China mainland in 1949, many were sure that Hong Kong would be swallowed up. The British, however, quickly recognized the new government and maintained their trading position in Hong Kong. The Korean War upset the colony's economy for a while, but it adjusted, as it was to do again and again in the next two decades. In the early fifties the first high rise buildings appeared on the Hong Kong bund, but the sixties were the time of the great construction boom. The cultural revolution in China tried to spill over into Hong Kong in 1967, creating a tense six months, but the majority of the people were unsympathetic. In each time of crisis and riots within the colony the communist minority has had to run for cover or face the fury of a populace with some old scores to even.

Since the crisis of '67 the economic inertia of motion seems to have given stability to the colony. The China-U.S. detente has lent encouragement to this. Hong Kong today rushes busily back and forth across its harbor, a modern, secular, commercialized tourist city, which is apparently indifferent to its precarious future.

Christian History

The first church in Hong Kong opened in 1842, shortly after the founding of the colony. The early colonial administration had close ties with the established Church of England. Saint John's Cathedral and a large number of Anglican churches and schools are evidence today of the early and strong start which they had on the island. Missions were early tolerated and respected, especially for their educational work, which provided bright, young clerks for the city's offices. Though the expatriate business community was not particularly interested in the conversion of souls, they did want chaplains to provide them with the religious services to which they were accustomed. Thus it was not long before the Methodists, Presbyterians, and Congregationalists had their places of worship too.

Some missionaries early reached out to the Chinese and preached the gospel, with the result that Chinese churches were planted. The Chinese Christian Churches Union was founded during World War I, and it subsequently sponsored many city-wide evangelistic campaigns and deeper life conferences. Later it provided homes for the aged and a burial association. The Hong Kong Christian Council was not formed until 1954, and it has succeeded in bringing together a number of overlapping service ministries. The council has gained acceptance with the government as the "voice of Protestantism" and thus receives free radio time on Hong Kong Radio to represent the Protestant community.

Roman Catholics have been slower than Protestants to develop Chinese leadership, and the first Chinese bishop of Hong Kong, Francis Hsu, was consecrated in 1967. Catholics and Protestants in Hong Kong have had many mutual contacts through their social agencies and in the field of Bible translation. Evangelical Protestants now have a separate Bible translation program underway in Chinese. In addition, two other groups are also working on a new translation.

The people of Hong Kong have a tender spot in their hearts for needy relatives and friends in mainland China. Nearly twelve million food parcels were sent from Hong Kong into China as early as 1961,[27] and this kind of help came from Christians and non-Christians alike. This consciousness of human need has caused Hong Kong residents to appreciate compassion wherever they see it in action. The opportunity to demonstrate such compassion has been seized by the church in Hong Kong. The result has been an openness to the gospel and a large response of faith.

Troubled times in the sixties turned many Godward. When riots and bombings disturbed Hong Kong in the summer of 1967, the attendances soared in vacation Bible schools. The Keswick conference was filled to its capacity of three thousand throughout the eight days of conferences. The virtual occupation of Macao by the Communists frightened many in Hong Kong. The threat was so real that six hundred doctors applied for visas for Canada. University students, who were in a better position than most to consider careers abroad, debated whether or not to leave. But a panel of seven Christian students declared that "each Christian ought to consider seriously the following questions before deciding to leave Hong Kong:

1. Why was I born a Chinese?
2. How does this relate to my responsibility to win my people for Christ?
3. Am I viewing the current situation calmly and from God's perspective? How does His Lordship fit in?
4. What are my present commitments?

5. If I should leave, who can readily take my place? Have I been training others to do this?
6. Could the present testing and future persecutions be God's plan for me to enter into the "fellowship of Christ's suffering"?
7. Will I be a misfit socially and spiritually if I were to settle down in another country?[28]

Thus there is seen a spiritual solidity and vigor among many younger Christians in Hong Kong today that bodes well for a continuous, expanding witness not only in the island but throughout the overseas Chinese communities for years to come. There are probably enough western missionaries to meet the needs of the church and opportunity there, observers feel.

NOTES

1. *HKCC Annual Report, 1971-72,* Chart 1 (Hong Kong: Hong Kong Christian Council, 1972).
2. *Hong Kong 1973,* p. 161.
3. Letter by Gordon T. Dunn dated Sept. 26, 1973.
4. *Hong Kong Directory, 1972.*
5. *HKCC Annual Report, 1972-73,* p. 9.
6. *Hong Kong Directory, 1972.*
7. Ibid.
8. *HKCC Annual Report, 1971-72,* p. 8.
9. Ibid.
10. *Confessing the Faith in Asia Today.*
11. *Alliance Mission Report.*
12. *HKCC Annual Report, 1972-73,* Appendix 2.
13. *Hong Kong 1973,* p. 53.
14. Ibid., p. 58.
15. *HKCC Annual Report, 1972-73,* p. 14.
16. Andrew T. Roy, *On Asia's Rim,* p. 127.
17. *Hong Kong 1973,* p. 4.
18. Ibid., pp. 100, 103.
19. Richard Hughes, *Borrowed Place, Borrowed Time.*
20. Mary Wang, *The Chinese Church That Will Not Die,* p. 120.
21. *Newsletter* (Singapore: Coordinating Office for Asian Evangelism).
22. *Hong Kong, 1973,* p. 13.
23. Angela Earnest, "Old Values Versus New," *Asia Magazine,* Nov. 26, 1972.
24. *Hong Kong 1973,* p. 1.
25. GIO, *Introduction to Hong Kong,* p. 3.
26. *Hong Kong, 1973,* p. 193.
27. Leslie Lyall, *The Church in Mao's China,* p. 10.
28. *The Way,* 1967, 4:25.

BIBLIOGRAPHY

General Works

Confessing the Faith in Asia Today. Hong Kong: Hong Hong Christian Council, 1966.

Christian Churches Union Jubilee. Hong Kong: Christian Churches Union, 1965.

Hong Kong 1973. Hong Kong: Government Press, 1973.

Hong Kong Church Directory. Hong Kong: Hong Kong Christian Council, 1972.

HKCC Annual Report, 1971-72. Hong Kong: Hong Kong Christian Council, 1972.

HKCC Annual Report, 1972-73. Hong Kong: Hong Kong Christian Council, 1973.

Hsueh, Theodore. *Involving Asians Fully in Complete Literature Programs*. Singapore: Asia Evangelical Literature Fellowship Conference, 1971.

Hughes, Richard. *Borrowed Place, Borrowed Time*. New York: Praeger, 1968.

Introduction to Hong Kong. Hong Kong: Government Information Offices, 1971.

Lyall, Leslie. *The Church in Mao's China*. Chicago: Moody Press, 1970.

Roy, Andrew T. *On Asia's Rim*. New York: Friendship Press, 1962.

Wang, Mary. *The Chinese Church That Will Not Die*. Wheaton: Tyndale House Publishers, 1972.

Periodicals

Asia Magazine. Hong Kong: Asia Magazine.

Challenger, The. Detroit: Chinese Christian Mission.

China Notes. New York: Asia Department, Division of Overseas Ministries, National Council of Churches.

Hong Kong Standard. Hong Kong.

Newsletter. Singapore: Coordinating Office for Asian Evangelism.

South China Morning Post. Hong Kong.

Way, The. Hong Kong: International Fellowship of Evangelical Students.

Hinduism continues, unchanged, to bind more than 550 million Indians; a priest and gods.

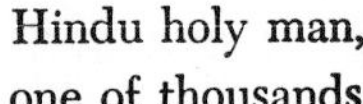

Hindu holy man, one of thousands

South Indian temple

10

INDIA, A SEETHING SUBCONTINENT

by Theodore Williams

Introduction

The world's largest free nation, one-sixth of the world, exploding toward a billion population in this century . . . a vast conglomerate of over five hundred thousand agrarian villages on an almost-certain collision course with famine in the decade of the seventies . . . the birthplace of four religions, two of which—Buddhism and Hinduism—are over two thousand years old and are among the world's largest, with its people still largely illiterate and plagued by a religion-hardened caste system . . . a country struggling to industrialize, with perhaps a dozen megalopolises of over ten million persons each by the end of the century. . . .

This is India, a great polyglot subcontinent whose terrain, languages, religions, cultural patterns, and climate are so varied that going from one state to another is like going from one country to another in Europe.

Yet in the midst of these staggering social and demographic problems, "The Christian church in India is a growing church," declares Dr. K. Baago of the United Theological College in Bangalore. The Christian population in India has increased at a greater rate in this century than in the last, mainly in Assam, Madhya Pradesh, Orissa, Punjab, Manipur, and Naga-

---

Theodore Williams is a Methodist evangelist and pastor in the Church of South India. Educated at the University of Madras (B.A.) and Serampore University (B.D.), Mr. Williams has taught for eleven years in the South India Biblical Seminary at Bangarapet. He is also currently general secretary of the Indian Evangelical Mission (an indigenous mission board) and chairman of the Christian Education Department of the Evangelical Fellowship of India. Mr. Williams is widely used as a Bible teacher and conference speaker both in India and abroad.

land. Growth of the church in other states has been normal except in Uttar Pradesh, which has experienced an 18 percent decline.

Unofficial returns from the 1971 census show that Christians have increased by almost three million persons in the last decade, growing from 2.44 percent to 2.60 percent of the total population. The Christian growth rate of 32.6 percent has been the highest of all religions during this decade, while Hindu population actually fell almost 1 percent to 82.72 percent during this same period.

The Church Today

Thus today the church totals over 14 million in India's 550 million-plus population. It is the home of the oldest church in Asia proper, the Mar Thoma church, which proudly claims the Apostle Thomas himself as its founder. As befitting its maturity, this totally indigenous church has seen thousands of its members migrate and establish congregations extending from Asia to certain Persian Gulf and east African countries.

Mass movements within the last century have greatly swelled the Indian church. But as a result two problems plague the church today: nominalism among many church members and a critical reaction against missionaries for allegedly exploiting the plight of the lower and disadvantaged castes who were in the majority of the mass movements.

Thus today for this and other reasons foreign missionaries are in steady decline in India. The government is promoting the indigenization of all foreign-related organizations, especially the churches, and laws against proselyting have been passed by some state governments. While missionaries from the British Commonwealth have gotten visas, it has become increasingly difficult for those from other nations to acquire them. Since 1966 it has become almost impossible for new missionaries from many countries, especially the United States, to enter India. Usually only those missionaries are permitted reentry who can demonstrate that they fill useful posts for which no Indian is available. The total missionary population has shrunk 40 percent in the last fifteen years.

But God is raising up His own instruments. A number of indigenous missionary societies (though not the hundred mistakenly reported in the U.S.) have arisen in India to evangelize crossculturally and internationally. More importantly, many churches are reaching out in evangelism, and interdenominational and extradenominational efforts are growing. Before reviewing these, let us look at the broad church picture throughout India.

The Christian population can be divided into three major groups: the Roman Catholics (55 percent), the Protestants (35 percent), and the Orthodox (10 percent). Nearly one-third of India's total Christian population (4.5 million out of 14 million) are in Kerala in the south, one of the poorest states and the largest one in communist loyalty. Approximately 2 million of the Kerala Christians are Roman Catholics, 1 million are Orthodox, and 300,000 are in the Mar Thoma church.

THE SYRIAN CHURCH

Historically the oldest, the Mar Thoma church (the reformed Syrian church) experienced a moving of the Holy Spirit which swept through the church during the last quarter of the nineteenth century. Out of this revival was born the Mar Thoma Evangelistic Association in 1888, which began with the purpose of evangelism and later came to be the missionary arm of the church. A large convention, with an attendance of fifty thousand or more, is held annually at Maramon on the sandbanks of a river in late February or early March by this association and is the largest Christian convention in India, if not the world. The Evangelistic Association has centers of work in different parts of India, in Nepal, and on the border of Tibet. Many educated young people have joined the association; they live together in Christian communities known as *ashrams,* composed of two or three families along with single people, and by life and service and proclamation they present the gospel. There are two major Mar Thoma ashrams in Madhya Pradesh and two in Mysore state. The Mar Thoma church also has a Voluntary Evangelistic Association consisting of lay people who pledge themselves to do systematic evangelism.

Since many Syrian Christians have gone out to other parts of India, Persian Gulf countries, Malaysia, Singapore, and parts of East Africa, they have kept their traditional form of worship and faith. A missionary bishop has a roving ministry to this diaspora. The potential of these groups as witnessing Christians in the places where they have settled is great, if only they have the spiritual life and vision.

CONTEMPORARY CATHOLICISM

The winds of change blowing in the Catholic church in other parts of the world are felt in India also. There is a new and friendly openness to talk about the faith with Protestant Christians. There is also much interest in the study and teaching of the Bible among the lay people. It is not uncommon to find Roman Catholic priests and nuns attending Protestant Christian conventions and revival meetings. There is also an eagerness to buy and read good evangelical literature. All these provide wonderful opportunities for witnessing to the Catholics in India today.

Ecumenical gatherings with Protestant and Catholic church leaders are becoming frequent in the cities. On special occasions like Christmas, Good Friday, and Easter combined services are sometimes held, with one sermon by a Catholic and the other by a Protestant.

CONTEMPORARY PROTESTANTISM

The major Protestant groups in India are the Church of South India (1,200,000), the Methodist church of Southern Asia (600,000), the Church of North India (700,000), the Lutheran and Baptist churches of the Assam hills, and the strong churches of Nagaland and Manipur in Northeast India (where half the population is Christian).

The Church of South India is a united church formed in 1947 by the union of the South India United church (the product of an earlier union between Congregationalists, Reformed, and Presbyterian churches), the southern diocese of the Church of India, Pakistan, and Ceylon (former Anglican church), and the British Methodist church. The Basel Mission churches (Lutheran) also joined later.

The Church of North India was formed more recently (November 29, 1970) by a union of the United Church of North India (formed in 1924 through the union of the Presbyterians and the Congregationalists in the north), the northern dioceses of the Anglican Church of India, Pakistan, and Ceylon, the Baptists, the Australian Methodists, the Disciples of Christ, and the Church of the Brethren in India. Besides these major groups there are different branches of Lutherans, Mennonites, and smaller conservative evangelical denominations and independent churches.

THE OUTLOOK OF THE CHURCH

The Indian church has come a long way in self-government, self-propagation, and self-support, yet its goals have not been completely realized. The government councils of most Christian organizations have a large majority of Indian members, and the administrative heads of most Christian institutions and theological seminaries are at present Indians. Of fifteen bishops of the Church of South India only two are westerners; all the bishops of the Methodist Episcopal church and the newly formed Church of North India are Indians; and the first Indian bishop of the Lutheran Church came into office in 1956. But unfortunately the transfer of leadership and responsibility has been much slower in the smaller and more conservative evangelical churches. In many evangelical Bible schools the leadership is still in the hands of western missionaries. The lack of able, trained Indian leaders may be a reason for this, but there is also a hesitation to recognize and trust such men when they are found.

There are still a number of missionaries today who are working with the Indian church in lay training, Christian education, seminary teaching, rural uplift, and other kinds of service. A happy relationship exists in many places between these missionary co-workers and the national church. In other areas and denominations many missionaries are engaged in pioneer evangelism and church planting.

Self-support has been realized in varying degrees from region to region and from denomination to denomination. Many of the dioceses of the Church of South India are self-supporting in the ordinary work of the church, though some still receive subsidies from the West. Some institutions also still depend on a large amount of support from abroad. The Methodist church is entirely self-supporting in some of its conferences; the city churches support themselves while the rural churches are subsidized from the central funds. But in its institutional work and its women's work the church still receives substantial aid from abroad.

Many of the younger evangelical churches went through much difficulty when grants from overseas were cut off and the churches were put on self-support. Several pastors had to leave and seek other employment, while others took up part-time jobs. Complete self-support is still far off.

One of the weaknesses of the church in India is the lack of lay witness. Evangelism still remains the responsibility of the full-time worker. The full implication of this can be realized only when it is pointed out that the ratio of full-time Christian workers to the population in India is 1 to 111,600; that there is a ratio of only 1 pastor for 8 churches and 400 villages; that in some places 1 pastor is responsible for 180 to 200 churches! These statistics make it obvious that every Christian must be a witness if the task of evangelizing India is to be accomplished. It is encouraging to note that in recent years there have been signs of new life in the bigger denominations through the impact of interdenominational, evangelical agencies, so that today there is a nucleus of active, earnest laymen in every denomination even though the church as a whole still remains cold and lethargic.

Evangelism-in-depth was tried a few years back in west-central India between Nagpur and Bombay, where there is a concentration of evangelical missions and churches grouped under the Berar-Khandesh Christian Council. The success was not as outstanding as in Latin America, but there are resulting signs of new life in the churches.

INTERDENOMINATIONAL EVANGELISM

In 1968 the Evangelical Fellowship in India initiated what was termed the "City Penetration Plan" in two major cities, Poona (in the west) and Shillong (in the northeast). Under this plan the city is visited by various evangelistic agencies for a period of two months. Evangelistic literature is widely distributed in homes, schools, and colleges, enlisting local Christians in this effort. Evangelistic films are shown and evangelistic campaigns conducted to reach the non-Christians. At the same time revival meetings are conducted in the various churches of the city, and these are followed up with Bible-teaching missions and Christian education seminars. The plan was a great success in Shillong where there is a large nominal Christian population, but in Poona, a strong center for philosophic Hinduism, the results were meager.

Many other extra-church agencies and ministries are also active in various parts of India, including the following.

The Ambassadors for Christ are a team of evangelists who make themselves available to the churches throughout India for evangelistic campaigns and conventions. Their work has been very effective.

The Union of Evangelical Students of India (UESI), related to the International Fellowship of Evangelical Students, evangelizes through active evangelical unions on college campuses. Such unions exist in all the states except Kashmir, Punjab, Haryana, Rajasthan, and Bihar. There are fourteen full-time staff workers and four associate staff workers in the UESI, of which fourteen are national and four are missionaries. Started in 1954, the UESI is the only effective, evangelical student movement among the 2½ million students of India. Campus Crusade has started work but has not made much impact thus far. The other student movement is the liberally oriented Student Christian Movement.

India Youth for Christ started in 1947 and has an effective program to win youth through Bible clubs, weekly and monthly rallies, and camps. Their influence and impact and their youth leadership training programs have inspired and helped many churches to start their own lively youth programs. But many denominations still do not have a youth department or a full-time youth worker.

Scripture Union is the oldest interdenominational effort among the children and youth. Working on pre-university levels largely through evangelistic missions in schools, inter-school fellowships, vacation Bible schools, holiday camps, and Scripture Union campus groups, they win the young people and build them up in the Word of God. Another organization with similar aims is the Child Evangelism Fellowship, which as a comparatively recent effort is in its beginning stages. Through their Good News clubs they sponsor a vital ministry among children in the slums and in poor neighborhoods.

Two widely known Christian education agencies in India are the India Sunday School Union, older and theologically liberal, and the Christian education department of the Evangelical Fellowship of India. The latter has adapted U.S. Gospel Light Sunday school material both in English and in many of the major Indian languages. CEEFI also serves to coordinate the work of others engaged in producing vacation Bible school and other Christian education materials.

In the last decade, two outstanding literature agencies have come into the country with very effective programs of literature evangelism. One is

Operation Mobilization, which sends out teams of young people, both Indian and foreign, to sell literature in many of the unevangelized and spiritually barren areas. Through the impact of this movement many Indian Christian young people have responded to the challenge to evangelize. Some have left lucrative jobs and comfortable positions and have gone out to live sacrificially in order to reach the masses.

The other literature agency is the India Every Home Crusade, sponsored by the World Literature Crusade. Their method is to cover each state systematically through church cooperation, reaching each home with two pieces of literature, one for the adults and one for the children. There are reports of many conversions in several areas through this effort. Converts are formed into small fellowship groups, called *koinonia* groups, in places where there are no churches to care for them.

Bible correspondence courses have also been effective in bringing many to Christ. The Light of Life Bible Correspondence Course, printed in English and in many Indian languages, is the most popular; it is sponsored by the Evangelical Alliance Mission (TEAM).

There are a number of evangelical publishing agencies in the country. Well-known among them are the Evangelical Literature Service in Madras, the Gospel Literature Service in Bombay, Masihi Sahitya Sanstha in Delhi, the Evangelical Literature Depot in Calcutta, and the Good News Literature Centre in Secunderabad. The Christian Literature Society and the Tract and Book Society are other literature agencies. All the evangelical literature agencies are members of the Evangelical Literature Fellowship of India, the literature agency of the EFI.

But all publishing agencies are handicapped by the great dearth of Indian writers. Most of the literature available is either imported from abroad or translated from English. The finding and training of Indian Christian writers is an immediate need. Khristiva Lekhan Sanstha, a Christian writers' institute in Maharashtra, is putting forth an effort to meet this need.

The Bible Society of India has been independent since 1956. Many streams of related societies have fed into the organization since the first Calcutta society was formed in 1911. Though the IBS is organizationally independent, substantial foreign subsidies are still needed as they face the task of Scripture translation in approximately eight hundred languages and dialects (recent Wycliffe Bible Translators' estimate). To date the entire Bible is available in only twenty-six languages, with portions in one hundred more. But in 1966 the Wycliffe Bible Translators entered India to aid the enormous task. They are targeting two hundred unreduced dialects for their ministry. Presently they are tackling the first eight to ten with over forty workers.

Christian films also play an important role in evangelism in India, and the Christian Association for Radio and Audio-Visual Service, associated with the National Christian Council of India, has the largest religious film library in Southeast Asia, at Jabalpur (in central India). Asian Screen Incorporated, an evangelically sponsored film agency, maintains a traveling team available to show Christian films in schools, public halls, and all churches; follow-up is left to the local churches.

Gospel Recordings, purposing to reach every Indian language group, especially the illiterate masses, erected a small production plant in Bangalore in 1961. Over thirty thousand records have been produced so far. A rugged, extremely simple player is sold in the villages at a price that all can afford.

In its edition of May 25, 1969, a Delhi newspaper reported that there were thirty-three times as many radio receiving sets in India than in 1947, when India became independent. What is being done in India to meet this challenge? The Far East Broadcasting Associates of India, with headquarters in Bangalore, produces programs for transmission from the Far East Broadcasting Company transmitters in both Manila and the Seychelles Islands in eight Indian languages and in English. Independently maintained by different churches and missions, fourteen studios produce programs for FEBAI, from which two thousand letters are received monthly from the listeners. Non-Christians who write are put in touch with a local church, but most of the response so far is from Christians.

In addition to the FEBAI-related studios, there are three NCC-related studios producing programs for the Radio Voice of the Gospel in Addis Abbaba, Ethiopia. Another recording studio is maintained by the Seventh-Day Adventists. Christian radio work in India is still largely in the hands of foreign missionaries and is dependent on overseas funds.

INDIGENOUS MISSIONS

Many of the dioceses of the Church of South India have their own missionary outreach: the Indian Missionary Society of Tirunelveli diocese in 1903 started missionary efforts in the vast unreached area of Dornakal (formerly Hyderabad state), resulting today in a numerically strong church there. It now works among the hill tribes in south India and Orissa. The Kerala diocese of the CSI has missionary work in Hyderabad (in Parakal) and in Thailand. The Coimbatore and Kanyakumari dioceses work among primitive hill people in south India. The Methodist church has a missionay family in Sarawak. The Church of North India and the Methodists both work in the Andaman and Nicobar islands, along with the Christian and Missionary Alliance. In the Northeast the Mizo churches have sent missionaries to the Assam hills, and the Nagas are reaching out to the Burma border and even into the restricted North East Frontier Agency, north of Assam.

Indigenous and interdenominational missionary movements began with the National Missionary Society, started in 1905 by sixteen Christian leaders in Serampore. The aim of the society was to evangelize India "by Indian Christians through Indian men and Indian money." Today there are twenty workers in seven fields, six within India and one in Nepal. A similar but older organization is the Indian Missionary Society.

A postwar indigenous agency with a strong evangelical emphasis was launched in 1965 during the fifteenth annual conference of the Evangelical Fellowship of India and is known as the Indian Evangelical Mission. Supported by funds from within the country, the IEM purposes to reach the unreached areas within India as well as outside and to stir up Indian Christians to shoulder their missionary responsibility. At present the IEM recruits and supports Indian missionaries working in four Indian fields and two foreign countries. There is a fresh awakening of missionary interest in many Indian churches, especially among Christian young people in south India.

CHRISTIAN ASHRAMS

Popularized in Western India by E. Stanley Jones, the Christian *ashram* is a unique contribution of Indian Christianity to the universal church. The term *ashram* is loosely used of any group of men and women who, living together in a community, practice simplicity of life and devoted service to their neighbors. The pioneers in the Christian ashram movement were two medical doctors, one an Indian (Dr. S. Jesudason) and the other a Scotsman (Dr. Ernest Forrester-Paton), who in 1921 founded the Christu Kula Ashram in a rural area southwest of Madras. The emphasis of this ashram was service to the poor villagers through educational and medical work. It consisted of a simple, communal, Indian-type life with regular worship, prayer, and meditation as well as celibacy for its members. Today there are Christian ashrams all over India—some for men, some for women, and some for families. The Orthodox Syrian church and the Mar Thoma Syrian church both sponsor a number of ashrams. Some seasonal ashrams function only at certain times of the year, serving as retreat centers. One of these is the Sat Tal Ashram, founded by Stanley Jones. Some of these ashrams emphasize evangelism as well as meditation and service.

INDEPENDENT, INDIGENOUS CHURCHES

Several independent Pentecostal denominations scattered throughout India are growing well; the two main groups are the Indian Pentecostal church and the Ceylon Pentecostal mission. These are in addition to the International Assembly of God and similar Pentecostal denominations. The Indian church consists of a group of indigenous, independent churches established since 1924 in various areas of India. The Ceylon Pentecostal mission (no longer connected with the island) maintains "faith homes," where men and women live in simplicity, giving up their own possessions and homes and being supported by the members of the mission. The pastors are celibate.

Another dynamic indigenous movement was founded by a Sikh engineer, Bakht Singh, who was converted while in training in Canada. Renouncing his profession, he came back to India to witness and preach among the sweepers of Karachi. Following this, God used him to bring revival and blessing to hundreds of nominal Christians in the large denominational churches in south India. In 1941 a group of believers who were converted under his ministry separated from the mainline churches and established an independent assembly in Madras, from where the work spread throughout India. Now there are two hundred independent assemblies in India and fifty in Pakistan; the largest is in Hyderabad, with a membership of two hundred families. Each assembly is autonomous, indigenous, and financially independent. These assemblies resemble the so-called "Plymouth Brethren" in the West.

CULTS

The Seventh-Day Adventists are the largest group among the cults in India, with a popular Bible correspondence course in several Indian languages and English, plus a college and a recording studio to prepare radio programs in Poona. Jehovah's Witnesses have spread mostly among nominal Christians, but their growth is not significantly large. There are also a few small groups here and there of Mormons, Christian Scientists, and Spiritualists.

THE ECUMENICAL MOVEMENT

After the World Missionary Conference held at Edinburgh in 1910, Dr. John R. Mott visited India and encouraged the formation of the National Missionary Council of India, which came into being in 1914; in 1923 its name was changed to the National Christian Council of India. Regional councils were later formed in state or language areas and affiliated with the NCCI. From 1956 full membership in the NCCI was restricted to Indian churches and regional councils. The NCCI now has committees for Christian literature, economic and social affairs, evangelism, etc., with an official organ called the National Christian Council Review. Doubtless the existence of the NCCI has encouraged the union movements throughout the nation.

Mention has already been made of church unions which brought into being the Church of South India in 1947 and the Church of North India in 1970. In 1926 the Federation of Evangelical Lutheran Churches in India was founded, which was not so much an organic union as a federation of nine autonomous Lutheran churches. There is now dialogue toward union between the Church of South India and the Lutherans, as there is between the CSI and the Mar Thoma church. There is also the possibility of union between the Church of North India and the northern Methodist and Lutheran churches.

Within these united churches there are many evangelical believers among both members and clergy, and their doctrinal bases are still orthodox. However, there are also many bishops and ministers, especially among the leaders, who give liberal interpretation to the church creeds.

EVANGELICAL COOPERATION

Concerned with the need for spiritual awakening everywhere (a concern heightened by the inroads of liberalism into Indian churches and theological colleges), a group of missionaries and Indian Christians met for prayer at Yeotmal (in central India) on January 16-18, 1951. The dominating motive was for revival in the churches in India. At this meeting the Evangelical Fellowship of India was born. The objectives of this fellowship can be summed up as 1) spiritual revival in the church; 2) active evangelism; and 3) effective witness to and safeguard of the evangelical faith in the church and all of its agencies.

Today more than a hundred evangelical bodies, including many churches and many missions, are members of EFI, as well as many individual persons. Members gather in an annual all-India spiritual life convention. EFI sponsors the universal week of prayer in India. It publishes a monthly prayer calendar as well as a monthly magazine called *Aim*. Pastors' conferences are organized throughout the country for all denominations, to which outstanding preachers and Bible teachers from India and abroad are invited. A monthly bulletin for pastors helps keep alive the burden and vision for revival.

Gradually EFI has branched out in many directions. In 1954 the Evangelical Literature Fellowship of India was organized to coordinate various evangelical literature agencies. An Evangelical Theological Commission was formed in 1962 to bring together evangelical theologians, pastors, and theological teachers in order to clarify the evangelical position on the sensitive theological issues which confront the church in India; this body is now called the Evangelical Theological Society. In 1962 a Christian education department was also formed to publish evangelical Sunday school materials, to train Christian education leaders and teachers, to promote Christian education, and to coordinate the efforts of various Christian education agencies in the country. EFI has also brought together a "Council of Evangelists," whom God is using widely in India and in other countries. Started by the EFI in 1954, the Indian Evangelical Mission was revived and renamed in 1965.

Another outstanding product of evangelical cooperation in India with which EFI is vitally linked is the Union Biblical Seminary at Yeotmal, Maharashtra, in central India. More than twenty-six evangelical bodies are cooperating in this effort, and the graduates of this seminary are recognized and ordained in the ministry of the larger denominations also. It has over a hundred students from various denominations all over India and other Asian countries who are working toward the B.Th., B.D., and B.R.E. degrees.

PRESENT HINDRANCES FACING THE CHURCH

Perhaps no other verse in Scripture is so applicable to the present situation in India as 1 Corinthians 16:9: "For a great door and effectual is opened unto me, and there are many adversaries."

Nominalism is one of the major obstacles to the church's fulfillment of its mission in India today. To a great extent this is the result of the mass movements of earlier periods. A vast majority of professed Christians have no personal knowledge of Christ. Petty rivalries and divisions, plus strife based on caste, language, and region, mar the witness of these churches. Litigation among believers is a common evil. Evangelistic zeal and missionary vision are sadly lacking in the larger part of the church.

Liberal theology, making inroads into the church and the theological institutions, has also blunted the sharp edge of evangelism. A false universalism which says that all men are already saved and need just the announcement of this good news is promoted by some Christian leaders in the ecumenical circles. Syncretism, tolerated by liberal theologians, claims that God is at work in all cultures and all religions and that one must discern Christ's presence and work in all religions and make the non-Christian see the Christ in his own religion. Thus the biblical Christ is replaced by a vague, mystical Christ who is in every religion. This is reflected in a recent book, *The Unknown Christ of Hinduism,* written by a Roman Catholic scholar. Another recent emphasis in Roman Catholic and liberal Protestant circles call for "equal dialogue" with men of other faiths instead of proclamation of the gospel. These dialogues are growing not only among Christians but also between them and Hindus and even some Muslims in Lahore.

Outside the church *militant nationalism,* propagated by Hindu political parties, has created a hostile attitude to Christian evangelism and conversions. Christianity is stigmatized as a foreign religion: "A true Indian and a patriot must be a Hindu." Political proposals have been forwarded to make India a Hindu country, to forbid all missionary work and conversions, and to take over all missionary institutions. Religions are frequently and wrongly identified with political communities, for it is feared that conversions may weaken a Hindu community and strengthen the Christian community, thus upsetting the balance of political power. Another accusation constantly put forth against Christian evangelism is that material benefits are offered to lure the underprivileged and less fortunate into the Christian fold. Two states in India, Orissa and Madhya Pradesh, have thus passed laws restricting conversions.

Scripture teaching and worship services are not allowed during working hours in the Christian educational institutions in many places, and even where they are allowed attendance must be completely voluntary. Some areas formerly open for Christian missionaries are now closed; in the North East Frontier Agency no Christian activity is permitted, whether by foreign missionaries or by Indian Christians. There are also pressures on the government to control the foreign funds coming into the country for missionary work.

Another serious external threat to the church in India today is *Communism.* In the state of Kerala a Communist-led coalition is in power. India's three communist parties have a large following in this state, including a number of nominal Christians. (Of these three communist parties in India, the Communist Party of India is pro-Russian; the Communist-Marxist Party is pro-Chinese; and the Communist-Marxist-Leninist Party, consisting of extremists advocating violent political revolution, is also pro-Chinese). In 1968 a revolt of the peasants was organized at Naxalbari, in West Bengal. Though this revolt was put down, the extremists, who since then have been known as Naxalites, have become a group to reckon with on the Indian political scene. The Naxalites are most active in Kerala, West Bengal, and Andhra Pradesh. Communist influence on the whole has been on the increase since the last general elections in 1967. Whether it be the leftist-communist forces or the rightist-Hindu parties who win in the future, times may become increasingly difficult for the Christian church.

Challenges and Opportunities

UNEVANGELIZED AREAS

Comparatively speaking, the Christian witness is weakest and the church is smallest in north India. Many villages and vast areas in several northern states are still without any Christian witness at all. The most needy state is Kashmir, where only one person in a thousand is a Christian, and in Himachal Pradesh, where only one in four thousand is a believer. In Kerala, in the south, there is one church for every two villages; in Gujarat, Madhya Pradesh, and Rajasthan there is one church for every thousand villages; but in Himachal Pradesh there is only one church for every two thousand villages!

The tribal areas of India offer another internal challenge to the Christian church. In the North East Frontier Agency, just north of Assam, there is no Christian work at all; since 1949 the government has forbidden any missionary work among any of the forty tribes living in this area. Though many of these tribes have not yet heard the gospel, among some there is a moving of the Holy Spirit that has come about through the witness of young people who have gone to mission schools in Assam and returned. As a result, many of these tribal people have been baptized and have taken up the responsibility to witness to others of their area. In spite of hostile attitudes and persecution from unfriendly government officials, it is reported that many of these tribespeople are faithful and active. Other tribal groups, like the Gonds (one of the three largest in central India), present a continuing challenge, while those in Madhya Pradesh are still without any witness at all.

Both to the east and the west of the Indian mainland lie groups of islands which are Indian territory. On the east are the Andaman and Nicobar Islands, comprising around 265 small, inhabited islands. The capital and chief seaport is Port Blair, which can be reached by sea or air from Calcutta. According to the 1971 census, the total population of the islands is 115,133.

The majority of the Andamanese are settlers from the mainland and Indian refugees from East Pakistan and Burma. During the British rule in India these islands served as a settlement for convicts sent from India and Burma to serve life sentences. Besides these, over seven hundred Karens from Burma settled in the north Andamans in 1925. These are nominally Baptist Christians with their own churches, though they show very little spiritual life.

Descendants of the original inhabitants of these islands are to be found here in very small numbers. The pure Andamanese, one of these aboriginal tribes, is fast disappearing; their latest number is about 30. The Onges tribe, about 130 in number, live in a small island called Little Andamans, located to the south of Port Blair. Two other tribes, the Jarawas and the Sentinelese, are hostile and have defied contact with civilization. Numbering about three to four hundred, these tribespeople attack all strangers and often raid unprotected villages and kill lonely passersby with their bows and arrows. Since these two tribes are hostile and since the government does not allow missionary contact with the Onges, the few aboriginals of the Andamans are left without the gospel.

The Andamans are divided into south, middle, and north Andamans. The Church of North India, the Methodists, the Syrian churches, and a few Pentecostal groups have congregations in and around Port Blair. But in the middle and north Andamans many villages and small islands have no Christian witness at all. The Indian Evangelical Mission, the Christian and Missionary Alliance, and an independent Baptist group work together in and around Mayabunder in north Andamans where the majority of the people are Bengali-speaking. (Other languages spoken are Malayalam, Tamil, Telugu, and Hindi.) A large number of Roman Catholics from Bihar have been settled there by the Catholic church. The total percentage of Christians in the Andamans is high, about 28 percent, but these statistics do not honestly portray a vital, growing church.

The Nicobar Islands, called "the coconut kingdom" because the graceful coconut palms provide the mainstay of Nicobarese life, are twenty-four in number and lie south of the Andaman group. The most important island in this group is Car Nicobar, with a population of about ten thousand. Unlike the Andaman Islanders, the Nicobar Islanders are tribespeople of Mongoloid stock who speak Nicobarese. Amazingly, 80 percent of the Nicobarese are in the Anglican church, and the majority of these Christians live on the Island of Car Nicobar. The story of their conversion is thrilling. A Tamil Christian government official, a convert from Hinduism, was interested in the Nicobarese, so he requested the British authorities in those days to station him on the Nicobar Islands. He and his wife took twelve young Nicobarese boys and taught them in their own private Christian school. One of these was a lad named Richardson, who later became bishop of the church there. Through these twelve trained young men many others became Christians, though it was only after World War II that a mass movement took place.

During the war the Japanese occupied the Andaman and Nicobar Islands, and the Nicobarese Christians underwent much persecution. At one time the Japanese shot a number of Christian young men, including bishop Richardson's son. Unafraid and undismayed, the bishop buried these young men while the congregation sang songs of the resurrection. This made a deep impression upon the people, and many of them became Christians. However, it must be said that their Christianity today is very nominal, and the people still retain many of their pagan customs. Just two years ago the translation of the Bible into the Nicobarese language was completed, and much of this work was done by bishop Richardson himself.

Foreigners are not allowed to visit the Andaman and Nicobar Islands, and Indian citizens need a permit to do so. With its sandy beaches, blue seas, and swaying palms, the Andaman and Nicobar Islands present an enchanting picture, but they still need Christ.

Another group of islands located off the Indian mainland in the Arabian Sea are the Laccadive, Minicoy, and Aminidivi Islands, positioned about two hundred miles off the west coast and accessible by boat from Calicut (in Kerals). Of the nineteen islands only ten are inhabited. The population according to the 1971 census is about 31,810, of which about 99 percent are probably Muslims. The islanders live in primitive conditions, with only a few primary schools and very inadequate medical facilities. The language spoken here is Malayalam, the language of Kerala. A government permit is needed in order to visit the islands, and unfortunately no missionary work is allowed.

India, with the world's third largest Muslim population—over 61 million—still has comparatively few missionaries giving full time to their evangelism; even fewer are the number of Indian workers who are engaged in the work of reaching the Muslims for Christ. The field is hard and the need is great.

INDUSTRIAL AREAS

India is rapidly industrializing. New industrial towns are springing up beside the old cities. The large steel plants which have sprung up in the last twenty years have given rise to large, modern industrial towns like Bhilai (in Madhya Pradesh), Tata Nagar (in West Bengal), and Rourkela (in Orissa). The new towns are usually located near older cities. Demographers predict that by the end of this century India may have ten or more great megalopolises of 20 million persons each!

The population in these new settlements is cosmopolitan, since thousands of people from villages have left their ancestral homes to come to these places for employment. Here in their new environment, away from the old communal ties, they are more open to change and to new ways of life. They represent an opportunity for Christian evangelism. Unfortunately, the churches in these cities and towns are very weak and are as yet indifferent to these opportunities.

FOREIGN MISSIONARY OPPORTUNITIES

"Are the doors of India closing to overseas missionaries?" The answer is both yes and no. It may be possible for new missionaries from abroad to come for direct missionary work. But it may become increasingly difficult to start new projects or new missions. Yet there are still many opportunities for gifted men and women who possess a profession or a skill to enter India, as lay missionaries. For example, a young printing technologist entered the country with a teaching appointment in a college of printing. His professional status opened up for him amazing opportunities among students and others, opportunities which he would not have had as a regular missionary. Others with technical skills may find a similar opportunity to serve, though regular missionaries under established boards are experiencing increasing difficulties in obtaining visas.

BIBLE TEACHING MINISTRY

Another challenge lies in the need of the Indian church for Bible teaching ministry. Very few pastors can preach expository sermons or teach the Bible adequately. The Christian education program is on the whole sadly neglected. Visiting Bible teachers, evangelical scholars, and Christian education experts can enter and make an important contribution to the growth and blessing of the Indian church.

The days of opportunity in India are certainly not over. India still remains by far the largest "open" mission field in the world. But the church both within and without India needs bold and innovative methods to meet the urgent need of its tragically booming population and the darkness of its traditional religions.

Nation and People

GEOGRAPHY

India is geo-structured into four natural, distinct regions: 1) the Himalayan mountain ranges bordering Nepal, China, and Pakistan in the north; 2) the central Indo-Gangetic plain; 3) the Deccan plateau in the south; and 4) the coastal belt. India's more sparsely populated Andaman and Nicobar islands (in the Bay of Bengal) and the Laccadive, Minicov, and Amindive islands (in the Arabian Sea) harbor more of India's racial and linguistic groups.

India's ethnos is like a great river fed by many streams. Dravidians, Aryans, Greeks, Mongols, Arabs, Turks, and others migrated to India beginning in 3000 B.C. and intermingled during the course of the centuries, until today it is not possible to distinguish clearly between these various groups. (The Dravidians are believed to have come from central Asia, and most of the people of South India are believed to have descended from them. From the same area the Aryan migration took place about 2000 B.C.)

HISTORY

These successive waves of immigrants brought drastic cultural, political, and religious changes to the vast subcontinent: the primitive Indus civilization reigned from 3000 to 1500 B.C., the Aryan civilization ruled from 1500 to 500 B.C., the Indian kingdoms were locally sovereign from 500 B.C.

to A.D. 1000, and the Muslim invasion established their government from 1000 to 1700. The British colonial rule brought western culture to India from 1700 to 1947. And India became the world's largest free, democratic nation on August 15, 1947.

At the time when independence from Britain was declared, the Muslim-controlled areas of old India were carved out in two great pieces, from which the nations of East and West Pakistan were created. India had left about 562 native states which were ruled by Indian princes not under the direct control of the British. These were first reorganized and merged with the other territories under British rule, and then in 1956 the states were again reorganized on a linguistic basis. At present the Republic of India has 19 states and Union Territories which are under the direct administration of the central government; the latter include the offshore islands of Nicobar, Laccadive, Minicoy, and Amindive. India has a parliamentary form of democracy, with her capital at Delhi. The legislatures, both national and state, are bicameral, elected by the people. Nehru's "Congress" party under his daughter Indira Gandhi consolidated their control of the government in a sweeping victory in 1971. An improving economy and food situation plus the rise of promising young leaders gives hope for future stability.

POPULATION FACTORS

India's population explosion began in 1850 and has increased alarmingly since about 1920. By the end of 1971 India's population was estimated to be over 550 million. This growth is due not so much to an increase in birth rate as to a decline in the death rate. Infant and adult mortality have been considerably reduced by the advances in medical science, control of epidemic diseases, improvement of living conditions, and control of famines and pestilences. As a result the annual growth rate is about 2.6 percent per year.[1]

At this present rate of growth in population India's people increase by nearly 14 million per year, or thirty thousand per day. At this rate the population by 1985 will be almost 800 million, and by 1990 over a billion! But since the present population is young (45 percent under fifteen years), the growth rate will naturally accelerate; therefore, unless the rate is cut the population could be 1.5 billion—one quarter of the world—by the year 2000! Right now the average density of population for the whole of India is about 370 people per square mile, but by 1990 it will be about 50 percent more, or a density equal to putting the entire 200 million people of the United States into the state of Texas![2]

It is said that every year India needs another 3 billion pounds of food, 2½ million extra houses, 126,500 new schools with three times as many teachers, 200 million extra yards of cloth, and 4 million new jobs. These needs are increasing yearly because of the largely youthful population now. Over 63 million youth will be added to the labor forces in the decade of the seventies.

Thus, despite the "green revolution" of new miracle hybrid grains, which has increased total food production 4 to 5 percent per year since 1965, India seems headed for a tragic collision with famine before the end of this decade. The only possible solution seems to be unfeasible—almost immediate stabilization of the population by birth control (each couple just replacing themselves), so that India may level off at a billion or less within this century.[3] But religious prejudice and ignorance will apparently bar this possibility.

Paradoxically, Christian missions may have contributed in part to India's present population problem, for under the favorable climate of British rule, missions greatly aided the modernization of the nation. Hundreds of mission hospitals (430 in the Christian Medical Association) have pioneered the treatment of epidemic disease and public health, resulting during this century in the drastically declining death rate which accounts for the burgeoning population.

India is still largely a rural population, with over 70 percent of its people engaged in farming. According to the 1961 census, there are 2,699 cities and towns and 566,878 villages in India. There are 107 cities with a population exceeding 100,000 of which greater Bombay is the largest (4,152,056). At present 82 percent of the people live in villages and only 18 percent in towns and cities. But like most other Asian countries, India also is urbanizing. One study predicts 10 cities of over 20 million each by the year 2000! In this century the urban population has gone from 11 percent in 1901 to 18 percent in 1961, and by 1976 it will be nearly 25 percent, or an estimated 157 million. While urbanization is shifting the population rapidly to the cities, these unfortunate millions are being neither culturally and socially assimilated nor evangelized with the gospel.

EDUCATION AND LITERACY

Sadly, even today only 24 percent of the people of India are literate, with 34 percent literacy among the men, a figure three times higher than the 13 percent among women. The lowest rate of literacy is found in the rural areas.

Since independence in 1947, however, the picture is brightening; not only has literacy increased but education is expanding, largely due to the first two "Five-Year plans," which stressed educational development. Between 1951 and 1961 the number of educational institutions doubled.

Leading in growth were universities, now totaling thirty-two. The oldest of these are the universities of Calcutta (120,000 students), Bombay, and Madras (60,000 students), founded in 1857. Total student population also doubled, increasing from 25.5 million (1951) to nearly 60 million (1962-63, and the number of university students was nearly tripled during this time to approximately two million.

NATIONAL LANGUAGES

The problem of literacy is compounded by the fact that no less than 720 (and probably more than 800) distinct languages and dialects are spoken in India. Of these, 14 major languages (along with Sanskrit) are recognized by the Indian constitution as national languages. With the exception of Tamil and Urdu, all trace their origin to Sanskrit, an ancient language of India with a rich literature, but which is hardly spoken or written anywhere in India today. Urdu, a joint product of Persian, Arabic, and Hindustani languages, is also rich in literature and is spoken mainly by the Muslims. Today for interstate communications and all-India affairs, Hindi and English have been declared the official languages of the nation, though not without much grumbling. In 1971, overall literacy was about 29 percent, and eight of ten children between the ages of six and eleven were in school.

MAJOR LANGUAGES OF INDIA

Language	*Speaking Population*
Hindi	133,435,450
Hindustani	
Telugu	37,668,132
Bengali	33,888,939
Marathi	33,286,771
Tamil	30,562,608
Urdu	23,323,518
Gujarati	20,304,462
Kannada	17,415,827
Malayalam	17,015,782
Oriya	15,719,398
Punjabi	10,950,826
Assamese	6,803,465
Kashmiri	1,956,115

NOTE: These figures are from 1961 and should be increased by about 25% for 1972.

SOCIETY

In Hindu social life the joint family system plays a dominant role. All brothers and sisters and even cousins operate as a single family unit. The joint family is the reference group for any matter of social, religious, or economic importance. Since the family normally consists of three generations, the benefit of wisdom and experience that comes with age is useful in making decisions. Family pressure is the most important instrument of social control; in certain cases of serious deviation from the norms an individual may even be disinherited. This fear keeps many Hindus from making an open confession of Christ and explains why there are very few conversions from the higher castes. But this condition emphasizes the need for reaching whole families. Urbanization and other social changes are breaking up this joint family system in some areas, however, thereby providing an opportunity for evangelism.

But by far the most important social factor dominating Indian social life has been the caste system. For over two thousand years this tragic division, rooted in Hindu superstition, classified all Indians into five socio-economic (occupational) strata. In order of importance these were the *Brahmins* (priests and intelligentsia); the *Kshatrivas* (rulers and soldiers); the *Vaisyas* (traders and merchants); the *Sudras* (laborers); and the *Pariahs* (commonly called "untouchables"). These latter were viewed as the dregs of society, left to eke out a living however they could.

Under the constitution of 1950 these classes were theoretically abolished when India became a democracy. Though caste-consciousness is gradually disappearing in the cities, it is still strong in the country and is a major obstacle to social and economic progress and evangelism. Traditionally the gospel has been most warmly received among the untouchables. But this in turn has militated against its reception by the higher classes.

MEDICINE

Due to increased medical care and facilities, the average life expectancy in India has increased from thirty-two years in 1947 to fifty years in 1970. It seems likely to rise another fifteen years within the century. The number of hospitals and dispensaries is now steadily increasing and the government is putting forth every effort to provide medical care in the rural areas; yet in spite of these efforts there are still many villages without even a clinic, and the shortage of trained doctors who are willing to go to the rural areas is acute.

The need for adequate facilities to treat leprosy and eye diseases is very appalling. In the northern areas of Punjab and Himachal Pradesh, eye diseases are widespread and serious. A missionary doctor who conducts eye clinics regularly in some of those areas reported, "If there are ten blind people in a village, seven of them could easily have sight with the proper treatment." But as yet there are no facilities for treatment in sight.

MASS COMMUNICATIONS

Broadcasting in India is under the control of the government's All India Radio, which has about fifty-one stations broadcasting in the regional languages as well as in Hindi and English. Transistor radios are becoming common even in the remote villages, though compared with some other countries of Asia the number of those who possess a radio is still small. Television, begun in 1959 in Delhi, is still unknown throughout most of India.

The Indian press is the second most developed press in Asia, and it is free. According to a recent report, the circulation of daily newspapers now stands at about seven million. The largest circulation is in the English language, though there are many newspapers and periodicals in the regional languages also.

National Religions

INTRODUCTION

Almost all the principal religions of the world are found in India. Among these Hinduism, Buddhism, Jainism, and Sikhism all claim India as their birthplace. Out of every hundred persons in India, eighty-three are Hindus, eleven are Muslims, two are Sikhs, and between two and three are Christians, both Protestants and Roman Catholics. The number of Protestants is estimated to be slightly less than that of Catholics. Oddly, though born here, Buddhism and Jainism claim less than 1 percent of the people. Other religions with small constituencies are Judaism, Zoroastrianism (the religion of the Parsees), and tribal religions.

Hindus are strong in the states of Orissa (97.5 percent) and Himachal Pradesh (96.9 percent), while Muslims dominate Jammu and Kashmir (68.3 percent). The highest percentage of Christians is in Nagaland (more than 50 percent), the Andaman and Nicobar Islands (28.3 percent), and Kerala (21.2 percent). The Sikhs have the highest percentage in Punjab (33.3 percent).

A comparison of the census records of 1961 and 1971 reveals that the percentage growth of Hindus in India is less than the general population increase, while that of Christians and Muslims is greater. Though there was a striking increase in the number of Buddhists between 1951 and 1961—from 180,000 in 1951 to 3,000,000 in 1961—this growth leveled off and actually decreased slightly between 1961 and 1971.

RELIGIOUS POPULATION OF INDIA, 1971

Religion	*Population*	*Percentage*
Hindus	453,292,086	82.72
Muslims	61,417,934	11.21
Christians	14,223,382	2.60
Sikhs	10,378,797	1.89
Buddhists	3,812,325	0.70
Jains	2,604,646	0.47

The following pages will deal briefly with the current trends in the major religious groups of India (see also chapter 28, "Important Religions of Asia").

HINDUISM

Over 450 million people of India are adherents of the Hindu faith, comprising a large majority in all states except Nagaland, Jammu, and Kashmir.

The question "What is Hinduism?" cannot be easily answered. Hinduism has no creed that sums up its tenets. It has no historical personality at its center. It cannot be traced to a clear beginning. An almost-proverbial saying has summed it up thus: "Hinduism brings under its sheltering wings all the religions, all the semi-religious and social practices, and all the observances of the Hindu race. Polytheism, monotheism, pantheism, and atheism have all flourished under Hinduism—not necessarily at different times—and still form an integral part of recognized Hinduism. Demon worship, hero worship, worship of animate and inanimate objects, worship of natural forces, and worship of God have all been woven into its web."

In order to know the strength of Hinduism in India today we must study its modern movements and the sects within Hinduism which exert a strong influence upon the Hindu people. Most of the following sects were founded to strengthen and reform Hinduism in order to safeguard it against the impact of the Christian gospel.

1. *The Arya Samaj.* Founded in the early nineteenth century, Arya Samaj began as a militant movement with a passionate zeal for the Hindu traditions. It opposes all attempts to convert the Hindu to any other religion. This movement was started by a Gujerati Brahmin, named Dayananda Sarasvati. It emphasizes a return to the religion of the Vedas (Hindu Scriptures) as a mark of ardent patriotism. Political and religious objectives are mixed, and thus the movement has a nationalistic appeal. The Arya Samaj has engaged actively in opposing Christian evangelism and in luring Christian converts back to the Hindu fold.

2. *The Ramakrishna Movement.* This effort was initiated by a Bengali ascetic known as Ramakrishna Paramahamsa (the second name being a title to denote his deep spiritual knowledge). Beginning in Bengal, this movement has spread throughout India and recently to other countries of the world, notably among American hippies. (In 1971 the American best-selling record "My Sweet Lord" referred not to Jesus but to "my Lord Krishna," though this was not made clear in the lyrics.) Ramakrishna is very popular among the intellectuals and has a missionary character. Though the movement owes its origin to the religious experiences and ecstasics of Ramakrishna, it was his ardent disciple Swami Vive-kananda who gave stability and worldwide recognition to the movement. Swami Vive-kananda established the Ramakrishna Mission, which now has about eighty-six centers in India and thirty-one in other parts of the world, including eleven in the United States. The Ramakrishna Mission is involved in educational, medical, cultural, and religious work and also publishes English translations of the Hindu Scriptures.

According to the teachings of Ramakrishna all religions are equally true; they are different roads to the same goal, the formless Reality, so there is no need for any man to change his religion. Many of the modern Hindu leaders, like the late Mahatma Gandhi, Dr. S. Radhakrishnan (former president of India), and Dr. Rabindranath Tagore have taken this line in their attitude to Christian evangelism. Thus this religious relativism is one of the obstacles to evangelism among educated Hindus today.

3. *Gandhi and the Sarvodaya Movement.* Among those most responsible for the renewal of Hinduism, making it more acceptable to the educated people, was Mahatma Gandhi.[4] Like many others, he combined politics with religion. Although in his earlier years he was influenced by Christianity, in later years he affirmed often that he found in the Hindu Scriptures, especially the *Bhagavadgita,* everything essential to his faith. With his emphasis on nonviolence (*ahimsa*) and truth (*sathya*), Gandhi gave a new impetus to Hindu ethics. To the worship of the cow (an ancient religious practice of the Hindus) Gandhi gave a new significance. He took this primitive reverence and sublimated it into something of a higher order based upon grounds of reason. He affirmed that cow-protection is the "central fact of Hinduism." Today cow-protection has become a symbol of Hindu patriotism in India.

Though he accepted the basic caste system, Gandhi fought for the removal of untouchability. His emphasis on social reform and social service gave a new look to the Hindu faith and prevented a large number of the backward community people from seeking security in other religions. Though after his death many of his teachings and emphases were forgotten, the Gandhian spirit is preserved in a movement called the Sarvodaya movement, whose present leader is Vinoba Bhave.

4. *Neo-vedanta.* India's philosopher-statesman, Dr. S. Radhakrishnan, a former president, stands out as a great exponent of the *neo-vedanta* (return-to-the-Scripture) movement in modern Hinduism. His greatest contribution has been to commend Hinduism and its philosophy to the West. The major emphasis of this movement is similar to that of the Ramakrishna movement, namely, that the nature of Absolute Reality transcends the powers of our human minds. Reality is far different from any view of it that we can form, and there is therefore no place for religious controversy. No religion can claim to be unique or to possess absolute truth. All religious truth is relative, and so there is no need for conversion from one religion to another. Radhakrishnan also tried to show that there are similarities in the truths and experiences which the various religions proclaim. The claims of Christianity as the unique, revealed religion is thus immediately rejected. This view is very common among the educated Hindus.

5. *Hindu Political Movements.* The Mahasabha, the Rashtriya Swayam Sevak Sangh, and the Jan Sangh are Hindu movements which have a political bias, seeking to make Hinduism the state religion. All three movements are opposed to any Christian evangelism and have vehemently fought to stop all Christian missionary work in India.

6. *Popular Hinduism.* The Hinduism of the masses in India, however, is still different from that of the Hindu thinkers mentioned above. While pantheism is accepted by the intellectual Hindu who believes in the Vedanta, the ordinary Hindu is still a polytheist. In the villages of India animistic features and magic practices are mixed with Hinduism. Blood sacrifices are offered to placate the deities. Spirit worship, with the inevitable fear of demons, provokes the use of charms, amulets, spells, and incantations for protection.

Vedic and philosophic Hinduism are generally unknown in the villages. Most village people have not read even the Bhagavadgita. Nominally they worship either Shiva or Vishnu, the two major Hindu gods, but it is the village deity which plays the larger part in their daily lives. Annual festivals for both national and village deities are celebrated, especially when there is need for rain or when there is an epidemic disease. The Brahman priest plays an important part in all family occasions, such as marriages and funerals.

7. *Other Trends.* Any report on modern Hinduism would be incomplete without mention of a modern rationalistic movement which arose within the Hindu society, the Dravida Kazhagam (Dravidian Assembly), chiefly a feature of the Tamil country. Its offshoot, the Dravida Munnetra Kazhagam (Dravidian Progress Assembly), is even more vigorous than the parent body. Though basically political in its goal, it has as one of its chief aims the reform of society. It condemns Hindu mythology and superstitions, advocating rather a rationalistic spirit. This movement has

attracted a large number of young people, students, and intellectuals in the Tamil area. Today the Dravida Munnetra Kazhagam is a powerful political party in Tamilnadu state. The effect of this movement has been to break the power of Brahmanic Hinduism in the Tamil country, thereby helping Christian evangelism, though the movement itself is against all religions.

ISLAM

One-third of all the Muslims of the world live in India and Pakistan. Even after the partitioning of India and Pakistan, India has continued to have the third-largest Muslim population of all the countries of the world (over 60 million). Islam in India has been open to Hindu and Christian influences more than in any other country, but there are still very few converts to the Christian faith from among Muslims. Followers of Islam in India belong to two main groups: those who claim to be descendants of the Muslim immigrants, and those who were converted to Islam, among whom the pure doctrine of Islam is somewhat diluted. India's relation with Islam began in A.D. 1001, when the first of a series of successive invasions through the northwestern passes took place. The main stream of Muslim invasion came from the central Asian plains in later years.

A unique element of Islam in India is Sufism, a pantheistic, mystical movement. These mystics, called Sufis, are among the more thoughtful Muslims in India and have a spirit of tolerance which is not found among any Muslims in other lands. Like Hindu pantheism, Sufism tends to the view that all religions are equally true.

A more aggressive modern movement in Indian Islam is the Ahmadiya movement. Originating in the Punjab in the late 1800's, this sect was founded by Mirza Ghulam Ahmad, who claimed to be the Mahid-Messiah who came into the world in the spirit of Jesus. The Ahmadiyas teach that Jesus died and was buried in Kashmir and that His grave is still there. This movement is very strongly missionary, carrying on zealous propaganda and attacking Christianity severely. It aims at working "not only for the reform of Islam, but for the regeneration of the Hindus, the Muhammadans, and the Christians." It is quite similar to the Ramakrishna movement.

A well-known Muslim educational institution in India is the Aligarh Muslim University, associated with the government of India. It has two divisions of Muslim theology. For Christian missionaries who desire to study Islam, the Henry Martyn School of Islamics in Lucknow, a Christian institution, offers more suitable courses.

BUDDHISM

Many Hindu intellectuals in India regard Buddhism as a part of the country's spiritual heritage and a movement within Hinduism, and Buddha as a reformer of Hinduism. Though this syncretistic approach has fostered much interest in Buddhism in India today, it has not flourished much in the land of its birth till the past fifteen years. There were mass conversions to Buddhism in 1956 among the depressed classes of people, who despaired of obtaining equitable treatment within Hindu society and so turned to Buddhism, in which social restrictions are less strict than in Hinduism. According to newspaper reports, some few Christians from the depressed classes also became Buddhists.

When the communist Chinese persecuted the Buddhists in Tibet, the Dalai Lama, spiritual head of Tibetan Buddhism, moved into India with tens of thousands of Tibetan Buddhist refugees in the fifties, thereby further swelling the Buddhist population. In 1961 it was seventeen times what it was in 1951.

JAINISM

The word *Jaina* is derived from *Jina*, meaning "the Conqueror," a title given to Mahavira, the founder of the Jain religion, who lived in the seventh century B.C. Jainism never wholly broke with Hinduism and even now is often regarded as a movement within it. Many of the Jains are merchants, money-lenders, and bankers, who are often wealthy and influential in society. Between 1951 and 1961 they too have increased by more than 25 percent.

The Jains have been generally a conservative group, found mostly in Gujarat. Though the standard of literacy and education is high among them, they have resisted the influence of western knowledge and culture upon their community.

SIKHISM

Like Buddhism and Jainism, Sikhism also has a close affiliation with Hinduism and is even regarded by some as a sect of the ancient Hindu system. Punjab is the home state of the Sikhs, many of whom are fine craftsmen, soldiers, and traders. Modern, educated Sikhs tend to give up the distinctive features of their community (such as untrimmed hair and beards and abstinence from tobacco) and instead adopt western ways. They also tend to accept traditional Hindu religious thought and practices. These practices have led to the revival of the Akhalis, a warrior sect within Sikhism, which in recent times has become quite powerful in the Sikh community.

PARSEEISM (ZOROASTRIANISM)

Although followers of Zoroastrianism today are found in Pakistan and Iran, India has the largest number. Here they are called Parsees and are descendants of the Zoroastrian fugitives who first flew to India from persecution by Persian Muslims in the eighth century. Headquartered in the Gujarat state, they are a very influential community in western India, noted for their business ability, their wealth, their zeal for the progress of their own community, and their philanthropy. Many have a high level of intelligence and education and number among the well-known industrialists and businessmen.

Though the Parsees are community-conscious, few are truly religious. It can be said that there are three classes of Parsees: the orthodox, who accept the traditional beliefs and practices; those who hold to the central principles of the religion while discarding what is unessential and obsolete; and the remaining majority, who neither practice nor profess the religion but take pride in their social community.

TRIBAL RELIGIONS

The tribal people of India are considered the original inhabitants of the country, those who were driven into the hills and forests by the Dravidians (who entered India through Baluchistan in prehistoric times) and later by the Aryans. According to government statistics there are about 414 main tribes, with a total population of over 35 million, or about 7 percent of the total population. This does not include the tribal population of the North East Frontier Agency (NEFA), which has 467,511 tribespeople (1971).

Indian tribal religion can be described as generally animistic, though the beliefs and practices vary from tribe to tribe. Also, many tribes are nominally Hindu. But in general these common characteristics can be traced in them:

1. A supreme or a superior Being is acknowledged.
2. Other spirits, mostly of a milignant nature with power to harm the people, are feared. These are believed to preside over the diseases, such as cholera and smallpox, and to live in hills, valleys, rivers, waterfalls, and even in trees or stones of unusual shape and size. Blood offerings are presented to placate them.
3. Guardian spirits which protect the village and bring prosperity are also recognized. Spirits of ancestors are invoked for the welfare of the clan.
4. Possession by spirits is common and is deliberately practiced on special occasions.
5. Witchcraft and sorcery are common. Sickness is thought of as being caused by evil spirits: unless the evil spirit causing the disease is appeased, no herb can effect a cure.

Among some tribes head-hunting has a religious sanction even today; the destruction of an evil person is considered a service to God and man. By cutting off an enemy's head he is deprived of the chance to live in paradise.

Some attempts have been made to assimilate the tribals into the Hindu religion. In some places this is done by absorbing the tribal deities into the Hindu pantheon. In others, Hindu deities are adopted by some of the tribals, where they are given a secondary place, next to the tribal deities. Some Hindu groups, such as the Arya Samaj, arrange religious celebrations in tribal areas and invite the people to take part. Revival movements in the tribal religions are syncretistic in nature, leading to the adoption of Hindu festivals and ceremonies.

Christian History

Though often branded as foreign and western, Christianity came to India earlier than Islam. Its long history is second only to that of Hinduism and Buddhism, and it did not come to India from the West.

SYRIAN CHRISTIANS

There is an ancient Christian community in the state of Kerala (in the south) known as the "Church of Saint Thomas," familiarly called the Syrian Christian community. It is the oldest church in Asia (barring Palestine). A long-standing tradition says that Thomas, one of the apostles, brought the gospel to this region in A.D. 52, founded churches in seven different places, and gained converts even from the highest Hindu caste, the Brahmins. Later, according to the tradition, he crossed over to the east coast of south India (now Madras city) and carried on a very successful evangelistic campaign, in which large numbers became Christians. This evoked so much hostility on the part of the Hindus that the apostle was martyred on a small hill eight miles from the city of Madras after twenty-five years of fruitful ministry with thousands of converts. This hill is even today known as Saint Thomas Mount. The body of Saint Thomas is supposed to have been buried in Mylapore, and over the tomb now stands the Roman Catholic Cathedral of San Thome. The reliability of this tradition is a matter of much controversy among church historians, many of whom maintain that this church is the fruit of the labors of Persian missionaries who came later. For a more extensive treatment of the Thomas tradition see chapter 7, "Christianity Comes to Asia."

Whatever its origin, there is no doubt that by the fourth century there was a Christian church in southwest India, and its affiliations were with Syria. When the Portuguese invaders came to this region at the beginning of the sixteenth century they reported about two hundred thousand Christians and fifteen hundred churches which paid allegiance to the Nestorian church of Persia. Under the Portuguese rule Roman Catholicism was forcibly imposed upon this community. But as soon as the Portuguese power was broken a large section of the Syrian Christians (who had already revolted against the Jesuit control) broke away from the Roman church and appealed to the Jacobite Patriarch of Antioch to accept their allegiance. These Syrian Christians came to be known as Jacobites and today are also known as the Orthodox church.

Another phase in the history of the Syrian church was the coming of British missionaries under the Church Missionary Society in 1816. At first the missionaries declared that it was not their intention to bring the Syrian community under the Anglican church, but that their only desire was to free it of the evil effects left by Rome and to bring it back to the purity of the gospel. After some time, however, difficulties arose, and the Church Missionary Society broke with the Syrian church to carry on its own program. In several places small Anglican congregations were formed of Syrian Christians and converts from the lower classes of Hindus.

The influence of the early Church Missionary Society was felt also in another direction. Some of the Syrian Christians who were influenced by the teachings of the missionaries wanted to continue in the Syrian church and to reform it from within. The leader of this reform movement was Abraham Malpan. A struggle arose between those who favored reform and those who opposed it, and the church finally split, with the group under the leadership of Abraham Malpan (the reform group) coming to be known as the Mar Thoma church. This group then declared itself independent of the Jacobite Patriarch of Antioch.

A further split occurred in the Mar Thoma church in 1961, when a section of its members who felt that the church was moving away from its reformation principles left and formed the Saint Thomas Evangelical church of India.

ROMAN CATHOLIC MISSIONS

Two Jesuit missionaries' names stand out in connection with the spread of Roman Catholicism in India: both were members of the Society of Jesus and both were devoted in their service, but each adopted widely different methods and appealed to widely differing groups of people. The two men were Francis Xavier and Robert de Nobili.

The dynamic Xavier, the first Roman Catholic missionary to come to India, arrived in 1542. He came not only as a missionary but also as the representative of the king of Portugal, and he was armed with considerable power and the right to correspond directly with the king. Christianity was part of the political equipment of the Portuguese government, and

Xavier used his powers to appeal often for the support of the government in his missionary work. No wonder Christianity in India is often associated with colonialism!

Xavier began in Goa (on the west coast) but soon moved to the east coast of south India. Here thousands of fishermen were baptized by the Portuguese in return for protection. These were poor and illiterate and were baptized without instruction or pastoral care. Among these people Xavier's method was simple: with the help of very imperfect interpreters he worked out a rough translation of the Lord's Prayer, the Creed, and the Ten Commandments. Then he taught these Christian elements by rote to the young people he attracted, who in turn instructed the older people. These were all then dubbed Christians!

Xavier also worked in Travancore (now Kerala) with spectacular results, as indicated by an excerpt from one of his letters: "In a month I baptized more than ten thousand persons." One of his fellow workers, who lived with him in Kerala for six months, said, "He [Xavier] went barefoot with a poor, torn gown and a kind of hood of black stuff. Everyone loved him dearly."

When Xavier left India in 1552 there were reputed to be sixty thousand Roman Catholic converts and thirty Catholic churches around Cape Comorin (at the southernmost tip of India).

Robert de Nobili, an Italian Jesuit, followed Xavier to India in 1605. After studying the Tamil language for a few months, he went to Madurai, a great center of Tamil culture and Hinduism in the south. Finding that the higher castes despised the Christian religion and the customs and manners of foreigners, de Nobili adopted a new policy. After making a careful study of Brahmin customs and prejudices, he gave up everything that would offend them (such as eating meat and wearing leather shoes) and instead adopted the robes of an Indian holy man, becoming an ascetic teacher and renouncing every form of attachment to the world. He mastered classical Tamil and then went on to learn Telugu and Sanskrit. His aim was to win the intellectual Brahmins, and he called himself a "Roman Brahmin."

Within a year or two de Nobili had baptized ten young men of the upper caste, and within four years the number of converts had risen to sixty-three, including a few Brahmins. His converts were not required to give up caste distinctions, and caste was thus accepted within the Roman Catholic church and continued as part of their missionary policy for many years. Their interpretation was that caste was merely a social distinction and had no religious significance. However, this policy later proved a handicap to the Catholic church, for the Brahmin converts were separated from the low-caste converts, who were usually left uncared-for.

There were even two classes of priests, one for the high caste and another for the low. There was also considerable accommodation to non-Christian practices, and it is now difficult to know just what the converts imagined themselves to have accepted in the act of baptism.

In spite of de Nobili's policy of accommodation, in 1643 the Jesuit *Annual Letter* stated that not more than six hundred of the higher castes had been baptized in thirty-seven years, and two years later it noted that not more than twenty-six Brahmin converts remained! It is also significant to note that, though the Roman Catholic missions were the first to come to India, it was the Protestant missionaries who first translated the New Testament into an Indian language and first entered the field of higher education.

During the latter part of the eighteenth century there was a decline in the number of Roman Catholics in India, and the activities of their missions had reached the point of collapse, partly due to the decline of Portuguese power. However, there was a remarkable recovery of zeal in the nineteenth century. In 1873 the Catholics entered the tribal area of Chota Nagpur, in central India, where by identifying themselves with the poor and distressed tribal people and by championing their cause against the cruel landlords they won many converts. The result was a mass movement in that area. Even many who had joined the Lutheran church earlier now came into the Roman church, and today the Catholic church has more members in this area than any other denomination.

EARLY PROTESTANT MISSIONS

To Tranquebar, a tiny colony of Denmark, on the east coast of south India, came India's first Protestant missionaries on July 9, 1706. Two young men, Bartholomew Ziegenbalg and Henry Plütschau, though sent by the king of Denmark, were Germans and products of German Lutheran pietism.

Although many modern missions would not have accepted him because he lacked two important prerequisites (he had neither a college degree nor good health), twenty-three-year-old Ziegenbalg was a natural leader, with outstanding achievements and ability. God took this man and used him to establish the first Protestant church in India. In one of his letters from Tranquebar he wrote, "Love makes light what to others seems hard and almost impossible."

Serious difficulties faced these first two apostles: the hostility of the local Danish community, harassment from the governor, the contempt of the Roman Catholics, and the indifference of the people. Having to learn both the Portuguese and the Tamil languages, they faced the additional difficulties of finding both a person willing to teach them Tamil and a place to live and study unmolested.

Bishop Stephen Neill observes that five principles stand out clearly in the pattern which these first missionaries set for their work:

1. Christians must be able to read the Word of God, and so all Christian children must be educated.
2. The Word of God must be available to Christians in their own language.
3. The preaching of the gospel must be based on an accurate knowledge of the mind of the people.
4. The aim must definitely be personal conversion.
5. As soon as possible, an Indian church with its own Indian ministry must come into being.[5]

With these goals in mind Ziegenbalg early began translating the New Testament into Tamil, a task he amazingly completed by 1711. Since there was no press in Tranquebar, the manuscripts had to be copied by hand with the common writing materials of those days—a pointed implement for a pen and palm leaves for paper. Three years later the Tamil New Testament became the first New Testament to be printed in any Indian language.

When Ziegenbalg died in 1719, just thirteen years after he had landed in Tranquebar, there were 350 Christians and the beginning of the Lutheran church in India. Unfortunately, these pioneer missionaries made the same mistake of the earlier Jesuits in recognizing and tolerating caste distinctions in the church.

After Ziegenbalg, other missionaries sought to move into other areas in south India, some of which were under British control, but the king of Denmark refused to support this move financially, so many of these mostly German missionaries began to receive support from the high church Anglican missionary society, called the "Society for Promoting Christian Knowledge" (SPCK). Most famous of these was Christian Schwartz, who served valiantly in India for forty-eight years without a break. Between 1706 and 1798, the year of Schwartz's death, over forty thousand people had been baptized and brought into the church!

NINETEENTH-CENTURY PROTESTANT MISSIONS

The nineteenth century is regarded by historians as the great century for missions. This was certainly true of missions in India. Though Protestant missions had already taken root in the south, William Carey, who landed in Calcutta in 1793, was the first Protestant missionary to come to north India. He was also the first missionary of the newly formed Baptist

Missionary Society, the first English mission to start work in India. The East India Company, governing India at that time, was suspicious of missionaries and did not favor their coming. This placed Carey in the position of an illegal immigrant, so to avoid this he moved to the interior and worked as the manager of an indigo plantation. Added to this inconvenience was the strain of having to put up with his mentally unbalanced wife. Yet in spite of these odds which were against him, Carey studied the Bengali language and in five years had translated the entire New Testament into that language.

In 1799 two other missionaries, Joshua Marshman and William Ward, came to India, and at their invitation Carey joined them. Together they moved to Serampore, a Danish colony sixteen miles from Calcutta, to escape the hostility of the British. Thus began the Serampore group, to whom the church in India owes so much.

Carey's strategy included widespread preaching of the gospel by every possible method, distribution of the Bible in the various Indian languages, the establishment of a church, and the training of an indigenous ministry as soon as possible. In thirty years the whole Bible was translated into six languages and the New Testament into twenty-three. Carey himself translated the Bible into Bengali, Sanskrit, and Marathi. In 1819 Carey founded Serampore College, which was later chartered by the king of Denmark. This college continues to train men for the ministry even today.

In 1813 the English parliament forced the East India Company to open its territories to missionary work; this led to a number of English missions coming to India. The Church Missionary Society began its work in Madras in 1814. Charles Rhenius, sent as their first missionary to the extreme south, introduced the teacher-catechist system. The church was built around the school in each village, and the village schoolmaster was also the catechist responsible to conduct the Sunday worship services. In fifteen years about eleven thousand people were brought into the church. The Society for the Propagation of the Gospel (SPG) also worked there along with the Church Missionary Society.

In 1813 the London Missionary Society began work in Madras. At the invitation of a new convert, Ringeltaube went to the Cape Comorin area (in the extreme south), where a mass movement took place in which about eleven thousand people became Christians in a few years.

EDUCATIONAL MISSIONARIES

With the coming of Alexander Duff to India a new period began in the history of missions in this land. Sent by the Church of Scotland, Duff arrived with the conviction that the gospel must be presented to the cultured sections of the community through higher education in English. Thus Protestant missions began to get involved in higher education.

Duff began his work in 1830 in Calcutta by opening a school with objectives that were educational as well as evangelistic. He made friends with young Bengalis of leading families, and in three years four young men were baptized. Though Duff did not see large numbers of converts, the thirty-three who were baptized during his eighteen years of service were notable in quality, and their influence in the church and its growth was very great.

Following Duff's effort many Scottish missionaries entered the field of education: in Bombay John Wilson founded what is now known as Wilson College, and Madras Christian College in Madras and Hislop College in Nagpur were started along similar lines. The first Anglican college was Noble College in Machilipatnam, in Andhra Pradesh. Though these institutions were started in the beginning with the aim of evangelism, the emphasis later shifted from conversion to service. Government restrictions have also made effective evangelistic outreach and witness difficult in these Christian institutions today.

CONTINENTAL AND AMERICAN MISSIONS

In 1833 permission to enter British India was granted to non-British missionary societies, resulting in a number of missions from Europe and America entering India. The American Congregationalists made a small beginning in Bombay in 1813 and came to south India in 1834. Among the first missionaries was Dr. John Scudder, who came from Ceylon; since then several generations of Scudders have served in India. Dr. Ida Scudder founded the training center for women doctors (later opened to men also) at Vellore, where today the Christian Medical College and hospital stand as a tribute to her great work.

The American Presbyterians came into the Punjab in 1833. The American Lutherans came to Andhra Pradesh (in the south) in 1841. The Methodist Episcopals came to the United Provinces of north India in 1856 and within thirty years had established fifty mission centers, mostly in south-central and north India. Today the Methodist Episcopal church is the second-largest denomination in north India.

Among the continental missions, the Basel Mission (Lutheran) worked on the west coast and the Leipzig Lutheran Mission worked on the east coast in south India. The Basel Mission more than any other paid attention to the economic development of the Christians, who came mainly from the destitute castes. Basel Mission tiles and textiles were famous throughout south India till the First World War.

In 1857 the Indian Christians went through the fiery trial of the War of Independence (commonly known as the Indian Mutiny). In the hatred and violence directed against all that was western, Christians and missionaries alike had to suffer. About thirty-eight missionaries and chaplains and at least twenty Indian Christians (doubtless many more) were martyred. This uprising was mainly in the north and did not affect south India to a great extent.

MEDICAL MISSIONS

Already in the eighteenth century the Tranquebar Mission had medical doctors, but they did not serve as missionaries. The first true medical missionaries came in the nineteenth century, of whom John Thomas, colleague of William Carey, was the first missionary doctor to India. These started their work with small dispensaries, and gradually large mission hospitals were established all over the country, followed by medical training centers for doctors, such as Vellore in the south and Ludhiana in the north. Christian medical colleges and hospitals are famous throughout the country even today.

"EVANGELICAL" MISSIONS

Toward the end of the nineteenth century smaller missions with explicitly evangelical goals began to enter India, most of them in central and north India. The Christian and Missionary Alliance, the Church of the Nazarene, the Free Methodist church, and the Wesleyan Methodists, all from America, have pioneered areas in Maharashtra, Gujarat, and Madhya Pradesh, establishing churches. The various branches of Mennonites also work in central and north India and in the Hyderabad area of Andhra Pradesh.

The first interdenominational mission to come to India was the Zenana Bible and Medical Mission, which sent women missionaries to work among the women as early as 1852. This mission now has both men and women, and is known today as the Bible and Medical Missionary Fellowship. Its work is almost exclusively service to existing churches and missions.

The beginning of the twentieth century saw the coming of many more evangelical denominational and interdenominational missions. Some of these established their own churches, while others worked with the existing churches. These have contributed significantly to specialized evangelism and service ministries, though in the main their churches are quite small.

MASS MOVEMENTS

The most notable feature of missionary effort in India during the nineteenth century was the mass movements, in which thousands of people, mostly of one community or caste, renounced their old faith and sought Christian baptism, both in the north and in the south.

The Roman Catholics first saw a mass movement in India in 1532, when about twenty thousand members of the fisher community on the east coast of south India were baptized. Later Francis Xavier added more than ten thousand to their number.

The first Protestant mass movement took place in the extreme south, in the Tirunelveli district. Between 1795 and 1805 more than five thousand converts were baptized in this area by Christian Schwartz and others. Later, through the efforts of the first missionary from the Church Missionary Society, about eleven thousand people were added from the upper-class Nadar community. In the same area the Society for the Propagation of the Gospel also baptized about four thousand people. In Kanyakumari (formerly south Travancore) another mass movement arose under the ministry of the London Missionary Society's Ringeltaube and his Indian co-worker, Vedamanickam. Although the first converts from this movement were all from the backward classes, later many of the Nadars (the higher-caste Hindus) also came forward.

The next mass movement in the south took place in Telugu country, now known as Andhra Pradesh. The American Baptist mission started there in 1840 and had so little success that the mission came to be known as the "Lone Star Mission." It was suggested that the work be abandoned, but a man from the lower caste who had been in touch with a missionary of the Church Missionary Society came from his village miles away and asked for baptism. The Baptist missionary visited his village and found that there were about 200 believers in that village as a result of the preaching of this one man. By 1882 there were 20,865 Christians in this area. American Lutherans saw a large mass movement in the coastal areas of Andhra; Anglicans, British Methodists, and Methodist Episcopals in the Hyderabad area also experienced mass movements in their work; and the Canadian Baptists and the London Missionary Society had similar movements in the northeast area of Andhra.

Though the mass movement in the Telugu country started with the lower castes, it later attracted high-caste people who were impressed with the change in the life and habits of the converts from the low castes. But in no area except Andhra has the mass movement included people of the higher castes.

The mass movements in the north also took place among the tribal people and the backward castes. The Gossner Evangelical Lutheran Mission started work in 1839 in the Ganges valley with very little success. Then they moved to the hill area, to the main tribal groups, the Oraons, the

Mundas and the Hos, and a mass movement started in 1850. By 1857, 900 converts had been baptized, and by 1914 the number had increased to 130,000. Another movement took place among the aboriginal Santals in this area, and within forty years 15,000 were baptized. In central India in Madhya Pradesh another aboriginal tribe, the Bhils, responded in large numbers to the preaching of the Church Missionary Society and the Canadian Presbyterian Mission. Today most of these tribal churches are self-governing and self-supporting.

For 30 years missionary work in the Punjab was marked by a small number of converts. Then around 1875 a lame Chuhra, one of the outcaste sweepers and landless laborers, came to a Presbyterian missionary and asked for baptism. The missionary was unwilling because the man wanted to remain in his own village to carry on his hereditary occupation of selling hides. The missionary's conviction was that unless a man came to live in the mission compound he could not stand firm in his faith. However, as the man persisted, he was finally baptized. After this he endured much persecution but stood firm, witnessing wherever he went. As a result, by 1900 half of the Chuhras in that district were baptized and later the entire community came into the church.

In Uttar Pradesh and Delhi the Chamars were the largest of the Hindu outcaste communities in the ninteenth century, their caste name coming from their traditional occupation of tanning leather. In 1859 a mass movement started among the Chamars in Delhi and spread through Uttar Pradesh, bringing a hundred thousand converts into the church.

In the follow-up of these Chamar converts in Delhi a new method was adopted: the converts were partially segregated, staying in their old community but living separately in little groups of houses surrounding a common courtyard called a *basti.* Usually there was a primary school and a chapel in each basti. These Christian bastis are seen in Delhi even today. In other parts of north India where mass movements took place, Christian colonies were started within the towns and cities. The disadvantage of this arrangement was that the Christians began to develop a ghetto complex, but in those days this was the best plan the missionaries knew to insulate converts from non-Christian customs and ways of life and to ensure purity of faith and conduct.

Another mass movement occurred in northeast India. In the hills of Meghalaya (formerly a part of Assam) live the Khasis, who are quite different from other tribes of northeast India in their language and cultural traits. It is believed that they came originally from Cambodia. In 1841 the Welsh Calvinists began work among the Khasi and after fifty years there were about ten thousand Christians. The Bible was translated into the Khasi language, and the mass movement spread throughout that area. The Welsh revival of 1904 and 1905 also had its effect on these people. The whole life of the hills was transformed and large churches came to be established. Even today there are churches in the Khasi hills with memberships of two or three thousand, and the latest reports show 47 percent of the tribe to be Christians, mostly Presbyterians. The Church of God is also growing there.

In 1892 the Welsh mission extended its work to the Mizo hills, where the English Baptists were already working. The mass movement in this area of Assam was characterized by waves of genuine spiritual revival, starting in 1906, when the Welsh revival in the Khasi hills spread to Mizo. Again in 1913, following a time of great famine when Christians by their helpfulness and concern made a profound impression upon the non-Christians, a wave of revival brought many more Mizos to Christ. In 1919 a third revival brought four thousand people to Christ. The last great revival of this area was in 1935. Today the Mizo hills have the highest concentration of Christians of any area in India, well over 50 percent. Originating in Burma of Mongolian stock and once headhunters, the Mizos today are earnest Christians, active in evangelism, and the Mizo church embraces practically the whole community.

The Nagas are another important tribe who became Christians in large numbers during this period. In 1840 an American Baptist missionary started work in Nagaland, and after eleven years the first Naga was converted. Then began the great movement which transformed thousands of these head-hunting tribals into strong, active Christians. Today, over 50 percent of the Nagas are Christians.* Dr. I. Ben Wati, grandson of a Naga headhunter, is now executive secretary of the Evangelical Fellowship of India.

After 1860 the American Baptists began work among the Garos, the Abors, and the Minis, all hill tribes, and mass movements among these people swept many of them into the Christian fold. One of the most recent mass movements was among the Konds, an aboriginal tribe numbering around two hundred thousand in the Kond hills of Orissa. Human sacrifice was practiced among the Konds until forcibly suppressed by the British Government in 1857.

John Goadby, pioneer missionary to the Konds, expressed his concern for these people: "Here I will stay even though my life may be spent without any token of usefulness. I will go on sowing all my days, though I myself may reap no harvest. But others assuredly will." Goadby spent only nine years in these hills and died at the age of thirty-five. The fruit

*In 1972, on the hundredth anniversary of Christianity in this area, Evangelist Billy Graham preached to a hundred thousand tribesmen who gathered for the celebration.

of his labors was reaped later, when the first Kond family was baptized in 1914 by his successors. Then followed a pattern of whole households turning to the faith. The break came with the starting of a school in the languages of the Konds. The schoolboys brought their parents and other relatives to Christ, and then whole groups came into the church. Some of these schoolboys, after being trained as teachers, went to work in isolated government primary schools in the hills. In the evenings and during weekends they went about teaching the gospel and establishing new groups of believers, which later were linked with the mission center. The first church to be built stands in a place near the hill where human victims were once sacrificed.

Though the first family in this area to take baptism was a Kond family, most of the above-mentioned results were among the Pans, the outcastes living among them. However, in 1951 a small group of Konds themselves asked for teaching. Then in 1956 this community suddenly burst into vigorous life, with its membership doubling in twelve months. Since the place was on an important trading route, the witness of these Kond Christians influenced many. The strong sense of family unity among the Konds led all the relatives connected to a converted household into the faith. Thus through the spontaneous witness of ordinary, lay Christians the movement spread. Many requests for teaching began to come from small groups in villages, and the new believers went from village to village telling the good news. Between October 1960 and July 1961 there were more than a thousand baptisms, and the church membership by 1962 was about five thousand. It is estimated to be nearly ten thousand at this writing, and the movement is still continuing. The great need there is for educated young men to enter the ministry and lead the church.

In south Orissa, where Canadian Baptists are working, there is currently a considerable movement among the Saoras, the publication of the Saora New Testament giving new impetus to this movement. There was also a mass movement in west Orissa among the weaver caste.

The question may be asked, "Are mass movements only a past phenomenon in missions in India, or are there such movements now?" As mentioned above, the movement still continues among the Konds and Saoras in Orissa. In the Krishna district of Andhra Pradesh there is a movement reported among the caste Hindus. In one area in west Orissa a hundred baptisms were reported last year. In former mass-movement areas there is still an openness to the gospel which could lead to new mass movements.

Bishop A. J. Appasamy (now retired) of the Church of South India has written, "From the depressed classes thousands of people are ready to become Christians, but we are unable to accept them, as it is very difficult to shepherd them adequately.[6] Bishop P. Solomon, another bishop of that church in a former mass movement area, writes, "If there were adequate financial help to carry on aggressive evangelism with all types of visual aids and with suitably qualified men, I am convinced that by the power of the Holy Spirit the mass movement will again revive."[7]

Sadly, the church in many places today is not able to take advantage of this opportunity because of lack of resources, personnel, and vision. The church is engaged so much in consolidating itself that there is little time and interest in evangelism. Then there is the attitude of the newly self-assertive Hinduism, which faces mass movements with hostility. Christians in many places have reacted to this hostility with timidity and caution.

A careful study of Indian mass movements reveals several facts.

1. It is not correct to say that the missionaries went at first to the outcastes and the tribals. In many cases they started work among the high castes and the educated people, but the results were few and slow in coming. Then through the conversion of one individual or through some other providential happening, an unexpected movement began among the tribals or the low castes in the same area, and the missionaries were drawn into it.

2. Most of the movements which have taken place among the outcastes, lower castes, or tribals can trace their human causes to serious economic conditions or famines, oppression from the higher castes, and a desire for security. Many of the churches in central India trace their origin to the great famine of the 1890's, when many were helped by the missions. Also, in many places the church started with orphans who were given refuge by the mission in times of need and famine. Nevertheless, it is not right to say that only material and economic motives led people to Christ in these movements. As Bishops Azariah and Whitehead have pointed out, "The motives that lead people to become Christians in mass movements are strongly mixed."[8] Spiritual motives did play a part, though they were admittedly mixed with other motives. Sometimes these motives were not so much personal as communal. A group of Bhil enquirers said, "What we need is a strong friend, one who can deliver us from sin, give us rest of heart and strength to live right lives. Jesus Christ is such a friend, and He only can save us as a people."[9]

3. Many of these movements have taken place in rural areas; in towns and cities where community life is not so strong, mass movements are rare. Also, in places where there is a strong political consciousness or a resurgence of Hinduism it has been difficult for people to step out for Christ.

4. The strength of the mass movements has something to do with the life of the Christian church in the area. Where the church is strong, the

Christians have demonstrated the transforming power of Christ in their individual and corporate lives; they have courageously faced and won the struggle against persecution and social ostracism and have established their own right to remain as Christians in their own communities. Wherever there has been a vigorous church with a spirit of evangelism the mass movement has been stronger.

5. In mass movements it is not the missionary who has played the main part but the converts themselves who have brought in the others.

Bishop J. W. Pickett says, "To object to mass movements is to place obstacles in the path along which an overwhelming proportion of Indian Christians, including more than 80 percent of those affiliated with Protestant churches, have come to profess faith in Christ Jesus."[10] However, it must be said in conclusion that mass movements have brought certain disadvantages to the church in India. Because of a failure to adequately emphasize personal experience and individual conversion among these masses, nominalism has become one of the major problems within the church. As a result, today in many places in India the church is as much a mission field as the unchurched masses. And pagan practices and customs still remain in the lives of large numbers of Christians, due mainly to lack of thorough teaching of the Word of God.

Continuing strife between Hindus and Muslims has brought much suffering to many. The recent East-West Pakistan war, with the resultant partition of Bangladesh, sent an estimated ten million refugees into northern India. Disease and starvation affected the entire area. Food is in shorter supply in many other areas also. One experienced Indian evangelist believes that this suffering is preparing India for the reception of the gospel, and that India might be the next great revival area.

Thus today India is one of the great open doors to evangelism in the world. A comparatively large Christian church waits to be revived, with millions of nominal Christians, unprejudiced against the gospel, ready to be reached with regenerating life. In India resides the greater single concentration of unredeemed humanity resident in any nation open to the gospel in this generation.

The call of India is "Come over and help us!"

NOTES

1. *Population Bulletin* (Washington: Pop. Ref. Bureau), Nov. 5, 1970, p. 2.
2. Ibid., p. 2.
3. Ibid., pp. 4, 9.
4. For Gandhi's life story see his autobiography, *My Experiments with Truth* (Ahmedabad: Navajivan Press), and Louis Fischer, *The Life of Mahatma Gandhi*, 2 vols. (Bombay: Bharatiya Bhavan, 1953).
5. Stephen Neill, *A History of Christian Missions*, pp. 229-30.
6. A. J. Appasamy, *The Church Among Tamils and Telugus*, p. 29.

7. Ibid., p. 30.
8. Azariah and Whitehead, *Christ in the Indian Villages.*
9. International Missionary Council, *Evangelism,* Tambran Series (Oxford Press), vol. 30.
10. J. W. Pickett, *Christian Mass Movements in India.*

BIBLIOGRAPHY

Agarwala, Dr. S. N. *Population.* India: National Book Trust, 1967.

Alter, James P., and Jaisingh, Herbert. *The Church in Delhi.* National Christian Council of India, 1961.

Azariah, V. S. *India and the Christian Movement.* Madras: Christian Literature Society, 1936.

Baago, K. *A History of the National Christian Council of India, 1914-1964.* The National Christian Council, 1965.

Boal, Barbara M. *The Church in the Kond Hills.* National Christian Council of India, 1963.

Campbell, Ernest Y. *The Church in the Punjab.* National Christian Council of India, 1961.

Chak, B. L. *Green Islands in the Sea.* New Delhi: Publications Division, Ministry of Information and Broadcasting, Govt. of India, 1967.

Estborn, S. *The Church Among Tamils and Telugus.* National Christian Council of India, 1961.

Facts About India. New Delhi: Publications Division, Ministry of Information and Broadcasting, Govt. of India, 1967.

Lehman, E. Arno. *It Began at Tranquebar.* Madras: Christian Literature Society, 1956.

Lloyd, J. Meirion. *On Every High Hill.* Liverpool: Foreign Mission Office.

Macnicol, Nicol. *The Living Religions of the Indian People.* Rev. ed. New Delhi: YMCA Publishing House, 1964.

Manorama, Malayalam. *Manorama Yearbook.* Kottayam, India, 1966.

Mathew, C. P., and Thomas, M. M. *The Indian Churches of Saint Thomas.* Delhi: ISPCK, 1967.

Neill, Stephen. *A History of Christian Missions.* New York: Penguin Books, 1964.

Paper No. 1 of 1963: Census of India. New Delhi.

Pickett, J. W. *Christian Mass Movements in India.* Lucknow, 1933.

Typical rural church

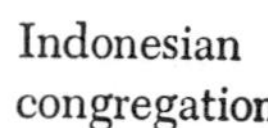

Indonesian congregation

Two national pastors of Indonesia

Photos by Audio-Visie Nederlandse Zendingsroad

11

INDONESIA

by Frank Snow

THE CHURCH TODAY

A NATION REBORN twice in one generation, Indonesia has captured the imagination of both the secular and Christian worlds. When it seemed that the country would fall inevitably into the Chinese communist orbit, a startling revolution established a modified form of government and set the nation on a new course.

Striking church growth in this nominally Muslim nation, reports of amazing revivals in remote islands, and unprecedented challenges to evangelism have encouraged Christians worldwide. Reports like Dr. Ebbie Smith's have focused prayer and interest on the three-thousand-mile-long archipelago with its polyglot of peoples.

FRANK SNOW, a graduate of London University and London Bible College, has served with the Overseas Missionary Fellowship in the Far East from 1958 to 1970, the majority of this time in Indonesia. There he served in both Central Java and the Celebes, majoring in Christian education work. In 1970 he returned to England to become candidate secretary of the OMF.

*Ed. note. In updating this excellent manuscript, completed two years ago by author Snow, I have relied heavily (and so indicated wherever possible) on recent information supplied personally by Dr. Frank Cooley, author of several excellent earlier works on Indonesia and associated with the Research and Study Institute of the Indonesia Council of Churches, and Dr. Ebbie C. Smith, author of an outstanding volume on Indonesian church growth, *God's Miracles: Indonesian Church Growth.* I am indebted to these men for their gracious and extensive cooperation.

Few regions have seen more remarkable church growth than has the Republic of Indonesia. One stands in awe of what the Holy Spirit has accomplished in these widespread islands. The marvelous stories of the Batak churches in northern Sumatra tell of the development of three separate churches with memberships of 819,000, 85,000, and 65,000. These accounts rank with God's mightiest deeds. The island of Nias, just off Sumatra's northwest coast, experienced one of the most productive revivals in Christian history—a revival that has resulted in a church of 225,000 members. Some of the truly noble servants of God have labored in Indonesia—men like Ludwig Nommenson, Gottlob Bruckner, Jabez Carey, Joseph Kam, Riedel, and Schwartz. Great chapters have been written by lay Christians, both European and Indonesian. People movements, such as took place in Minahasa, have resulted in areas that are predominantly Christian. No other area already under the sway of Islam has experienced anything like the church growth seen in Central and East Java.

Not all the miracles of church growth in Indonesia were written in the past. Since the upheaval of 1965, when the Indonesian Communist Party was defeated in its attempt to seize power, unusual responsiveness has been experienced among some of the peoples of Indonesia. The Karo Batak church doubled its membership in two years, reaching 65,000 in 1967. Thousands were baptized in east and central Java during the same period. The church on the island of Timor, under the stimulus of a tremendous spiritual awakening, baptized 200,000 into its fellowship in 1965 and 1966 alone. Southern Baptists on Java and Sumatra saw their membership triple by 1969.

The only term for such blessings is *miracle*. The works of God in Indonesia are among His mightiest deeds.[1]

Between the years of 1964 and 1971 the Protestant church membership doubled, from four to over eight million. One knowledgeable national observer believes that the number may actually be closer to twelve million. Since Indonesia as a whole is nominally 84 percent Muslim, the growing strength of the church there is all the more remarkable, even when allowing for the fact that much of the Christian growth is in the non-Muslim areas. But the gospel has also been making strong inroads into Islam in several areas.

The story of the East Java church is one of the inspiring stories of Christian missions. Nowhere else have such results attended missions in a Muslim country. While the 95,000 members is small in proportion to the total population, it is a cause for praise in a country already brought under the banner of Islam. We can but regret the lost opportunity of the vital two hundred years between 1650 and 1850, when to all appearances great harvest could have been reaped had the Dutch been willing to put in the scythe.[2]

Other accounts from Muslim areas in the Celebes, Timor and its surrounding small islands, and other areas witness to hundreds and even thousands turning to Christ from nominal Muhammadanism. Possibly the most dramatic of the evangelistic efforts took place in the island of Timor. Controversy has surrounded its authenticity, but missionary Smith reports:

> Around 1964 one of the truly miraculous movements of the Spirit in modern times broke out in Timor. Much has been written about this movement, but much is still unclear. Among factors that are both clear and substantiated are the following: the movement began around 1964, before the communist failure (Bryan, 1968:48); it has been largely accomplished by lay evangelistic teams (Bradshaw, 1967:83); it has been accompanied by signs and miracles (Bryan, 1968:48); it has spread from the coastal regions to the largely unevangelized interior tribes (van Capelleveen, 1968:29); it has added over 200,000 members to the church in three years' time (Bradshaw, 1967:83). . . .
>
> The authenticity of this awakening has been substantiated. Detmar Scheunemann, a missionary to Indonesia who recently visited Timor, reports continuing fruit from the movement. Christians are beginning to tithe, animistic practices are vanishing, and spiritual progress is continuing in many areas. One community, long a center of drunkenness and black magic, has become law-abiding since conversion. Emphasis in the movement is changing from miraculous elements to the education of the converts. While some problems did develop during the movement, they were minor and have been overcome (Scheunemann, 1969:3-8). Obviously a genuine movement of the Spirit has been experienced on this little island. . . .
>
> Four factors stand out concerning the Timor awakening. It has been largely a lay movement. Secondly, it has moved from an awakening in the coastal churches to evangelization among the interior tribes. Thirdly, it has added greatly to the church and is continuing to produce development in Christian graces. Fourthly, it has been a genuine movement of the Spirit. Future study will add to our present knowledge of this wonderful movement.[3]

Dr. Frank C. Cooley, author and student of church history and growth in Indonesia, terms the movement in Timor

> a classic revival movement characterized by widespread confession of sin and repentance, yielding up and destruction of charms and fetishes, intense witnessing, and praying and preaching by youth teams called by the Holy Spirit to leave their homes to preach the gospel. . . . It is an unquestionable fact that a real revival did occur in central Timor, bringing blessing and renewal of spiritual life to thousands of people. . . . But after researching the matter in detail and on the spot the writer reached the conclusion that claims for extraordinary church growth . . . resulting

> from the movement of the Spirit are greatly exaggerated, and that such increase as there was must be explained at least equally as a result of the radically altered political-religious atmosphere following the abortive September 30 Movement. . . . It might be said that the Timor revival was more of a revival of nominal individual Christian awakening and spiritual deepening than a revival of the churches. (From a letter to the editor dated February 1973)

In the tropical, primitive jungles of Kalimantan (formerly Borneo) an amazing work has also been going on among the Dayaks, many of whom were formerly headhunters. One report describes twenty-four hundred Dayaks coming to Christ after twenty months of work in thirty-seven villages. The entire formerly pagan village of Beirung, population two hundred, professed Christ in one two-day meeting, followed by the healing of the chief's daughter after a three-year illness with yellow fever.

Thus, though revival in the sense of a renewal of the spiritual life of the church has not occurred in the majority of Indonesian churches, nevertheless there have been undeniable movements of the Holy Spirit both inside and outside the membership of these churches. One major church, renowned for its formalism and lack of spiritual life, has experienced such a powerful work of the Holy Spirit within the ranks of its leadership that today it is leading in the promotion of evangelistic effort, Bible reading, and lay training programs. Reports which are difficult to verify have come from remote areas describing miraculous phenomena such as the restoration of a dead person to life. And the neo-Pentecostal movement has spread in Indonesia. It is sadly true, however, that the vast majority of church members still show only a formal and outward acquaintance with the contents of their faith, and national evangelistic concern and efforts are still relatively small.

Yet throughout Indonesia there has been widespread interest in Christianity following the failure of the communist coup in 1965 and the subsequent emphasis on religion in the government's moral and educational programs. Non-Christians have frequently pressed for membership within the church in large numbers. And for a variety of motives large sections of the populace suddenly became open to Christian instruction, causing reports to circulate of tens of thousands of "conversions." This makes Indonesia the single most hopeful evangelistic opportunity in Asia today, in view of its large population and its relatively open door to Islamic peoples.

A brief statistical survey of national church populations and church growth in the major denominations will help Indonesia to tell its own story.

According to the nationwide census completed in 1971, the total population was 119,232,000. The religious breakdown of Indonesia's population is as follows:

Muslims	100,120,000 =	84.0%
(All persons not enumerated under another specific category are listed as Muslims. Census figures on religious affiliation have never been released by the Indonesian government.)		
Protestant Christians, including Pentecostals.... (Ministry of Religion figures for 1971)	8,104,000 =	6.8%
Roman Catholic Christians (based on R.C. sources)	2,538,000 =	2.1%
Total number of Christians in Indonesia........	10,642,000 =	8.9%
Hindus	4,000,000 =	3.3%
(Estimating 2,000,000 for Bali and 2,000,000 for Java)		
Buddhists and Confucianists	2,970,000 =	2.5%
Mystical sects and tribal religions	1,500,000 =	1.3%
	119,232,000	100.0%

The story of the church is told in the table on page 266.

Church growth figures for twenty-two Indonesian churches have also been compiled in detail from 1948 through 1971 by Dr. Cooley (see Appendix 1). Examining these figures objectively, Cooley points out that for the twenty-two major churches in the island there has been a growth of 127.4 percent during the postwar period. This was accompanied by a 112 percent increase in the number of congregations and a 250 percent increase in the number of ordained Indonesian ministers. The growth has been substantial and continuous, and all of these churches are autonomous bodies led and served by Indonesians. Looking even more closely at some of the churches, we find that between 1948 and 1971 four churches registered a growth of more than 500 percent, nine exceeded 250 percent, and seven were between 100 and 250 percent. The lowest growth rate among these churches for that period is 17.7 percent and the highest is 935.6 percent.

Cooley also points out that there is a widespread assumption abroad that the Indonesian churches began to grow phenomenally following the

Region	Population End 1971	PROTESTANTS, 1971				ROMAN CATHOLICS, 1969			
		Baptized Christians	*Churches*	*Ordained Clergy*	*Percent Christians*	*Baptized Christians*	*Parishes*	*Priests*	*Percent Christians*
Sumatra	20,812,682	3,154,989	4,176	949	15.16	331,096	93	208	1.59
Java	76,102,468	1,151,825	1,163	1,077	1.51	410,285	153	514	0.54
Kalimantan	5,152,166	325,846	360	239	6.32	106,284	45	130	2.06
Sulawesi	8,535,164	1,572,334	2,855	1,099	18.42	179,179	91	135	2.10
Moluccas	1,088,945	616,564	903	252	56.62				
S.E. Indonesia and Bali	6,617,616	685,966	328	201	10.36	1,073,911	191	336	16.22
West Irian	923,440	596,737	207	216	64.62	119,673	87	112	12.97
Totals 1969						2,220,428	660	1,435	2.16
Totals 1971	119,232,481	8,104,261	9,992	4,033	6.80	2,575,474			2.15

SOURCES: Statistics compiled by Dr. Frank C. Cooley, with the following explanations:

1. Protestant statistics are from the Ministry of Religion, 1972. The term "churches" indicates church buildings, not congregations; the latter figures would be larger.
2. Catholic statistics are from a report prepared by them for the World Christian Handbook in 1972.
3. To make the two figures compatible for 1971, the 1969 Catholic total was increased twice by 7.7%, the average annual increase for the years 1967-69. A comparable percentage increase for the number of parishes and priests was unavailable.

1965 coup. But the figures do not bear this out as a whole. For example, the annual rate of growth for the churches studied in the chart show it to be 4.4 percent both in the four years preceding the coup (1960-64) and the years since then. Even more disturbing is the fact that for the same twenty-three-year period (1949-71) the Catholic church grew 220.9 percent, nearly double the Protestant figure. Their annual rate of growth was 5.65 percent for 1960-64 and 8.4 percent for 1964-71. Though only one-third the total number of the Protestants now, the Catholics seem to be increasing numerically much more rapidly.

But to return to the Protestant picture, what generalizations can be drawn regarding the fastest-growing churches? To summarize Cooley's findings (see analysis in Appendix 1), we find that five of the six rapidly growing churches are in distinctly non-Christian cultural areas with three of these actually in Muslim communities. Secondly, geographically these rapidly growing churches are located in east and central Java, in Karoland in north Sumatra, and in east and west Kalimantan (Borneo). It is interesting to note that all of these lie in the western half of the archipelago. Finally, Cooley points out that five of the six fastest-growing churches are regional churches rather than national ones.

Along with heartening numerical church growth in postwar Indonesia, Cooley again points to a number of other encouraging factors for the future of the church there:

1. Not only has the number of ordained clergy more than trebled, but there has been a marked increase in the quality of ministerial preparation.

2. Lay interest and activity is also being notably advanced in the life and the work of the churches by the development of effective lay training centers in at least eight regional churches.

3. In the years since 1965 at least sixty-five unique Indonesian "foundations" or evangelistic organizations have been organized, composed almost wholly of laymen and functioning separately from (though often through) the churches. These are particularly strong in Java.

4. Educational ministries have grown rapidly, with more than ten thousand church-operated schools all over the islands today. Thirteen Christian colleges and universities have been organized since 1953.

5. The church has emerged from being a ghetto community into a recognizable force in Indonesian society, participating actively in national and community affairs.

6. Specialized ministries have increased sharply: through student evangelistic movements, student centers, and university student pastors; through political prisoners and their families; through people in urban and industrial situations; through social and economic development; through family welfare centers; through family planning and responsible

parenthood programs, etc. All of these new types of service and ministry have been initiated since 1960.

7. Theological training schools have increased in number, until now there are more than thirty-five, a large percentage of which have been established since 1960.

8. Among the mainline denominations there has been broadened and deepened cooperation in the areas of common witness and service.

The Indonesian National Council of Churches is one of the strongest and most vigorous anywhere. These groups, in cooperation with their overseas churches, have examined carefully and critically the nature and quality of ecumenical relations, and they have been active in the World Council of Churches and the East Asia Christian Conference and have cooperated with their respective worldwide confessional bodies: Reformed, Lutheran, Mennonite, Methodist, and Pentecostal communions. But some of these growth factors should be examined briefly and more critically. Theological seminaries in Indonesia tend to be of a fairly high academic standard. Three seminaries which are recognized by the Foundation for Theological Education in southeast Asia give students the equivalent of a B.D. degree. Many smaller ones also train pastors. Lack of theological perception and disinterest in western theological debate has frequently opened the door of these schools to foreign personnel who hold more liberal theology without awareness of the possible consequences. Though the seminaries may not be called fully "liberal" in the western understanding of the term, unconcern and unguardedness do characterize them. Conservative Indonesian scholars still dominate most of these seminaries, but the door is open to both liberals and conservatives. It is not too late for conservatives to answer this challenge.

With regard to Indonesian ecumenism, more than 80 percent of Indonesian Protestant Christians are in churches nominally within the National Council of Churches in Indonesia (*Dewan Geredja di Indonesia*). Of the thirty-nine member churches, fourteen are also members of the WCC. Lack of any other superdenominational fellowship until recently has left the question uncomplicated.

The desire for a united front against a hostile environment has been the major motivating force behind the ecumenical involvement of the majority of churches. Also, there have been very real advantages in united Christian representation before the government to preserve the religious freedom for the Christain minority. The NCC has also ensured a vital link with the Christian world outside Indonesia, a psychological boost to a minority group that lives in a society imposing countless minute pressures upon them. Cooperation between churches in theological education, literature production, and Bible translation have been profitable ventures that have maximized the limited resources of all churches. Inter-church aid has channeled help to areas where natural disasters have necessitated Christian action. Joint Christian capital development projects have been attempted in areas where lack of communications and development have impoverished both the church and society in general. There has also been cooperation with the government scheme in family planning clinics and transmigration programs, with a view to overcoming the exploding population with its overcrowding problems.

Relationships between Roman Catholics and Protestants have undergone radical changes in the last two or three years. Unabashed competition and mutual distrust in many regions has changed almost overnight to dialogue, cooperation in Bible translation, and frank discussion of problems. Indonesian Roman Catholic church leaders have been quick to reflect the liberalizing movement and the revolt against the conservative elements of papal leadership within that church. Thus the ordinary church members on both sides have been bewildered by the sudden change of climate. Protestant attitudes have varied from uncritical and wholehearted acceptance to stubborn refusal to believe any change possible. The Protestant church leadership's desire for a united front has frequently resulted in a less critical evaluation of the situation than is necessary at this stage. One is tempted to wonder whether the Roman Catholic attitude might be different were they a majority rather than a minority.

In 1970, evangelical missions, some churches, and many individuals united to form the Indonesian Evangelical Fellowship. The largest numerically and the most important of the constituent members of this fellowship are the majority of the sixty-five "evangelical foundations" engaged in both intra-cultural and cross-cultural evangelism throughout the islands. The president of the Fellowship is Dr. Petrus Octavianus, the board chairman is Rev. Ais Pormes, and the general secretary is Rev. Stephanus Damaris. Though not primarily polemic in their purpose and orientation, this group nevertheless has been alarmed at the liberal trends in the ecumenical movement. Currently they are planning a congress on evangelism for all Indonesia.

Mission bodies working postwar in Indonesia generally fall into two classifications. Because they are committed to complete cooperation with the longstanding Indonesian churches, the Netherlands Reformed church, the United Presbyterian church in the U.S.A., the United Church of Christ, and other ecumenically-minded bodies have provided workers and substantial funds for institutional work, especially seminaries and universities, and for the National Council of Churches in Indonesia. These workers have tended to be of a more latitudinarian theological background than many of the Indonesian churches, though this generalization doubtless has exceptions. The sixty-three workers of the Overseas Missionary Fellowship (formerly the China Inland Mission) have also chosen to cooperate with existing churches and institutions who are considered to be of "like faith" with this Fellowship, loaning their workers at the request of the church concerned to engage in various kinds of ministry, ranging from lay training to teaching in schools and colleges.

At the other end of the spectrum are such conservative bodies as the Southern Baptist Mission, whose policy has been not to cooperate with the existing churches, thus producing considerable friction between them and the older churches. The World Evangelization Crusade has also largely ignored the older churches (though the WEC offshoot in Batu has been much more open), but their concentration of work in more virgin areas has resulted in less suspicion and friction. In this latter category are also the work of The Evangelical Alliance Mission, the Regions Beyond Missionary Union, the Go Ye Fellowship, the Conservative Baptist Missionary Society, the Unevangelized Fields Mission, and several others. Most of these bodies do not cooperate with existing churches (though there is intermission comity between some of them), but their work in Central Kalimantan and west Irian have seldom brought them into contact with the older churches.

Deserving special note is the Indonesian Gospel Institute (*Institut Indjili Indonesia*), located in Batu (near Malang) in East Java. An offshoot of the WEC, this evangelistic training school is now fairly independent of its parent mission. Foreign participation, a strong evangelistic emphasis, and the phenomenon of glossolalia have tended to prejudice the Institute in the eyes of some churches, but many (over 80) of its graduates are already accepted in some of the older churches, and their evangelistic emphasis is appreciated. There are currently 130 students in training at this school. This group has attracted several able Japanese missionaries to work with them.

Before concluding this section on the church in Indonesia today, a word of the marvelous work of God in the romantic Irian Barat (formerly Dutch or West New Guinea) area is necessary. Though there has been more than a hundred years of missionary history in this area, World War II opened up the highland interiors in a revolutionary way, exposing this stone age culture to modern civilization. But even before then, "the progress of the gospel in the highlands of Irian Barat demonstrates the power of people movements in discipling the multitudes of the earth. The accounts of God's miracles in New Guinea must stand as some of the most inspiring of all missionary victories. God has richly blessed the noble and sacrificial efforts of his people, both missionary and national, who have labored in this fertile field and brought from it the abundant harvest prepared by the Lord."[4]

Shortly after the close of World War II, this geographically large but demographically small area (860,000 persons) saw the influx of several aggressive evangelistic missions. In addition to the Dutch societies, with their hundred-year history, and the Christian and Missionary Alliance, which entered in 1939, The Evangelical Alliance Mission, the Unevangelized Fields Mission, the Regions Beyond Missionary Union, and the Australian Baptists began new work there, largely in the interior.

Martyrdoms, physical hardships, initial transportation difficulties (until tiny airstrips could be hacked out of the mountain jungles), and other problems beset the early pioneers.* But there gradually began a series of remarkable people movements in the small tribes which are unequaled in magnitude throughout the Indonesian islands. Dr. Frank Cooley believes that the end result (subsequent to the 1971 census) has been that at least 60 percent of the population of Irian Barat are now Christian and overwhelmingly Protestant evangelical. The interior peoples are roughly divided into the Kapaku, the Moni, the Uhuduni, and the east and west Dani tribes. The first of the sweeping people movements took place in the Uhuduni tribe, through the ministry of Christian and Missionary Alliance missionaries. After careful cultivation and many weeks and months of thinking, tribes and smaller groups came one by one to Christ. "In January of 1958 four groups of about a thousand people burned their charms and declared for Christ."[5] An interesting feature of this conversion phenomenon was the fact that the converts testified that they had been given prophecies that eternal truth would come to them.

Sunda further relates that on February 13, 1960, over eight thousand Dani tribesmen gathered in the North Balim valley. Their own preachers, baptized only a few months before, conducted the service. At the end of the service, some five thousand Danis prepared a pyre and placed their charms on it, giving a shout of joy as they did. When all was prepared, the fire was lit. But another three thousand of those assembled were afraid to burn their ancestral fetishes. Yet before the night was over many of them had decided to do so, and on the following day they too participated in this outward demonstration of commitment to the new "Jesus way." In two days' time eight thousand people had burned their charms and declared for Christ.[6]

Commenting on these people movements, Smith says that, "The Dani miracle points to two principles, both enormously important to church

*Missionaries Walter Erickson and Edward Tritt of TEAM mission were martyred there by their native carrier on an exploratory trip in 1952. Erickson was a former college roommate of the editor.

growth: first the gospel crossed a bridge of relationships from the Uhuduni tribe to the Dani tribes. . . . Then the experience of the Uhuduni and Dani churches also demonstrates the importance of a decisive encounter and commitment in conversion. For the animist to retain his animistic charms, fetishes, or idols is to face the extreme danger of reversion."[7]

A similar response was found in the Bird's Head area of western interior New Guinea, where The Evangelical Alliance Mission missionaries have labored. The greatest response to the gospel there followed a fetish-burning in the Manikion tribe in 1962. The uprisings after the revolution in 1965 slowed down growth there, but it has picked up since then. All in all God's blessing on evangelism and church growth in Irian Barat is a microcosm of the best evidence of the Spirit's working in Indonesia in this generation.

Challenges and Opportunities

What are the present spiritual needs of Indonesia? Three fields of opportunity may be differentiated at the present time. First, there are still the almost completely untouched areas and ethnic groups where little or no Christian witness has yet been known. There is a challenge to the church to redeem the long neglect of certain solidly Muslim areas such as Atjeh (north Sumatra), the Minangkabau territory of central Sumatra, Banten (west Java), and Madura, as well as some of the unreached tribal groups in west Irian, Kalimantan, and Sulawesi. It is questionable that a foreign evangelist can directly meet this need, because of intense nationalistic feelings and fanatical prejudice against Christianity. The great need is for neighboring churches, or churches that have isolated congregations of their own ethnic groups within these areas, to exercise evangelistic concern toward their Muslim fellow citizens. In 1971 an all-Indonesian Consultation on Evangelism made the following statement:

> Indonesia must truly be regarded as a mission field, and all churches must undertake cooperation in evangelism. The cooperation is also made necessary by the extensiveness of the regions not yet touched by the gospel. The extensiveness must not be seen only in geographic but also in sociological terms, e.g., functional groups, Pedicab drivers, farmers, fishermen, ethnic groups, beggars and vagrants, etc. It is necessary that information be shared about evangelistic activities and that intercessory prayer schedules be prepared for unevangelized or closed areas.

Bali illustrates the pressing need: "Many are in a condition of loneliness and are powerless to destroy the evil of darkness which has pervaded the islands of Bali and Madura."[8] A Balinese pastor says, "few Christians seem able to stand against this onslaught and are crying out for help." More than 42 percent of the people of these islands are under fifteen years of age, and they are being dehumanized by the pleasure-seeking tourists. In the rapid growth of the church in Indonesia these islands have resisted the penetration of the gospel. In a population of three million only ten thousand people are Christians. Such enclaves of unreached people are still scattered throughout the island.

Secondly, there are large areas of Indonesia with existing churches which are either insufficiently concerned or else numerically too weak to make an adequate witness to the area. Java may be taken as typical. A 1971 census in Java[9] revealed 1,151,825 Protestant Christians (plus another 495,290 Roman Catholics) out of a total population of 76,102,468. A less than 2 percent concentration of Christians, together with the weak and immature nature of much of this Christianity, indicates the evangelistic need here among a people nominally Muslim (in central and East Java) but whose present openness offers a challenging opportunity. The existing churches in these areas claim that the role of the foreign worker is to strengthen the church to do the task of evangelism rather than for him to evangelize directly.

The third field of opportunity is to be found within the older Indonesian churches' membership itself. Second, third, and fourth generation Christians have often not taken the decisive step taken by their forefathers in renouncing a former religion to "enter Christianity." The practice of infant baptism has encouraged the philosophy of "I was born a Christian." Personal faith and a living relationship to Jesus Christ often appear to be lacking. Alongside this need are the many "converts" that have flooded into the church in recent years without adequate teaching and also without any personal experience of salvation. Some perceptive church leaders recognize these needs and are more than willing to accept foreign participation in bringing these people to a vital faith in Jesus Christ and a sense of spiritual responsibility for their non-Christian friends and relations. This may be the greatest of the evangelistic needs in Indonesia, since it could result in a church revived and renewed to carry out a witness to the rest of the population.

Other specialized needs challenge the church in Indonesia today. To the tremendous challenge of the postwar era, especially the post-revolution era, the Indonesian church is just beginning to respond. To the opportunities among students as yet only minimal response is being given, although the teaching of religion to 17.5 million children in primary and secondary schools has engaged the efforts of a special commission on religious education from the National Council of Churches.

While the rapid urbanization of the population has created the need for a radical new approach to the spiritual needs of the large cities, industrial evangelism has scarcely been explored, and mass media witness has only recently received attention. Christian publishers are beginning to adapt some of their programs to the semiliterate section of the population that is on the boundary of Christian witness and influence. A Christian newspaper and Christian magazine have sought to meet the needs of the more literate and educated. But the surface is merely being scratched by existing efforts, and the churches are appealing for foreign experts in these various realms to adapt western methods and ideas to the Indonesian scene.

Is it possible to summarize the spiritual and religious situation of Indonesia when each island, region, and church presents its own unique challenge, when each faces its individual problems, and when each experiences the multifaceted grace of God differently within its witness, worship, and service? One can only return to the Indonesian motto, "Diversity becoming Unity," to describe God's church in this country. While the Ambonese church, with a history of 350 years, wrestles with the problems of self-renewal in a new age, the South Sulawesi church has yet to celebrate its thirty-fifth birthday. The Toba Batak church can number its membership at 819,000, while the Balinese church has a mere 6,000 members. The Karo Batak church is baptizing new members by the hundreds and thousands, while the West Java Pasundan church advances at a less spectacular but nonetheless sure pace. Some missionaries struggle to bring the gospel to primitive, stone-age-culture tribes in West Irian, while others run sophisticated programs for university students in Java and Sumatra. Yet all of these are part of Christ's body in Indonesia.

The call to the non-Indonesian Christian is for a greater interest, concern, and involvement in this country, its people, and its weak Christian community. The answer is not quite so simple as to merely send more money or more missionaries. There is a pressing need to seek creative means whereby God can unite our western churches with Indonesian churches (rather than merely with missionaries) in a common sense of calling and responsibility to evangelize this country and to pastor its Christians. Much intercessory prayer is urgently needed. Christians can profitably correspond with an educated Indonesian who also feels the need to widen his Christian interests. Imaginative programs for training Indonesian Christians according to the needs of their own culture in methods of evangelism are more valuable now than many new missionary efforts, I believe.

This land of challenge and opportunity that has drastically experienced the providential intervention of God in the last few years should stand high in the priorities of western Christians in the immediate future.

Nation and People

With its declaration of independence in 1945 this large but comparatively little known nation's bold action caught the attention of Asian and African countries, released a chain reaction of revolt against colonialism, and set the pace for a succession of new nations to be born throughout the world.

With an estimated 119 million population in 1971,[10] Indonesia is fifth among the world's largest nations. Its 739,000 square miles of land contain some of the world's richest deposits of oil, tin, bauxite, and nickel, while its plantations of tea, coffee, rubber, sugar, tobacco, and copra seldom find their equal in potential production. Paradoxically, the average income per capita of $85 is one of the world's lowest.[11]

Indonesia is a *big* country, vast in its tropical rain forests covering high mountains and separated by large and impenetrable coastal swamps. Incalculable natural resources remain yet untapped, mocking the present poverty of its immense population. It is big in problems that have tumbled one after another upon relatively untrained and largely inexperienced government leaders.

Indonesia is a *beautiful* country, its conical volcanoes producing so rich a soil that luscious green rice fields creep high up the mountainsides in a fantastic array of terraces. Blue skies and seas blend with green coral and waving palms. Freshwater lakes mirror the surrounding mountains and picturesque houses on stilts. It continues to attract an unending stream of tourists from the world over.

Indonesia is a *diverse* country. *Bhinneka Tunggal Ika*, the motto on the national emblem, has been translated "Diversity becoming Unity,"† and is a fair summary of the Indonesia of today, combining in a succinct phrase both the problems faced and the progress made toward their solution in this far-flung archipelago that straddles the equator for three thousand miles. Over three thousand inhabited islands, 250 languages, seventeen large ethnic groups (plus many smaller ones), and four major "official" religions make for diversity. But the unity of purpose that has been the driving force of the Indonesian revolution cannot be denied, creating out of this widely diverse, miniature United Nations a political unity that is impressive.

The Indonesian language, a modern development of the ancient Malay language, has been one of the unifying forces in this young state. Needing a practical alternative to the colonially-imposed Dutch language used officially until 1941, the new nation could not choose any of its regional languages despite their rich literary heritage. But Malay was a neutral trade

†I owe this translation to Dr. Frank Cooley. The more usual translation is "Unity in Diversity."

language which could be enriched by uninhibited borrowing from foreign and regional languages alike. Thus the rapid development of Malay-Indonesian into a medium for technical, educational, and government communication has been one of the miracles of the past forty years. It is rapidly replacing regional languages among youth, and even older people in isolated villages are able to use it in a modified form.

The past twenty-five years in particular have been ones of radical social ferment and change, but they have gradually served to further unify the island kingdom. The basic impact of western modernization upon a largely agrarian society has been uneven but great. In even the most isolated areas the transistor radio links its listener with the rest of the world. In the cities the latest style in clothing is only a few days behind that of America or Europe. The scramble for higher education has become the consuming passion of increasing numbers of young people. Impressive are the quantitative strides that Indonesia has made in the realm of education, where, despite the rapid growth of population, the literacy rate has jumped from 6 percent in 1940 to around 50 percent in 1968.[12] Before 1945 there were no universities in Indonesia; currently there are 206,000 university students in twenty-four government universities, ninety-eight academies, and numerous private institutions.

The interplay of cultures within the country, rapid urbanization, inflation, and political instability have thrown modern Indonesia into a vast cauldron of new ideas and impressions. (An example of rapid urbanization is the city of Djakarta, whose population in 1930 was 300,000 and is now around 4.5 million.) Old values and norms no longer apply, and the situation has given birth to a spiritual vacuum. The challenge to the Christian church is great, and the question is whether it can respond adequately with active and vigorous plans of evangelism to meet this new situation.

Economic turmoil has marked these postwar years also. Despite lack of capital investment and the inexpertise of ethnic Indonesians, the country's economy has revealed a remarkable resilience. Nevertheless, the slow deterioration of the nation's finances under Soekarno gradually developed into galloping inflation accelerated by the burgeoning population.‡ A 40 percent increase in the real income of the country during the period 1951-65 was outstripped by a 45 percent increase in population, from 75

‡Cost-of-living increases during the period 1951-66:

1951-53	10%	increase per annum
1954-57	20%	average increase per annum
1958-60	50%	average increase per annum
1961-65	205%	average increase per annum
1966	634%	average increase per annum

These and the other figures on this page from Cooley, *Indonesia: Church and Society*, p. 27.

to 109 million in the same period, meaning that the per capita income actually dropped 5 percent per year.

Fortunately, the future appears brighter at present. Since the overthrow of the communist bid for power, there has been increasing confidence in the country on the part of western nations, bringing support in the form of long-term loans, capital investment, and expert financial advice. Inflation has been curbed, rises in cost of living have been limited, and wages have increased. Given time, political stability, and patience (an Indonesian trait fortunately in abundance), there are hopes that Indonesia may yet achieve the prosperity promised by her natural resources.

National History

Indonesia owes its character to successive waves of immigrants and cultural influences that have in turn impressed themselves upon the archipelago for millennia. The present Java Sea was probably dry land until the millennium before Christ, and over this vast plain came the various waves of immigrants from India and northern Asia that were to form the "original" inhabitants. They were Negritos with a stone-age culture. Their relationship to the "Java Man" (*homo soloensis*) has yet to be established. Prehistoric man left his footprints in Indonesia's volcanic soil at least six hundred thousand years ago, scientists claim. Fossil remains, *Homo Modjokertensis,* dating from the early Pleistocene age, were found near the east Java city of Modjokerto. The *Pithecanthropos erectus,* discovered in 1890, was thought to have lived some three hundred thousand years ago. Eleven skulls found in central Java near Solo (*Homo Solensis*) were judged to be some forty thousand years old (Vlekke). The Wadjak skulls were thought to be of late or even post-pleistocene age and related to proto-australoid man. The contention that *Homo Modjokertensis* and *Pithecanthropus* resemble *Sinanthropus* (Peking man) has been refuted by authorities (Hall). It is extremely doubtful that modern Indonesians descended from these prehistoric races (Vlekke).[13] The immigrants from India and northern Asia settled in the (now) coastal plains of Sumatra, Java, Bali, Borneo (Kalimantan), and Celebes (Sulawesi) and were followed by a further wave of immigrants (probably from Ceylon), the Veddoids or Dravidians.

Later came the Proto-Malays from southern China via the Malayan peninsula, and in the millennium before Christ yet a further movement followed, the Deutero-Malays, of Mongol origin. This last movement brought a more advanced culture with them, which commenced the wet rice cultivation that has become so integral a part of western Indonesian culture to this day.

During the first thousand years of the Christian era Indian and Chinese influences molded Indonesian life. From India came the religious and literary traditions of the *Ramayana* and *Mahabharata* sacred writings which, implanted into Indonesian soil, flowered into powerful empires and magnificent cultures, considerable traces of which can still be found in Java and Bali today. Music, drama, dance, and literary expression were at their peak from the eighth to the seventeenth centuries.

Next on the scene, from the twelfth century onward, were the Arab traders, who brought another set of cultural patterns along with their Islamic faith. But until the advent of European traders, Arabic influences were slow to gain ground in Indonesia; where Islam was accepted it was in a compromised form rather than in its exclusive purity. But European threats drove many Indonesians into the arms of Islam in the sixteenth and seventeenth centuries, and Arabic culture added yet another layer to the multi-stratified way of life in the islands.

Finally, European influences from the sixteenth century onward contributed to this general amalgam of cultures. Portuguese, British, and Dutch traders came to trade but eventually stayed to rule and control. Even today Indonesian life, language, and culture bear the indelible stamp of Europe, chiefly that of 350 years of Dutch trade monopoly that gradually developed into 120 years of active colonial control (1820-1942).

One further immigration, coming in waves over the past 150 years, has also made a significant impact on Indonesia, particularly on its economic life. Today there are about three million inhabitants of Chinese extraction in Indonesia. Half of this number are officially classed as aliens, of which more than a million are stateless. Those born in Indonesia (about 70 percent) usually speak only Indonesian and are termed *Peranakan.* Many among this group have Indonesian citizenship and have even taken Indonesian names in an effort to identify themselves with the country. Mutual suspicion and discrimination by ethnic Indonesians is slowing the process of assimilation despite the government's avowed policy to promote and facilitate it. Those born in China are the hard core of older and more conservative Chinese, who often can speak only Chinese and who often retain their mainland Chinese citizenship. They are known as *Totok* Chinese. It has been from among the Paranakan Chinese that the larger interest in Christianity has come.[14]

The twentieth century was to witness the first birth pangs of nationalism and revolt against colonialism. Dutch control had not gone uncontested before then, but in the second decade of this century were born the first national political movements and parties (including the Indonesian Communist party, founded in 1921, which was ostensibly dedicated to unifying the country in its struggle for independence from foreign control). The Dutch colonial administration pursued a definite policy of "divide and rule," limiting educational advancement and curtailing participation in government. But this control came to a precipitous end with the Japanese invasion and conquest in 1941.

During their occupation the Japanese for their own purposes encouraged the nationalist movement and appointed Indonesians to many government civil jobs. Thus with the sudden capitulation of Japan in August 1945, Indonesia took advantage of the hiatus of outside control to proclaim her independence on August 17, 1945, with the watchword *Merdeka!* ("Freedom"), just three days after the Japanese surrender. Lack of experience and trained personnel and equipment as well as repeated Dutch efforts to retake the country by armed force could not daunt the new nation. Finally, after a bitter four-year struggle, and helped by United Nations pressure, national sovereignty was conceded on December 27, 1949. The hero of that struggle was the charismatic Soekarno, who continued to lead the nation in an increasingly despotic manner until his downfall in 1966.

The subsequent twenty-five years of independence have been characterized by the word "revolution"; strife, change, and unsettled conditions have predominated over the Indonesian scene. Independence was followed by rebellion in some of the outer islands against the kind of government laid down by Djakarta; in turn Ambon, Minahasa, and North Sumatra were reluctant to bow to the central government. Fanatical Islamic groups were anxious to turn the secular state into a religious one and resorted unsuccessfully to armed terrorism in west Java and south Sulawesi to achieve their aims. And the campaign to wrest West Irian (former Dutch New Guinea) from the reluctant Dutch was painful and expensive.

At the outset of his regime President Soekarno tried to weld the divergent forces and interests of nationalism, religion, and Marxism into an all-embracing state ideology and government patterned after western European parliamentary systems. But by the late fifties he was convinced that this type of government was not suited to Indonesia. He replaced it in 1959 with what he called "guided democracy," concentrating powers increasingly in the hands of the president at the expense of the legislative and judicial branches. When Malaysia was formed as an independent nation in 1963, Soekarno's government party fought it bitterly, claiming its formation to be a part of a "neocolonialist plot" to encircle Indonesia.

Under the new guided democracy the Indonesian Communist party rapidly expanded its influence, and the government's foreign policy increasingly leaned toward Red China, though maintaining nominal neutralism. Intoxicated with this, the Communists staged an abortive coup to seize the government on September 30, 1965. It was blocked by the army assisted by Muslim youths and others. As a result tens of thousands of alleged Communists and their supporters were slain, eliminating the Communist party as an overt political force. In the chaos which followed, President Soekarno was replaced in office by a five-man presidium headed by General Suharto, on July 25, 1966.

Major reforms have been initiated since then, and the unity of the country seems to be increasing slowly. The Communist party has been banned, but until his death in June 1970 Soekarno remained a shadowy figure in detention. The superior resources, training, and skill of the armed forces still supply a large percentage of necessary personnel for government at all levels, but the country has stabilized and seems to be moving ahead democratically.

National Religions

ANIMISM

The original animism of primeval Indonesia is nominally strong only in the many isolated mountainous areas, comprising about 1.9 percent of the population. But this figure does not adequately portray the wide influence of animism on national thought. In actual fact animistic beliefs and practices are reflected in a thousand different continuing practices in Javanese life, including Christian superstitions, Balinese rites, and a syncretistic Islam. Christianity's most spectacular gains have been among animists with frequent mass movements, but poor follow-up has tended to allow many animistic practices to carry over into the lives, worship, and beliefs of the new Christians. Such practices have frequently been taught hand-in-hand with more orthodox Christianity when evangelism has been carried out by Indonesian Christians from the older churches. An isolated example would be the magical use of the Bible to protect the owner from misfortune or to cure illness, a practice found frequently among Ambonese Christians.

The lack of official recognition of animism has at times placed its adherents at a disadvantage under the present order. In the post-communist-coup purge, not to be a member of one of the four recognized religions was to be in danger of being listed as "atheist," a term synonymous with "Communist." Thus in some animist areas the past four years have witnessed a distinct movement toward Christianity. Ulterior motives cannot be ruled out, and there are those who feel that the church has sometimes been tempted by numbers of seekers and has neglected wisdom in this situation.

HINDUISM

Hinduism propagated by Indian traders during the first few centuries A.D. came first to the western islands of Sumatra, Java, and Bali and tended to be syncretistic additions to the primitive animistic faith. But under the influence of this religion a flourishing culture reached its peak in the eighth and ninth centuries in the Shailendra and Srawidjaja empires, to which many monuments still bear witness today. The decline of these empires coincided with the coming of Arab traders from the twelfth and thirteenth centuries onward, bringing their Islamic faith, which influenced the local sultans and rulers. The result was that certain areas in west Indonesia became firm followers of the Prophet (e.g., Atjeh, Sunda, and Madura) while other areas (central and eastern Java) merely assimilated Islamic doctrines into their multi-stratified faith.

Original Hinduism has maintained its exclusive hold only upon the island of Bali. Today this "isle of the gods" has fifteen thousand village temples for its two million population. It presents the picture of a society permeated in every sphere of life with the admixed religious practices and beliefs of Hinduism and Buddhism—truly a unique pocket of Indian influence from another age.

BUDDHISM

Buddhism in Indonesia has received external stimuli in the past two centuries from two sources. Chinese immigrants over the past 150 years have brought their faith from the mainland, often mixed with Confucianism, Taoism, and Shintoism. Animistic and materialistic influences have further weakened the purity of this religion, and Indonesians of Chinese extraction have frequently found themselves accused of Communism in recent years. It is not surprising that considerable numbers of this long-harassed minority have turned to the Christian faith in the past four or five years for a variety of reasons. But since 1968 Thai priests have been entering Indonesia as missionaries and have been spreading Buddhism among the Javanese. It is as yet too early to estimate the significance of this new challenge to the larger faiths of Islam and Christianity, but it illustrates the spiritual vacuum to be found in the post-communist-coup era of Indonesia.

ISLAM

The rapid spread of Islam eastward to Indonesia in the thirteenth century, following on the heels of Arab traders, was rivaled in some areas by Catholic Christianity brought by Portuguese traders and missionaries. But the alliance of priest and soldier in the latter religion often proved to be an advantage for Islam, for the reluctant people frequently sought the help and protection of neighboring kingdoms which had already turned to Islam.[15] Following the Portuguese and then Dutch control of the area, Arabic influence waned but Islam continued to grow. By the middle of the nineteenth century, when active Protestant missions began to take this country seriously, Islam was already firmly established in many areas and had spread its influence over the whole country.

Present-day Indonesian Christian leaders study Islam with great concern but are naturally reluctant to publish their views. Indiscriminate and irresponsible publishing of facts and figures about Muslim conversions, though often true, has served to heighten the tension already felt between the religious groups in Indonesia. Attempts to build churches in some predominately Muslim areas have been thwarted; occasional riots and violence have been directed against churches; and a steady stream of invective against Christianity comes from Muslim publishing houses. But the miracle of Indonesia is that so small a minority of Christians in a predominantly Muslim society does have equal rights, even to the point of government aid in the teaching of "religion" in day schools, which for Christians can mean the teaching of the Bible and the Christian faith.

The basic reason for this freedom is found in the postwar constitution. Faced with the problem of unifying a newborn nation in its struggle for freedom in 1945, President Soekarno together with other politically liberal leaders met the question of religious unity with characteristic compromise: in the *Pantja Sila*, the five principles of the constitution, a statement of belief in "divine unity" was inserted, leaving each religious group to interpret this phrase according to its own beliefs.§ Because Indonesia was to be a religious state only in the sense that it believed in the importance of religion apart from any established religion, the official government Department of Religion was to include representatives of all the major recognized faiths within the country: Islam, Bali Hinduism, Protestantism, and Catholic Christianity. The anomaly of this move was that the only "indigenous" faith was not represented; primitive beliefs that came under the general heading of "animism" had no official recognition. However, the leaders were not blind to the fact that the statistics showing religious adherents by no means represented the actual influence of the respective religions.

CHRISTIANITY

The Christian minority has had a far greater effect upon society than the combined 8 percent-plus figure of Protestant and Roman Catholic church members would indicate. Moreover, the leaders of the country were aware that, despite its minority position as a whole, Christianity actually formed a majority in some areas. To have proclaimed a Muslim state, then, would have been to invite secession, bloodshed, and violence,

§The five pillars or principles are a) divine omnipotence, b) humanity, c) national consciousness, d) democracy, and e) social justice (W. B. Sidjabat, *Religions Tolerance and the Christian Faith,* p. 20 ff.).

to say nothing of playing into the hands of Dutch colonial desires to retake the country by splitting its ranks in the 1945-50 era. A recent proposal in government circles to maintain the status quo in present religious conditions is obviously aimed at forbidding change of religion, but Christian leaders have been unshakeable in their insistence that "freedom of religion" must mean freedom to worship, freedom to propagate, and freedom to change one's religion. It has been a healthy sign to see the insistence which Indonesian churches have placed on evangelism as an integral part of the Christian faith.

SUMMARY

A final note on religion must mention the present strong anti-communist sentiment of both government and people. During the past two or three years the recognition of religion, originally embodied in the Pantja Sila constitution, has been strongly emphasized as the antidote to atheistic Marxism. The teaching of religion in all educational institutions is now compulsory, the particular religion taught depending on the religious background of pupil and teacher and the availability of teachers. The promise of government support for such activity has awakened the enthusiasm of church and mosque alike to this opportunity.

Christian History

CATHOLIC MISSIONS

In recent years there have been efforts to prove a "Christian presence" in Indonesia antedating even the advent of Islam in the thirteenth century.[16] Though possibilities are strong, convincing proof is still lacking; for practical purposes it will be better to regard the first active Christian evangelism as taking place when Portuguese traders and missionaries arrived in Ternate (the Moluccan isles) in 1512, with the first Catholic mass being celebrated there in 1522. However, "The Moluccan Protestant church, founded around 1537, is the oldest church in Asia. At least seven congregations were functioning in 1546 when the Jesuit, Saint Francis Xavier, arrived in Ambon."[17] The sixteenth century proved to be a time of considerable activity from Jesuit, Dominican, and Franciscan orders. No less a personality than Francis Xavier spent nine months of his indefatigable missionary endeavor in the Moluccan area in 1546, and it has been estimated that up to two hundred priests played their part in establishing a church that numbered forty-five thousand in Ambon, eighty thousand in Halmahera, ten thousand in Minahasa and Sanghir, and twenty-five thousand in Timor by 1580. However, the work was without plan or order, and frequently the recipients of mass baptism were unable to receive any further attention. Rival Muslim efforts resulted in many martyrdoms, including foreign priests. However, the estimated figure of sixty thousand martyrs is probably grossly exaggerated, as are all the above-quoted figures.[18]

Methods of evangelism were often based on promise of Portuguese protection against troublesome neighboring kingdoms, meaning that the king and his subjects frequently submitted to baptism without any deeper understanding of what they were doing. Consequently, when Portuguese power declined at the end of the century, church membership correspondingly decreased. When Dutch traders ousted the Portuguese, Roman Catholic workers were also driven out, and their former work continued only in some of the smaller southeastern islands (principally in Flores) until they were once more given limited access to Indonesia, in the nineteenth century.

Catholic missions have continued with varying success until the present time. In recent years the Roman Catholic effort is impressive in its planned and effective impact upon the country, emphasizing institutions as usual. Catholic membership had reached 275,000 in 1923, though of these 64,000 were Europeans. This number grew to 1.9 million in 1967 and over 2.5 million in 1971, according to Catholic estimates (per Cooley). The annual increase in Catholic church membership has never been less than 5 percent since 1961, outstripping on the average all Protestantism since that time.

But the Catholic church has been slow to indigenize. National leaders are still few: of 30 bishops, only 4 are nationals; of 1,356 priests, only 220 are nationals; of 700 brothers, only 272 are nationals; and of 3,270 sisters, only 1,360 are nationals. Their current emphasis on education will probably rectify this soon.

PROTESTANT MISSIONS

The Dutch East Indies Trading Company era (1605-1800). The year 1605 saw Portuguese power replaced by the newly formed Dutch East Indies Trading Company. The crusading zeal with which Holland had freed herself from Roman Catholic domination in the sixteenth century was carried over to the new area under her control. Moreover, the principle of *cuius regio eius religio* ("who reigns, his religion") in Europe was also applied in Indonesia, with the result that Roman Catholic church members were expected to embrace the Protestant faith forthwith. The shallow nature of the faith of most Indonesian Christians at that time aroused no problems of conscience in such a move. The trading company claimed absolute rights and authority over the whole area, including its spiritual welfare; and until the disbanding of the company in 1799 the placement of all ministrers and church workers was controlled by the "Seventeen Gentlemen" (company directors) in the Dutch headquarters.

Pastors and workers were chosen from the state Reformed church of Holland, and their numbers varied greatly through these two centuries. Most of these (with a few notable exceptions) were concerned only with their European flock, as the terms of their engagement stipulated. Nevertheless the numbers of baptisms among Indonesians were far in excess of church attendance.|| But a work which was hamstrung by outside control,

||Compare the following statistics from Muller-Kruger, *Sedjarah Geredja di Indonesia,* p. 40.

Year	*Island*	*Baptisms*	*Regular church members*
1708	Seram	1132	33
1710	Ternate	432	39
1741	Roti	964	4
1754	Kisar	425	0
1754	Banda	1088	72
1762	Ambon	27311	963
1771	Sangir & Minahasa	12396	34

which was chronically short of workers, and in which spiritual concern for the native population was the exception rather than the rule was hardly able to produce a strong and virile church. Despite all this, it must be recorded that the roots of at least four present-day churches in Indonesia (the Moluccan Protestant church, GPM, the Timor Evangelical Christian church, GMIT, the Minahasa Evangelical Christian church, GMIM, and the Western Indonesia Protestant Church, GPIB), are in this period of work. Of these, the Moluccan church probably had the largest impact on its surroundings, for today almost half of the Moluccans are Christian. There were several attempts to make the Bible available to Indonesian readers, the first translation being as early as 1629 (the gospel of Matthew). By 1733 the whole Bible had been published in Malay by Dr. Melchior Leydekker and Rev. Van der Norm and had been officially approved for circulation, but Trading Company regulations delayed its printing for ten years!

The Mission Society era (1800-1942). The demise of the Trading Company in 1799 also coincided with the nadir of Protestant missions in the country. At the turn of the century, out of 500,000 Christians only 15,000 were communicants, and the 240 congregations had only four Dutch ministers and about 300 Indonesian schoolteachers.[19] But the effects of the pietistic movement in Europe during the eighteenth century were profound the world over, particularly in their renewed emphasis upon missionary concern and endeavor. In 1797 the Netherlands Missionary Society (*Nederlands Zendeling Genootschap*) was founded, but the wars in Europe at that time temporarily thwarted any expression of this new zeal in the direction of Indonesia. Not until 1814, with the aid of the London Missionary Society, was it possible for them to send three workers to Indonesia, though these three were giants.

The brief interregnum of British control (1811-16) saw the beginning of the Indonesian Bible Society (1814) and a brief interest in Indonesia by British and American societies; but following the return of Dutch control after 1816 the existing church (the Reformed church) was put under direct state control, and missionary work was largely restricted to societies from Holland (and later from Germany and Switzerland).#

From 1820 onward the history of missionary endeavor in Indonesia becomes too diverse and widespread to record in detail. The impetus of the pietistic movement and the general revival of personal and spiritual religion in Europe in the nineteenth century gradually saw its fruit in an ever-increasing stream of missionaries going from Holland (and later from Germany) to the Indonesian archipelago. Many of these initiated missionary work independent of state church support. Thus in this new era the state church was no longer the only Protestant church, and the link between evangelism and colonialism was not as close as it is sometimes made out to be. If the missionary sometimes followed on the heels of colonial troops, there were also examples where the missionary preceded them (for example, Kruyt and Adriani in central Sulawesi). Moreover, many instances can be quoted where missionaries did not always enjoy the favor of the colonial government. Actually, missionary activity in certain areas was either discouraged or definitely forbidden by the colonial administration. Fears of unrest and disturbance to a profitable trade were at the back of such prohibitions in Java and Bali.

It is much to be regretted that Dutch exclusivism and Anglo-Saxon provincialism have combined to result in the comparative ignorance of much of the Christian world about the lives of notable missionaries in Indonesia whose names rank with Livingstone, Carey, Judson, or Morrison. It is dangerous to single out three names, but I do so with the understanding that they represent many other equally praiseworthy efforts and names that deserve to be better known and honored in the Christian world.

A figure of apostolic dimension was that of Joseph Kam (1769-1833).[20] Of Swiss stock, his parents settled in Holland in the late eighteenth century and were profoundly influenced by the Moravian movement. Kam offered himself to the newly formed Netherlands Missionary society in 1808, but war conditions made it necessary for him, together with two other recruits (Supper and Bruckner) to go first to England and then to Indonesia with the aid of the London Missionary Society. Appointed to Ambon, Kam broke his journey with a six-month stay in east Java, where

#The French occupation of the Netherlands during the Napoleonic wars became the opportunity for Stamford Raffles to seize the Dutch East Indies for the British crown in 1811. After the defeat of France the territory was handed back in stages through negotiations between Britain and the Netherlands in 1816.

his ministry profoundly affected the lives of several members of the state church in that city. A group was formed, mockingly known as the "Surabaja pietists," and through them Kam indirectly played a part in the evangelism of east Java. In Ambon, Kam found twenty thousand Christians (who had been visited only twice by a minister in the last seven years) and a Christianity that was a syncretism of Roman Catholicism, animism, and Protestant beliefs and practices, all entwined with deeply ingrained superstitions. In seventeen years he went as far afield as Minahasa, Sanghir, Halmahera, and Timor, and wherever he went the reviving effects of his ministry were to continue throughout the rest of the century. His call for workers opened the eyes of the Dutch church to the missionary opportunities in Minahasa and Timor. Few missionaries could ever claim to have influenced so wide an area in so deep a manner. Still relevant today, Joseph Kam's effective ministry witnesses to the value of helping revive the Indonesian church rather than commencing a new work in areas where that church already exists.

Ludwig Ingwer Nommensen (1834-1918)[21] commenced his work in the highlands of north Sumatra in 1862. Sent out by the Rhenish Missionary Society to their newly opened field, Nommensen was not the first missionary to seek the conversion of the Batak people; two American missionaries, Henry Lyman and Samuel Munson, had been killed and ceremonially eaten in 1834 by these fierce people. And the Dutch Bible Society had already made a rough translation of several New Testament portions. But Nommensen envisioned the whole hinterland conquered for Christ. Early attempts to murder him failed, and, deeply impressed, several chiefs professed their interest in the new religion. The flood of new converts during the next four decades took Nommensen and his co-workers by storm. From 52 church members in 1866 the figure rose to 2,056 in 1876, 7,500 in 1881, and 103,525 in 1911. (In 1971 the Batak Protestant Christian church claimed a membership of 916,000.)

Nommensen's work was characterized by an unusual (for that age) appreciation of the need for an indigenous church, one that could retain its tribal characteristics and the best of its customs. As early as 1868 the first training school for Batak workers was opened, and in 1881 (only twenty years after the first converts were baptized) a form of church order was fixed. Stephen Neill lists four major advantages that greatly aided this early Rhenish missions work: a single language and customs pattern throughout a large area; one missionary society free from competition until late in the history of the work; subsequent colonial control of the area that was willing to help Christian schools in their educational program; and a prior language exploration which meant that the whole Bible was quickly available for the entire area.[22] Ludwig Nommensen is rightly known as the "apostle to the Bataks."

Dr. Albert C. Kruyt,[23] the third missionary statesman, together with Dr. N. Adriani of the Dutch Bible Society, laid the foundations of the church in the Poso area of central Sulawesi (Celebes). Richly experienced as the son of a missionary in east Java, Kruyt's two avowed principles of work were that the animistic tribes of north and central Sulawesi should be reached with the gospel before Muslim emissaries reached the area and that the gospel should be preached in indigenous terms that would win the whole of society for Christ, rather than a few isolated individuals.

On these two principles Kruyt made two bold decisions at the commencement of his work. One was to leave an area in north Sulawesi to which he had been sent in 1891 and in which Islam was already firmly entrenched, and instead move to Poso. This was the gateway to the whole of central Sulawesi and an area where lived many fierce animistic tribes, who knew neither the control of colonial forces nor the influence of any outside religion. Kruyt did not regard Islam as impregnable, but since he was the only worker his society could afford to place in that region, he felt it more profitable to precede the rapid Islamization of animistic tribes rather than follow it.

Kruyt's second decision was to delay the baptism of any converts until, having fully acquainted himself with the customs, culture, and languages of the people, he was satisfied that there were sufficient numbers of converts from the upper strata of society. He was wisely concerned that the society as a whole should know the leavening influence of the gospel. On Christmas day, 1909, Kruyt baptized 180 people of a single tribe, including the influential headman, Papa i Wunte. Then followed a staggering succession of tribe after tribe desiring to become Christian.

Today, sixty years later, the church is still reaping the fruits of those patient years, and the healthy independence of the church is adequate testimony to the way the gospel has found its roots in central Sulawesi society. The church now numbers more than a hundred thousand members, though communication difficulties have necessitated the division of part of this church. (In 1967, before division, membership numbered 126,000.)

Indonesian church history records not only the Herculean labors of foreign missionaries but also remarkable stories of gospel triumphs in the indigenous church. The beginnings of the church in east Java is an outstanding example of the coordination by the Holy Spirit of several factors, not the least of which is the part that laymen played. Until 1849 the evangelization of Java's indigenous population was forbidden by the colonial government. A shipment of Javanese New Testaments, translated by Bruchner in Semarang, was confiscated in 1830; but handwritten copies of parts of this publication were privately circulated by some of the "Surabaja pietist" laymen in east Java (the cosmopolitan group founded by Kam in 1815), despite efforts of the government to intimidate them. A parallel movement was commenced by the Eurasian, Coolen, who evangelized his plantation workers in Ngoro with his own indigenous brand of Christianity. Though little publicized, his work was tremendously important for the future work in that area.

It fell to the lot of later missionaries (1840 and onward) to labor in the train of these two endeavors and to unite their unfortunately different methods and ideas. The Surabaja group had insisted on their converts adopting western dress, customs, and habits a la "Dutch Christianity," while the Ngoro group had "indigenized" the gospel to the extent of denying the necessity of the sacraments and identifying Javanese folklore characters with gospel truths.[24] It says much for the statesmenlike qualities of the early missionaries (Jellesma, Harthoorn, and Kruyt) that a single church ensued. (However, the early promise of a mass movement to Christ was never realized, unless the events of the past two years be called such. In 1971 the membership of the east Javanese Church, GKDW, was 126,000. A rather similar situation in central Java was handled far less diplomatically, with the consequence that both missionary work and indigenous efforts were split.)

It was the suggestion of the Dutch missionary statesman, Hendrick Kraemer, upon his visit to Bali in 1933 that the East Javanese church take upon itself the spiritual responsibility for the entire two-million population of this world-famous island. The occasion for this suggestion was the furor created in 1932 among artists, anthropologists, tourists, and Balinese religious leaders by the baptism of 113 Balinese people by the ex-China missionary and pioneer, Robert Jaffray, of the Christian and Missionary Alliance. Previously, in 1873, a single Balinese had been baptized after seven years of work by the Utrecht Missionary society, but his involvement in the murder of the missionary eight years later caused the Dutch government to proclaim the island closed to further missionary activity.

But CMA work (commenced in 1929) was permitted with the understanding that a Chinese colporteur would confine his efforts to the Chinese population. However, family ties widened the scope and influence of his witness, with the result that the ethnic population also became involved. Jaffray's baptisms caused the government, anxious to please all but the church, to once more close the island to foreign efforts. But inconspicuous Javanese and later Balinese evangelists, trained in east Java, have since then been able to reap a significant, if yet limited, harvest on Bali.** Since independence (1945) the CMA workers have followed up their former success. In 1967 there were sixty-nine hundred members in thirty-two congregations in the Balinese Protestant Christian church.

Here it may be well to mention that historically, missions of Anglo-Saxon background in Indonesia have made limited and more circumscribed contributions, for until the postwar period the only significant work was done by the American Methodists, the Christian and Missionary Alliance, and the Salvation Army. Earlier English and American work in Ambon, west Kalimantan, and Sumatra was short-lived, with no visible results. In 1903 in Java and in 1906 in west Kalimantan the American Methodists commenced a work that concentrated on English language schools, but subsequent pressures from the government and financial stringency in the 1929 depression caused them to withdraw and concentrate in north Sumatra instead. The churches left behind were predominantly Chinese and received sporadic help from Singapore for a while. The west Kalimantan work, now fully independent, has undergone a radical renewal and revival in recent years, during which time the Overseas Missionary Fellowship has loaned it a limited number of workers. The Methodist church, centered in north Sumatra, became autonomous in 1964 and presently numbers forty thousand members.

One major and continuing Anglo-Saxon ministry in Indonesia has been the Christian and Missionary Alliance. After an initial survey conducted by several Chinese Christians together with Dr. R. A. Jaffray, who commenced in 1929 and rapidly expanded in Bali, the lesser Sunda islands (Lombok, Sumbawa, and Flores), Kalimantan, and later (in 1939) to west Irian. In 1938 work was begun in some of the larger cities of Java. In 1971 these workers reported 84,000 baptized members and regarded themselves reponsible for 109 missionaries and a total constituency of 6.7 million. The policy of believer's baptism and the careful examination of candidates for baptism makes these churches approximate more closely the American and British evangelical patterns. Church membership figures also represent a deeper degree of Christianity than do comparable figures for churches of continental background.

The Salvation Army opened work in Indonesia in 1894, soon after a branch of this group had been opened in Holland. Extensive social work has concentrated upon hospitals, leprosariums, orphanages, and the rehabilitation of homeless beggars in the large cities. This latter type of work resulted in a Christian colony near Salatiga (in central Java), which

**H. Kraemer, *From Mission Field to Independent Church,* pp. 159-86, and Muller-Kruger, *Sedjarah Geredja di Indonesia,* pp. 124-26. Both accounts are critical of CMA work on account of their lack of discretion and their reluctance to advise the Balinese converts to associate with the east Java church.

later resettled many people in a transmigration move to central Sulawesi (Palu area). This area has thus become a recognized field of evangelism for the Salvation Army. A large officer training school in Djakarta continues to supply their work with considerable numbers of Indonesian workers.

Before concluding this brief historical review it may be profitable to cast a brief glance at the methods used by the major continental missionary societies during these 150 years of rapid church growth. Failure to sympathetically understand the different approaches to evangelism has caused many evangelicals of Anglo-Saxon background to pronounce Indonesian church members "unsaved" or "not converted." Kruyt's aim—to evangelize the society rather than the individual in central Sulawesi—has been fundamental to much later missionary strategy. In other places a limited force of missionary workers faced with a large-scale interest in Christianity chose the expediency of mass baptisms rather than lose this opportunity to rival religions. The pioneer's dilemma of choosing between a deliberate personal decision by a few people or a widespread but more shallow acceptance of Christian teaching by many people is not an easy one for an evangelist to make. Moreover, the eastern pattern of community decision rather than the individuality of western society is a major consideration.

The emphasis upon external ceremonies by other religions has naturally given a great importance to Christian baptism, so that often the convert to Christianity is thought to have relinquished his former belief only after he has submitted to this rite. In practice this means that until the time of baptism the former religion still claims the allegiance of the person concerned. This consideration has often led to the policy "baptize now, teach later" (note the similar order in Mt 28:19, 20). The real and obvious dangers of such a policy must be offset by the possibility that if the church waits until all have been adequately taught, possibly many will be drawn back into their former religions or be attracted to other competing faiths.

These early Protestant missions also emphasize institutional work in order to reach society as a whole. Schools, hospitals, hostels, and orphanages have been time-honored methods used by most Dutch, German, and Swiss missionaries. It has been estimated that between 70 and 80 percent of converts to Christianity have had some contact with a Christian school. Widespread emphasis upon Bible translation also often went hand in hand with the first missionary labors, and Christian literature has been incalculable in its results, though it is still limited.†† But other methods have

††The Indonesian Bible Society (*Lembaga Alkitab Indonesia*) report of 1967 records eight Indonesian languages that have the whole Bible, twelve more that have the New Testament, and a further twenty-eight that have portions of the Bible. In 1969 more than 1¼ million portions of Scripture were printed on the new press installed in

been of less obvious spiritual value. The formation of Christian villages in east Java during the latter part of the nineteenth century had limited results, and there were even fewer results in central and western Java. The redemption of slaves in south Kalimantan and the formation of Christian plantations in Sumatra, though of supreme importance, likely attracted converts for ulterior motives.

How is one to evaluate the church in Indonesia produced by these often-disputed methods? There are many paradoxes. Lack of assurance of salvation among these Christians goes together with a staunch loyalty to Christ that has often been demonstrated in times of persecution and hardship. The absence of evangelical shibboleths, the term "entering Christianity" (*masuk Kristen*), syncretism, church politics, and the poverty of Christian giving have given unfavorable impressions to many a visitor. It is easier to condemn the deficiencies than to recognize and commend the very real signs of God's grace within the lives of many. Indonesian churches would be the first to admit their need of an even deeper work of God's grace within both individual lives and the church as a whole. The neat category of "saved" and "unsaved" is a divine distinction that the visitor to Indonesia may be too anxious to make himself. The present writer admits the desperately shallow and superficial nature of the faith of many church members but is still unprepared to claim on these grounds that they cannot rightfully be called Christians.

Thus with often differing and sometimes conflicting patterns of operations, missionary work in Indonesia is built on church foundations that for the most part were laid scores if not hundreds of years ago. Shortly before World War II broke out, radical changes began to take place in missionary-church relationships, as national churches one by one proclaimed their independence and autonomy. The Japanese occupation further radically disrupted these relationships. Thus when the war ended, the churches were largely autonomous in direction, though fraternal workers were loaned by mainline denominations to assist the churches' witness and service, and a considerable number of churches then and now still depend to a greater or lesser degree on financial help.

The Christian history of Indonesia is rich with examples of courageous heroism and pioneering work, successfully creative missionary methods, and stirring revival movements. Much can be learned from Indonesian churches which will guide the dynamic movements of the Spirit in the operation in the island today.

Bogor in 1966, and demand exceeds production. The Christian Publishing Body (*Badan Penerbit Kristen*), based in Djakarta, publishes a variety of evangelistic, theological, and educational material. In 1965 they published 137 titles, representing more than a million pieces of literature. Rising prices have caused a slight decrease in these figures in recent years.

APPENDIX 1

Church Growth Figures for 22 Indonesian Churches
Compiled by Frank C. Cooley in February 1973

		1948[a]		1953[b]	1960[c]	1964[c]
Name of Church	*Baptized Members*	*Organized Congre-gations*	*Ordained Ministers*	*Baptized Members*	*Baptized Members*	*Baptized Members*
1. Karo Batak Protestant Church	7,000	20	2	13,808	20,000	30,000
2. Batak Protestant Christian Church	502,855	1,000	67	650,000	742,000	800,000
3. Nias Protestant Christian Church	145,650	197	23	161,565	191,000	205,000
4. Pasundan Christian Church	5,000	20	17	8,234	9,400	10,000
5. North Central Java Christian Church	6,485	58	4	n.a.	('54) 3,500	('65) 5,000
6. Java Christian Church	17,875	58	25	24,813	38,000	41,760
7. Evangelical Christian Church in Java	4,343	13	1	5,565	7,000	17,562
8. East Java Christian Church	40,000	64	56	55,000	46,000	62,890
9. Kalimantan Evangelical Church	18,261	22	24	29,644	36,000	46,000
10. Bali Protestant Christian Church	1,914	9	2	2,700	3,000	4,748
11. Sumba Christian Church	6,540	20	16	14,230	17,000	22,000
12. Sangihe Talaud Evang. Christian Church	90,515	164	52	135,000	130,000	154,523
13. Minahasa Evangelical Christian Church	293,815	435	97	335,000	450,000	489,672
14. Bolaang Mongondow Evang. Christ. Ch.	16,175	61	4	23,729	25,000	25,132
15. Central Sulawesi Christian Church	77,598	359	20	80,000	143,000	105,000
16. Toraja Christian Church	30,000	205	11	120,000	110,000	171,726
17. South East Sulawesi Protestant Church	3,119	n.a.	6	23,359	3,000	3,786
18. Halmahera Evangelical Christian Church	30,000	128	2	32,140	45,000	45,000
19. West Irian Evang. Christian Church	100,000	350	n.a.	100,000	n.a.	160,000
20. Timor Evangelical Christian Church	200,000	170	75	253,501	375,000	450,000
21. Moluccan Protestant Church	200,000	n.a.	n.a.	276,813	290,000	275,000
22. Gosp. Tab. Church of Indonesia (CMA)	17,014					37,692
TOTALS	1,816,159	3,353	494	2,305,106	2,683,900	3,161,991
Roman Catholic Church[f]	791,014 (1949)			929,435	1,302,732	1,596,575

a) Issued by the Church and Mission Publishing House, Kwitang, Batavia (Jakarta).
b) Cooley, F. L., *Indonesia: Church and Society* (New York: Friendship Press, 1968).
c) From publication issued by the Indonesia Council of Churches.
d) Compiled by the Research and Study Institute, Indonesia Council of Churches.
e) Incomplete report for 1966 of The Christian and Missionary Alliance.
f) From The Roman Catholic Institute of Social Research and Development.
g) 1953-61.

ANALYSIS

by Frank C. Cooley

What do these figures tell us about church growth in Indonesia?

Taking the sample as a whole, these twenty-two churches have grown in numbers 127.4 percent during the postwar period. However, if we look at the figures for individual churches in the sample we note that between 1948 and 1971 four churches register growth of more than 500 percent,

APPENDIX 1 (*Continued*)

1967[b]			1971[d]					
Baptized Members	*Organized Congre-gations*	*Ordained Ministers*	*Baptized Members*	*Organized Congre-gations*	*Ordained Ministers*	*Percent Growth 1948-71*	*Average Annual Percent Growth 1960-64*	*Average Annual Percent Growth 1964-71*
65,000	200	19	72,492	300	30	935.6	12.5	20.2
819,172	1,365	232	916,363	1,467	276	82.2	1.9	2.1
220,000	390	35	220,000	350	53	52.4	1.8	1.1
15,500	40	25	18,890	38	21	277.8	1.6	12.7
n.a.	('65) 14	10	7,896	43	16	17.7	7.1	5.2
76,500	149	130	121,500	174	136	588.9	2.5	27.2
27,000	16	33	38,000	22	32	775	37.7	16.6
85,000	79	70	126,000	92	74	215	9.2	14.4
67,667	300	66	90,000	301	60	332.6	6.9	13.5
6,900	32	17	5,000	33	11	161.8	14.5	0.76
31,934	371	44	43,121	52	50	559.3	7.3	14.10
200,000	275	108	170,000	305	84	87.8	4.7	1.4
500,000	502	110	500,000	525	110	70.2	2.2	2.1
30,600	95	7	34,833	100	14	109.2	0.0	5.5
126,467	339	56	125,000	254	68	61.1	—6.6	2.7
185,000	297	43	162,700	347	60	442.2	14.0	—0.75
6,611	32	13	9,000	36	14	188.5	7.4	19.7
50,000	240	20	82,000	280	25	173.3	0.0	11.6
180,000	800	70	360,000	800	77	260	8.6[g]	17.9
650,000	1,258	125	517,779	1,253	106	158.9	12.5	2.15
380,000	673	403	425,000	648	407	112.5	—1.2	7.8
65,873[e]	834	170	84,320			390.0	n.a.	18.9
3,789,224	8,299	1,797	4,129,894	7,220	1,727	127.4	4.4	4.4
1,907,227			2,538,070			220.9	5.65	8.4

This chart represents a sample of half the churches in the Council of Churches, those on which comparable statistics could be assembled. In the writer's judgment it represents fairly the situation of the larger and older church bodies in Indonesia, except that none of the nine churches in which Chinese Indonesians predominate is included in this sample. These are all relatively small and young churches compared with the others.

nine exceed 250 percent, and seven are between 100 and 250 percent. Six are well below 100 percent. The lowest growth rate for this period is 17.7 percent and the highest is 935.6 percent. For the period 1960-64, before the coup, five churches registered 10 percent growth per year. But at the other extreme seven churches were below 2.5 percent per year, the rate of natural growth for Indonesia. Thus it is clear that the growth rates for the churches vary greatly due to a variety of factors.

For the post-coup period (1967-71) two churches (the Karo Batak and central Java churches) registered an annual growth rate in excess of 20 percent, while ten churches grew over 10 percent per year. Seven churches, however, were below 2.5 percent. Ten churches showed a substantially higher annual growth rate for 1967-71 than for the pre-coup period. Twelve churches were above the average annual growth rate (4.4 percent) for 1960-64, showing conclusively that a large numerical increase was already underway in the period before the coup. For the period 1967-71, however, fourteen churches were in excess of the average rate of 4.4 percent.

What generalizations may be drawn regarding the fastest-growing churches? Of the six churches with an annual growth rate exceeding 15 percent, two are on Java—the Christian Church of Java (Christian Reformed) and the Evangelical Christian Church on Java (Mennonite)—and one is on Sumatra—the Karo Batak Protestant church (Reformed in background). These three are all ethnic churches using the vernacular language rather than Indonesian in most church activities. The other three—the Southeast Sulawesi Protestant church, the Evangelical Christian church in West Irian, and the Gospel Tabernacle church—are composed of people from several ethnic groups and generally use the Indonesian rather than the vernacular language; the first two are Reformed in background and the third is Christian and Missionary Alliance related, and they are all in east Indonesia. Five of these six churches are in areas where the majority is not Christian, three of them being in strongly Islamic regions. The one exception is the West Irian church, where Protestants already constitute 64.6 percent of the population (and Roman Catholics another 14.3 percent). Only one of these six is a national rather than a regional church—the Gospel Tabernacle church, which concentrates on Kalimantan and West Irian but also has congregations in southeast Indonesia, Bali, and Java. Four of these six churches have strong evangelism programs.

Can any generalizations be made regarding the seven churches whose growth rate is below the population growth rate for Indonesia (2.5 percent)? Five of the seven are ethnic churches in regions where the population is already largely Christian, nominally at least. They are the Nias and Toba Batak churches in north Sumatra, with German national church (including Lutheran) backgrounds; the Minahasa and Sangihe-Talaud churches, and the Timor church, all with Dutch Reformed background, the first two in north Sulawesi and the third in southeast Indonesia. The final two are also ethnic churches in the Dutch Reformed tradition, but they are located in areas where the population is predominantly non-Christian (the Toradja and Balinese churches). Only two of these seven have a vigorous mission and evangelism outreach (the Batak and Balinese churches).

To examine the growing churches from the standpoint of geography, those areas where relatively large numbers of people are becoming Christians and the church is growing rapidly are east and central Java, Karo-land in north Sumatra, and east and west Kalimantan (Borneo).

The four Javanese churches in east and central Java are neither large nor, with one exception, small in numbers. They are well organized and fairly competently led, and they all have a very active evangelistic outreach. Their witness takes place among a people overwhelmingly Islamic in tradition. For many that tradition is weak, being heavily mixed with Javanistic (Hindu-Buddhist-animist) beliefs and practices. It is from this grouping that most of the converts have come. The other major grouping, perhaps numerically somewhat smaller, holds strongly and practices vigorously its Islamic traditions and beliefs. It is from this quarter that the Javanese churches receive strong pressures and often open antipathy. Following the coup this group tried to force all nominal Muslims to deepen their belief and faithfully practice the five pillars of Islam. But in many towns and villages this "hard-sell" approach backfired, leading significant numbers—at times whole villages—to opt for Christianity and to request instruction from the church. Also, social and political factors—nationalism, rapid social change, modernization, and urbanization—have contributed to creating a spiritual climate receptive to the Christian evangel. Thus in east and central Java active witness by word and life by the Christian community and a favorable, open environment have combined to lead many to accept Christ. The quiet but solid witness of church schools, medical programs, and social-economic outreach has touched at one time or another many of the Javanese, who later opt for Christian faith and the church.

The second region which has witnessed large-scale turning to the church is Karo Batak-land in north Sumatra. The Karos are one of the smaller Batak ethnic groups and inhabit an area perhaps somewhat less advanced than that of either their Batak or Malay neighbors on the east coast. The drive for education and political, social, and economic advancement is very strong among them. They see in the Christian faith and church a new and open way, a means of modernizing and giving positive content to their daily lives. In seeking to understand the widespread turning of the Karo people to the gospel and the church, the political situation immediately preceding and following the September 30 (1965) movement must be properly assessed. In the clashing competition and infighting prior to the coup the Christian community—a very small, vulnerable minority—stood steady and firm. Then in the profound turbulence following the coup, when many were seeking a new orientation and loyalty and a modern faith to replace tribal religion, the Christian gospel and community presented an attractive alternative. Again the educational, medical, and social witness of the church was a contributing source for the swelling stream of Karos coming into the church.

The third major area of new church growth is west and east Kalimantan. The situation there is significantly different from the two areas described above. Due to the impact of political events and struggles already referred to, the economic exploitation of the rich timber and mineral resources, and the evangelistic witness of many new missionary groups—including the Christian and Missionary Alliance, Regions Beyond Missionary Union, Conservative Baptists, Overseas Missionary Fellowship, and various Pentecostal groups—many Chinese and Dayaks are turning to Christ and joining His church. The major church body on this huge island is the Evangelical Church of Kalimantan, with headquarters in Banjarmasin, south Kalimantan, whose outreach until recently has been concentrated in central Kalimantan. Under the new, promising conditions that have already opened up, however, pastors and evangelists are being sent to west and east Kalimantan as well. The people to be reached live in isolated areas and have their own language and traditions. Many are ready to turn from their tribal beliefs and practices to the Christian gospel. The wide field of Kalimantan is "ripe to the harvest," but the laborers are few and the small Dayak settlements spread over east and west Kalimantan are difficult to reach.

In addition to these major areas of substantial new church growth there are two regions of less extensive but no less exciting opportunity: Bengkulu on the west coast of south Sumatra, and south Sulawesi, especially the Salayar island. These are regions where Islam is deep-rooted and claims the loyalty of the majority, but the manifest spiritual hunger on the part of small but significant groups of people is being fed by the churches. Since the Minangkabau in west Sumatra and the Buginese-Makasarese in south Sulawesi are famous for their fanatic adherence to Islam, many people are watching the spread of the gospel in these two areas with intense interest and concern.

Several books have been published recently which highlight "revival in Indonesia," "miracles in Indonesia," and "movements of the Spirit." Much of their content can be considered descriptions of new church growth and outreach. However, there is one area which has experienced what may properly be called a revival—namely, the island of Timor.

Beginning in late 1965, under the influence of the preaching and leadership of teachers and students from the Indonesia Evangelists' Institute in Batu, east Java, there broke out, largely within the Evangelical Christian church of Timor, a classic revival movement, characterized by widespread confession of sin and repentance, yielding up and subsequent destruction of charms and fetishes, intense witnessing, and praying and preaching by youth teams called by the Holy Spirit to leave their work and homes for a time to serve the gospel. Hundreds and hundreds of people of all ages, both male and female, were engaged in this revival movement, which was centered in the mountain communities of central Timor. The movement was termed "classic" because it was accompanied by a wide range of spiritual phenomena: a variety of "miracles" were reported, covering all the kinds of miraculous happenings recorded in the Bible; during the height of the movement, from 1966 through 1969, many team members reported receiving direct and specific guidance from the Holy Spirit by voice, vision, or dream. These gifts of the Spirit were earnestly sought by many people through intense private and group prayer and fasting.

It is much easier to describe a movement such as the Timor revival than it is to evaluate it. With regard to the writings by outsiders, there is without doubt much exaggeration and glorification of the spectacular, especially as regards the so-called miracles reported to have taken place. However, it is an unquestionable fact that a real revival did occur in central Timor, bringing blessing and renewal of spiritual life to thousands of people. Scores of young people gave themselves for full-time witness to the gospel, left Timor for training at Batu, and then scattered to preach and witness in the power and blessing of the Holy Spirit.

> This is not a new phenomenon. Revivals of this kind, and even larger, have occurred several times this century in Timor. The last revival occurred during the last year of the Second World War. Indeed, many of the people who threw away their idols in this revival were the very people who were "converted" in the last one. A revival may count for little unless the people touched by it can be taught, encouraged, brought into the fellowship of the Church, and established in a close and deep relationship with the Lord. There are many parallels between this revival and the last. . . . The movement has, for the time being, run its course. One may say it is finished, because when revival comes again it will be seen as a new movement. In the meantime the work of teaching and consolidation, of pastoral and spiritual care, must go on. (From a personal letter to the editor from Rev. Gordon Dicker, experienced former missionary to New Guinea from Australia.)

APPENDIX 2

Recommendations for Church Growth

The facts of church growth amid the Indonesian religious situation drive irresistibly to several conclusions. These will be stated in the form of recommendations to the Baptists of Indonesia.[25] The recommendations are purely personal.

1. Make full use of survey materials and insights.
2. Win the winnable now.
3. Plant churches in homogeneous units. The statistics have demonstrated that unusual growth is taking place in those churches planted among the homogeneous units of Indonesian population.
4. Accept the idea of home churches and unpaid pastors.
5. Design theological education to meet the demands of growth. There must be developed some form of extension training that can equip the pastors in their own locality to better lead their people and disciple their neighbors.
6. Use heart languages.
7. Encourage local church outreach.
8. Produce indigenous literature.
9. Come to grips with subsidization. All subsidy is not wrong. Even Nevius, the champion of self-support, used mission funds for his month-long training courses. The great danger of subsidy is that the churches will continue to be dependent on mission funds for their day-to-day needs.
10. Seek service opportunities. The natural result of genuine revival and true church growth is an increasing social awareness.
11. Nurture churches in developmental growth. As new churches multiply in ever-increasing numbers they must not neglect the nurture of the congregations already planted.
12. Adjust church polity to Indonesian life.
13. Find valid contact with the animistically oriented peoples of Indonesia. It has been seen that the Indonesian religious scene is at least in major respects animistically oriented, even among followers of one of the great religions. . . . In approaching animistically oriented peoples the missionary must keep in mind the need for functional substitutes. To reject cultural ways of providing peace in the face of felt needs is to leave a cultural void and invite relapses to pre-Christian ways and/or syncretistic adaptations of the Christian message. Functional substitutes supply the felt needs of the people without non-Christian meanings. They not only satisfy the felt need but also bring about a closer congregational involvement in the act of worship itself.

NOTES

1. Ebbie C. Smith, *God's Miracles*, p. 13.
2. Ibid., p. 105.

3. Ibid., pp. 81, 83. Citations in parentheses refer to other works listed in bibliography.
4. Ibid., p. 119.
5. James Sunda, *Church Growth in the Central Highlands of West New Guinea*, pp. 16, 17.
6. Ibid., pp. 26-28.
7. Smith, p. 117.
8. *COFAE Newsletter*, Oct. 1971.
9. Taken from the National Social and Economic Survey (1971) and quoted in the daily newspaper *Berita Yuda*.
10. *1971 Census Report*.
11. Frank L. Cooley, *Indonesia: Church and Society*. Other sources quote as low as $50 for the year 1969.
12. "Indonesian Educational Planning" (1968 UNESCO report). Other sources, using different literacy standards, show literacy rates of 45-60%.
13. Smith, pp. 3, 4.
14. G. W. Skinner, *The Chinese Minority*, ed. R. McVey, p. 97.
15. W. B. Sidjabat, ed., *Panggilan Kita di Indonesia dewasa ini* [Our Calling in Indonesia Today] (Djakarta: Badan Penerbit Kristen, 1963).
16. Ibid., p. 30.
17. Cooley, "Altar and Throne in Central Moluccan Society," p. 343.
18. Muller-Kruger, *Sedjarah Geredja di Indonesia* [The History of the Church in Indonesia] (Djakarta: Badan Penerbit Kristen, 1959).
19. Ibid., pp. 52, 59; see also Stephen Neill, *Colonialism*, p. 179.
20. I. H. Enklaar, *Joseph Kam*.
21. Nellie Dewaard, *Pioneer in Sumatra*. This may be the only English-language account of Nommensen's life.
22. Ibid., pp. 349-50.
23. Muller-Kruger, pp. 112-14.
24. Hendrick Kraemer, *From Mission Field to Independent Church*; David Bentley-Taylor, *The Weathercock's Reward*.
25. Smith, pp. 194-200.

BIBLIOGRAPHY

Bentley-Taylor, David. *The Weathercock's Reward*. London: Overseas Missionary Fellowship, 1967.

Beyerhaus, Peter, and Lefever, Harry. *The Responsible Church and Foreign Missions*. Grand Rapids: William B. Eerdmans, 1964.

Bradshaw, Mac. "A Hand Moving in Indonesia." *East Asia's Millions* 75 (1967): 6:81-83.

Bryan, Gainer. "Indonesia: Turmoil Amid Revival," *Christianity Today* 12 (1967):312-13.

———. "The Pacific: Scene of Miracles Today." *Christian Life* 29 (1968), 12: 47-49.

Cooley, Frank L. "A Church Reformed and Reforming." *IRM* 51 (1962: 26-32.

———. "Altar and Throne in Central Moluccan Society." Ph.D. dissertation, Yale University, 1966.

———. *Indonesia: Church and Society*. New York: Friendship Press, 1968.

———. Letter to Ebbie C. Smith, 1970.

Dewaard, Nellie. *Pioneer in Sumatra*. London: China Inland Mission.

Enklaar, I. H. *Joseph Kam*. Djakarta: Badan Penerbit Kristen, 1960.

Kraemer, Hendrick. *Agama Islam*. Djakarta: Badan Penerbitan Kristen, 1952.

———. *From Mission Field to Independent Church.* The Hague: Boekencentrum, 1958.

Middelkoop, Pieter. *Curse—Retribution—Enmity.* Amsterdam: Jacob van Campen, 1960.

Muller-Kruger, Th. *Sedjarah Geredja di Indonesia* [The History of the Church in Indonesia]. Djakarta: Badan Penerbitan Kristen, 1959.

Neill, Stephen. *Colonialism and Christian Missions.* London: Lutterworth Press, 1966.

Scheunemann, Detmar. "Our God Is Marching On." *Thrust* 6 (1969), 5:1-3.

Smith, Ebbie C. *God's Miracles: Indonesian Church Growth.* Pasadena: William Carey Library, 1970. This work contains an excellent bibliography on pages 201-14. Numerous other works on early Indonesian missions are available in the Dutch language.

Sunda, James. *Church Growth in the Central Highlands of West New Guinea.* Lucknow, India: Lucknow Publishing House, 1963.

Tari, Mel. *Like a Mighty Wind.* Chicago: Creation House, 1971.

Warneck, G. "The Growth of the Church Among the Bataks." *IRM* 1 (1912): 20-43.

Warneck, John. *The Living Christ and Dying Heathenism.* Translated by Neil Buchanan. New York: Fleming H. Revell Co.

Shinto priest walking on bed of hot coals

Photo by Stars and Stripes; T. Varnel

12

JAPAN: A BRIEF CHRISTIAN HISTORY

by Gordon H. Chapman

Introduction

Dynamic Japan, a tiny island chain now throbbing with over a hundred million people, a land with only meager mineral resources and with only 16 percent of its land arable, is almost impossible to explain by usual canons. Former U.S. ambassador Edwin Reischauer suggests that Japan's very geographic isolation has been the most important determinant throughout its history.

This isolation has protected Japan from military and other external pressures. It has preserved her divergences from the general trends and cultural patterns of east Asian civilization. It has allowed her civilization to develop under her own internal evolutionary forces. For only twice—during the period of the Chinese T'ang dynasty (A.D. 618-906) and during the past hundred years of western influence—has Japan drawn heavily from the outside for her own culture and economy.

Though the Japanese have keen eclectic gifts and are highly innovative in their own right—not merely copycats—their isolation has contributed to a rare degree of culture conservation, with the result that the old is retained along with the new. But there was a high degree of selectivity in the historical process, and only those elements of foreign culture were welcomed which seemed good for Japan. Thus, although the Japanese embraced Mahayana Buddhism along with Chinese culture in the seventh and eighth centuries, parliamentary government introduced from the West in the Meiji period (1868-1912) was minus the underlying Christian presuppositions.

Geographic isolation may also account for the fact that the Japanese constitute a highly homogeneous race and culture, representing an ancient

For information on author, see chapter 8, "Christianity Comes to Asia."

blend of diverse elements which are not now easy to identify. However, it is now generally agreed that they are mainly Mongoloid, with a fairly close kinship to the Chinese and Koreans.

Japan has been called "the department store of religions," for here numerous sects, tailored to meet the emotional and practical needs of the natural man, are available in great abundance. This apparent religiosity has been characterized by a broad tolerance or even indifference to alien faiths, except as these seem to violate accepted social custom or are deemed inimical to the state, and persecution has been rather rare (the notable exception being the widespread persecution of Christians in the sixteenth and seventeenth centuries). In the absence of strong metaphysical and philosophical gifts, both religious response and expression tend to be empiric and practical, and the varied needs of an individual Japanese have often been met by adherence to several faiths. Thus the grand totals of religious adherents every year are considerably in excess of the total population.

Buddhism first commended itself to the Japanese mainly as an attractive vehicle of Chinese culture and an aid to political consolidation, rather than for its mystic and ascetic practices. Confucianism was attractive because of its ethical system, rather than for its philosophy and its attitudes toward governmental institutions. Even Roman Catholic religion was tolerated in the latter half of the sixteenth century because of Japan's desire to trade with certain Christian nations, and it was later suppressed only because their colonial expansion seemed to be closely associated with a missionary effort. But the introduction of alien religions has always involved the demand for some degree of accommodation to the native cult of Shinto, especially throughout the prewar period. This has presented a special problem for Christians because of the exclusive claims of the gospel.

Traditional Religious Heritage

It is not without significance that there was no clear differentiation between the religious and governmental functions in early Japanese society, and this is reflected in what is known as State Shinto. Thus the shamanistic animism and ancestor worship which are basic to the ceremonies, practices, and beliefs of Shinto became constituent parts of the state system. Shinto installed a reverence for nature, all of whose parts and phenomena were identified as spirit beings, or *kami* (the generic term for divinity). As there was no necessary distinction between the things of nature and man, superior men (especially the emperors) were regarded as divine until disavowed by the present emperor. There was little or no ethical content to this primitive cult, except for the emphasis on ritual purity as symbolized by bodily cleanliness.[1] Confucianism provided the ethical standards for Japanese societal structure, while Buddhism fostered notions of holiness through ascetic practices and came to terms with Shinto by designating the members of the Shinto pantheon as Bodhisattvas or Buddhas-to-be.[2] Thus the three religions were viewed as Shinto being the root, Confucianism the leaves, and Buddhism the flower and fruit of Japanese civilization. They became so interwoven during the centuries that they are now regarded as part of the common cultural heritage of the nation.

The Christian Movement in Japan

It is quite likely that Japanese visitors to China in both the T'ang (618-906) and Yuan (1260-1368) dynastic periods were influenced by Christian teaching, and it is even possible that missionaries visited Japan.[3] However, the first successful missionary effort of any proportion was that of the Roman Catholics in the latter half of the sixteenth and early part of the seventeenth centuries. Then followed a period of about 250 years when the country was secluded and all Christian activity ruthlessly suppressed. The modern Protestant missionary effort was inaugurated in the latter half of the nineteenth century.

The dynamic Jesuit Francis Xavier brought Christianity to Japan first in 1549. He found what seemed a most attractive and promising field of service and was soon reinforced by the arrival of colleagues of both his and other catholic orders, such as Franciscans and Dominicans. Their efforts met with quick and considerable success, for by 1582 there were said to be about 250 churches with 150,000 communicant members to show for the labors of 85 foreign priests and their 120 Japanese colleagues.[4]

Church membership doubled before the end of the sixteenth century and reached a peak of half a million by 1615, when the working force included 116 foreign priests and about 250 Japanese priests and catechists.[5] However, before 1650 what had been regarded as the most promising Christian movement in Asia was cruelly suppressed. Aside from a company of crypto-Christians in the neighborhood of Nagasaki (whose descendants came to light more than 200 years later), the church was exterminated and its gospel light extinguished for two centuries.

Factors in Catholic Success and Failure

How can we account for both the initial success and subsequent frustration of this early missionary enterprise? The Jesuit missionaries, who bore the brunt of the work in the formative years, were noted for their devotion to the pope and their strict discipline, scholarship, and thorough training for active accomplishment, including political intrigue. They were closely associated with the rather militant Portuguese and Spanish traders and received a considerable portion of their support from these governments and from trading operations.[6] Thus some of the feudal lords who became Christians were doubtless motivated by trade interests, and the initial toleration of the central authorities was aimed at securing the continuance of profitable trading operations. Also, the Japanese who had borrowed so much from China were still receptive to foreign ideas and other innovations, and for a time there was a rage for things Portuguese, which contributed new words to the language, such as *pan* for bread.

However, to most Japanese of this period Christianity appeared as a new Buddhist sect: the terminology resembled that of Buddhism; there were similarities in ritual, worship of images, processions, and even teachings; and the Jesuits even dressed like Zen priests. Because of their feudalistic background, the missionaries appreciated the martial skills, ideals, and chivalrous attitude of the Japanese warrior class and thus concentrated much of their effort on this select group. Also, in return for official patronage and protection the missionaries supported the familiar code of feudal ethics imposed on the lower classes and helped instill political loyalty by teaching the principles of Catholic hierarchical absolutism.[7]

Today there is no way of knowing how much of the true gospel was effectively communicated by the early Romanist missionaries. But the combination of official permission, missionary zeal, and a popular spiritual thirst bore results, some of which must have been sincere, for a goodly company of ardent believers later refused to renounce their faith and consequently suffered martyrdom under cruel torture.

The early popularity of Christianity soon provoked questions for many reasons. The Japanese converts no longer submitted easily to coercion. Roman Catholic Christianity, which had once seemed so loyal to feudalism, was now revealed as anti-feudal because of its emphasis on the rights of a person under God. With the arrival of Spanish, Dutch, and English traders in the area (in addition to the Portuguese) it became apparent that these European nations were engaged in a global trade war and a scramble for new colonies. Further, the Jesuits' opposition to the Dominican and Franciscan orders under Spanish auspices revealed that the Christians were by no means a unified body. Thus the competing nations, priests, and faiths of the West undermined one another's position and prestige in Japan and paved the way for the drastic proscription of the Christian faith.

Beginning with Hideyoshi in 1587, increasingly severe anti-Christian decrees were issued, effectively banning the western faith. Between 1597 and 1660 thousands suffered martyrdom after slow burning, crucifixion, hanging upside down, and other fiendish tortures. This climaxed with the

Shimabara rebellion, when about thirty-seven thousand Christians were slain at one time.[8] Public opinion was also turned against Christianity by increasingly bitter polemics on the part of Confucian and Buddhist writers, with the result that Christian faith came to be regarded with great fear and as an evil to be avoided.

Thus the Catholic century came to a tragic end with doors closed to the West. However the Japanese, desiring to keep at least one small window open to the West, permitted the Dutch (who had refrained from missionary activity) to maintain a small trading post on the small island of Deshima (in Nagasaki harbor) to transmit information concerning the new science and technology. This set a precedent for accepting western civilization minus Christianity, which has influenced Japanese eclectic activity since that time. The failure of the first Catholic mission to Japan reveals the fallacy of appealing to secular motives to elicit response to the gospel and also calls attention to the many dangers inherent in a policy of accommodation or compromise.

The Century of the Whole Church

INTRODUCTION

The reentry of Christian missionary forces in the mid-nineteenth century roughly coincided with the reopening of Japan to western relations and the inauguration of the modernization process. It was also contemporaneous with, and in part influenced by, the revolution which overthrew the Tokugawa hereditary and military dictatorship and ushered in the imperial restoration and elaborate reforms of the Meiji era (1868-1912).

Commodore Peary's black ships first forced open Japan's doors to the West again by visits in 1853 and 1854. He insisted on trade treaties, but these early treaties made no reference to missionaries as such and provided only for the residence of foreigners in three treaty ports (except for those in the employ of the Japanese government. But these had the right to practice their own religion and erect suitable buildings for worship. As far as the Japanese were concerned, Christianity remained a prohibited religion, punishable by death; and though the anti-Christian edict boards were removed in 1873, these penal laws were not actually rescinded until the promulgation of the new constitution in 1889, with its "freedom of religious belief" clause.[9]

But in spite of the rather unpromising situation, as soon as the treaties were ratified, not only Roman Catholic but Protestant and Eastern Orthodox missionaries almost immediately took up their residence in the treaty port cities. Though evangelistic activity during the early years was practically impossible, much was accomplished by way of preparation, and the foundation for a future fruitful enterprise was effectively laid. Of the three main branches of Christianity which entered Japan, the Protestant churches were to have the greatest growth and to exercise the most effective influence on Japanese society.

THE PROTESTANT MOVEMENT

Highly gifted men in various fields—men of spiritual depth and experience—were the first to pioneer the Protestant work in Japan, in 1859. These included James C. Hepburn, M.D. (Presbyterian), a physician, linguist, lexicographer, Scripture translator, educator, and winsome evangelist;[10] Channing M. Williams (Episcopal), the pioneer bishop and founder of Saint Paul's University and Saint Luke's Hospital of Tokyo,[11] Guido F. Verbeck (Reformed Church of America), a versatile linguist, musician, and hymnologist and a trusted counsellor of leading Japanese statesmen as well as the first head of the incipient Imperial University and a theological educator, Scripture translator, and eloquent gospel preacher;[12] and Samuel R. Brown (Reformed), pioneer of theological education, greatest of the early schoolmen, inspirer of young men to become leaders of the church, and a Scripture translator.[13] Each of these men except Verbeck was an American, and each set a pattern of American characteristics.

In the face of severe restrictions the missionaries moved with prayerful caution. At first the government authorities, anxious not to offend the treaty powers, regarded the missionary effort with a kind of permissive disapproval. Missionary activities were largely confined to the regions of the several treaty ports: Nagasaki in the southwest, Yokohama and Tokyo in the east-central area, and Hakodate in the north. The first Japanese contacts were with ambitious young samurai (warriors), bred alike to letters and to arms, who were seeking knowledge of English and occidental culture.

Dr. Guido Verbeck, the historian of the first quarter-century of missions, later summarized the achievements of this difficult period: missionaries gained the confidence and respect of many Japanese; thousands of copies of Chinese Scriptures and some Japanese tracts and Scripture portions were circulated among eager inquirers; some missionaries who had diligently studied the Japanese language were able to use it in teaching, preaching, and Scripture translation; medical dispensary work, with attendant opportunities to train Japanese physicians in western medicine, helped to disarm prejudice by the demonstrations of Christian love; and Christian schools for both sexes were established in the several areas.[14]

So within fifteen years of the arrival of the first missionaries eight foreign mission societies had twenty-nine missionaries on the field. But the number of Japanese who had been baptized was small—only ten up to 1872, though there were many more inquirers in the several communities.

The year 1872 was epochal in the history of Japanese Protestantism, for it marked the founding of the first church and the beginning of the Presbyterian and Reformed movement in Japan. A group of students in Yokohama, sons of sumurai families, had been receiving instruction from Brown, Hepburn, and J. H. Ballagh and had become increasingly interested in the Christian faith. During the New Year series of prayer meetings, held under Evangelical Alliance auspices at Yokohama, they expressed the desire to continue the prayer meetings in Japanese, in conjunction with a study of the Book of Acts, led by Dr. Ballagh, a man of devout character and deep prayer life. Something like a spiritual revival took place, for nine of the young men were soundly converted on the spot and were baptized the following March.[15]

The prayer meetings continued until the summer. This group became the nucleus of the first church, with Dr. Ballagh as the pastor. Though under the influence of Presbyterian and Reformed missionaries, it was actually established as an independent, self-supporting church with a creed based on the articles of the World Evangelical Alliance and with the name "The Church of Christ." This name was later appropriated by the Presbyterian and Reformed denomination, with which some seven missions eventually cooperated.*

The following September the missionaries of all societies held a meeting in Yokohama, at which time they approved of the undenominational character of the first church and agreed to work for such identity of name and organization in all future church developments (a unity principle which was soon violated).

When the Japanese government learned through its special mission to the western powers, originally suggested by Verbeck, that religious freedom was a prerequisite to revision of the unequal treaties, the notice boards proscribing Christianity were removed in 1873. Thus the way was open for the unfettered propagation of the gospel. As a result a new surge of interest in the evangelization of Japan spread throughout the churches of the West; the number of missionaries doubled in the year of 1873 alone, and seven new societies had entered the field by the end of the decade.

CHRISTIAN STUDENT BANDS

The government mandate to overtake the western nations by mastery of their culture and technology opened to the missionaries the channel of education as a means of circumventing the official proscription of evangelistic activity. Thus the pioneer workers focused their efforts on groups

*The seven missions were the Presbyterian Church USA, Presbyterian Church US, Cumberland Presbyterian Church, Reformed Church in America, Reformed Church in the U.S. (German), the Women's Union Missionary Society, and the United Presbyterian Church of Scotland (H. Ritter, *History of Protestant Missions in Japan,* p. 183).

of young samurai who were bent on taking a lead in the modernization movement. As a result the early indigenous leadership of the Protestant churches was mainly recruited from these elite groups of students. Five such Christian student bands were raised up within this decade and, in part at least, determined the formation and character of as many important Protestant groupings.

The Yokohama Band furnished the nucleus of the first indigenous church in Japan and was the spearhead of the evangelical movement. As disciples of the early outstanding Presbyterian and Reformed missionaries, these young men gave leadership to the Church of Christ in Japan, the largest of the prewar denominations. From among these men came eminent leaders of the church: Masahisa Uemera, pastor, theologian, writer, and editor; Masatsuna Okuno, hymnwriter and forerunner of a long succession of nationwide evangelists; and Kajinosuke Ibuka, president of the Presbyterian Reformed college, voluminous writer, preacher, and evangelist.[16]

Meanwhile, in extreme southwest Japan, on recommendation of Dr. Verbeck, Capt. L. L. Janes, a former instructor of West Point, was employed in 1871 to head a clan school which was to be paramilitary in character. He and his devout and praying wife immediately impressed the young samurai students, and after the ban against Christianity was lifted he openly used the Bible and prayed for Japan and the students. As a result within five years, by 1876, thirty-five of these samurai were converted and in their own blood signed a solemn covenant to stand fast in the faith and go forth to enlighten the darkness of Japan with the gospel of Christ.

Fierce persecution broke out but the majority did not flinch even under threat of death. But Janes was discharged and the school was closed. Fortunately, just at that time Rev. Jo (Joseph Hardy) Niishima, with the cooperation of the American Board (Congregational), was struggling to get a Christian college started in Kyoto on land adjacent to the palace grounds. Janes commended a substantial number of the most promising students to Niishima, and they constituted the first class of what came to be known as Doshisha University, where they were nicknamed the Kumamoto Band. This group included at least a score of the early leaders of Japanese Protestantism and was influential in establishing the Japanese Congregational church. These young men started well but were animated by a strong spirit of nationalism. Many later became liberal and turned Doshisha University in that direction.[17]

The third influential Christian student group was raised up on the northern island of Hokkaido, the fruit of an effective lay witness by Dr. W. S. Clark, world-renowned botanist and president of the Massachusetts Agricultural College, who in 1876 established a similar institution at Sapporo. An earnest Christian, Clark was determined to make the most of his opportunity, and he successfully insisted that he could not teach ethics without the Bible. As a result of his faithful Christian witness during a stay of only eleven months, the whole of the first class of fifteen students was converted and applied for baptism. Such was the Christian enthusiasm of these sons of the samurai families that the sixteen members of the second class were also led to Christ; these were the Sapporo Band of thirty-one, who signed the "Covenant of Believers in Jesus," written by Clark himself on March 5, 1877.

The most outstanding member of this group was Kanzo Uchimura, the founder of the so-called *mukyokai* or "non-church," an individualistic type of Japanese Christianity. Uchimura was a devout student of the Word, an accomplished expositor and Bible teacher, and the editor of a magazine called *Bible Study,* which became the most widely read Christian journal in Japan. Uchimura's twenty-seven books have been repeatedly reprinted and continue to inspire sound Bible study. Hundreds of non-church related Bible study groups have been meeting regularly since his day, with a total nationwide attendance at times ranging from thirty to fifty thousand.[18]

Less well-known, yet influential in the development of early leadership for particular denominations, the Osaka Band included the students chiefly influenced by Bishop Channing M. Williams, an Episcopal pioneer, from which were recruited leaders for the *Seikokai* or Anglican Communion in Japan. Another Christian student group developed at Hirosaki, in north Honshu, from which more than two hundred men and women went into full-time Christian service with the Methodist church. Most influential among these was Yoichi Honda, a member of the original Yokohama Band, who became first bishop of the denomination.[19]

The decade of the 1870's was one of remarkable growth for the infant church. By the end of the decade Protestants had established about a hundred churches, with some five thousand members, 150 missionaries, and fifty Japanese-ordained clergy, not to mention many evangelists and Bible women. There were also seven theological schools, about seventy other educational institutions at various levels, numerous medical dispensaries and clinics, and many growing Sunday schools. Christian literature was being published in Japanese—the New Testament in 1880 and the Old Testament in 1888—and the first popular Christian periodical appeared in 1875.

But there were still potent forces in society which continued to oppose the Christian movement. Anti-Christian laws were not repealed until the promulgation of the new Constitution in 1889. Nationalism, based on a Confucian ethic centered in the person of the emperor, was being fostered through the general education system and the official rites of state Shinto.

The Buddhists charged that Christianity was an alien religion which was opposed to the traditional ancestor worship and was inimical to the Japanese spirit and customs. Furthermore, Christians tended to sympathize with and support the cause of the poor and afflicted rather than that of the government, which was inclined to support big business and rich landlords.

REVIVAL AND RAPID GROWTH (1883-89)

So as the Christian forces prepared for the special conferences to be held in 1883, it was in a spirit of high expectation and yet with deep concern over the mounting opposition, especially from reactionary forces in the government. The annual week of prayer, sponsored by the World Evangelical Alliance, found all the Japanese churches uniting in prayer meetings, which in some cases continued for a month or more. As a direct result the fires of revival began to burn, first in the churches and Christian schools of Yokohama and then in Tokyo and later Osaka.

Continuous prayer was especially offered for the Second General Conference of Protestant Missionaries, to be held in Osaka in April, and the meeting of the Evangelical Alliance of Churches at Tokyo, in May. The tone for the former conference was set by the powerful opening address of Dr. James H. Ballagh on "the need and promise of the power of the Holy Spirit in our work as missionaries, as we carry out the great commission." The spirit of unity and heartfelt expectation and enthusiasm evidenced among the 107 missionaries, representing eighteen missions and four Bible societies, deeply impressed the Japanese brethren present, whose hearts had already been warmed by the fires of revival. This conference marked a shift from missionary domination to indigenous leadership, for many churches were already standing on their own feet.

At the communion service which climaxed the meetings of the Evangelical Alliance of churches in the following month (attended by some six hundred Japanese brethren and a goodly number of missionaries) all the people burst into tears and their hearts were melted in mutual love, with perfect unity between the native brethren and the missionaries, who were happily united in the Lord. Proud and successful ministers confessed their faults to one another, especially the sin of prideful self-seeking and ingratitude toward the missionaries. The delegates returned to their praying churches like new men who had received fresh light, grace, and power from on high.[20] Soon letters and reports reflected the joyful accounts of nationwide revival. Certain constantly recurring features stood out: the genuine conversion of nominal church members; restitution made for wrongs; the experience of the filling of the Holy Spirit with a passion for the souls of the lost; and renewal of evangelistic witness and service.

But these revivals often were the prelude to persecution instigated by the Buddhists. Churches were attacked with rocks, which in one case were so large as to provide suitable "persecution stones" for the foundation of the new church structure. Christian schools also experienced revival; Doshisha College, for example, was obliged to suspend its classes to give converted students time to return to their homes to witness.

Within three years the number of churches had doubled, church membership had increased by 300 percent, and the number of communicants of the average congregation had tripled. By 1890 there were some 297 Protestant churches, with a membership of about thirty-four thousand, representing more than a threefold increase in the number of churches and an 800 percent increase in church membership within a decade. Professor Yasuo Furuya of the International Christian University regards this time of renewal as an important part of the "maturing process" in the Japanese church, "the important turning point in the understanding and the grasping of the truth of the Gospel among Japanese Christians."[21]

Meanwhile, anti-Christian philosophies and liberal theologies were troubling the church. Unitarianism and the radical German theology with its destructive criticism were being advocated among the intelligentsia, not only by Unitarian missionaries from abroad but also by the Japanese who had studied in western lands. Reaction to this western rationalism within the church, however, stimulated the first Christian apologetic in Japan.

The renewal and rapid growth of the eighties proved to be preparation for a period of testing and persecution. The nineties was perhaps the most crucial period of all for the development of the Christian movement during the next fifty years. When the latest efforts to secure revision of the unequal treaties with western powers failed, a wave of disillusionment and disgust with all things western swept the nation. Christianity as a part of western culture was regarded by many as incompatible with the new nationalism.

The new constitution, granted under popular pressure and patterned largely after the Prussian model, was promulgated by the emperor Meiji in 1889. It actually repudiated both the concept of the natural rights of man and the equality of all men before God. It established an official cult of national absolutism and legalized state Shinto, based on emperor worship, with twenty-nine shrines given special status as "national shrines." This strengthened the concept of a national family-state centered around the emperor as the father-head, who according to the constitution was "sacred and inviolate." The Imperial Rescript on Education was issued in October 1890 and further aggravated the inevitable conflict with Christianity. It referred to the imperial throne as "coeval with heaven and earth" and asserted that the "way set forth" was "the teaching bequeathed by our Imperial Ancestors—being infallible for all ages and true in all places." The government distributed to the schools copies of the rescript, together with the imperial portraits, which were regarded as sacrosanct.

As the custom of worshipping before the imperial portrait or rescript spread, people increasingly felt that anyone who refused to do so was disloyal. Kanzo Uchimura ran afoul of the rescript when as a schoolteacher he refused to bow in obeisance before it and was obliged to resign from his post. Thus the small and struggling church in Japan was confronted with the problem of idolatrous bowing to the portrait or else facing imprisonment—a problem of conscience which was to perplex it until after the Pacific War.

In addition, the designated national shrines were placed under the jurisdiction of the Home Ministry of the government, though religions were usually under the Ministry of Education. Thus Shinto ceremonies which were patently religious were construed as non-religious, and pressure was imposed on all loyal Japanese to participate in shrine visitation as a patriotic duty. This severe test to the Christians was augmented by resurgent Buddhist opposition. And within the church rising tides of liberalism provoked controversy. Though most church members were not greatly influenced by the new theology, there were several prominent leaders and many nominal Christians who fell away. This brought the orthodox churches to the defense in lengthy theological discussions which prepared the way for the formulation of several brief but sound confessional statements. The pressures literally brought the church to its knees during the week of prayer in 1894. Revival resulted in the Nagoya churches, spreading to Yokohama, Kobe, and other places. Christians whose faith had grown cold confessed their sins and were spurred to new evangelistic endeavors. Moreover, with the inauguration of successful negotiations for the revision of the unequal treaties with western powers, missionaries were freed at last from the restrictions which had limited their extensive evangelistic endeavor in the interior provinces for about forty years. The clouds appeared to be lightening.

There were two fields in which the Christian forces showed great vitality and which served to commend Christianity to the unbelieving world, namely, education and social welfare. The majority of those who became Christians in that era did so while students in Christian schools.

Thus for a decade some government officials attempted to stop the schools with restrictive laws, but these were withdrawn in 1901, and the schools continued aggressive witnessing. Sunday schools were another very flourishing aspect of Christian growth in the 1890's, and their increase was practically threefold. The YMCA movement, under the leadership of

Dr. John R. Mott, developed in this period, and annual summer conferences conducted after the manner of the Northfield Student Conferences (founded by D. L. Moody) were productive in training such leaders as Gumpei Yamamuro, who was to head the Salvation Army in Japan.

Christians pioneered much of the social welfare work in Japan during this period, with lasting results far out of proportion to the Christian community. Christians were usually foremost in rendering aid in times of natural disaster, as in the great Gifu earthquake. Christian medical work continued to develop, though the rapid progress of Japanese medicine led later to an almost complete withdrawal from this type of missionary work except for leprosariums, TB sanitariums and medical care for the poor. The visit of George Muller to Japan awakened Christian concern for the many orphans, and soon orphanages and nurseries for unfortunate children were established and have been an important part of Christian effort since that time. The WCTU was organized throughout Japan and had a great impact for temperance, purity, and peace, establishing numerous homes for the rehabilitation of unfortunate girls. The Salvation Army joined in the rescue of victims of licensed prostitution and in other works of mercy. Thus in this rather difficult period the association of the Christian faith with acts of mercy and moral reform contributed to the development of a more favorable public opinion.

By the end of the century the picture was not totally dark; the wave of opposition had subsided. New missionaries, particularly many of "holiness" persuasion, had swelled the force of evangelists from 583 to 723, and the Japan Holiness church had burgeoned, becoming the fifth-largest denomination. Church growth in the decade of 1889-99 had increased from 32,354 to 43,273 Protestants, who met in 416 churches and preaching places. The church marched on![22]

Japan entered the twentieth century having already achieved a high degree of modernization. The industrial revolution had been accomplished with a minimum of dislocation to the societal order. Capital had been amassed to finance a large-scale military outlay. A victory over China had brought Japan into direct confrontation with Russia as both nations sought to exploit their territorial and economic advantages in northeast Asia.

But the unsatisfactory nature of the terms of the settlement following the victory over Russia, the denial of equality to Japan at the Versailles Conference in 1919, and the anti-Japanese legislation in the U.S. in 1924 all contributed to anti-Christian sentiment. Indeed, what gave Japanese nationalism its special character is that it represented basically a reaction against western cultural expansion and therefore, in some measure, a reaction against Christianity as one phase of this expansion.

So hard days for the church began to return. Japan's expansionist policies throughout Asia kept her at war for almost thirty years. These aggressive policies aroused adverse public opinion in the other nations, with the result that Japan became virtually isolated and ostracized. So the ruling oligarchy of Japan promoted the idea of a theocratic state based on the teachings of state or shrine Shinto, which demanded implicit loyalty to the throne and obedience to the authorities. Its rites were declared to be patriotic and non-religious and therefore obligatory for all citizens, Christians included. Efforts to secure government control of all religions through legislation had been going on from the beginning of the century. The instrument which finally achieved the control was the "Religious Bodies Law" of 1939, which was enforced the following year. Thus the totalitarian pattern of militaristic Japan included the regimentation of religion, with control facilitated by the forced union of all religious sects. Thus the twentieth century brought steadily increasing pressure on the church, with ultimately disastrous effects.

But notwithstanding these mounting problems the Protestant churches continued to grow and were numerically the largest and most active wing of Christianity in Japan. By 1913, the end of the Meiji era, Protestants numbered 102,790, more than Roman Catholic and Eastern Orthodox churches combined.[23] In the next twenty years Protestants doubled again, until by 1941 there were 233,463 listed, the majority being in the big five: Presbyterian-Reformed, Congregational, Methodist, Episcopal, and Holiness churches (the number of missionaries peaked at 1524 in 1925.)[24]

For mutual encouragement, strength, and witness, for many years Japanese Protestant churches had banded together in the Evangelical Alliance, patterned closely after the World Evangelical Alliance, of which it was a member. This became a Federation of the Japanese Churches in 1911, which in turn was superseded by the National Christian Council in 1922, which continues to this day. Of all the Alliance's cooperative efforts the most conspicuously successful during the first thirty-five years of the century were the united evangelistic campaigns. These had the support of virtually all Protestant bodies. The Twentieth Century (or Forward Evangelistic) Campaign lasted for three years and had the participation of most churches, with laymen serving as personal workers both in house-to-house visitation and at the meetings, and the follow-up was thoroughgoing. The total attendance was between three and four hundred thousand, and decisions for Christ numbered about sixteen thousand.

During this campaign and thereafter such well-known evangelists as R. A. Torrey, William Booth, H. Gratten Guinness, John R. Mott, and Sherwood Eddy held meetings in Japan. Another Japanese evangelist of nationwide influence emerged, Seimatsu Kimura, and became known as the Billy Sunday of Japan. Regional campaigns were held, the most notable being the one conducted in connection with the Osaka National Exposition in 1903. Some 246,000 people attended these meetings out of a total exposition attendance of about three million.

Denominations conducted their own "forward drives," with wide lay participation. In 1907 so-called "concentration evangelism," comparable to the modern "evangelism-in-depth," was introduced with the slogan "one Christian teach the one gospel to one person."

The Church Federation launched another nationwide evangelistic effort from 1914-16, an effort which proved to be the most determined and comprehensive united Christian witness yet launched. More than a hundred prominent ministers and laymen undertook preaching tours to the various needy areas of Japan, and fifteen hundred workers in Tokyo distributed gospels and tracts to every home in the City. This campaign was marked by the first use of newspaper evangelism on a national scale, with articles on the Christian faith inserted in the secular press, together with an invitation for inquirers to correspond with a central office and enroll in Bible correspondence courses. At least 90 percent of the Protestant churches cooperated in this campaign and were encouraged by many professions of faith, increased church attendance, and the deepening of spiritual life. During this period another outstanding evangelist of nationwide influence was raised up, Tsurin Kanamori of the Kumamoto Band. For years he packed the largest available halls throughout the land with eager listeners to his three-hour sermon on "God, Sin, and Salvation." Having once been led astray by the new theology, he often said, "our country needs the true and pure Gospel of Jesus Christ and Him crucified, and not a counterfeit or diluted one."

This era witnessed a new dimension of evangelism in the person and work of Toyohiko Kagawa, whose activity continued until 1960. In a unique manner, Kagawa's ministry combined a basic biblical gospel proclamation with a life of identification with the needs of the poor, the outcast, and the fallen. Kagawa became an ardent advocate of people's rights, and exerted himself on behalf of downtrodden minorities, organizing cooperatives for farmers and fishermen. To conserve the results of his evangelistic campaigns, Kagawa also gathered inquirers into "Friends of Jesus" societies, a number of which eventually became churches which combined Bible study with subjects calculated to help build up a more wholesome rural life. These churches became a permanent part of the Christian impact on rural Japan. In the late 1920's Kagawa set the goal of a million souls for Christ, which developed into a "kingdom of God" movement emphasizing both individual conversion and the social application of the gospel.

In spite of several imprisonments during the Pacific War and multiple health problems, Kagawa did not lose his evangelistic vision and took the initiative immediately after the war in launching another nationwide evangelistic effort. More than two hundred thousand people signed decision cards, and inquirers were enrolled in Friends of Jesus societies when the fellowship of a nearby church was not available.[25]

Kagawa was a unique and controversial figure. Though at times neither conservatives nor liberals would claim him, he quickened the social consciousness of the Christian forces. Furthermore, Kagawa preached the gospel and made immeasurable contributions to the lower classes of Japanese, with the result that they were given a favorable impression of Christianity.

JAPANESE OVERSEAS MISSIONS

As the Japanese empire gradually enlarged its borders, the Church Federation sent outstanding Christian leaders to explore the possibilities of foreign missionary work during this same period. Their reports were favorable, though they chiefly envisioned missionary work among Japanese emigrants. Soon Japanese denominations were sending missionaries to countries where their sister denominations from the West had missions. Thus the Presbyterians went to Taiwan after 1895, when it was ceded to Japan. The Congregational church organized the Hawaiian Missionary Association in 1903 and sent missionaries to the South Seas in 1920.

With a view to unifying these overseas missions and giving greater emphasis to work among non-Japanese in Taiwan, Manchuria, and the mandated islands, the Overseas Evangelistic Association was constituted in 1931, and by 1934 had extended its operations to China, the Philippines, Brazil, and Peru—countries where there were substantial numbers of Japanese emigrants. With the outbreak of the Pacific War, overseas missionary efforts were merged under the government-sponsored Greater East Asia Bureau. The missionaries were instructed to cultivate the goodwill of the various churches in the overseas territories. Thus the value of the work of the Japanese overseas churches during this difficult period varied according to the evangelical character and courage of the particular minister in a given occupied area; some were loyal to their spiritual principles while others were over-zealous in their enforcement of military directives.

During the ensuing years before the Pacific War, mission societies and churches continued to be heavily involved in all levels of education except the compulsory primary school years. The prestige of Christian schools was greatly enhanced when in 1919 the government recognized their status as special schools for vocational and professional training, with the result that privileges hitherto restricted to the government schools were now extended to Christian schools, and the way became open for Christian colleges to achieve university status. As indicated above, the most vexatious problem for Christian schools, especially in the last decade before the Pacific War, was the government policy to use schools as a principal instrument of nationalistic indoctrination based on participation in the rites of state Shinto. Fortunately, almost to the end of the period the government did not strongly enforce its indoctrination policies in Christian schools, which continued to conduct chapel services, teach Bible, and engage in various Christian activities. For example, it was not until December 1941 that the seminary where the writer was a professor was closed by government order for its failure to possess itself of the sacrosanct Imperial Rescript on Education and Imperial Portrait, and to participate in state Shinto ceremonies.

Theological trends in prewar Japan were influenced not only by theology from the West but also by the ultranationalism of the day, and various forms of liberalism had their spokesmen. But the large sale of not only Scriptures but also works by Uchimura and Uemura, and the translations of such classics as the writings of Augustine, Calvin, Luther, and Wesley, gave a certain theological stability to a majority of the churches.

The social gospel, with its optimistic view of human progress, influenced many, especially in the Congregational and Methodist churches. Perhaps the most significant development among the evangelical churches of the holiness type was a revival movement inspired by a book entitled *Japan in the Bible,* by Jyuji Nakada, bishop of the Holiness church. In this he declared that the Japanese were God's chosen people and that the military forces were raised up of God to chastise the western nations for their apostasy. This contributed to dissension and disunity in the Wesleyan groups at a crucial time. Though this Christian form of nationalism at first found favor with the chauvinists in the government, its emphasis on Christ's second coming was rightly deduced to be contrary to the eternal rule of the emperor god, and more than 150 pastors were imprisoned in 1942.[26]

Japan's increasing involvement in the war with China and with the totalitarian forces of Europe, as well as the steady decline of Japanese-American relations, contributed to an atmosphere of hostility toward Christianity. To promote the nationalistic aims of the "Spiritual Mobilization Movement," launched by the government in 1937, the "Great Unity League of Religions" was organized with the support of the non-Christian religions and even the Roman Catholic church. This plan aimed at securing the participation of all Japanese in the rites of the state Shinto cult, not only at the shrines but also in schools, homes, and even churches. With the Roman Catholics setting an example of patriotism by ready participation in the prescribed Shinto rites, Protestant Christianity alone came under attack; believers were stigmatized as unpatriotic and anti-Japanese, and missionaries were regarded as spies. J. J. Spae states, "The Ministry of Education asserted that official worship at Shinto shrines was of a non-religious, patriotic nature. This declaration, together with other considerations, became the basis of a subsequent Roman decision which allowed Catholics to offer obeisance at shrines as a matter of civic duty. This decision still stands."[27] Sadly, in the interest of demonstrating their loyalty the churches agreed to support the general aims of "The New Order in Asia" and the "Co-Prosperity Sphere," which increasingly involved churches and ministers in activities which were definitely outside their Christian duties.

As a result there was a steady decrease in attendance and participation in church activities. All Christian schools were forced to cooperate in the nationalistic indoctrination and to regiment the students for various wartime tasks. With all news strictly censored, it is not surprising that Christian people succumbed to the constant pressures to which they were subjected. In 1936 the National Christian Council declared that "Christians should recognize the national character and value of the state Shinto shrines and as loyal citizens pay homage to those whose memories are enshrined there. Christians should accept the government's interpretation that these shrines are not religious—and understand the difference between the obeisance paid at these shrines to the nation's notables and the worship of God."[28] Though a courageous minority of pastors and laymen of various groups had steadfastly refused to conform and participate in the Shinto rites or become agents of nationalistic propaganda (later suffering persecution and imprisonment), the majority of Christians accepted this official interpretation.

The 2600th anniversary of the legendary date of the founding of Japan was celebrated in 1940 and became the focal point of nationalistic propaganda. A "New Structure" abolished the last vestiges of parliamentary democracy and also brought all phases of Japanese life under one totalitarian system. To secure official recognition and the right to exist, a given sect or denomination was obliged to have a minimum of fifty churches and five thousand members. Since only eight denominations could meet this standard, the smaller ones had to unite with other congenial groups, with the result that the thirty-odd prewar denominations were reduced to eleven blocs of related churches. All ties with western churches and their mission societies had to be severed.

In the interest of complete control, the authorities later demanded complete organic union, in which the National Christian Council concurred; this was ratified by action of the respective denominational groups at their final assemblies. A mass meeting of all the constituent groups was held on

Foundation Day (October 17, 1945), when all pledged themselves to unite in a single church and also to put forth greater efforts on behalf of the national purpose.

GOVERNMENT HARASSMENT OF THE CHURCH

Thus there finally came into being the Church of Christ in Japan (afterward known as the *Kyodan*) in 1941. Since the Kyodan was unwilling to sacrifice the basic doctrines of the Christian faith, the bureau of thought control of the Ministry of Education refused to sanction any of the drafts of credal standards submitted during the war period.

Even though the Kyodan had yielded to official directives, many Christian individuals and institutions suffered harassment and persecution. The Salvation Army, both for the military character of its structure and for its ties with a British headquarters, suffered the arrest of its leaders. The Episcopal church also experienced harassment because of its Anglican connections. Christian clergy and laymen were arrested and detained, often for extended periods. Others were arrested for neglect of prescribed Shinto rites and in a few cases charged with *lese majesty* for failure to ascribe divinity to the emperor and the imperial ancestors. To this end, homes, schools, and even churches were pressured to accept a *taima*, or paper amulet, of the Grand Shrine of Ise with the inscribed name of the original imperial ancestress or sun goddess, to be placed in a god-shelf or miniature shrine. The churches were pressured to indoctrinate their members in the nationalistic ideology, with special emphasis on harmonizing ancient Japanese tradition with Christian doctrine. Several Christian leaders even sought to find a primitive monotheism in Shinto mythology or to develop a kind of Japano-Israel theory.[29] The work of missionaries came to a complete standstill; the majority of those caught in Japan by the outbreak of the war were interned and later repatriated.

As the enemy bombing raids wrought havoc in the cities of Japan, about five hundred church buildings and parsonages were completely destroyed, and many were damaged. Furthermore, the conscription of pastors and lay leaders for the various forms of wartime labor seriously hampered the regular meetings and activities of the churches, and the work of the churches was further hindered by the arrest of loyal ministers and some laymen who had refused to cooperate with the wartime government. Thus it is little wonder that the Christian community, like the proverbial bamboo, bent before the storm winds of Shinto-inspired jingoistic nationalism, but did not break and die. However, by the end of the war the total Christian community of about 350,000 had been reduced by about one-half through death, dispersion, and some lapses; but in spite of all her trials and difficulties, the church did survive the war and was ready to resume building on the one foundation, which is Jesus Christ the Lord.[30]

THE ROMAN CATHOLIC CHURCH

With the reopening of Japan to the West after 1854, Catholic missionaries joined Protestants in early establishing beachheads in the port cities. First to come were the French, and then other missionaries of the several orders and societies which had been represented in the evangelism of the sixteenth and seventeenth centuries.

The most moving and encouraging event for the Roman church was the unexpected discovery of crypto-Catholic communities in the neighborhood of Nagasaki in 1865. Ten thousand Christians surfaced and put themselves under the instruction of the French missionaries. A much larger number, chiefly in the nearby Goto islands, were found to hold a quasi-Christian faith in separation from the Roman church. The government tried to force the crypto-Christians to recant, and several thousand were deported to distant regions. But though this persecution was protested by the western treaty powers, the exiles were not permitted to return to their former homes until 1873.[31]

The rapid success which the Catholic missionaries apparently hoped for was thus not only inhibited by the incubus of a formerly proscribed form of Christianity, but also by the general restrictions which applied to Protestants as well. So during the early years they concentrated their efforts more on the rural class, of which the crypto-Christians were a part, and on the poor. It was not until the Christian heyday of the 1880's that work was undertaken on a larger scale among members of the new middle and upper classes. By 1885 there were about 30,000 Christians; in 1895 over 50,000; and at the end of the Meiji era (1912) Roman Catholics numbered more than 66,000 (including baptized infants), drawn mainly from the lower classes. At this time there were 152 foreign priests, 33 Japanese priests, 133 lay brothers, 232 nuns, and about 165 catechists, with the preponderance of the foreign workers coming from France.[32]

In the post-Meiji period the Roman Catholic church continued to develop its work in Japan with great caution, enjoying a fairly steady though slow growth. In the next two decades its membership increased from about 66,000 to nearly 109,000. The church greatly strengthened its educational program at all levels, including the establishment of Sophia university; with a view to appealing to the more intellectual classes, extensive use was made of books, journals, and pamphlets produced by its scholarly institutes.

The authoritarian structure of the Roman church and the fact that the vast majority of its foreign workers were from European countries with which Japan was not at war greatly simplified its adjustment to the various vicissitudes of the mounting wartime climate. The transition to a national organization with Japanese bishops was quickly made under the terms of the Religious Bodies Law, and Archbishop Tatsuo Doi, later the first Japanese cardinal, became the head of the church. Its policy with reference to participation in the rites of state Shinto, not to mention certain pagan rites of family religion, was one of almost complete conformity. Possibly with the memory of its former suppression in mind, the church decided to avoid all confrontations with the government and sit out the storm while waiting for a better day.

THE RUSSIAN OR EASTERN ORTHODOX CHURCH

The mission of the Russian Orthodox church in Japan has been commonly regarded as a phase of the eastward expansion of the Russian Empire within the nineteenth century, and as such has often been misunderstood in Japan. However, more than is the case with the other branches of Christianity, the establishment and growth of this church is quite largely due to the versatility and devotion of one man, Ivan Kasatkin (archbishop Nicolai). He first came to Japan as a Russian consular chaplain in 1861 and subsequently devoted himself to missionary work for fifty years, seeing his beloved church grow from nothing to more than thirty thousand members.[33] Nicolai constantly emphasized the principle that Christianity must be spread by Japanese, and he early translated all the service books and other literature into the vernacular. Thus the Russian staff was always very small, but before Nicolai's death, at the end of the Meiji era, there were about two hundred Japanese workers—priests, deacons, and evangelists—serving churches which stretched all the way from Japanese Sakhalin on the north to Formosa on the south. The headquarters of the church were established at the great Nicolai Cathedral, which stands on a prominent hill in Tokyo.

Growth inevitably slowed during the Russo-Japanese War, but by 1932 membership was about thirty-two thousand.[34] Growth was still further retarded during World War I. And with the communist takeover of Russia in 1917 the Japanese church separated from the supporting Orthodox church of Russia. By 1937 the actual membership was reduced to between thirteen and fourteen thousand. The Russian Archbishop Sergius resigned at this time and, though succeeded by a Japanese bishop, the outlook was not bright. Like the other branches of Christendom the Orthodox church suffered and shrank as the Russian War intensified.

NOTES

1. E. O. Reischauer and J. K. Fairbank, *East Asia, The Great Tradition,* pp. 472-73 *et al.*
2. H. Nakamura, *Ways of Thinking of Eastern Peoples,* pp. 572-75.
3. P. Y. Saeki, *The Nestorian Monument in China,* pp. 61-62, 220-24.
4. M. Anesaki, *History of Japanese Religion,* p. 244 et al.
5. R. H. Drummond, *A History of Christianity in Japan,* p. 51.
6. K. S. Latourette, *A History of the Expansion of Christianity,* 3:330.
7. Reischauer and Fairbank, *East Asia,* pp. 581-82.
8. J. Murdoch, *A History of Japan,* 2:642-62.
9. Drummond, pp. 162 ff.
10. W. E. Griffis, *Hepburn of Japan.*
11. H. S. Tucker, *History of the Episcopal Church in Japan,* pp. 75-94.
12. Griffis, *Hepburn of Japan.* See also this author's article in *Concise Dictionary of the Christian World,* pp. 636-37.
13. Griffis, *A Maker of the New Orient.*
14. G. F. Verbeck, "History of Protestant Missions in Japan," pp. 740-897.
15. Ibid., pp. 764-65.
16. H. Kishimoto, *Japanese Religion in the Meiji Era,* pp. 180-82, 200-01.
17. Ibid., pp. 204, 209.
18. Ibid., pp. 209-11, 300-03.
19. Drummond, p. 172.
20. Otis Cary, *A History of Christianity in Japan,* pp. 168-69. (Reported in a letter from Dr. Jo Nishima.)
21. *Japan Christian Yearbook, 1968,* p. 10.
22. *Proceedings of the GCPM in Japan, 1900,* pp. 987-91.
23. *The Christian Movement in Japan,* 1914.
24. *Japan Christian Yearbook, 1926.*
25. Drummond, pp. 227-41.
26. C. W. Iglehart, *A Century of Protestant Christianity in Japan,* pp. 196, 255-58.
27. Joseph J. Spae, *Catholicism in Japan* (Tokyo: ISR Press, 1963), p. 112; see also Jan Swyngedouw, "The Catholic Church and Shrine Shinto," *The Japan Missionary Bulletin,* Nov. 1967, pp. 579-84, Dec. 1967, pp. 659-63.
28. D. C. Holton, *The Political Philosophy of Modern Shinto,* pp. 95-98.
29. Iglehart, pp. 233-35 ff.
30. Ibid., pp. 253-57.
31. Ibid., pp. 109-17, 301-08.
32. *Japan Catholic Directory, 1967,* p. 451, and Drummond, pp. 308-20.
33. Latourette, 6:279-418, and Drummond, pp. 339-55.
34. Drummond, pp. 355-59, and Latourette, 7:383-84.

BIBLIOGRAPHY

Japanese History and Background

Beardsley, R. K.; Hall, J. W.; and Ward, R. E. *Village Japan.* Chicago: University Press, 1959.

Beasley, W. G. *The Modern History of Japan.* New York: Praeger, 1963.

Benedict, R. *The Chrysanthemum and the Sword.* Boston: Houghton Mifflin Co., 1936.

Brown, D. M. *Nationalism in Japan: An Historical Analysis.* Berkeley: University of California Press, 1955.

Dore, R. P. *City Life in Japan.* Berkeley: University of California Press, 1958.

Fujii, J. *Outline of Japanese History in the Meiji Era.* Tokyo: Obunsha, 1958.

Fukutake, T. *Man and Society in Japan.* Tokyo: University of Tokyo Press, 1962.

Kawai, Kazuo. *Japan's American Interlude.* Chicago: University Press, 1960.
Murdoch, J. *A History of Japan.* 3 vols. London: Routledge & Kegan Paul, 1949.
Nakamura, H. *Ways of Thinking of Eastern Peoples.* Tokyo: UNESCO, 1960.
Reischauer, E. O. *Japan, Past and Present.* New York: Alfred A. Knopf, 1964.
———. *The United States and Japan.* Rev. ed. New York: Viking Press, 1957.
Reischauer, E. O., and Fairbank, J. K. *East Asia: The Great Tradition.* Boston: Houghton Mifflin Co., 1960.
Reischauer, E. O.; Fairbank, J. K.; and Craig, A. M. *East Asia: The Modern Transformation.* Boston: Houghton Mifflin Co., 1965.
Sansom, G. B. *Japan: A Short Cultural History.* New York: Appleton-Century, 1944.
———. *The Western World and Japan.* New York: Alfred Knopf, 1950.
———. *A History of Japan from 1334 A.D. to the Present.* Palo Alto: Stanford University Press, 1958.
Scalapino, R. A., and Masumi, J. *Parties and Politics in Contemporary Japan.* Berkeley: University of California Press, 1962.
Tsunoda, R.; de Bary, W. T.; and Keene, D. *Sources of Japanese Tradition.* New York: Columbia University Press, 1958.

Japanese Religions, General

Anesaki, M. *History of Japanese Religion.* 1930. Reprint. London: Chas. Tuttle Co., 1963.
Bellah, R. *Tokugawa Religion.* Glencoe, Ill.: Free Press, 1957.
Bunce, W. K. *Religions in Japan.* Tokyo: Chas. Tuttle Co., 1959.
Hammer, R. *Japan's Religious Ferment.* New York: Oxford University Press, 1962.
Kishimoto, H. *Japanese Religion in the Meiji Era.* Tokyo: Obunsha, 1956.
Kitagawa, J. M. *Religion in Japanese History.* New York: Columbia University Press, 1966.
Yanaibara, T. *Religion and Democracy in Japan.* Tokyo: Institute of Pacific Relations, 1948.

Japanese Buddhism

Callaway, T. H. *Japanese Buddhism and Christianity.* Tokyo: Chas. Tuttle Co., 1958.
Eliot, Chas. *Japanese Buddhism.* 3rd ed. New York: Barnes & Noble, 1959.
Lloyd, A. S. *The Creed of Half Japan.* New York: E. P. Dutton & Co., 1912.
Reischauer, A. K. *Studies in Japanese Buddhism.* New York: The Macmillan Co., 1917.

Japanese Confucianism

Hall, R. K. *Shūshin: The Ethics of a Defeated Nation.* New York: Columbia University Press, 1949.
Smith, W. W. Jr. *Confucianism in Modern Japan: A Study of Conservatism in Japanese Intellectual History.* Tokyo: The Hokuseido Press, 1959.

Shintoism

Aston, W. G. *Shinto, the Ancient Religion of Japan.* London: A. Constable & Co., 1907.

Holtom, D. C. *The Political Philosophy of Modern Shinto.* Tokyo: Asiatic Society, 1922.

———. *The National Faith of Japan.* London: Kegan Paul, 1938.

Holtom, D. C. *Modern Japan and Shinto Nationalism.* Chicago: University of Chicago Press, 1943.

Kato, G. *A Study of Shinto: The Religion of the Japanese Nation.* Tokyo: Meiji Japan Society, 1926.

———. *What Is Shinto?* Tokyo: Maruzen, 1935.

Japanese New Religions

McFarland, H. N. *The Rush Hour of the Gods: New Religious Movements in Japan.* New York: MacMillan Co., 1967.

Offner, C. B., and Van Straelen, H. *Modern Japanese Religions.* Tokyo: Enderle, 1963.

Thomsen, H. *The New Religions of Japan.* Tokyo: Chas. Tuttle Co., 1963.

The Christian Movement in Japan

Aoyoshi, K. *Masahisa Uemura: A Christian Leader.* Tokyo: Maruzen, 1940.

Axling, W. *Kagawa.* New York: Harper & Bros., 1946.

Berry, K. F. *A Pioneer Doctor in Old Japan: The Story of J. C. Berry, M.D.* New York: Revell, 1940.

Bolshakoff, S. *Foreign Missions of the Russian Orthodox Church.* London: SPCK, 1943.

Boxer, C. R. *The Christian Century in Japan, 1649-50.* Berkeley: University of California Press, 1951.

Braun, N. *Laity Mobilized: Reflections on Church Growth in Japan.* Grand Rapids: Eerdmans, 1970.

Cary, Otis. *A History of Christianity in Japan.* 2 vols. New York: Fleming Revell Co., 1909.

Drummond, R. H. *A History of Christianity in Japan.* Grand Rapids: Eerdmans, 1970.

Griffis, W. E. *A Maker of the New Orient: S. H. Brown.* Chicago: Revell, 1902.

———. *Hepburn of Japan.* Philadelphia: Westminster Press, 1913.

———. *Verbeck of Japan.* New York: Revell, 1900.

Hardy, A. S. *Life and Letters of Joseph Hardy Neesima.* Boston: Houghton Mifflin Co., 1891.

Iglehart, C. W. *A Century of Protestant Christianity in Japan.* Tokyo: Chas. Tuttle Co., 1959.

Jennings, R. P. *Jesus, Japan, and Kanzo Uchimura.* Tokyo: Kyo Bun Kwan, 1958.

Kanamori, T. *Kanamori's Life Story.* Philadelphia: Sunday School Times Co., 1921.

Kozaki, H. *Reminiscences of Seventy Years: Autobiography of a Japanese Pastor.* Tokyo: Christian Literature Soc., 1933.

Latourette, K. S. *A History of the Expansion of Christianity.* 7 vols. New York: Harper & Bros., 1938-45.

Ritter, H. *History of Protestant Missions in Japan.* Tokyo: Methodist Publishing House, 1892.

Spae, J. J. *Christian Corridors to Japan.* Tokyo: Oriens Institute for Religious Research, 1967.

———. *Christianity Encounters Japan.* Tokyo: Oriens Institute, 1968.

———. *Japanese Religiosity.* Tokyo: Oriens Institute, 1971.

———. *Christians of Japan.* Tokyo: Oriens Institute, 1970.

Thomas, W. T. *Protestant Beginnings in Japan: The First Decades, 1859-1889.* Tokyo: Chas. Tuttle Co., 1959.

Van Hecken, J. *The Catholic Church in Japan Since 1859.* Tokyo: Agency, 1963.

Verbeck, G. F. "History of Protestant Missions in Japan" in *Proceedings of the General Conference of Protestant Missions in Japan, 1900.* Tokyo, 1901.

The files of *Japan Evangelist* (now out of print), *Japan Christian Quarterly, Japan Harvest,* and *Japan Catholic Yearbook* (all published in Tokyo yearly), together with the annual report volumes of *The Christian Movement in Japan, Korea and Formosa,* and its successor, *The Japan Christian Yearbook,* contain invaluable material for the study of Christianity in Japan.

Typical rush hour scene in a Tokyo commuter station

Christian church on the grounds of a leper colony in the rural part of Tokyo

Photos by Stars and Stripes; T. Varnel

13

JAPAN'S POSTWAR RENAISSANCE

by Alvin D. Hammond

LIKE THE LEGENDARY Oriental phoenix, an eagle-like bird which rose from the ashes of fiery death to new beauty and power, Japan's economic and political resurrection has surpassed the wildest dreams of both her own people and her conqueror.

In the closing months of World War II this amazing little island nation saw her major industries destroyed, her cities razed with fire, her territorial acquisitions torn from her, and six million discouraged soldiers dumped back into the destitute economy. To crown it all, her god-king denied his divinity in an epochal broadcast on January 1, 1946. General Douglas MacArthur, regent of the Allied occupying powers, rightly assessed it as a theological crisis. Old ideals and false hopes had been abruptly shattered. The nation was cast trembling into a vast economic, social, and spiritual vacuum. Darkness had fallen over the land of the rising sun.

So MacArthur called for ten thousand new missionaries to minister to the poverty of spirit and replace the old, false, ethical ideals with Christian ones. Thus opportunely began the third great Christian missionary invasion of this complex Oriental nation in which Christian evangelism has seen meteoric successes burn out in bloody persecutions in its four hundred year history.

ALVIN D. HAMMOND, a church-planting missionary with the Churches of Christ in Japan from 1954 to 1970, has grappled firsthand with postwar church and mission problems. For ten years he also edited the periodical *Christian Mission Today*. He holds the B.A. degree from Sophia University (Tokyo) and the M.A. degree in Asian Studies from the University of California. He is currently Director of Missions at San Jose Bible College, California.

In this new era of opportunity, how has the church fared?

When the smoke of battle was cleared from Japan in August 1945 it revealed almost half of her Christian church buildings destroyed, largely in the cities. Most pastors were moonlighting or had left the ministry. All but two or three missionaries had long since been repatriated, most never to return. The populace was frightened and despairing. Christians were bewildered.

Into this materially and spiritually destitute wasteland the first missionaries began to come in 1946. Some few veterans of the large denominations and older societies were the first to survey the need. Then a trickle of new missionaries from almost sixty smaller denominational and interdenominational societies soon swelled to a stream. And a new era of evangelistic opportunity dawned promisingly.

During three contrasting periods of Japanese history the church, representing three general types of Christianity, has had interrupted opportunities to make the Christian message known. The period from 1549, when Saint Francis Xavier introduced the Catholic form of the faith, until 1639, when it was forcibly rejected, can be designated "the Catholic century." The second period, beginning in 1859, when the first Protestant missionaries entered an awakened Japan following her two hundred years of self-imposed isolation, may be referred to as "the Protestant century" because of Protestant prominence in evangelism.

The third opportunity came to the church with the close of the war in 1945 and the resumption of Christian missionary activity. Because of the large number of new missionaries from committedly evangelical boards that entered Japan during this time it may be called "an evangelical opportunity." It is this period of unparalleled opportunity that I will emphasize here.

Protestant Reconstruction

Mission boards that had been involved in the prewar efforts were eager to return in order to estimate their losses and to help the shattered Japanese church rebuild. The most critical problem confronting the Protestant movement at that time was the future of the *Kyodan* or United Church of Christ, which owed its existence to government pressure just before the outbreak of the Pacific War. The majority were agreed that the United Church should continue. However, a substantial minority had been opposed to church union from the beginning. Though a constitution which provided an effective blend of Congregational, Methodist, and Presbyterian polity elements was early adopted, over a decade passed before a minimal creed for the church was agreed upon.

Thus various groups withdrew from the Kyodan soon after the war for various reasons. The Anglican church and the Salvation Army were followed by the Baptist churches of the American and Southern Baptist missions. The churches founded by the United Lutheran Mission and several smaller societies were reconstituted as the Evangelical Lutheran church. The churches of the holiness group, such as the Nazarene, Free Methodist, and most of the Holiness church itself, also withdrew, not to mention the various Alliance churches and several other smaller groups. About one-third of the Presbyterian Reformed churches later seceded to reconstitute the prewar church, while earlier a smaller group of churches organized the Reformed Church of Japan.

The formation of the Kyodan in 1941 and the attainment of full self-support and autonomy by the larger Japanese denominations dictated the need for a different mission strategy. Thus in anticipation of the renewal of relations with Japan and reopening of mission work, the foreign mission boards of some eight denominations (Congregational-Christian, Disciples of Christ, Evangelical and Reformed, Evangelical and United Brethren, Methodist Episcopal, Presbyterian U.S.A., Reformed Church of America, and United Church of Canada) agreed on a united approach with a view to a policy of joint planning and cooperative action before the war ended. The basic plan for future cooperation between these boards and the Kyodan went into effect in 1948, with the official representatives of the constituent agencies constituting what is known as the Interboard Committee for Christian Work in Japan (IBC).

Relief, rehabilitation, and reconstruction were initially emphasized. The Church World Service sent 5.5 million pounds of relief and reconstruction supplies in 1948 alone, valued at $1.5 million.[1,2] For reconstruction of churches and schools $3.5 million was sent, with which 242 churches were rebuilt in the initial years. These large amounts of emergency aid diminished as the Nippon Kirisuto Kyodan (United Church of Christ) grew. Through the Interboard Committee (liaison organ of eight U.S. mission boards working with the Kyodan), $500,000 annually was channeled to the Kyodan.[3] In more recent times the United Church is said to be self-supporting in its internal affairs, and the continuing U.S. aid is used largely for building new churches as the denomination strives for total self-support by 1980.

Separate estimates of the growth achieved by Japan's older Protestant bodies identified with the National Christian Council have been made. These estimates are inclusive of four main groups: the Interboard Committee-Kyodan, the American Baptists, the Lutherans, and the Episcopalians. In 1968 there were an estimated 270,485 church members, 1,772 churches, and 2,440 ministers in these groups.[4] The high number of ministers in comparison to churches may indicate the great number involved in institutional work. Also, the ratio of ministers to church members points up the sociological fact that in Japan the churches tend to plateau between 40 and 50 adult members.[5]

Despite the adoption of a minimal doctrinal statement by the Kyodan several years after the war, it has been plagued by doctrinal, political, and social dissension. This climaxed in the annual conference of 1969, when young radicals, largely pastors, disrupted the meeting, physically assaulting one older leader. They claimed that the church had failed to condemn the Vietnam war, had been mistaken to erect a pavilion at Expo 70, and in general was not sufficiently activistic. By 1973 the entire denomination had still been unable to hold its annual conferences and some regional synods.

The churches of the National Christian Council sponsor nine universities, seven postgraduate schools, nine colleges, twenty-eight junior colleges, sixty-seven high schools, two commercial high schools, and twelve junior high schools, as well as various Bible schools, language schools, and rural training centers. Their benevolent program includes eight old people's homes, twelve centers for the handicapped, fifty-two orphanages, widows homes, and nurseries, seventeen neighborhood centers, twelve hospitals (inclusive of clinics), five homes for delinquents and prostitutes, one center of rehabilitation for ex-convicts, and one employment center.[6] Perhaps the YMCA and YWCA, involved largely in educational youth work, should be included in this listing also.

Following the war, not only were the existing mission universities rebuilt, but a new multi-million-dollar project, the International Christian University, was undertaken by cooperating Protestants. These college-level schools, and to a lesser degree the high and middle schools, have had a steadily lessening Christian impact. Probably less than 5 percent of the students graduate as Christians. The national average shows less than 50 percent of the faculties even nominally Christian. And prolonged campus disruptions initiated in recent years by minority student power groups in a number of the liberal arts Christian colleges, including ICU, have caused further misgivings regarding their value as Christian organizations.

Christian Social Welfare Work

In Japan the Christian forces were from the beginning the pioneers in the various forms of welfare work. Often the Christians first became aware of some area of human distress and promptly set the example of meeting the need, after which public agencies became active in the field. In fact, many of the early workers in government social service departments were Christians, and a high degree of collaboration between Christian social work projects and the Ministry of Welfare has been the usual pattern. As mission support of Christian social work has decreased and the Japanese church has failed to assume the main burden of financial support, inevitably Christian social welfare agencies and institutions have become heavily dependent on public subsidies. This has unfortunately caused some to become secularized and lose their evangelistic outreach, except as they are associated with the work of a live church or agency like the Salvation Army.

The present dimension of Christian social welfare work in Japan is clearly indicated in the 1969-70 volume of the *Christian Yearbook.* It lists some eighteen agencies with central headquarters which engage in a variety of projects: twenty-nine social settlements; eight homes for the rehabilitation of women (under the auspices of the WCTU, German Midnight Mission, and Salvation Army); seventeen homes for women and children; sixty-six orphanages; thirty-two homes for the elderly, including a home for elderly atomic bomb victims at Hiroshima. There are fifty-one church- or mission-related medical facilities, including thirty-six hospitals, ten medical clinics, and five TB sanitariums under Christian auspices.

New Missions and Activities

The early postwar period, however, offered an especially golden opportunity for evangelism. The favorable conditions brought about by the American occupation, the emotional needs of the times, and the abrogation of emperor worship opened the hearts of the Japanese to the propagation of the Christian message to a degree unprecedented in the entire history of the church. Challenged with the idea that a spiritual vacuum existed and urged on by reports of the ideal political environment and of receptive response, over 2500 new and largely evangelical missionaries poured into Japan and eagerly began evangelizing. Unhindered by institutional ties they dispersed throughout Japan, though most were blissfully ignorant of cultural problems and the remaining pockets of feudal tradition. They proclaimed the Christian message with boldness and authority. From a prewar peak of 60 societies with twelve hundred missionaries in 1931, the postwar influx swelled the number of missions to 140, though many had less than ten missionaries.

Every type of evangelistic method was tried, since the missionaries had complete freedom. In the early postwar years street meetings drew large crowds, and respondents were urged into Bible classes. Gospel teams and tent meetings were used effectively by The Evangelical Alliance Mission and the Oriental Missionary Society, among others, to plant churches in rural areas. Rented halls were used for city-wide campaigns by Youth for Christ, Pocket Testament League, and others.[7] The PTL also distributed twelve million gospels of John nationwide.

These efforts peaked in the Bob Pierce Crusades in Osaka in 1957 and in Tokyo in 1959, and in the Billy Graham Crusade of 1967 in Tokyo. In the latter alone there were 15,854 inquirers, all of whom were contacted by the nearest cooperating churches and kept on the mailing list of the Crusade headquarters for a year after the end of the meetings.[8] One veteran missionary estimates, however, that of those making decisions in the first ten years of intensive mass evangelism, only 10 percent went on to baptism and church membership.

Mass communication was early stressed, and the Pacific Broadcasting Association (PBA) set up a radio studio in Tokyo in the early fifties. In 1954 Akira Hatori returned from America, where he had received his theological training, and took up the work of broadcasting the gospel message to an estimated six million Japanese listeners weekly. PBA now broadcasts over as many as ninety-two radio stations with four weekly and three daily programs. Several thirteen-week TV series have been tried, along with special Christmas and Easter programs. Evangelicals have also developed audio-visual aid centers, making filmstrips and movies available to the churches. Moody Science films with Japanese sound tracks have been shown on television and in many churches throughout Japan since 1968. Among NCC-related groups, AVACO, HOREMCO, Lutherans, and Southern Baptists have used radio and some TV time as well.

The training of an indigenous leadership for the Japanese evangelical churches was soon emphasized by the missions and churches as being of central importance. The Southern Baptists, Nazarenes, Oriental Missionary Society (Holiness), and Churches of Christ built and staffed their own Bible colleges or seminaries. Perhaps the most representative of the interdenominational efforts was the Tokyo Christian College (formerly Japan Christian College), headed by Dr. Donald Hoke of TEAM mission, which opened its doors in April 1955 not only to its original TEAM Bible school students but to all evangelical groups. It gradually developed into an accredited theological college. Hoke also organized the Association of Evangelical Theological Schools, which recognizes fifteen members plus another fifteen schools which train Christian workers in Japan.

The Kyodan rebuilt its Union Seminary soon after the war. It peaked at two hundred students in the early sixties, then began to suffer from increasing organizational strife in the denomination. In 1970 it was closed by radical students who occupied the administration building for more than six months. When Union Seminary finally reopened in 1971, it was with half the former student body and a truncated program. The Kyodan also trains ministers in theological departments of its mission schools. The combined Lutheran churches rebuilt next to the Union Seminary and operate a small federated training program in cooperation with the seminary.

Evangelical literature of every type and description has been produced through a number of evangelical publishers. Word of Life Press, Christian Literature Crusade, the Evangelical Publishers, New Life League, and the Conservative Baptist's Bible Library Publishers began work postwar. Under the leadership of Ken McVety, director of Word of Life Press, and the WLP facilities, the Every Home Crusade (sponsored by World Literature Crusade) has visited nearly every home in Japan twice with evangelical literature packets.[9] In 1970 the WLP became Japan's largest Christian publishing house.

A Japanese-language *Gospel for the Millions* magazine began from a humble beginning in 1952 and grew to be a recognized evangelical magazine with a subscribed readership of over twenty thousand. Billy Graham's book *Peace with God* became the Word of Life Press's best seller and is representative of the numerous books being translated into the Japanese language.

The postwar period represents a new era in Bible production and distribution, marked by the proliferation of translations in the modern colloquial language. Since 1950 there has been an almost incredible output of modern Japanese translations, both Catholic and Protestant, including three complete Bibles and one revision, a New Testament, two new versions of the gospels, and a number of translations of individual books. The Japan Bible Society has distributed more than seventy million Scriptures (Bibles, New Testaments, and portions) since the war, with nearly nine million copies in 1970, ranking it second only to the U.S. The Gideons have concentrated on the distribution of bilingual New Testaments among high school students, English being the second language in Japan.

In the spring of 1970 a new translation of the entire Bible in Japanese was published after seven years of work by forty-two evangelical Japanese scholars. The New Testament was finished in late 1965 and received wide acclaim for its fidelity to the original languages and excellent, contemporary style. By the end of 1972 over four hundred thousand copies had been sold. Supervised by a six-man editorial board, the draft of the manuscript went through five stages of careful scrutiny in order to insure both accuracy and naturalness of expression.[10]

Evangelicals have taken the lead in evangelistic student work through such groups as the Inter-Varsity Christian Fellowship and Campus Crusade for Christ, which have organized cell groups on the campuses of many universities. Hi-BA (High School Born-Againers) is a vigorous club and camp program with extensive outreach among high school students in Tokyo and Osaka. The Ochanomizu Student Center, located in the heart of Tokyo's clustered university settlement, occupies a modern office-building complex, where Bible classes are held and various conference rooms are made available to the evangelical community. Many key evangelical agencies also have offices within its spacious construction.

In spite of the great diversity in the nearly one hundred evangelical mission societies operating in Japan, there has been a willingness to cooperate in witness to the oneness of the Lord's church and in evangelism. The Evangelical Missionary Association in Japan (EMAJ), organized in 1949, formed a rallying center for fellowship and informal cooperation.

For more effective cooperation and liaison between missions, the Japan Council of Evangelical Missions was organized in 1961 and later consolidated with the EMAJ to form the Japan Evangelical Missionary Association (JEMA). *Japan Harvest*, a quality quarterly, is their official publication. JEMA is presently made up of over forty member missions and a number of associate independent members, totaling over eight hundred missionaries. As well as its spiritual undergirding of evangelical endeavors, JEMA has offered such practical services as charter flights for furloughing missionaries, disaster relief, cooperative evangelistic luncheons for women in many cities, etc.

Paralleling this mission-cooperative agency, evangelical super-church groups also developed soon after the war. In 1948 the Japan Evangelical Fellowship was formed by seven denominations for spiritual fellowship and cooperation. These included Christian and Missionary Alliance, Nazarene, Free Methodist, Evangelical Alliance, Holiness, and others.

In preparation for the centenary of protestantism in 1959 almost two thousand pastors banded together for an evangelical witness and conference. This group later became the Japan Protestant Conference of evangelicals, in which membership is on an individual basis. In 1968 the JPC, the JEF, and the JEMA all united under the banner of the Japan Evangelical Association, providing a united vehicle for fellowship, cooperation, and liaison among all evangelicals in Japan.

In the spirit of cooperation crystallized by the evangelical and ecumenical effort of the Billy Graham Crusade International in 1967, plans were soon begun for a Japan-style evangelism-in-depth program. Arousing interest was difficult, however, so it was decided to divide the nation into areas. Japan's smallest island, Shikoku, with four states, was chosen for the pilot project in 1970. This was followed by a program in the major city of Kobe in 1971, Japan's newest state, Okinawa, in 1972, and five states in southwestern Japan in 1973. Under the leadership of the national committee, headed by Dr. Akira Hatori (radio evangelist and key younger evangelical of the nation), enthusiasm mounted gradually during the years.

Starting with 65 percent of the churches cooperating in Shikoku, the figure rose to 90 percent in Okinawa in 1972. In some churches 200 to 300 percent growth was reported in one year. Reports of these area experiments began to spread, and reports are now coming in from all over Japan of extending the program to other areas.

The increasing success of this Total Mobilization Evangelism program, greatly modified to meet the needs of Japan, has charged Chairman Hatori with a broader vision for an All-Japan Evangelistic Missionary Movement. Without centering in any one organization, including even the Total Mobilization Evangelism program, Hatori visualizes mobilizing all Christians for an all-out evangelistic movement for the country, just as the nation was mobilized for war thirty-five years ago. It will be a multi-year, goal-centered program with a vision to reach all schools, all institutions, and all strata of society. Hatori hopes to embrace all para-church organizations in cooperation with local churches and all evangelistically minded denominations in order to accomplish this task.

In late 1973 four leadership training programs for both pastors and laymen are projected for four areas of Japan. Hatori feels that a more ambitious and thoroughgoing program must also be developed to train new converts after the various efforts. His widely respected leadership and enthusiasm promises success to the program.

An important factor in the program will be the Japan Congress on Evangelism, projected for June 1974. Here a thousand evangelical leaders from all groups across the country will be gathered in the ancient capital city of Kyoto to make plans for extending the evangelization of the nation in this generation.

Another hopeful evangelical postwar development was the formation in 1972 of the Japan Overseas Mission Association. Again with Hatori as chairman and with Rev. Andrew Furuyama as executive secretary, this group has drawn together fourteen small mission-sending organizations in cooperation, much like the Interdenominational Foreign Missions Association of the U.S. Embracing approximately half of all missionaries now currently serving overseas from Japan, this group hopes to fire greater missionary vision in all evangelical churches and theological institutions, with a view to sending Japanese missionaries in increasing numbers throughout the world.

The growth of the strictly evangelical church community in postwar Japan has contrasted favorably to that of the traditional Protestant churches. The members of evangelical churches which have already become totally indigenous number 115,936. The number of those yet in mission-related evangelical churches (95,322), added to the indigenous church count, brought the total in 1969 to 211,258 evangelical church members.[11]

By 1972 this figure had probably increased 20 to 25 percent. Sub-orthodox missions and indigenous churches are excluded from this total. When it is remembered that more than half of the missions represented in this classification were new on the scene in postwar Japan and that most of their related churches were begun in this period, it can be seen that the rate of growth far surpasses that of the older bodies.

The 1972 membership figure of 300,000 for the five older Protestant churches (all of which had early prewar beginnings and massive postwar aid) does not greatly exceed the total number of 242,463 estimated to exist in the peak prewar period.[12] Even granting heavy losses because of the war, their growth has still been relatively slower. Professor Masatoshi Doi of Doshisha University warned the NCC-Kyodan leadership that some of the evangelical churches have enjoyed as much as 320 percent growth increase over a measurable fourteen-year period while the National Council churches have had only 70 percent and the Catholics 90 percent.[13] By 1972 total membership figures for all Protestant churches was 722,742.

The largest of the National Christian Council members is the Japan Church of Christ, an ecumenical church formed during the war and continuing to the present. Its 1972 membership included less than 40 percent of all Protestants in Japan. Beginning with its annual conference in 1969, when a group of radical theological students and younger pastors physically attacked the chairman in one session and caused the conference to close down, the United church has been unable to have its annual conference. All efforts to mediate the problems between the left-wing radicals (whose activities largely center on political action and peace movements) and the remainder of the church have failed. As a result churches have been losing ground, and around the country in many places total disorganization has appeared. A senior evangelical statesman of the church was appointed by an acting executive committee in late 1972 to bring the church together. He reported nothing but failure and discouragement concerning the prospects of healing the breach in the church. Thus Japan's example of Protestant ecumenicity, hailed as a worldwide example in the decade following the war, has come to a chaotic standstill within its first generation.

Because of the emphasis of the evangelical groups on evangelism, the number of their institutions of higher learning and benevolent agencies is less impressive than that of the traditional Protestants and Catholics. However, in view of their comparatively short history in Japan their contribution has been significant, including five colleges, four junior colleges, five senior high schools, four junior high schools, one primary school, and innumerable kindergartens.[14] As well as a number of orphanages and rest homes which operate on a small scale, the Southern Baptists, the Southern

Presbyterians, and the Seventh-Day Adventists (if they may be included as evangelical) operate full-size hospitals which perform top-level service largely to the Japanese and the foreign community. (The Seventh-Day Adventists have been accepted as evangelical in the thinking of many because of their high view of the Scriptures and their restraint in overt proselytization.)

About half a dozen churches, some of them indigenous movements and some mission-related, are difficult to fit into any simple category. The mission-related non-orthodox groups are more familiar to westerners, including the Church of the Latter Day Saints (10,790 members) and the Watchtower Society (6,909 members). But several Japanese sub-orthodox, indigenous groups show vigorous growth. Among these are the "non-church" movement (estimated at more than 25,000 members), which has no formal churches or organization and refuses to observe baptism and the Lord's supper. The Original Gospel Movement (Genshi Fukuin), claiming 45,000 members, is a Japanese charismatic movement that is usually placed in the heretical-sect category by Japanese churchmen. The Holy Spirit Association for Unification of World Christianity, known popularly by the Japanese as "Genri Undo" (117,020 members) is a semi-political, anti-communist organization with heterodox views of the Godhead and other doctrines.

The Roman Catholic Church

The growth of the Catholic work since the war has in many respects paralleled that of the Protestant movement. The Catholic population has more than doubled, and the various branches of its effort have greatly expanded. Though the church now enjoys a more favorable public opinion, the more rapid advance experienced earlier in the period has since leveled off, with the same annual leakage of membership reported by many Protestant groups in this time of population mobility. The number of new orders or missionary societies working in Japan is unprecedented—a total of forty-three for men and seventy-four for women.

The administrative structure of the Catholic church is divided into 15 dioceses with 964 churches and chapels, with a total membership of 345,074 (exclusive of clergy, seminarians, and members of secular institutes). Under the jurisdiction of the 15 Japanese bishops are 1,881 priests (716 Japanese and 1,165 missioners); 376 brothers (204 Japanese and 172 missioners); 6,127 nuns (5,125 Japanese and 1,002 missioners); and a large number of Japanese catechists and other lay helpers. In 1972 total Catholic church membership (including children) was listed as 371,148.[15]

Like the older Protestant groups, the Catholic church has a well-balanced educational system at all levels, which has done much to commend the church to the general public. There are 11 theological schools which prepare for the diocesan clergy and various religious societies of priests, with a total of 805 students. Schools giving a general education include 11 universities, 29 junior colleges, 114 high schools, 100 middle schools, 57 primary schools, and 34 special schools, for a total of 345 schools with 153,378 students.

The Catholic social welfare program is equally imposing, with thirty-three hospitals and sanitariums, twenty clinics, sixty-two orphanages, twenty-seven homes for the elderly, ten institutions for the handicapped, and four social settlements, not to mention agencies in the field of social action.[16]

The Eastern Orthodox Church

It is difficult to estimate the strength of this church, which has been languishing during the postwar period—in fact since the communist take-over, when the support of the home church was largely cut off. The latest report gives the Orthodox population as 24,500, including baptized infants, children, and adults. With no authorized translation of the Old Testament, and with the New Testament and prayer book in difficult classical Japanese, the church suffers from a dearth of usable Christian literature. The number of active clergy is quite inadequate even to man the forty-two churches and thirty-six chapels. Seminarians are few and the majority of the priests are over sixty-five years of age. The church has very little educational work, and social welfare work is unknown.

Ecumenical Activities

Interest in Protestant-Catholic ecumenical cooperation had been current on both sides for many years prior to the first Ecumenical Roundtable, which was held in July 1966 with officials of both the Kyodan and the Catholic church. Out of this came suggestions that a joint "Faith and Order" study group be established, that ecumenical dialogue be begun, and that they prepare together a new version of the Bible. Following this, in 1968, the *Japan Christian Yearbook* became a joint publication of the NCC and the National Catholic Council.

The formation of the Japan Ecumenical Association in 1972 was a prelude to the erection of a joint Protestant-Catholic pavilion at Japan's Expo '70. The low-key exhibit in a dramatic, modern building featured music, drama, and a daily worship hour presided over alternately by Catholics and Protestants. Evangelicals as a whole boycotted this effort.

Although a groundswell of ecumenical interest is present in Japan, drastic internal problems in the Kyodan and apathy on the part of other NCC members have limited further developments following Expo '70.

Nation and People

To understand the church's initial postwar spurt and subsequent leveling off, a brief analysis of the postwar social, economic, and political scene is illuminating.

As a chain of small islands which extend two thousand miles from northeast to southwest and fence off the mainland of the Asian continent from the expanse of the Pacific Ocean, Japan's four main islands and 3,300 smaller islets comprise only 147,000 square miles, less than that of the state of California. Since four-fifths of the country is mountainous, agriculture and industry compete for the sparse coastal plains.

On the slopes of these volcanic isles Japan must now support 104 million people, the seventh-largest national population in the world. Japan's geographical setting and isolation are probably the most important determinants of its destiny, giving rise to a highly homogeneous race and culture. Japan has developed a unique combination of self-reliance, aggressiveness, and ability to assimilate from nations round about her.

Thus for fifteen hundred years Japan has absorbed widely from other cultures and metamorphosed into something distinctly Japanese. First to be assimilated was the culture of the ancient Chinese T'ang dynasty (A.D. 618-906). Simultaneously with this Japan took to her heart with lasting, ineradicable influence Mahayana Buddhism, in the seventh and eighth centuries.

During the Tokugawa era (1603-1867) Japan adopted with her own unique modifications the Confucian concepts of social and personal ethics. During the Meiji era, in the close of the nineteenth century, she adopted parliamentary government from western models.

And now in the tumultuous postwar era Japan has assimilated western technology with a vengeance. From her capital, Tokyo, the largest city in the world (population twelve million in a metropolitan area of twenty million in 1972) to the remotest village a superficial western culture seems to ride easily on the shoulders of this ancient oriental kingdom. Her technical society has become a microcosmic model for underdeveloped nations to follow.

Aided by the beneficence of her U.S. conquerors and by much strategic aid, an economic explosion has taken place in Japan. Her gross national product has gone from 7 billion in 1949 to 262 billion in 1972. In recent years her economic growth has averaged 15 percent yearly. The cost of living has risen an average of 10 percent yearly for over ten years. The best trading partner of the United States from both standpoints, Japan has aggressively sought and captured the markets of the world today, resulting in an unhealthy excess of export trade (over $16 billion in late 1972).

"Salesman to the world," Japan ranks first in world shipbuilding, second in production of radio and TV sets and automobiles, and third in the production of steel, electric energy, and petroleum refining.

Where her military invasion of east Asia ultimately failed, her economic invasion seems to be succeeding with no end in sight. This is being called in economics "the Japanese century." Futurist Herman Kahn, on a visit to Japan in late 1971, predicted that her gross national product would surpass that of Russia and even the United States before the end of the century!

But this economic colossus balances precariously on a narrow footing. With almost no raw materials, Japan is dependent for her very life on both import and export goods. An international war or determined blocking of her sea lanes could bring quick collapse to her fantastic economy. And Japan's rapid economic growth has already brought strong complaints from opposition politicians that public works have been slighted and internal problems compounded, and that Japan must begin to look inward rather than outward in the decade ahead.

During this time Japan has rapidly changed from the traditional pyramidal structure with the emperor at the top to a diamond-shaped society with a large middle class, to which the emperor as a human being has now been drawn much closer.

The modern educational system of Japan, begun over a hundred years ago, is also a responsible factor in her prosperity. Based on the western pattern of education which she emulated, the free educational system offers six years of elementary school and three years of junior high school, plus three years of high school. Colleges have boomed—from 50 universities and colleges prewar to 852 institutions of higher learning in the present period, with 1½ million students. Approximately one-third of all high school graduates go on to college.

Linguistically, the Japanese people are blessed with a common language, and Japan's 99 percent literacy rate is the highest in the world, despite the fact that it is rated by U.N. interpreters as the world's most difficult language. Because Japanese must be adapted to the social level of the person addressed and because of its highly subjective, emotional nature, some feel that it is a major hindrance to communicating the Christian message.

Within Japan during this time political attitudes have changed radically from those of expansionist, aggressive, warlike feelings to those of passionate, pacifistic sentiments, especially among the students and intelligentsia. Under the strong leadership of MacArthur a new peace constitution was written which forever renounced war as an instrument of diplomacy. Of all things in the constitution, this has evoked the most enthusiastic support from the majority of the Japanese people, who were the first to experience an atomic holocaust. The gradual expansion of the "self-defense forces" has been bitterly opposed by students, labor, and various pressure groups. But in recent years a subtle change in basic public attitude has been taking place. One newspaper poll in 1969 revealed that 65 percent of the population had come to believe that the nation should have its own meaningful defense force. For it has only been behind the strong shield of American bases scattered throughout the islands that the Japanese economic power has been able to develop. In 1962 Japan spent less than 3 percent of her gross national budget for "defense."

The postwar constitution followed the British model of parliamentary democracy, with the emperor reduced to a symbol of national unity. State Shinto was forever abolished, and the Shinto shrines were reduced to sectarian religious status.

Freedom of the press was instituted, but it was abused, and now the overwhelming majority of all mass media are strongly left-leaning. In April 1972, following the visit of President Nixon to China the month before, a secret agreement was brought to light whereby the major newspaper and radio chains in Japan had servilely agreed not to print any anti-communist news or information of any sort in exchange for the privilege of stationing correspondents in Peking.

In the twenty-seven years since her surrender, Japan's Diet (a bicameral house in which the upper house is largely honorary) has been in control of the conservative Liberal-Democratic party for all but one two-year period. In late 1972 a dynamic new prime minister, Kakuei Tanaka, came to power under the LDP banner. At age 52 he was the youngest prime minister in Japan's history. Opening doors to diplomatic recognition of Red China, he called for a general election. Surprisingly, the LDP lost ten seats, and the strongest gains were made by the Communists and left-wing socialists, who largely displaced the Sokka Gakkai party delegates.

Religious freedom, the cornerstone of the new constitution, has provoked some of the most dramatic changes in Japan, with political repercussions as well. In the post-occupation period the nationalism that lay dormant at the base of the social structure since the end of the war surfaced and formed new combinations having vestiges of old Japanese culture. Resurgent indigenous faiths began to claim the allegiance of their own people. Some of the prewar religious symbols, like the Grand Ise Shinto shrine, were restored to legal status, alarming the Christian community. But for the most part these were calculated measures taken by the government to reestablish Japanese national identity.

Japan's traditional forms of the Shinto and Buddhist faiths, although they both claim the allegiance of a majority of the population and serve important social functions, lack vigor and are not taken seriously by the greater number of Japanese. The typical Japanese person is still married in a Shinto ceremony and buried by a Buddhist priest, but the real issues of life are considered simply a matter of fate. The present opposition to Christian evangelism came not from the old, inflexible forms of the Japanese indigenous faiths but from the fast-growing, so-called "new religions."

When the restrictive "Religious Bodies Law" of 1939 was repealed by the new constitution, scores of so-called "new religions" sprang into being, and within a few years seven hundred of them were registered! These new religions' phenomenal growth and continued influence in national politics has made them a topic of vital concern. The majority are not exclusive faiths but sects of Buddhism and Shintoism. The fastest-growing and most powerful groups are outgrowths of the nationalistic Nichiren sect of Japanese Buddhism. These are nearly all completely lay movements. The heyday of the Nichiren sects (especially *Sokka Gakkai*) was the late fifties and early sixties. During this time their membership increased 4367 percent, to over fifteen million.[17]

At the time of Nichiren (A.D. 1222-82) the older Buddhist sects had become formal and decadent. The reformer, Nichiren, preached a distinctively Japanese Buddhism, identifying religion with national life. At that time the Mongol hordes of Genghis Khan had attempted to invade Japan. Nichiren claimed the credit for overcoming the enemy through his prayers, which had supposedly brought the kamikaze (divine wind) that wrought havoc with the Mongols' invading ships. Since Mongol barbarians had been expelled by faith in the "true religion," then why cannot the foreign threat of war be dispelled today, reason the followers of Nichiren.

The postwar Nichiren sect that has been most successful is Soka Gakkai (Value-Creation Education Society), which grew from 20,000 in 1945 to 1,270,000 members in 1958, when Daisaku Ikeda, the present leader, took over the reins. Ikeda, a young man (then in his early thirties) with charismatic charm, rapidly demonstrated his ability to attract young Japan. He instituted a dramatic program of sports clubs, Madison-Avenue-style publicity, and hypnotic mass meetings. The sect mushroomed, claiming over 15 million adherents in 1972.

Ikeda, popularizing Nichiren's idea that they were to establish a golden age worldwide, started a political party, the Komeito. In April 1959, in the local elections in Tokyo, all 76 of the Soka Gakkai candidates were elected, and 261 were successful in other areas of the nation.[18] In July 1968 the sect's political party won thirteen upper house seats in the national government and 6½ million votes of the national constituency even though the sect's formal religious adherents were estimated at only 2½ million people.[19] By the time of the December 1969 Diet Parliament elections, the Komeito succeeded in securing the third-largest political party position in both upper and lower houses of the national government, with forty-eight members.[20] In the elections of late 1972, however, the Komeito suffered a disappointing defeat, losing over half their seats in the lower house.

Soka Gakkai is militantly anti-Christian. Until the late sixties the sect practiced "shakufuku" ("break and destroy"), a form of brainwashing and psychological pressure designed to intimidate men into conversion.[21]

Risshoo Kocei Kai, another lay offshoot of Nichiren's teaching, is less militant and more oriented toward restoring the "pure teachings of the past." Appalled at the number of Japan's postwar problems, such as juvenile delinquency, growing crime, and the constant threat of nuclear war, Kosei Kai leaders began promoting the teachings of the Nichiren "Lotus Sect" and endorsing ancestor worship.[22, 23] But another secret to the rapid rise of Risshoo Kosei Kai (which has grown to over three million adherents) is that, although oriented to the past, it emphasizes the practical values in religion. Thousands visit their fifteen-million-dollar-temple daily, where small groups of from fifteen to twenty members receive group counseling for personal and social problems.

Christians are not the only ones who are concerned about the rapid growth of the new religions. The general secretary of the Soto branch of Zen Buddhism remarked, "Buddhism is now beset by a danger such as it has never known since its beginning. This danger comes from the new religions and their astonishingly effective propaganda methods."[24]

These sects seem to represent what many Japanese refer to as the mercenary-minded, ruder elements of society. Little original creative thought is to be found in their literature. The teachings are basically nationalistic, hedonistic, and materialistic. Heaven is here and now. And, as the opposing candidates of the Liberal Democrat party pointed out about Soka Gakkai's political candidates, "All the Komeito candidates say the same things, as if they were speaking from the same script. Even their faces look alike."[25]

Thus in this changing, developing milieu of social, economic, and political values, the Christian church has been experiencing a painful renaissance since World War II. What does the future hold?

Conclusion

Complex, dynamic, changing Japan a generation after World War II challenges the best in the church of Jesus Christ. This brief summary of postwar conditions suggests certain conclusions regarding the future of the church, evangelism, and missions here.

1. Japan is still an open door. Therefore, although classified as a "resistant field," Japan should be retained high on the priority list as a potenial harvest field of high yield.

2. Japan may well be the key to reaching Asia through Asians. Her acceptance by many countries she formerly ruled has been amazing. The apparatus and technical know-how for mass communication of the gospel is here, and the miracle of rebirth could add the necessary spiritual power to these material forms. In the early years of the seventies the rapid growth of new overseas mission organizations has been a harbinger of this hope.

3. Japanese nationalism is mainly positive and does not yet appear to be a major threat to missionary evangelism. But its existence does mean that missionaries must increasingly work in the background, encouraging the development of virile indigenous churches. Many evangelicals need to develop a stronger church consciousness and a more effective program for cooperating with national leaders in church planting. Missionaries of oldline denominations might well rethink their church-missions relations and press for renewed recognition of the missionaries' role in their churches.

4. Urbanization, likely to continue unabated for the foreseeable future, calls for fresh strategies to reach the millions clustering in Japan's huge, high-rise apartment complexes. Population flow is irresistibly from country to city. (It is estimated that by 1980 over one-third of Japan's population will be housed in these complexes, severed from old family webs and lost in the lonely, crowded cities.) These require innovative evangelistic methods, as yet undiscovered. New missionaries have unlimited opportunities in these for the indefinite future.

5. This changing life-style of the people calls for the development of new patterns of church life. Urban land is so fantastically expensive that the traditional pattern of a central church building—now demanding parking space as well—seems to be an economic impossibility. Thus home churches, cell groups, and other patterns seemingly must be developed, for these have often been the key to the growth of new religions.

6. Statistics in the postwar period reveal that evangelical churches have the greatest potential for church growth. But some form of biblical ecumenicity is urgently required in order to maximize the limited resources of Christian personnel and funds.

7. Renewal and revival of the church is a prime necessity. Old prejudices and outmoded patterns of church life must be swept away by the wind of the Spirit in order to allow the life of the body of Christ to express itself fully and creatively in modern Japan. When the church is revived and the laity are restored to a position of responsible authority, then, I believe, the latent potential of this great people will be realized and the church will grow.

NOTES

1. C. W. Iglehart, *A Century of Protestant Christianity in Japan*, pp. 282-84, 300.
2. John M. L. Young, *The Two Empires in Japan*, p. 141.
3. Tomonobu Yanagita, *Japan Christian Literature Review*, p. 78.
4. Hallam Shorrock, "The Protestant Christian Movement in Japan," *Japan Christian Yearbook, 1968*, p. 98.
5. Donald McGavran, "Church Growth in Japan," pp. 15-22.
6. Shorrock, pp. 97-98.
7. Dorothy Pape, "A Branch of God's Planting," *Japan Christian Yearbook, 1968.*
8. *Tokyo Crusade News*, Oct. 20-29, 1967.
9. Pape, pp. 123-31.
10. Kenneth McVety, "The New Japanese Bible."
11. *Japan Christian Yearbook, 1969 and 1972.*
12. Ibid., 1939.
13. James Gittings, "Gotemba Meetings, A Possible Beginning of Japanese 'Mission in Unity' Effort," *Japan Christian Yearbook, 1967*, p. 145.
14. Shorrock, p. 93.
15. Koki Nakazawa, "Churchless Christianity in Japan," pp. 154-59; James Gittings, "Genri Undo," *Japan Christian Quarterly*, Summer 1968, pp. 194-98; Kirisutokyo *Nenkan, 1970; Japan Catholic Yearbook, 1969 and 1972.*
16. All Catholic statistics from *Japan Catholic Directory, 1972.*
17. *Japan Statistical Yearbook*, Oct. 1, 1965, quoted in C. B. Offner and H. Van Straelen, *Modern Japanese Religions* (Tokyo: Enderle, 1963), p. 35.
18. Harry Thomsen, *The New Religions of Japan*, p. 97.
19. Yasuo Furuya, "The Current Scene," *Japan Christian Quarterly*, fall 1968, p. 270.
20. *Asahi Evening News*, Dec. 30, 1969.
21. Kiyoaki Murata, "The *Soka Gakkai* Today," *Japan Times*, Feb. 13, 1964.
22. *Kosei Kai* Information Booklet.
23. Thomson, p. 117.
24. Thompson, p. 31, quoting 1957 annual report of Soto Sect.
25. Quoted in "Tensei Jingo" (Vox Populi, Vox Dei), *Asahi Evening News*, Dec. 30, 1969.

BIBLIOGRAPHY

(See also bibliography following chapter 11, "Japan, a Brief Christian History")

Bellah, Robert N. *Tokugawa Religion: The Values of Pre-Industrial Japan.* Glencoe, Ill.: Free Press, 1957.

Japan, Miracle '70. London: Longman Group, 1970.

McGavran, Donald. "Church Growth in Japan." *Japan Harvest,* Winter 1968.

McVety, Kenneth. "The New Japanese Bible." *Japan Harvest,* Winter 1969.

Michell, David. "The Christian's Attitude to Student Activism." *Christian Mission Today,* Summer 1970.

Nakazawa Koki. "Churchless Christianity in Japan," *Japan Christian Yearbook, 1954.*

Storry, Richard. *A History of Modern Japan.* London: Penguin Books, 1960.

Takenaka, Masao. *Reconciliation and Renewal in Japan.* New York: Friendship Press, 1957.

Yanagita, Tomonobu. *A Short History of Christianity in Japan.* Sendai: Seisho Tosho Kankokai, 1957.

Young, John M. L. *The Two Empires in Japan.* Tokyo: Bible Times Press, 1958.

Refugee camp in Phnom Penh before communist take-over

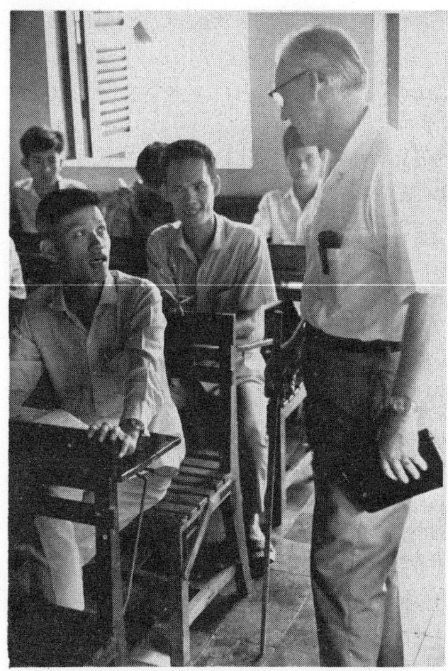

Missionary Merle Graven teaching in CMA Bible School

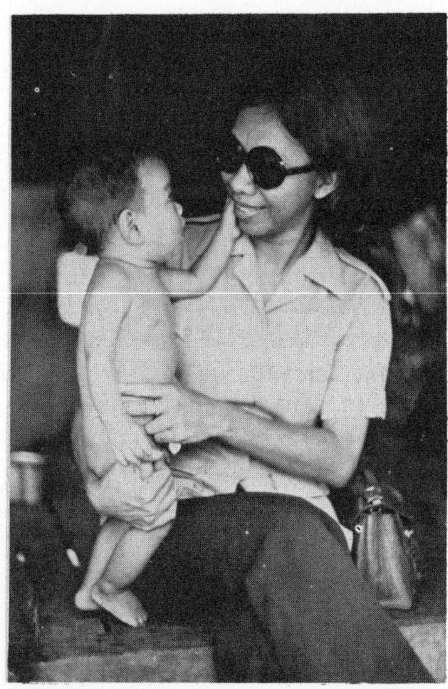

Camp worker with refugee child

Photos by Billy Bray

14

THE KHMER REPUBLIC

(CAMBODIA)

by Edward A. Cline and Billy Bray

The Church Today

"Constant change is here to stay" describes the current situation of Cambodia. While other parts of southeast Asia progress toward stability, the Khmer republic continues to be enveloped in war and day-to-day uncertainty. But what is going on in Cambodia with regard to church growth is truly remarkable; there may not be a parallel situation anywhere in the world. As this chapter is being written (October 1973) people are coming to Christ daily. The faith and experience of the new Christians is on the same level as the book of Acts; their joy in the Lord is thrilling to witness. Between 1970 and 1973 the church doubled in numbers, and it is still continuing to grow. World Vision, the Christian and Missionary Alliance (the only mission in Cambodia for fifty years until recently) and the national church are all effectively cooperating with the government to serve the tremendous human needs of the people who have been caught

---

Edward A. Cline, now regional secretary of the United Bible Societies for the Asia-Pacific region, began his missionary career with the Christian and Missionary Alliance in Cambodia in 1959. Two years later he was loaned to the British and Foreign Bible Society, and in 1969 he became the area director, administering Bible translation and distribution work from Lebanon to French Oceania from his headquarters in Singapore.

Billy Bray, author of chapters 4 and 23 of this volume ("Bhutan" and "Sikkim"), and Rev. Merle Graven, currently senior Alliance missionary in Cambodia, also contributed much valuable information to this chapter.

Ed. Note: As this book goes to press, Cambodia has been captured by the Khmer Rouge Communists. Hundreds have already been murdered, but the latest report tells of more than 3,000 evangelical Christians in and around Phnom Penh. Their fate is unknown.

Due to recent happenings in Cambodia, a brief updated report is given on page 366.

up in the war between government and insurgent forces. Along with the relief and medical assistance is a clear gospel witness, and the Lord Jesus Christ is being glorified.

In 1965, after over thirty years of dedicated ministry, missionaries from the U.S. were forced to leave the country. During the next five years the tiny Protestant church was assisted by the sacrificial service of the Jean Fune and Jean Clavaud families from France, and by Mr. and Mrs. Jean-Jacque Piaget from Switzerland. Daily the church faced misunderstanding, mistrust, and opposition. Some church leaders spent months in prison, and many Christians were afraid. The future looked dark. But the Lord gave strength and courage, and the church gained a deep spiritual maturity.

In 1970 the Lord brought his people through this trial into an experience of spiritual blessing and unprecedented opportunity to share the good news of the Christian message. Former missionaries from the U.S. returned to join the growing number of Christians in ministries of evangelism, Bible teaching, and medical assistance to the thousands who were suffering and displaced because of the war. With a new atmosphere of freedom, with a new confidence and assurance of God's faithfulness, and with a new maturity and depth in spiritual experience, the church of Jesus Christ was prepared for the dawning of a new day of opportunity. In the ensuing months other CMA missionaries returned, reinforced with a medical doctor and nurses; Christians then rallied and relief programs were initiated. Thus a new spirit of hope and euthusiasm has been born. Church attendance has multiplied and continues to increase. In a country torn by years of war—with almost half of Cambodia controlled by the Communists in 1973—the Evangelical church and the Christian and Missionary Alliance mission have responded to the tragic needs of the people and have earned a new position in the Khmer society. Recently other Christian missions have joined the Alliance in efforts to evangelize.

With refugees pouring in from outlying areas after the 1970 coup, five Cambodian Christians met together in 1970 to discuss how they could minister in the name of Christ to the needy masses. With a belief that God would supply funds, they organized a relief committee. Outside assistance was appealed for and received from the Christian and Missionary Alliance and from World Vision. To bring the church into an active part in this ministry, they started a school to teach English and used the proceeds to assist in refugee relief and evangelism. These plus individual gifts enabled the church to distribute dried fish, soya sauce, soap, salt, beds, mats, blankets, mattresses, mosquito nets, and food packs to thousands of individuals. On each gift was inscribed the name of the church, and a gospel tract was placed inside. The missionary doctor and nurses work with the church and mission relief program.

World Vision secured a tradition-shattering contract with the government in 1972 to build a new hundred-bed, $800,000 hospital project, the first mission hospital in the history of the country. The building is to be constructed on a ten-acre site across from the university in Phnom Penh, and the Alliance will staff and operate it. Through these and scores of unheralded acts under God's guidance, the Alliance, World Vision, and the national church have made scores of new friends at all levels of a government and society which had formerly been suspicious and even hostile to the gospel.

When the Phnom Penh church was closed by police in 1965, the believers moved to a less conspicuous youth center. In 1970, with unparalleled opportunities and abundant open doors, the Christians and missionaries alike were quick to seize the initiative, and by 1971 they were experiencing great blessing from the Lord. No longer content with one Cambodian church in a city expanding at a phenomenal rate, the mother church gave birth to twins in February 1971. By the end of the year she had recouped most of her membership loss, and one of the twins had outgrown her mother! A third group constructed its own church building in 1971, making a total of four Cambodian churches in this capital. Other congregations have since been organized in the rapidly growing refugee suburbs of Phnom Penh, and in October 1973 nine groups were meeting.

Thrilling conversions have stimulated the church to greater witness and work. A strong lay group has emerged to set the pace in church leadership and soul-winning. The hunger for and openness to the gospel is unprecedented. All levels of society are responding—schoolteachers, students, doctors, soldiers, government officials, and laborers.

Most encouraging are the young intellectuals in the church. One of the outstanding lay leaders was converted in the U.S. Another leader is prominent in the national bank. The young archeologist who directs the National Museum has believed with his wife, and they have been holding home Bible studies and seeing the gospel spread in the family. It is interesting to note how naturally these intellectuals fit in and identify with the national church. As a result, one church which opened in February 1971 is led entirely by qualified laymen and is filled to near-capacity each week, with souls finding Christ regularly.

Another ministry, the International church, was resumed in October 1971 for the English-speaking population of the city.

The opportunity for the evangelization of tribespeople has been brought to the church by the war. In 1971 approximately two thousand Mnong tribesmen came to Phnom Penh as refugees and settled on the other side of the Mekong River. (It is estimated that there may be as many as five hundred thousand refugees in and around Phnom Penh.) They first left Mondulkiri province and went to Vietnam, where they came in contact with the gospel. About forty of these refugees became believers. When they reached Cambodia, the church gave them relief supplies on a number of occasions. In October 1971 a Sunday school was begun among the refugees, and many more have confessed Christ, including a witch doctor who burned his fetishes. The Cambodian national church constructed a simple chapel on property prepared by the Mnongs themselves, thus becoming the first Mnong church in Cambodia. When on February 20, 1972, approximately thirty Christians were baptized in Phnom Penh, fourteen of these were Mnong tribesmen.

While this ministry has been growing, the Vietnamese church in Cambodia has practically disappeared. The members of at least three Vietnamese congregations returned to their homeland in 1970, leaving behind only a few scattered Christians, who were assimilated into the Cambodian churches. The Vietnamese church building in Phnom Penh was taken over by one of the new Cambodian congregations.

In Phnom Penh in 1970 the church for the first time in its history began planning large evangelistic rallies in downtown auditoriums. At Christmastime 1971 the national church took the initiative in renting an auditorium in downtown Phnom Penh. Seventy young people from both Cambodian and Chinese churches gave a choral background to the four speakers, who presented aspects of the Christian message. More than seven hundred overflowed the auditorium, with as many or more turned away.

But in April 1972 occurred "the greatest single manifestation of the working of the Lord in the history of the Cambodian church," according to CMA chairman, Merle Graven. It turned out to be only the first in a series of dramatic evangelistic breakthroughs. Sponsored by the national church, an evangelistic team composed of Dr. Stanley Mooneyham (president of World Vision) and a black women's quartet from the U.S. (the Danniebelles) held a three-day crusade in a twelve hundred-seat auditorium in Phnom Penh.

The young national Christians did not know quite what to expect but planned ambitiously, scheduling the meetings for 4:00 P.M. to enable people to get home before curfew in the besieged city. Military police surrounded the hall for security, planning to search every attendant. By 2:00 P.M. the first day hundreds had started to gather. As each person entered he received a Scripture portion chosen for that service and prepared by the Bible Society. When the doors were finally opened, the crowd rushed past the guards. When the seats were full, police had to allow the overflow to sit in the aisles to prevent a riot.

Mooneyham's simple messages were greeted with cheers, laughter, and jeers. After each mention of the miraculous, some people left. When Dr. Mooneyham gave the invitation, he was greeted with a burst of laughter—then two-thirds of the crowd rose. He repeated the invitation twice, then asked the seekers to come forward. With cheers and laughter more than five hundred people came. Apparently the laughter was more embarass-ment than mocking.

By the end of the brief campaign, 654 people had signed decisions for Christ, and 369 more had indicated a desire for more instruction. Of these, 90 percent were men between the ages of eighteen and thirty. The next Sunday eighty of these men were in churches. "If by some miracle the majority of those who professed faith could be gathered into the life of the church, the total membership of the Cambodian church will have nearly doubled," observed Malcolm Bradshaw from the OMF's church growth study office in Singapore, on hand to assist. "These could influence the whole future of the church and evangelism there, for the Mooneyham campaign established beyond a shadow of a doubt that the atmosphere is ripe for the church to grow. . . . When I talked to the museum director about the meetings, he said that the response of the young men reflects the groping of their age group, desperate for answers to life's perplexities. The older generation, he continued, rests on Buddhist belief. But men his age are looking for alternatives."

The results of this first mass evangelism effort were so surprising that follow-up preparations were inadequate. Some of the converts were drawn into the Catholic church, though about 10 percent were successfully led to discipleship in the evangelical churches. CMA chairman Merle Graven reported in October that the church had a record number of baptisms of sixty-six already that year, of which twenty-nine resulted from the Mooney-ham campaign.

Preparing for better follow-up, the church welcomed Dr. Richard Har-vey (from CMA in the U.S.) in July for six days of evangelism out of which came 95 more professions of faith. Then in October a Campus Cru-sade "Lay Training Institute" enrolled 105 Christians, mostly young peo-ple converted within the year. On a single day of witness after the train-ing they reported that 83 people had prayed for salvation.

A still greater harvest was gathered in November 1972, when Dr. Mooneyham of World Vision returned for another six-day campaign. De-spite a sunset curfew and a rigid search of all who entered the twelve hundred-seat auditorium, the hall was filled daily. Large quantities of Scriptures were again distributed by the Bible Society. Over twenty-five hundred responded to the invitation to receive Christ, of whom more than 75 percent were youths under twenty-five. More intensive follow-up began with these. Church leaders in Cambodia feel that Indian and Indonesian missionaries could be a boon in assisting this follow-up and nurturing the converts because of their cultural and educational affinity.

During the five-year period of oppression in Cambodia (1965-70), prayer for a new entrance for the gospel was offered around the world, especially at the Asia-South Pacific Congress on Evangelism in Singapore in November 1968. God has answered wonderfully. The return of the missionaries in 1970 was marked by wise planning and careful training of the few church leaders. Mission-church relationships were resumed in a healthy and well-balanced framework, with full mission cooperation in church projects but with church financing in the hands of the nationals.

"The servant role of the missionaries is noticeable," Bradshaw reports.* "The initiative for governing the church is firmly in the hands of the nationals, and the missionaries are careful to leave it with them. The passive dependence on the foreign leadership so often present on mission fields seemed to me to be absent. The national leaders want other missionaries, assuming, of course, that they will serve with them as the present ones do." Thus joint church and mission expansion programs for both Bible school and publications show promise. Though teenage evangelism is just beginning, new Sunday schools have already been opened. A new effort is being made to compose Cambodian tunes and hymns, and local musical instruments are being used to some degree in the churches. And in the 1971 annual church conference, the infant church of less than seven hundred decided to send missionaries to countrymen in Vietnam, Laos, and Thailand. In August 1973 a small team visited Vietnam (where there are an estimated five million Cambodians) in cooperation with the Evangelical Church of Vietnam for a witness to the large Cambodian-speaking population in the southern part of the country. The Lord wonderfully blessed their witness, and a group of new believers was established. Plans are now underway for a more permanent missionary effort among the Khmer-speaking people of South Vietnam.

Throughout the years of opposition, quantities of Bibles, Testaments, and Scripture portions were kept available by the United Bible societies. In step with the response of the church, special editions have recently been prepared to support its growth and witness with a solid base of the Word of God in the language of the people. In January 1972 a joint church-Bible society-mission training seminar launched pastors, Bible school students, and dedicated laymen on an unprecedented program of witness with literature and the Word of God. Thus today Scripture distribution in the Khmer Republic is rapidly increasing. The Bible Society

*Malcolm Bradshaw is an Overseas Missionary Fellowship worker doing research on church growth in Asia.

recently supplied a van to assist teams of young people in Scripture distribution and witness in the large refugee communities surrounding the capital. The number of Bibles distributed, as seen in the statistics below, reveals the zealous outreach of the very small Protestant Christian community in the Khmer Republic.

SCRIPTURE DISTRIBUTION

	1970	*1971*	*1972*
Bibles	137	173	396
New Testaments	50	237	718
Portions	15,595	29,463	37,084
Selections	632	25,845	93,911
Totals	16,414	55,718	132,109

Mass literature production has been limited by high costs, but translated books and tracts are selling increasingly. Gideons International has also assisted in supplying some eighteen thousand New Testaments in recent months.

Since Cambodia is nominally a Buddhist state, gospel broadcasts have not been permitted over the three national radio stations and one TV station (there are over a million radios and seven thousand TV's in the country). Thus the televising of the Mooneyham meetings was another significant breakthrough, spurring hopes that radio and TV may now be open to other gospel efforts. These and other providential happenings in Cambodia in recent months have brought new life and hope to evangelism.

In 1970 the tiny "Khmer Evangelical church had only 640 members and about 1,000 communicants spread among nineteen organized churches, seven unorganized ones, and three outstations in nine provinces. (The only other church is a small Seventh-Day Adventist group and a recently organized Pentecostal group). These are served by seven ordained pastors, eighteen other workers, and five elected lay leaders. But growth is accelerating encouragingly, particularly since the evangelistic efforts in 1972. The membership had more than doubled by 1973, and there are expectations of continued multiplication.

A good precedent for church growth has been established. The concept of branch churches is well accepted and will in time lead to a multiplication of members. Within six months of the new era the mother church spawned off two new congregations, called the "sister churches." Since then other new congregations have started. The sister churches will also very likely give birth to new congregations in the near future.

Challenges and Opportunities

With apparently unlimited opportunities and an atmosphere of freedom and friendliness, the Protestant church by itself is not yet strong or large enough to meet all its challenges. Therefore wide doors of missionary opportunity beckon, not only to the Christian and Missionary Alliance, but also to other sympathetic evangelical groups. The currently few CMA missionaries and pastors are overworked and overwhelmed by staggering spiritual and physical needs. (One other couple, the Clavauds, formerly French missionaries with the CMA but now independent, have continued in Phnom Penh since 1965, supporting themselves as teachers.) For years the Alliance has sought assistance from other evangelical missions with sympathetic views on evangelism and the establishment of a self-supporting church policy. They would welcome help today in the face of challenges like these:

1) The population is still largely unevangelized. Eight of the nation's seventeen provinces are still without a Christian church or witness and represent a fertile field for pioneer, church-planting evangelism. Numerous literature and radio opportunities offer a challenge to new missionary involvement.

2) The war has disrupted the educational system, forcing almost half of the schools to close. This presents new opportunities for the churches to establish schools which combine education and evangelism in the days ahead.

3) A missionary society was recently formed by the church, and national efforts are underway to reach geographical and social segments of the country which have never heard the gospel of Christ. The Alliance Bible School, founded in 1938, has an enrollment of twenty young people, who are being trained for future leadership in the new churches. Theological Extension Education (TEE) was organized in September 1973, with a beginning class of twenty-eight students. This program is intended to equip laymen for leadership roles in the new congregations and to carry on the expanding efforts of evangelism.

Following the April '72 evangelistic campaign, Malcolm Bradshaw made a penetrating critique of Cambodia's spiritual needs for the immediate future:

> 1) First comes feeding the hundreds of enquirers. Ways should be found to gather them into "new believers' cells." There are too many new people and too few workers available to accomplish this in one-by-one fashion.
> 2) There needs to be emergency training of leadership for these cells from among the new believers themselves.
> 3) The momentum must be maintained. New believers must be intro-

duced to soul-winning right away. The challenge is for the congregations to keep evangelism going as their way of life, and not as a special feature.

4) The policy of multiplying new congregations all over the Phnom Penh area and in all the occupation-free areas should be pressed very hard now.
5) New forms of pastoral training—lay and full-time—need to be discussed. Theological extension education that would train laymen to pastor congregations may be part of the answer. But full-time pastors will also be needed.
6) The recent great influx was among young men of marriageable age.
7) Outside help will be needed for the Cambodian Church without swamping it. There is a danger that publicity about the harvest potentiality in Cambodia might bring a deluge of evangelists and independent missions down upon Phnom Penh. That happened in Indonesia. What is needed is for new groups to enter *only* if they are willing to build the one indigenous church instead of introducing sheep stealing, shepherd-hiring, and the unfortunate image of a divided body.

Thus today Cambodia is happily one of the most opportunely open doors to evangelism anywhere in the world. With official pressure against the Christian community suddenly and dramatically relieved and with anti-Christian sentiment almost completely forgotten, church and mission leaders are excited about the opportunity to reach Cambodia in this time of desperate need. Since God has answered prayer so miraculously since 1970, the prospects for a spiritual breakthrough in the days ahead seem great. But laborers are urgently needed.

Nation and People

A proud nation with a long and rich history, Cambodia was a part of the Funan Empire at the time of Christ. The dominant regional ethnic group, the Khmers, began moving down the Mekong Valley from their kingdom of Chenda during the early part of the Christian era, and by the sixth century they had overthrown Funan. Brilliant architects and builders, they proceeded to construct the enormous Ankor Wat, a beautifully exotic temple city, and then consolidated the Khmer empire there in the ninth century. The Khmers' military victories subjugated much of what is now modern Thailand, Laos, and Vietnam by the twelfth century.

Cambodian law, religion, and civilization spread throughout mainland southeast Asia during that period. Even today Cambodian music, dance, and paintings are the basis of many classical art forms in all the surrounding countries. Khmer temples are found as far away as northeast Thailand and Laos. But her two most aggressive neighbors, Vietnam and Thailand, steadily ate away at Khmer power, until the Thais finally ended the Angkor civilization in 1431, leaving the magnificent city to be reconquered first by the jungle and later (in 1972) by communist forces.

Thus by the beginning of the nineteenth century Cambodia had shrunk to its present size, and it was ripe for French colonial takeover in 1863. The French colonial rule lasted until Japan in World War II shook the French grip. It was resumed in 1945, but independence efforts soon began to gain power. Norodom Sihanouk, elected king, in 1951, when he was only nineteen years old, forced French forces to hasten the relinquishment of Cambodia, so that it became an independent, neutral state in 1953. But in practice Sihanouk turned increasingly to the left. He abdicated his throne to his father in 1955, devoting his time to organizing a new political movement, the Popular Socialist Community. When Sihanouk's father died the young man announced himself not king but chief of state, and began a program of "Buddhist Socialism"† with a left-leaning foreign policy. By 1965 eastern Cambodia had become a military supply funnel for the Viet Cong attempt to take over South Vietnam. North Vietnamese army units had built a large infrastructure there. Nervous Cambodian leaders began to feel that a bloodbath was soon to come.

So in March 1970, while Sihanouk was vacationing in Paris, Marshall Lon Nol, deputy prime minister, led a parilamentary coup d'etat and deposed Sihanouk. The new government took a strong anti-communist stand, began drafting a new republican constitution, and appealed for U.S. aid to drive out the increasing number of Viet Cong invaders. In October 1970 Cambodia was declared the Khmer Republic. In May, Prince Sihanouk set up a government-in-exile in Peking, with a mock cabinet of former Cambodian Communists. Most observers feel that he will probably not return to power.

After the brief U.S. foray of sixty days (at the invitation of Marshall Nol) to destroy Viet Cong supplies and supply lines in 1970, guerilla fighting intensified. Communist forces captured much of the north, including the old capital at Ankor and the four northeastern provinces. While these comprise a large land area, they are the most sparsely settled

†Sihanouk is quoted as having said, "Our socialism does not stem from Karl Marx, Engels, Lenin, Stalin, or Mao Tse-Tung, but from the Buddha. It is our own form of socialism—one that corresponds to our needs" (*Is Cambodia Next?*, Russell Press). He himself has written a book, *Our Buddhist Socialism* (Cambodian Ministry of Information), in which he says, "Buddhism, contrary to certain other religions, does not make its followers aggressive in respect to others. On the contrary, it does not extol proselytism but perfect respect for the beliefs of others. That is why our state, of which the religion is Buddhism, protects just as steadfastly the other religions established in Cambodia, Islam, and Catholicism in particular. . . . This explains our attitude toward Communism, which, in our eyes, is simply a different religion to ours. We find in it many merits, and we do not belittle it. But we should follow our own Buddhist way. As long as it does not attack us, we accept with pleasure to coexist with it in a friendly way."

area of the country. Thus in early 1973 about 80 percent of Cambodia's land area was under communist control, though no more than 25 percent of the people are under their domination; over 75 percent remain free in the southern areas.

Then strong man Marshall Lon Nol, in a surprise move in early March 1972, abruptly seized full control of the government. Deposing the titular head of state, he declared himself president, dissolved the national assembly and cabinet, and stopped work on the new republican constitution, saying that he would revert to the twenty-five-year-old royalist constitution. At the time of takeover Lon Nol declared that he would give the nation a new system of government under a powerful president who would appoint his own sixteen-man cabinet. This he has done. But in mid-1973 the war conditions worsened. Communist forces moved southward to the borders of the capital, cutting off major supply roads and even the Mekong River for a brief time. With American support bombing scheduled to stop in October, the whole future of the country at this writing is precarious.

While 85 to 90 percent of Cambodia's 7,400,000 population are ethnic Khmer, there are large minorities of Vietnamese, Cham, and Chinese. Before the mass Vietnamese exodus in 1970 there were about 375,000 of these in the country, but by 1972 almost all are believed to have joined the refugees returning to South Vietnam. Many of the 400,000 Chinese in the country fled with the Vietnamese. The Cham minority group, which once formed a great kingdom of their own in South Vietnam, remains as a Muslim enclave numbering about 90,000. Smaller groups of Thais, Laotians, and Europeans complete the picture except for 80,000 primitive tribal people in the northeastern provinces of Ratanakire and Mondulkiri, mostly in Khmer-Loeu, Raday, and Mnong.

Cambodia's population is youthful; about 44 percent are under fifteen, and the country is growing at the rate of 3 percent per annum. While nearly 20 percent of the population lives in the booming capital city of Phnom Penh (almost tripled to two million population since the intensification of communist hostilities), most of the people are still concentrated along Mekong waterways and the great freshwater lake of Tonle Sap. None of the other major urban centers have populations of over forty thousand.

Most of the people speak Khmer, but all the ethnic minorities speak their own languages or dialects as well. French and more recently English are the languages of the educated classes, though Chinese and Vietnamese once predominated in the markets and commercial centers. Pali and Sanskrit, upon which the Khmer language is based, are the languages of the temples. Tribal languages are scorned by the Cambodians, although there has been increased interest in understanding them in an effort to assimilate the hill people into Cambodian society. Literacy in the country is high; about 60 percent of the population can read Cambodian, according to the government. About 10 percent of the population is literate in both Khmer and French.

About the size of Missouri or Washington, Cambodia is largely a nation of very well watered rice plains dominated by the Mekong River and Lake Tonle Sap. A tropical, monsoon country, its rainfall averages fifty-eight inches a year, and annual floods from the Mekong irrigate the phosphate-rich fields. The country is therefore ideally suited to agriculture, and most of the Cambodians are farmers. Except for some people on the hilly border area with Thailand, most Cambodians live by rice farming on the plains, which are seldom higher than ten feet above sea level. High plateaus lie in the south and west, peaking at the Elephant Mountain range, which runs to the Gulf of Siam, where the granite Cardomom mountains reach five thousand feet. Two-thirds of the land is forested.

Although Cambodian spokesmen choose statistics to show great progress in several areas of development, there is little doubt that the outbreak of the war has seriously set back progress in economic, educational, and medical development. The $300 million American aid grant in 1971 is a drop in the bucket compared to the country's great needs. The economy is severely crippled. The per capita annual income in 1970 had slumped to $120, one of the lowest in Asia. Rice production is down, as well as rubber, jute, coffee, and tea, all of which were once major export earners. Transportation on the nation's 16,381 kilometers of roads was largely severed by military activity, forcing prices up by as much as 200 percent in less than a year. Subsequent devaluation of the currency has forced prices up still further. Transport of lumber and other products of light industry has also been paralyzed, so production has gone down. Light industry had grown from 650 factories in 1955 to 3,700 in 1968 and was producing textiles, rubber, plastic, and paper as well as electrical, leather, and metal goods. But with the mass exodus of Vietnamese skilled labor in 1970, much valuable administrative and technical assistance has been lost. Tourism, also a valuable source of national income before the war closed off Angkor Wat as a tourist attraction in 1970, has dropped to almost nothing.

Education, probably the top national priority before the war, has suffered severe setbacks. Half of the 6,037 primary and secondary schools in the country were closed or destroyed by communist activity in 1970. In the first fourteen years of independence, the student population had jumped from 317,000 to 1,161,000, but tens of thousands of the students have now been mobilized into the armed forces.

Modern medicine in Cambodia saw progress after World War II, but having fewer than five hundred doctors, forty dentists, seven hundred nurses, and six thousand five hundred hospital beds, the country still faces a chronic medical crisis. Almost all these medical personnel were drafted into military service, so civilians are forced to go largely without medical attention. In all areas of preventive medicine and social welfare the country is still in the most primitive stages of development. Cambodian officials have invited missionaries to begin work in leprosy treatment, preventive medicine, and medical education and to open a hospital in Phnom Penh. Thus World Vision's projected hospital will alleviate a desperately great need. Cambodian officials have also asked for help in refugee housing, war victim relief, and other pressing needs.

National Religions

While Cambodia's indigenous religion is usually considered Theraveda Buddhism, animism and Hinduism were strong influences early in its history. Today Hinduism still lingers pervasively along with ancestor worship and Cao Dai-sm—a popular religion of the masses which is actually a mixture of Buddhism, Brahmanism, and animism (see chapter 28, "Important Religions of Asia). In theory, explains one Cambodian, the people worship Buddha for morality ("Buddha teaches us how to be good"), though the people usually follow Brahmanic and animistic customs in everyday life. In times of death and distress, for example, the people turn to Brahmanism for Vedic chants and prayers. They worship and recognize the powers of the mythical Hindu Naga serpents and the holy cow, and Brahmanism is the religion of art, architecture, music, and drama.

Overall, however, as in nearby Thailand and Laos, the fear of spirits dominates the daily lives of the people. Placating these evil forces and paying homage to protecting "angels" is the true religion of the masses and the home. It is this mixture of beliefs and superstitions that is referred to by most Cambodians when they declare that they are Buddhists.

Cambodia has a remarkable geographical feature with deep religious connections. The Tonle Sap (Great Lake) drains into the Mekong River at Phnom Penh most of the year, but during the monsoon months the flood waters of the Mekong back up into the lake and flood large areas of the surrounding plains, with the 100-square-mile lake then covering up to 770 square miles. When the wet season ends and the moon is full, the water in Tonle Sap begins to flow back toward the distant sea again. This moment when the water reverses itself was the occasion for the famous "water festival," whose time was fixed by the lunar month of Kadek, which means that it fell over a three-day period in either late October or early November. The water festival was a celebration of harvest and fertility, a time when monks came back from their annual retreat and a signal for revelry among the whole population. The queen took up residence in her floating house, a beautiful barge in front of the royal palace, and there were colorful races and processions of brightly painted, great canoes day and night for three days.

Historians are not sure about the origins of this major Cambodian festival, but its religious significance is great. It is clearly linked with a desire to pay tribute to the mighty Mekong and the part it plays in everyone's daily life—the richness of the soil along its banks, the wealth of fish in its waters, and the approaching harvest of the crops watered by it. The Kadek water festivities are a dramatic demonstration of the closeness of the people and their religion to the land and spirits that dominate the life of all the southeast Asian nations.

Cao Dai, Confucianism, Roman Catholicism, and ancestor worship are largely of Vietnamese and Chinese origin; thus with the mass exodus of the Vietnamese they have lost the little power that they had. A large Cao Dai temple was left half-completed at Phnom Penh, probably never to be finished.

Islam remains quite strong among the minority Cham group (numbering only 90,000) and a number of mosques dot Phnom Penh, Kompong, and Battambang.

Christian History

CATHOLIC MISSIONS

Into this milieu of religions the Catholic church came with the Christian message in the sixteenth century. Members of the French Foreign Mission of Paris were the pioneers and still dominate the work today. Their work has customarily been more institutional than evangelistic, and has been until present almost completely foreign-led, flowering under the protection and promotion of French colonialism.

Orphanages and schools were soon founded, and three hundred years later, at the beginning of this century, communicants were numbered at sixty-six thousand. Just before the climax of the recent political crisis in the late 1960's, Catholic schools numbered eighty and had an enrollment of about fifteen thousand, which was divided into eighty-four parishes under a reputed seventy priests. But since the beginning Catholic work majored on French expatriates and the large Vietnamese community in the country. Thus when guerilla activity by the Viet Cong and North Vietnamese caused most of the Vietnamese to flee in the late 1960's, the Catholic community was decimated. Though in 1966 there were eighty-four Catholic parishes with seventy priests, the Catholic church lost fifty-two thousand Vietnamese members in the 1970 migration and all seventy of its Vietnamese priests; sixteen Roman Catholic churches and seventeen schools were completely closed as a result. According to Catholic sources, only two or three thousand Vietnamese Catholics are still left in Cambodia. Thus Catholic estimates, which their officials say are optimistic guesswork, put their total church membership today at twenty thousand. Few are practicing Catholics, and less than three thousand are true Cambodians.

Catholic leaders are now planning a shift in emphasis to work among the Cambodians themselves. A relief commission has been set up to help the country in the present crisis, and Catholic leaders are working desperately to set up a lay-training program among their handful of Cambodian members. Since their two seminaries have been closed, seminarians are sent to Malaysia. Few of the Catholic missionaries have a command of the Cambodian language, and they have done little work in translation or other efforts for the Cambodian church, though they are now purchasing Protestant Bibles.

PROTESTANT MISSIONS

Protestants first penetrated Cambodia in 1923. For years Robert Irwin of the American Bible Society in Bangkok had been urging missionaries to enter Cambodia—first the Oriental Missionary Society and then the Christian and Missionary Alliance, which had worked across the border in Vietnam since 1911. Early petitions to enter Cambodia were opposed by both the Buddhists and the French. But finally Rev. A. L. Hammond, who had been assigned to work among the Cambodians in Vietnam, received permission from the new French resident superior, and in 1923 as the first Protestant missionary he entered Phnom Penh. Later that year the David Ellisons joined the Hammonds and opened a work in Battambang near Thailand.

These two missionaries plunged immediately into translation work and education, while trying to get a grasp of the language themselves. Thus the first three decades of the work resulted mainly in the translation of the Scriptures into Khmer, a small handful of converts, and the opening of the first Bible school in 1925. The New Testament was completed in 1934 and printed by the British and Foreign Bible Society in Hanoi. In 1940 the Old Testament was finished, but the war prevented the whole Bible from appearing until 1954. Thus early evangelism went painfully slowly. Churches had been weakly established in only eight of the seventeen provinces when in 1933 the French (Catholic) government decreed that missionary work could be carried on only in those areas occupied prior to

1932. This restrictive policy continued until the end of World War II, when the first new constitution provided religious liberty.

Yet even after the war the fruits of religious liberty and peaceful evangelism were hard-won. In 1946 a movement called "Issarak" was organized to obtain complete independence for Cambodia from French rule. For several years a period of unrest and danger set in. It was unsafe for the Cambodians themselves to live in country areas, and it was impossible to visit the Christians in such places. In the daytime the Cambodian government and French troops patrolled the main roads and centers, but at night the Issaraks were in complete control of everything outside the principal towns. During this time, Christian pastor Yan and elder Yieng were murdered by the Issaraks.

But through a postwar missionary activity a printing press was established in 1947, the Bible school moved to the capital of Phnom Penh in 1949 and evangelism accelerated to the limit of the available presonnel. Contact with the remote Kony Antra tribe was made in 1955. The national church grew slowly to a membership of six hundred baptized believers in eighteen organized churches in 1961. Continually hampered by lack of personnel, the CMA sought help from friendly missions. The Far Eastern Gospel Crusade sent one couple from the Philippines in 1961, but they were able to stay only two years. Other missions' plans to help did not materialize.

By 1965 Prince Sihanouk's steady moving to the left caused him to cut off diplomatic relations with the U.S. With the excuse that missionaries were doing nothing for the country, the government canceled all visas, and the U.S. missionaries sadly left. All responsibility for the churches, Bible school, and press was turned over to the tiny Protestant church, which had less than a dozen ordained pastors. In 1967 the Bible school was forced to close because of political pressures, but it reopened a year later. Meanwhile, the American missionaries who had to leave the country asked the Alliance Chretienne Missionaire (French branch of the CMA) to continue their work because the French could easily go to Cambodia. Into this critical breach the Clavauds, Piagets, and Funes stepped with sacrifice and faith, courageously serving the young church as it grew to selfhood through suffering. In all this the Holy Spirit was later seen to have been preparing them for the new days of opportunity following the revolution.

Yet even in these difficult times a number of Christians bore a heroic witness that strengthened the entire church. Every day the radio attacked the U.S. for helping South Vietnam, and to Sihanouk's government "evangelical" meant pro-American! Thus several times the church elders and pastors were summoned by the government for questioning, and a general summons asked the church to stop all activity. But the church committee believed it better to obey God rather than man, and the services went on. Later those in charge of the church services in Phnom Penh were again summoned by the police, and four of them were put in jail without any trial. One of those jailed was the Bible school principal, who had never stopped serving the Lord openly and who had refused to sign a statement that he would stop preaching.

The testimony of another of these men, Son Sonne, a full-time staff member of the Bible society, records the courage, the joyful faith, and the fruit of these new Christians during this trial:

> On 13th August 65 at 10 A.M. I was working in the Phnom Penh Church bookroom; there were two policemen who came to invite me to their office in urgent. So I closed the door and went with them. I knew there would be some difficulties, but I felt I am in the Lord and He's in me.
>
> At 1 P.M., after questioning me, two other policemen led me and one of my Christ friends (we two were accused the same time) to the jail.
>
> The iron door shut, and the accused men and women gathered around us and asked "What's about you?" We answered them smiling, for that was the testimony we made. There were many difficulties, such as bad smell, darkness, bad food, not enough water, bedbugs, and so on. I thought this was a type of hell, but the Word of God gave us enough strength to live. In that circumstance, I knew that the Word of God in Psalm 119:72 is very true.
>
> We had enough time to pray together, for we had no work to do. Oh! Praise the Lord, the watchmen had given us a small chamber filled with darkness and bedbugs, but it's a good place for prayer.
>
> One thing very noticeable for prisoners and watchmen was that when they were worshipping Buddha, we two were worshipping One True God; they had one time per day while we had several times per day.
>
> God had helped us during the two months, and one by one our small chamber had no place for the receivers of Christ to worship. There were eight when we left there!

As this chapter is being edited, three years from the founding of the Khmer Republic, suffering Cambodia presents a stark, Rembrandt-like picture. In the background are the dark shadows of communist encirclement and attack, the bleak tragedy of the whole Indo-Chinese war, and the grave uncertainty of Lon Nol's future course. But shining with glowing light from an unseen source is the central figure of the tiny, heroic church. Born in suffering and nurtured by the bitter fare of recent persecution, it is a vital, growing church. To speed and enlarge the evangelistic harvest now being reaped, workers are urgently needed; new missionaries are welcome. But above all, intercessory prayer is imperative to undergird church and mission and to preserve the suffering, embattled nation.

Since this chapter was edited in late 1974, Cambodia has fallen to the communist forces. Until the last moments there were reports that the spiritual awakening begun four years ago was continuing. The tiny national church—exclusively Christian and Missionary Alliance related—grew over 300 percent in 1974. Christians reportedly numbered up to 5,000, with over 100 professions per week being reported until the bamboo curtain fell. Churches had increased to thirty-eight, twenty-seven in Phnom Penh alone. In one refugee area of the city (whose population had swollen from 600,000 to 2,000,000 in the last three years), 1800 conversions were reported. One church enjoyed a weekly attendance of 300 worshipers. Laymen, including the president of the Supreme Court, the commissioner of the national police, and other prominent figures, courageously led the churches.

But the news blackout of the church since the communist takeover has been complete. The forcible evacuation of the entire civilian population of Phnom Penh was probably a shrewd way to eliminate the sick, weak, young, and aged; only the hardy survived the march. Many youth converts in the last three years are believed injured or dead as a result of the bittter fighting in early spring. The fate of the 125-bed World Vision hospital is unknown, although missionary workers were evacuated. Minh Voan, former oil company executive and lately World Vision leader in the country, chose courageously to stay. Only twenty-six Christians are known to have escaped to Thailand. It may be years before the fate of the church and Christians is known. But a vital, growing, glowing church, born in suffering and war, was boldly witnessing when the bamboo curtain fell around the ancient Khmer kingdom.

DONALD E. HOKE
June 23, 1975

BIBLIOGRAPHY

Cambodia and Its Industry. Edited by the Sangkum. Phnom Penh, 1967.

Cambodia under the Sangkum's Administration. Edited by the Sangkum Reastr Niyum. Phnom Penh, 1968.

Irwin, E. F. *With Christ in Indo-China.* Harrisburg, Pa.: Christian Publications, 1937.

Kambuja Magazine, Oct. 15, 1968 (15th Anniversary Issue).

Kingdom of Cambodia. Publication 7747. Washington: U.S. Government, Department of State Background Notes, Office of Media Services, Bureau of Public Affairs, July 1969.

Light in Their Dwellings. Phnom Penh: Gospel Press of Cambodia (CMA), 1963.

Rollin, P. Vincent. *Historie de la Mission du Cambodge (1555-1967).* Phnom Penh: Grand Seminaire St. Ignace, 1968.

Sihanouk, Norodom. *Our Buddhist Socialism.* Phnom Penh: Ministry of Information, 1969.

Personal witness is the secret of Korean church growth. Korea's Protestant church is the strongest in Asia. It hosted Billy Graham in 1973 when the evangelist held the largest public Christian meeting in history.

15

KOREA

by Samuel Hugh Moffett

The Church Today

Christianity came late to the ancient country of Korea, but it has found in the Korean heart an openness and receptivity almost unmatched in the history of modern missions. The country has become famous for rapid church growth, indigenization, and faithfulness during persecution.

Evidences of the impact of the gospel are visible everywhere in South Korea, even to the casual tourist. The capital, Seoul (fifth-largest city in the world) is a city of churches. There are said to be more than sixteen hundred Christian congregations in the capital city alone. Steeples and crosses are prominent on the skyline in all directions. At four or five every morning church bells all over town call the faithful to daybreak prayers. Even the national assembly, the Korean Parliament, has an early prayer-breakfast once a month for the sixty-eight Christian assemblymen who comprise one-third of the total membership of the Assembly.

A climactic display of Christian strength in Korea was the outpouring

---

Samuel Hugh Moffett, son of pioneer Presbyterian missionaries to Korea, is currently dean of the graduate school of the Presbyterian seminary in Korea, the oldest Protestant seminary in the country. After serving in pastoral and national youth work in the United States, Dr. Moffett began his missionary career in China after World War II under the Presbyterian USA board, teaching at Yenching and Nanking universities until the communist takeover. Reassigned to Korea in 1951, he did rural evangelism and Bible school teaching before assuming his present responsibilities. Dr. Moffett has authored two books on Korea, *Where e'er the Sun* (1953) and *The Christians of Korea* (1962), and has coauthored (with his wife) *Joy for an Anxious Age*, a Bible study guide on Philippians. He is a member of numerous church and university boards and learned societies. Dr. Moffett holds the degrees of B.A. (Wheaton College), B.D. (Princeton Seminary), and Ph.D (Yale University).

of support for the Billy Graham Crusade in the summer of 1973. More than 4.5 million people attended the meetings in six cities, and on the last day alone, in Seoul, more than a million Koreans packed the Yoido Plaza in a tide of humanity which was perhaps the largest crowd ever gathered at one time and in one place to hear an evangelistic message. More than eighty thousand decisions were recorded, and Christian unity in faction-torn Protestant circles was visibly reinforced by the nationwide cooperative effort.

The Christian church is growing at the rate of nearly 10 percent a year, more than four times as fast as the general Korean population (see the church growth table in Appendix 2). Protestant and Roman Catholic total adherents now number 3,037,047 in a total South Korean population of 31,000,000. If the marginal sects are included, the number of Christians is over 4 million, or about 13 percent of the population, which is one of the highest percentages in Asia.[1]

In the armed services the proportion is even higher. A continuing revival spearheaded by Korean chaplains has brought thousands of ROK troopers to Christ. At one mass service in April 1972 some 3,478 officers and men were baptized in a single afternoon. Since January 1971 a total of more than 20,000 Protestant and 2,000 Catholic military have been baptized, and it is reported that the percentage of Christians in the armed services has risen from about 16 percent in 1965 to 25 percent in 1972.

An impressive network of Christian schools undergirds this growing church and feeds Korea's youth. Half of South Korea is under twenty-five. Open doors welcome them to 11 Protestant colleges and universities (out of a national total of 173), 85 Protestant high schools, 79 Protestant middle schools, and innumerable Christian primary schools—not to mention the sixty thousand boys and girls from underprivileged families who are enrolled in the church day-schools called Bible clubs.

The rapid growth of the church has also sparked an explosion in theological education. Korea now has eighty listed theological schools, of which three are Roman Catholic. Most of these are at the high school level, though there are twelve major seminaries accredited as colleges and at least three designed primarily for college graduates, as in the American system. Two denominational and one interdenominational graduate school of theology offer Th.M. degrees, and an international, evangelical center for advanced theological studies is projected for Seoul in 1973 or 1974.

The Korean church has been among the first of the younger churches to shoulder its own responsibility for foreign missions and world outreach. Presbyterians organized a mission to China as early as 1912, at the same time they formed their first Korean general assembly, because, they insisted, a true church must have its own missionaries. Today there are at least forty Korean foreign missionaries supported by Korean denominations with their own funds and working in nine foreign countries—Thailand, Brazil, Mexico, Taiwan, Ethiopia, Sarawak, Hong Kong, and Japan. There is also one Korean missionary in the United States.[2]

Christianity has penetrated the life of the nation at all levels. Protestant hospitals are scattered across the peninsula. The impressively growing Presbyterian medical complexes in Taegu and Chonju lead the way in successfully linking medicine to evangelism and in taking medicine out to where it is most needed, the rural countryside. It is estimated that only 6.5 percent of the rural population ever gets modern medical attention. Chonju's Presbyterian medical center has developed a vigorous rural health program, and Taegu Presbyterian Hospital, where converted patients have started more than a hundred new churches, has pioneered a satellite system of subsidiary Christian country hospitals.* Yonsei University's huge Severance Hospital and medical school, and its counterpart, the Catholic medical center in Seoul, continue to inject a significantly large percentage of Christians among Korea's physicians. And there is a significant Christian experiment in low-cost health care at Koje Island Community Health and Development Project.

Korea's mushrooming cities are another of the many focuses of special Christian concern. Christians have not only performed some of the best research on urban social problems but have also provided direct leadership in slum clearance, resettlement, family planning, and industrial relationships. Sogang (Jesuit) University has what has been called in a recent report "the best labor-management school in Korea."

The same report notes other recent evidences of the Christian presence throughout Korea. The church has already transformed the role of women in Korea, led by Christian heroines like the late Dr. Helen Kim of Ewha University. Thus prominent Christians were among the twenty-eight women honored for contributions to Korean society at the tenth anniversary of the National Federation of Women's Association. Christian power was made evident when church protest forced the withdrawal of a banknote bearing a portrait of Buddha. Korea's first Christian opera, *Esther* (composed and directed by the leader of a famous church choir) packed the country's largest auditorium in Seoul for three nights running.

The mass media in Korea are wide open to Christianity. The first Christian broadcasting network in the world is HLKY, operating under the Korean NCC and blanketing the country with the gospel from five substations. TEAM Radio's HLKX from its base in Korea beams the uncon-

*Ed. note. The Taegu hospital and its outreach is one of the most effective medical evangelistic projects in modern mission history. It has been prayerfully engineered by the author's brother, Dr. Howard Moffett, also born and educated in Korea.

quered good news through bamboo and iron curtains into Red China and Russia. Christians also have a strong foothold in Korean television.

But perhaps in the long run the most significant manifestation of the Christian presence in Korea will prove to be the fact that four of the seven South Korean delegates, including the chairman, in the crucial North-South Red Cross talks in late '72 were Christians (two Presbyterian, one Methodist, and one Roman Catholic).[3] For in the midst of all the rejoicing over church growth and influence in South Korea, it must not be forgotten that in North Korea there is apparently not a single organized church left.

When in August 1972 the tightest border barrier in the world opened briefly to permit a cavalcade of South Korean Red Cross negotiators and reporters into the north to discuss the problem of the 10 million Koreans whose families have been separated by the division of the country, for the first time in twenty-two years reporters were able to interview a professing Christian in North Korea. Kang Ryang-uk, now a high communist official and uncle of Premier Kim Il-sung, is probably the last Christian minister left alive in communist Korea. He was asked about the state of the church. Rather defensively he asserted that North Korea has freedom of religion and that he was still a Christian, but he knew of no churches left standing or of any Christian meetings. "The churches," he said, "were all destroyed by United States bombers during the war." Asked about Bible distribution, he said there was none because "not many people want them."

But South Korea's Christians look at the churchless north and wonder. If there is really freedom of religion in North Korea, why does Seoul, which was also destroyed in the war, today have sixteen hundred Christian churches, while P'yongyang, once known as "the city of churches," has none?

Before surveying in more detail the Christian situation in Korea, let us glance briefly at the nation, its historical and religious background, and the history of Christianity in "the land of high mountains and clear water."

Nation and People

Surrounded by three giant neighbors—China, Russia, and Japan—the ancient nation of Korea juts like a thumb from the eastern rim of the Asian mainland. Its mountain-studded peninsula covers only 84,579 square miles—about the size of Minnesota—but holds a combined population, north and south, of 44,839,000. In mission history its church is famed for rapid growth, indigenization, and faithfulness in persecution.

Racially homogeneous and united politically for more than thirteen hundred years, Korea has been badly used by the twentieth century. First it lost its freedom to Japan for forty years (1905-45). Then, when World

War II restored Korea's independence, it lost its unity to the Communists. Since 1948 the peninsula has been cut in two politically at about the thirty-eighth parallel: North Korea is communist; South Korea is free. The two republics are about the same in area (each roughly the size of Indiana), but South Korea has two and a half times the population of its communist sibling in the north: the Republic of Korea (South Korea) has a population of 31,139,000 while the Democratic People's Republic of Korea (North Korea) has a 13,700,000 population. Seoul, the capital in the south, has a population of well over 6 million while P'yongyang, the northern capital, has less than a million.

National History

Korea's legendary past stretches back more than four thousand years to a mythical founder, Tan'gun, miraculously born to the earth-descended son of the heavenly father and a bear-woman. The traditional date is 2333 B.C. Archeological evidence more matter-of-factly suggests even earlier paleolithic inhabitants and important tribal migrations from Siberia and Mongolian central Asia beginning about 3000 B.C. Recorded history begins much later, in the first century B.C., with the rise of three kingdoms competing for power in the peninsula and driving Chinese colonists from its northwest corner. Under one of these kingdoms, gold-rich Silla, the whole country was unified in the seventh century. For a while the Silla capital of Kyŏngju was perhaps the fourth-largest city in the world, after Constantinople, Baghdad, and T'ang China's Changan.

From the seventh century to the twentieth Korea was ruled by three dynasties: *Silla* (A.D. 668-935), famous for gold and chivalry; *Koryo* (935-1392), renowned for its blue-green celadon pottery; and *Yi* (1392-1910), which gave the world movable metal type, armored battleships, and the most scientific phonetic alphabet ever used. The Korean throne was sovereign and independent, but it stood in a typically Confucian associate relationship to the mighty Chinese Empire, much like that of a younger to an older brother.

Late in the nineteenth century the old order in east Asia was broken by the meteoric rise of Japan and the collapse of China. As a national proverb puts it, Korea was caught "like a shrimp among whales" in the clash of her huge neighbors. After Japan defeated China in 1895 and Russia in 1905, she stayed on in Korea, finally annexing the country as a colony in 1910. When in 1882 the western powers entered Korea, it was too late to secure an open-door policy, which might have saved her.

Japanese colonialism ended in 1945, but Korea's troubles were not over. The war ended with Russian troops in North Korea and United States occupation in the south. The country never regained its unity, for the

Russians claimed the thirty-eighth parallel as a new international boundary. In 1948 Russia installed Kim Il-sung as premier of a communist dictatorship north of the parallel, while the people of South Korea elected a famed freedom-fighter and Christian, Syngman Rhee, as their first president. Two years later, in June 1950, the north attacked, and for three years the peninsula was ravaged by the Korean War. Its end at P'anmunjŏm in July 1953 was an armistice, not a peace, and the armistice line was one of the tightest-sealed borders in the world until the summer of 1972, when South Korea's President Park made a surprising move to open negotiations with the North Koreans. At this writing diplomatic talks have begun, but their future is uncertain.

The artificial division has been economically crippling, separating the country's industrial resources in the north from its agricultural assets in the south. This unbalance at first gave the industrial north an economic edge; but the remarkable economic boom in the south since 1960, combined with the comparative failure of North Korea's doctrinaire communist economy, has now closed the gap.

South Korea's gross national product (GNP) has been rising at one of the highest rates in the world: 8.9 percent in 1967, 13.1 percent in 1968, and a record 15.9 percent in 1969, the world's highest. The average per capita GNP has jumped in ten years from about $80 (1960) to $195 in 1969 (compared with $48 in Malawi, $495 in Hong Kong, and $4,255 in the U.S.) and to $252 in 1971. Perhaps the best overall indication of the striking improvement in South Korea's living standards is the lengthening life span of its citizens. In ten years, six years have been added to the average Korean's life expectancy. Twenty years ago he could expect to live only to fifty-two, and ten years ago to fifty-eight, but today he can expect to live to sixty-four.[4]

National Religions

The old religions are not, at least on the surface, a significant factor in Korea today. Historically, the country is Buddhist and Confucian. Buddhism came into the country from China in the fourth century and has dominated the country's art and folk literature. Confucianism came in the seventh century and has molded its ethics and academic disciplines. Both have been politically powerful, Buddhism in the Koryo dynasty up to the fourteenth century and Confucianism in the Yi dynasty up to the twentieth. But today they are largely ignored by all but the old and the sick—and foreign tourists. Most of modern Korea professes no religious faith, and the largest organized religion in the country, according to actual spot surveys if not by official report, may well be Christianity.

Beneath the surface, however, the unorganized, felt religion of the masses is still animistic shamanism, with all its related superstitions—fortune-telling, geomancy, and folk healing. There are said to be over twenty-seven thousand practicing shamanist sorceresses registered in the country. This primitive tribal religion was probably brought by the Korean people into the peninsula from their place of origin in the Siberian or Mongolian steppes millenniums before Christ.

In the cities, however, shamanist rites are giving way to a brash import from the West, modern materialism. The religion of the people as a whole might best be described as an uneasy tension between the old animistic-shamanist superstitions touched by Buddhist-Confucianism and a new, secularized, self-centered preoccupation with material progress. But neither the old fears nor the new obsessions are organized religions, and the country is virtually wide open to the evangelistic presentation of the gospel.

Statistics on religious membership as reported by the Ministry of Culture and Information are somewhat misleading. Its *Handbook of Religions* simply repeats the membership claims of the country's religious bodies and is not a critical assessment of actual membership. As the chart indicates, Buddhists and Confucianists claim more members than the Christian churches, but recent survey samplings suggest that in organized membership as well as in popular preference Christianity has now overtaken both of these older, traditional religions. Chondokyo, the "Heavenly Way Religion" (shown in fourth place) is a late nineteenth-century "new religion" combining Korean nationalism wth elements of Confucianism, Buddhism, and Christianity. Despite its listing in some encyclopedias as a major Korean religion, it has been virtually moribund since the 1920s. Shamanism is not charted at all, for despite its underground vigor it is neither organized nor publicly admired.

KOREA'S RELIGIONS

	Believers	*Places of Worship*	*Clergy*	*Property Value*
Buddhism	5,562,278	2,266	15,420	$20,200,000
Confucianism	4,423,000	231	11,831	2,800,000
Christianity	3,943,838	13,235	17,026	41,000,000
Chondokyo	636,067	119	977	2,460,000
Others	1,136,853	629	3,149	

SOURCE: *Chongkyo P'yonlam* (*Handbook of Religions*, in Korean only) (Seoul: Ministry of Culture and Information, 1969, p. 15). "Others" includes such sects as Taechongkyo, Chonrikyo, Bahai, etc.

CHRISTIAN HISTORY

Compared with Buddhism and Confucianism, Christianity in Korea is very young—a handicap in a land where age and tradition mean much. It has therefore been very tempting to try to trace Korean connections with seventh- and eighth-century Nestorianism in China, but so far the evidence is disputable. Not until the sixteenth century did a Roman Catholic reach Korea, and the first Protestants were shipwrecked Dutch sailors (and one Scot) in the seventeenth century. Though Catholicism entered Korea in earnest in 1784, the Protestant church is such a recent arrival that the first infant to receive Protestant baptism is still alive. Yet despite its youth, Christianity in its vigor, influence, and perhaps numbers has already decisively overtaken its older rivals. One great secret of Christianity's success in Korea has been the indigenous nature of its expansion.

THE CATHOLIC CENTURY (1784-1884)

Father Gregorio de Cespedes may have been the first Roman Catholic in Korea, but he was not the father of Catholicism in that land. He came more as a chaplain to invading Japanese troops in 1593 than as a missionary to Korea. It was another two hundred years before the church in Korea was founded, and then it was planted not by a foreigner but by a Korean.

At the request of a small circle of Korean scholars a young man, Lee Seung-run, went to Peking in search of missionaries to ask them more about the strange Catholic doctrines which had been filtering across the border since 1631 in smuggled Christian literature. He returned, was baptized, and a few months later, in 1784, began to spread the faith. When the first priest and foreign missionary arrived ten years later, a Chinese named Chou Wen-mo (baptized James or Chu Mun-mo in Korean), he found to his surprise that there were already 4,000 Catholics in Korea. Not for another forty years, until 1835, was a western missionary able to enter the country successfully for residence—Father Pierre Maubant of the Societe des Missions Etrangeres.

But the price of success for those early Catholic missionaries was martyrdom. Four great persecutions decimated the church in 1810, 1839, 1846, and 1866. Father Chou died in the first persecution and Father Maubant in the second. More than 8,000 Christians are said to have perished in the greatest persecution of all, that of 1866. But though driven underground and scattered, Catholics could still count some 17,500 believers in Korea at the end of their first century.[5]

PROTESTANT BEGINNINGS (1884-95)

As the Catholics ended their first century in Korea, in 1884, the first resident Protestant missionary arrived, a physician, Dr. Horace N. Allen, who was transferred from China by the Presbyterian Church USA (Northern). However, as with the Catholics before, it was not a missionary but a Korean convert who gathered together the first group of Protestant believers in the land.

The earliest Protestant missionary contacts, beginning fifty years before Allen, had been either impermanent and exploratory or else conducted from across the Manchurian border. In 1832 Carl Gutzlaff, a German who had begun evangelism in Thailand, distributed Scriptures along the eastern coast; and in 1866 a Welshman, Robert J. Thomas, lost his life in a similar attempt. He was killed at P'yongyang in the act of offering a Bible to the man who beheaded him and is revered as Korea's first Protestant martyr. Two Scots, John Ross and John McIntyre, baptized the first Korean Protestant in Manchuria in 1876 and produced the first Korean translation of the New Testament between 1882 and 1887.

It was thus one of the Koreans baptized in Manchuria who established the first worshiping Korean Protestant congregation. So Sang Yun, who helped Ross in Manchuria translate the New Testament, returned to Korea in 1883 and won over a hundred believers to Christ before Dr. Allen ever set foot in the country.

Six months after Allen's arrival, on Easter Sunday of 1885, the first ordained Protestant ministers reached Korea together. They were Horace G. Underwood, a Presbyterian, and Henry G. Appenzeller, a Methodist. Within fifteen months, in 1886, Underwood had baptized a convert (the first Korean baptized in Korea) and Appenzeller had opened a school, Pai Chai. This was symbolic, in a way, of the subsequent emphases of Korea's two largest denominations: the Methodists tended to stress education, the Presbyterians evangelism. The first two missions were soon joined by others: Australian Presbyterians and Independent Baptists in 1889, Anglicans in 1890, Southern Presbyterians in 1892, Southern Methodists in 1896, Canadian Presbyterians in 1898, Seventh-Day Adventists in 1903, the Oriental Missionary Society in 1907, and the Salvation Army in 1908. These remained the major Protestant bodies in Korea until World War II.

FIRST EXPLOSION OF CHURCH GROWTH (1895-1910)

Beginning in 1895 and continuing about fifteen years, a dramatic explosion of Protestant church growth in Korea startled the Christian world. It was spearheaded by the evangelistic work of Samuel A. Moffett and his colleagues in Presbyterian churches in northwest Korea,[6] and it was spread and reinvigorated nationally by the Great Revival of 1907.[7] Early emphasis on lay witness and Bible study began the expansion, which reached its climax in the large evangelistic meetings of the revival. Denominational barriers were broken and Christians were moved to join together in witness. "Some of you go back to John Calvin," said one

Korean leader to the missionaries, "and some to John Wesley, but we can go back no further than 1907, when we first really knew the Lord Jesus Christ."[8]

In those important fifteen years the Protestant community in Korea (total adherents) grew from only 802 in 1895 to an astonishing 167,352 in 1910. Comparative Roman Catholic figures for the whole period are unavailable, but from 1900 to 1910, while Protestants reported a phenomenal 900 percent increase in adherents (from 18,081 in 1900 to 167,352 in 1910), the number of Catholics rose only 25 percent, from 60,000 to 75,000.[9,10]

Many reasons have been given for the amazing Protestant growth, which was particularly notable in the Presbyterian church. The most important reasons seem to have been a stress on people-to-people evangelism, Bible training for the entire church membership, the adaptation of the Nevius method (which promoted self-support, self-government and self-propagation), and the unique outpouring of the Holy Spirit in revival. Presbyterians also strategically deployed their missionaries to take advantage of and to follow up areas of growth, whereas the Methodists for a time were forced to reduce the number of their missionaries.

The development of Christian institutions in this same period not only contributed to the spread of the faith but also helped to conserve and train new believers. Methodists pioneered in education for women with Korea's first school for women, Ewha, as early as 1886. By the beginning of the twentieth century Christian schools were the most popular and crowded schools in the country. In 1906 Presbyterians and Methodists cooperated in opening the country's first Christian college, Soongsil, in P'yongyang, and four years later Ewha Girls' School shocked the old-fashioned by introducing college grade education for women. Medical work also, which under Dr. Allen had been the opening wedge for all Protestant missions in Korea, continued to contribute not only to Korea's evangelization but also to her modernization. In 1908 the nation's first Korea-trained doctors graduated from Severance Medical College, which had begun as Allen's Royal Hospital. By 1910 it seemed to many thoughtful Koreans that the wave of the future was with the Christian faith.

HARASSMENT AND PRESSURE (1910-45)

But in 1910 the tide turned not only against the church but against the country itself. Two thousand years of Korean independence ended when Japan, victor over China and Russia, formally annexed the peninsula as a Japanese colony. The church soon felt the pressure of the new government's distrust, and growth slowed perceptibly. Christians, not without reason, were accused of independent nationalist sentiments. In the Independence Movement of 1919 fifteen of the thirty-three signers of the

Korean Declaration of Independence were Christians. Economic depression in the 1920s was a further blow to Korea's self-supporting churches.

Finally, in the 1930s the revival of Japanese militarism brought violent persecution upon the church for its resistance to Shinto shrine ceremonies demanded by the Japanese. The number of Christians who suffered imprisonment for their faith is estimated at about 3,000, of whom some 50 were martyred. The crushing climax came between 1943 and 1945, when Korea's great independent Protestant churches were ordered abolished and melted down into one government-controlled organization, "The Korean Christian Church of Japanese Christianity." The Christian community on the eve of World War II (1940) numbered 372,000 Protestants and 150,000 Roman Catholics.[11]

PRESENT SITUATION (1945-70)

The restoration of Korean independence at the end of World War II did not end the church's time of troubles, but it did, by the grace of God, usher in a new period of church growth. Yet troubles began at once. North Korea, where the church had once been the strongest and largest, was held by the Communists, who lost no time in destroying the church as an organized body. They first tried to control the church through a puppet "Christian League." When that failed, they moved to exterminate it by ruthless, direct persecution. By the summer of 1950, when the Communists attacked South Korea, the organized church in the North had almost ceased to exist. So when United Nations' armies advanced to the Yalu River, then reeled back south under Chinese onslaught, 4.5 million North Koreans fled south to freedom. With them came all the Christians in North Korea who were able to leave.

Today some of the largest congregations in South Korea are refugee congregations from the north. The most famous is the great seven thousand member Yong-nak Presbyterian Church in Seoul, where attendance on a regular Sunday morning passes nine thousand. The pastor, Dr. Han Kyung-chik (now retired), was a featured speaker at the Berlin World Congress on Evangelism and chairman of the Asian South Pacific Congress on Evangelism in Singapore in 1968. But back in the north, so far as we know, there are no organized congregations left. It is estimated that more than four hundred Protestant ministers were murdered by the Communists, and Roman Catholic sources give the names of over a hundred martyred priests.[12]

CHURCH DIVISION

In the south the greater enemy proved to be weakness and division inside the church rather than communist persecution from without, and this weakness lost the church its greatest opportunity. During the years of Japanese occupation, it was only in the Christian church that Korea could produce free and vigorous leadership. It was no accident, therefore, that, when the country regained its independence, it turned to Christians for its first three presidents: Syngman Rhee, a Methodist (1948-60); Chang Myon, a Catholic (1960-61); and Yun Po-son, a Presbyterian (1961-62). Most of Rhee's first cabinet and 25 percent of the early National Assembly were Christians. It was a time for decisive, united spiritual leadership by the Korean church. But the church failed. The years from 1950 to 1960 were not years of leadership; they were a decade of division. Controversies and schisms split all the major denominations, and the reputation of the Christian churches was critically tarnished throughout the nation.

Before World War II, in 1940, there were only six nationally recognized Korean Protestant denominations: Presbyterian, with 173,738 communicants and catechumens; Methodist, with 25,661; Anglican, 10,120; Holiness (Oriental Missionary Society), 7,332; Salvation Army (no figures); and Seventh-Day Adventist, 7,370 (Federal Council Prayer Calendar, 1940). Today, however, there are fifty-seven denominations in Korea. Until 1940, 90 percent of the Protestants were cooperatively organized in a Federal Council, and the two largest bodies, Presbyterian and Methodist, had divided their areas of work in a comity agreement in order to avoid undue competition and the appearance of disunity. Today less than half the Protestants and only six of the fifty-seven denominations belong to the National Council of Churches. All semblance of organized unity is gone. Presbyterians, who make up two-thirds of the country's Protestants, are divided into four major and eight splinter denominations. Only the Roman Catholics and the Salvation Army seem to have escaped schism or duplication, as a 1969 table of the larger groups in Korea today shows:

MAJOR RELIGIOUS GROUPS IN KOREA

Confessional Bodies		*Total Adherents*	*Churches*
Presbyterian	(12 groups)	1,415,436	5,814
Roman Catholic	(1)	751,217	369
Methodist	(4)	300,107	1,517
Holiness	(2)	217,289	727
Baptist	(4)	64,191	434
Salvation Army	(1)	40,604	102
Seventh-Day Adventist	(2)	35,091	656
Pentecostal	(6)	30,790	143

SOURCE: Compiled from *Chongkyo P'yonlam*, pp. 16-19.

Actually, since 1950 an entirely new dimension of Christian division has been added to the picture with the emergence of what may be called "marginal sects." It could be said, therefore, that for all practical purposes Korean Christianity is grouped into three or four categories, depending on how deep is judged to be the current division between ecumenical and nonecumenical Protestants. Each of the four groups described below has roughly a million adherents.

Roman Catholics (839,711 members in 1970). After the century of persecution, Catholics emerged from hiding in 1890 and reorganized. Membership increased, though more slowly than for the Protestants. In 1830 the Societe des Missions Etrangeres de Paris had been given exclusive jurisdiction in Korea, but in 1909 the French missioners were joined first by German Benedictines, then in 1923 by American Maryknoll Fathers, and in 1933 by Irish Columbans. The Korean priesthood grew even more slowly than the membership and the foreign missioners. In 1941 there were 102 foreign missioners and only 103 Korean priests.[13]

But after World War II membership began to rise with increasing rapidity, more than matching the rate of growth (though not the actual numbers) of the Protestants. In 1969, 185 years after the baptism of Lee Sung-hun in Peking, Korea received its first cardinal when Stephen Su-hwan Kim, archbishop of Seoul, was elevated to the rank of prince of the church.

Ecumenical Protestants (1,013,035 adherents). Six Korean denominations comprise the Korean National Council of Churches, and through that body they are related directly or indirectly to the World Council of Churches. The bulk of the membership is old-line Presbyterian and Methodist of evangelical and conservative persuasion, as well as the Salvation Army, but also included are the Anglicans of Korea and a moderately liberal Presbyterian denomination (ROK), together with a tiny indigenous body, the Korean Gospel church.

Non-Ecumenical Protestants (1,184,035). For both theological and ecclesiastical reasons an equal number of Korean Protestants do not choose to belong to the Korean National Council of Churches. To them, that ecumenical body seems too liberal theologically and too inclusivist ecclesiastically. Three main groupings are discernible in this important segment of Korean Protestantism. One consists of independent but cooperative evangelical bodies, like the Christian Korean Holiness church (Oriental Missionary Society), the Korea Baptist Conference (Southern Baptist), the Missouri Synod Lutherans, and the Evangelical Alliance Mission. Another is the small but growing group of Pentecostal denominations. The third and largest part is more outspokenly antiecumenical and independent. It includes two of the largest and most influential Presbyterian bodies (the Haptong and Koryo Presbyterian churches) as well as smaller Holiness and Methodist schisms.

The Presbyterian divisions are important enough to deserve separate notice (see Appendix 1, "The Presbyterian Church Controversy in Korea"). These divisions trace back to a decade of division, 1950-60, when Korean Presbyterianism splintered into its present four main churches. The parent Korean Presbyterian church (Tonghap) was founded in 1907 and is related to the American United Presbyterians, the US Southern Presbyterians, and the Australian Presbyterian church. Since the schisms, the church is popularly known in Korea as the Ecumenical or Tonghap (i.e. United) Presbyterian Church. The first division occurred in 1951. It began as a protest against what were considered to be compromises in Korean Presbyterianism on the shrine issue, combined with charges of theological liberalism, and it culminated in the formation of the Koryo Presbyterian church. Three years later the parent body was accused again, this time of fundamentalism, in a controversy over Bible interpretation and seminary control, and its liberal critics separated in 1954 to form the Presbyterian Church in the ROK, which is related to the United Church of Canada. The most violent schism of all occurred in 1959, the division between what is now known as the Tonghap Presbyterian church and the Hapdong Presbyterian church. Hapdong Presbyterians are antiecumenical but have now largely discarded their connections with the Reverend Carl McIntyre and the ICCC. They are sometimes called "NAE" Presbyterians, but their relationship is not so much with the American National Association of Evangelicals as with the US Orthodox Presbyterian church and the Reformed Presbyterian church (Evangelical Synod).

It is encouraging to be able to add to this sad record of discord a hopeful note. By 1972 the tide was beginning to turn away from division and, if not to reunion, at least to cooperation. In September, for the first time since the beginning of the schisms in 1950, the moderators and general secretaries of the four leading Presbyterian denominations met together, representing a constituency of about 1.5 million Korean Presbyterians, and made plans for a Presbyterian Federation in Korea.

Marginal Sects (1,014,275 estimated, probably exaggerated). Though classified by the government as Protestant, these semi-Christian sects are unacceptable to most Korean churches. The largest is the "Olive Tree church," founded in 1955 by a former Presbyterian elder turned faith healer, Pak Tae-son. An industrialist as well as an evangelist, Pak has established two heavy industrial complexes near Seoul as "heavens" or "Christian towns" for his followers, who must surrender all their capital to him. The second-largest sect is the bizarre "Holy Spirit Association for the Unification of World Christianity," popularly known as "Ong' il-kyo" or "Unity." This was started in 1954 by Moon Sun-myong, who claims to be a Korean Jesus Christ. The Jewish Christ failed, he says![14] (This sect is also rapidly growing, oddly enough, among university students in Japan.)

Something of the comparative size and denominational complexity of all these Protestant and semi-Protestant bodies can be seen from the listing in Appendix 2 of the thirty largest Korean denominations.

Conclusion

What the new foment on the political scene will mean to Korea in days to come is as yet unknown. Some normalization of relations with North Korea might mean an opportunity for the churches to be reestablished and evangelism to begin again there aboveground, though the churches in other Asian communist nations have not taken this direction. The new prosperity of Korea also may affect church growth, as it has in nearby nations like Japan.

Whatever the political and economic conditions, Korea presents a great challenge to its strong churches to increase their evangelism and to the world church to continue its prayer and wise missionary assistance.

APPENDIX 1

The Presbyterian Church Controversy in Korea

by Harvie M. Conn

Ed. note. In view of the worldwide publicity given to the controversy in the Korean Presbyterian church since the war, I asked a representative of another large body of Presbyterians there to share his view of the difficulties. Dr. Conn, presently professor of missions at Westminster Theological Seminary, Philadelphia, Pa., was for many years a missionary under the Orthodox Presbyterian Mission in Korea. Dr. Moffett, author of this chapter, has graciously consented to the addition of this appendix to the chapter.

The years 1910-45 were ones of harrassment and pressure for the Korean church as both church and nation adjusted to the harsh Japanese military dictatorship. Liberal spokesmen in the church gained ascendancy in leadership roles. The long, vigorous domination of liberalism and neoorthodoxy in Japan now made itself felt among those Korean students who had to turn to Japan for theological training. Liberation in 1945 found a church that, for some years, had been controlled by liberal hands.

It is this background that forms the sad years of church division in Korea (1945-60), as the church turned its strength to the question of renewal and reformation. What steps were to be taken about Shinto shrine collaborationists? What about the theological liberalism that had taken control? Within the Methodist church, the conflict was not so acute. But within the Presbyterian church, the struggle produced at least four major church divisions.

Almost the first program to be initiated centered in the far southwest around a newly established school (1946), the Koryo Theological Seminary. Calling for the church to exercise discipline against the Shinto shrine collaborationists and against the liberal leadership of the church, the Koryo Seminary circle commended itself to many for the consistency of its demands, the tested piety of its leadership, and the politicking of its opponents. But without the support of the church's liberal element or of those conservatives who felt their demands to be too "purist," the circle was rebuffed time and again by the church as a whole. In May 1951 the General Assembly cut off the presbytery from which the circle gathered its main strength.[15] Those presbyterial commissioners continued to attempt to be seated at the Assembly until 1954, when the Assembly reiterated its action of 1951 and the delegate from the presbytery "formally withdrew from the General Assembly."[16]

Unwilling to support the Koryo Seminary, the Assembly also found itself increasingly uncomfortable in its official support of the Chosun Seminary, erected in 1940 as a neoorthodox reversal of the prewar seminary policy and tradition.[17] The institution had been made the official General Assembly seminary of the rebuilding church when the southern part of the country had nowhere to turn for leadership training. But student protests concerning the theological liberalism of the school in 1947 forced the issue before the Assembly, and mediating conservatives then sought to avoid a showdown by erecting a third school, obtaining recognition for it as well in 1949. Then they proposed a merger with the liberal Chosun seminary; when this failed, in 1951, the Assembly withdrew their recognition of both schools and proceeded to erect still another new institution. The conservatives demanded the suspension of Chosun Seminary's neoorthodox president and barred its graduates from ministry without further study in the Assembly's now recognized seminary. In 1953-54 the Chosun Seminary (now called Hankuk Seminary) circle withdrew, taking with it approximately one-fourth of the original Assembly.

In 1959 the most violent eruption occurred within the mediating group, now the largest of the three. Increasingly the question of continuing membership in the World Council of Churches had come to the fore. The Koryo Seminary circle had expressed their concern for the theological latitudinarianism of the council when the church had first joined in 1948. And conservatives were not reassured by the strong support of the liberal-oriented Chosun Seminary faction toward the WCC. This concern grew with the report of the two delegates to the 1954 Evanston Assembly, enough so to erect an "Ecumenical Study Committee." Its 1957 report noted two streams of thought within the WCC—those said to be seeking a united world church and those interested merely in wider fellowship. The report urged continued cooperation as long as it intended merely the latter.[18]

By the time of the 1958 Assembly, however, the question exploded again, this time coupled with charges of unethical use of funds against the conservative president of the General Assembly seminary. Attitudes toward the WCC became inextricably linked with attitudes toward the president's continuing in office. "The assembly seemed to be deadlocked over the Korean church's relationship to the ecumenical movement. Finally a compromise position was adopted which left the Korean church in the WCC but qualified its participation in it to matters where faith might not be compromised."[19] The formula did not resolve the issue.

During the year, tension continued to mount; the conservative group began a systematic campaign to discredit the WCC on three grounds—liberalism, superchurch ambitions, and pro-Communism. The 1959 Assembly met with this unsettled question, as well as many internal ones now linked to it rightly or wrongly. The result was violence, politicking on both sides, and strong paternal and financial pressures from western groups both for and (later) against the WCC. In an atmosphere of pandemonium, with obstructionist tactics used by both groups, the Assembly was adjourned by its anti-WCC moderator to meet again in a few weeks. Immediately after, the pro-WCC "former stated clerk rushed to the platform, made a motion that a vote of nonconfidence be declared in the moderator, . . . put his own motion, which he announced as being passed.[20] The room was cleared out by anti-WCC and pro-seminary president forces, and weeks later two adjourned Assemblies declared themselves in session.

Both groups withdrew their membership from the WCC, one in strong opposition to the liberal leadership of the movement, the other in hopes that withdrawal would bring unity to the national church. The strongly anti-WCC body (the Haptong group) has continued to maintain a firm stance, supported by missionaries of the Orthodox Presbyterian church and the Reformed Presbyterian church, Evangelical Synod. The other body (Tonghap group), supported by the major boards mentioned by Dr. Moffett, at their 1969 Assembly voted to join the WCC again. Conservatives now predict that union is inevitable between this group and the 1953 division.

APPENDIX 2

Korean Protestant Denominations and Marginal Sects

Denomination	*Adherents*	*Ministers and Evangelists*	*Churches*
(Olive Tree) Evangelistic Society#	700,520	1,515	1,768
Presbyterian Church of Korea (Hapton, NAE)	550,790	2,096	1,991
Presbyterian Church of Korea (Tonghap, Ecum.)*	504,728	2,580	2,281
Holy Spirit Assn. for Unification of World Christianity (Tong'ilkyo)#	304,750	1,013	936
Korean Methodist Church*	289,024	1,507	1,350
Presbyterian Church in the Republic of Korea*	194,188	788	689
Christian Korean Holiness Church (OMS)	145,773	639	581
Korean Presbyterian Church (Koryo)	102,125	702	513
Jesus Korean Holiness Church	71,516	185	146
Korean Baptist Conference (Southern Baptist)	51,613	353	378
Salvation Army*	49,635	236	206
Seventh-Day Adventists	33,596	748	627
Christian Korean Assemblies of God	27,348	150	117
Korean Bible Presbyterian Church (Non-ICCC)	21,190	62	58
Jesus Korean Methodist Church	19,960	70	41
Korean Church of Christ (instruments)	19,813	87	97
Korean Bible Presbyterian Church (ICCC)	13,951	91	89
Korean Bible Baptist Church	12,108	61	49
Nazarene Church	10,880	59	60
Anglican Church in Korea*	9,826	38	64
Jehovah's Witnesses#	8,911	657	219
Christian Korean Reformed Church	8,225	58	51
Korean Jesus Reformed Presbyterian Church	7,260	187	139
Jesus Free Methodist Church	6,788	48	45
Korean Gospel Church*	5,900	19	12
Korean Jesus Presbyterian Church (Head Presbytery)	5,016	17	14
Church of Christ Evangelical	4,490	107	87
Church of God	3,637	24	17

#Marginal Sect
*Member of N.C.C. of Korea

Reconstructed Church	3,449	35	53
Choson Christian Church	3,030	20	13
Others (24 bodies)	24,414	..	285
Total	3,214,454	14,152	12,976

NOTE: The Roman Catholic Church in Korea reports 839,711 members, 3,042 priests and church workers, and 368 churches.

SOURCE: *Kidokyo Yonkam, 1970* (Korean Christian Yearbook, pp. 511-521, with exception of number of adherents of Presby. Ch. of Korea (Tonghap) taken from *Report of the 1971 General Assembly of Presbyterian Church in Korea.*

NOTES

1. *Kidokyo Yonkam, 1970* [Korean Christian yearbook], (Seoul: National Christian Council, 1970), pp. 511-21.
2. Ibid., pp. 537-40.
3. Stanton R. Wilson, "Narrative Report on Korea, 1972" (submitted to Commission on Ecumenical Mission and Relations of the United Presbyterian Church in the U.S.A.), pp. 19-24.
4. Statistics from *Pick's Currency Yearbook, 1969;* Korea Herald, July 17, 1970, and Jan. 29, 1970; *Korea Times,* Dec. 2, 1969.
5. Joseph Chang-mun Kim and John Jae-sun Chung, *Catholic Korea Yesterday and Now.*
6. Roy E. Shearer, *Wildfire,* pp. 108-35.
7. William Newton Blair, *Gold in Korea,* pp. 63-74.
8. J. Fowler-Willing and (Mrs.) G. H. Jones, *The Lure of Korea,* p. 21.
9. Charles D. Stokes, "History of Methodist Missions in Korea, 1885-1930," pp. 10-15.
10. *Le Catholicisme en Coree* (Hong Kong, 1924).
11. "Survey 1947," in *Report of the Joint Deputation to Korea* (Far Eastern Joint Office, 1948).
12. Kim and Chung, *Catholic Korea,* pp. 341-384.
13. Ibid.
14. Spencer J. Palmer, ed., "The New Religions of Korea."
15. Harvie M. Conn, "Studies in the Theology of the Korean Presbyterian Church—I-IV," *Westminster Theological Journal* 29-30 (1966-68).
16. Kim Yang-sun, *History of the Korean Church in the Ten Years Since Liberation,* pp. 159 ff.
17. Kang Won-yong, "The Korean Church in the World Community," *Koreana* 3, no. 1 (1961): 123.
18. Kan Ha-bae, "Korean Theology: Where Is It Going?", *Themelios* 7, no. 1:41.
19. George T. Brown, *A History of the Korea Mission, Presbyterian Church USA, from 1892 to 1962,* pp. 715 ff.
20. Ibid., p. 730.

BIBLIOGRAPHY

General Works

Blair, William Newton. *Gold in Korea.* Topeka, Kan.: H. M. Ives & Son, 1957.

Brown, George Thompson. *Mission to Korea.* Nashville: Board of World Missions, 1962.

Campbell, Archibald. *The Christ of the Korean Heart.* Columbus, Ohio: Falco Publishers, 1954.

Clark, Allen D. *History of the Korean Church.* Seoul: Christian Literature Society, 1961.

Fenwick, Malcolm C. *The Church of Christ in Korea.* Seoul: Baptist Publishers, 1967.

Harrington, Fred Harvey. *God, Mammon, and the Japanese.* Madison: University of Wisconsin, 1944.

Hunt, Bruce F. *For a Testimony.* London: Banner of Truth, 1966.

Kim, Helen. *Grace Sufficient.* Nashville: Upper Room, 1964.

Kim, Joseph Chang-mun, and Chung, John Jae-sun. *Catholic Korea, Yesterday and Now.* Seoul: Catholic Korea Publishers, 1964.

Moffett, Samuel Hugh. *The Christians of Korea.* New York: Friendship Press, 1962.

Paik, George L. *The History of Protestant Missions in Korea, 1832-1910.* Seoul: Yonsei University Press, 1970.

Palmer, Spencer J., ed. "The New Religions of Korea," *Transactions of the Korea Branch Royal Asiatic Society.* Vol. 43. Seoul, 1967.

Rutt, Richard. *Korean Works and Days.* Tokyo: Tuttle, 1965.

Shearer, Roy E. *Wildfire: Church Growth in Korea.* Grand Rapids: Eerdmans, 1966.

Voelkel, Harold. *Behind Barbed Wire in Korea.* Grand Rapids: Zondervan, 1953.

Sources for Statistics

Beach, Harlan P. *Geography and Atlas of Protestant Missions.* Student Volunteer Movement, 1901.

Christian Literature Society. *The Korea Missions Yearbook.* Seoul: Christian Literature Society, 1932.

Clark, Allen D. *Prayer Calendar of Christian Missions in Korea.* Seoul: Christian Literature Society of Korea, 1959.

Clark, Charles A. *Nevius Plan for Mission Work in Korea.* Seoul: Christian Literature Society, 1937.

Dennis, James S.; Beach, Harlan P.; and Fahs, Charles, eds. *World Atlas of Christian Missions.* New York: Student Volunteer Movement for Foreign Missions, 1911.

Koons, E. W. "Mission Statistics." *The Korea Mission Field,* January, 1941, p. 15.

L'Aunay, Par Adrien. *Memoire de la Societe Des Missions: Etrangeres 1658-1912.* Paris Seminaire: De Missions Etrangeres.

Missions Advanced Research and Communication Center. *North American Protestant Ministries Overseas Directory.* 9th ed. New York: Missionary Research Library, 1970.

Rhodes, Harry A., ed. *History of the Korea Mission, Presbyterian Church U.S.A., 1884-1934.* Seoul Chosen Mission Presbyterian Church USA, 1934.

Rhodes, Harry A., and Campbell, Archibald, eds. *History of the Korea Mission Presbyterian Church in the U.S.A., 1935-1959.* Vol. 2. New York: Commission on Ecumenical Mission and Relations of the United Presbyterian Church in the USA, 1965.

Stokes, Charles D. "History of Methodist Missions in Korea 1885-1930." Ph.D. dissertation, Yale University, 1947.

Swinehart, M. L. "Statistics with Comparison of Work Done by Different Missions in Korea." Private printing. Kwangju, Korea, 1920.

Laotians receive medical aid from mobile clinics.

Photos by Armand Heiniger and Jerry Tergerson

Gospel recordings minister to the tribal Laotian churches in their own languages.

16

LAOS

by G. Edward Roffe

The Church Today

INTRODUCTION

How is the church faring in the most vulnerable nation on the embattled Indochina peninsula, the focus of a bitter "secret" war paralleling that of Vietnam in the early 1970's?

Romantically called the "Kingdom of the Million Elephants and the White Parasol," Laos is the poorest, most divided nation in southeast Asia. A landlocked inland isle, it has been battered by the waves of six warring border nations for centuries, and with increasing intensity during the last twenty years. Laos lacks the binding unity of common race or culture. A large minority of its people have been uprooted and shifted during the last two decades. Communist invaders from North Vietnam and Cambodia have surged across its borders in waves, demoralizing the isolated, rural tribes and keeping the weak, tripartite government constantly off balance and defensive.

And the church has not escaped their vicious raids. Early in the morning of October 28, 1972, Pathet Lao (Communists) and North Vietnamese attacked the small town of Kengkok in southern Laos. One Christian family escaped across a large lagoon, but two single girls, Evelyn Ander-

---

G. Edward Roffe was the first resident Protestant missionary in North Laos, and has served there since 1929 with only furlough and wartime interruptions. He has been chairman of the Christian and Missionary Alliance Mission, has served as the first missionary pilot in that area, has been a linguist and Bible translator, and has authored numerous articles on linguistic and biblical subjects. Dr. Roffe is a graduate of McMaster University (Toronto) and Nyack Missionary College, and has studied in the Language Institute of Paris, the Summer Institute of Linguistics, and Cornell University. He was honored with an LL.D. by Eastern Baptist College and Seminary in 1971.

son, and Beatrice Kosin, were seized and bound to a post, and their house was burned down around them, martyring both. Two men, Samuel Mattix and Lloyd Oppel, were captured and marched barefoot seventeen miles to the town of Don Hene. No word has been heard from them since. All were Americans associated with Christian Missions in Many Lands.

Evangelism, begun almost a hundred years ago, has progressed slowly on two fronts, north and south, resulting in two national churches, the "Christian Church of South Laos" and the "Evangelical Church in Laos," both thoroughly conservative. All missionary work until the present has been done by a few groups: Swiss Brethren in the south and early pioneer Presbyterians and Christian and Missionary Alliance in the north. Since World War II these have been reinforced notably by the Overseas Missionary Fellowship (largely in the south) and several smaller service groups.

Historically a suffering buffer state in the heart of the Indochina peninsula, tiny Laos, with less than three million population, became a target of communist activity from 1950. Before this activity became overt in the north, God prepared the church there with a minor mass movement, a sovereign moving of the Holy Spirit that saw over a thousand people come to Christ in a single remote northern area within weeks and witnessed the conversion of whole villages within months.

The drama actually began during the days of the Japanese occupation. Pastor Saly, the first Alliance-ordained pastor in Laos, was forced from his church in the royal capital of Luang Prabang by Japanese pressure in 1942. He fled to a nearby tribal village and began to minister to a few believers, but soon was forced to flee to his home in the south. A zealous tribal elder then took over responsibility for the church. When the missionaries returned after the war, practically the whole village had been converted. Another earnest believer, cast out of his village for his faith, had left a lasting impression in his home town. When the missionaries arrived there, some seventy of these villagers soon made professions of faith. Another simple tribesman in the area, with only one term of school behind him, led two hundred of his fellows to Christ.

The real break, however, came in the form of a mass movement that began in 1950. The entire Alliance mission staff was absent, attending the annual field conference in Vietnam. Bible school students were out in vacation ministries, mainly serving Christian communities. One tribesman who had been in school only four months, Kheng, had been sent over to Xieng Khouang, where there wasn't a single Christian, in the hope that he would undertake colportage work and, at best, effect a limited witness. But when the missionaries returned some eight weeks later, Kheng reported a thousand converts among the high-altitude Meo tribespeople!

One of Kheng's neighbors, a retired Meo sorcerer, had watched the young lad, inquired about his activity, listened to his message, wondered how he could live with apparent impunity in a haunted house, and then made a convincing profession of faith. The converted sorcerer then led Kheng to many of the mountaintop villages where he was well-known and respected. They came to one village where two years earlier a sorceress had made the unusual announcement, "Within two years the village will be visited by a messenger of the God of grace. If the village receives the message and recognizes this God, then He will become their God and they will be His people."

In the simplest possible terms Kheng told these primitive people the basic truths of the gospel. They turned to the sorceress and asked, "Is this what you told us about two years ago?" Her unhesitating reply was, "Yes, and to prove it, I'll be the first one to believe!" The entire village followed suit. The message spread from village to village until, within a few weeks, a thousand Meo villagers had made a profession of faith.

With only two couples having completed language study, the mission was overwhelmed. Steps were taken to meet the situation. Pastor Saly had gone to minister to the Vientiane congregation during vacation. School was about to reopen, but he was sent to Xieng Khouang as soon as possible to acquaint the ever-increasing number of converts with the simple basics of their newfound faith. Soon a delegation of nearby Khamou villagers visited Pastor Saly to inform him that they too had received a message from the spirits, claiming that the coming of "The God of grace" was to result in the departure of the spirits. He lost no time in responding to their invitation to preach in their villages and was overjoyed to find many ready to turn to Christ. Again the message spread from home to home and was accepted by entire villages.

The flame of faith among the primitive peoples of the mountainous hinterland spread in every direction until it became humanly impossible to keep pace with the ever-multiplying conversions. The entire student body of the Bible school was released to help Pastor Saly in Xieng Khouang. A senior missionary couple was transferred to carry on a shorttime Bible school for the new believers. Eventually the central Bible school was moved into this area to strengthen the new churches there.

This people's-movement revival precipitated the formalization of the national church structure in north Laos after twenty-five years of missionary evangelism. The church was first organized on a provincial basis in Xieng Khouang and then in Luang Prabang, in 1954. The church formation happened just in time, for these two areas soon became the center of communist infiltration activity, and the entire area fell behind the bamboo curtain a few years later.

But the church was established, with a constitution adopted in 1956. The "Evangelical Church of Laos" held its first assembly in Xieng Khouang in March 1957. Pastor Saly, the first ordained minister of the Alliance church, became its first president, while other officers in the church represented the Khamou, the Meo, and other tribal groups (plus the national Lao, who, though they comprise 50 percent of the population, form only two percent of the church).

PRESENT STATUS OF THE CHURCH

The new church was granted corporate status by the Royal Lao government in 1960, making it possible for her to own property in her own name and to deal with the government. Today, apart from special projects the Evangelical Church of Laos is self-supporting, with no foreign mission funds going to support any national worker under church authority. Where committees exist in the field of radio, literature, Bible school, etc., they are generally of mixed church-mission membership, looking forward to growing participation by the church in all phases of endeavor and, ultimately, to the day when church initiative will assume all these responsible ministries.

The church is indifferent to statistics, and the continuing politico-military upheaval in Laos makes it impossible to secure accurate figures. However, the church claims a Christian community of some ten thousand believers, about half of them baptized in about fifty organized churches and many more of them belonging to unorganized groups of believers. There are five ordained pastors and some fifteen not yet ordained.

In some ways communist persecution has resulted in blessing. Following the fall of Xieng Khouang to the Communists in 1960, the Bible school in the midst of the new tribal movement was lost. But it reopened in 1961 in Vientiane on a refugee basis. It now has a growing campus and student body and a higher-level program in a permanent location.

The small and scattered Christian villages in the border area, previously neglected because of inaccessibility, have now in many instances been relocated together in larger communities by the government with foreign aid. Some have a Christian population of several hundred, and one numbers at least twelve hundred baptized believers. An Alliance plane began visiting the remote villages as early as 1949, for no other transportation or even roads were available. Now a Missionary Aviation Fellowship plane courageously serves the churches in the few village centers in the still-free areas of the north. In some few instances the plane has been able to dip down over the curtain and renew contact with small groups of believers isolated over a decade. Throughout the country the plane ventures in and out of twenty barely accessible landing strips in jungles and mountains, ferrying missionaries and supplies.

Reports indicate that among believers in the tribes farthest north (those contacted almost a hundred years ago) martyrdoms have occurred. The pastor of one group, one of the first four graduates of a training program begun before World War I, was murdered by communist dissidents. Tragic, yet possibly hopeful, is the report that this persecution is due to the western and American connotation of Christianity rather than to antagonism toward Christianity itself.

Churches and missions operating in southern Laos are also suffering from communist harassment and occupation. Evangelism there was begun in 1902 by a young Swiss brother, Gabriel Contesse. He and his successors began widespread evangelistic itineration but soon saw the strategic need of preparing literature and beginning Bible translation. Their heroic work eventuated in 1932 in the first publication of the entire Bible in Lao.

In this southern boot-shaped area the population of Laos is most dense. Here a three-pronged evangelistic effort has been directed toward town dwellers, lowland rural communities, and upland tribal peoples. Growth has been slow but steady. A feature has been the gravitating to the mission stations of considerable numbers of socio-religious outcasts. Accused by their neighbors of having the power to cause misfortune, illness, and death, they are hounded and harried until in desperation they seek the refuge afforded by the mission station. Patently, many of these make a confession of faith as a matter of convenience, but some are truly converted.

In 1957 the Overseas Missionary Fellowship entered south Laos under John Kuhn to work side by side with the Swiss Mission. It was hoped that the new mission could assume responsibility for work among the upland peoples living along the border of Vietnam and in the southern highland, thus releasing the Swiss Mission for work among the lowland Lao. Increasing military activity, however, has caused a definite modification of this program. Of seven stations opened, six have had to be closed. Thus there has been considerable fusing of territorial responsibility and a joining of hands in such projects as a Bible school that serves the entire church in the area.

Ten tombs remain as a witness to the sorrow and sacrifice woven into the tapestry of Swiss missionary endeavor in the south. But now the "Christian Church of South Laos" has a membership of seven hundred baptized and two thousand non-baptized communicants, many of whom are now behind the bamboo curtain in the southeast. The churches are mainly small, organized in the simple Brethren pattern and ministered to by five "pastors" and five young women Bible school graduates partially supported by the churches. The total missionary force now stands at sixteen in the Swiss mission and thirty-six in the OMF, twelve of whom are nurses.

CHURCH PROBLEMS

These two major churches of north and south Laos reflect the linguistic, racial, and geographic divisions in the tiny nation. But in the main their problems are the same for both evangelism and church growth.

The outwardly dominant Buddhist religion has been strengthened in recent years by nationalistic incentives: loyalty to the state has been declared to be loyalty to Buddhism.

Literacy is as low as any country in southeast Asia, only 15 percent. In addition is the problem of many tribal language groups. Efforts are being made to increase literacy and to translate the Scriptures into Meo and other languages beside Lao. The church in the north also faces the problem of assimilating the three linguistic and ethnic groups that make up its composition. The Lao exercise an influence out of proportion to their 2 percent of the overall membership.

Catholicism in Laos has a history antedating that of Protestantism by two hundred years (see later paragraphs headed "Christian History"), but its numbers today total only about thirty-two thousand, approximately twice that of the Protestant community.

Sects have invaded Laos in recent years. Jehovah's Witnesses, with their assiduous house-to-house visitation, have in part provoked a positive reaction on the part of the Christian community, who have turned to the Bible for a clearer understanding of their faith. Seventh-Day Adventists received permission to build a hospital in 1969 but first sent a Filipino pastor to establish residence in Vientiane for evangelistic work, with medical work and education to follow later.

Generally speaking, the church needs to show deeper concern for the unbelieving and unreached community throughout the land. Unable to provide pastors and trained workers in sufficient numbers to shepherd existing groups of believers, she has tended to concentrate on pastoral work to the neglect of evangelism. It is a matter of priorities, and the mission must lay emphasis on outreach. As this is done and as vision filters down to the local level—and there are signs that this is beginning to take place—the thrust of the church's ministry ought to shift to an outward direction. Attendance at the 1968 Asia-South Pacific Congress on Evangelism (to mention only one church meeting) should bear fruit in an awakened conscience and a desirable enthusiasm for evangelism.

In the north recent events have contributed to the emergence of nascent theological problems. Foreign aid channeled through the East Asia Christian Council has been invested in a Protestant Christian elementary school in the north. The EACC motive is laudable, but evangelicals fear lest the church be enamored of the pottage of social benefits, thereby placing decreasing value on their spiritual ministry. The low level of education of church leaders makes them vulnerable to non-evangelical teaching and emphases.

One evidence of this has been the influence of a prominent layman of the northern church who was sent on an all-expense-paid, five-month visit to the World Council of Churches' Ecumenical Institute in Switzerland. There he became thoroughly indoctrinated in the basic concepts of ecumenism and has been propagating these with great influence in the church since his return.

These incipient signs of danger in the northern church have caused some mission leaders in the south to be cool toward cooperative efforts to bring union between the two churches.

At one time a central and joint program for the training of workers was proposed, but basic differences existing between the north and the south on ecclesiastical and other concerns caused each area to set up its own facilities at considerable duplication of expenditure, personnel, and time. A single, jointly-operated facility could have strengthened fellowship between missions and between leaders of the churches and laid the foundation for a truly national church. Thus at present the development of a single church organization seems to be ruled out by the differing ecclesiastical patterns, apprehension that the relatively small church in the south would be submerged by the overwhelmingly larger northern body, and fear that the church in the north may become penetrated or even split by the theologically liberal influences to which it may be subjected on an increasing scale.

In the absence of a single, nationwide, organized church, some kind of structural evangelical fellowship has been proposed. As far as the missions are concerned, it would be both welcome and feasible. But the church in the north sees no need for any organization of this nature, and some fear that such an association might cut them off from sources of material and social aid. But there has nevertheless been much fruitful joint effort to alleviate wartime suffering and to reach this unfortunate nation's people effectively for Christ in the postwar period.

EVANGELISTIC OUTREACH

A type of limited "saturation evangelism" was undertaken in the south for the three-year period from 1966 to 1969. This was a program of considerable promise, and future undertakings should be fruitful, though early efforts produced only minimum results.

Literature has been a traditional concern in both the south and the north. Audetat's work in literature and Scripture translation in the south has been paralleled by Alliance work in the north through the years. A completely new translation of the entire Bible is currently under way, sponsored by the United Bible Society. When I reached retirement age and was serving as senior translator for the new Bible, the Bible Society requested the Alliance to release me for full-time work in 1965. After the completion of the new text of the New Testament and its adoption by the interchurch, intermission consultive committee, it was suddenly decided to reconsider the entire project and do a further stylistic revision. Much of this has now been accomplished, and this entirely new New Testament in Lao will hopefully be on the market late in 1972. The Old Testament translation work is progressing slowly under a younger team of nationals, with a Swiss missionary supervising and a Catholic priest assisting.

A recent cooperative effort involves the Alliance, the Overseas Missionary Fellowship in Thailand (which has put much constructive effort into literature in recent years), and the Bible societies, which have united to produce a scientifically sound writing system for the Meo language, based on an adaptation of the Lao system. Mark has been published as a Meo-Lao diglot and a hymnal has been produced. Literacy campaigns will soon be launched. This is the first significant breakthrough in the field of literature and Scriptures for the minority languages. A similar script has long been prepared for Khamou, but the teaching aids have not been developed, although missionaries are learning this language too.

Local radio facilities have not been open to gospel broadcasting, but for many years tapes have been prepared in Laos in the studios of both the Swiss and the Alliance missions and have been broadcast over the facilities of the Fast East Broadcasting Network in Manila in the Lao and Meo languages. In the last few years films produced by Moody Institute of Science and the Billy Graham Association have been shown though only on a limited basis due to a lack of equipment. Gospel Recordings' records by the thousands and simple recorders by the hundreds have been placed in widely scattered villages, bringing the gospel in the local language in the absence of any human messenger.

While much has been done in the way of traditional children's meetings, organized Sunday schools have been almost unknown. Early 1969 saw printed materials used for the first time in Vientiane. Results have been most encouraging, for the church is showing a gratifying interest. Youth work, particularly in the capital city (where education draws young people from all over the country) presents a challenge to Christian ministry. Enthusiasm for this is mounting as youth teams fan out to more remote church centers.

National leaders are becoming increasingly adequate in the fields of preaching and witnessing but exhibit shortcomings in pastoral activity and administration. When Bible schools were started, the only entrance requirement was the ability to read and write Lao (the only written language). But now in the north, entrance requirements are constantly being raised and curriculum upgraded to meet the challenge of the emerging nation.

Lay activity is an important element in the Lao church, since many groups are without an official pastor and are dependent on elders to shepherd the local congregation. This is particularly true in the south, where the Brethren tradition is strong. The northern church holds elders' institutes and short-term Bible schools to provide teaching and training at this critical level.

Unfruitful Alliance efforts have been made to bring Asian missionaries to northern Laos from the Philippines. In 1969 there were missionary candidates from among the Chinese in Hong Kong. For over ten years a small band of ten to fifteen Japanese missionaries has been working sacrificially in Laos. Since these workers are entirely independent in both their home and Laotian affiliation, little is known of the extent and success of their efforts. Further Asian personnel came in through the recently adopted policy of the Overseas Missionary Fellowship, which has opened its doors to nonCaucasians.

In an underdeveloped land, decimated by almost twenty years of vicious warfare, the social and physical needs are understandably tremendous. Unfortunately, Protestant missions have done little in the way of institutional or social work historically. A small dispensary was established in the south by the first missionaries, and a second is now in operation. A leprosarium in Paksé was recently turned over to the Protestant church by the government and is staffed by Swiss missionary personnel.

Several Alliance missionary nurses labor in north Laos, and funds have been expended generously in recent years for refugees. The church is now operating a hostel in Vientiane for students from rural areas. After years of appeals, other agencies are now joining the established mission groups in meeting pressing physical and social needs. World Vision has signed an agreement with the government to carry on relief and social activity at many levels, and two experienced couples have now set up operations in Vientiane. The EACC came in on the heels of World Vision with a similar government agreement with a multi-national staff of fifteen, including agriculturalists, nurses, social workers, and home economists. In the south a former OMF doctor is central in plans for a new hospital. But much remains to be done in the face of the continuing poverty, sickness, and injuries provoked by the omnipresent guerrilla warfare.

Evangelism among minority groups in Laos has been going on for more than a generation. The Alliance began it among Vietnamese in the early 1930's and continued until they fled the country after World War II. Their little chapel has been used and rebuilt in subsequent years by French, Chinese, and English-speaking congregations, until the Chinese erected their own building in 1968. Both of these churches are, however, a part of the Evangelical Church of Laos, and the Chinese and Vietnamese in particular have carried on limited evangelism among their compatriots in various areas of the country.

FUTURE CHALLENGES

An objective overlook of the church here indicates (as is true in other countries on the Indochina peninsula) that the bulk of the church members have been recruited from the tribal groups of animistic religious background. Laotians of Buddhist background are a majority group in the country but comprise only a 2 percent minority in the church. Reaching them is the greatest challenge facing the church of the future.

Second to this are the needs of literacy and literature for the tribes, the accelerated training of national leadership, and the training of specialists in the fields of radio, literature, student work, urban evangelism, etc.

The impending arrival of the Southern Baptists is viewed with some concern because of their generally exclusivist and non-cooperative policies.

Ecumenical encounter between Catholic and Protestant missions has been only on the personal level, where relationships have generally been correct and cordial. Catholics, however, have made wide use of the Protestant Lao Bible and have demonstrated increasing interest since Vatican II in the forthcoming new translation.

Nation and People

For centuries the western world was in almost total ignorance of the land of Laos, which actually dominated the whole inner stretches of the fertile Mekong Valley. But when communist troops from North Vietnam joined forces with communist dissidents within Laos and threatened to overrun the entire northern half of the nation in 1953, world attention dramatically re-focused on this tiny buffer state. The red invasion was but the latest act in the ever-recurring dramatic conflict of rival interests which have warred over Laos for centuries.[1]

In the mid-fourteenth century King Fa Ngoum united Laos, established his capital at Luang Prabang, and ruled an area that today would encompass not only Laos but also much of northeast Thailand and part of the southern Chinese province of Yunnan. But within a hundred years the Vietnamese began invasions which continue until today. By the eighteenth century Thailand entered the competition, wresting control over much of what is now Laos. This Thai rule continued until the French incursion into the Indochina peninsula. Laos became a French protectorate in 1893, and her present boundaries were defined in the Franco-Siamese treaty of 1907.

But the peace was short-lived. The Japanese began border invasions in 1941 and completely subjugated the country in 1945. French troops returned in 1946, reoccupying Laos. Then began a series of negotiations climaxing with Laos' independence in 1949 as a sovereign state within the French Union. When the French Indochina war ran to its bloody end in 1954, Laos became an independent member of the United Nations the following year.

But internal communist forces (the Pathet Lao) were organized under North Vietnamese auspices and began bloody power plays, which have continued to the present. An uneasy half-peace was achieved by the creation of a tripartite government composed of three Lao fractions: conservative (the government), neutralist (the Viet Minh under the Communists), and Pathet Lao (the Communists), all under the premiership of Prince Souvanna Phouma.

A new Geneva agreement was reached in 1962, which sought to guarantee independent and neutral status for Laos. The results have been ineffective. The communist Pathet Lao, almost completely a minion of the North Vietnamese (who finance and direct it) soon withdrew cooperation. With increasingly close cooperation from the neutralists and conservatives, Souvanna Phouma has tried to hold the country together in the face of widespread North Vietnamese guerrilla warfare and Pathet Lao activity. A bamboo curtain of these forces has been drawn around much of northern Laos and some of southeastern Laos, so that today Communists occupy perhaps a third of the land area and control 20 percent of the population.

The almost impossible complexity of administering the constitutional parliamentary monarchy established by the king in May 1947 is made apparent by examining the nature of the nation's people. Laos is an ethnographic kaleidoscope of racial and linguistic groups, delineated as much by altitude as by latitude and longitude throughout the country. Various political pressures for centuries sent successive waves of peoples sweeping down through Laos, India, Burma, and China. These migrations usually followed the great watercourses of Indochina: the Irawaddy, Salween, Menam, Mekong, Black, and Red rivers. Early nomads settled in the valleys. Later comers often dislodged these, who then moved up from the riverbanks into the hills. Still later groups forced the nomads even higher into the highlands, where they became isolated from progress and prosperity, leaving enclaves of primitive, minority peoples.

The most significant of the migrations were those of the Thai, who had occupied southern China since before the Christian era. Driven out by the Mongols in the thirteenth century, these became the majority group in the southern end of the peninsula and were merged into the confederation of Lao states under King Fa Ngoun in the fourteenth century. Thus modern Laos is a racial melting pot in which the pure Lao, descendants of the early Thai, comprise about 49 percent of the population and live largely in the valleys. In the highlands live the Meo and Yao tribes of Sinitic origin, the Akah and Lahu tribes of Tibeto-Burman origin, and other smaller scattered tribes of Malay and Indonesian ancestry. In addition there are resident minorities of Vietnamese, Chinese, Cambodians, Indians, and Pakistanis in Laos, plus an influential enclave of French from the days of colonialism.

The unifying geographic factor of modern Laos is the rambling Mekong River, which with its tributaries starts in the far north and exits in the southernmost tip of the country, some seven hundred miles to the south. In the northeast is the Xieng Khouang plateau with its Plain of Jars (named for the hundreds of large, earthenware burial jars which dot it), surrounded by mountains towering up to nine thousand feet. Another plateau marks the south. And on all sides are the far-ranging highlands. The total area is ninety-one thousand square miles, slightly larger than Great Britain. Six nations, at least half of them militantly hostile, border the tiny country.

In Lao's monsoonal climate lives a population never accurately measured but estimated to be nearly three million people, probably evenly divided between the upland and lowland. Since World War II expanding medical facilities and the introduction of modern hygiene have lowered the death rate and given an annual population growth of approximately 2.4 percent.

The nation's economic potential is unknown, unsurveyed, and unexploited. Forests cover two-thirds of the landscape and hold tremendous commercial possibilities. But Laos is handicapped by its isolation from the sea and an almost total lack of internal transport: there are no railroads, and the Mekong River is navigable only by small boats. Hence 85 percent of the people are subsistence farmers, making even their own cloth for clothing. Once self-sufficient in rice, the nation now has to import a large share of its food, along with all other manufactured products, because of the war. Its per capita GNP of $72 is one of the lowest in Asia. Over a quarter million refugees from Communism add to the poverty, while the disproportionately high percentage of men in the armed forces robs the economy of productive workers.[2]

The nation's only economic hopes are for increased regional cooperation and massive foreign aid in order to stimulate rapid development of its potentials, such as mineral resources. But this will take many years even after peace is achieved.

A brief look at the present racial division of the country reveals that the majority Lao occupy the favored position along the lowland rivers on the central Mekong valley. United linguistically, the Lao dominate Laos both politically and economically. Until recently they denied to the various minority groups even the relatively limited educational facilities that existed in the country, making the divided tribal groups vulnerable to exploitation by communist propaganda. This policy has made it difficult for any central government to win tribal loyalty, be it to the loosely linked nation or to the Crown as symbolic of national unity.

A complete catalog has never been made of the at least forty tribal peoples who represent divergent ethnic, linguistic, and cultural backgrounds, most of which antedate (in some cases by long centuries) the coming of the Thai-speaking Lao. The largest and latest to arrive were the Miao (Meo), who moved in from high-altitude homelands in south China. Settling in the highest reaches of north Laos about 150 years ago, the Miao have since then spread south, east, and west, for their slash-and-burn culture requires ever new areas of exploitation. Other large tribes include the Mau, Kwa, and Yao tribes, which in general inhabit the less fertile highlands in north and south and have been the forgotten peoples of the Indochina hinterland until recently.

Today urbanization is changing Laos. Until the country achieved national status towns were few, far between, and relatively small. Luang Prabang, the ancient royal capital in the heart of the north, had a population of only 10,000. Today all cities have grown, but none so much as Vientiane, the administrative capital, whose population is currently estimated to be about 150,000. The location of the central government in Vientiane has brought in a large government bureaucracy, diplomatic missions, the country's first banks, burgeoning commercial interests, and schools with thousands of students. But a major factor also has been the influx of refugees seeking security.

This urbanization is forcing radical changes on the nation's economy and society. From simple two-to-ten-family village life the rural people must readjust to competitive cities. The present low literacy rate of 15 percent must be rapidly raised in order to facilitate the urban transition and to enable the people to determine their political destiny. The old slash-and-burn rice culture must be eliminated in order to raise argricultural production. These needs put an almost impossible burden on the weak government and the inadequate foreign aid programs.

Yet there is this bright hope: left to their own choice, and with sympathetic treatment by the ruling class, the vast majority will opt for the monarchy and a viable form of the democratic process, I feel.

National Religions

Though the constitution provides for religious liberty, modern Laos is a Buddhist state. Conservative Theraveda Buddhism is the state religion, and the king as its chief protector is required by the constitution to be a fervent Buddhist. But long before Buddhism was introduced animism held sway, and it continues to exist as a strong undercurrent of fear and superstition.

The early Lao princes of Luang Prabang were vassals of the Indianized state of the Khmers and consequently were probably exposed to Hinduism. These Indian beliefs may also have been introduced through Burma around the year 1000. So when Cambodian influence was restored in the Mekong valley in the fourteenth century, it brought Buddhism for the first time. Buddhism is therefore a foreign religion, a fact often overlooked by the Buddhist Lao, who reject Christianity on the ground that *it* is a foreign religion!

However, eight centuries of Buddhist influence have indelibly marked community life, centering it around the monastery. Every male is expected to spend some time wearing the saffron robes of the mendicant monk. Until recently all village education was in the hands of the monks. Girls received no formal education. Boys were taught at least to read and write, if only the sacred *tham* writing system, which they often gave up before mastering the secular writing system used for ordinary communication. Illiteracy is thus widespread, but it is now beginning to give way under the impact of a modern education system (though still only 15 percent of the people are literate). Some problems are encountered when zealous teachers attempt to force non-Buddhist school children to do obeisance to Buddha.

The typical Lao belongs to a tightly-knit, extended family unit which leaves little room for individual initiative. This makes it very difficult for anyone to step out of the group and profess faith in Christianity. But Laotian Buddhism is generally tolerant, and the government, whether at the national or local level, has put very few obstacles in the path of Christian missions. The writer back in 1930 was authorized by His Majesty Sisavang Vong, king of Luang Prabang, to preach the gospel without hindrance throughout the length and breadth of the realm. The very best of relations, based on mutual respect and consideration, have been maintained through the succeeding years.

Upland peoples are bound by agelong animistic traditions which are unmodified by any of the concepts of an ethnic religion. Hedged in on every side by fear and superstition, the people are at the mercy of the sorcerer. Animal sacrifices, often of considerable monetary value, are required to conciliate offended spirits. Added to this is a fee paid either in cash or in kind to a go-between, who determines the cause of the particular misfortune—crop failure, accident, illness, death—and prescribes the remedial action to be taken. This practice helps to keep the people in relative poverty and in bondage to the powers of darkness. Thus men are in Satan's grip, robbed of much which they might otherwise enjoy in the way of material comforts. With both household and village spirits to be conciliated, it is a rare family and a much rarer individual who will dare to take any step to flout tradition and customs.

Christian History

CATHOLIC MISSIONS

Though he was not a missionary, the first Christian to set foot in the remote interior of Laotian Indochina was Jerret von Wusthoff, an "anti-papist" and "honest Puritan merchant" who reached Vientiane in 1641. The romantic account of his travels for the Dutch East India Company tells of the pomp and ceremony of the court of Souligna Vongsa, the last of the great kings of Laos to rule over both the north and south of the country.

A year later, however, Jean deLeria, a courageous Jesuit, set out from Cambodia for Laos on the first mission of evangelism. His scholarly reputation earned him a reception by the king, but the hostility of the Buddhist monks apparently made his stay of five years totally unfruitful. Catholic fathers tried to penetrate Laos from Northeast Thailand and Bangkok in 1683 and again in 1866, but they were met only with rebuffs. Finally, in 1878, a mission was established in the northeast. It came to a tragic end with the martyrdom of twelve priests in 1884, and five more five years later.

And so the strategy was changed; exploratory trips were begun from Bangkok. From then until 1940 the main thrust of Catholic missionary endeavor has come from the south, concentrating on the most densely populated areas on the right bank of the middle Mekong River. Through the early years losses were heavy and work slow. But the latest official statistics (1967)[3] indicate that Catholics now number 31,978 Christians, 5,807 catechumens, approximately 100 priests, 9 lay workers, 188 nuns in three major orders, and between 80 and 100 catechists. They follow the traditional pattern, operating twenty-seven primary and three secondary schools, which have a total of 255 teachers and over 10,000 students.

It is probable that the catechists will be main instruments of direct Catholic evangelism in the future, with foreign personnel progressively forced out of many areas as a result of increasing military activity.

Several priests are working among lepers. Others have sought to set up model farms to promote substitute economies for opium growers, to train skilled artisans and tradesmen, and to provide instruction in home economics. Two convents are in operation, and there are at least two orphanages. Two Catholic seminaries, survivors of several others, serve the entire mission in Laos, but a total of only ten nationals have been ordained. Many more have gone out into various levels of government service and other areas of civilian life. Training at catechist level is provided in various centers for different language groups: Lao, Meo, Khamou, etc.

PROTESTANT MISSIONS

Inhabitants of Luang Prabang, the royal capital, were startled one day in 1880 to see a large elephant plodding through the streets of their remote city with a white man on his back. All the way from north Thailand and across northern Laos Dr. Daniel MacGilvary (a Northern Presbyterian) had come as God's spy to investigate the land for the gospel. On then and other occasions as he itinerated primarily among the Khamou tribal people, it is possible that close to a hundred came to Christ and were baptized as a result of MacGilvary's pioneer work.

At the turn of the century another Presbyterian from North Siam (presently Thailand), Dr. Hugh Taylor, followed in MacGilvary's elephant tracks and made numerous evangelistic trips to the Khamou, among whom at least two groups turned to the Lord. This Christian community continues today, with possibly 290 adult Christians among them. One of the men from this area, the only Khamou to be ordained to date, is currently on the faculty of the Laos Bible Training Center. (He had his first taste of formal education when Dr. Taylor took him across the border to north Thailand for limited schooling.) The fruit of MacGilvary and Taylor's work has been nurtured in the Evangelical Church of Laos, and I personally have had the privilege of meeting Dr. Taylor and of visiting and instructing many of his and MacGilvary's converts.

Meanwhile, in the south of the tiny country French Indochina's first Protestant missionaries established residence. A devout young Swiss missionary, Gabriel Contesse, received in the mail one day an unpretentious piece of literature from the Christian and Missionary Alliance appealing for missionaries for Annam. It fascinated him. He read widely on the races, customs, languages, and religions of the entire area. As a result he offered himself to the Swiss Brethren Assemblies to pioneer for Christ, not in Annam or Vietnam, but rather in the inaccessible interior area of little-known Laos. So in company with a Mr. Willy, Contesse sailed from Genoa in September 1902 and settled in Song Khona a few months later.

It was three years before he baptized his first convert at Easter, 1905. Their little missionary community had grown to seven by 1908, but by 1910 only Fritz Audetat was left. (Others of the early party had been stricken by fever, fatigue, typhoid, and cholera, including Mr. and Mrs. Gabriel Contesse, Mrs. Willy, and Mr. and Mrs. Charles Contesse. Mr. Willy returned alone to Europe.) Audétat's labors were amazing: he carried on regular services locally, undertook extensive evangelistic trips, dabbled in medical relief programs, and took up the translation work begun by Contesse and which had seen the gospels of John and Luke printed in 1908. His work was crowned with the publication of the New Testament in Laotian in 1926 and the Old Testament on the Alliance Press in Hanoi in 1932. Many other smaller books and pamphlets flowed from his fertile pen and dedicated zeal in those early years.

Annual weeks of Bible study and fellowship were begun in 1911. These evolved eventually (in 1955) into a small Bible school, currently carried on in Savannakhat, headquarters of the Swiss Mission. In the early 1900's north Laos was without a resident Protestant missionary or Christian worker. But infrequent trips from the south in the early 1920's brought Audétat providentially into contact with Dr. Taylor on one of his itinerant evangelistic journeys, and Taylor pleaded with the Swiss Mission to include north Laos in their program, but they had insufficient personnel. So in the mid-twenties these men began negotiating with the Christian and Missionary Alliance, who were established in Vietnam and Cambodia and enjoying good relationships with the French colonial administration.

Thus in 1928, while studying in France preparatory to going to French Indochina, I was asked to open up this new field as a part of the Indochina mission of the Alliance. Like Contesse some thirty years before me, I eagerly consulted the meager sources of information available in Paris about a land which until then was completely unknown to me but for the next forty-five years was to be my home.

Reaching Saigon in late 1928, I journeyed by horseback and river steamer with D. I. Jeffrey (then field chairman of the Alliance Mission in Indochina) up through Vientiane to the royal capital, arriving at the end of February 1929. I thus became the first person from the western hemisphere to establish residence in Laos, to which home I brought my bride in 1929 and remained, with short interruptions, until 1951.

We were joined two years later by old friends from youth, Rev. and Mrs. Frank Grobb. Upon completion of formal language study and with newly granted permission from the king himself, we started direct evangelism with the help of two Laotian Christians, generously loaned to us from the southern church for three months. Open air meetings were held, homes were visited, tracts and gospel portions were distributed (Swiss Mission-produced), and regular church services were started in their homes.

The coming of these two young Laotian witnesses was far more providential than we realized. One of them, Saly, is today chairman of the northern Evangelical Church of Laos and chief consultant for the completion of the new Bible translation.

As war shadows gathered over both Europe and the Far East in the late 1930's, two other couples joined the mission working there. But in 1940 the Japanese swarmed into north Laos, and missionary work came to a standstill. A new couple was hastily transferred to the Philippines; due for furlough, we were able to leave in September. A third couple was put under house arrest and then exchanged for prisoners in 1942, and the Grobbs were interned in Saigon, where Frank Grobb died just before the end of the war.

With the close of the war two of us finally obtained passports and transportation, enabling us in early 1947 to visit Vientiane and Luang Prabang by military plane. All mission and church property had been stolen or destroyed as a result of successive occupations by French, Japanese, and Chinese forces. But within a few months the two key cities were reoccupied by missionaries, and after many discouraging delays two couples resumed evangelistic activity in north Laos.* The Alliance missionary roster grew and peaked at twenty-eight in 1969.

Conclusion

Laos today lives in an atmosphere of political and military crisis. Linked inevitably to the larger problem of Vietnam, it is unlikely that any real solution will be found to the problem of Laos until and unless that of Vietnam is satisfactorily solved. Likewise, the church in Laos faces a crucial period in her history. Thousands strong, she could go forward if only she could be united and doctrinally stabilized. Many people in both the mission and the church are earnestly praying and working to this end.

In the meantime much remains to be attempted in terms of Christian endeavor. While not all areas are accessible to missionary occupation or activity, there is an expanding need for specialists in the fields of radio, literature, youth and student work, urban evangelism, etc. To do this

*Postwar political developments resulted in a breakdown of the Indochina complex, with its component parts being granted the status of independent nations. In line with this movement the Alliance Indochina Mission divided into separate fields; in 1953 Laos started out as an autonomous unit, with its own administrative structure and its own budget.

missionaries are needed and welcome. In the south the OMF is cooperating with the Swiss Mission. In the north and northwest they collaborate with the Alliance workers in literacy and literature programs for the Meo and other remote tribes. Thus both specialists and church planting missionaries who can relate to the existing missions and churches of suffering Laos are a desperate need of this open nation in the opportune seventies.

NOTES

1. Hugh Toye, *Laos: Buffer State or Battleground,* pp. 3, 22, 24.
2. *Kingdom of Laos: Background Notes,* p. 2.
3. *La Mission Catholique Lao.*

BIBLIOGRAPHY

Challenge of Laos. CMA periodical. New York: Christian and Missionary Alliance.

Corthay, Charles. *Le Laos: Decouverte d'un Champ Missionnaire.* Yverdon, Switzerland: Imprimerie Henri Cornaz, 1953.

Decorvet, Jeanne, and Rochat, Georges. *L'appel Du Laos.* Yverdon, Switzerland: Imprimerie Henri Cornaz, 1946.

Dodd, William Clifton, D.D. *The Thai Race: Elder Brother of the Chinese.* Cedar Rapids, Iowa.

*Dommen, Arthur J. *Conflict in Laos.* Rev. ed. New York, Washington, London: Praeger, 1971.

Fall, Bernard. *Anatomy of a Crisis.* Garden City, New York: Doubleday & Co., 1969.

*Human Relations Area Files. *Laos: Its People, Its Society, Its Culture.* New Haven: HRAF Press, 1960.

Hunter, J. H. *Beside All Waters.* Harrisburg: Christian Publications, 1964.

Kingdom of Laos: Background Notes. Washington: U.S. Dept. of State, Aug. 1970.

*"Kingdom of Laos: The Land of the Million Elephants and of the White Parasol." *France-Asie* (Saigon), 1959.

La Mission Catholique Lao. Vientiane, Laos: Historique, 1969.

Le Boulanger, Paul. *Histoire du Laos Francais.* Paris: Plon, 1930.

Pradith, Khamchan. *Place Historique du Laos en Asie.* 2nd ed. Vientiane, Laos: Press Education, Royal Government of Laos, 1969.

Semailles et Moisson. Periodical. Yverdon, Switzerland: Imprimerie Henri Cornaz.

*Toye, Hugh. *Laos: Buffer State or Battleground.* London: Oxford University Press, 1968.

*Extensive bibliographies are to be found in these publications.

Aerial view of central Singapore

Photo by Lee Tuck Soon and Singapore Housing Board

17

MALAYSIA–SINGAPORE

by W. O. Phoon

Introduction

Romanticized by exotic legends and adventure tales for centuries, modern Malàysia drips from the Asian land mass onto the northernmost isle of the great Indonesian archipelago, which curves in a great crescent five thousand miles to New Zealand. Throughout the history of sailing ships the Malay Peninsula—particularly the straits of Malacca —was a convenient haven for the voyagers between the Indian Ocean and the China Sea.

Malaysia's early inhabitants migrated from south China twenty-five hundred years before Christ. Other groups joined them from India on the north in succeeding centuries, bringing with them Buddhism and Hinduism, which soon engulfed the animism of the earlier inhabitants. In the thirteenth century Islam was swept in from Sumatra on the west and soon dominated the peninsula. It was at the end of that century that a few adventurous souls crossed the straits of Johore and first settled in Singapore.

The early years of the sixteenth century saw successive flotillas of colonial ships sail greedily into the strategic straits of Malacca: first the Portuguese (1511), then the Dutch (1641), and finally the British (1786-1824). With them came the first Christian missionaries, each with the faith of his homeland.

W. O. Phoon, currently professor and head of the Department of Social Medicine and Public Health at the University of Singapore, serves many important posts as an active evangelical layman. A lay reader of the Anglican Diocese of Singapore, Dr. Phoon is president of the Fellowship of Evangelical Students, vice-chairman of the Scripture Union, vice-chairman of the Overseas Missionary Fellowship for Singapore-Malaysia, and a key leader in the evangelical church life of the island.

Much additional material was contributed later by Singapore Anglican pastor James Wong, Rev. Russell Self of the United Bible Societies, and the editor, with information being kindly supplied for East Malaysia by the Borneo Evangelical Mission.

Thus Malaysia and Singapore were originally pioneered and evangelized as one nation. But the Malaysia of today is composed of two areas as a result of the addition of Sarawak and Sabah on the island of Borneo in 1963. And Singapore, expelled from the Federation of Malaya in 1965, is an independent republic. Brunei, carved out of East Malaysia, is also independent. West Malaysia, East Malaysia, and Singapore are disparate in culture, people, and religious character: Singapore is a sophisticated, prosperous cosmopolitan city; Brunei, a rapidly developing, oil-rich state; West Malaysia, a struggling, emerging country; and Sabah and Sarawak, a tropical conglomerate of primitive tribes in which the church of Christ is nevertheless the most dynamic of the four areas.

The Chinese diaspora in all these countries has played a very significant role in the spread of the gospel in these areas. In West Malaysia they constitute about 45 percent of the population, in Singapore at least 75 percent, in East Malaysia about 30 percent, and in Brunei about 25 percent. They have been the backbone of church growth. But tribal work in East Malaysia has shown phenomenal growth since World War II. And there has been recent interest in the gospel in West Malaysia also. Thus the story of the church in this area is a diverse and fascinating one. Each of the Christian movements in these four areas (and nations) will be treated separately. Because of the 20 percent density of Christians in East Malaysia and the dramatic growth of the church there in the past four decades, we shall deal with this area first.

At the outset a word about Singapore-Malaysian church relationships may be helpful. Though originally evangelized as one territory, since the political separation a few years ago free interchange and cooperative activity are increasingly limited. Thus churches in the two areas are gradually drifting apart into two autonomous entities which operate independently.

The Church Today in East Malaysia

A remarkable work of the Holy Spirit in this generation has sparked rapid church growth despite opposition and almost total illiteracy in primitive East Malaysia, once the British colonies of Sarawak and Sabah on the island of Borneo. The result is that an amazing 18 percent of the total population is Christian!*

Government permission to evangelize the highland Murut tribe in central Borneo was denied to the enthusiastic missionaries of the new Borneo

*Ed. note. Statistics on Malaysia are confusing for several reasons:

1) No official governmental census is taken of various Christian communities.
2) Denominations often do not have accurate nor up-to-date records, so much estimating is guesswork, and the definition of what constitutes membership varies.
3) Several of the West Malaysian and some of the East Malaysian churches are tied in with Singapore, and therefore it is difficult to separate these statistics.

Evangelical Mission in 1933. The Dutch considered them virtually hopeless; a survey revealed that the Muruts were drunk one hundred days out of the year! But fellow tribesmen from Dutch Borneo across the invisible boundary witnessed to them late that year, and when British government officials visited them in 1938, after five years of isolation, they were astounded to find that the formerly disease-ridden, intoxicated tribe which was bound by fear of evil spirits had been transformed into a clean, upright, and courageous people! Their leisure time was spent praying. Missionaries of the Borneo Evangelical Mission entered to train and help them, but the Japanese occupation in 1941 forced these into internment, once again leaving the Muruts to themselves. They were now organized, however, in six churches, with indigenous leadership and portions of New Testament manuscripts in their own language. Visits to the Muruts in 1945, after the war, revealed that the church had not only stood and grown but had reached the Kelabit tribe further inland and had brought these also to Christ. And two other tribes were also asking for teaching.

I am indebted to Rev. Duain Vierow of Malaysia, who has painstakingly tried to collate and enlarge all available statistics for both East and West Malaysia from the best available sources, including the work of Thomas Heng of West Malaysia and James Wong of Singapore. The following are his totals, probably the best available. (Please note that the last-listed "Baptist and others" division for each of the islands was made by the editor. The total for both is probably accurate.) The population estimates are for 1974, projected from the 1970 census by Vierow and the church statistics from 1973.

	General Population		*Christian Population*
Sarawak	1,170,000	85,000	Catholics
		40,000	Methodists, tribal and Chinese
		30,000	Anglicans
		35,000	SIB related to Bornea Evangelical Mission
		5,000	Baptist, Adventists, and others
		195,000	Total
Sabah	690,000	86,000	Catholics
		20,000	Anglican
		39,500	Lutheran Basel Mission, tribal, and Chinese
		22,500	Baptist, Brethren, Adventists, and others
		168,000	Total
East Malaysia totals	1,860,000	363,000	

From this auspicious beginning the Sidang Injil Borneo church was born. Fraternally related to the Borneo Evangelical Mission, today it works in ten tribes with an estimated thirty-five thousand Christians meeting in two hundred congregations under a hundred pastors. Nationals run the central Bible school in Lawas, Sarawak. Nationals and some missionaries staff short-term itinerant deacons' schools for lay Bible training throughout the tribes, with the result that today there are a thousand deacons serving the totally indigenous churches and electing their own national church officers. Meanwhile, the Borneo Evangelical Mission continues its basically pioneer work in the tribal longhouses of ten tribes with fifty missionaries. Language reduction and Bible translation is the second major emphasis of their work.

This work among the Muruts has been the most dramatic of the peoples' movements in North Borneo. Methodist work had an early, healthy start but was largely centered in the cities. But an encouraging movement among the Iban tribe began among Methodists just before the war.[1] The first missionary was a Batak tribesman from Sumatra. Since 1952 an Iban Methodist conference has been set up, with a current estimated membership of over sixteen thousand in sixty-two churches with thirty-eight pastors. (Older Methodist churches, largely among Chinese, total twenty-five thousand.) The Iban conference is reputedly the most rapidly growing Methodist church in the world. Next in size are the Anglicans, who report twenty-nine thousand members and twenty clergymen in Sarawak and six thousand members and twelve clergymen in Sabah.[2] (However, Vierow reports twenty thousand Anglican Christians in Sabah.) Recent encouraging growth, spurred by evangelicals from the Church Missionary Society of Australia, has necessitated the division of the work into two dioceses.

Dating from the late nineteenth century, the Basel Mission Lutheran churches now approximate eight thousand Chinese members in twenty congregations and fifteen hundred tribal Christians, principally the Dusun in Sabah, where work began in 1952. In smaller Sabah, where there is a higher percentage of Chinese than Malay population, the Chinese church is generally the larger. Actually the first Chinese who immigrated to Borneo were Hakka Christians from Foochow in the late nineteenth century. Thus the bulk of the Anglican, Methodist, and Lutheran Basel mission Christians are Chinese. However, one Methodist missionary estimates that though as many as half of the Chinese in some areas may profess to be Christian, many of these are only nominal.

Plymouth Brethren also work among the Chinese, as do the Southern Baptists, who began an aggressive work in 1970. A number of independent missionaries are pioneering among the tribes but largely associating themselves with the BEM national church. And the omnipresent Bible societies are currently supervising translation work in seven or more languages. Thus Protestant Christians in Sarawak and Sabah today number over 160,000. Catholics, however, have also been energetically working among the receptive Murut and other tribes, and they now claim over 170,000 believers. Converts among the large Iban tribe have been fewer for both Protestant and Catholic.†

Though somewhat abated, the enthusiastic tribal evangelism of the Muruts and others continues. Generally the future for church growth is hopeful. But a number of serious problems are present. Language is the foremost. In addition to the almost total illiteracy among those tribespeople who are untouched by missions (government efforts at education and literacy are still largely limited to the cities), it is estimated that there are more than 150 different dialects in use throughout the country. Admittedly many of these are in very small tribes numbering only in the hundreds. Transportation to reach these remote tribes is a second serious problem. Traditionally rivers, broken by dangerous rapids, have been the only roads, and these constitute expensive means of travel in terms of both time and money. The BEM pioneered gospel invasion by planes after World War II. But there are still only approximately ten airstrips open to missionaries in the interior, and only four commercial airstrips.

A third problem is the serious tension between tribespeople and Chinese people caused by growing nationalism. Though a smaller group, the Chinese are the traders and businessmen and control the majority of the wealth. This tension between Chinese and tribesmen and Malays is mounting. In Sabah the Malays are a more influential group, and, though there is nominal religious freedom, they are pushing to make Islam the national religion, as it is in West Malaysia. A more recent problem has been the incursion of communists, particularly in Sarawak, where the extreme poverty and primitiveness of the people may prove fertile ground for communistic appeals. Finally, though missionary work has been welcome since World War II, the government now seems to be pursuing a policy of subtly forcing out missionaries. Though it is not official and though no dates have been set, missionary visas are now limited to a ten-year period,

†The failure to win more Ibans for Christ is perhaps due to the value we have placed on certain aspects of Western culture and a corresponding neglect of local culture. Our activities have often stifled the natural development of local communities by overemphasizing materials and money. The creative power of the Ibans has been stifled and the germ (always there) which could produce a responsible, God-fearing community has been sterilized. The Ibans are still in their own Old Testament, but the fact that they are already a people, a recognizable social and cultural group with their own structures, economy, and customs, indicates that they could be led to Christ and to a way of life which is truly Christian and truly Iban." Chandu Ray in *COFAE Newsletter,* 1973.

including two brief furloughs. Extension of religious liberty in East Malaysia may depend on the aggressiveness of the Islamic government and West Malaysian headquarters.

The extreme primitiveness of the tribal people and their superstitious animism have as a whole been advantageous to the preaching of the gospel there in this generation. With the progress of Bible translation and literacy in these areas the future for the church is bright, if both city and tribal churches rise to the challenge. And a work of the Holy Spirit in renewing the older church could bring a new day for them in this decade.

The Church Today in West Malaysia

On the surface the 2 percent of Christians (of which Protestants may number about one-quarter) in West Malaysia seems similar to the other Christian minorities of Asia. But closer analysis reveals a tragic difference. Of the 10 million population of West Malaysia, 55 percent are Muslim Malaysians, and the other 45 percent are Chinese and Indian immigrants (in a ratio of approximately 3½ to 1). The estimated 50,000 Protestant Christians and 148,000 Catholics are almost exclusively among the minorities. This means that within the 5½ million parent population of Malaysia, there is no true indigenous church, no discipled group bearing witness within their own ethnic community. In some of the Malay states inquirers from Islam must get a court declaration before they are allowed to convert to Christianity. In other states family ostracism, persecution, and physical threats are reported by the few Malay Christian converts. Some leave the country; others, converted abroad, do not return. Thus the Malay indigenous church is pitifully weak.‡

What of religious freedom in West Malaysia? Since the country holds a charter membership in the United Nations, it is nominally committed to religious freedom. The problems occur within individual states. Each is at liberty to make up its own rules and regulations on religious affairs. In one state it is reliably reported that if a person leads a Muslim to Christ, that person must go to jail for three to six months or is asked to leave the country. The Malay making the decision may lose all his privileges as a citizen, including his rights to a job, etc.

An informed observer of the Asian scene met with an interdenominational group of church leaders in 1971 to inquire more deeply into the whole problem. In no place was there a total ban on Christian evangelism reported to church leaders. A small subcommittee of the various churches is supposedly watching legal issues and collecting information about any local enactments which would curtail religious liberty. Nevertheless, open

‡Thomas Heng, local Inter-Varsity staff worker, has contributed valuable material for this section.

evangelistic work among the Malays is usually prohibited, and many Chinese Christians feel that open evangelism would endanger their position and be a breach of peace.

As a result there is currently a severe reduction in missionary forces, due in part to Malaysia's rule that no foreign missionary may stay more than ten years; in fact, there is no guarantee that he may stay even that long. One reliable missionary source reports that a number of Indian pastors in the Tamil Methodist churches are having to leave due to the ten-year rule, and there are no pastors to replace them. However, at the latest count there were still at least sixty-one Protestant missionary workers laboring in West Malaysia. These had come from many countries—not only from North America and Europe, but also from Asia. The majority of these, however, have been laboring with the Chinese and Indian minorities.

Yet there is a vital, growing, witnessing church in West Malaysia despite these problems. Total Protestants probably number about 50,000 in 363 churches, with 219 full-time pastors, evangelists, and missionaries related to more than a dozen denominations.§ Even with this small number of

WEST MALAYSIAN CHRISTIANS

Anglicans	7,500
Seventh-Day Adventists	3,500
Baptists	2,000
Brethren	3,200
Presbyterian	6,000
Evangelical Lutheran Church in Malaysia and Singapore	2,000
Lutheran Church in Malaysia and Singapore	2,300
Mar Thoma Church	1,500
Syrian Orthodox	500
Evangelical Free Church	200
Assemblies of God	3,000
Methodists	15,000
Roman Catholics	148,000
Others	2,500
Total	197,200

Protestant Christians, full-time national pastors and evangelists are in short supply: at present they average only 1 worker to more than 220 members. The Roman Catholic church, whose total members probably exceed 140,000, report 76 churches with 148 priests, some of whom are missionaries.

An accurate assessment of the churches and their growth in West Malaysia is difficult, since statistics have not been regularly kept. But one informed, interdenominational, parachurch evangelistic worker reports briefly as follows.

Presbyterians are now in their fourteenth year of an evangelistic plan

§The following statistics were compiled by Vierow et al.; see footnote *.

aimed at doubling their membership by twenty years. They are optimistic about reaching this goal. They are using mass evangelistic efforts, working particularly closely with Campus Crusade for Christ. Good growth is being experienced in the country churches. The Presbyterians are working mainly with the Chinese and with English-speaking persons.

Lutherans, whose main evangelistic efforts have been in the postwar period, are using mass and personal evangelism, but the bulk of their small growth has come through biological development within the church, fostered by the Sunday school and youth movements.

In more recent years other groups have begun aggressive programs in the nation. Baptists report steady growth, primarily through youth and Sunday school departments. Brethren do not report an optimistic picture of growth through evangelism, although they are one of the older groups in the community. The Evangelical Free churches now number three, having grown mainly through young people from smaller towns who moved to the city. The Assembly of God has reported rapid growth in the last two or three years through "a work of the Holy Spirit." The Church of Christ claims to have added 30 percent to its church membership through evangelistic meetings and personal work in the past two years. No groups report outstanding church growth or large numbers of conversions through any direct evangelistic means.

However, two major mass evangelistic efforts have been tried in the last several years. The Asian Evangelistic Commission sponsored an evangelistic campaign in the capital city of Kuala Lumpur in 1967, using a large amphitheater. This is the first time that a large, united Christian meeting had been held in such a public place with city-wide advertising. No disturbance from the Muslim majority was reported, and there were professions of faith. Two years later Dr. Grady Wilson of the Billy Graham Evangelistic Association held a similar type of meeting there (and in Singapore), and with similar results. The very permission to hold such a meeting in the nation was a hopeful harbinger of future wider evangelistic efforts.

Currently three parachurch, youth evangelistic organizations are now working in West Malaysia. The first on the scene was the Fellowship of Evangelical Students (related to the International Fellowship of Evangelical Students), which began work in 1962. It has a current membership of five hundred and is making attempts at grounding believers and doing student evangelism. Conversions are few but apparently permanent. Most of the converts come from youths in their late teens and early twenties. Campus Crusade for Christ has also reported good response to evangelism and is working among lower grades and university students, and in close cooperation with some of the denominations. The Navigators report three hundred converts since 1966 and two hundred current members in their work among college students. Thus it appears that evangelistic efforts to reach the large non-Christian population are being made mostly by para-church youth groups.

Problems and needs in Malaysian evangelism are numerous. On-the-scene observers report the following major problems:

1. The Malaysian Muslim majority is not being effectively reached.

2. The poorer members of the community and the adults are also being ineffectively reached. Most of the converts are from among middle-class youth.

3. The multiplicity of languages throughout the relatively small country is a major problem of gospel communication. Literacy is less than 50 percent in the cities and still less in rural areas, magnifying this problem.

4. The dropout rate of professing Christian converts is high, due to persecution in every dimension of life.

5. Inadequate Bible teaching in the churches has produced weakness. One widely traveled Christian worker reports that "the teaching programs in the churches of Malaysia need evaluation and tremendous overhaul if there is to be a real thrust forward in sound evangelism and a steady growth of membership with a minimum dropout rate."

6. Finally, the lack of evangelistic vision seems to characterize most of the churches, due in part to the hostile environment.

Yet despite all this God has been working in Malaysia, primarily among the youth. Among the Indians and Chinese the religions of the older generations no longer strongly grip the young. Despite the attraction of materialism and secularism, many young people are open to the gospel and have been responding. The fruit among these youths needs to be more carefully conserved, however.

The picture is not totally dark in Malaysia today. The doors for evangelism among the Chinese and Indians are still open. People are coming to Christ. The church is growing slowly. But a revived church with a vision of evangelism is desperately needed to exploit the open doors among the semireceptive peoples there. And God himself may sovereignly open a door into the majority Malay community in the near future in answer to prayer, as he has done in Indonesia in recent years. Some few new missionaries are being admitted, especially from Asian countries, and their ministry in renewing and teaching in the national church may be a key to a forward movement in the days ahead.

The Church Today in Singapore

The unique, polyglot island-city-republic of Singapore contains one of the largest Christian communities in Asia, conservatively estimated at 8 percent of the population.[3] It is rapidly becoming a center of evangelical activity in the Far East. The total Christian population is probably slightly greater than 50 percent Catholic, though of an estimated two hundred congregations meeting in 150 church buildings and homes, probably 85 percent are Protestant.

Singapore's churches are largely organized along ethnic and linguistic lines, with 97 percent of the Christians in Chinese congregations (since 75 percent of the population is of Chinese origin). The second-largest group is Europeans. Little evangelism is being done among the Malays, who comprise 14.5 percent of the population. The majority of Singapore's laity are conservative, says Dr. Sng Ewe Kong.[4] Having had to pay a large personal price for their faith as first-generation converts from traditional religions, these laymen now oppose the liberal trends in many denominations, Dr. Kong reports. Harry Haines observes, "Many of the Chinese Protestant churches in southeast Asia are almost as isolated from the ecumenical thinking and activities of the last decade as their brethren in China."[5]

Singapore enjoys complete religious freedom and has no official religion, as is promoted in neighboring Malaysia. There is an evangelistic spirit in most churches. But church growth is slow, having averaged approximately 30 to 50 percent in the postwar transitional period. With half of Singapore's 2.3 million population under twenty years of age and another 15 percent in young adulthood, opportunities for youth evangelism have been fruitful. It is estimated that a sharply higher percentage of Christians is found among university students than in the general population. Singapore is rapidly urbanizing; government high-rise developments already house 40 percent of the population, and by 1979 it is estimated that they will contain 80 percent. To meet the spiritual needs of these concrete jungles, the Church Growth Study group of the Graduates' Christian Fellowship in Singapore estimates a need for some fifteen hundred house-churches by 1980. These would be centered in the towering apartment developments.

This commercial center of central Asia is also rapidly becoming headquarters for many Christian religious organizations,|| so much so that the government began restricting visas for foreign religionists in 1971. It has become a Buddhist center as well, serving as the regional center for the World Fellowship of Buddhists and other organizations. But despite the fact that many Buddhist temples are going up and many pilgrims crowd them on holy days, most of the converts to Christianity still come from Buddhism. As in other urban-industrial societies in Asia and around the

||Overseas Missionary Fellowship, Scripture Union, Coordinating Office for Asian Evangelism, Evangelism International's leadership training school, etc.

world, however, the biggest problem facing the church and evangelism in Singapore today is materialism and secularism.

In a population of 2,050,000 (75 percent Chinese, 14.5 percent Malays, 8 percent Indians and Pakistanis, 3 percent other in 1971), Christians total over 160,000, with estimates running as high as 200,000 (since the number of independent Christians and church groups and sects is unknown). The number of Protestant churches is over 170, and there are seven Bible schools and seminaries on the island. The major Christian denominations look like this:

Denominations	*No. of Adherents*	*No. of Churches*
Roman Catholic	80,000+ (incl. children)	27
Methodists	13,000	24
Anglicans	7,200 (baptized members)	17
Presbyterians	4,570	17
Brethren	2,000	8
Bible Presbyterians (ICC group)	1,500	10
Baptists	1,500	12
Assemblies of God		12
Pentecostals	?	6
Independents	7-14,000	17+
Church of Christ	550	5
Christian Nationals Evangelism Commission	250	6
Orthodox	770	2
Salvation Army	230	3
Lutherans	700	5
Evangelical Free Church	200	3
Bible Church	90	4

SOURCE: Compiled by James Wang for "Church Growth Study Group" of Singapore Graduate Christian Fellowship.

Ministering to the more than 170 Protestant congregations are between 120 and 130 full-time ministers, of whom 75 are local nationals. But only 7 are university graduates (1970).

Singapore's first missionary landed in 1822, Rev. G. H. Thompson of the London Missionary Society. Probably the greatest single spiritual impact on Singapore was made by the Chinese evangelist Dr. John Sung, who made six visits to Singapore in the 1930's. In his first campaign alone he preached forty times, and thirteen hundred persons professed conversion. The Singapore Evangelistic League, the Chin Ling Bible School, and the Chinese-speaking Methodist Conference (paralleling the existing English-speaking conference) were founded as a result of Sung's ministry. Today,

150 years later, there are seventeen Protestant mission groups with 138 missionaries laboring in Singapore. The largest of these include the Seventh-Day Adventists, the Overseas Missionary Fellowship, and the Methodists. The Overseas Missionary Fellowship (the former China Inland Mission) shifted its headquarters first to Hong Kong and then, in 1952, to Singapore, when the communist takeover in China forced their exodus. Currently about thirty missionaries are in church planting and other evangelistic work in Singapore alone, with the program of its other hundreds of missionaries scattered throughout southeast Asia being guided from its headquarters there.

Ministering to the 50 percent youth population are a number of active youth organizations. Oldest is the local branch of the Scripture Union, which currently has over five thousand people studying the Bible in three languages, sponsors ninety-two interschool Christian fellowship groups in schools, and has ninety branches in churches. Youth for Christ has an indigenous work featuring rallies, Bible clubs, follow-up and training programs, camps, and their own magazine in the city.

Varsity Christian Fellowship was born on the campus of the University of Malaya when it was located in Singapore in 1950. Disillusioned with the liberalism of the old Student Christian Movement, four students began meeting for Bible study and prayer (two of these subsequently became university professors). In 1952 the VCF was formally organized there. Four years later chapters were organized at the University of Singapore and Nanyang University, when communist-inspired riots kept the students from their own churches on Sunday.

Graduates of these groups formed the Graduate Christian Fellowship in 1955. In 1959 the Fellowship of Evangelical Students was formed as a coordinating group of the other local fellowships. Today over four hundred students meet regularly with these various groups. A large number of graduates hold high positions in government, universities, businesses, and professions. The openness of the students and their expanding population in many schools of the city offer a tremendous challenge to future evangelism, but outside help is probably needed in order to capitalize on this opportunity.

Theological education for the old-line denominations is largely centered in Trinity College, begun by Anglicans but now shrinking in size and influence. Singapore Bible College has grown slowly since the war as an evangelical, college-level training school. In the late sixties David Adeney, former OMF missionary and International Fellowship of Evangelical Students' far-eastern director, began the Discipleship Training Center to provide seminary-level education for young people from all over Asia.

Classes are conducted in English, and students are qualified for examinations on the B.D. level from London University.

The Bible societies have been active for decades in Scripture distribution in all the major languages in Singapore, mainly through the churches. Currently the local Bible society is erecting a new headquarters. Singapore also houses the regional headquarters, now under the strong evangelical leadership of Edward Cline. Former Presbyterian missionary Russell Self is promoting dramatic, creative publication and distribution efforts throughout southeast Asia with great effectiveness. Local Gideons are also active in distributing Bibles, largely through the hotels at present.

A unique indigenous missionary organization, the Malaysia Evangelical Fellowship, was founded in 1964 by Dr. G. D. James, a Singapore national but a Tamil-speaking Malaysian by birth. In addition to his own evangelistic ministry, Dr. James sponsors full-time missionaries in East and West Malaysia and in nearby countries. Other excellent independent and indigenous ministries have also developed. An example is Rev. Peter Ng, director of the Jesus Saves Mission, who operates four centers among Singapore's poor people with a contagious exuberance.

The Singapore Council of Churches is an outgrowth of joint Protestant worship services conducted during the Japanese occupation of Singapore between 1942 and 1945. Anglican Bishop John Wilson first established a "Federation of Christian Churches," for which he was interned. Following the war the first NCC of Malaysia was organized, in 1948. (From this came eventually Trinity College). Today the council works largely with the old-line denominations and is not primarily evangelical in emphasis. It has been active in establishing a church counseling service and the "Samaritans of Singapore," a twenty-four-hour-a-day telephone service designed to thwart suicides through telephone and counseling friendships. The Far Eastern Council of Christian Churches, an affiliate of the International Council of Christian Churches, was formed in 1956. It is largely supported by the few Bible Presbyterian churches and is vigorously opposed to the Council of Churches in Malaysia and Singapore.

Across the horizon in Singapore there are thus many strong churches and interchurch organizations executing and projecting excellent plans to meet the needs of this unique city-community. But several problems hinder the church in these organizations. One is the still inordinately large foreign influence within the church. This has tended to stifle initiative on the part of local churches, so that until very recent years the church and its related organizations have not been adequately indigenized. Progress is being made now, however. The shortage of pastoral and evangelistic leadership is also great; even the vital Varsity Fellowship has not contributed the expected number of Christian leaders.[6] A third problem is the lack of adequate lay leadership, though strides have been made here. In most of the interdenominational, extrachurch organizations, as well as in church councils, the laity are now taking an increasing grip on leadership. One strong lay ministry is that of Koo Siaw Hua. Starting in one prison, he now preaches in all four government prisons. Koo has baptized over a hundred men whom he has led to Christ while they have been in detention. Only recently was he ordained a lay Methodist preacher.

Language differences in the polyglot community are also a barrier. Of the 80 percent Chinese in the community, probably half of these are bilingual in both Chinese and English. But many of the older people speak a number of Chinese dialects (six commonly), rather than the standard Mandarin. Widespread evangelistic efforts thus often strike these barriers. Though there is a tendency for greater participation among both evangelical and nonevangelical Christians in the community, Christian social efforts are also still inadequate.

Other problems facing the church include the lack of adequate plans and policies for church growth and systematic extension in the face of expanding opportunities, a lack of missionary zeal, and a need for better understanding and closer cooperation among evangelical bodies. Newer groups, bringing newer methods, have also conflicted with older, more established groups in the community (e.g., the invasion of Campus Crusade and Navigators in areas formerly served only by the Fellowship of Evangelical Students).

Despite these problems the future for evangelism in the church in Singapore is bright with hope and incipient activity. Two great challenges are before Christians: the youth opportunity—over 50 percent of the growing population—and the increasing centralization of the population in urban high-rise apartments. These large-scale urban developments challenge the church to be realistic, relevant, and rightly related to the needs of these new communities. During the next five to ten years the lives of more than half of Singapore's population will be uprooted, demanding necessary social and economic adjustments. Evangelical Anglicans are planning for a multiplication of house-churches in these high-rise enclaves. Along with these goes the steadily mounting literacy and its opportunity for literature evangelism; already Christian book sales are growing hopefully, but more must be done.

Facing the future, I would note the following factors:

1. The ecumenical movement will probably gain momentum. The Singapore government is keen that Christians should speak with one voice rather than many. It is generally agreed that there is little justification for

the existence of so many independent denominations and autonomous groupings along linguistic lines.

2. Evangelical, interdenominational evangelistic efforts are needed and will probably grow.

3. In the light of the urban crisis, much greater social involvement among evangelicals will doubtless be done.

4. The church must help combat the dangers of materialism and communalism. To do this she will need both financial and personnel help from Christian organizations outside the community.

5. Many new churches must be planted to meet the needs of the uprooted peoples and the growing population, particularly in the high-rise apartments. Mac Bradshaw proposes that "a basic objective in strategy should be the bountiful planting of house-churches." Only these can be reasonably expected to meet the needs.[7] To do this, Dr. Kong of the Fellowship of Evangelical Students suggests the development of three trends:

a. Transdenominationalism–transcending denominational differences to get the job of evangelism done, particularly in the high-rises.
b. Multilateralism–affiliating Christians with small house-churches in their apartments and then meeting their larger needs by relating them to established churches outside their apartment communities.
c. Destratification–promoting lay leadership to advance evangelism on every level.[8]

If the churches can rise to the broad challenge of Singapore's great opportunities, the future is bright. The church is at a crossroads. If evangelical Christians see the ample opportunities to take the lead, they can mold the history of the church and make the church in Singapore a great center of Christian witness and missionary activity. If they do not, others may determine the future of the church here and in Malaysia.

Malaysia-Singapore and Its Peoples

Frequent changes in the composition of the nation itself has made Malaysia difficult to understand since World War II. But the nation today is made up of two parts, which include the eleven states of former Malaya on the tip of the Malay peninsula and the states of Sarawak and Sabah on the island of Borneo, 400 miles southeast. Together they cover over 128,000 square miles, an area larger than the British Isles. Malaysia is 80 percent dense tropical jungle, mountains, and swamps. Sarawak and Sabah are coastal plains rising rapidly to mountains. Lying close to the equator, the nations' climate is damp tropical.[9]

The total population at the end of 1973 was 11.8 million.[10] The ethnic breakdown is Chinese, 36 percent; Malays, 48 percent; Indians and Pakistanis, 9 percent; tribal peoples, 7 percent, the bulk of whom are in Sarawak and Sabah.[11] The national language is Malay, though the many Chinese people, largely immigrant descendants from south China, speak a number of Chinese dialects. The Indians largely speak Tamil. Literacy is low, 25 to 35 percent, in Sarawak and Sabah but is over 50 percent in Malaya. The various ethnic groups largely maintain their own identities.

The island-city-republic of Singapore, nestling off the tip of the peninsula, is only 225 miles square, yet it houses 2.3 million persons. Of these, 78 percent are Chinese, 15 percent Malays, and 7 percent Indians and Pakistani. Though the language here too is officially Malay, about half of the people are bilingual in English and Chinese. Currently 60 percent are under thirty years of age. With increased public health measures in both Malaysia and Singapore, population is booming (2.7 percent per year in Malaysia, 2.2 percent in Singapore).[12]

The West Malaysian economy depends to a large extent on the production of natural rubber and tin, but in recent years timber and palm oil exports have also become important. Industrial development, encouraged by the government, is going ahead well. East Malaysia is faring less successfully. Her major industry is agriculture, though some rubber is grown, along with a rare nut (*illipenut*) used in making cosmetics. The gross national product for the entire area in 1973 was only $380 per person, while in Singapore it was over $920.[13]

Until the late sixties Singapore's major income came through its entrepôt trade, for Singapore is the world's fourth-largest port. But hundreds of new industries have now sprung up, particularly the huge industrial park built just ouside the main part of the city. In 1970, 30 percent of the gross national product came from manufacturing. In the last few years Singapore has become a major center of foreign exchange and trade throughout all of central Asia, attracting hundreds of million dollars of foreign investment and boosting the economy significantly.

Singapore's unique nature as a city-nation deserves special note. Over 80 percent of its people live on 25 percent of the land. The government housing board has built huge satellite towns, the largest of which has 180,000 persons in high-rise flats. About 40 percent of the population live in such low-cost apartments. Within a decade over half of Singapore's population will have been uprooted and moved into huge concrete jungles.

History of Malaysia-Singapore

Long before the advent of European powers, the two great ancient civilizations of India and China had indelibly influenced Malaya. From

India in the pre-Christian era had come the religions in Hinduism and Buddhism, though they were fused with the animism of the indigenous population. Indian and Chinese commercial and political influences were strongly exerted upon the peninsula as early as the fourteenth century. And Islam, which arrived at the end of the thirteenth century, when the Malacca sultanate was established, soon came to dominate the political and religious atmosphere of the entire area.

Malaya, as it was then known, early had an appeal to the European powers. Since the days the Portuguese first ventured into the region, the long, thin peninsula jutting out from the mainland of Asia occupied a strategic position as the crossroads of all of southeast Asia. To the west lies the long island of Sumatra, to the east is the China Sea, and to the south lies the great, curving crescent of the Indonesian archipelago. From Malacca, the Portuguese discovered, they could control all commerce between the Indian Ocean and the sea of China.

The advent of the white man marked a turning point in the history of all Malaysia. In 1511 D'Albuquerque captured Malacca for Portugal from the Malay sultanate. The Dutch seized the straits from the Portuguese in 1641. Finally the British appeared on the scene, hoisting the Union Jack in Penang in 1786 and later trading the former British colonies in Java and Sumatra for Malacca in 1824. From that moment on Britain gradually extended her influence through war and treaties until the whole of modern West Malaysia and Singapore came under her control.

Sir Stamford Raffles recognized the strategic value of a beautiful harbor on the small (225 square miles) tropical island of "Singapura" (Lion City) at the tip of the Malay peninsula, so he acquired it as a port for the English East India Company in 1819, 20 years before Hong Kong was founded. Thus Britain's colonial rule over the peninsula and northern Borneo to the south continued till the Japanese invasion in 1941. The British returned at the end of World War II, but only to pave the way for transfer of sovereignty. After 175 years of British rule, in 1957 the Federation of Malaya was born after a long and bitter postwar struggle with communist insurgents.

Present-day East Malaysian ports, located on the northern and western sides of Borneo (the third-largest island in the world), were also trading stops for Chinese and Indians for centuries. Europeans first landed in the sixteenth century, followed shortly by several French Roman Catholic missions. In the early nineteenth century the British founded the North Borneo Company, taking over Sabah and later turning it over to the crown as the colony of British North Borneo. Meanwhile, her sister area of Sarawak, long under the rule of the ancient sultanate of Brunei just to the south, came under British colonial influence until, in 1844, the famous

"White Rajah," James Brook, made himself the expatriate ruler, gradually expanding it at the expense of Brunei. All three—Sabah, Sarawak, and Brunei—became British protectorates in 1888 and finally full-fledged British colonies in 1946. In 1963 they became part of the new nation of Malaysia.

The establishment of the Malaysian nation in 1957 heralded a political and military confrontation with its southern neighbor, Indonesia. Though full-scale war was averted, forays and battles claimed many lives. The tension was quieted somewhat when the Indonesian coup deposed Sukarno in 1966. In 1965 Singapore was forced out of the restive federation because of the increasing disagreement between the Malay leaders of Malaysia and the Chinese leaders of Singapore, and Brunei withdrew at the same time.

Today Malaysia is a constitutional monarchy with a king elected from among the hereditary rulers of the component states. Actual rule is in the hands of an elected prime minister. Islam was proclaimed the state religion, and freedom to practice other religions is nominally guaranteed in the constitution. But tension between churches and government is increasing, and gospel preaching is being restricted and missionary visas are becoming more difficult to obtain.

In May 1969 a series of riots claimed unknown thousands of lives, particularly in Kuala Lumpur. The cause was apparently bitter communist opposition to the established government. This resulted in a tightening of restrictions over all activities of the country and the issuance of special rights to the Malays, who comprise a 45 percent plurality of the population. Between them and the Chinese, who are often the intellectual and business leaders of the country, there has been tension historically. So the departure of Singapore from the federation saw many of the leading Chinese in all fields trek southward to that tiny republic. There their wealth and acumen have made the economy boom. Under the energetic leadership of Prime Minister Lee Kuan Yew and the mild socialism of his People's Action party, Singapore has forged ahead, sweeping away slums and encouraging new industry.

Religions of Malaysia-Singapore

The religions of the immigrants determined the early allegiance of the inhabitants of the Malay Peninsula until in 1276 the sword of Islam swept in. Today as a result 46 percent of the people are Muslims, and most of the Chinese are classified as Buddhists, though their religion is usually diluted with mixtures of Taoism and Confucianism. The few Indians are mostly Hindu. The animist religion of the aboriginal tribes has to some degree corrupted all of these religions.

The Muslim Malays belong to the ancient Sunni sect, and since they enjoy political and restricted economic privileges, they have remained strong. The Hindus are numerically weak in the entire area. But their colorful festivals, particularly the *Thai Pusam,* has become a popular tourist attraction. Penitents skewer their cheeks and bodies with metal spikes and walk barefooted on hot embers at this time. Because of their syncretistic tendencies, there has not been strong opposition by the Hindus to Christianity. The few Sikhs stand out in the general population, their tall figures, full beards, and red turbans marking them. Though they were traditionally policemen and money lenders, now many are professional people, businessmen, and soldiers. Their wealth and influence is far in excess of their numbers.

Mahayana Buddhism is practiced in Malaysia, and the largest number of Christian converts in that area come from among them. In East Malaysia and Brunei the tribespeople are superstitious animists, the Chinese are both Buddhist and Christian historically, the Malays are Muslims, and the few Indians are mostly Hindus. Singaporeans claimed to be 40 percent Buddhist, 15 percent Muslim, and 8½ percent Christian in a government survey taken in 1969, but some feel that this Christian percentage is unrealistically high.

Christian History of Malaysia-Singapore

ROMAN CATHOLIC BEGINNINGS

Into this melting pot of religions the first Christian missionaries followed the traders and colonizers from their mother countries, as is mentioned in the introduction.# The advent of the Roman Catholic missionaries coincided with the conquest of Malacca in 1511. In the invasion fleet itself were eight chaplains, of whom six were Franciscan. These remained behind to minister to the Portuguese garrison founded there. But the arrival of Francis Xavier in 1545 heralded a great era of expansion. He founded a school from which Roman Catholic missionaries eventually spread to Burma, Siam, and the entire Malay archipelago.

When Portuguese influence declined at the end of the sixteenth century, the French Catholics took over. They established a seminary in 1806 at Penang, from which more than five hundred missionaries have gone to other Asian countries. Singapore was entrusted to them for evangelism in 1830, and they are still the predominant foreign group among the Catholics in East Malaysia, to which they went around 1870. The expansion of the Roman Catholic church has been rapid in the last hundred years. Dur-

#Ed. note. Because until 1965 Malaysia and Singapore enjoyed a common historical heritage, the early Christian history of the two nations will be reviewed as a unit.

ing the period from 1885 to 1905 the Chinese Catholic congregations trebled in numbers. In 1953 the diocese of Malacca was elevated to an archdiocese. Under the government Malayanization policy of "independent Malaysia," the ecclesiastical hierarchy has been to a large extent taken over by local clergy.

PROTESTANT BEGINNINGS

Protestant missions at first followed the British flag. The first Protestant missionary to come was a Presbyterian working under the newly organized London Missionary Society, constituted to help Robert Morrison go to China. Then William Milne of the LMS arrived in Malacca in 1814, wisely concentrating on education and printing. He started the first mission station in Singapore in 1819. But the most significant Presbyterian figure in that era was Benjamin Keasberry, who came with the LMS to Malaya in 1839. He pioneered a church in Singapore in 1841: "In regard to our little church, we now have seven Malays, one Chinese, and two country-born members," he wrote. They dedicated a church two years later, with an attendance of almost sixty. When the LMS abandoned the Malaya work officially in 1847 to go to China, Keasberry remained, supporting himself with a printing press, which he also used to print the Scriptures and Christian literature. During his lifetime he also founded the first Chinese church in the smaller city of Bukit Timah.

After the LMS officially left, expatriate Britishers petitioned their home church for a chaplain. MacKenzie Fraser came in 1856. He not only built a church for his parishioners but showed enthusiasm for evangelism among the Chinese. Thus in 1881 J. A. Cook arrived to work among them. When he retired in 1925 there were nine congregations with eight hundred Christians among them. Today the Presbyterians number around seven thousand in Malaysia and Singapore, with forty clergy.

On the heels of the Presbyterians came the Anglicans, whose first churches were established in Penang, Malaysia, in 1819 and in Singapore in 1834 (a church named Saint Andrews, successor to the cathedral today). The Anglican mission to the Chinese and other nationals was launched first in 1856. The breadth of the work gradually expanded to various Chinese and other language groups in the city. Until 1970 Malaysia and Singapore were one diocese; in that year they were divided into two, and the first national bishop, Chiu Ban It, was appointed over Singapore.

Though small in number, the Brethren are significant in their spiritual influence throughout the area. Their first assembly was probably held in Singapore in 1864, when Philip Robinson, founder of the present prestigious department store, met for worship with his wife and two other people. A Chinese catechist, formerly a Presbyterian, joined them, and in 1866 the Bethesda church hall was built, which continues as a thriving assembly till today. A Chinese assembly followed in 1867. In 1859 Brethren work was begun in Penang by a Mr. Chapman from Bristol. It spread slowly to other major cities of the peninsula. And in the closing years of the nineteenth century J. W. Moore worked among the Malays, wearing their clothes and living in a Malay-style hut. But he was soon forced to stop evangelism among them. Emphasizing open air preaching, Bible study correspondence work, literature, and lay evangelism, the Brethren work has had a strong and steady growth. Today many of the leaders in interdenominational movements in both areas come from this small group.

Methodists were the next to begin in Singapore. Burdened for the whole area, J. M. Thoburn of the South India Methodist Conference called for two volunteers for Singapore; twenty responded, but all were turned down. Eventually he and William Oldham, with two others, arrived in Singapore in 1885 without support. Convinced that they were called of God, however, they began with two weeks of evangelistic meetings in the town hall and promptly established a church. Schools for boys and girls followed.

In 1891 the work spread to Malaya, again with the school, and in 1900 the Methodists went to Borneo, laboring at first among the Chinese immigrants from Foochow, who settled around the city of Sibu. From there the work spread to the Ibans, who have had a people's movement to Christ in recent years. Differing from the Presbyterians and Anglicans, the Methodists from the outset majored on the Asians. They often started schools even before congregations. Today the Methodists probably constitute the second-strongest church group in the area.

Lutherans of the Basel Mission went to Sabah when a number of Lutheran Chinese migrated there in 1882. The work has continued strongly among them to the present, branching out after World War II into the largest Dusun tribe there. Early in the twentieth century the Lutheran church was planted in western Malaysia among the Tamil Indians. In 1907 the first church was begun in Kuala Lumpur, and a number of smaller groups scattered throughout the area. Missionary pastors from India found it difficult to labor there and often returned in broken health. Finally the Tamil church called on the church of Sweden for help, but the first missionary did not arrive until 1961. The following year the Evangelical Lutheran church of Malaya and Singapore was formally constituted. American Lutherans from the United Lutheran Synod began work in Malaysia in 1953. The missionary force grew to a total of thirty-two by 1959, including workers from Hong Kong. Lutheran work, however, has not been strong, and probably still numbers not more than fifteen hundred members.

In addition to the recognized older churches, a number of vital, aggressive smaller groups and individuals have been laboring in all three areas being considered here. When veteran Overseas Missionary Fellowship missionaries came out of China in 1949, they were joined by many new recruits. Over a hundred of them are now working in the Malaysia-Singapore area, mostly in direct evangelism and many with the Anglican church. The Evangelical Free church of the United States is working in both Malaysia and Singapore, with a Japanese missionary in the former. The Southern Baptists have come in strongly and have approximately fifteen hundred Christians in the Singapore area. Numerous other groups, almost all of them evangelical and evangelistic, are contributing to church growth there now. And of course along with them have come the sects: Seventh-Day Adventists, Mormons, Jehovah's Witnesses, etc.

But overall the picture is spiritually encouraging. Despite the stubborn presence of Islam, a babel of languages, and the unsettled political conditions of the last decade, the church is on the move in the Malay peninsula. Diverse as they are, these three equator-straddling countries nevertheless contain thousands of warmhearted Christians who are zealous to evangelize their own nations. Barring further oppression by the West Malaysian government, open doors for effective evangelism beckon to nationals and to missionaries in Singapore and in the ripe tribal areas of East Malaysia.

NOTES

1. *COFAE Newsletter,* 1973.
2. West Malaysia Council of Churches.
3. Wong, *Urbanization and Church Growth in Singapore,* p. 8.
4. Ibid., p. 11.
5. Harry Haines, *Christians of the Diaspora.*
6. *Logos,* May 1970.
7. Wong, *Urbanization,* p. 17.
8. Ibid., pp. 11-14.
9. *Background Notes Malaysia* (Washington: U. S. Dept. of State, Oct. 1969), p. 1.
10. *1973 World Population Data Sheet* (Washington: Pop. Ref. Bureau, 1974).
11. *Background Notes Malaysia,* p. 1.
12. *1973 World Population Data Sheet.*
13. Ibid.

BIBLIOGRAPHY

Anderson, G. H., ed. *Christ and Crisis in Southeast Asia.* New York: Friendship Press, 1968.

Area Handbook for Malaysia and Singapore. Washington: U.S. Government Printing Office, 1965.

Finlay, M. H. *1864-1964: The Story of 100 Years of the Lord's Blessing.* Singapore. Centennial brochure of Bethesda Gospel Hall.

Fleming, John R. "Singapore, Malaysia, and Brunei: The Church in a Racial Melting Pot." In *Christ and Crisis in Southeast Asia,* edited by Gerald H. Anderson. New York: Friendship Press, 1968.
———. *Some Notes on the History and Development of the Malayan Christian Council.*
From Every Tribe. Essex, England: Borneo Evangelical Mission.
Glass, Ernest W. "Christian Missions in Malaysia." In *Malaysian Baptist Mission Seminar on Philosophy and Strategy for Christian Missions,* 1965.
James, G. D. *Missionary Tours in Malaya.* Singapore: Malaya Evangelistic Fellowship, 1961.
Lee, F. G. *The Catholic Church in Malaya.* Singapore: Eastern Universities Press, 1963.
Lim Chong Yah. *Economic Development of Modern Malaya.* London: Oxford University Press, 1967.
Logos, vol. 10. Singapore: Varsity Christian Fellowship, 1970.
Loh Keng Aun. *The Anglican Church in Singapore Island, 1909-1959.* Singapore: University of Singapore, 1960.
Loo Choo Kheam. *The Methodist Impact on Malaya, 1885-1953.* Singapore: University of Singapore, 1955.
McDonald, Nelson. *Borneo Peoples.*
Milne, R. S. *Government and Politics in Malaysia.* Boston: Houghton, Mifflin Co., 1967.
Moore, D. and J. *The First 150 Years of Singapore.* Singapore: Donald Moore Publications, 1956.
Morrison, H. *Sarawak.*
Morrison, N. *Life in the Longhouse.*
Nyce, Ray. *The Kingdom and the Country.* A Singapore area research project presented to the Lutheran Church in Malaysia and Singapore and the Board of World Missions, Lutheran Church in America, 1970.
Ooi, J. B., and Chiang Hai Ding, eds. *Modern Singapore.* Singapore: University of Singapore, 1969.
Singapore: The Island Republic. Singapore: Ministry of Culture, 1969.
Statistics, vol. 9, no. 3, Mar. 1970. Singapore: Department of Statistics.
Tregonning, K. *Malaysia and Singapore.* Melbourne: F. W. Cheshire, 1966.
Wong, James, ed. *Urbanization and Church Growth in Singapore.* Singapore: Graduates Christian Fellowship, 1971.

18

THE REPUBLIC OF MALDIVES

by Lennie de Silva

Introduction

A TINY CHAIN of coral atolls in the Indian Ocean may be the only nation in all of Asia where there are no known national Christians. A fanatical Muslim police state, these islands have never had a church, so far as is known.

Christianity (or for that matter any religion other than Islam) is anathema to the Maldivians. To them anyone of another faith is an infidel, and according to the Muslim brotherhood to help an infidel is a heinous crime and a deadly sin. Among the foreign residents there are some Christians, the majority of whom are Roman Catholics. The few nonconformists (Protestants) meet on Sundays for worship in a private residence, though not regularly. A short service is led in turn by the members. In October 1971 they tried holding a Christmas carol service for the first time, but activities even of this nature are not viewed with much favor by the local people.

No kind of Christian propaganda is permitted. Anyone attempting too active religious work would face the certainty of immediate deportation. The hatred of the Maldivian people toward other religions is unadulter-

---

LENNIE DE SILVA was a member of the tutorial staff of Royal College, Colombo, Ceylon, for twenty-five years. A professor of English and mathematics, Mr. de Silva also served as a senior housemaster and the president of various club activities. Upon his retirement he accepted a short-term teaching assignment in the Maldives for two years.

ated, and Christianity in particular is most repugnant to them. Thus there seems little hope for evangelism in the Maldive islands for the foreseeable future.

Virtually unknown in the western world, the Republic of Maldives is one of the smallest members of the United Nations (it was admitted in 1965), and its 107,000 residents[1] are proud of this fact. The more than two thousand isles are a chain of twelve lush coral atolls which stretch 550 miles from the equator northward to a point a few hundred miles from the southern tip of India and Ceylon. The islets are small (none is larger than five square miles), and they average only five or six feet above sea level. Tropical vegetation covers the isles, from scrub palms to dense forests of coconut palms and fruit trees. The climate is hot (the average temperature is eighty degrees), humid, and unhealthful, with widespread malaria.

The capital of the isles is Male. On its 1¼ square miles of area lies the seat of government and live about sixteen thousand Maldivians.

What has the Muslim political and cultural monopoly produced in the Maldives after more than eighty years of British protection and modest economic aid?

Literacy is low—no accurate assessment has yet been made—and government positions even at the highest level are held by men and women with little or no education. An educational program with English as the medium of instruction was started ambitiously a little over ten years ago. Three government schools were founded at that time with the assistance of teachers from Ceylon with little or no teaching experience. Salaries and general living conditions are not attractive enough to draw more qualified personnel, and even the present salaries are frequently changed.

The people would be considered poor—the per capita annual income is well under a hundred dollars. All rice and grain must be imported, so the staple foods are fish and fruit. The government is currently seeking to attract and build industry. The average dwelling is small, usually a thatched tuft affording little or no privacy, with plumbing unknown except in the homes of high officials or well-to-do foreigners.

But employment is no problem, for the warm tropical seas surrounding the islands abound in fish. Thus fishing is a major occupation. But the next most important occupation is sex. Marriage ties are very flimsy, and divorce in the islands is an extremely common feature. Instances of a person divorcing as often as twenty-five times are not unusual. Sex life among girls starts at the age of about twelve, and among boys a year or two later. Thus the school careers of many girls are often jeopardized through unwarranted interest in sex. The recently imported western influence has not helped. Miniskirts, stovepipe trousers, expensive foreign cigarettes, wristwatches, and transistor radios have captured the hearts of the teenagers, no matter how difficult these items are to obtain.

Nation and People

Long ruled by a native sultan under successive Portuguese, Dutch, and British protection (beginning in 1887), the Maldive islands became a fully independent republic in November 1968. Former Prime Minister Nasir, who served under the sultan, Amir Ibrahim, was named president when the constitution was revised. A legislative council of fifty-four members elected by popular vote for a five-year term was installed, along with a cabinet. "The new president is a young modernist who is especially interested in education, public health, and the fisheries industry."[2]

But the islands are still essentially a police state. Penalties even for the most trivial offences are inhuman. Fundamental human rights are unheard of, and the freedom of speech is totally absent. Banishment, exile for indefinite periods, and the death sentence keep the entire population in constant fear and anxiety. It would be no exaggeration to state that there is hardly a single household where at least one of its members has not been banished or exiled. However, the twenty-four hour surveillance by the police and army has resulted in the lessening of major crimes, though larceny is not uncommon. The police are invested with authority to apprehend anyone without question, and, once arrested, it is difficult to prove one's innocence.

Despite this the average male Maldivian is proud of his country, though not of the state. He is very conscious of the fact that the country is a member of the UN, but he regrets its absence of freedom of speech and action. From time to time there have been political upheavals, resulting in assassinations and abdications of rulers in the past. Today, however, the strictest measures are taken regarding the personal security of the president, who is the sole authority for every action in the state machinery and especially for the dispursement of the finances of the country. The nominal cabinet ministers seem to have no executive powers. Yet Communism under the existing system of government is unthinkable with these tight controls. The mounting level of education and the paucity of employment for the English-educated young people now coming from the schools with the knowledge of other nations and constitutions portends the possibility of unrest in the near future.

Fishing is the mainstay of the economy, and 95 percent of the catch is exported by the state. Coconuts and local crafts are the next most important exports. The government operates a small merchant fleet on the Indian Ocean and is trying to introduce industry. All real property is held by the government, and the land is rented out to individuals. Similarly, all imports are state-owned, and all these goods are retailed through a chain of state-owned stores plus a very few private dealers. There is no direct taxation, but state income is largely provided through import duties. An additional source of income are the paid Voice of America broadcasts over Radio Maldives.

National History and Religion

Presumably of Aryan descent with some Arab admixture, the first Maldivians are traditionally reputed to have descended from an Indian Sinhalese who was stranded with his bride near one of the islands and stayed on to become the first sultan. Thus the language is a dialect of Sinhalese, and the most ancient religion was Buddhism.

But Arab traders began to visit the islands in the twelfth century, and their influence resulted in the "conversion" of the entire population to Sunni Islam (conservative) within a few years. Islam remains the religion of almost the entire population to the present day.

Though the Didi clan has nominally ruled the islands for the past eight hundred years, they have been successively "protected" by the Portuguese, the Dutch, and the British, finally becoming a self-governing British protectorate in 1887. The subsequent relationship has been marked with tension because of a British air facility on one of the islands, but the British have in turn supported the government with substantial grants.

The law of Islam is the law of the land, by which the Maldivians are expected to pray five times a day, observe an annual fast, and repudiate all other religions. Humanly speaking, there seems to be no hope for the evangelization of these isolated people in their squalid but beautiful tropical ghetto. Apparently only a miracle can open the doors to this tiny, neglected nation. The Christian world can only pray for this.

NOTES

1. *Background Notes,* Jan. 1969.
2. Ibid., p. 3.

BIBLIOGRAPHY

General Works

Agassiz, Alexander. *The Coral Reefs of the Maldives.* Cambridge: Harvard Museum, 1903.

Bell, Harry Charles Purvis. *The Maldive Islands: Monograph on the History, Archeology, Epigraphy.* Colombo: Ceylon Government Press, 1940. Without doubt the definitive work on the islands. A general survey of Maldivian history and archeology.

Hockly, Thomas William. *The Two Thousand Isles.* London, 1935. A short account of the people, history and customs of the Maldive archipelago.

Ibn Batuta. *Ibn Batuta in the Maldives and Ceylon.* Translated by Albert Gray from the French edition by de Fremay and Sanguinetti in *Journal of the Royal Asiatic Society, Ceylon Branch,* 1882. Ibn Batuta was a Moroccan Muslim who travelled extensively between China and Africa, visiting the Maldives in 1343 and 1344.

———. *The Rehla,* tr. by Mahdi Husain, Baroda, Oriental Institute, 1953.

Pyrard de Laval, Francois. *The Voyage of F. Pyrard.* Translated by A. Gray and H. C. P. Bell. London: Hakluyt Society, 1887-90. Pyrard was a French adventurer held captive on the islands from 1602-07.

Pamphlets

Background Notes. Washington: Dept. of State, Jan. 1969.

Progress of the Colombo Plan, 1968. Colombo: Colombo Plan Bureau, 1968.

The Maldive Islands Today. Colombo: Information Department, Office of the Maldivian Government Representative, n.d.

Ministry of External Affairs, Maldive Islands. *Ladies and Gentlemen . . . The Maldive Islands.* Colombo: M. D. Gunasena & Co., 1949.

———. *The Maldive Islands.* Colombo: M. D. Gunasena & Co., 1952.

Villiers, Alan. "The Marvelous Maldive Islands." National Geographic Magazine, June 1957, pp. 829-49.

Nomadic life continues in Mongolia. Early missionaries were unable to plant a lasting church there.

Missionaries Dr. David Johnson, A. Gunzel, and Fred Nelson visit with Mongols outside their tent.

Photos by Stewart Gunzel

19

THE MONGOLIAN PEOPLE'S REPUBLIC

by Stuart Gunzel and Donald E. Hoke

Introduction

Cold, remote, and practically unknown to the outside world, Outer Mongolia is tragically distinguished in the 1970's as the only country in Asia—possibly the world—without a single Christian church, witness, or assembly of any kind.

It is possible that the nation has never had an indigenous Christian church,[1] although when Outer and Inner Mongolia were one, just before the outbreak of World War II, there may have been as many as nine Protestant and four Roman Catholic groups meeting among the Mongols. Even then the scattered Christians totaled less than five hundred Catholics and three hundred Protestants. Missionaries working with the Mongols have never numbered more than forty, possibly during the same period; and the number of Mongol Christian workers, both Protestant and Catholic (usually converted outside the land) was probably even less than this. Thus when Communism slammed shut the door to both Outer and Inner Mongolia in 1949 it is likely that 95 percent of the estimated three million Mongols had never heard the gospel.

Stuart Gunzel first went to Mongolia in 1933, where he lived for over a year in the home of a Mongolian prince before marrying a fellow missionary. Mr. and Mrs. Gunzel then continued their ministry in Mongolia until 1946, but were subsequently forced out by the Communists and took up residence in Hong Kong. There Mr. Gunzel was active in the revision of the Mongolian New Testament and the production of a Mongol-English dictionary and grammar. In his last visit to the Far East, in 1966, he was instrumental in getting Mongol gospel radio programs broadcast on a regular basis over station HLKX from Korea. A missionary under the Evangelical Alliance Mission, Mr. Gunzel has through the years kept close touch with the Mongolian situation and his fellow workers there while working as Canadian secretary for the Mission.

The basic reason is obvious: Outer Mongolia lies in the cold heartland of central Asia and was accessible only by horseback, camelback, or foot until the mid-twentieth century. Its few people, roving in tiny bands over the Gobi Desert and mountain slopes, were diffident and difficult to reach. Since the days of her glory, when the Mongol Empire stretched from the Pacific Ocean to the Danube—the largest empire in the history of man—the nation has shrunk to an area one-third that of the United States. For almost two hundred years now, Mongolia has been a shifting battleground between Russia, China and Mongol nationalists. In the past twenty-five years Communism has quelled what appeared to be a rising spiritual interest during the late forties, so that today there is no church and probably not a single Christian family in the Mongolian People's Republic. Thus today perhaps the greatest significance of this tiny nation of 1½ million people is the absence of any witness in relation to the prophetic plan mentioned in Matthew 24:14: "This gospel of the kingdom shall be preached in all the world for a witness unto all nations; and then shall the end come."

Nation and People

The present-day Mongolian People's Republic comprises what was formerly known as Outer Mongolia, an area of six hundred thousand square miles between Siberia on the north, China on the south, and Manchuria on the east. The fabled Gobi Desert occupies much of the southeastern area, and mountains ranging to fourteen thousand feet rim the northern borders. Salt lakes dot the central area and earthquakes shake the entire kingdom frequently. Current population probably numbers 1.4 million. The nation's racial origins are indistinct but have given name to a whole strain, the Mongoloid peoples. They are characterized by small, wiry bodies, dark or yellowish skin, black hair, and black eyes. The present language is 90 percent Khalka Mongol (completely distinct from Chinese), and under communist leadership during the past two decades literacy has soared to an estimated 80 percent.

Traditionally the Mongols have been nomadic herdsmen who fed, clothed, and housed themselves with the products of their sheep, camels, cattle, and horses. The women have been the beasts of burden, performing all the manual work and even caring for the cattle while the men gave themselves to soldiering and the priesthood. (It was estimated at one time that close to half the men were priests.) But under communist rule, beginning with independence in 1945 but gaining strength by 1948, there have been full-scale efforts to introduce agriculture, to collectivize all animal husbandry, and to industrialize. "Under Soviet tutelage the Mongols have turned to the raising of grain corps, the catching of fish, the extraction of minerals, including crude oil, the manufacture of consumer goods and construction materials, and the development of the food-processing industry. A railroad was built in the mid-1950's, traversing the country from north to south and providing a shorter route between Russia and China. . . . There is now also an internal and international airline service, and trucks have largely replaced the camels on the domestic freight routes."[2]

As a pawn in a tug-of-war between Russia and China in recent decades, Mongolia has faced increasingly to Russia. Russian aid to the tune of over half a billion dollars, plus technical assistance and loans, has spurred the primitive Mongolian economy. Russians believe that the number of livestock can be increased to 35 or 40 million, that dependence on foreign trade can be reduced, and that the nation can be industrialized. Already people are flocking to the cities from their former nomadic existence—the capital, Ulan Bator, now houses 20 percent of the population.

Long scattered under roving "Leagues and Banners" (divisions of the population), the people have now been organized into eighteen major provinces. The tight rule is headed by a nine-man communist politburo, supported by a forty-seven thousand member Communist party. Once a year for three days the Great People's Hural, the congress, meets. In the interim the Council of Ministers, appointed by the Hural, rules and legislates. The chairman of the Council is Yunjaagiyn Tsedenbal, who has survived a number of upsets in the infant government. The Mongolian People's Republic is a member of the United Nations, but has not been recognized by or had diplomatic relations with the United States.

National History

It was during the brilliant T'ang dynasty of China (A.D. 618-906) that the Mongols were first recognized as a people, though they did not become a nation until several hundred years later under Kubal Khan, grandfather of the famous Genghis Khan. Shrewd, ruthless, ambitious, and a strict disciplinarian, Genghis unified the scattered Mongol tribes into the most famous fighting force of his day. Moving first to the south, he conquered north China in 1215. From there he moved westward into central Asia and eastern Europe, charging up the Steppes of Russia across the Moslem lands and destroying much of Islamic-Arabic civilization before he stopped within reach of Constantinople. The Mongols were probably the most ruthless and fearless conquerors of history, systematically slaughtering the population of entire cities.

When Genghis Khan died in 1227, his son Ogotai pushed the battle into Hungary and Poland and threatened all of western European civilization. But his untimely death caused the Mongol generals to return to Mongolia, where they elected Genghis Khan's grandson, Kublai Khan, as their emperor. He immediately moved southward and completed the conquest of China over the reigning Sung dynasty. Kublai Khan then founded the Yüan dynasty, which continued from 1279-1368, setting up his capital at what is present-day Peking. His was the greatest land empire in history, stretching from the Pacific Ocean across all of China and central Asia into eastern Europe. At one time he had four thousand five hundred ships, yet he failed to conquer tiny Japan—his defeat credited by the Japanese to a divine wind.

There are varying tales of Kublai Khan's religious interest. Some say he was converted to the lama type of Buddhism, which subsequently became the religion of the land. However, it is known that Marco Polo visited Kublai Khan and returned to Europe with his request for missionaries to be sent to China, after which Dominican and Franciscan monks were welcomed by him in his capital. After Kublai Khan's death the empire soon began to disintegrate through lack of a unifying culture and governmental system over the far-flung, multiracial area. A hundred years later the great Tamerlane, descendant of Genghis Khan, briefly joined some of the Mongol empires together. A mogul (derived from the Persian word for Mongol) emperor of India built the Taj Mahal in the early 1600's.

By the end of the seventeenth century the Manchu empire had shrunk to the area south of Siberia and east of Manchuria, embracing part of northern China. The Manchu emperors of China brought the area of Outer Mongolia under their suzerainty in 1691. A few years later the Russians moved down from the north, and in 1727 the Treaty of Khalta settled the area of Outer Mongolia and the Russian borders, which have continued approximately the same until today. From that time on Russia supported Mongolia against China, until Mongolia proclaimed herself independent of China for the first time in 1911, but the Russian Revolution loosened her hold on the area for a few years, from 1919 to 1921. The long struggle for independence which led to the eventual formation of the Mongolian People's Republic began in 1924 and was partially realized as one of the terms of the Yalta Declaration at the end of World War II, in 1945. The Chinese border agreement, separating the two countries, was not signed until 1964. Shortly after 1966 the twenty-year agreement of assistance and friendship with Russia was signed. Since then Mongolia has looked to Russia in the cold war between the communist giants.

National Religions

Lamaism was introduced into Mongolia from Tibet in the late twelfth or early thirteenth centuries, possibly through Kublai Khan. Lamaism is basically a form of Buddhism corrupted by tribal animism and doubtless also containing certain Hindu influences. One economic result of Lamaism was that until this generation Mongols never plowed the land for fear they would injure the resident spirits. Through the influence of Lamaism the lives of the Mongolians have been centered on the worship of spirits located in objects of wood and stone and the worship of many idols.

The Buddhist ideas of the transmigration of the soul through endless centuries and the belief that merit earned in this life can hasten one's progress through the endless reincarnation prompted the people to make significant sacrifices and even long pilgrimages in search of merit. Among some Mongols a colorful ceremony in the fourth month of the Chinese year used to see thousands paying large sums of money to ambitious Chinese traders for live fish which were released in a nearby lake, thus saving the lives of the fish and getting much merit for the devotees. Prayer wheels, prayer beads, and prayer flags were traditionally an important part of the daily life of the people for centuries. At least one son in every family was dedicated to the lamasery, the local Buddhist monastery, until a generation ago.

But now the forced communist educational program has largely eliminated much of the superstition. Agriculture is competing with animal husbandry as an occupation. And travelers report that the trappings of traditional Lamaism are now largely gone. Doubtless the younger generation worship only an atheistic materialism.

Christian History

Whether or not zealous missionaries of the church of the East ever reached the area of Outer Mongolia when they made their deep impression on China in the seventh century, no one can state with certainty. One early report stated that there were several hundred Christians in the Mongolia of the seventh century,[3] and it is at least possible, if not likely, that these eastern missionaries (commonly called Nestorians) either visited Mongolia themselves or else that some of their converts did so during the T'ang era (A.D. 618-906). (See the section on China in chapter 7, "Christianity Comes to Asia.") A possible interesting corroboration of this is the fact that during the succeeding Sung dynasty of China (A.D. 960-1280) Christianity was regarded as the faith of the hated Mongols and was suppressed for this reason.

More authentic is the record that these missionaries in the twelfth century penetrated well into the northern part of Mongolia, north of the Gobi desert, and there successfully evangelized the Kerait tribe,[4] with the result that the ruler and some of the people became Christians. Thus when the mighty Genghis Khan came to power early in the thirteenth century he first allied himself with the Keraits, then overpowered them and made their capital at Karakorum his own capital. It has been reported that at that time there were small Christian groups present in the city. Though the great Khan himself was apparently indifferent to Christianity, good authority reports that one of his daughters-in-law was converted and became the mother of Kublai Khan, Genghis Khan's grandson, who eventually succeeded to the empire. Though Kublai Khan himself apparently never became a Christian (though two of his brothers did) he was friendly to the faith. After the establishment of his capital in Cambaluc (Peking), missionaries from the church of the East in some numbers (along with a few Roman Catholic and Greek Catholic missionaries) evangelized successfully in China, with the result that a special government bureau was established to supervise their churches and monasteries. Apparently, however, the bulk of these converts were foreigners enjoying the patronage and confidence of the Mongol emperors as against the Chinese themselves. Thus when Kublai Khan's Yuan dynasty fell, opposition to Christianity quickly followed, and the curtain on gospel witness was drawn for another five hundred years in remote Mongolia. (For further details see chapter 7, "Christianity Comes to Asia.")

In 1815 a copy of the gospel of Matthew, translated by a Professor I. J. Schmidt in the Kalmuck language (used by Mongols on both the Siberian and Mongolian side of the northern border) was published by the British and Foreign Bible Society. Some of these gospels came to Irkutsk and were discovered by some of the Buriat tribesmen. Though they could only partially understand the message, the tribesmen's interest was keen. Together with a high lama they began to gather funds to have this and other New Testament books translated into Mongolian and printed. These were given to the Russian Bible Society, and two Buriat leaders were sent to Saint Petersburg to assist Professor Schmidt in translating the gospels and the book of Acts into Mongolian. As a result both of these officials were converted, and one was baptized shortly before his death.

Viewing this growing interest, the Russian Bible Society appealed to the London Missionary Society for missionaries, and in the year 1817 Kornelius Rahmn from Sweden and Mr. and Mrs. E. Stallybrass from England opened a mission station in the city of Selenginsk (on the Siberian-Mongolian border) on land supplied by the Russian emperor. Other missionaries from the LMS followed shortly, and two new stations were opened. Stallybrass and one of the later missionaries, Swan, translated the whole Bible, so when the missionaries were forced out they left behind the entire Bible in Buriat-Mongolian (published by the British and Foreign Bible Society) along with tiny groups of Christians on both the Mongolian and Siberian sides of the borders.[5]

James Gilmour, best-known of all Mongol missionaries, was sent out by the London Missionary Society in 1870. After staying a few weeks in Peking he moved into Mongolia, where for twelve uninterrupted years he spent his summers with the nomadic Mongols, learning their language, adopting their dress, living in their tents, and as far as possible fully identifying with them. His simple knowledge of medicine greatly endeared him to the primitive peoples. During the winters he lived in Peking, ministering to Mongols there. Whether Gilmour actually ever saw a church born in Mongolia itself is not known. But he traveled throughout the entire area of the present Mongolian People's Republic, saw the tombs of Stallybrass and Swan (who had died over thirty years before), and visited the areas in southern Siberia where the first missionary work to the Mongols had begun.[6]

In 1895 the first of several Scandinavian Alliance missionaries (later the Evangelical Alliance Mission) began itinerant work in Mongolia. David Stenberg was joined in 1896 by Carl Suber and in 1897 by Hilda and Clara Anderson, Hannah Lund, and N. J. Friedstrom. Little success marked their work, and all but Friedstrom (who escaped across the Gobi desert) were martyred in the Boxer Uprising of 1900.[7] Friedstrom and his wife later returned to build an extensive missionary colony in Inner Mongolia. Meanwhile two Norwegian missionary brothers named Naestegard opened a work in the capital of Urga (present-day Ulan Bator) in 1896. They fled the Boxer uprising and never returned. But missionary work began again in Urga in 1919; a clinic was reopened, and more missionaries came in 1921. Young people seemed interested, and many youth and soldiers came for Scripture portions, but this soon attracted the attention and opposition of Russian officials, who searched the mission station, confiscated the books, and killed the interest. In May 1924 the missionaries left Urga in Outer Mongolia for good.

Some forays into Outer Mongolia were made in the years immediately before and after World War II by members of the Swedish Mongol Mission, TEAM (including the author), and possibly others, but no aggressive evangelistic work has been carried on there for over half a century. When the earlier Swedish missionaries left in 1924 they reported no open converts, though there were some inquirers.

The largest of the groups working in Inner Mongolia (located just south of the Mongolian People's Republic in the northern and northwest provinces of China) was the Swedish Mongol Mission, which began work in the entire area in 1905. They were preceded by the missionaries of TEAM, who first entered in 1895, and by missionaries of the Assemblies of God, the Mongolian Indian Mission, the Brethren, the Seventh-Day Adventists, and some independents. Probably most successful was the work of the Swedish Mongol Mission, which reported, "In 1942 we had three stations and some over 100 converts. The last contact we had with some of them was 1947-48, when some of us had returned after the Japanese occupation."[8] In 1955 the Christian Workers Mission reported, "A Chinese brother in Inner Mongolia had been continuing his travels and had found earlier converts (Mongols) going on well. . . . In the provincial capital, following special meetings for the Christians, there had been a small-scale revival resulting in the start of a nightly meeting for Bible study and prayer. . . . In another district of 80,000 Mongols many were turning to the Lord through the witness of another China Bible seminary graduate. At Manass, where the leader was a Russian, God had visited the church in cleansing and quickening power."[9] No other word has apparently been heard since then.

One of the most significant projects carried on in the postwar period was the revision of the entire Mongolian New Testament by missionaries of TEAM, the Swedish Mongol Mission, and two national Mongol refugees in Hong Kong. Completed in 1949, the New Testament was mailed out in numbers through a Christian contact in north China for at least 10 years. Then in January 1968 radio messages in the Mongol language began to be aired over the TEAM radio station, HLKX, from Korea. These witnesses have continued to the remote Mongol nation despite the absence of any known Christian evangelist.

Thus in modern times for 150 years missionaries have nibbled at the cold edges of this inland empire with few discernible results. Though there have been tiny congregations of believers in the north China areas of Inner Mongolia, it is doubtful that a true Christian church has ever existed in what is now the Mongolian People's Republic. This country may thus be the only national and racial enclave in the world today where no Christian witness of any kind exists.

NOTES

1. C. R. Bawden, *The Modern History of Mongolia.*
2. *Background Notes,* p. 4.
3. O. C. Grauer, *A Burning and Shining Light,* p. 123.
4. *Vid Gobioknens Gränser.*
5. Ibid.
6. W. P. Nairn, *James Gilmour of the Mongols.*
7. Grauer, p. 123.
8. Letter from Mr. Joel Eriksson.
9. L. T. Lyall, *Come Wind, Come Weather,* pp. 69-73.

BIBLIOGRAPHY

Background Notes. Mongolian People's Republic, Sept. 1969.

Barnett, Doak. *Communist China and Asia.* New York: Harper, 1960.

Bawden, C. R. *The Modern History of Mongolia.* New York: Praeger, 1968.

Grauer, O. C. *A Burning and Shining Light.*
Hibbert, R. A. "The Mongolian People's Republic in the 1960's." *The World Today,* Mar. 1967.
Letter from Mr. Joel Eriksson, former SMM missionary.
Lindholm, A. G. "Light in the Regions Beyond." *Youth Christian Companion,* Nov. 1945.
Lyall, L. T. *Come Wind, Come Weather.* Chicago: Moody Press.
Murphy, George G. S. *Soviet Mongolia.* Berkeley: University of California Press, 1966.
Nairn, W. P. *James Gilmour of the Mongols.* London and New York, 1892.
Rupen, Robert A. *Mongols of the Twentieth Century.* Bloomington: University of Indiana Press, 1966.
Sanders, A. J. K. *The People's Republic of Mongolia.* New York: Oxford University Press, 1968.
Vid Gobiöknens Gränser. Stockholm: Swedish Mongol Mission Publication; Chicago: Evangelical Alliance Mission.

One of the nation's few church buildings

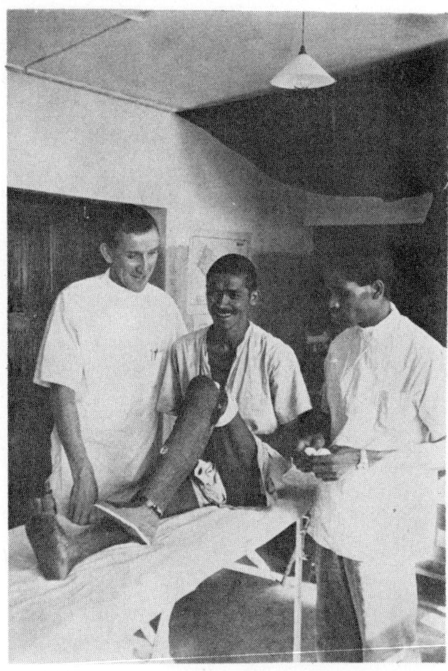

Doctors fit a locally made artificial leg.

Villages hear a gospel recording in a community clinic.

20

NEPAL

by Samuel R. Burgoyne and Jonathan Lindell

Introduction

In Nepal today one may still see a manner of life that goes back to the dawn of recorded history. The social structures and religions are reminiscent of ancient Sumer in Egypt. And the Bible student sees illustrated the life and times of the Old Testament in scores of communities in the valley. "The surrounding mountains have protected them. The rich valley has sustained them. They are kings of isolationism. And while the rest of the world is evolved on its way to modern technological civilization, the valley of Nepal, deep in the Himalayan mountains of central Asia, has lived on in its age of clay."[1] Suddenly, in 1951, a revolution opened the long-closed land. Visitors stepped in, and Nepal stepped out to fraternize with people in many lands. For the first time in Christian history Protestant

---

Samuel R. Burgoyne began his missionary career in India under the Bible Churchmen's Missionary Society in 1927. An Anglican and Canon of the Cathedral at Lucknow, he served for many years after the war under the United Methodist Board. Following a three-year service in Nepal, Mr. Burgoyne is now retired in the United States.

Jonathan Lindell, born and reared in China of missionary parents, began his missionary service in North India under the World Mission Prayer League in 1941. He went to Nepal in 1956 with the United Mission, first in teaching and then for eleven years in administration as executive secretary.

Helpful information updating this chapter was provided in late 1973 by Rev. Frank Wilcox, new executive secretary of the United Mission to Nepal.

missionaries were permitted to enter, though for one brief period of sixty years in the eighteenth century Catholic Capuchin fathers had worked in the Newar city-states of the valley.

The Church Today

Nepali Christians from India, Bhutan, and Sikkim joined the missionary messengers. Today, two decades later, in this "last home of mystery" Christ's church has been firmly planted. Christians, though persecuted, are witnessing, and God is "adding to the church such as should be saved." Though no accurate census has been nor can be taken, it is conservatively estimated that there may be some 450 Christians scattered in thirty small congregations throughout the nation. And the number of Christians in Bhutan, Sikkim, and Indian border cities may total 10,000. In the capital city of Kathmandu there are three church buildings, with a possible total membership exceeding 150. One pastor estimates that there are at least 150 baptized Christians from the Santali tribal group. Wherever Christians live, they form themselves into small groups or congregations and carry out the normal activities of the church. Their organization is simple. There is no official national church body or denomination. However, Christians have formed the Nepal Christian Fellowship, to which both groups and individuals may belong. The Fellowship has officers and holds an annual conference, seeking to foster unity, prayer, and cooperative work. It sponsors short-term Bible schools in different places. Literature is distributed. Book shops have been opened, and among them six or eight pastors instruct and baptize seekers.

It is illegal for anyone, Nepali or foreigner, to do overt Christian evangelism. But leaders and members of the churches continue with effective colportage ministries—occasional preaching tours to outlying towns and villages, where the home of a Christian family becomes the center and gathering place for people interested in hearing the gospel. Personal encounter and conversational witness are used widely by the Christians to win others to Christ. And the regular services of the established congregations are open to visitors and are effective evangelistic opportunities.

The Christians boldly carry on their worship and quiet witness, because the constitution of Nepal permits a man freedom to worship and practice the religion of his father, but forbids conversion to another faith. That crime, and the related crime of urging or assisting a man to change his ancestral faith, are punishable by law. But of the many Nepali citizens who have been converted to Christ and baptized, only a very few have been arrested, brought to trial, and given jail sentences. His Majesty's government has chosen to take an attitude of "benign neglect" toward the law. Conversion to Christ is considered a "non-cognizable" offense, and arrest and prosecution will be made only if someone makes a definite and determined complaint and charge against the new Christian.

So the church continues to grow slowly under pressure and prays for the day when the law will be changed to allow full religious liberty. Nepal, after all, is a member of the United Nations and subscribes to the Universal Declaration of Human Rights. Thus Christians are being baptized every few months, and always several are preparing for baptism in the little congregations scattered across the country. In late 1972 seven men were in prison for three months because they had been baptized, but they were released in March 1973, rejoicing that they would then be allowed to witness openly. The evangelist who had led them to Christ was sentenced to jail for nine months, and others who had been previously sentenced were not released at this writing. Those released in April '73 brought new dedication and unity to their home church, it was reported.

The unofficial status of the church creates many difficulties. There are problems of assembly, marriage, baptism, income tax, and, not the least, burial. One elderly man who had become a Christian was sentenced to one year in prison for providing a Christian burial for his wife. The Nepal Christian Fellowship is seeking on behalf of the churches to obtain this official recognition as a legitimate minority religious community.

But meanwhile the tiny churches carry on in New Testament fashion. Pastors of congregations have gone out with small teams during the winter months, encouraging isolated Christian groups and individual believers. One team went as far as Sikkim. Three-month Bible schools have been held in one of the Kathmandu churches, with students from the local church and surrounding towns averaging about twelve to each school. Unrecognized and under constant surveillance and threat of prison, Christians are nevertheless witnessing and seeing fruit in Nepal today.

The missionary organizations which have entered Nepal since the revolution are not intentionally creating or building the church in the traditional missionary pattern, for they are forbidden to do so. Missionaries as individuals join the local church group and function as members. Mission and churches are organizationally independent of each other, and each congregation is fully responsible for its own faith and order. With a healthy relationship to the churches, mission organizations in the past two decades have given an excellent example of evangelical ecumenicity in the wise prosecution of their work in Nepal.

The largest mission organization is the United Mission to Nepal (UMN), formed in 1954. It is a cooperative effort of twenty-eight missionary societies spanning all continents, many denominations and interdenominational mission bodies, and almost a score of nations.* Over 180 missionaries serve in this cooperative fellowship. Its first beachhead of service was the establishment in 1954 of a hospital at Tansen, a busy mountain town accessible to both India and Kathmandu by highway. Medical work has continued to be the UMN's largest ministry, with three more hospitals, several dispensaries, area health service units, and a community health advisory team which coordinates community health work throughout the nation. Land has recently been given by the government to erect another new hospital.

The educational services of the UMN are significant: it is building and staffing a twenty-acre campus for a vocational, boarding high school. In the Gorkha district it staffs a high school, a middle school, and five village primary schools. The girls' high school of 600 (180 boarding) in Kathmandu has helped raise the standard of girls' education throughout the nation. The UMN's Institute of Technology and International Development in Butwal has pioneered on-the-job apprentice training in the trades, fostered a hydroelectric power scheme, and built Nepal's first plywood factory. And in addition to these major works, it maintains a rehabilitation work for Tibetan refugees, a student community center, a building department to direct construction programs, a language orientation school for new workers, and an administration center and hostel in the capital city.

Though much smaller, other missionary organizations are carrying on significant work. First to enter the country was the International Nepal Mission, which centers its work in the nation's second-largest city, Pokhara, 125 miles from the capital. There the mission sponsors a hospital, a leprosy sanitarium, and other growing ministries with both foreign and national personnel. Thriving churches have grown from this work. The oldest continuing Nepal mission is the Nepal Border Fellowship, which was made up of a few missionaries plus Indian and Nepali Christians decades ago in India. They prayed for the opening of the country, and a national missionary society was formed by Indian Christians, among them Sadhu Sundar Singh, famous Indian mystic and evangelist. This fellow-

*Member bodies of the United Mission to Nepal: American Friends Mission; Bible and Medical Missionary Fellowship; Central Asian Mission; Church Missionary Society of Australia; Church Missionary Society, UK; Church Missionary Society of British Isles; Committee for Service Overseas of the Protestant Churches in Germany; Baptist Missionary Society, UK; Disciples of Christ; India and United Christian Missionary Society; Service Association of the Christian Church (Disciples); Church of Scotland; Episcopal Church of USA; Free Church of Finland; General Assembly, United Church of North India; International Christian University Church, Japan; Japan Overseas Cooperative Service; The Leprosy Mission; United Church of Canada; Mennonite Board of Missions and Charities; Mennonite Central Committee, Pax Service; World Division of United Methodist Church, USA; Norwegian Free Evangelical Mission; Regions Beyond Missionary Union; Swedish Baptist Mission; Swiss Friends for Missions in India and Nepal; United Presbyterian Church, USA; Wesleyan Methodist

ship sent workers into Nepal in the early fifties and still continues quietly. Other missions currently working in Nepal are the Evangelical Alliance Mission at Dandeldhura (in the far west), the Nepal Christian Fellowship at Pokhara and several other small villages, the Gorkhpur Nurseries at Semri, the Seventh-Day Adventists at Bannepa, Operation Mobilization, and the International Leprosy Mission.

Supporting the churches and missions are several extremely helpful agencies. The Bible Society is currently revising the Old Testament, along with publishing Scriptures. The Giwan Jyoti Prakashan, a Christian publisher, is printing several kinds of Christian literature in Nepali. The Bible Correspondence Institute has distributed thousands of Bible courses in Nepali to seekers both in and out of the country. The Darjeeling Hills Bible School in India offers a two-year course of study, from which a good number of students have graduated and returned to live and work in Nepal.

Challenges and Opportunities

What is the future for missions and evangelism in Nepal in the days ahead? It is difficult to assess accurately, particularly with regard to missions, yet the future is modestly hopeful. The United Missions' agricultural work has been closed, and there is some pressure against school work in spite of the fact that the schools have never been more popular and are crowded. Leaders of the United Mission have launched it into a new phase, in which the mission is shifting over to work in various forms of close cooperation and integration with the government. After careful study, they have approved wise guidelines for the road ahead. Whereas projects up until this time have been operated pretty much independently under mission management, they are now being incorporated into planned government development projects and put under government management. Missionary workers are being offered to the government and being given appointments to continue in these projects, though under government appointment and management. Mission money is going the same way. Thus the broad trend is from relatively independent management of projects, people, and money to integration under government management. As far as can be judged at present, there is a prevailing (though not 100 percent) attitude on the part of the government that Christian missions may continue to live and work in the country if they work for and in the government-planned programs for national development. What the ultimate results of this will be in the future cannot be fully predicted, but the UMN is proceeding prayerfully, believing for the best.

Church of America, DWM; Woman's Union Missionary Society; World Mission Prayer League, USA; Den Norske Tibetmisjon, Norway.

Nepal's churches are vital and growing. Christians are witnessing joyfully in the face of persecution and imprisonment. Tiny home congregations are springing up. So after two thousand years of closed doors in this tiny, landlocked kingdom, the future for Christ's church there is hopeful.

Nation and People

GEOGRAPHY

Forming an approximate rectangle 500 miles wide from east to west and 100 miles deep, the 54,000 square miles of Nepal (about the size of Florida) are pressed between the subcontinent of India and the great Himalayan plateau of Tibet. In this small kingdom of great diversity are

> three distinctly different physical regions, each running latterly the length of the kingdom. In the south a flat, fertile strip of territory called the "Teari" is part of the Ganges Palan and shares the extreme heat of India. About a third of Nepal's ten million inhabitants [now twelve million, ed. note] live in the Teari. Central Nepal, known as the hill country, is criss-crossed by the lower ranges of the Himalayas and by swift-flowing mountain rivers. The majority of Nepal's population lives in this temperate region, which also contains the Kathmandu Valley, focal point of the nation's political life. The Himalayas, the world's highest mountains, run the length of northern Nepal. This high mountain area has few people and frigid, arctic winters.[2]

The watersheds of the Nepalese rivers lie not along the line of the highest peaks of the Himalaya but far to the north, on the Tibetan plateau. These rivers have carved their way across high elevations, running through awe-inspiring gorges of great depth. Over the centuries there have been communication and interchange of rice, salt, and other goods along the steep trails which cross high passes and river torrents.

ANTHROPOLOGY

Nepal's twelve million people are descendants of three major migrations from India, Tibet, and central Asia. They are divided into many tribes (formerly called castes), major among which are the Gurungs and Magars in the west, the Tamangs and Newars in the center, the Bhotais in the north, the Rais, Lambus, and Sherpas in the east, and the Thaius in the south. Of these, the Newars have the oldest clear history (going back to the neolithic period) and a disinct literature and language, as well as high skills in iron and wood craftsmanship, beautifully evidenced in the tiered pagodas of the capital, Khat Mandu. A unique, ancient community, these Newars form 55 percent of the population of the Kathmandu valley (but number only 383,000 in the country as a whole) and speak a distinct language, Newari. As one author writes, "Their valley is a little world of itself, and in the past this kind of isolation was primarily responsible for the undisturbed flowering of the Newar culture."[3] Anthropologists state that this was a complex civilization in the very early stages of man's development. The Newar artisan has left his mark all over the country, and there is good foundation for the claim that some of these craftsmen were taken to Peking in the thirteenth century and at that time introduced the tiered pagodas to China. Intricate designs, carved skillfully in wood and stone, are found everywhere in this Himalayan kingdom, and today the descendants of the Newar artisans of the past century maintain their traditions.

LANGUAGE

The national language is Nepali (derived from Sanskrit) and is used in the courts and all government work, though it is actually spoken by only 48.7 percent of the people. Unfortunately, nationwide literacy, according to the 1971 census, is only 13.8 percent. This percentage is rising as a nationwide educational program gains momentum, and Nepali will gradually replace Nepal's thirty-five or forty tribal languages,† which are especially numerous in the Kathmandu valley. The government regards this national language emphasis as vitally important to produce a national consciousness. The Summer Institute of Linguistics (Wycliffe Bible Translators) is cooperating with the government university in their language and literacy program.

ECONOMY

Throughout its known history Nepal's economy has been almost totally agricultural, with the majority of the population located in the central, temperate area. Still today agriculture provides more than two-thirds of the country's income. If irrigation facilites can be provided, more intensive and productive farming will be possible. At present Nepal's crops in order of importance include rice, corn and millet, wheat, potatoes, oil seeds, tobacco, jute, sugar cane, and vegetables. Jute is gaining importance as a money-making export crop.

Postwar foreign aid has been spent largely for the cutting of roads to link the eastern section with the west and to encourage connections with neighboring countries. Indian aid built the road from Rexau north to the capital; Chinese engineers drove south linking Lahsa with Kathmandu across rugged mountains; and the Russians are building a seventy-five-mile road in southern Nepal. U.S. aid, which has been by far the greatest (totaling over $120 million since 1951, about $10 million annually), has

†Wycliffe Translators' estimate. Major ancient languages still in use are Newari, Sherpa, Magar, Gureeng, Rai, and Bhojpuri.

been concentrated on providing basic economic and social needs through programs of agriculture, education, health, and rural development. In addition, scholarships have enabled the training of professional and skilled manpower in many fields by the sending of Nepalese students to other Asian countries. Peace Corps workers have promoted several excellent programs in Nepal to assist development and agriculture, education, etc.

A five-year plan for the economic development of the nation was launched in 1969. Since Nepal is still very much a developing nation, it is difficult to see tremendous advance at this stage. This plan, the first of its kind, has perhaps succeeded in establishing the basic framework for later nation-building.

Thus today a country-wide education program is underway. A university has been established. Malaria has been brought under control. Several hydroelectric projects have been completed. A system of internal finance and public administration has been established. A start has been made toward a rational exploitation of Nepal's three major economic resources—forests, hydroelectric potential, and tourism . . . .

Nepal's foreign trade, almost entirely with India, has grown in recent years as the pace of development has accelerated. . . . Nepal is seeking to lay the basis for a modern economy, a task made difficult because of the country's rugged terrain and its recent emergence from the traditional feudal society. Maintenance of a sufficient rate of economic progress to keep pace with the rising aspirations of the population is now, and is likely to continue to be, a primary task for Nepal.[4]

GOVERNMENT

In 1961 the present King Tribhuvan established a unique new government which he called Panchayat democracy. Under this system authority flows in a line running from village councils to district councils and thence through zonal councils to the summit of the pyramid, the national council, meeting in Kathmandu. Late in 1968 His Majesty reformed the council of ministers again with his own appointee, the prime minister, making the choice of his cabinet colleagues. Early 1969 saw the king appointing another new prime minister with more energetic attitudes, obviously to encourage a more vigorous drive toward the development of the country. (On international issues Nepal usually follows the non-aligned and neutralist nations, voting with the Afro-Asian group at the United Nations customarily.) An official government publication offered this revealing statement about the new Panchayat democracy.

> The objective of the Panchayat system of democracy is to establish a spiritual, partyless, and decentralized democratic society which is also free from exploitation. To this end it has provided for an Election Commission

> to ensure fair and free election. In national interests this system wants to fulfill its objectives without recourse to class struggle. Equality before the law and equality of opportunity to prove their worth and rise to the highest positions up to the ministerial level for Nepalese nationals of all classes and races are among its dominant characteristics. That nobody is entitled to enjoy any right without fulfilling the corresponding duty is the main contention of the Panchayat philosophy and way of life. The Panchayat philosophy is based on the firm conviction that "moral, intellectual, and spiritual values ever preside over the destinies of the universe and its passers-by. And that the perennial well-being of every one of us lies in never for a moment losing sight of this fundamental truth even in the midst of the most dazzling, even moon-meeting, achievements of the physical sciences" (His Majesty King Mahendra). In other words, the Panchayat philosophy of life believes that human beings can prosper and advance politically, economically, and socially only to the extent they live by moral, intellectual, and spiritual values. In this connection, the five directives given by His Majesty the King as guidelines for all Nepalese deserve mention. They are: (1) Study well and work hard. (2) Produce more scientifically and distribute equitably. (3) Earn cleanly and spend properly. (4) Act promptly and be true to your thoughts, words, and deeds. (5) Be responsible, dutiful, and impartial, and enjoy or suffer unitedly for the benefit of the country, culture, and society.

In Nepal today newspapers, books, civics texts, history books, etc., all speak of and distinguish between the government (His Majesty's government, the king-run and -appointed structure which includes the army, cabinet, civil service, police, courts, and zonal commissioners with their assistants—in other words, the actual government power at work) and the other thing, called the Panchayat system. This second, people-elected system has only a limited measure of responsibility—mainly to undertake development and community improvement projects. This is a structure for learning and experiencing the democratic process and putting it to work to a limited degree in the running of the affairs of society and government.

National History

Before the eighteenth century Nepal was the name applied only to the Kathmandu valley, which was itself divided by the rivalries of the small states represented by the three capitals of Kathmandu, Patan, and Bhaktapur (Bhatgaon). The country as a whole was divided up by numerous chieftains, most of them Buddhist Newars—a community dating back to neolithic times, whose dynasties maintained close relationships with the rulers of Tibet. For centuries India had pressed in upon the small buffer state, forming "a frontier zone of acute international tension."[5] This remains to the present day and is made more acute by the uneasy relationship between India to the south and China (formerly Tibet) to the north.

Nepal as a united country has its origins in the middle of the eighteenth century, when a Hindu clan with a capital in Gorkha began a determined drive to overcome all rivals. The Gurkhas' leader, Prithwi Narayan, conquered one chieftain after another and quickly became the master of the three principalities of the Kathmandu valley. The final victory took place in 1769, and by the end of the century the new king's territory extended from the Indian Punjab to Sikkim.

However, there were also uneasy relationships with Tibet, and these rapidly deteriorated between 1788 and 1792, when the Gurkhas made several incursions northward until the Chinese felt it necessary to intervene in strength. Nepal was compelled to accept tributary status to China and to send a mission to Peking every five years. Any plans for expansion were then limited to the west, east, and south. Unsuccessful skirmishes with the British in India from 1814 to 1816 forced a further definition of boundaries upon the Gurkhas, and a British resident was then established in Kathmandu, though he did not interfere in internal affairs. Meanwhile, with the end of the Manchu dynasty the tributary relationship with China lapsed.

In the 1840's the Rana family seized the reigns of the divided country, increased their power at the expense of the king, and gradually established a line of hereditary prime ministers. For a hundred years this continued, and the unprogressive Ranas controlled enormous wealth. Then came a popular "palace revolt" of 1950, followed in February 1951 by King Tribhuvan's proclamation of a constitutional monarchy. It was a startling change in a country wholly unprepared for political freedom. There was no past history of democracy, and very soon political immaturity became evident. As a result of the first general election in 1952 a Nepali congress government took over, but instability marked the next six or seven years. King Mahendra, who in March 1955 succeeded his father King Tribhuvan, became thoroughly dissatisfied with the political leadership and in December 1960 took over the reins, dissolved parliament, and imprisoned the leaders. He appointed himself chairman of a council of ministers and later proclaimed the present form of government, Panchayat democracy.

National Religions

Hinduism is the constitutionally protected state religion of Nepal, but Buddhism shares this protection; and in the lower valleys, particularly the Kathmandu, it is difficult to separate them. One writer states that they have "become more or less fused, the practices and beliefs, as well as the gods and shrines of both being equally worshipped by the people."[6] And this mixture is further confused by the presence of ancient animistic practices. Historically, ethnic and geographical links of the Nepalese and Teari in the central hills contributed the Hindu religion to that area, while the strong minority Buddhist population is located in the northern part of the country bordering Tibet.

Religion is tightly interwoven with the fabric of everyday life. Since some of the larger temples are approachable only through narrow alleyways between houses or through low tunnels under dwellings, the life of the people in the surrounding houses overflows into the temple quadrangle. The precincts of the place of worship are the children's playground, the family laundry, the tradesmen's market, and the gossips' corner. No one views this as incongruous, not even when the wandering cattle lick up the clarified butter offerings from the bowls on the rails surrounding the shrine.

Through the crowds thronging the early morning markets press many men and women carrying brass worship trays filled with temple offerings of rice, coconuts, and flowers. A young man in a fashionably-cut European suit on his way to a desk in a government office wears flower petals in his hair, remnants of the morning's devotional *puja* (worship). Book satchel under her arm, a modern schoolgirl pauses at the archway of a house, touches the vermilion-painted figure of Ganesh, the elephant-headed god seated in a niche, and goes on. The king and his queen show their devotion by frequent visits to the most revered temples, for not only is the king the head of state, but to every Nepali he is a divine incarnation of the Hindu god, Vishnu.

In such a stronghold of orthodox Hinduism mixed with Buddhism it is not surprising that the law makes any change of religion an offence and applies stiff penalties of imprisonment to both the convert and the "messenger." These penalties have been invoked in recent years in relation to a pastor and a group of converts, though the king's clemency granted release before the full term was completed.

Foreign aid in its varied forms has brought to this long-closed land scores of intellectuals and experts, many of them to develop and liberalize higher education. Inevitably the tide of young people rushing into university life (at present largely concentrated in Kathmandu) creates problems. One result of this has been the breaking of family bonds and the habits of orthodox religion. Books, newspapers, films, and the usual ultra-radical discussions on the campus are producing in many young people a cynical attitude toward family religion and a rebellion against the easy acceptance of primitive conditions of life.

Christian History

EARLY CATHOLIC MISSIONS

The earliest Christian contact with Nepal took place in 1662, when Italian Capuchin priests passed through enroute to Tibet. Possibly encouraged by these visitors, in 1703 the Capuchin fathers were assigned by the Roman Catholic church to evangelize in North India, Nepal, and Tibet. From their base at Patna in north India several went to work in the Kathmandu valley city-states of the Newars from 1707 to 1769. However, when the Gorkha Prithwi Narayan Shah conquered Nepal, he expelled the priests and the group of Newar Christians they had won, accusing them of being agents in the expansionist plans of European colonial powers.

From then until modern times (1769-1951) a firm policy excluded all foreigners and Christians. This was based on two main considerations: 1) independence must be maintained, since foreigners and their influences might lead to invasion and occupation; and 2) the Hindu kingdom must be kept undefiled and the Hindu structure of society kept intact. Hence foreign religions must be excluded. This closed inland Nepal to Christian missions for almost two hundred years and limited the evangelism of Nepalese to the large community domiciled in India, mainly in the border cities of Darjeeling and Kalimpong in India and Gangtok in Sikkim. Mission stations were established at places of useful contact where Nepalese came in and out of the country, and workers prayerfully waited for the opportunity to enter the country. For two hundred years many missionary agencies and individuals thus stood praying and knocking at the door of Nepal.

EARLY PROTESTANT MISSIONS

The Serampore missionaries, inspired by William Carey, must have been in touch with Nepal, because they published the New Testament in Nepali in 1821. The Church of Scotland mission started work in 1870 in India, in the Darjeeling "wedge" district among predominantly Nepali people. They continued work on the Bible, and with the help of the British and Foreign Bible Society published revisions of the New Testament and in 1914 the Old Testament in Nepali. One hundred years of work by mission and church in this border area has seen the growth of quite a large Nepali church, which has continually carried a prayer burden for the evangelization of Nepal. For fifty years they have sung and prayed this song in their hymnal:

O Lord, hear our petition,
  Open the door of salvation for the Gorkhalis.
Father, Son, Holy Spirit, hear our petition,
  Show us the way by a cloudy, fiery pillar.

Peoples of different religions are to east, west, and south;
Tibet is north, and Nepal, our home, in the middle.
There are cities: Thapathali, Bhatgaon, Patan, Kathmandu:
Our desire is to make them your devotees.
Up, brothers, we must go, ignoring hate and shame,
Leaving wealth, people, comfort, to do the holy task.

These Christians early formed a Gorkha mission, which undertook to preach and sell Scriptures at border points. Some went into Nepal to live and work and witness, but they were soon expelled.

At the beginning of the twentieth century, all along the northern border of India missions opened work for the Nepali, generally at the railheads through which traffic passed. Some fifteen to twenty groups undertook preaching, distribution of literature, and in some places medical work. The famous Indian itinerant mystic and evangelist, Sadhu Sundar Singh, entered Nepal from the Darjeeling side into the eastern Ilam district briefly in 1914. He was immediately arrested, jailed, and tortured, a basket of leeches being poured over his naked body. Fortunately he was released the next day, and he returned to Darjeeling.

During this period there are stories of occasional Nepali in whose heart the Word of God bore fruit, but such converts could not return to their own country for long.

A colporteur was able to enter Kathmandu for a season and sell books there (1908). In the capital city he hired a shop from a Mohammedan for Rs. 5 per month and spread out his books, which consisted of Nepali and Hindi translations of the Bible. For the first few days little was done, but thereafter, leaving his shop and moving about among the people, he made sales freely. He was visited at his shop by Nepali men and women of the upper classes, who made purchases of books. In the space of some days he sold several hundred books. Then he received a summons and was interrogated about his work in the presence of the Maharajah. As a result an order was passed requiring him to sell no more books and to depart from the country, and this order he obeyed.

These were long years of waiting for the missionaries; some waited a lifetime and were not able to enter. But many labored in prayer for this country. In the 1930's a Nepal Border Fellowship of missionaries and Indian and Nepali Christians was formed, through which many shared news and prayed for Nepal to open. Thus when the revolution of 1951 brought a new regime to power, the question was asked: Will this bring an opening for missions to Nepal? It did. The country opened its doors to the world family of nations and embarked on a vigorous program of national development. Foreign agencies were welcomed to assist in this work.

Thus in late 1951 Christian missions were permitted to enter the country, but only under certain conditions. They were to serve the people in such useful ways as would further the cause of nation-building; they were to follow the rules of the department to which they were connected; they were to travel and live only as their visas allowed; but they were not to propagate their religion or convert the people. The religious laws remained substantially the same, protecting Hinduism and forbidding conversion. But these agreements applied only to foreign mission organizations; Indian and Nepali Christians could now freely enter and live in Nepal.

The first missions to take advantage of the new opportunity in Nepal were the Catholic Jesuits from Patma, who opened an English boys' boarding school near Kathmandu in 1951, following it with a similar school for girls later. The story of the first evangelical Protestant mission to enter is a thrilling one of waiting patience and answered prayer.

In the early 1930's Dr. Lilly O'Hanlon and a Christian friend in England felt strongly called of God to work in Nepal. Though the doors were closed and there were many discouragements, they left England in 1936 and began a small dispensary in the Indian border town of Nautanwa, four miles from the Nepalese border. Under the initial name of the Nepal Evangelistic Band, Dr. O'Hanlon and her colleague (plus other medical personnel) later studied the Nepalese language and operated a dispensary for the itinerant Nepalese who traveled the trail. Gradually a tiny church was born among the Nepalese living in Nautanwa. In 1951, when the revolution brought the king to power and established provisional democracy, Nepal was opened to the foreign entrepreneurs for the first time in two hundred years. Since the first British ambassador had known Dr. O'Hanlon in England, in February 1952 he invited her and her colleague to visit the capital city. It was an exciting time for them—their first glimpse of that country on whose border they had prayed, waited, and worked for sixteen years.

During their visit there the ambassador arranged for them to meet various ministers to discuss the possibility of opening a hospital in Pokhara, a country town one hundred miles west of Kathmandu. Though no permission was immediately given, the officials did permit them to visit Pokhara in the king's private plane, along with the British ambassador. While they were in the needy town God confirmed to them that this was the place where they were to begin work, even though permission was not yet given.

After returning to Nautanwa Dr. O'Hanlon again opened negotiations with the Nepal government. And finally, in November 1952, they were given permission to proceed to Pokhara and build a hospital. Amid excitement and rejoicing a party of six missionaries, five Nepali Christians, and nineteen coolies shortly thereafter began the eight-day trek over four ranges of hills and rivers into Pokhara. And there in temporary buildings in March 1953 the "shining" hospital was opened—so called by the natives because of the glint of the sun on the aluminum roof. The work has continued until today and is currently called the International Nepal Fellowship. Today the work has grown to include a leprosarium and two outstation dispensaries, with a foreign staff of over forty workers. Associated with the mission is a group of Nepali Christian workers, through whom a church has been formed with a national pastor.

The largest foreign mission to enter Nepal was the United Mission to Nepal, formed in 1954. Prior to the granting of official permission to enter, Drs. Robert L. and Bethel Fleming used to visit Nepal in their winter vacations from Woodstock School in Mussoori, India. When the door was finally opened they were invited to open hospitals at Tansen and Kathmandu. Realizing that their Methodist mission alone was unable to meet the challenge, they helped organize the United Mission to Nepal, which began with ten missions from India under commitment to work as one body of Christians to build one church in the country. The mission negotiated a five-year term to take medical work in two places initially. It grew rapidly. Agreements were negotiated for new projects, and the initial agreement was extended for a further period of ten years. In 1969 it entered a third agreement with the government for five years. By now the UMN had grown to about thirty different member bodies from a dozen countries, with more than 180 missionary workers assigned to ten provinces throughout the country. Their work embraces medical, public health, education, agriculture, industrial development, and training projects.

Thus since the open door of 1951 other mission groups and individuals have entered the country from overseas and from neighboring India, and the church has been planted in Nepal. The large reservoir of missionary vision, concern, and prayer which had been building up for so many years has now been flowing into Nepal for two decades.

NOTES

1. *Nepal on the Potter's Wheel,* pp. 9, 10.
2. *Background Notes,* p. 1.
3. G. S. Nepali, *The Newars,* p. 4.
4. *Background Notes,* p. 4.
5. Alastair Lamb, *Asian Frontiers,* p. 132.
6. Pradyumna P. Karan and William M. Jenkins, *Nepal, a Cultural and Physical Geography.*

BIBLIOGRAPHY

Background Notes. Department of State Publications 7904, revised Oct. 1967.

Bista, Dor Bahadur. *People of Nepal.* Kathmandu: His Majesty's Government of Nepal, 1967.

Fletcher, G. N. *The Fabulous Flemings of Kathmandu.* New York: Dutton & Co., 1964.

Hagen, Toni. *Nepal, the Kingdom in the Himalayas.* Bern: Kummerley and Frey; Calcutta and New Delhi: Oxford Book and Stationery Co., 1960.

Hitchcock, John. *The Magars of Banyan Hill.*

Karan, Pradyumna P., and Jenkins, William M. *Nepal: A Cultural and Physical Geography.* Lexington: University of Kentucky Press, 1960.

———. *The Himalayan Kingdoms: Bhutan, Sikkim, and Nepal.* Princeton: D. Van Nostrand Co., 1963.

Kazami, Takehide. *The Himalayas: A Journey to Nepal.* Tokyo: Kodansha, 1968.

Lamb, Alastair. *Asian Frontiers.*

Miller, Luree. *Gurkhas and Ghosts.*

Nepal: An Interesting Account for Foreigners. HMG, Nepal: Department of Information, 1971.

Nepal and the Gurkhas. London: Her Majesty's Stationery Office, 1965.

Nepal Himalayas, The. HMC, Nepal: Dept. of Tourism.

Nepal on the Potter's Wheel. Kathmandu: United Mission to Nepal, 1970.

Nepali, G. S. *The Newars.*

Northey, W. Brook, and Morris, C. J. *The Gurkhas: Their Manners, Customs and Country.* London: John Lane, 1928.

Reed, Horace and Mary. *Nepal in Transition.*

Sekelj, Tibor. *Window on Nepal.* London: Robert Hale, 1959.

Shaha, Rishikesh. *Heroes and Builders of Nepal.* London: Oxford University Press, 1965.

Snellgrove, David. *Himalayan Pilgrimage.*

Tichy, Herbert. *Himalaya.*

Tucker, Sir Francis. *Gorkha, the Story of the Gurkhas of Nepal.* London: Constable and Co., 1957.

Weir, Tom. *East of Kathmandu.*

A street scene typical of Chinese communities in many parts of the world

21

OVERSEAS CHINESE

by David Woodward

"WHEREVER the ocean waves touch there are overseas Chinese," the Chinese commonly say. Excluding mainland China and Taiwan, but including Hong Kong, there is a total of 23,000,000 Chinese outside of China, 15,000,000 of whom are in Southeast Asia. (Of the remainder 740,000 are in the Americas, 112,000 in Europe, 61,000 in Africa, and 68,000 in India and other parts of Asia.)[1] Protestant Christians number almost 200,000 in Hong Kong and over 300,000 in other southeast Asian Chinese communities. These Christians are easily identifiable, since they tended to have their own churches and church associations until recently. But the external pressures of society have kept them in a position of low profile, and many of them are now making determined efforts to identify with the national churches in some countries.

Roman Catholic Chinese have been tabulated at 400,000 in southeast Asia.[2] In Singapore and Malaysia, "the Chinese form the strongest body of Christians."[3] Chua quotes Dr. J. Harry Haines of the WCC as reckoning that 1 out of 28 overseas Chinese in southeast Asia is a Christian. Then he adds, "If we include Hong Kong and Taiwan, where the percentage of Christians is higher, I believe that we shall discover that 1 out of every 20 Chinese is a Christian. In other words, 5 percent of the Chinese of the diaspora are Christians, and the rest are unchurched."[4] Many of these overseas Chinese are having difficulty maintaining their Chinese culture and are being rapidly assimilated into the nations where they live. They often hold citizenship or have been born in countries where they now reside. These acculturation problems have produced an identity crisis among them. An overseas Chinese student, Swee Hwa Quek, writing from the University of Manchester in England, asks, "Is the unifying factor among Chinese today our Chinese language, or is it our Chinese birth

For information on author, see chapter 28, "Taiwan."

and upbringing?"[5] Many overseas Chinese no longer read or even speak Chinese. Jonathan Chao, an overseas Chinese theological student in the United States, points out:

> Chinese today no longer have a homogeneous culture, but many subcultures, determined by a locality. . . . Taiwan is probably the most Chinese locality insofar as Chinese culture or subculture will emerge. So birth and upbringing do not necessarily determine whether one is Chinese or not, but perhaps "certain degrees of Chinese characteristics."[6]

These problems have created a more favorable climate for evangelism, for the effect of this assimilation into the national cultures seems to increase the number of Chinese turning to Christ, judging by a study in Indonesia by Dr. Frank L. Cooley. Of the total Chinese community of 3,000,000 there, at least 263,000, or 8.8 percent, are Christians (counting both Protestants and Catholics); but among the Chinese born in Indonesia twice as many, 17.5 percent, are Christians.[7]

Overseas migration started as early as the Han Dynasty (A.D. 206-22), and the majority of the emigrants went from the southern provinces of China. They left because of overcrowding, lack of land, or a desire for a new start. Southeast Asia attracted most of them, and they found themselves at an advantage in many of these lands because of their creative industry. Within a generation many of them were transformed from day laborers to small businessmen, though colonial powers sought to curb or use these entrepreneurs. "The Chinese were 'middle men.' They set up their own schools and formed their own communities. . . . If we were to stop the clock of history at 1939, we would discover that the overseas Chinese formed a monolithic group,"[8] states Chua Wee Huan, general secretary of the International Fellowship of Evangelical Students. He continues, "Today there is no longer this monolithic group of overseas Chinese who think alike or act alike." What has happened?

The newly emergent nations bitterly resented the economic power and the resistance to assimilation of the Chinese living among them. When from 1949 communist China tried to use overseas Chinese to extend its influence and to promote Communism in Malaysia, Singapore, and Indonesia, the policy backfired and left the local Chinese suspect of being communist sympathizers. The result has been a new willingness on the part of most overseas Chinese to disassociate themselves clearly from mainland China and to look toward fuller assimilation into their host cultures. There were about three thousand Chinese schools in southeast Asia in 1957, but most of these have by now changed their curriculum to conform to local systems of education, with Chinese language studies only elective.[9] Even where national governments have not forced this issue, there has been a surprising change; in Singapore, for example, 70 percent of the young people, mostly of Chinese extraction, are now in English schools by personal choice.

The admission of Red China to the U.N. and the expulsion of the titular Republic of China—Taiwan—from it has hastened the assimilation process in most southeast Asian countries. In Japan, for example, some of the more affluent Chinese emigrated to the U.S. when the Taiwanese embassy was closed, while the majority took out Japanese citizenship. Despite this political identification, however, the more educated and wealthy Chinese remain a small international enclave which will not soon lose its Chinese identity.

The major Chinese Christian communities outside the mainland have been chronicled either in separate chapters, as those on Taiwan, Hong Kong, and Singapore, or within the chapters on such nations as Indonesia and Malaysia. One further colonial community, however, deserves mention here since its population is almost exclusively Chinese.

Located forty miles by water from Hong Kong, tiny Macao is a Portuguese enclave on the Pearl River estuary leading up to Canton. Like Hong Kong, it is a colony permitted existence by Red China for trade and communication purposes. Some 275,000 people, largely Chinese, are crowded into its six-square-mile area.

Macao was the first beachhead for Catholic missions in the Orient almost five hundred years ago. Today about 15 percent of the population is nominally Catholic and about 1 percent, an estimated two thousand eight hundred, are Protestant. Almost no western missionary personnel are involved in the Portuguese schools (with seven thousand students), orphanages, or relief programs. There is a shortage of Chinese personnel as well, and few are permitted or are willing to go there from other Chinese communities.

When the Macao government planned the celebration of its four hundredth anniversary in 1960, Chinese Communists trumped up a labor dispute, forcing the Portuguese governor to make humiliating concessions, including the closing of the Chinese Nationalist consulate.

By 1967 the Communists covertly sought control of the schools, the majority of which were run by Catholic orders. The resistance of the Roman Catholic archbishop was more adamant than that of the governor. Nevertheless, even in the schools certain concessions had to be made, with Chinese gunboats dominating Macao's harbor and red flags festooning its streets. The people of Macao say, "China sneezes, and we tremble; China spits, and we drown."

APPENDIX

Overseas Chinese Protestant Communities, 1968

	No. of Chinese	*No. of Churches*	*No. of Christians*
A. *Mainland China*	700,000,000		700,000

This figure has been given by leaders of the Three Self Movement. The 1951 official figure was 1,000,000 Christians, but the total community may have been closer to 2,000,000.

	No. of Chinese	*No. of Churches*	*No. of Christians*
B. *Chinese Diaspora*	38,500,000	(1973)	
1. Taiwan, Republic of China	15,500,000	2,000	300,000
2. Japan		10	1,200
3. Korea		8	650
4. Okinawa		1	70
5. Hong Kong		400	179,000
6. Macao	275,000	6	2,800
7. So. Vietnam	860,000	8	1,000
8. Laos	45,000	1	50
9. Cambodia	435,000	2	400
10. Thailand	2,700,000	17	3,500
11. Philippines	500,000	54	7,000
12. Burma	400,000	10	5,000
13. Malaysia (excluding No. Borneo)	3,500,000	250	77,000
14. Singapore	1,500,000	137	38,000
15. Sabah, Brunei, Sarawak			20,000
16. Indonesia[a]	3,000,000	130	150,000
17. India		2	600
18. Ceylon			14
19. Pakistan			47
20. Australia, New Zealand		6	1,200
21. Canada		24	2,500
22. United States[b]		190	11,000
23. Costa Rica			15
24. Panama			10
25. Cuba		1	25
26. Jamaica		1	100
27. Trinidad		1	50
28. Surinam		1	250
29. Ecuador		1	20
30. Peru			20
31. Brazil		5	2,000
32. England		6	1,000
33. France		1	100

a) Many Chinese in Indonesia are in Indonesian-speaking churches.

b) Many campus Bible classes conducted by Chinese in North America also operate as church fellowships. There are at least 160 of these in the U.S. and 15 in Canada.

34.	W. Germany	1	30
35.	Netherlands	1	40
36.	Mauritius	1	150
37.	South Africa	1	150
			804,991

NOTES

1. Moses Chow, *Reconciling Our Kinsmen in the Golden Mountain,* p. 3.
2. Carlo Melckebeke, *Diaspore Winicae Staticarum Testamen,* p. 12.
3. Gerald Anderson, "An Impartial Glance at our Church in Southeast Asia," *Teaching All Nations,* Aug. 1970, p. 26.
4. Chua Wee-hian, "Evangelizing the Chinese of the Diaspora," *Evangelical Missions Quarterly,* Fall 1971, p. 25.
5. "Bulletin No. 4," The Christian Fellowship for Christian Studies.
6. Ibid.
7. Frank L. Cooley, *Indonesia: Church and Society* (New York: Friendship Press, 1968), p. 99.
8. Chua Wee-hian, p. 24.
9. *Herder Correspondence,* Mar. 1967, 4:90-92.

22

PAKISTAN

by Warren Webster

Introduction

CARVED from the Muslim-majority areas of East Bengal and the northwestern provinces of British India in 1947, Pakistan was born with a tremendous handicap. From 1947 to 1971 it struggled to exist in two sections, known as East and West Pakistan, which were separated not only by a thousand miles of India but also by languages which were not mutually intelligible. The peoples of East and West Pakistan reflected different racial stocks. They lived in vastly different climates, raised different crops, dressed differently, and ate different diets. Their culture and life-style differed considerably. Seemingly only the religion of Islam—and later, the Pakistan International Airline—linked the two widely separated provinces of this ideological state, whose name meant "the land of the holy."

To many people it was not surprising that in less than twenty-five years this strangely bifurcated nation was further divided and broken by civil war, resulting in the independence of East Pakistan as Bangladesh in 1971. The present state of Pakistan, reshaped by secession and reduced in size

---

WARREN WEBSTER was appointed general director of the Conservative Baptist Foreign Mission Society in June 1971 following fifteen years of active missionary service in West Pakistan. As a missionary there, he was active in literature and linguistic ministries, and helped establish the Pakistan Bible Correspondence School, a cooperative effort among evangelicals designed to reach middle- and upper-class Muslims. He also served as editor and consultant for two Christian literature societies publishing in different languages and was active in Christian witness among both Hindu and Muslim peoples. Dr. Webster is a graduate of the University of Oregon and Fuller Theological Seminary, and has taken advanced studies in Islamics, missionary medicine and linguistics. He has taught missions at Fuller and Gordon-Conwell Seminaries. Dr. Webster holds the honorary doctorate of divinity degree from Conservative Baptist Theological Seminary in Denver.

and population from what it originally was, still retains its importance, however, as a bridge between East and West, as a leader in the Muslim world, and as a continuing challenge to Christian evangelism.

The Church Today

Christians comprise the largest religious minority in Pakistan, numbering nearly a million people, of whom approximately 60 percent are Protestant and 40 percent are Catholic. While the total Christian community accounts for less than 2 percent of the population, the number of Christians has been increasing slowly but steadily. A 1961 government census reported, "Christianity has grown fastest of all religions in Pakistan. Between 1901 and 1961 Christians have increased about 23 times."* Most of the growth of Christianity in this area in the twentieth century is attributable to early group movements from Hinduism sustained by a high birthrate within the Christian community. Accessions from Hinduism and Islam continue to some extent, particularly in Hindu scheduled castes, from which four to five hundred baptisms a year are being reported. The largest number of Christians is located in the central province of the Punjab.

The Pakistan Christian Council began in the 1920's and now loosely links about half a million Protestants in common concerns. Its largest constituent member is the Church of Pakistan, which was formed in 1970 through the merger of Anglicans (110,000), United Methodists (60,000), Presbyterians of the Sialkot Church Council (20,000), and Lutherans (2000) into an episcopal type of church union, with four bishops presiding over four dioceses which take in all of Pakistan. The total Christian community served by this united church now numbers approximately 216,000. The United Presbyterians (170,000), who previously constituted the largest Protestant denomination, Presbyterians of the Lahore Church Council (47,000), and the Associate Reformed Presbyterians (20,000), declined to enter the final plan for church union work alongside the Church of Pakistan in the Pakistan Christian Council, which also includes the Salvation Army (40,000). Protestant groups outside the council include the Seventh-Day Adventists (14,000), Brethren (11,000), Pentecostals (8,000), and various other independent or nondenominational groups (6,000). At the time the Church of Pakistan came into existence, some churches in the uniting bodies chose to remain outside church union. This gave rise to several small new separatist groups, such as the National Virgin Church of Pakistan, the Orthodox Church of Pakistan (Anglican), and the Methodist Church of Pakistan, whose constituencies are somewhat fluid and indeterminate because pastors and laymen return to their former church bodies from time to time.

**The Census* (Government of Pakistan, 1961).

Taking advantage of theological and personal differences that arose before and during church union negotiations, leaders of the International Council of Christian Churches have made inroads into most of the major denominational bodies, dividing congregations, separating pastors, and taking over some church and mission properties. In the process Pakistan's oldest theological seminary, a cooperative institution at Gujranwala, was split into three competing schools. Other Bible training centers, however, have opened in each region of the country to equip pastors and laymen for Christian service and witness.

World War II and the postwar era, which brought Pakistan into being, saw many Christian groups come for the first time to work alongside the established denominations. Some entered into comity agreements with the older missions. Others went to neglected areas or the major cities. They included the Full Gospel Assemblies, Afghan Border Crusade, World Mission Prayer League, the Evangelical Alliance Mission, Bible and Medical Missionary Fellowship, Pakistan Christian Fellowship, Conservative Baptists, International Missions, Women's Union Missionary Society, Worldwide Evangelization Crusade, Baptist Bible Fellowship, Church of Christ, and others. The personnel of these new groups, as of the older missions, came primarily from the United States and the United Kingdom. European churches, however, have assumed a growing responsibility and are represented by Danish, Finnish, and German Lutherans, German Brethren, Swedish Pentecostals, and missionaries of the Netherlands' Gereformeerde Kerken. More recently Asian churches, particularly in Korea, Japan, and Indonesia, have sent missionaries and evangelistic teams to share the gospel with fellow Asians in Pakistan.

For the most part the newer missions are unrelated to any sizable body of Pakistani Christians and so have majored in evangelism, church planting, and literature outreach, with a minimum of institutional involvement. Being independent, or interdenominational, as well as somewhat separatistic, the newer evangelical missions have not generally joined the major denominations in the Pakistan Christian Council, though some of them cooperate with member bodies. These newer groups tend to work alone or cooperate in the Evangelical Fellowship of Pakistan, which was organized for joint sponsorship of prayer conferences, pastors' seminars, evangelistic programs, and literature distribution. Through such encouragement Pakistani believers have formed groups for evangelizing border areas, such as Swat, Gilgit, and Azad Kashmir, which are closed to the ministry of missionaries for other countries. While the newer mission organizations directly represent only a small percentage of Pakistan's Christian community at present, they are at work on the growing edge of mission, where some of the most encouraging developments are taking place.

Roman Catholics, comprising the largest single Christian body in Pakistan, are found in six dioceses across the country and, like other church groups, are growing slowly but steadily. In 1970 they reported 338,511 communicant members—an increase of 12 percent in four years. The total Catholic community is somewhat larger.

While there is little concerted planning for nationwide evangelistic thrusts in Pakistan, much sharing goes on quietly at many levels of city, village, student, and tribal life. Overall the greatest current response is from among the "scheduled castes," who are neither Muslim, Christian, nor caste Hindu. They are people of outcaste origin whose religious beliefs and practices are more animistic than Hindu. Increasingly restless and dissatisfied with their socially degraded position, these people are on the move to something better. In general they are not inclined toward Islam, whose followers have despised and oppressed them as idolators. Caste Hindus do not want them. But the love of Christ and the concern of Christians has found a response among them. The scheduled castes number around three-quarters of a million people scattered throughout the province of Sind and the southernmost districts of the Punjab. In recent years some thirteen thousand baptisms have taken place among them (five thousand Protestants and eight thousand Catholics) in a growing movement despite the lack of any really concerted effort to win them to Christ. Though they are presently the most receptive people in Pakistan, only about fifteen of the approximately four hundred Protestant missionaries in the country are working even part-time for the evangelization of these Hindu tribal groups.

One hindrance to more effective evangelism among the scheduled castes is their division into some thirty distinct tribal units, which speak a wide variety of languages and dialects. In an effort to meet their needs, the Sindhi Bible translation is being revised and reprinted as a medium for evangelism and teaching among those who are bilingual in that language. At the same time new translations of Scripture portions are being undertaken in Kohli, Marwari, and Odki dialects. In several cases alphabets are being designed to write these languages for the first time, and adult literacy materials are meeting a need among scheduled caste people, of whom only about 2 percent are literate. They have not been greatly welcomed in most schools and until now have not been keen on getting an education. Literacy has enhanced their interest in the gospel, which in turn has stirred them to see the values of education. This is one more way in which the churches of Pakistan are making a significant contribution to the development of the country. At the same time there are still many tribes in Sind, Baluchistan, the Northwest Frontier, and the foothills of the Himalayas which have no Scripture portions of any kind in their language. A great deal remains to be done.

Specialized ministries serving many churches and missions include the Pakistan Bible Society, Punjab Religious Book Society, Christian Publishing House, Student Christian Movement, Pakistan Fellowship of Evangelical Students, Campus Crusade for Christ, Church World Service, Child Evangelism Fellowship, and the Children's Special Service Mission. The Pakistan Bible Correspondence School, with four branch centers, serves churches and interested inquirers throughout Pakistan with Bible courses in three languages. Christian broadcasting is not possible over the government-operated radio and television stations except for a few hours made available at Easter and Christmas. Christian programs can be heard daily, however, in several languages from India, the Seychelles Islands, and Sri Lanka, but only on shortwave radios, which most people do not possess.

Christians have long pioneered in education in the Indo-Pakistan subcontinent. In Pakistan, church and mission bodies have operated boarding schools, technical training schools, teachers' training institutes, colleges, and hundreds of primary and secondary schools, both rural and urban. In October 1972 the new government nationalized most private educational institutions without compensation, including nine Protestant and Catholic colleges, two teachers' training centers operated by Protestants, and most other church and mission schools. Some urban English medium schools of high standards were at least temporarily exempted from nationalization, as were some small Christian schools maintained entirely by and for the Christian community without receiving aid from any public funds. This nationalization of private schools, including most Christian institutions, led to strong protest demonstrations on the part of many Christians, who saw this as a threat to their job security or the future of the Christian community. Initially almost all Christian faculty and staff were retained in their jobs. For the most part their salary and allowances actually increased under the higher pay scales prevailing in government schools. However, through retirement and resignation some of these positions are being lost to members of the majority community, as was originally feared. There is no doubt that the church and mission schools had provided employment and status for many Christians, and their loss through nationalization has been a blow to the pride and morale of some people in the Christian community.

Other Pakistani Christians, however, view the government takeover of Christian school as advantageous. While these schools had a certain value for educating the Christian community, in most cases the majority of students were Muslims. Long before the teaching of the Bible to non-Christian students was prohibited and the teaching of the Koran made obligatory for Muslim students, most church and mission schools had ceased to have much, if any, effective value in explaining or demonstrating the Christian faith to others. Some sensed that a disproportionate amount of limited Christian resources was going into minimally useful institutions, which had frequently become storm centers of politicking and controversy, especially among Protestant leaders. To this extent nationalization has freed the churches of a continuing problem, financial and otherwise, while putting Christian students and teachers into the mainstream of national life. Competition may be greater here, but so also are the opportunities for incorporating Christian values into the framework of nation-building.

Christians have also had a prominent role in the development of medicine and public health. There are some twenty Protestant hospitals and clinics and a similar number of Catholic institutions scattered across Pakistan, providing a high level of medical service at nominal cost to the public. Training schools for nurses and midwives are maintained in several centers. Christians have pioneered in the development of eye surgery and the treatment of leprosy. There are also homes for poor children and a training school for the blind.

Christians have further contributed to community development through land reclamation and settlement projects involving land-leveling, tubewell installation, and the development of irrigation. Farmers' cooperatives, small loan schemes for starting simple businesses, improved seed and breeding stock, and the encouragement and marketing of handicrafts have all been used to contribute to the economic uplift of developing rural areas.

In Karachi, the former capital and Pakistan's largest city, with a population of over 3.5 million, Christians sponsor an organization which deals with labor-management relations and provides both job training and job placement services for Christians who have migrated to this port city in search of employment. Lahore, the cultural center of Pakistan and the largest city in the Punjab, with 2 million people, is also a center of Christian activity to which large numbers of village Christians have migrated. Recently Christian social workers have undertaken studies to facilitate a successful transition from rural to urban life for these thousands of people.

Despite the gradual growth of Christian influence in Pakistan, the church's effectiveness in recent years has been greatly limited by three factors.

1. Unlike Indonesia, where the churches include a hundred thousand or more converts from Islam, the churches in Pakistan are largely the product of a mass movement from the lower castes of Hinduism which dates back two or three generations. Now they find themselves in the center of an al-

most exclusively Muslim culture but with relatively few Muslim converts in their membership to provide a natural bridge for communicating the gospel to the dominant religious community. Moreover, by virtue of having come from a predominantly Hindu background, most Christians have little inside knowledge of Islam and little interest, perspective, or ability for effectively witnessing to their Muslim neighbors. The Christian Study Center in Rawalpindi now assists churches in understanding their responsibility for witness to non-Christian friends while actively engaging in dialogue with Muslims on many levels.

2. The Christian community in Pakistan is one of the few in Asia which on the whole ranks socially, economically, and educationally below the national average. This is somewhat understandable in terms of the extremely depressed background from which most of the early Pakistani Christians came. One must not forget, of course, the number of local Christian doctors, nurses, teachers, college principals, lawyers, businessmen, and government servants who have risen from very humble beginnings as evidence of the type of transformation which the gospel can effect. But the present status of the nominal Christian community taken as a whole does not always commend itself to others. For example, whereas the national literacy rate in Pakistan is about 20 percent, only 10 percent of those classed as Christians are able to read and write. Although nearly 50 percent of Pakistani children between the ages of five and eighteen attend school, the percentage of Christian children in school is only half that, and a mere 0.4 percent of Christian young people get as far as college.

3. The spiritual life of many churches in Pakistan reflects a failure to adequately teach and evangelize each succeeding generation that has grown out of the earlier group movements. Now poverty, ignorance, and spiritual neglect are so interrelated as to require simultaneous attention if the church is to move ahead.

Today in Pakistan, church and mission bodies are working together with a renewed emphasis on laying solid foundations through stressing personal Christian commitment. The cell-group, the house-church, and lay leadership offer viable patterns for an uncertain future. A "Literacy House" is effectively promoting programs to teach children and adults to read the Scriptures. Bible study materials have been simplified and translated into Urdu for giving foundational teaching to spiritually awakening people within the nominal Christian community. Lay institutes for evangelism are also stimulating response. Saint Andrew's Brotherhood provides a temporary home and Christian teaching for new converts. These ministries are accompanied by programs for improving health, teaching trades, encouraging cottage industry, and improving agricultural production—all designed to meet the needs of the whole man while strengthening the church and nation of which he is a part.

Nation and People

INTRODUCTION

A land of great ethnic and linguistic diversity, present-day Pakistan stretches from the snowclad Himalayas in the north to the sprawling plains of the Indus valley and includes vast expanses of desert on the west and south, where it adjoins Afghanistan and Iran. Geographically and culturally Pakistan has much in common with the semiarid lands of the Muslim Middle East. The average annual rainfall is less than ten inches and temperatures range from below freezing to 120 degrees Fahrenheit.

For thousands of years migrants and invaders from central and western Asia entered the Indo-Pakistan subcontinent from the northwest, settling and mixing with the earliest inhabitants. Successive waves of Aryans, Greeks, Persians, Arabs, Turks, and Mughals have produced a racial and linguistic admixture that is reflected in the differing cultural and linguistic groupings of the country: Pushtu is spoken in the northwest frontier territories, Punjabi in the upper Indus plain, Sindhi in the lower river basin, and Baluchi and Brahui in the barren regions toward the western border. Urdu has become increasingly popular as the national language for unifying government and commerce, particularly since the influx of refugees from north India following partition in 1947. But the well-established regional languages still dominate the life of the home and family in most places. English is also used extensively in government and education, although the national languages are progressively, and rightly, playing a dominant role in schools and colleges.

Pakistan has some 70 million people and an annual growth rate of about 3 percent. The population is predominantly rural (80 percent), and only 17 percent of those over five years of age are literate. While the literacy rate is somewhat higher in the cities, nationwide for women it is less than 10 percent. These two factors—expanding rural populace and a high rate of illiteracy—help to account for the low per capita income, which averages barely $100 per year.

The economy is primarily agricultural, although significant steps toward industrialization have been taken. A shortage of raw materials and such natural resources as oil, coal, iron, and other minerals has impeded the process of industrialization. Pakistan does, however, possess large reserves of natural gas and ample water for irrigation and hydroelectric power from the Indus—one of the largest river systems in the world. The "green revolution" holds out hope that in time Pakistan may attain self-sufficiency in such essential food grains as wheat and rice. Other important crops for export and domestic consumption are cotton, sugar, tea, and tobacco.

The development of modern Pakistan has been unquestionably hindered by three wars with India and the accompanying military buildup, as well as by internal political struggles, in which religious factors have often played a part. The role of religion in the creation and continuation of Pakistan cannot be minimized.

GOVERNMENT

Pakistan's new capital is located at Islamabad, a modern city specially planned and built since 1960 on a previously farmed plateau in the temperate climate of the country's northern region. The capital city is the administrative center of the nation, and its name means "the city of Islam." Pakistan is divided administratively into four Provinces—Punjab, Sind, Northwest Frontier, and Baluchistan, each with its own provincial parliament, governor, and chief minister.

Since the 1971 civil war and subsequent secession of East Pakistan as Bangladesh, the government of Pakistan has been concerned with bolstering the morale of its people, who were shocked by their military defeat and the loss of half of their nation. Prime Minister Zulfikar Ali Bhutto took a popular step in lifting martial law and effecting a return to democratic rule. He launched a new constitution for the Islamic Republic of Pakistan which went into effect on August 14, 1973—twenty-six years from the date that Pakistan first became an independent nation. The constitution provides for a parliamentary form of government with a bicameral legislature and a president as ceremonial chief-of-state; the actual governing power, however, resides in the prime minister, who is elected by a majority of the national assembly. The present prime minister is also the founder and leader of the majority Pakistan People's party, which came to power on a platform of "Islamic socialism." Under his direction a number of economic and social reforms have been enacted, including a modest redistribution of land holdings, restrictions on banking and corporate activities, and extension of health and educational benefits.

Education in all government schools, including those newly nationalized, is now provided free of charge through high school. Hundreds of new primary schools are under construction as part of a program to attack illiteracy with a school ultimately in every village.

RELIGION AND FREEDOM IN PAKISTAN

When Pakistan declared itself an "Islamic republic" in 1956, it was something unique on the world scene. No Muslim state in the modern world had heretofore presumed to use this title. Many Muslims as well as non-Muslims have questioned whether it is possible for a state to be both truly Islamic and a republic. Two of Pakistan's most eminent jurists concluded in a lengthy report that a government founded on the Koran could not be democratic. Nevertheless, the new constitution of 1973 officially proclaimed Islam as the state religion. (Previous attempts to do so were complicated by the presence of 10 to 12 million Hindus in East Pakistan.) The constitution stipulates that only a Muslim can be president or prime minister. The state is to facilitate Muslims in understanding the Islamic way of life by making the teaching of Islam and the Holy Koran compulsory for them. The government will also oversee the operation of mosques and the proper distribution of funds which they collect for charitable and other purposes. Another clause calls for bringing all existing laws into conformity with Islamic principles. Inasmuch as the numerous sects of Islam do not agree on specific interpretations of the Holy Koran, and even less on the other three sources of Islamic law, it appears to some observers that this may open the door to an interminable series of religio-political struggles.

Despite these thoroughly Islamic provisions, the constitution of 1973 follows the previous constitution in guaranteeing the basic right of citizens of any faith to *profess, practice,* and *propagate* their religion. Pakistan from its inception has provided for freedom of religion. The flag of Pakistan symbolizes this guarantee to minorities within the country: a green field with white crescent and star stands as a traditional symbol of the Islamic faith, and a broad white strip on the left fittingly represents the minority communities—Christians, Hindus, Buddhists, and others (since white is a combination of all colors in the spectrum).†

FOREIGN RELATIONS

In the aftermath of the war in 1971 Pakistan has been concerned with

†This is all the more commendable when viewed against the background of traditional Islamic understanding of religious freedom as the right to remain what you are by birth, or to become a Muslim. Because Islam is regarded by traditionalists as the world's last and final religion, it is inconceivable to them that any Muslim would wish to forsake it; and the option to do so does not, in their thinking, validly exist. It is this mentality which has kept several Muslim states in the United Nations from agreeing to the Universal Declaration of Human Rights, whose paragraph on freedom of religion includes the freedom of conscience to change one's faith, and not simply freedom to remain in the religion of one's parents. It is to the lasting credit of Pakistan that at the time religious freedom and the Declaration of Human Rights were being debated in the United Nations, Sir Zafrullah Khan, then foreign minister of Pakistan, stood before the general assembly to affirm Pakistan's belief in the right of all religions to peaceful propagation within an Islamic state on the ground that Islam is itself a missionary religion. Since Muslims desire the right to propagate their faith and receive adherents in other countries, they should be willing to extend the same privileges to other faiths. For that reason, the foreign minister affirmed, Pakistan would vote for full freedom of religion, including freedom of conscience to change one's faith.

reordering its relations with both India and newly independent Bangladesh. For some time the People's Republic of China has enjoyed a particularly favored position as a result of consistently giving diplomatic, political, and military support to Pakistan. An all-weather road linking Pakistan with China's Sinkiang Province is under construction in the far north to facilitate trade and communication, including future military assistance, if needed. The Chinese presence in Pakistan is increasingly evident. Pakistan's relations with the USSR have continued correct but not close, since the Soviet Union's growing concern over China led to their support of India during the 1963 Indo-Pakistan war in Kashmir and again during the conflict over Bangladesh in 1971.

Despite the fact that Pakistan has received military and economic aid from both Russia and China, the small Communist party, as such, is not permitted to operate in Pakistan. While Muslims tend to insist that they could never become communists because of their belief in Allah, there is a good deal of evidence to the contrary. It appears that once Islam's spiritual roots are undermined, whether by nationalism, materialism, or secularism, its control over the totality of life may be replaced without too much difficulty by the type of totalitarianism which communists espouse.

The United States and Pakistan established diplomatic relations in 1947, when the new nation first came into existence. In the intervening years the U.S. has committed some $5 billion to Pakistan in economic assistance over and above military aid. Some Pakistanis criticized the U.S. for suspending military and economic assistance to both Pakistan and India during their fighting over Kashmir in 1965 and again during the clash of 1971. But the peaceful endeavors of the United States to bring hostilities to an end while seeking for political solutions to the crises, coupled with continuing large-scale technical and economic assistance for the country's development plans, have clearly indicated to the government of Pakistan that the U.S. is concerned for the present and future well-being of her people. The U.S. further demonstrated her friendship by tacitly siding with Pakistan in the civil war of 1971. Apart from India, relations with other countries which were originally part of the British Commonwealth have been generally good. Pakistan is particularly committed to preserving and strengthening fraternal relations among Muslim countries while supporting the common interests of other peoples in Asia, Africa, and Latin America and fostering good relations among all nations.

National History

While Pakistan became recognized as a political entity on August 14, 1947, its roots lie deep in antiquity. Before the time of Abraham highly organized cities along the Indus River in what is now Pakistan were carrying on trade with Sumer in ancient Babylon. Centuries before Christ, Alexander the Great led his army into the fertile Indus valley through the Khyber Pass. A thousand years later in A.D. 711, an Arab army conquered the lower Indus basin, gaining a firm foothold on the Indian subcontinent for the followers of Muhammad. In the course of centuries Islam became the dominant force over all of northern India, from west to east. But the emergence of Pakistan as a political entity cannot be understood apart from the struggles between Muslims and Hindus, which go back for centuries. Within less than a hundred years of Muhammad's death, in A.D. 632, the message of Islam had been carried to India by the example and missionary spirit of Arab travelers and traders. The Arab conquest of Sind, now a province of Pakistan, established the Muslims on the subcontinent. By the mid-seventeenth century, when the Mughal emperor Shah Jahan built the famous Taj Mahal, most of India was under Muslim rule, and the Hindus were a subjugated majority.

The cultural contacts between Muslims and Hindus were mutually beneficial, however. They did not hesitate to learn from one another in the fields of arithmetic, astronomy, medicine, and philosophy. It was from the Hindus that Arab mathematicians learned the concept of zero, which they subsequently passed on to the rest of the world. In turn the Muslims introduced historiography to India. But the Muslims were the first invaders of the subcontinent who did not ultimately merge into Hindu society. Instead, parallel cultures grew up face-to-face, which divided Indian society into two powerful forces with minimal intermingling of life between them. During these centuries of coexistence and mutual influence neither Muslim nor Hindu society fully accepted the other, however, and the tensions which ultimately led to the partition of India and Pakistan into two separate nations were present since the advent of Islam.

In the eighteenth century the Muslim empire in India began to decline under attacks by Hindu and Sikh armies, but it did not come to an end until the British occupation and administration of India. The first British conquest was the state of Bengal, including what became East Pakistan. Muslims resented this intrusion from the west, but Hindus saw it as an opportunity to escape from Muslim rule and to redress the imbalance of power in the subcontinent. While orthodox Muslims retired to their mosques and Koranic schools and warned their children of the dangers of British education, Hindus were quick to learn English and to find positions in the new civil service. In general, the British tended to favor the Hindus because of their greater cooperation and responsiveness. Moreover, since the British had taken over the administration from Muslim rulers, they were anxious to ensure that the Muslims did not regain their lost power.

After a century-and-a-half of British rule, as independence approached

Indian Muslims grew understandably uneasy about being outnumbered three to one by a Hindu majority in a free democratic India. Because Islam is not merely a religious faith but a total way of life which has always sought to express itself politically, socially, and religiously, the Muslims feared they would not have full freedom to develop and express themselves in a secular state dominated by Hindus. The All-India Muslim league under the capable leadership of Muhammad Ali Jinnah began to work for the creation of Pakistan as a separate religious homeland for the hundred million-plus Muslims of the Indo-Pakistan subcontinent, an independent state where they could order their lives fully in keeping with the Koran and the traditions of their prophet.

When Pakistan came into being as a self-governing dominion within the British Commonwealth of nations in 1947, the partition from India was accompanied by bitter hatred and Muslim-Hindu communal rioting, in which perhaps half a million people fell victim to the uncontrolled religious passions of crazed mobs on both sides of the borders. During the nine months that followed partition some six to eight million Muslims fled Hindu-dominated areas to start a new life in Pakistan, and a similar number of Hindus and Sikhs escaped to India in one of the greatest mass migrations of history. Christians distinguished themselves at this time on both sides of the borders in providing medical assistance and humanitarian service impartially to the uprooted, the hungry, the sick, and the wounded during the migration. The settlement of these hordes of refugees continued for twenty years to be a major problem on both sides.

Both India and Pakistan benefited immensely from the British institutions and traditions inherited at the time of independence. Pakistan, however, received fewer developed institutions and had fewer experienced political leaders than India. While Jawaharlal Nehru in India lived for many years after independence and helped establish a stable government, the political development of Pakistan was dealt a serious blow when the "Father of Pakistan," Muhammad Ali Jinnah, died the year following partition, and his successor, Liaquat Ali Khan, was assassinated three years later. After the death of its two most outstanding leaders the Muslim League was progressively split by internal dissension. Cabinets changed overnight, and the political situation progressively deteriorated, aggravated by economic problems. When a series of politicians failed to agree upon a constitution and offered no hope of establishing a stable, progressive government, a group of senior military officers took over the administration in October 1958 under the leadership of the commander-in-chief of the army, General Muhammad Ayub Khan, who assumed the presidency.

The "peaceful revolution" which began at this time continued for more than a decade under President Ayub. With firmness and military precision but without undue force or oppression the martial law government attacked a series of unresolved problems which the politicians had permitted to accumulate. The new administration, drawn largely from the military, initially cracked down on smuggling and tax evasion, hoarding and black marketing, and general corruption in government and society at large. The problems of rehabilitating refugees, which had previously dragged on for years, were promptly tackled by settling property claims, providing compensation to displaced persons, and undertaking housing developments. Some land reforms which attempted to limit the land holdings of wealthy absentee landlords were only partially successful. But other agrarian reforms contributed to the "green revolution," which offered promise of self-sufficiency in food grains provided that population growth could be held in check. However, an extensive nationwide birth control program met with relatively little success, for in Pakistan's traditionally agrarian economy large families are valued for the free labor they contribute to the fields and for the honor and security they supposedly afford to elderly parents under the joint-family system. In addition, many educated people among the orthodox Muslims purported to find in the *Koran* prohibitions against birth control of any kind, and the less educated saw it as a communist or Hindu plot to limit the growth and influence of Islam.

Educational reforms were aimed at creating a balance between traditional Islamic values and the advances of modern science and technology needed in a developing nation, where a single family may bridge a gap of centuries between village parents living in an oxcart culture and a son studying jet-age physics in a nearby college. Commendable progress was made in providing elementary education at government expense in every town. A new beginning was also made by opening technical and vocational schools to train technicians for growing industrialization.

Undergirding this decade of reform was a political structure called "Basic Democracies." President Ayub saw some of the difficulties inherent in trying to have a meaningful democracy in a land where more than 80 percent of the people lived in villages and only 15 to 20 percent of the people could read. Ayub saw that the situation would not be quickly changed, since less than 50 percent of the primary age group were attending school, and he became one of the first national leaders of Pakistan to clearly sense that the type of parliamentary democracy which worked in Great Britain was not necessarily best suited to Pakistan.

While the ten years from 1958 to 1968 marked a significant era of advance for Pakistan, Ayub Khan's programs sowed the seeds of his ultimate undoing. The politicians had been alienated by their fall from influence and prestige. Large landlords and capitalists were not happy over property and power which had been lost. Orthodox religious elements had been offended by modern innovations and a scientific approach to such problems as birth control. Students became increasingly disenchanted with Ayub's government when they discovered that there were too few jobs for all the new graduates being turned out of colleges and universities. Further disillusionment arose on the part of youth, peasant farmers, and laborers over corruption in government and the disclosure that twenty-two wealthy families, mostly in West Pakistan, controlled 60 percent of the banking, insurance, and large business interests of the country.

Meanwhile, in East Pakistan disaffection was mounting even higher against the Ayub government. The Bengalis charged that the government, the military, and industry were all dominated by West Pakistanis, who comprised 85 percent of the central government bureaucracy and 90 percent of the army. They resented the national capital being at Islamabad, in West Pakistan. Even when the country was under military control, since the army was dominated by Pathans, Punjabis, and Baluchis from the west, the more populous eastern province continued to be shortchanged in development projects and allocations for industrialization. The Bengalis complained that while their region produced 60 percent of the nation's foreign exchange earnings, they seldom received more than 30 percent of the nation's imports and foreign aid. So the cumulative effect of these grievances led to widespread rioting and demonstrations against the governments in both wings, with the result that in March 1969 Ayub Khan relinquished his office as president to the commander-in-chief of the army, General A. M. Yahya Khan.

President Yahya Khan held out hope that the long-subservient Bengalis would have a greater voice in national affairs. By this time Sheikh Mujibur Rahman's majority Awami ("People's") League in East Pakistan was demanding greater regional autonomy, with the right to handle their own taxation, foreign trade, and foreign aid. As a result of free national elections in December 1970, the Awami League under Sheikh Mujibur Rahman won 167 of the 169 seats allocated to East Pakistan and an overall majority of the 313 seats in the proposed national assembly. When military and political leaders in West Pakistan saw that the balance of power was about to shift to East Pakistan, possibly permanently, they persuaded the president to postpone convening the national assembly. This incensed the Bengali leaders, and their demonstrations of protest were ruthlessly repressed by the army. Late in March 1971 President Yahya Khan's negotiations with key political personalities broke down, and he secretly flew back to West Pakistan, from where he ordered the banning of the Awami League, the arrest of Sheikh Mujibur Rahman, who was charged with treason, and the unleashing of the Pakistani army in a brutal attempt to repress the revolution in East Pakistan. During the night of March 25-26, 1971, three battalions of the Pakistani army moved into Dacca and out across the province using tanks, rockets, flamethrowers, rifles, and machine guns in an attempt to smash all Bengali resistance. The Awami League leadership responded on March 26 by proclaiming the independence of East Pakistan as the "People's Republic of Bangladesh." The Pakistani military, supported by Sabre jets, followed a systematic course of strafing, killing, burning, and looting defenseless towns and villages, thereby decimating unnumbered thousands of students and other civilians and driving millions of Bengali refugees over the border into India.

This time it was not primarily a struggle between Muslims and Hindus. This was a clash between two Muslim majorities. The religion of Islam (which once formed almost the only common link between the two disparate provinces of East and West Pakistan) in this time of civil war was no longer adequate to preserve unity in the face of nationalistic pressures for independence. The ruthless slaughter of Muslims by fellow Muslims signaled the beginning of the end for Pakistan as it had been created in 1947. The Pakistani army in East Pakistan, cut off from supplies and reinforcements from its base a thousand miles to the west, was overwhelmed in less than two weeks. On December 16, 1971, it surrendered to the combined forces of India and Bangladesh. In the west General Yahya Khan, disgraced by this defeat, stepped down on December 20 as president to be replaced by a civilian, Zulfikar Ali Bhutto, leader of the majority Pakistan People's party, thus bringing sixteen years of military governments to an end. A truncated Pakistan now faced reconstruction.

National Religions

Approximately 97 percent of the people of Pakistan are at least nominal adherents of Islam. The majority of Pakistani Muslims belong to the Sunni or orthodox sect of Islam, which traces itself back to the Arabian prophet through his immediate successors, although a sizable minority follows the doctrine and practice of the Shi'ah sect, which originated later in what is now Iraq. But several smaller and more recent sects of Islam are also represented in Pakistan; the most significant is the Ahmadiyyah movement, which was founded earlier this century in India and then moved to Pakistan following partition. While this movement is regarded as heterodox by most other Muslims, the Ahmadiyyahs from their international headquarters in Rabwah carry on an active worldwide missionary program, with centers in every continent for the propagation of their particular interpretation of Islam.

Bitter communal rioting broke out between Ahmadiyyahs and orthodox Muslims in 1974, in which many people were killed and numerous mosques were burned or desecrated. The clash ultimately led to a demand that Ahmadiyyahs be declared a non-Muslim minority sect.

The Ahmadiyyahs are probably best known for the attempt of their founder, Mirza Ghulam Ahmad Qadiani, to blunt Christian expansion in the Muslim world by claiming to have discovered through research and divine revelation that Jesus did not die in Jerusalem, but merely swooned. Once revived in the cool tomb, he purportedly set out in search of the ten lost tribes of Israel and eventually found his way through Afghanistan and northern India to Kashmir, where he lived to be over a hundred. Having completed his mission, Jesus allegedly died a natural death and was buried in Srinagar in a tomb which can still be visited on Khanyar Street. The local Kashmiri Muslim residents of Khanyar Street, however, reject the Ahmadiyyah claim and believe that the poorly maintained tomb is just what its inscription claims—the burial place of a local holy man named Yuz Asaf, who was buried there several centuries ago.

The power and prestige of Islam as the religion of the rulers, coupled with Muhammad's egalitarian teachings and the absence of caste in Islam, early had an attraction for the lower classes of Hindu society, especially the so-called "untouchables," so these sought to improve their status by becoming Muslims. It has been authoritatively estimated that approximately 90 percent of the Muslims in India and Pakistan are descendants of low-caste Hindus who changed their religion in the hope of finding greater human dignity in the caste-free brotherhood of Islam.

Thus today Hinduism in Pakistan ranks below Christianity in number of adherents, for the majority of Hindus and Sikhs who were living in the provinces of northwest India prior to partition migrated to India. This was due in part to the fanatical opposition of Muslim Pathans and Punjabis in the north. Only in Sind to the south (where a famous syncretistic poet and mystic, Shah Abdul Latif, had long preached communal harmony) did large numbers of Hindus (several hundred thousand) remain, most of them belonging to the poorer scheduled castes living near the border with India. It is among these tribal peoples that a recent group movement to Christianity has begun. Many of their religious beliefs and practices are basically animistic, though they appear outwardly to be Hindus. Islam has also been influenced by this animism and superstition, especially among the semiliterate masses of town and village peoples. The interplay of Islam and Hinduism at the popular level is seen in the number of devotees who venerate each other's saints and shrines.

Still, Hindu and Muslim society in Pakistan and India have coexisted for centuries without losing their cultural distinctives. Muslim women have traditionally been veiled or secluded, while the wives and daughters of Hindu families experience greater freedom. Customs, ceremonies, holidays, and even the calendar differ between the two faiths. Caste and dietary restrictions have tended to keep them from eating and drinking together in homes, schools, and restaurants. While the cow is sacred to Hindus, it is killed and eaten by Muslims. But most Hindus, unless they are vegetarians, will eat pork, which Muslims are forbidden to eat by their holy book. Endless murders and riots have stemmed from passions inflamed by the violation of one another's taboos and the slaughter of totem animals. Even at the end of life the two communities go their separate ways to cremate the Hindu dead and bury the bodies of Muslims.

Among smaller religious groups in Pakistan is a tiny but economically important community of about five thousand Parsis,‡ whose ancestors migrated from Iran—a remnant of ancient Zoroastrianism. A scattering of indigenous Jews, Buddhists, and Baháis will also be found.

Overall, the record of the Islamic Republic of Pakistan in dealing with its religious minority communities compares very favorably with the record of India as a secular state. While he was still a cabinet member under a previous government, Prime Minister Bhutto earned the appreciation of minority groups for repeatedly defending their rights as full and equal citizens of Pakistan, including their freedom to practice and propagate their faiths. After the independence of Bangladesh he again affirmed that his government would uphold the rights of all minorities and not discriminate against them. A minister of minority affairs in the cabinet is charged with sympathetically attending to the legitimate rights and interests of minority groups, and safeguards for minorities are written into the constitution.

Christian History

The history of Christianity in Pakistan was until 1947 necessarily part of church history in India. It is possible, however, to trace something of the early contacts of Christianity within those regions which now constitute Pakistan. The Christian church here is much older than the nation!

The ancient church of the so-called Thomas Christians in south India staunchly maintains that the apostle Thomas himself brought Christianity to India in the first century. While the claim cannot be positively substantiated, neither can it be denied; and there is strong historical evidence that by the third century A.D. parts of India had been Christianized.§ Then for most of a thousand years the rise of Islam cut India off from the West, and the Thomas Christians in south India were largely unknown to the rest of the world apart from such occasional travelers to the Orient as

‡See chapter 31, "Important Religions of Asia."
§See chapter 8, "Christianity Comes to Asia."

Marco Polo, who repeatedly reported the presence of long-established Syrian or Nestorian Christians in Persia and India.

Catholic, European Christianity next found its way to the subcontinent when Vasco de Gama sailed into the Indian Ocean in 1498. In the century that followed, the Roman Catholic Portuguese opened enclaves along the Indian coasts while the Muslim Mughals were spreading over much of the interior. Jesuit missions began early, with the arrival of Francis Xavier in Goa in 1542. In the Punjab of northwestern India, which much later became part of Pakistan, Portuguese Jesuits from Goa built a church in Lahore around 1600, when the Mughal Emperor Akbar looked with tolerance upon some of his subjects accepting the Christian faith. To the south an Augustinian friar is chronicled to have died in Sind in 1598, and by 1618 Portuguese Carmelites arrived from Persia to found a church and mission at the important trading center of Thatta (near Karachi) as a link between their missions on the Persian Gulf and in Goa. By 1672 the mission had come to an unfruitful end, and no more trace of Christianity is found in the area until after the British conquest of Sind in 1842-43.

Protestant missions in Pakistan trace their origin to the initiative of the Church of England and Presbyterians from the United States. In the fall of 1833 Rev. and Mrs. John C. Lowrie, American Presbyterians, arrived in Calcutta bound for the Punjab to establish a mission to the Sikhs. Mrs. Lowrie died of tuberculosis shortly after arriving, but her husband decided to proceed alone to the Punjab. He believed that the Sikhs, having discarded the old idolatry of Hinduism and to some extent the system of caste, should be potentially responsive to the Christian message. The following year he founded an American Presbyterian mission at Ludhiana, from where he visited Lahore in 1835. The Sikh ruler of Lahore, Maharaja Ranjit Singh, invited him to open a school there, but ill health and repeated attacks of malaria forced him to return to the United States, where he became secretary of the Presbyterian board of foreign missions. It was left to his successors, John Newton and Charles Forman, to begin Protestant missionary work at Lahore in 1849, the year after the second Sikh war brought the Punjab under British rule. Forman spent more than forty years in the Punjab, founding the college in Lahore which is still known by his name.

While British army chaplains had preceded the American Presbyterian mission in the Punjab, the first resident British missionaries came in 1850 with the Church Missionary Society and settled in Karachi, where the first resident Roman Catholic priest in the modern era had preceded them in 1843. In a few short years CMS had branched out across Sind, Baluchistan, the Punjab, and the Northwest Frontier, frequently at the request of British civil officers. Dr. Karl G. Pfander, a German scholar and polemicist who had worked successfully among Muslims in the Middle East and India, opened a CMS station in Peshawar on the Afghan frontier in 1854. Pfander's Mizan-ul-Haqq ("Balance of Truth") was long a classic of Christian-Muslim controversy, and he saw a number of learned Muslims converted to Christianity through his writings and public disputations. Along the borders of Afghanistan the Church Missionary Society established a string of hospitals as evangelistic outposts, which were distinguished by men like Dr. Theodore Pennell, who, at the end of the nineteenth century, was almost alone among British missionaries in adopting Indian dress. In the twentieth century a CMS doctor, Sir Henry Holland, performed cataract operations which gave sight to more than a hundred thousand people in Sind and Baluchistan during his long lifetime of Christian witness and service.

While English missionaries under CMS (later assisted by the Society for Promoting Christian Knowledge, the Society for the Propagation of the Gospel, and the Church of England Zenana Missionary Society) were more widely spread over northwest India than those of any other group, Presbyterian missionaries soon increased in number. In 1855 Andrew J. Gordon arrived to begin what became known as the Sialkot Mission of the United Presbyterian Church of North America. In 1856 the Church of Scotland (Presbyterian) also began work in Sialkot district with the arrival of Thomas Hunter to start a Punjab mission. After just six months Hunter, his wife, and their baby boy were killed by an escaped prisoner during the Indian Mutiny of 1857. Although the Scottish mission was resumed by others in 1861, progress was slow. By the 1880's they had fewer than 200 Christians. The Presbyterians from America and the English CMS missionaries did not generally have any more to show for their labors. After twenty years Andrew Gordon and the United Presbyterians could count only 153 adult communicant members, most of whom had been disowned by their upper-class families.

In most of India during this period, missionary work was directed toward winning educated and high-caste people, largely in urban centers through schools and orphanages as well as through preaching. Medical work followed later. Visible results were almost microscopic. The converts, mostly young single men expelled by their families, were housed in or around mission compounds, where they were given food and work or land. In general these attempts were rather unsuccessful because they separated new believers from their own people and created a spirit of dependence on the mission. A change in emphasis came to the Sialkot district in 1873 with the conversion of Ditt, a partly crippled, dark-skinned seller of hides from the outcaste Chuhras. He had been somewhat instructed in the Christian faith by a weak and rather unsatisfactory Hindu convert before he appeared at the door of the Presbyterian mission house requesting baptism. The missionary wanted him to stay for further teaching, but Ditt insisted on going back to his village. Three months later he brought his wife and daughters for baptism, but instead of remaining on the mission compound they too returned to their people. Ditt's occupation took him from village to village, where he started to witness to his relatives. Despite a good deal of persecution he remained firm. As others believed, they continued living in their own villages. Ditt never did learn how to read and write, but he memorized the Word and preached until half the Chuhras in Sialkot district had been baptized under his example and spiritual leadership. By 1935 nearly all of Ditt's people had become Christians, and today some 90 percent of the Christians in Pakistan trace their ancestry to this Chuhra caste.

Whereas the United Presbyterian Mission gained fewer than 200 followers during their first twenty years in Pakistan within the next two decades more than 6,000 people were baptized, and by 1915 another 25,000. This group movement to Christ spread to other areas and missions. The Church of Scotland, which had only 192 members in the 1880's, grew to 8000 by 1892. The Anglicans and American Presbyterians also began to turn from concentrating primarily on educated, city dwellers to more responsive peoples in the rural areas. Itinerant preaching received new emphasis. As the group movement developed, village schools were opened primarily for the education of Christian children, and not for evangelistic purposes among non-Christians, as had previously been attempted.

In 1904-05 the famed Sialkot Convention revival was at its height under the spiritual leadership of John "Praying" Hyde. This resulted in a deepening of spiritual life among the growing congregations. Many pastors volunteered to be supported by their churches instead of by the mission, and this gave further impetus to the Christward movement among the Chuhras.

American Methodists opened work in Karachi in 1873, the year of Ditt's conversion, and also moved into the Punjab to participate in shepherding the group movement among the depressed classes. The Salvation Army entered in 1883. In 1910 the Associate Reformed Presbyterian Mission from America started work in the Punjab, from where the vast majority of Pakistani Christians have come. These seven Protestant bodies, together with the Roman Catholics, claim the allegiance of more than 95 percent of the Christians in Pakistan today.

Smaller groups which have had an important role in the evangelization of Pakistan before its independence from India include the Brethren (1892), Danish Lutherans (1903), Seventh-Day Adventists (1917), and the Church Missionary Societies of Australia and New Zealand, which have worked closely with the British CMS. The Australian and New Zealand societies have been particularly active in the evangelization of Hindu tribal peoples.

Christians and the Future

Since the founding of Pakistan in 1947 at least fifteen new missions and Christian organizations have begun ministries alongside the older church and mission bodies. Despite many pressures and political changes during the last three decades the Christian community, in common with others, continues to enjoy freedom of worship and the right to preach, practice, and propagate its faith. While some restrictions and difficulties have been experienced by missionaries in recent years in obtaining or renewing visas, there are still about four hundred Protestant and a thousand Roman Catholic missionaries in the country. What is more disconcerting than the gradual decline in number of Protestant missionaries is the indication that less than one-tenth of them spend as much as half their time presenting the gospel to Muslims, who constitute 97 percent of the populace. Even after due allowance has been made for the continuing need to train Pakistani Christians to carry on the church's primary task of evangelism, it remains true that much of the training must come from the example of leaders, both missionary and local.

For the new era in Pakistan new methods are needed for communicating the gospel to both Muslims and Hindus. New patterns of church-mission partnership must be sought, in which every church becomes the base for a continuing mission to those around. Experience has shown that only an actively evangelizing church is able to provide a warm, receptive fellowship, in which those who respond to the gospel feel at home and progress to the point of sharing their newfound faith with others. In the process, churches should make new efforts to establish fellowship groups for inquirers and new believers, groups which are relevant to cultural and religious backgrounds from which the converts come.

While the followers of Christ in Pakistan may seem relatively few, it has been well said that "Christians weigh more than they count." True Christians bear an influence out of proportion to their number. Today in Pakistan there is not a major city without a church and hardly a town without a Christian representative in private business, government, or municipal service. This vast Christian dispersion has the potential for great growth if believers, indwelt and empowered by the Spirit of God, will move forth in faith to outlive and outlove their neighbors in proclaiming the good news that "God was in Christ, reconciling the world unto himself."

APPENDIX 1

Religions of Pakistan

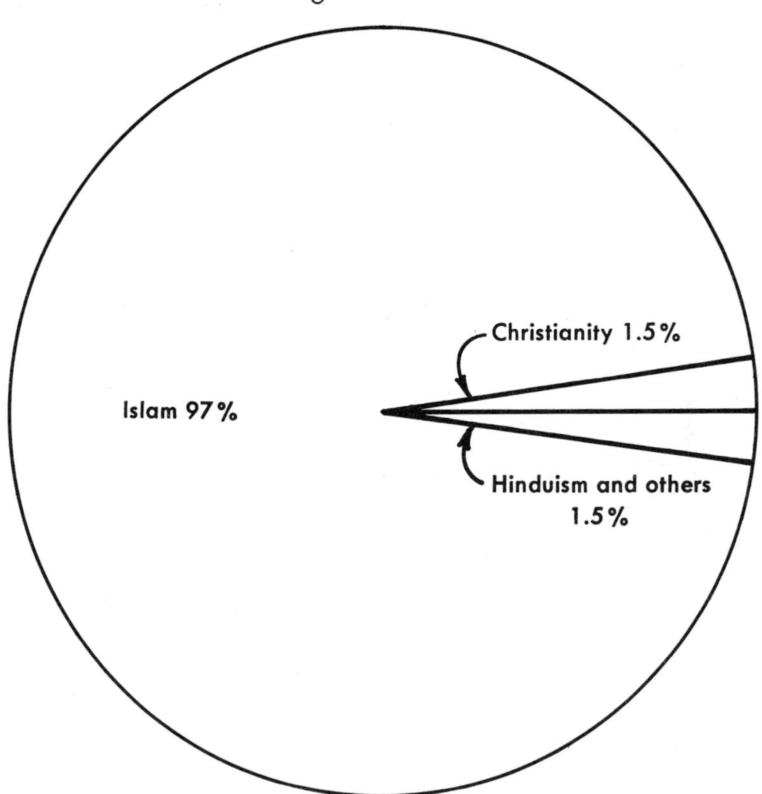

APPENDIX 2

Major Christian Groups in Pakistan

Group	Number
Roman Catholic	360,000
Church of Pakistan	216,000
United Presbyterian Church	170,000
Lahore Church Council (Presbyterian)	47,000
Salvation Army	40,000
Associate Reformed Presbyterians	20,000
Seventh-Day Adventists	14,000
Brethren	11,000
Full Gospel Assemblies	8,000
Pakistan Mission IFMA	2,000
Pakistan Christian Fellowship	2,000
Indus Christian Fellowship	800
TEAM	700
Protestant	533,500
Roman Catholic	360,000

Church of Pakistan includes Anglican, Methodist, Sialkot Church Council (Church of Scotland), and Lutheran

Figures estimated from earlier statistics (Dec. 1973) by F. E. Stock

BIBLIOGRAPHY

Akhtar, Rafique, ed. *Pakistan 1973 Year Book.* Karachi: East and West Publishing Co., 1973.

Background Notes on Pakistan. Washington: U.S. Department of State, 1973.

Binder, Leonard. *Religion and Politics in Pakistan.* Berkeley: University of California Press, 1961.

Goddard, Burton L., ed. *The Encyclopedia of Modern Christian Missions.* Camden: Thomas Nelson & Sons, 1967.

Kane, J. Herbert. *A Global View of Christian Missions.* Grand Rapids: Baker, 1971.

Loshak, David. *Pakistan Crisis.* New York: McGraw-Hill, 1971.

Neill, Stephen. *The Story of the Christian Church in India and Pakistan.* Grand Rapids: Eerdmans, 1970.

Qureshi, Ishtiaq Husain. *The Struggle for Pakistan.* Karachi: University of Karachi, 1968.

Rafe-uz-Zaman, ed. *Pakistan Year Book, 1971.* Karachi: National Publishing House, 1971.

Stacey, Vivienne. *Focus on Pakistan.* London: Bible and Medical Missionary Fellowship, 1969.

Stephens, Ian. *The Pakistanis.* London: Oxford University Press, 1968.

Stock, Fred E. *Profile on Pakistan.* Monrovia, Calif.: MARC, 1974.

Wilcox, Wayne Ayres. *Pakistan: The Consolidation of a Nation.* New York: Columbia University Press, 1963.

Bible College graduation in Taguru Tabernacle.

Bible school student engaged in personal evangelism.

Children receiving food at clinic in Fugwa.

Photos courtesy Gen. Dept. of World Missions, The Wesleyan Church

23

PAPUA NEW GUINEA

by Geoffrey Smith and John Hitchen

Introduction

One of the most amazing people's movements in modern history and probably one of the greatest untold stories of modern missions is the conversion of the interior of Papua New Guinea to Christ in one generation. In an estimated population of 2½ million persons, 92 percent are reported as Christians in the latest government census.*

All society has been drastically affected by the sweeping movement of the Spirit. All but two of the indigenous members of the House of Assembly (elected by universal suffrage in 1968) claimed to be adherents of one or another of the Christian missions and their related churches. Parliament sessions are opened by all reciting the Lord's Prayer! All indigenous troops in the Pacific islands' regiment are classified as Christians. In the government's annual report to the United Nations the prime educational objective is stated as "The voluntary acceptance of Christianity by the indigenous people." This report also stated that there is "the absence of any other indigenous body of religious faith founded on teaching or ritual" in the islands. Only 7 percent of the population are listed as followers of

---

John Mason Hitchen is dean of the Christian Leaders Training College of Papua New Guinea, an evangelical and interdenominational theological college which serves many evangelical churches in the western highlands of the island. Mr. Hitchen completed his education in the University of New Zealand (B.A.), New Zealand Bible Training institute, and Melbourne College of Divinity (B.D. Hons), and served as pastor before going to New Guinea.

*See Appendixes 1-4. The figure of 92 percent is an estimate of professing Christians, many of whom are not baptized church members.

"indigenous religion," an indefinable hodgepodge of traditions and animism.

The Church Today

And there is a bright future for the church in Papua New Guinea, for the movement is still growing. Christians, both nationals and the large number of expatriate missionaries, are making frontal attacks on the numerous social and economic problems of this long-neglected area, where some tribes in the interior were still living in a stone age culture within this generation.

All of this has happened within 125 years. Following initial Christian beachheads established by the Roman Catholics in 1847, Dutch Reformed, Australian Methodists, and British Anglican missionaries came to the islands. Both Methodists and Anglicans brought with them South sea island Christians from Fiji, Samoa, and Rarotonga. Thus European and south Pacific island martyrs mingled their blood on these islands under attacks by headhunters and tropical disease during the first 50 years. The Rhenish Mission's first eight years saw ten missionaries die, and in the first 25 years thirty-seven of forty-one missionaries either died or were forced out by virulent sickness. Probably named nowhere in the annals of the church are many South sea island martyrs, but their sacrifice, no less than that of the Europeans, became the seed of this great but simple church in our generation. Biskup, Jinks, and Nelson have this relevant comment in their *Short History of New Guinea:*

> Speaking of the island teachers in 1895 to an audience in Scotland, Sir William MacGregor, the first lieutenant-governor of British New Guinea, said, "He, poor simple soul, leaves at our call his own little world and warmhearted friends in the South seas to devote his efforts to his fellowmen in an unknown country. I believe some eight of the society's (LMS) teachers have been murdered by our natives. How many of you have heard of those eight men? Had they belonged to our own race we should all have known much about *their career, their suffering, their martyrdom.*"[1]

The great period of growth which has resulted in this church has occurred almost entirely since the end of World War II, when new means of transportation, especially missionary planes, penetrated the long-unknown highlands which literally cover most of Australian New Guinea. But it was actually during the absence of the missionaries that the spiritual chain reaction appears to have begun, at least in the southern highlands, during World War II.

The first interdenominational mission to commence work in Papua New Guinea was the Unevangelized Fields Mission (now the Asia Pacific Christian Mission). The first UFM missionary, Albert Drysdale, took over an LMS plantation at Madira near the mouth of the Fly River in 1931. From here Drysdale and Len Twyman penetrated inland up the Fly and Aramia rivers. The first four men were baptized at Balimo in 1940, but the missionaries were forced to leave in 1942. But there followed a remarkable, spontaneous turning to the Lord Jesus Christ, so that when missionaries returned in 1944 they found a young, growing church already in existence among the Gogadala tribe. From this Gogadala church in postwar years over sixty national missionaries have gone out to evangelize the upper reaches of the Fly River and parts of the southern highlands.

Summary statistics do not reveal the full drama of God's working there, but they are significant pointers to the fifteen years of thrilling advance that has taken place throughout the highlands and islands of this area. The Roman Catholic and Lutheran missions had slowly penetrated the eastern highlands and parts of the western highlands districts prior to the war, but the following brief summary indicates something of Protestant advance between 1948 and 1963.

> By 1963 the Lutheran missions had seventy-three missionaries working in the eastern highlands and claimed ninety-six thousand adherents. In the western highlands thirty-one missionaries listed sixteen thousand adherents, and in the southern highlands nine missionaries had a thousand adherents. The Missouri Synod of the Lutheran church began work in the western highlands in 1948, and after twenty years the Wabag Lutheran church had thirty-two thousand members.
>
> The Australian Methodist Overseas Mission expanded its work into the southern highlands in 1950 and estimated fifteen thousand adherents by 1963.
>
> The Anglicans moved into the highlands from the Madang district in 1953 and into the eastern highlands in 1955, and they too saw rapid growth to over eleven thousand by 1963.
>
> The Asia Pacific Christian Mission (UFM) moved into the southern highlands in 1949 from their established work in western Papua. Like the Lutherans, Methodists, and Anglicans, APCM made strategic use of national missionaries in this new outreach into the highlands.

But this postwar period also saw the advent of a host of new mission groups. The Australian Baptist Missionary Society established work in the western highlands in 1949 and among the Min tribesmen of the Star mountains in 1951. The Swiss Evangelical Brotherhood Mission moved into the western and eastern highlands in 1954. Several American missions representing the Wesleyan doctrinal position, such as the Church of the Nazarene Mission, began missionary work in the period 1955-61. During this same period the highland people of the western part of the island (then Dutch New Guinea) were being contacted by UFM, Baptists, Christian and Missionary Alliance, and Regions Beyond Missionary Union.

In the lowlands of Australian New Guinea the inland regions of the Sepik River were entered between 1949 and 1951 by the Assemblies of God Mission, South Seas Evangelical Mission, and missionaries from the Christian Brethren Assemblies (known as Christian Missions in Many Lands). The Australian Churches of Christ Mission brought missionaries from the New Hebrides to establish their work in the Ramu River area in 1958.

Thus today, in place of the six missions established in the territory in the prewar period, there are now thirty-three missions (or as many as fifty-two if the subdivisions within some denominations, such as the different Catholic orders, are counted). To these must be added specialized missionary agencies in Bible translation, aviation, broadcasting, and linguistics. Expatriate missionaries in 1966 totalled 3,246 (or 1 to every 670 of the total population, probably the highest ratio in the world). The Australian Council of Churches[2] estimated the number of indigenous mission staff workers as at least five times the number of expatriates (and in some missions the ratio is substantially higher), giving a total of approximately twenty thousand full-time Christian workers in the country. (In 1969 about five thousand of these were teachers in mission schools.)

The majority of these missions working in the western and southern highlands have seen rapid church growth in the years up to 1968, movements often characterized as "people's movements" toward Christianity. One example is the Australian Baptist work, which began in 1949. The first converts among the Enga people were baptized at Baiyer River in 1956. Just ten years later membership of the Enga church had reached over six thousand (or approximately a quarter of the total population of that area) and is still growing, though not quite so rapidly since 1968. This movement is taking place in the context of multiple Christian initiative in Enga society. Practical educational and medical work are in progress via manual training in a junior technical school and on the mission's agricultural station. A Bible school and translation work have spurred missionary evangelism by the Enga church. Indigenous leadership and responsibility are developing as some churches fully support their own pastors, while others work with decreasing mission contributions.

Viewing this remarkable church growth, one must acknowledge the existence of important cultural and economic factors, along with the spiritual principles and wise methods employed. A summary of these factors would include:

1) The traditional patterns of group decision-making in the close-knit highland community;

2) The almost total absence of any strong, sophisticated, religious system;

3) The enlightened approach to the highlanders by the government, which has created mutual trust between expatriates (government and missionary) and indigenous peoples;

4) The rapid economic development in some areas, which has undermined the whole animistic philosophy of the highland people, thus making them more responsive to the new message;

5) The belief in some areas that religion is the key to material progress (see below concerning the "cargo" religion);

6) The large concentration of missionary personnel, probably the greatest in the world;

7) The concerted attack by missions and churches alike on the many problems of the peoples, thus identifying the church with the felt needs of the community.

This last factor must be stressed. Early missionaries expressed concern for the social and economic conditions of the native people, and this concern has broadened into imaginative schemes. C. W. Abel, pioneering the Kwato mission around the turn of the century, used to argue "the need for us to teach the natives to be industrious" and so developed a program including carpentry and needlework. In the 1960's the Lutheran church established NAMASU (Native Marketing and Supply), a vigorous commercial enterprise managing many trade stores, vehicles, and even shipping in New Guinea. Its ownership is mainly indigenous shareholders. This and similar programs are being continued with wider and more creative applications today, specially emphasizing education. The older established missions in the territory are also changing their concerns and institutional structures. Increasing weight is being given to education in the traditional partnership of medical and educational activity,† and whole socio-economic conditions of rural and urban life are receiving increasing attention.

Problems of urban local government and racial discrimination are also active concerns of the churches, and some of the increasingly educated

†Expenditures by religious missions on health and education in Australian dollars, including grants received from government. The missions' share in these is usually from 55 to 65 percent (in both Papua and New Guinea). These figures are taken from the Australian government annual reports to United Nations.

Year	*Health*	*Education*
1959-60	$ 826,700	$1,614,184
1961-62	1,231,738	2,169,546
1963-64	1,106,038	2,792,000
1966-67	1,225,000	4,087,000
1968-69	2,894,000	5,377,000
1970-71	3,005,000	4,812,000

and elite people have indicated that they will write off Christianity as irrelevant unless it expresses a social conscience on such issues. The Catholic mission has developed plantations in the highlands to raise the level of the village economy, and not just to support its own work. Nevertheless, this last aim is a major incentive for some missions to undertake commercial activities, for they see it as one method of making the local church self-supporting.

In a climate of rapid change and unexpected, almost unmanageable, church growth it is natural that increasing attention has been paid to the structure of the churches and their relations to one another. Three interrelated trends have appeared: one toward cooperation in specialized ministries, another toward church union, and another toward the transfer of authority from mission to church.

The need for concentration of special facilities and expertise has given rise to the use of specialized missionary agencies serving many missions. These include the Summer Institute of Linguistics, the Missionary Aviation Fellowship, Christian Broadcasting Service (or Kristen Redio) and Kristen Pres, the Lutheran printing and publishing organization, which includes representatives of other churches on its board. Similar cooperation is seen in the sharing of teachers' college facilities on the part of the Lutherans and Anglicans and in the ministry of the APCM teachers' college, which serves all the churches linked with the Evangelical Alliance.

Growth in these specific areas of cooperation has been part of a movement toward wider association between the churches in response to the mood of ecumenism and the awareness of the need for cooperation in negotiations with the government over education and other social services. One stream of cooperation began at an ecumenical Bible study conference held at Bumayong in June 1963; it prepared the way for the inauguration of the Melanesian Council of Churches in 1965. The members of the Council until 1971 included the Lutheran church, the Church of England (Anglicans), the United church (formerly Methodists and LMS), the Australian Baptist Mission, and the Salvation Army.

During the same period another movement toward closer fellowship was taking place between other missions and churches which shared an aggressive evangelical faith. This led to the formation in 1964 of the Evangelical Alliance of the South Pacific Islands. The foundation members included the Austrian Baptist Mission, Christian Missions in Many Lands (Brethren), South Seas Evangelical Mission, UFM (APCM), Australian Churches of Christ Mission, Assemblies of God Mission, and a number of service organizations. It has since expanded to include a number of national church organizations and other missionary groups, notably those holding a Wesleyan doctrinal position. The Alliance serves as a forum for fellowship and witness to the evangelical faith and has worked cooperatively in such areas as education, Bible teaching, and convention ministries.

From 1965 to 1970 relationships between the Melanesian Council of Churches and the Evangelical Alliance were marked by cordiality, consultation, and cooperation on matters of mutual concern.‡ In fact, out of a desire to insure close working relationships with the Evangelical Alliance, the MCC in its original constitution stated that it would not formally affiliate with international bodies, such as the World Council of Churches. The strong evangelical emphasis of large groups within the membership of the Melanesian Council of Churches was a major factor in this early cooperation.

Steps to union have been taken by some denominations at the same time as they have moved from control by missions to indigenous denominations. Thus several Lutheran groups united to form the Evangelical Lutheran church of New Guinea in 1956, and the London Missionary Society handed its churches to the Papua Ekalesia in 1962, which in turn joined with the Methodists to form the United Church in 1968.

The most recent developments, however, have concerned relationships with the Roman Catholic church. Since Vatican II there has been a change in attitude on the part of that church's local leaders, which stands in marked contrast to the long-standing antagonisms at village church level. This has led to quite unprecedented situations in which the Roman Catholic church is avidly using evangelical literature, Bible translations, cassette Bible teaching programs, and the like. In 1971 evangelical onlookers were somewhat taken aback when with Rome's approval the Roman Catholic church said it agreed with the constitution of the Melanesian Council of Churches and accepted membership within the Council. Unfortunately, there has also been a marked tendency in recent years for a small but influential minority in the larger denominational churches to reinterpret the church's mission in terms of social, economic, and political development instead of evangelistic proclamation.

Thus in the last few years the Evangelical Alliance has been forced to reevaluate its previous close working relationship with the Melanesian Council of Churches. Following two major joint efforts—the World Vision Pastors' Conference 1971 and the Ralph Bell Evangelistic Crusade 1972—there has been a noticeable slowing down of this cooperative effort, coupled with increasing pressure from both government and MCC sources for the MCC to be recognized as the official voice of the churches. Some

‡In 1966 the relative memberships were: MCC, 1,011,000; EA, 150,000. But this figure is deceiving, since the majority of EA missions include only church members, whereas most other churches include all the residents of their geographical areas.

recent moves have indicated a tendency to ignore or bypass EA viewpoints on important issues, particularly in the field of media communications. However, EA involvement is still a force to be reckoned with, and a number of national church leaders in MCC circles have recently begun to voice disapproval of some expatriate missionaries' disregard for EA opinion. The situation is still in a state of flux, and the increasing transfer of authority from mission to church within both groups is still the most important factor which will influence future developments. Thus the years ahead could see a polarizing of the different viewpoints. The long-term position, however, will be determined by the developments in the third trend, that toward the transfer of authority from mission to church.

The handover from mission to church has followed several different patterns of transfer: An Anglican autonomous church has been constituted in Papua and New Guinea, but it remains largely under expatriate influence. The Evangelical church of Papua, which is the outgrowth of the old UFM work, is now under indigenous leadership but has virtually no control of funds raised outside the country. Whatever their constitutional position, most churches are in various stages of indigenizing their staff by the lateral withdrawal of expatriate workers.

Challenges and Opportunities

While expatriates remain, their primary task must be the training of indigenous workers. Bible school training, adult literacy programs for the illiterate majority of the people, Christian literature for the student generation, the use of opportunities to broadcast the message of God over the administration radio stations—all of these must be included in the ongoing work of evangelism.

The needs in these directions should compel a review of the churches' commitment to the government's education program. Is this the most effective way to use the churches' resources, or is the bureaucratic machinery which this commitment requires an unnecessary burden for an independent church? On the other hand, to what extent would gradual withdrawal from this commitment increase the problems of training Christian leadership for the church and nation?

This is just one of several pressing problems which the amazing church of Papua New Guinea faces today. As mentioned above, probably the greatest challenge to the church is its need for creating further indigenous Christian leadership. Evangelism has outstripped leadership training programs. This, together with the high percentage of expatriate Christian workers, suggests that the domination of Christian organizations by expatriates may be discouraging the development of Christian indigenous initiative and responsibility in Papua New Guinea. A comparison with the priority given to indigenization by secular organizations (government administration and more especially private enterprise) underlines the urgent need for indigenous church leadership if current evangelism is to be fruitful in the church of an independent nation. The immensity of this leadership training task is highlighted by the fact that theological education at a post-secondary school level has become a reality only since 1964. The English-language denominational colleges and the Christian Leaders' Training College (which serves the churches of the Evangelical Alliance) have all commenced since that date.

Still another problem is the fact that despite the reported 92 percent Christian population, there remain vast, isolated areas of New Guinea where pioneering is still necessary, missionary Richard Loving of the Wycliffe Bible Translators reports. He feels that economists, educators, and government officers have generally written off or ignored these isolated enclaves. Though they may represent only a minority of people, as individual linguistic groups these tribes create a tremendous and difficult challenge. They may not be easily accessible, but scores if not hundreds of these tribes must be reached, their language reduced, and Scriptures produced if they are to be truly converted and brought into the church of Jesus Christ, Loving points out.

Nominalism is undoubtedly also a major concern of the growing church in Papua New Guinea. The very vagueness of government statistics granting to the church total villages and tribes highlights the latent need for Bible teaching and pastoral care to insure that these nominal Christians, the fruit of people's movements, are truly converted and led into discipleship. One missionary observer estimates that only 40 to 50 percent of these are committed Christians. An emerging generation gap between the older tribesmen and the more educated younger people also seems to point in this direction. Here again the need for young, indigenous leadership is imperative.

Still another critical problem lies in the fact that until now the church's strength has been in the rural areas. Churches are not adjusting to and reaching the booming urban societies. Christians are being lost when they move to the cities. The Evangelical Alliance is wrestling with this problem, seeking to promote unity and cooperation among the churches in order to minister to the needy, growing towns.

Prospects for future church growth are good, provided relevant biblical answers can be given to these and other pressing problems of the hour. The high caliber of the young men entering ministerial training and the mature evangelical experience of key national leaders in both the MCC and EA groups suggest that under God Papua New Guinea could become a center for Christian influence throughout Asia.

Nation and People

GEOGRAPHY

Geographically Papua New Guinea is a widely disparate island kingdom. It includes the eastern half of the world's second-largest island, New Guinea, plus the large islands of New Britain and New Ireland in the Bismarck archipelago, Bougainville in the Solomons group, and several hundred smaller islands. Papua New Guinea's nearest neighbor is the Indonesian (western) half of New Guinea, now called Irian Barat. And Australia's boundaries come within a few miles of southern Papua.

From east to west Papua New Guinea extends about 1,000 miles and has a total area of about 180,000 square miles, which are almost equally divided between the two original territories of Papua and the Trust Territory of New Guinea.[3]

ANTHROPOLOGY

The indigenous inhabitants of Papua New Guinea are generally classified as Negroid racial stock of the Negro or Melanesian and Papuan subgroups, but they share physical characteristics common to various racial groupings and exhibit considerable diversity of features. The highlanders are small, averaging only five feet in height, and have very dark skin. Lowlanders tend to be lighter-skinned and taller. Being preliterate societies, the various tribes have no recorded history in the modern sense.

HISTORY

The historical origins of these small, dark peoples are shrouded in mystery. Their known history begins with the initial contacts made by Indonesian, Malaysian, and Chinese traders who touched on the western part of the island centuries ago. The earliest reference to New Guinea in literature dates from the eighth century A.D. Clearer records begin with the Portuguese and Spanish traders who sailed along the coasts between 1526 and 1545. They named the island "New Guinea" and the inhabitants "Papuans" (from a Malay term for "frizzy-haired men"). Then followed successive explorations by the Dutch East Indies voyagers in the seventeenth century, followed by the English (who in the eighth century had discovered the Bismarck archipelago). During the next hundred years British and French navigators charted most of the coastline of New Guinea. In 1884 the British declared the southern half of the island a British protectorate, and the same year the Germans claimed the northern half and the Bismarck islands. In 1906 the British ceded their claims to Australia, who renamed the area Papua. Little was done by either of the nations to develop the territory. In World War I Australia took over German New Guinea. Following the war, in 1920, the League of Nations gave Australia a mandate to govern the former German territory, including Buka and Bougainville in the Solomon islands group.

Between the two world wars there was little economic or commercial development in Papua. In the mandated Territory of New Guinea the discovery of gold and the introduction of light airplanes led to considerable economic progress for the expatriate settlers, though native welfare, health, and education was virtually left to the Christian missions. But the entire area became a focus of world interest with the outbreak of World War II in the Pacific. New Guinea became the center of fighting following the Japanese invasion early in 1942, and the Japanese defeat when attempting to take Port Moresby marked the turning point of the war in the Pacific for the allies. Following the war Australia was given a new mandate over the Trusteeship Territory of New Guinea by the United Nations, and Papua was reaffirmed as an Australian territory.

A United Nations trusteeship council mission in 1962 gave the impetus to more recent political development; until that time government was administered by a legislative council dominated by expatriates. But in 1964 a sixty-four member parliament known as the House of Assembly was elected democratically. This was extended in 1972 to one hundred elected members.

However, during 1971 two further significant steps were taken toward nationhood. The Australian government announced that "self-government" would be granted during the life of the 1972-76 House of Assembly as the next step toward independence. And in June 1971 the House of Assembly passed a "National Identity Bill," giving the former Territory of Papua and New Guinea a new national name of "Papua New Guinea," a national flag, and a national emblem. Thus the stage has been set for the growth of national unity. Rapid and possibly dramatic changes in the near future are expected.

Since the war, in marked contrast to the prewar situation, the Australian government has initiated rapid development among the indigenous population economically, educationally, and politically. This plus the Australian government's immigration policy for Papua New Guinea has enabled careful control of outside political influence, and to date there has been no evident communist activity. It would be unwise, however, to predict limits or even trends for the next few years.

POPULATION

Just how many people inhabit the new nation cannot be exactly determined, but the 1971 census enumerated 2,520,118, including over 50,000 expatriates from Australian, German, Chinese, and American stock. The 1966 census was the first real census ever made, and since registration of births and deaths is not compulsory, accurate figures for population growth are not available.§ The 1966 census showed that 95 percent of the people live in the rural areas, commonly in villages of less than three hundred inhabitants in the highland districts. Though only 5 percent live in urban centers of over five hundred population, cities are rapidly beginning to rise, with shanty settlements growing on the urban fringes. Even in these city ghettos the migrants tend to maintain their linguistic and tribal identities.

LANGUAGES

According to Dr. Stephen Wern of the National University of Australia, approximately seven hundred distinct languages are spoken in Papua New Guinea, dramatically indicating the cultural diversity of the people. In the coastal areas of New Guinea, language groups which include more than five thousand people are unusual; only thirty-four languages have more than ten thousand people, and only one over one hundred thousand. In the highlands small tribes living in the same or adjacent valleys may have languages that are mutually unintelligible. Early mission activity was generally in the local vernacular, although in some instances (notably under the Lutherans in New Guinea) the vernacular was transferred from another tribal area.

The lingua franca include Pidgin English (or neo-Melanesian) and Motu, formerly current in Papua but now in decline. Pidgin, on the other hand, is spreading rapidly and making inroads even in Papua, although it retains closer identification with New Guinea and is most widely spoken in the New Guinea island region. Its spread has been encouraged by some missions, by government field staffs, by movements of labor groups, and by the growth of road communication. "Pidgin is primarily an internative lingua franca; and because of its extensive use by indigenes in matters relating wholly to the native cultural sphere, it has developed into a very rich and elaborate language whose grammatical and semantic structure parallels and reflects native languages rather than English."[4] The publication of the New Testament in Pidgin in 1969 and the use of Pidgin by most speakers in the House of Assembly mark significant stages in its development as a national language. English, however, is the official language of

§A 1972 report by the government Department of External Territories (with accurate figures only for 1966 and 1971) shows the growth slower than expected:

POPULATION FIGURES

Year	*Indigenous*	*Non-Indigenous*	*Total*
1950	1,439,664	13,060	1,452,724
1960	1,880,326	23,870	1,904,196
1966	2,150,317	34,669	2,184,986
1971	2,466,986	53,132	2,520,118

Papua New Guinea. It is used in all recognized schools, and the expressed education policy since 1955 has been "teaching all children in controlled areas to read and write in English."||

EDUCATION

"Modern" education had a late start in Papua New Guinea. Early mission efforts attracted some subsidy, but there was no coherent education policy or large-scale administration support before the Second World War. Since 1962 attention has been concentrated on expanding the secondary schools. A university was established in 1965, as well as other tertiary institutions to teach education, medicine, and agriculture. Therefore education is still greatly retarded. In 1968 less than half the children of primary school age were attending school, and in the southern highlands this proportion was as low as 14 percent. The 1966 census showed 77 percent of the indigenous population over the age of ten as illiterate and 55 percent as able to speak only in the vernacular. Literacy in English and Pidgin was assessed at 11 and 12 percent respectively, with three times as many able to speak in Pidgin as in English.

ECONOMY

Most of the people in Papua New Guinea are engaged in subsistence agriculture, though many grow some crops for sale. Less than a fifth of the total indigenous work force is employed wholly or mainly in money-raising activities. Copra, cocoa, and coffee are the major crops. Tea, beef cattle, pyrethrum, and palm oil have recently been introduced. Total dependence on a plantation-agricultural economy has been avoided by the commencement of large-scale copper mining in 1969 on Bougainville. This has encouraged other mineral exploration. Some secondary industry has developed, principally in Lae and Port Moresby, but more than half the regular and capital expenditures by government authorities are supplied by the commonwealth government of Australia. This heavy reliance on external aid, coupled with a similar reliance on expatriate manpower at upper-middle and high levels, raise difficult questions in the light of growing political awareness. These factors underline the urgency of economic development programs for Papua New Guinea, involving especially the training and localization of staff.

National Religions

The original religions of these primitive peoples were relatively simple

||Translators from the Wycliffe Bible Translators assert that Pidgin and English are nowhere near widely enough used or understood in many tribal groups to make it satisfactory for adequate communication of the gospel.

forms of animism and totemism. The spirits of ancestors, dead people, trees, and other mysterious or useful inanimate objects received rudimentary worship from the peoples. The men in the interior, particularly in those bordering what is now called West Irian, were frequently headhunters for partly religious reasons. Thus the unsophistication of this truly primitive religion, existing in what anthropologists call one of the most primitive living societies in the world, made the simply-understood but profound truths of the gospel more readily and quickly acceptable to the peoples.

The best available statistics today list only 7 percent of the population as followers of these indigenous religions. But such statements give no impression of the extent to which traditional beliefs and magico-religious practices underlie the thinking of the people, including Christians, in all levels of education; nor does it reveal the different and often conflicting codes of moral values followed. "Traditionally," Lawrence has stated, "the natives regarded their cosmos as a finite and almost exclusively physical realm in which man was the focal point of two systems of relationship: actual relationships between human beings (social structure) and putative relationships between human beings and deities, spirits of the dead, and totems (religion)."[5] Many of these spirit-beings are localized in rivers, rocks, and other features of the environment. The cooperation of such spirit-beings is regarded as being fully as important as the cooperation of human beings in any work undertaken.

Thus the supernatural is both very real and nonexistent in traditional religion, since gods and spirits are so involved in the world of physical reality that no distinction between the natural and the supernatural can be maintained. Illness, misfortune, loss of crops, and the outcome of war are all attributed in traditional thinking to the intervention of deities and ancestors who may be manipulated by ritual action and observance of taboos. This traditional form of animism has been described as "a technology rather than a spiritual force for human salvation."

This way of thinking has also been applied in relation to the material possessions of the white man, giving rise to "cargo" cults—the belief that Europeans have a secret which brings them cargo from heaven, and which, if known by the native people, could enable them to obtain loads of cargo brought from their ancestors by ship or air. In *Road Belong Cargo* Lawrence has described how cargo beliefs in the Madang district incorporated pagan belief in the local deities within a framework of Christian doctrine and ritual. Some sincere indigenous Christians and mission workers helped to promulgate an expectation of the second coming of the Lord and with Him the arrival of cargo—western goods—if the customs of which the missionaries disapproved were eradicated. Such outbreaks of cargo belief under native leaders have generally been fairly brief and localized in their impact, but traditional magico-religious beliefs and the fear of sorcery persist widely even in Christian communities.

Christian History

CATHOLICISM

The first beachheads for the Roman church in Papua New Guinea were established in 1847 with incredible difficulty by the Marists, a Roman Catholic mission. They were succeeded by Italian, French, and German speaking priests in mission work there and in New Ireland, New Britain, and the Papuan coast during the 1880's. Plantations, workshops, and schools were established, along with mission stations along the Sepik River and on the islands of Bougainville and Buka before the turn of the century.

PROTESTANTISM

Dutch Protestants began work in West New Guinea in 1855. It has been said that during the first twenty-five years, more of their missionaries died of fever than natives were converted, such were the problems faced by these pioneers! In the 1870's two other Protestant missions entered what is now Papua New Guinea: from the Australian Methodist church Rev. George Brown came to the Bismarck archipelago, and the London Missionary Society sent missionaries S. McFarlane, W. G. Lawes, and J. Chalmers to Papua and the New Guinea islands. Both the Methodists and the LMS employed South sea islanders (mostly Fijians, Samoans, and Rarotongans) as teachers and mission workers, and some of these shared the martyrdom of some early missionaries. Without doubt it was these South sea islanders who carried the larger share of the burden of bringing Christianity to Papua and New Guinea. Brown secured the support of a notable local leader, Topulu, and opposed some European traders who were recruiting laborers for plantation work in Queensland.

Early contact with foreign labor recruiters made the islanders suspicious in the Louisiade and d'Entrecasteaux group when Methodist missionaries arrived in 1891. But W. E. Bromilow and his fellow workers soon won acceptance, and the Methodist mission expanded both among the islands and on the mainland of the Milne Bay district.

In the same period the work of the Lutheran Mission was established by missionaries from two German missionary societies. Dr. Johannes Flierl of the Neuendettelsau Mission arrived at Finschhafen in July 1886, six months after the German "New Guinea Company" had established a post there. Rev. W. Thomas of the Rhenish Missionary Society arrived in 1887 and commenced work from Madang. Like the Catholics, the Lutheran mission developed plantations to support its work, which was later carried to the interior by explorers and students from the schools. But a turning point in the Lutheran work after the turn of the century can be traced to the methods of missionary work introduced by Rev. Christian Keysser, who

> . . . revolutionized the mission's evangelical system. He realized that the policy of singling out individuals for conversion was useless, for individual converts could not resist the pressures of their own communities and relapsed into paganism as soon as they left the mission station. The wisest approach would be to move out into the village and remould whole native societies as Christian congregations. The most energetic converts should become leaders, serving as congregational elders and evangelists or teachers in other pagan villages. This system of group approach soon proved its worth: it enabled the natives to adopt Christianity on their own terms and increased the mission's effective field staff.[6]

Keysser was one of the great, farseeing pioneers of nineteenth century missions, though unheralded by any western biographer. His vision and sacrificial efforts resulted in tremendous fruit on both sides of New Guinea, and it was his work which laid the foundation for the peoples' movements on the Papuan side in the postwar period.

In 1891 the Church of England in Australia established the Anglican Mission to New Guinea. Headed by Rev. Albert Maclaran and Rev. Copeland King, they commenced work at Wedau in the northern district of Papua. Thus the last half of the nineteenth century saw beachheads for the church established along the coastal fringes of the New Guinea mainland and the smaller islands only. In the early years of the twentieth century European secular and missionary explorers began probing the interior. But the great growth of the church has been a feature of postwar history, a building on the foundations of the martyrs, sacrifices, and wise experiments of earlier years.

This phenomenon of evangelism in Papua New Guinea is cause for praise to God and study by missiologists. But the continuing need of the islands belay any complacency. All the problems of urban, secular society are facing them. As objects of intense missionary activity in the past by other south Pacific islanders like themselves, the church in Papua New Guinea now has the potential of becoming a mission-sending source to other areas of swelling Asia.

APPENDIX 1

General Christian Population in Papua New Guinea

Year	Roman Catholic	Seventh-Day Adventist	Other Protestant	Total
1898	3,435	....	10,314[a]	13,749[a]
1906	4,600	....	n.a.	n.a.
1912	7,000	....	n.a.	n.a.
1927	12,000	....	n.a.	n.a.
1931	85,064	816	88,834	174,714
1935	165,335	3,038	102,360[b]	270,733[b]
1940	186,196	3,856	220,413[b]	410,465[b]
1959-60	n.a.	n.a.	n.a.	906,274
1961-62	n.a.	n.a.	n.a.	1,018,729
1963-64[c]	508,149	51,762	687,374	1,247,285
1966[d]	563,504	48,762	841,357	1,453,623

a) Not complete—no Anglican figures available.
b) Not complete—no UFM figures available.
c) Figures taken from Papua and New Guinea Annual Reports for 1963-64.
d) Figures taken from June 1966 Census figures, thus computed differently from c.

Different missions use different methods of determining "adherents," and thus these figures are only a rough guide. The discrepancies between this chart and the following one are due to this fact plus inadequate reporting.

Figures for 1898-1940 are taken from P. Ryan, ed., *Encyclopaedia of Papua and New Guinea* (Melbourne: 1972) and for 1959-71 from Australian Govt. Annual Reports on Papua New Guinea.

APPENDIX 2

Christians in Papua New Guinea by Denominations, 1966

Christian	*Males*	*Females*	*Total Persons*	*Proportion of Total Population (Percent)*
Baptist	23,034	21,585	44,619	2.07
Brethren	1,922	1,496	3,418	0.15
Roman Catholic	354,149	317,300	671,449	31.23
Church of Christ	1,120	954	2,074	0.10
Church of England	54,994	49,409	104,403	4.86
Congregational	18	14	32	....
Evangelical Alliance	59,113	55,548	114,661	5.33
Lutheran	303,042	291,057	594,099	27.63
Methodist	96,841	85,837	182,678	8.50
Orthodox	28	35	63	....
Papua Ekalesia	67,475	63,024	130,499	6.07
Presbyterian	46	10	56	....
Protestant (undefined)	116	50	166	0.01
Salvation Army	205	212	417	0.02
Seventh-Day Adventist	37,803	33,468	71,271	3.31
United Church (undefined)	56	40	96	....
Other Christians	32,300	31,900	64,200	2.99
Total Christian	1,032,262	951,939	1,984,201	92.27
Total Non-Christian	81,628	72,225	153,853	7.16
Total Indigenous	1,120,306	1,030,111	2,150,417	100.00

Responses in the 1966 census to the question on religious denomination yielded the above data for the indigenous population. This table should be interpreted with caution, as no criteria were cited for adherents, and the table may include double entries for respondents who cited two denominations. The 1973 total population is estimated at 2,500,000, with Christian proportions of the total at approximately the same percentages as shown in the table.

APPENDIX 3

Foreign Missionaries in Papua New Guinea

Year	*Roman Catholic*	*Seventh-Day Adventist*	*Other Protestant*	*Total*
1898[a]	58	...	31	89
1906	70	...	54	124
1912	79	...	74	153
1927	99	...	67	166
1931	363	17	97	477
1935	445	13	143	601
1940	500	9	167	676
1959-60				1,905
1961-62				2,372
1963-64	1,180	189	1,284	2,653

Year	*Roman Catholic*	*Others and Independents*	*Melanesian Council of Churches*	*Evangelical Alliance Churches*	*Total*
1968[b]	1,574	505	829	469	3,377
1969	1,613	382	755	586	3,336
1970	1,702	384	767	558	3,411
1971	1,709	356	710	613	3,388

a) Figures for 1898-1927 are for Europeans only (not including Polynesian missionaries); from 1931 onward the figures include all expatriates.

b) Since 1968 the figures have been published by organizational groups. "Others and Independents" therefore includes SDA and some evangelical missions for these years.

Foreign Missionaries Serving in Papua New Guinea by Nationalities (1966)

British (incl. Australian)	1,884	Italian	8
Dutch	106	Swiss	71
French	79	U.S.A.	569
German	396	Others (incl. Tonganese)	109
Irish	24		

APPENDIX 4

Indigenous Church or Mission Workers in Papua New Guinea

Year	*Roman Catholic*	*Seventh-Day Adventist*	*Other Protestant*	*Total*
1898[a]	3	. . .	163	166
1906	7	. . .	338	345
1912	22	. . .	321	343
1927	113	. . .	489	602
1931	859	24	642	1,525
1935	1,158	61	1,503	2,722
1940	1,433	138	1,783	3,354

Year	*Roman Catholic*	*Others and Independents*	*Melanesian Council of Churches*	*Evangelical Alliance Churches*	*Total*
1968[b]	5,378	1,367	1,880	499	9,124
1969	5,329	1,211	1,803	767	9,110
1970	5,359	1,447	1,964	588	9,358
1971	4,387	1,330	3,002	592	9,311

a) Figures for 1898-1927 include Polynesian missionaries; after that date Papua New Guineans only.

b) Since 1968 the figures have been published by organizational groups. "Others and Independents" therefore includes SDA and some evangelical missions for these years.

NOTES

1. P. Biskup, B. Jinks, and H. Nelson, *A Short History of New Guinea*, p. 30.
2. "Responsibility in New Guinea," p. 2.
3. Howlett, "Geography," *Papua New Guinea: Prospero's Other Island*, ed. P. Hastings, (Sydney: Angus & Robertson, 1971), pp. 4-5.
4. S. Wern, "A Thousand Languages," *Papua New Guinea: Prospero's Other Island*, pp. 86-87.
5. Peter Lawrence, *Road Belong Cargo*, p. 9.
6. Ibid., p. 52.

BIBLIOGRAPHY

General Works

Biskup, P.; Jinks, B.; and Nelson, H. *A Short History of New Guinea.* Sydney: Angus & Robertson, 1968.

Hastings, Peter, ed. *Papua New Guinea: Prospero's Other Island.* Sydney: Angus & Robertson, 1971.

Lawrence, Peter. *Road Belong Cargo.* Melbourne: University Press, 1963.

Lawrence, P., and Meggett, M. J., eds. *Gods, Ghosts, and Men in Melanesia.* OUP, 1965.

Morton, Harold. *Below Me the Mountains: Flying for God in New Guinea.* Punchbowl, N.S.W.: Jordan Books Ltd., 1964.

Souter, Gavin. *New Guinea: The Last Unknown.* Sydney: Angus & Robertson, 1963.

Ward, R. G., and Lea, D. A. M., eds. *An Atlas of Papua New Guinea.* University of Papua New Guinea and Port Moresby: Collins-Longner, 1970.

Literature by the Asia Pacific Christian Mission (UFM)

Horne, Shirley. *Out of the Dark.* London: Oliphants, 1962.

———. *Them Also: First Mission Contacts with the Primitive Biamis.* Port Moresby: UFM Press, 1968.

Lea, Frank B. *Papua Calling.* Melbourne: S. John Bacon, n.d.

Missionaries of the U.F.M. *Papuan Triumphs.* Auckland: Institute Printing & Publishing Society, 1959.

Price, Rhys. *Papuan Victory.* Melbourne: UFM, n.d.

Twyman, Eva. *The Battle for the Bigwigs.* Auckland: UFM, 1961.

Literature by the Australian Baptist Missionary Society

ABMS: Statement of Policy, Organisation, Etc. Melbourne: ABMS.

After Three Years: Oksapmin. Melbourne: ABMS.

1959-1969 The Church Grows at Telefolmin. Melbourne: ABMS.

Enga Baptists: After Twenty Years. Melbourne: ABMS.

The Enga Church: First Decade. Melbourne: ABMS.

Himbury, Mervyn. *Discovering the Church in New Guinea.* Melbourne: ABMS.

Morling, G. H. *Impressions of New Guinea.* Melbourne: ABMS.

Watson, E. E. *This Fire.* Melbourne: ABMS, c. 1962.

Literature by Christian Missions in Many Lands (Brethren)

Liddle, K. W., ed. *God at Work in New Guinea.* Palmerston North, N.Z.: Gospel Publishing House, 1969.

Marsh, L. A. *The Wind Blows.* Palmerston North, N.Z.: Gospel Publishing House, 1969.

Pethybridge, J. *From Fear to Faith.* Palmerston North, N.Z.: Gospel Publishing House, 1971.

LITERATURE BY THE CHURCH OF ENGLAND

Tomkins, Dorothea, and Hughes, Brian. *The Road from Gona.* Sydney: Angus & Robertson, 1969.

LITERATURE BY THE CHURCH OF THE NAZARENE MISSION

Berg, A. *Arrows of the Almighty.* Kansas City: Beacon Hill Press, 1972.

Blowers, Bruce L. *The New Guinea Frontier.* Kansas City: Beacon Hill Press, 1969.

Knox, Wanda. *Pioneer to New Guinea.* Kansas City: Beacon Hill Press, 1969.

LITERATURE BY THE LUTHERAN CHURCH

Flierl, Johannes. *Forty-five Years in New Guinea: Memoirs of the Senior Missionary.* Columbus, Ohio: Lutheran Book Concern, 1931.

Frerichs, Albert and Sylvia. *Anutu Conquers in New Guinea: A Story of Mission Work in New Guinea.* Rev. ed. Minneapolis: Augsburg Publishing House, 1969.

Koschade, Alfred. *New Branches on the Vine: From Mission Field to Church in New Guinea.* Minneapolis: Augsburg Publishing House, 1967.

Vicedom, G. F. *Church and People in New Guinea.* London: USCL, 1961.

LITERATURE BY THE UNITED CHURCH

Bromilow, W. E. *Twenty Years Among Primitive Papuans.* London: Epworth, 1929.

Butcher, Benjamin T. *We Lived with Headhunters.* London: Hodder & Stoughton, 1963.

"The History of the United Church." Mimeographed. Port Moresby: United Church, c. 1969.

Lennox, Cuthbert. *James Chalmers of New Guinea.* London: Andrew Melrose, 1902.

McFarlane, S. *Among the Cannibals of New Guinea: Being the Story of the New Guinea Mission of the London Missionary Society.* London: London Missionary Society, 1888.

LITERATURE BY OTHER EVANGELICAL MISSIONS

Daimoi, Joshua. "CLTC Notes on History of Missions. Unpublished lecture notes covering work of member missions and churches of the Evangelical Alliance of the South Pacific Islands, Banz, W. H. D., Papua New Guinea.

Division of Mission of the Australian Council of Churches. *Responsibility in New Guinea: Report of an Ecumenical Visit to New Guinea, June, 1965.* Sydney, 1965.

Ridgway, Kingsley. *Wesleyan Mission in New Guinea.* Marion, Ind.: Wesleyan Methodist Church, 1966.

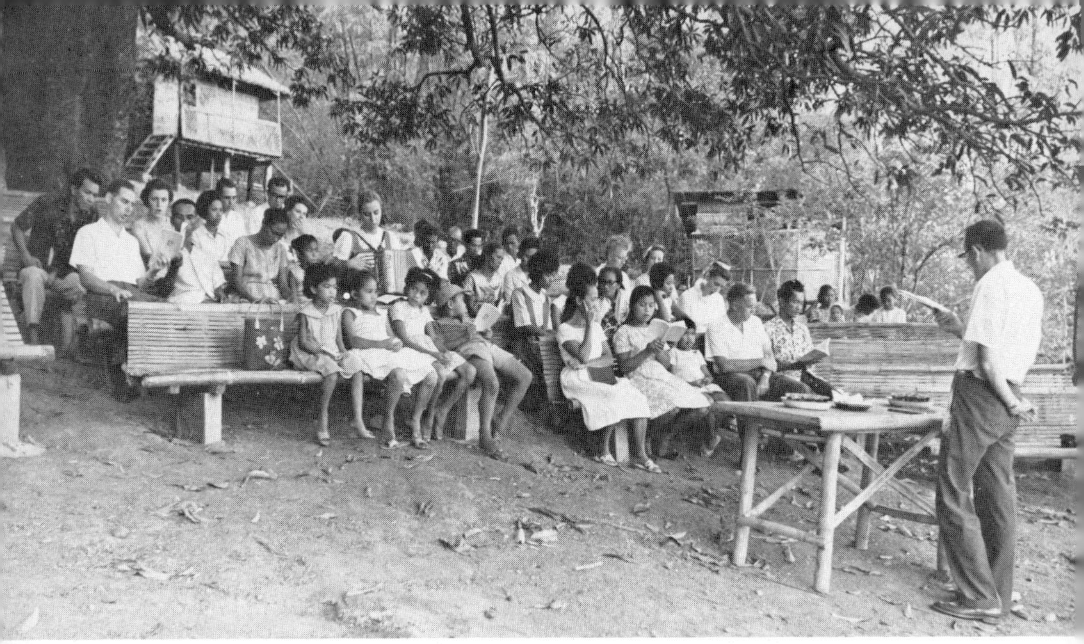

Christian campers celebrate their first communion.

Goat stew is featured in a church camp.

OMF missionary Barbara Reed works in Bentaugvan language with informant.

Photos by Russell Reed

24

THE PHILIPPINES

by Ralph Tolliver

Introduction

The Philippines are like an onion. The thin outside skin of the onion is American: the first things that impress the visitor to Manila are the American technology, products, and language—potent reminders that the Stars and Stripes flew over the Philippines for forty-eight years, from 1898 to 1946 (interrupted by four years of Japanese occupation, from 1942 to 1945).

Peel off the outside skin of the onion, and the next layer is Spanish. He who delves into life in the Philippines soon discovers that its religion, music, social customs, and commercial systems of telling time, counting money, and weighing vegetables all come from Spain. Among these enduring emblems of the 377 years of Spain's rule in the Philippines (1521-1898), the most important is the nominal Catholicism, which claims almost 85 percent of the people still today.

Then peel off the Spanish layer and you come to the hard and durable core of Filipino life, which is Malayo-Indonesian. Proverbs and values, the family system, and personal relationships—the real game of life—is played by ancient tribal rules.

Ralph Tolliver, a missionary to China from 1938 to 1951 under the China Inland Mission, moved to the Philippines after the communist takeover in China. Under the banner of the Overseas Missionary Fellowship he has carried on an evangelistic ministry. This article is in part a result of his three-year study, along with A. Leonard Tuggy, of church growth in the islands; this survey was published in 1972 in the volume *Seeing the Church in the Philippines.* Mr. Tolliver had previously authored *They Found the Way of Victory* (1963) and co-authored (with Ramon Cenit) *Smuggler's Story* (1966).

But this make-believe onion is still an organic unit, for "Juan de la Cruz" (the Filipino "Joe Doe") functions during office hours as an American, goes to mass on Sunday morning like a Spaniard, and rules his home like a traditional Filipino. He is a mixture of East and West, old and new. Sometimes the conflict disturbs him, but most of the time he does not stop to think about the disparate influences which mold his life.

In this interesting multi-layered cultural milieu Protestant Christianity has a scant seventy-five year history. As of 1972, it numbered 1,443,000 members in the Christian community apart from the quasi Protestant Aglipayan church. Latourette notes that the Protestant population grew twice as rapidly as even the burgeoning general population from 1914 to 1957. There exist in the Philippines complete freedom of worship and evangelism, maturing indigenous evangelical churches, diverse missionary activities, and sparks of revival here and there.

The Church Today

OVERALL PICTURE

There are evidences that the evangelical faith has just begun in the Philippines, and that great days lie ahead.

1) There is a wide open door. The very fact that 368 religious bodies exist is evidence in itself that Filipinos are open to religious change.
2) There is a growing corps of mature leaders among both Filipinos and Chinese churches. Sixty-five seminaries and Bible schools, most of them conservative, hold good promise for training future leaders.
3) There is more mutual understanding and cooperation among conservatives.
4) Some of the newer churches, particularly the Baptists and Pentecostals, are seeing much fruit and rapid church growth. There is no real reason why this fruitfulness should not also be enjoyed in other communions.
5) For the first time since the evangelical message arrived in 1899, the attitude of the dominant Roman Catholic church is one of tolerance. Whether evangelicals allow themselves to be lulled to sleep in this new, comfortable atmosphere or whether they will make the most of their new opportunities will greatly alter the future of the Protestant church in this land.

In these days of opportunity for the Philippines God has been raising up numerous new programs to reap the harvest.

In late 1968 Baptists sponsored a nationwide "New Life Crusade" in 181 churches. Over six thousand first-time decisions for Christ were recorded.

Growing out of the Asia-South Pacific Congress on Evangelism in 1968 has been a unique, indigenous, five-year evangelistic thrust designed to cover the entire nation. Customarily called the COW movement ("Christ, the Only Way"), it is an interdenominational, many-pronged thrust to revive the church and evangelize the nation in the period 1970-75. Starting with an All-Philippine Congress on Evangelism in May of 1970 (attended by 250 delegates from fifty-six Protestant denominations and organizations), the first stage of the program featured a series of twenty-three regional congresses on evangelism to stir zeal and increase vision. Church renewal campaigns, visitation evangelism, and local evangelistic crusades are being held.

A key element of the five-year plan is the LEGS program, "Laymen's Evangelistic Group Studies," with a goal of ten thousand study cell groups established throughout the islands by the end of 1973. All these efforts will come to a focus in 1974, when it is hoped that Billy Graham will conduct a city-wide crusade in Manila. COW has already accomplished what has never been done in Philippine Protestantism before—the uniting of large numbers of evangelicals from seventy denominations and church groups for evangelism. Is this the beginning of the revival and reformation so sorely needed in the Philippines today?

Stirred in part by the activities of the COW movement, many Catholics have become interested in Bible study, with priests urging their people to study the Scriptures. Many have joined with the Protestants in these cell groups. Missionaries from the ultraconservative denominations are in a quandary, but some are suggesting that their people cooperate in the study groups without trying at this stage to bring Filipino Catholics into Protestant churches.

The Philippines, particularly Manila, have become a hub of radio and television evangelism in the postwar years. Best-known and most evangelistically effective is the extensive facility of the Far East Broadcasting Company, founded in 1948. Now it has seventeen stations in the islands beaming programs in several scores of languages across all Asia. To serve remote areas of the Philippines, they have distributed over two thousand pre-tuned transistor radios in forty-eight provinces. In addition to the evangelical FEBC, the National Christian Council operates three medium-wave and two smaller FM and shortwave stations. An ecumenical venture, the Southeast Asia Radio Voice began broadcasting in 1968 with a 50,000-watt voice to southeast Asian countries. The Roman Catholics had twelve stations on the air by 1969, and in the Manila area they are experimenting with TV for educational use. The large Iglesia ni Cristo sect also operates a station.

Thus in the Philippines today there is a welter of prewar and postwar, church and para-church, mission organizations at work. As a result, many denominations are in varying stages of growth and vitality. In some the cutting edge of evangelism is already keen in the national church itself, and missionaries have either stepped into the background or withdrawn (unfortunately). In other groups, however, missionary leadership in pioneer evangelism and church planting is still vital for growth. Let us take a brief look at these churches.

THE UNITED CHURCH OF CHRIST

Since the Second World War the country's largest Protestant denomination has been the United Church of Christ in the Philippines. Its present membership is more than 145,464, distributed in almost twelve hundred churches with some seven hundred pastors. They claim a total Christian community of over 350,000.

This ecumenical church is the result of two mergers, one which formed the United Evangelical church in 1928 and a final one creating the UCCP in 1948. The UCCP embraced Presbyterians, Congregationalists, United Brethren, Disciples, independent Methodists, and other small missions and churches. During the first ten years the upper echelon of leadership in the UCCP was so involved in internal organization that little time was left for evangelism and church planting.* Later, social action emphasis claimed the attention of many church leaders. This emphasis along with ecumenism have become the warp and woof of the denomination, eventuating in increasing dialogue with Roman Catholics. Joint meetings have been arranged: "Rally for Christian Unity," "United Prayer Meeting," and "Ecumenical Rally for Peace." Since Roman Catholics often include a mass in any kind of religious gathering, it was not long before Protestant pastors were finding themselves involved in Roman Catholic masses.

This kind of ecumenical rapprochement has been going on largely in the cities. Many pastors and local church leaders at the grass roots level view these developments with concern, for a sizable number of local churches and some leaders are strongly evangelical. A practical question that many pastors are asking is, "If the Roman Catholic church is a sister communion, then is it proselytizing to evangelize Roman Catholics?" The result has been to downgrade, if not to eliminate, evangelism among Roman Catholic Filipinos by the liberals. Thus growth of the UCC has been slower in the postwar period.

SEVENTH-DAY ADVENTISTS

Second-largest of the Philippine Protestant groups is the Seventh-Day Adventists, who total 114,296 in one denomination. Despite the fact that theirs was a slow start—only five converts in the first six years (1905-11),

*"One of the weaknesses of Philippine Evangelical Protestantism has been its preoccupation with its own organizationism," (Peter G. Gowing, *Island Under the Cross*, p. 233).

during the decade of the sixties they grew at an annual rate of 8 percent a year, more than double the growth rate of the general population. A brief study of their methods may provide some keys to understanding methods for church growth in this culture.

The SDA's have not grown because of a popular doctrine, for they demand abstinence from pork, shrimp, and crabs, all of which are delicacies to the Filipino. A Filipino desires to be socially accepted, yet Filipino SDA's hold a belief concerning prophetess Ellen G. White that tends to alienate them from other Christians, and their worship on Saturday sticks out like a sore thumb in a Catholic, Sunday-oriented populace. But this very apartness has resulted in built-in advantages which have brought to the SDA's a strong sense of both unity and identity. Add to this an amazing amount of very thorough planning, hard work, efficient organization, and tight financial control, and one can understand the success of this second-largest mission-founded Protestant church in the Philippines.

One very significant factor in SDA growth has been literature. During 1968 alone they sold $750,000 worth of literature in the Philippines through a thousand colporteurs; sixty people are employed at their printing establishment. Probably no other church group in the Philippines, or perhaps even in all of east Asia, can top this literature record. Another secret is their coordinated use of radio, correspondence courses, campaigns, Sabbath school, secular education, relief work hospitals, and clinics. Still another key is their promotion of home Bible study courses. Their course "The Bible Says" is, significantly, under their department of lay activities. "Eighty percent of our converts are the work of laymen: twenty percent are the direct work of the ministry," says Pastor F. M. Arogante of the Visayan headquarters in Cebu city.

These laymen who do the work of ministers are undoubtedly the greatest factor in SDA success. There is only one paid worker for every fifteen to thirty preaching places. The paid district pastor supervises these enterprising lay pastors, possibly visiting any one place only three times a year. A district pastor may be a woman, after the tradition of the SDA prophetess, Ellen G. White. In the provinces of Cebu, Bohol, and Masbate there are 116 SDA churches and preaching places, with only seven district pastors supervising an average of seventeen churches each.

This system neatly solves an insistent and nagging problem in the Philippines, the support of the ministry. The men in charge of local work are, in effect, self-supporting pastors. Yet despite this, SDA authority is remarkably centralized and individual members are disciplined. Finances, for instance, are strictly controlled. All collections go into the central office, and all salaries are paid from the central office, resulting in a unique combination of local initiative in the churches and recognized authority in the central office. An observer of the Philippine scene who opines that "Filipinos cannot be regimented" should examine the power structure of the SDA's. The marvel of their growth is an object lesson for other churches in the Philippines today.

METHODISTS

Before the war the largest denomination in the nation was the Methodists, who recorded a postwar high of 74,000 members in 1952.† Their growth since then has been widely different according to location. For one reason, a significant decision of postwar Methodism was to break away from comity and go nationwide. Just after the war tens of thousands of Ilocano farmers migrated to the open and beckoning frontier of Mindanao, and among these were thousands of Methodists. The denomination followed its own members and established Methodist churches in the near areas. The new conference there grew by leaps and bounds, from 746 members in 1955 to 3,135 members in 1965, a growth of almost 500 percent in a decade. This growing edge of Methodism is found not only in Mindanao but also in Nueva Ecija, Palawan, and suburban Manila. But while the Methodists are expanding into new areas they are losing ground in some old centers. They are plagued with the "third-generation" problem of how to keep their young people in the church and how to continue to experience that "heart strangely warmed" which changed the life of John Wesley.

Post-World War II Methodism in the Philippines might have been considerably different except for the leadership of one man, C. L. Spottswood. The "flying parson," with a Bible in one hand and a joystick in the other, pioneered gospel work in northern Luzon, Mindanao, and Palawan, always taking with him aggressive Filipino workers. "Spotty," as he is affectionately called, is an example of the kind of spiritual leader around whom Filipino Christians will rally.

BAPTIST MISSIONS

The nearest thing to a Protestant town in the Catholic Philippines is Ilog, on the western shore of Negros island. The Protestant church in town has 736 members and there are eight daughter churches in the surrounding barrios (villages). These are the American Baptist churches, or "Convention Baptist," as they are commonly called. Their churches total 289 nationwide, with 28,627 members. Working largely in the west-

†It is difficult to reconcile this with the fact that between 1948 and 1968 the number of ordained ministers jumped from 185 to 305 and the number of local congregations almost doubled, from 358 to 648. The answer is that Methodist pastors after the war began to quietly drop the deadwood from their rolls, with the result that there was an apparent but not real loss in members.

ern islands, these Baptists have been traditionally among the most evangelistic believers in the islands, though suffering problems and splits.

As with all churches, the Second World War brought destruction to Baptist chapels and dislocation and death to many Christians. But the war threw believers directly on God for safety and guidance, thus setting the stage for self-reliance, aggressive evangelism, and postwar increase. And increase they did. Convention Baptist membership doubled between 1954 and 1968. Most of the growth was in Negros Occidental (the west side of Negros island), the sugarland of the Philippines. In Bacolod city, Convention Baptist churches increased to six in the five years from 1953 to 1957, and local churches throughout the province doubled, principally through a systematic outreach from town and city churches into the surrounding countryside. A leader in this program was Rev. Greg Tingson, who in later years traveled as an evangelist to other Asian lands and to the U. S. through Youth for Christ.

While other older denominations are cutting back their Bible school training programs, the Convention Baptists are expanding theirs. Among pastors and workers in Occidental Negros, 65 percent have been trained at the Convention Bible Institute in Bacolod city. Since of the 129 organized Convention Baptist churches in the province 109 are barrio and mountain churches, it is obvious that the denomination's growing edge is in the rural areas, and it is precisely in these areas that the Bible institute graduates are notably successful.

Meanwhile, an offshoot of the Convention Baptists, the Fellowship Baptists, have also been growing in the same general western area. The Association of Baptists for World Evangelism mission organized this church in 1928, after splitting from the American Baptists during the war. Several of their missionaries were interned by the Japanese. After the war Mr. and Mrs. Paul Friederichsen pioneered a new type of evangelism with a tent and house trailer, beginning campaigns that became a standard method of evangelism by conservatives. These were particularly fruitful in the Visayas and Mindanao during the 1950's, resulting in a corps of able evangelists who have continued effective work through the 1960's. As of 1970, ABWE-related churches are geographically more widespread than any other Baptist group in the country. With approximately sixteen thousand members, they are the largest separatist group in the Protestant spectrum. As a result, by 1970 there were in the Negros Occidental province alone 129 Convention Baptist churches and approximately the same number of Fellowship Baptist churches (ABWE-related), along with newer groups, such as Maranatha Gospel Fellowship (also Baptist). The total number of Baptist churches in that one province comes to some 260. The appraisal of church-growth researchers in the Philippines is that, as of 1970, the prospects for future growth of evangelical churches in this province are possibly more promising than for any other single province in the Philippines.

THE PHILIPPINE INDEPENDENT CHURCH

The most controversial of the nation's non-Catholic churches is the Philippine Independent church, commonly called the Aglipayan church (after its founder, Gregoreo Aglipay, who was excommunicated from the Catholic church in 1899 for his anti-Spanish activities). In ritual the Aglipayan church is Catholic but not Roman; it doesn't acknowledge the pope, it uses the vernacular in its ritual, and its priests marry.

In 1948 its priests were acknowledged by the American Episcopal church, thus giving the church nominal Protestant status. In the early postwar years many of these churches threw open their doors to evangelism by the Overseas Crusade teams, leading some to think that the entire church might be revived. Though doubtless many were converted, wholesale revival has not occurred. But if they be counted as Protestants, the Aglipayans are the largest Protestant denomination in the Philippines, with between one and two million members.

POSTWAR CONSERVATIVE GROUPS

After the Second World War a plethora of new foreign missionary societies arrived in the Philippines, most of them from the U. S. A. Among these were many older missions, especially those forced out of communist China: Southern Baptists, Conservative Baptists, Overseas Missionary Fellowship (formerly China Inland Mission), Free Methodists, International Missions, Advent Christian Mission, the Church of the Nazarene, and the Lutheran Church, Missouri Synod. But several missions new to east Asia also arrived, with evangelism and church-planting as their basic aim: Far Eastern Gospel Crusade, Baptist General Conference, Evangelical Free Church Mission, Church of God (both Anderson, Indiana, and Cleveland, Tennessee, branches), Baptist Bible Fellowship, Berean Mission, and General Baptist Mission.

Also arriving in force were service and specialty organizations, a phenomenon in full flower immediately following the war: Far East Broadcasting Company, Inter-Varsity Christian Fellowship, Wycliffe Bible Translators (Summer Institute of Linguistics), Campus Crusade for Christ, Child Evangelism Fellowship, Missionary Aviation Fellowship, Navigators, Servicemen's Centers, Philippine Overseas Crusades, Back to the Bible Broadcast, Christian Literature Crusade, and others. The fact that the Philippine government has allowed a multiplicity of groups to set up shop in the country is evidence of the religious liberty enjoyed here.

Summarizing the missionary picture, of the 1,250 Protestant missionaries currently assigned to the Philippines, 84 percent belong to non-ecumenical societies[1] while only 16 percent belong to member groups of the National Christian Council—a reversal of the situation that prevailed before the war. Missionary-wise, a new day has dawned in the Philippines. But the question is, "Are these missionaries producing live believers and viable Christian churches? And are those Christians and churches reproducing themselves?"

The answers to these questions are as varied as the names of the different organizations. Analysis is necessary. In the first place, one-third of the postwar groups are specialist organizations or auxiliaries set up to serve the national church or even to serve other missions—Far East Broadcasting, Missionary Aviation Fellowship, etc. Others are semi-service, such as the Far Eastern Gospel Crusade and the Overseas Missionary Fellowship, which are helping the Christian community at large by training workers and producing and distributing Christian literature.

The majority of the postwar missions, however, are church-planting organizations. As of 1970 the thirty missions listed above had been in the Philippines an average of seventeen years each. Yet the Christian community of the new conservatives totals only about 150,000 people. "Church-growth Research in the Philippines" estimates that the Protestant community is now 3.5 percent of the general population, or 1,443,000[2] out of 40,800,000. If this estimate is correct, then nine-tenths of the Protestant community would belong to the older, prewar denominations and to indigenous churches that have grown up without mission connections, while one-tenth would be associated with the postwar conservatives. This is not a large figure. It seems to say that orthodoxy alone does not guarantee effective evangelism.

But these comparative percentages are now in the process of changing. The growth of member groups of the National Christian Council has leveled off and is not keeping abreast of the 3.3 percent annual[3] growth rate of the general population, while the growth rate of many conservative denominations is far in excess of that of the general population. Examples are the Foursquare Church, the Assemblies of God, and the Southern Baptists. The latter grew from 2,552 in 1959 to 11,458 in 1968, a phenomenal average yearly growth of almost 35 percent.

Most of the non-ecumenical conservative groups find fellowship and corporate expression in the Philippine Council of Evangelical Churches, founded in 1966. Including some prewar conservatives, such as the Christian and Missionary Alliance and the Assemblies of God, by 1972 the Council embraced thirty-two denominations and organizations and had an office and executive secretary in Manila.

THE ROMAN CATHOLIC CHURCH

As the Philippines is a land of contrasts, so is the Roman Catholic church. It is the most progressive of churches and the most backward, the most modern and the most medieval. Here, for instance, is a Jesuit priest, a Ph.D. in anthropology from an American university, dressed in sport shirt and slacks, on his way to give a lecture on family planning. And here is an Austrian priest dressed in black cassock down to his ankles, pausing before a well-dressed lady as she presses the back of his hand to her forehead and mumbles the traditional *Manu-po,* "Your right hand, sir." A mass in a new-styled chapel features circular seats looking toward an immaculate altar in the center of the floor. A few blocks away in a dusty, candle-smoke-clouded church, the faithful inch their way on their knees to the altar while others line up to kiss the foot of a dark image called "The Black Nazarene."

On an average Sunday, only two men and five women out of a hundred Filipino Catholics attend mass. One reason for low church attendance is the absence of pastoral care, for even at this late date the number of priests is woefully inadequate—only one priest to 6,500 members on the average. But half of these priests are assigned to Catholic seminaries, colleges, orphanages, and other institutions, so there is only one functioning parish priest to every 12,500 members! As one parish priest remarked to me, "When I have married the youth, baptized the babies, and buried the dead in any one day, I don't have time for anything else." I remarked to him, "Your city has forty thousand people. How many priests do you have?" "Three," he replied.

A Belgian priest made a survey to find out how much the average Catholic knows about his faith. He walked along the street and stopped a young man with a crucifix on a string around his neck, obviously a Roman Catholic. "Who is that on the cross?" the priest asked. "I don't know," the young man replied. The answer was not uncommon.

One reminder of the medieval matrix of the church is the Good Friday spectacle of penitents and flagellants, still staged in many places. Stripped to the waist, their back already ripped by knives or broken pop bottles, the flagellants walk slowly through the streets, whipping their backs with thongs while the blood runs down their trousers and drips off onto the ground. On the same day other men are tied or nailed to a cross and lifted high for all to see.

"Why have you allowed them to nail you to a cross?" a missionary once asked a crucified penitent.

"So my sins will be forgiven," the crucified man replied.

The situation, however, is changing. For the first time in its 415 years in the Philippines, the Roman Catholic church appears to be modernizing and adopting a live-and-let-live policy toward other faiths. In the spirit of Vatican II, images are being reduced in number and toned down in significance. Roman Catholic priests (some of the brave ones!) are demanding that the hierarchy sell the church's extensive rice lands to the tenants who farm them. And a new interest is being shown in translating, distributing, teaching, and reading the Bible. Some priests are attending evangelical home Bible study groups.

Protestant reaction to all this varies widely, from appreciation for reformation in the Roman Catholic church to suspicion that these are political moves to snare the unsuspecting. Both of these extreme reactions can hardly be correct at the same time. Wherever the truth may lie, the main issue is not what Protestants think of the situation inside the Roman Catholic church but what Protestants will do to further evangelism in this obviously improved climate and to insure that evangelical churches are scripturally sound and spiritually alive.

CULTURAL MINORITY EVANGELISM

Any survey of the Christian scene in the Philippines would be incomplete without a look at the cultural minorities: the Chinese community, the aboriginal tribes, and the Muslims of Mindanao and Sulu. The Muslims make up about 4 percent of the population, and both Catholic and Protestant missions are notably unfruitful among them. Congregations in which most of the members are Muslim converts total only four or five. Philippine Muslims, therefore, may be likened to the Muslims of Malaysia and south Thailand in their resistance to the gospel message—far cry from the responsiveness of Indonesia, where thousands have been baptized into the Christian church in the last few years.

Protestants have found a better reception among the Chinese, who total some four hundred thousand (see chapter 19, "Overseas Chinese"). The Chinese Protestants have forty churches, the largest of which in Manila and Cebu have a Sunday morning attendance of 450. While some belong to denominations, most of these churches are financially independent and only loosely identified with American missions or churches. Many are composed of mainland refugees. The Chinese churches are theologically conservative, and their involvement in both home and foreign missions has increased since the Second World War.

The Protestant church is also spreading among the tribal people. (Tribal churches are those among the approximately half million Filipino people whose background is animism and who, for the most part, live high in the mountains or deep in the jungles of Luzon, Mindanao, Palawan, and Mindoro. "Lowlanders" comprise the vast majority of Filipino people, who come from a Roman Catholic background.) Two pioneer missions chose to work among the cultural minorities—the Christian and Missionary Alliance and the Episcopalians. While to this day the principal evangelical testimony to Muslims is borne by the Christian and Missionary Alliance church in the Philippines (CAMACOP), most of their 20,031 members (as of 1968) are among the tribes and lowland settlers. The Episcopal church has continued to minister among the tribes of north Luzon and Mindanao and reports a current communicant membership of 22,536. Interestingly enough, the "Concordat of Full Communion" which Episcopalians entered into in 1961 with the Aglipayan or Philippine Independent (Catholic) church has had the effect of spreading the interest of the Episcopalians in the general lowlands population. This trend promises to increase during the decade of the seventies.

Some whole tribes or sections of tribes have become evangelical Christians: the Davao Bagobos through the ministry of the Christian and Missionary Alliance, the northern Palawanos of Palawan island through the New Tribes mission, and the Binokid of Bukidnon, Mindanao, through the ABWE. The usual Protestant approach, however, is extractive (emphasizing individual conversion and baptism) rather than holistic. This is true, for instance, of New Tribes mission work among the Ilongots of Eastern Luzon, the UCCP work among the Kalasan of Northern Luzon, and Overseas Missionary Fellowship work among the Mangyan of Mindoro, where the Christian community makes up 10 percent of the total tribal population of twenty thousand.

On the other hand, the Missouri Synod Lutherans are using a holistic approach among the tribes of Mountain province, northern Luzon. It is too early, however, to evaluate their methods. The approach of the Summer Institute of Linguistics, though basically technical (language reduction, literacy, and Bible translation), has nevertheless brought eighteen local churches into being among the tribes.

The aboriginal tribes of the Philippines are moving, finally but fast, into the twentieth century, with an openness to change and innovation as never before seen in their history. Now it is time for the evangelical church to reexamine its extractive approach and to press hard for the conversion of whole tribes with the prayer that, under the empowerment of the Holy Spirit, the tribal people will move into the full stream of Filipino life with the full blessing of the gospel of Christ.

It would be misleading to close this postwar summary of the Philippine church picture without pointing out that all is not promising. There are disquieting, obstructive factors.

1) The evangelical church is still too American to be truly Filipino. Unfortunately, the more conservative a church is, the more American it appears.

2) The closing of some Bible schools which had trained men and women on the lower education levels threatens to cut the nerve of evangelism in many barrios, where the majority of the Filipinos (80 percent of whom are farmers and fishermen) still live. It is estimated that of all the churches in the Philippines, over 50 percent have no pastor; most of these are barrio churches. "Theological education by extension" may be the answer—evangelicals training workers and lay leaders for these churches after the pattern of the successful Seventh-Day Adventists.
3) No program has yet been devised by any evangelical group to adequately meet the challenge of the inner cities, particularly Manila.
4) Perhaps the most disturbing fact on the Protestant scene in the Philippines today is fear of the future. Riots and demonstrations since 1970, the new constitution in 1972, the insistent threat of communist guerrillas in the hinterland and of communist intellectuals in the universities—all these have produced a pessimism that threatens to paralyze evangelistic and church-planting initiative.

Nation and People

Lying off the southeast coast of the Asian mainland are the seven hundred islands of the semitropical Philippine archipelago. Here in the sixth-largest nation of non-communist Asia live over forty million people, increasing at the remarkable rate of 3.3 percent, or over a million a year (though it is still not a critical problem, for Japan supports almost three times this many people on the same land area).

The capital city of the isles is greater Manila, a sprawling, brawling, boiling metropolis of 3½ million people. One Filipino in ten lives within a radius of fifteen miles of the Manila city hall. Factory work, white-collar jobs, and the many universities, colleges, and high schools of the metropolitan area are the magnets which draw the people in an unending stream from the hinterlands. Once in the big city, "Juan de la Cruz" refuses to turn back the clock—or his steps—to the barrio (village) life he knew as a child. To care for this influx of humanity, many new housing developments are springing up in cornfields and rice paddies on the edges of the city, and new shacks appear daily in already-overcrowded slums, such as Tondo and San Andres Bukid. Unfortunately, the Christian church has been slow to adjust to this kaleidoscopic change, and today there are areas in greater Manila larger than many an American city with no evangelical witness.

Other cities are also bursting at the seams: Cebu city, Baguio, Bacolod, Davao, Iligan. Yet even today, in spite of the rapid urbanization the average Filipino (more than 55 percent) is a farmer plodding behind a plow pulled by a reluctant water buffalo . . . or a fisherman throwing his net into the sea like Peter, James, and John did on the Sea of Galilee. But universally the ambition of farmer and fisherman alike is to scrape enough from nature to send his children to school in hopes of a better life for them than he himself has had. Even the poorest Filipino is mesmerized by the magic of education, feeling that it is the key which will open the door to a bright new tomorrow. Perhaps this idea came from forty-five years of American tutelage. Now every barrio has its school, and there are no truant officers. One cannot keep the children *out* of school! Education is the largest single item on the budget of the Philippine government; half its entire income goes for schooling. The teachers form a tight little segment of society, respected and admired, the spearhead of a growing, knowledgeable, influential middle class.

To single out teachers as representatives of the middle class emphasizes how really small it is when compared, for instance, to the predominantly middle-class societies of Canada, Australia, or New Zealand. Filipino society falls into four divisions: the wealthy, comprising perhaps 3 percent of the population; the comfortable, 15 percent; the common man, 80 percent; and the very poor, about 2 percent.

Thus in Filipino society the laboring class, Juan de la Cruz and his friends, totals four times the three other economic classes combined. Even though poverty in the Philippines is not the harsh, hopeless condition of the very poor in some other Asian countries, still four out of five Filipinos are poor by western standards. The contrasts are shocking: a palatial concrete palace with extravagant baroque decorations sits beside a demi-house of forty metal drums, flattened out and thrown together to form the walls and roof of a squatter's hut.

Lack of communication, transportation, and lack of confidence in each other and in the future have held back the Filipinos. Accidents of geography have been partly to blame for this. Living on seven hundred different islands hinders the people from mingling freely and knowing each other. Formidable, stark mountain ranges rise to ten thousand feet, further fragmenting and dividing the country. Over the centuries this isolation bred by sea and mountain has produced a cacophony of languages. Dr. Richard Pittman, pioneer Wycliffe Bible translator in the islands, estimates that there are sixty-seven languages in the Philippines, subdivided into hundreds of minor languages and dialects. This babel of voices has fostered still more isolation and seriously increased the difficulty of spreading the gospel.

Though Tagalog is the official national language, English is the real lingua franca of the Philippines, for it is used in government, business, education, and communication. Only three other languages are used widely—Ilocano, Ilongo, and Cebuano, the heart language of more people than any other. Fortunately, the Bible has been translated into all four of these major languages.

Class and social position in the Philippines is determined mainly by wealth. Since government is the biggest business in the islands, the greedy seek political office for gain, a situation which has produced widespread graft, corruption, nepotism, and inefficiency. One FEGC missionary was an apparent victim of this in 1970. A local police chief stopped the missionary's panel truck and asked for his driver's license. When he reached for it, the policeman shot him dead. A political appointee of the president, the policeman's trial dragged on over two years, until he was finally acquitted fully.

National History

Historians opine that in the dim predawn of Filipino culture a land bridge connected the mainland of southeast Asia with what we know today as the Philippine archipelago, and that the first ancestors of present-day Negritos (pygmies) walked across the land bridge to the Philippines. By this theory the "little blacks," as the word "Negrito" means, would be the original inhabitants of the country.

Then came waves of migrations from what are today Indonesia and the Malay peninsula—the Malayo-Polynesian people—in canoes hewn out of great trees from the tropical forests. These migrants felt their way along the coasts of Borneo, then wound through the myriad islands of the Sulu archipelago up to Mindanao. Or they braved the austere coasts of Palawan island to land on Mindoro or Luzon. Chinese arrived from south China in great seagoing junks. Even to this day many cultural and vocabulary items and even some physical characteristics betray the Chinese ancestry of perhaps 10 percent of the Filipino people.

Ferdinand Magellan introduced the Philippine islands to the western world in 1531, when he claimed them for Spain and the Catholic religion on his historic globe-circling voyage. The Spanish hold on the islands was strengthened in the next two generations, resulting in a centralized colonial government and social system which was strongly influenced by the church. Under this the Filipinos rebelled periodically but with little success.

The man who did the most to further the cause of Filipino nationalism, however, was a man of peace who never lifted a hand against Spain. He was Jose Rizal, a medical doctor and author of two great Filipino novels, *Noli Me Tangere* and *El Filibusterismo*. These novels dramatically articulated the complaints of the Filipino people against Spain and led to the public execution of their author by Spanish authorities. His martyrdom provided what nothing else could at that time—a rallying point for a people deeply emotional but traditionally isolated from one another.

The third era in Filipino history began with the destruction of the Spanish fleet in Manila Bay by Admiral Dewey in 1898, ending the Spanish-American War. As a result, Spain ceded the islands to the U.S. in 1898, which immediately began to develop institutions, schools, and civil service with an eye to the eventual establishment of a free, democratic government. In 1935 the Philippines became a self-governing commonwealth under President Manuel Quezon and functioned effectively until the Japanese conquered the isles in May 1942. Under their occupation, with the rough guerrilla warfare and the devastating battles of liberation, the country suffered tragic physical and economic damage and complete governmental breakdown. Despite this, however, a year after liberation from the Japanese the restored Philippine islands became the independent Republic of the Philippines in accordance with the original U.S. mandate (Tydings-McDuffie Act) of 1935. The new government, patterned largely after the U.S., has functioned democratically since that time, though with great centralization and vast power in the hands of officials in Manila. The communist Huk rebellion in 1945-53 was suppressed, and the nation has continued to progress since then.

Headed toward free enterprise and with two billion dollars of U.S. assistance, the economy has performed impressively. The GNP has grown an average of over 5 percent a year for the last eight years. Thanks to "miracle rice" and government development programs, the country is now largely self-sustaining in food. Industry and foreign trade are growing, though too slowly. The U.S. is still the Philippines' major trading partner.

On the international scene the new nation has been aligned solidly with the West as an active member of the UN, SEATO, and other free-world groups. The nation's major international tension arose in the sixties over the recognition of the new state of Malaysia, which incorporated into itself the province of Sabah in North Borneo—an area which the Philippines claim.

To consolidate these seven hundred islands with their poor communication and to unite the language groups has demanded a strong national government and leadership. Many inexperienced and often unscrupulous men have been brought into power. Though neither coup nor revolution has marred the brief history of the new R.P.I., as a result of reputed corruption in 1970, opposition to the government erupted in many protest marches and riots. These disorders bore the marks of communist manipulation. After a generation of little better than bandit-band survival in the rural areas, the communist guerrillas (Huks) suddenly found that disorders on the streets were tailor-made to their designs. Significantly, the armed forces remained loyal to the government, a fact which has not always been true among Spain's ex-colonies in Latin America.

Continued unrest and bloodletting riots in Mindanao climaxed in late '72 with President Ferdinand Marcos declaring the nation under martial law.‡ Almost coincidentally this act followed the adoption by referendum of a totally new constitution, the result of two years of work on the part of an elective constitutional convention. Under the referendum's provisions the president may indefinitely succeed himself. Tight as the new rule was, life continued largely undisturbed except for an apparent diminution of crime in the cities. The military also aided and accelerated the Manila urban renewal and relocation programs. Thus by early 1973 the nation was enjoying a restive peace which was welcomed by the churches, for many of the demonstrations had anti-American and anti-Chinese overtones, affecting the churches and missions.

Christian History

THE ARRIVAL OF ROMAN CATHOLICISM

When Ferdinand Magellan discovered the Philippines for Spain in March 1521, he landed on the small island of Limasawa, erected a wooden cross, and symbolically claimed all the islands for the Roman Catholic church. A few days later he raised another cross in what is now Cebu city. But Magellan lost his life there; his decimated force limped back to Spain; and the conquest of the Philippine islands temporarily lapsed.

The Roman cross did not plant its lengthening shadow on Philippine soil until forty-four years later, when Father Andres de Urdaneta and four other Augustinian missionary monks arrived with Conquistador Miguel Lopez de Legaspi. These five Augustinian monks landed behind the muskets, cannon, and armorplate of the conquering Spanish forces, and this relationship continued for three centuries of Spain's rule with church and state, cross and crown, cassock and cannon interlocked and interdependent. Any tourist today can see this relationship depicted in the Legaspi-Urdaneta Monument at the southwest corner of the old city wall, which shows the armor-clad conquistador grasping the flag of Spain and the monk holding the cross high over the two of them.

The early missionaries began their work in Cebu and Manila, two cities that remain strongholds of Catholicism to this day. But these pioneer missionaries did not stay in the cities. As reinforcements arrived from Spain they fanned out into the hinterland. The amazing record is that

‡Ed. note. This was apparently not a "religious war," as has been reported by some, but a struggle of the minority community to have equal rights. In this struggle both Muslims and Christians stood shoulder to shoulder. Unfortunately, however, outside powers have attempted to take advantage of this unrest to woo people to anti-government and violent-action camps.

within forty-five years of Urdaneta's arrival the entire country at least nominally was in the fold of the Roman Catholic church, with the exception of the aborigines in their mountain bastions and the Muslims of Mindanao and the Sulu archipelago. (To this day these aboriginal peoples in the high mountains and deep jungles of North Luzon, Mindoro, Palawan, and Mindanao hold to the pre-Spanish animism of the original Filipinos, while the Muslims in the southern isles of Sulu and Mindanao still hold to the Islamic faith first introduced from Arabia via Malaya in the fourteenth century.)

In their definitive compilation Blair and Robertson observe that the many Catholic religious orders were the real rulers of the lands during these centuries.

> From the beginning the Spanish establishments in the Philippines were a mission and not in the proper sense of the term of a colony. They were founded and administered in the interest of religion rather than of commerce or industry. . . . In examining the political administration of the Philippines, then, we must be prepared to find a sort of outer garment under which the living body is ecclesiastical.[4]

From the standpoint of the evangelical Christian, several factors in the early history of the Roman Catholic church are noteworthy:

1) The Bible was withheld from the people. Spanish Bibles were restricted, and no translation into a local language was permitted.
2) Filipino priests were not promoted to positions of eminence. Indeed, as late as 1870 less than 25 percent of the ordinary parishes were in the hands of the Filipino priests.
3) The average member was not taught the doctrines of the church. His daily life continued to be governed by beliefs carried over from the animism and spirit-worship of pre-Spanish days.
4) There was no religious liberty. It was not merely that Roman Catholicism was the preferred faith: the propagation of any other faith was forbidden under pain of imprisonment.

The mainstay of Spain's control of the Philippines was the friar. An old viceroy of colonial Mexico used to say, "In each friar in the Philippines the king had a captain-general and a whole army."[5]

On the local level such a position meant great power. One of the sorest points was the church's large land holdings. The friars were the absentee landlords and the Filipinos were the tenants, so many of the friars came to be cordially hated by the Filipinos. This was one of the provocations that led to the revolt against Spain in 1896, a revolt which eventually involved the United States and led to independence and the opening up of the Philippines to the gospel message.

THE ARRIVAL OF THE EVANGELICAL FAITH

As in 1565 Roman Catholic missionaries arrived behind Spanish armor, so in much the same way Protestant missionaries rode the supply wagons of the United States army to carry the gospel message to the Filipino people, after Commodore George Dewey won the battle of Manila bay on May 1, 1898. Only three weeks after the battle, Dr. George F. Pentecost laid before the 1898 General Assembly of the Presbyterian Church in the U.S.A. the responsibility of American Christians to evangelize the Filipino people. Baptist and Methodist leaders met with Presbyterians to discuss how to begin missionary work, and the first Presbyterian missionary, Rev. James B. Rodgers, arrived in Manila a few days less than a year after the battle of Manila bay.

Did these early missionaries merely hold onto Uncle Sam's coattails, following wherever American military forced open a door? Hardly, unless Paul and Barnabas could be accused of merely cashing in on the imperialism of ancient Rome when they walked the military roads to preach the gospel throughout the Roman empire.

In 1899, with Spain's hold on the Philippines breaking, a number of Protestant missions moved into the country within a decade, almost all from the United States.§ This unusual circumstance of eight church-planting missions beginning work in one country in the four years from 1899 to 1902 set the stage for one of the classic comity agreements of mission history, laying out a non-competitive plan to evangelize the islands. In a fresh, vigorous, and optimistic atmosphere the early missionaries met in Manila in April 1901 to organize the Evangelical Union, to choose a common name for all Protestant churches, and to fix geographical areas for each mission. The name chosen was Iglesia Evangelica (Evangelical Church). With later adjustments, the areas allocated to different missions were:

Methodists	most of Luzon north of Manila
Presbyterians	Luzon south of Manila and eastern Visayas

§When Spain lost its hold on the Philippines, the following missions were able to enter:

Missions	*Dates Entering the Philippines*
Presbyterians	1899
Bible Societies (American, British, and others)	1899
Methodists	1900
Northern Baptists	1900
United Brethren	1901
Disciples of Christ	1901
Protestant Episcopals	1901
Congregationalists	1902
Christian and Missionary Alliance	1902
Seventh-Day Adventists	1905

United Brethren	Mountain Province and La Union Province
Disciples of Christ	Ilocos, Abra, and some Tagalog towns
Northern Baptists	western Visayas
Congregationalists	Mindanao, except the western
Christian and Missionary Alliance	western Mindanao and the Sulu archipelago
The city of Manila	open to all groups

Of the early missions, two did not enter into comity agreements: the Seventh-Day Adventists, who decided they would go to all sections of the country, and the Episcopalians, who held that the Roman Catholic church was a sister communion among whom they would not proselyte. They decided to go to the non-Catholics—the Muslims, the Caucasians, the Chinese of the cities, and the non-Christian tribes of the mountains. The comity agreements worked well at first but with diminishing effectiveness after World War I; after World War II the comity agreement died.

Though most missions began their work in Manila, which was even then the hub of the country, it was not long before they fanned out from Manila and set up centers throughout the islands. The missions went to work in earnest. Their preaching was dogmatic and iconoclastic. With the exception of the Episcopalians, the pioneer missionaries looked upon the Roman Catholic majority as people in need of the transforming experience of the new birth and therefore in need of the message they had come to deliver. By and large the initial thrust of all Protestant missions was evangelism and church-planting.

American Presbyterians have the distinction of sending the first Protestant missionary to live and work in the Philippines. James B. Rodgers sailed into Manila Bay on April 21, 1899. He was destined to spend forty years in the Philippines. "As Augustinian friar Urdaneta had arrived with Spanish cannon and muskets, so Presbyterian missionary Rodgers arrived under the protection of American artillery and Springfield rifles" (Tuggy and Tolliver, *Seeing the Church in the Philippines*, p. 18).

Soon other Presbyterian missionaries arrived. They pushed evangelism and church planting so effectively that within ten years communicant membership totalled 10,000. During the next decades, however, the rate of growth faltered and slowed—to 16,661 by 1919 and to only 19,430 by 1929. This decreased rate of growth coincided with the placing of attention, time, personnel, and money on institutions rather than on direct evangelism and Bible teaching.

By 1929, too, much energy of the leaders among the Presbyterians was being channeled into efforts at merging. Indeed, this was no new stance for the Presbyterians. They were prime movers in the founding in 1901 of the Evangelical Union, a loose association of Protestant missions which set the comity bounds of evangelical missions in the Philippines. Organic union on the church level was finally achieved during the first general assembly of the United Evangelical church, held in Manila in March 1929. The Presbyterians brought in two-thirds of the total membership of 27,827 (1931 total); other members came from the United Brethren, Congregationalists, and the United Church of Manila.

This church was the forerunner of the United Church of Christ in the Philippines, finally and formally organized at a conference held in May 1948 at Ellinwood-Malate Church, Manila. Others joining the original United church were Disciples of Christ, Philippine Methodist church (independent), and individual congregations of various denominations. In the earlier union movement missionaries took most of the initiative,[6] but of the leaders forming the new church in 1948, 80 percent were Filipino. The mission boards which were involved discontinued their operation per se and set up an "Interboard Office" to care for foreign personnel and finance. The missionaries became "fraternal workers," serving in support capacities or doing special jobs. All local financing, from the deaconesses through the moderators, is Filipino, but projects, institutions, and the central office in Quezon City (including salaries of the four bishops) are still heavily supported from abroad.

Noticeably absent from both the 1929 United Evangelical church merger and the 1948 United Church of Christ merger in the Philippines were American Baptists and Methodists. To this day they remain separate and distinct bodies.

The first count of members of the United Church of Christ in the Philippines (1951) showed 96,261. By 1966 the merged church totaled 145,464 members and was the largest Protestant church in the country. Today the United Church of Christ in the Philippines and most other National Christian Council-related churches are still growing, but not at the remarkable rate of Presbyterians and Methodists in their first decade, nor as fast as some non-NCC-related groups are growing today, notably Seventh-Day Adventists, Assemblies of God, Southern Baptists, and Foursquare Gospel church.

Among pioneer Protestant churches in the Philippines the Methodists got off to the fastest start. By 1911 they had baptized twenty thousand members, more than all other Protestants combined. They maintained this lead up to World War II, when they were the largest single denomination in the country. The early Presbyterian missionary, James B. Rodgers, gives one reason for the large additions:

"Our Methodist brethren have devoted themselves almost exclusively to evangelistic work and to the development of the churches."[7]

The Methodists have had no secular educational institutions comparable to Central Philippines University of the Baptists or to Silliman University of the Presbyterians—projects that have demanded a tremendous input of missionary manpower and money. And Philippines Methodists have not been too concerned about ecumenism; they did not merge with the United Evangelical church in 1929, nor did they join the United Church of Christ in the Philippines in 1948. They have, however, cooperated freely in such cross-denominational projects as Union Theological Seminary in Manila and in umbrella organizations, such as the National Christian Council. Their major emphasis has been on evangelism, which has paid off in consistent growth to the present.

Pioneer Baptist missionaries began work in 1900 in Jaro, near the port of Iloilo on Panay island. Shortly afterward, W. O. Valentine started the Jaro Industrial School, later to develop into the prestigious Central Philippines University. The mission then established a chain of private academies (high school level) on neighboring Negros islands, plus a dormitory school in Bacolod, capital of Negros Occidental. Valentine was committed not only to education but also to evangelism, so Baptist churches sprang up in and around the academies.

In 1912 the American Baptist Foreign Mission Society adopted the "intensive policy"—that already-opened work should be developed in depth before beginning new work in new places. This meant the development of institutions, particularly Central Philippines University and its related Iloilo Mission Hospital, and the concentration of manpower, money, and interest in the Iloilo area rather than exploiting the evangelistic possibilities of Negros island. This policy led directly to the resignation of Dr. Raphael Thomas, director of the Iloilo Mission Hospital, and to the founding of what later became the Association of Baptists for World Evangelism (ABWE) in 1928.

Following their split with the American Baptists, members of the new Association of Baptists for World Evangelism opened the Doane Evangelistic Institute, which quickly gave them the nickname "Doane Baptists." Their Bible school graduates and foreign missionaries fanned out to such far places as Palawan island (the southwesternmost isle in the archipelago) and the typhoon-plagued Bataan islands, between the Philippines and Taiwan.

Despite the decision, however, many American Baptists and their related Convention Baptist churches continued extensive rural evangelism with an aggressive Bible school training program in the western Negros Occidental province alongside the Fellowship Baptists of the ABWE. Both have seen above-average growth in that area.

Arriving a couple of years after the big nine missions, the Seventh-Day

Adventists had a very slow start. They baptized less than one member a year for the first six years. But the first missionary, R. A. Caldwell, was a diligent colporteur, as were all his successors. Soon the trickle of Adventist literature swelled to the flood described earlier. Concentration on literature and a strategic use of many related methods has made the SDA's possibly the most successful of all Protestant missionary ventures in the Philippines.

STRATEGIES AND TRENDS

An early analyst of Protestant missions would soon have detected differences in method: the Presbyterians became involved in hospitals and schools; the Christian and Missionary Alliance emphasized spiritual fellowship and was slow to formally organize a national church; the Methodists put into effect their historic program of a graded leadership. Despite these differences Protestants met a cold reception among the upper class, but found a better hearing among those of middle and lower income brackets. But even though it was from the lower income class that converts were being won, not all missions made large efforts among them. It is hard to escape the impression that the Protestants by default left the poor to the native cult, the Iglesia ni Cristo, which was to gather large numbers of low-income converts in the decades following World War I.

Strangely enough, the battles for the living were often fought out among the dead. Cemeteries became a live issue in the Protestant-Catholic conflict. Before 1898 every burying ground was owned by the Roman Catholic church. Only by great effort under the American rule was a new law passed that every town should have a public, non-sectarian cemetery. Still today there are scores if not hundreds of towns with only a Catholic cemetery. A potent taunt in the mouths of both priest-in-pulpit and people-in parish is, "If you join the Protestants you will have no one to bury you!"

One day I asked an elderly woman who seemed soundly converted, "Aling Maria, when are you going to be baptized?"

"Oh, I can't be baptized as a Protestant," she said; "we do not have a public cemetery here, and there would be no one to bury me!"

Early in the century two diametrically opposed forces were at work in Philippine Protestantism (as seen above)—a drive toward unity and a drift toward division. The first split of note was among the Methodists in 1909, led by Rev. Nicolas Zamora, resulting in the formation of the Iglesia Evangelica Methodista en las Islas Filipinas. Later a parallel split from the Presbyterian church saw the formation of Iglesia Evangelica Unida de Cristo, or "Unida." Both Methodist and Presbyterian splits were due more to personal differences than to doctrinal devotion. On the other hand, the urge to unite, articulated as early as 1901 in the founding of the Evangelical Union, continued on through the years and later found fruition in such bodies as the Federation of the Christian Churches and the United Church of Christ in the Philippines.

Until the Second World War the original nine missions had almost a clear field. The only other Protestant missions arriving between 1905 and 1941 were the Salvation Army, Pilgrim Holiness, Assemblies of God, Christian Missions in Many Lands (Plymouth Brethren), and several branches of the Church of Christ. The Association of Baptists for World Evangelism was organized in the Philippines by missionaries breaking from the American Baptists. They were later officially recognized by the General Association of Regular Baptists (GARB) in North America and then spread to other lands.

INDIGENOUS CHURCHES AND SECTS

While not many new American missionary societies appeared in the Philippines until after the Second World War, during the first four decades of the century a unique phenomenon was developing which, even to this day, has not been adequately recognized by either Roman Catholic or Protestant church leaders. That was the beginning of many religious groups which often could not be properly called either Catholic or Protestant, but were sometimes mixtures of both, plus generous additions of spiritism, nationalism, Masonic doctrines and practices, philosophy, theosophy, Unitarianism, humanism, and a multitude of ancient indigenous beliefs. A whopping total of 368 religious groups are registered with the government.[8] Of this total, 38 indigenous groups list their origin between 1899 and 1941. This was a mere trickle, however, compared to the spate of indigenous groups that have flooded the Philippine religious market from the Second World War until the present. Elwood lists 179 groups organized between 1942 and 1967.[9]

What do these churches and sects believe and practice? Some represent natural and vigorous church growth along indigenous lines, e.g., Philippine Missionary Fellowship, Chinese Christian Gospel Center, Fellowship of Christian Churches of Southern Luzon, and the Association of Baptist Churches in Luzon, Visayas, and Mindanao. But the very names of many others conjure up their unusual beliefs and practices: "The Church of God Economic Production and Brotherhood"; "Wheel of the Life of Faith in God"; "Philippine National Schismatic Church"; "Patriotic Church of our Lord Jesus Christ"; "The Sacred Philippine Church of the Five Vowels and Virtues Holy Land of Jerusalem"; "Association of Three Persons, One God: National Prayer for the Peace of the Country"; "Universal Religion of Universal Equality, Fraternity, and Liberty"; et al. Anyone familiar with the Filipino trait of *ningas cogon* (flash-in-the-pan) would expect that many of these organizations may long since have sputtered into a well-earned oblivion. But all have not died.

The Iglesia ni Cristo, whose elaborate church buildings with their pseudo-Byzantine spires stand out on the skyline of most towns and cities of importance in the Philippines, dramatizes this. Founded in 1914 by Felix Manalo, this group lists a total of 2,228 local congregations in its official yearbook.[10] The "Church Growth Research in the Philippines" organization in a report published in 1972 estimates that the current membership of this group may be as high as 430,000, or approximately three times the size of the largest single Protestant denomination, the United Church of Christ.[11]

What, then, is the Iglesia ni Cristo? Felix Manalo was converted in 1902 and aligned himself successively with the Methodists, the Disciples of Christ, and the Seventh-Day Adventists. He then came into contact with the Unitarians, from whom he adopted the view that Christ was only man. Manalo's eschatology reflects the Jehovah's Witnesses, but with the peculiarity that he himself was the "angel ascending from the east" (Rev 7:2). The Iglesia ni Cristo is syncretistic, simplistic, unitarian, and nationalistic. Just now it is giving the Roman Catholic hierarchy more concern than all Philippine Protestantism lumped together because of its dogmatic proselyting. It garners its members principally from the lower-income brackets, among whom its belligerent propaganda methods are most effective.

While dramatic, the growth of the Iglesia ni Cristo is not an isolated phenomenon. Among the 179 native churches and cults that have sprung up since 1942, another, the "Crusaders of the Divine Church of Christ," claims a hundred thousand converts in the last fifteen years. This growth is nativistic and nationalistic, partaking of elements of both Catholicism and Pentecostalism. Some rural Baptist churches in the Ilocos area have been wiped out by mass movements into this group.

The Philippine Independent Church (Aglipayan) dates from the tumultuous days that marked the close of the Spanish era, when a revolutionary faction revolted against Spain, headed by one Isobelo de los Reyes. Identifying himself with them as chaplain was the Filipino priest Gregorio Aglipay. When he refused to recant and return, he was excommunicated by Archbishop Nozaleda in 1899. As a result Roman Catholics stampeded out of the church, until by 1906 one Filipino out of four had joined the Independent Church as the movement rode the flood tide of resentment against Spain and the friars. An intriguing and unanswerable question in Philippine church history is, "What would have happened if the Protestants and the Philippine Independent church had early joined hands?" Strangely enough, it was Aglipay's apparent acceptance of certain Unitarian doctrines introduced to him by American Governor-General William Howard Taft that later closed the door to such rapprochement.

All his life Aglipay was plagued by the problem of apostolic succession. Being Catholic, he accepted this as a tenet of faith, but no bishop had defected with Aglipay. Finally he was consecrated "Supreme Bishop" by a council of priests—not by a council of bishops. The gap was finally bridged after Aglipay's death by the American Episcopal church, which bestowed their own apostolic succession on three priests of the Independent church in 1948.

The Independent church ran aground and almost foundered on the shoals of a 1909 Supreme Court decision stating that regardless of the defection of priest or people in any parish church, the property still belonged to the Roman hierarchy. Until this day the Independent church has not recovered from that blow. Probably the majority are still as ignorant of evangelical truth as their Roman forebears.

Conclusion

In the onion-layered culture of the Philippines today there are stirrings in the heart. It is undoubtedly a day of opportunity for both established churches and missions. Certain strategies, notably literature and home Bible study groups, have proven effective. Concentrating on these, the nationwide COW movement may be God's tool to unite all evangelicals in a truly nationwide, in-depth thrust that will see the psuedo-Christian Philippines biblically evangelized in this generation.

NOTES

1. Douglas J. Elwood, *Contemporary Churches and Sects in the Philippines,* p. 28.
2. Leonard Tuggy and Ralph Tolliver, *Seeing the Church in the Philippines,* p. 163.
3. *World Population Data Sheet* (Washington: Pop. Ref. Bureau), 1972.
4. Kenneth Scott Latourette, *A History of the Expansion of Christianity,* 5:266.
5. Emma Helen Blair and James Allen Robertson, *The Philippine Islands,* 1:41-42.
6. Walter N. Roberts, *The Filipino Church,* p. 142.
7. James B. Rodgers, *Forty Years in the Philippines,* p. 3.
8. Elwood, *Churches,* p. 124.
9. Ibid., pp. 75-124.
10. *55th Anniversary of the Iglesia ni Cristo,* 1969.
11. *Seeing the Church in the Philippines* (Manila, 1972), p. 140.

BIBLIOGRAPHY

Achutegui, Pedro S. de, and Bernad, Miguel A. *Religious Revolution in the Philippines: The Life and Church of Gregorio Aglipay, 1860-1960.* 2 vols.

Anderson, Gerald H., ed. *Studies in Philippine Church History.* Ithaca: Cornell University Press, 1969.

Blair, Emma Helen, and Robertson, James Alexander. *The Philippine Islands.* 53 vols. Cleveland: Arthur H. Clark Co., 1903 et seq.

Brown, Arthur Judson. *The New Era in the Philippines.* New York: Fleming H. Revell Co., 1903.

———. *One Hundred Years: A History of the Foreign Missionary Work of the Presbyterian Church in the U.S.A., with some Account of Countries, Peoples, and the Policies and Problems of Modern Missions.* New York: Fleming H. Revell Co., 1936.

Coxill, H. Wakelin, and Grubb, Sir Kenneth, eds. *World Christian Handbook, 1962.* London: Lutterworth Press, 1962-68.

Dean, John Marvin. *The Cross of Christ in Bolo-Land.* Chicago, New York, Toronto: Fleming H. Revell Co., 1902.

Dick, William McCullough. "Home Bible Studies Paper." A paper read before the Lowland Workers' Conference, Philippines Field, Overseas Missionary Fellowship, Balayan Bay, April 3, 1968.

Elwood, Douglas J. "Contemporary Churches and Sects in the Philippines." *The Southeast Asia Journal of Theology,* Oct. 1967.

———. *Churches and Sects in the Philippines: A Descriptive Study of Contemporary Religious Group Movements.* Dumaguete City: Silliman University, 1968.

Gowling, Peter G. *Islands Under the Cross: The Story of the Church in the Philippines.* Manila: National Council of Churches in the Philippines, 1967.

Hibbard, D. S. *Making a Nation.* New York: The Board of Foreign Missions of the Presbyterian Church in the U.S.A., 1926.

Higdon, E. K., and Higdon, I. W. *From Carabao to Clipper.* New York: Friendship Press, 1941.

Jagor, Feodor. *Travels in the Philippines.* London: Chapman and Hall, 1875.

Laquian, Apriodicio A. *Slums Are for People.* Manila: DM Press, 1969.

Latourette, Kenneth Scott. *A History of the Expansion of Christianity.* Vols. 1-4. New York and London: Harper and Bros., 1939.

Laubach, Frank C. "The Missionary Significance of the Last Ten Years: A Survey, Chapter IV in the Philippines." *International Review of Missions, Volume the Eleventh.* London: Edinburgh House, 1922.

———. *Seven Thousand Emeralds.* New York: Friendship Press, 1929.

Lim, Manuel (Bureau Secretary). *Handbook: Census, Philippine Statistics, 1903-1959.* Manila: Bureau of the Census and Statistics, 1960.

McGavran, Donald Anderson. *Multiplying Churches in the Philippines: Church Growth in the United Church of Christ in the Philippines.* Manila: United Church of Christ in the Philippines, 1958.

———. "The Independent Church in the Philippines: the Story of a Spiritual Quest." *Encounter,* Summer 1958.

Montgomery, James. *Why Churches Grow: the Foursquare Church in the Philippines.* Unpublished manuscript, 1968.

Neill, Stephen. *A History of Christian Missions.* Harmondsworth, Middlesex: Penguin Books, 1964.

Oliphant, Bill, ed. *Seventh-Day Adventists Today: A Report in Depth.* Nashville: Southern Publishing Assoc., 1966.

Olsen, M. Ellsworth. *A History of the Origin and Progress of Seventh-Day Adventists.* Washington: Review and Herald Publishing Assoc., 1925.

Osias, Camilo, and Lorenzana Avelina. *Evangelical Christianity in the Philippines.* Dayton: United Brethren Publishing House, 1931.

Philippine Missionary Directory. Manila: Philippine Crusades, 1966.

Presbyterian Church in the U.S.A., The. "Minutes of General Assembly which met the third Thursday of May, 1898." New York: The Presbyterian Church in the United States of America, 1898.

———. "Minutes of the General Assembly Board Reports." New York: The United Presbyterian Church in the United States of America, 1900 to 1966.

Roberts, Walter N. *The Filipino Church: The Story of the Development of an Indigenous Evangelical Church in the Philippine Islands as Revealed in the Work of "The Church of the United Brethren in Christ."* Dayton: Foreign Missionary Society and the Women's Missionary Society of the United Brethren in Christ, 1936.

Robertson, James Alexander. "Catholicism in the Philippine Islands." *The Catholic Historical Review,* Jan. 1918.

Rodgers, James B. *Forty Years in the Philippines: A History of the Philippine Mission of the Presbyterian Church in the United States of America.*

Sanger, J. P., Bureau Director. *Census of the Philippine Islands, 1903: Taken under the Direction of the Philippine Commission in the Year 1903.* 4 vols. Washington: U.S. Bureau of the Census, 1905.

Snead, Alfred C., ed. *Missionary Atlas: A Manual of the Foreign Work of the Christian and Missionary Alliance.* Harrisburg: Christian Publications, 1950.

Sobrepena, Enrique C. *That They May Be One: A Brief Account of the United Church Movement in the Philippines.* Manila: United Church of Christ in the Philippines, 1955.

Stuntz, Homer C. *The Philippines and the Far East.* New York: Eaton and Mains, and Cincinnati: Jennings and Pye, 1904.

Tolliver, Ralph E. *They Found the Way.* Manila: Overseas Missionary Fellowship, 1963.

Tolliver, Ralph E., ed. *Smuggler's Story: Ramon Cenit of the Philippines.* London: Overseas Missionary Fellowship, 1966.

Tuggy, Leonard, and Tolliver, Ralph. *Seeing the Church in the Philippines.* Manila: Overseas Missionary Fellowship, 1972.

Utt, Richard H. *A Century of Miracles.* Mountain View, Calif.: Pacific Press Publishing Association, 1966.

Whittemore, Lewis Bliss. *Struggle for Freedom: History of the Philippine Independent Church.* Greenwich, Conn.: Seabury Press, 1961.

Worcester, Dean C. *The Philippine Islands and Their People: A Record of Personal Observation and Experience, with a Short Summary of the More Important Facts in the History of the Archipelago.* New York: The MacMillan Co., 1899.

Zaide, Gregorio F. *Philippine History for High Schools.* Manila: The Modern Book Co., 1958.

Tiny Sikkim's only church building

Rev. C. T. Pazo, respected pioneer and leader of the Sikkim church

Photos by Billy Bray

25

SIKKIM

by Billy Bray

Introduction

Cradled in the heights of some of the world's loftiest peaks and virtually unknown to the world till her god-king married an American girl in 1963, tiny Sikkim is a lonely outpost of the church of Jesus Christ.

Though it is completely landlocked, with no airport and only a few roads recently opened . . . though it was almost overlooked by the great missionary movements of the nineteenth century . . . though like Nepal, Tibet, and Bhutan, Sikkim has on the whole successfully prevented the few Christian missionaries that have entered it from evangelizing its hundreds of tiny hamlets . . . yet a tiny church has taken root there and both grown and prospered. Christian Sikkimese play a significant role in government and other areas of influence. The so-called *Lepcha* or Sikkimese church is probably the most well-established Himalayan church.

The Church Today

Today there are fifteen hundred Christians in Sikkim (in a total population of two hundred thousand) and most of these are Lepchos by race.* Since evangelism in Sikkim was pioneered by the India mission of the Church of Scotland, this Lepcha church went with her sister Indian Presbyterian church into the United Church of North India in 1970. But this relation was criticized so strongly by the Sikkim government that now all references to the Indian church have been removed from letterheads and other publications.

A Lepcha boy from a good family went to Darjeeling on the Indian border to study early in this century; there he came to Christ under the

*Ed. note. There are also reasonable estimates of up to a thousand Nepalese Christians in Sikkim, some of whom may have been assimilated into the Sikkim churches.

For information on author, see chapter 4, "Bhutan."

guidance of pioneer Scottish missionaries. He later returned to Sikkim as a catechist to teach in a girls' school. Because he was a Lepcha, he was able to move in royal circles; his fine education and brilliance made him a trusted advisor and later a magistrate and member of the king's council. But all the while he was witnessing for Christ, and in reality he was the first pastor of the Sikkim church, though he was not recognized as such for some years.

Today Pastor C. T. Pazo is in his seventies, having guided the Christian community for over forty years. His tireless diplomacy has earned official recognition for the growing Christian community by the government. During his time the Christian church in the country has grown steadily both in influence and numbers. But there seems no one to replace him, and the whole church faces a leadership crisis. There are only two ordained ministers for the fifteen hundred Christians scattered over a wide area; 92 percent of these are Presbyterians related to the Scottish mission. There is at present no seminary or Bible institute in the country. Church services are largely based on a foreign liturgy and are conducted in languages other than Lepcha. While the government has encouraged the use of the Lepcha language, only a few gospels and portions of the Old Testament are in the mother tongue. Thus the Nepali Bible has largely replaced Lepcha in the national church.

Sikkim's small, scattered churches have youth and women's organizations. Ten Sunday schools have been established in the country, but hundreds could be established or supplemented with youth clubs, neighborhood Bible clubs, and youth centers, since there are reports of considerable enthusiasm among the youth for evangelism. In Gangtok, the capital city, the youth group of the only church in the city has an active, regular pattern of evangelism. Church growth, however, has come mainly through births into Christian families and from migration from India. In past years, when missionaries played a larger role, the church was involved in widespread social activities, primarily medicine and education. Today many individual Christians are still in the professions, but the church has turned over all its institutional work to the government except for a few schools. Thus it might be fair to say that while the established church has built up a large reservoir of goodwill from past social work and is now a recognized part of the religious establishment, evangelism by the church is very limited.

But recently smaller, newer Indian groups have won a few to Christ and established fellowship groups. The *Elsadai,* a Plymouth Brethren-type movement founded by Bakht Singh in India, has a handful of believers in the country who often hold street meetings and preach in the bazaars. Others, mostly Pentecostals from across the border in India, come in occasionally to preach and to blitz the bazaars with Christian literature. These activities, according to official church sources, frequently cause embarrassment to the recognized church leaders, who, when questioned by the government, are unable to explain exactly who the secret evangelists are.

The "All India Prayer Fellowship" in recent years has also added to church growth, along with some witness by Indian Christians on military bases in the country. Also hopeful for the church has been the return of some Sikkimese Christians from Kalimpong and Darjeeling in India.

Recently, Roman Catholics from India have also gained permission to have a priest and have opened a small Catholic center in an office building in downtown Gangtok. There the priest holds church services and a small catechetical school, but it is too early to report results.

Overt evangelism is naturally viewed as alien and suspicious by Sikkim authorities, who fear that it will cause division among Sikkim's predominantly Buddhist population. Thus open preaching in the bazaars and proselytism is usually forbidden, though anyone is permitted to change his religion (unlike nearby Nepal and Bhutan, where becoming a Christian is illegal). Particularly resented by the Buddhist Sikkimese are attacks upon their demon worship and idols, and church leaders in Gangtok have consistently urged Christians to preach the gospel without attacking Buddhism. Thus, to date there have not been any reports of violent opposition to Christians. Christian schools, clinics, and other institutions have been nationalized as a part of the nation's development, but this is not viewed as reflecting any special anti-Christian feeling.

Pressure from the Indian government has forced the gradual withdrawal of Scottish missionaries. Only one now remains, and as missionaries on the Sikkim borders disappear India is not allowing new ones to take their place. Scottish financial support is also gradually being phased out. There is little hope of foreign missionaries playing an increased role in Sikkim, say local people, unless they can provide specialized skills that both the Indian and Sikkim governments judge valuable. Gospel literature, radio, and audio-visual techniques have not been introduced to Sikkim, for the country is largely without a developed mass media. There is not a single radio station in all of Sikkim. Thus in this area modern Christian missions might possibly make an impact with specialized personnel not labeled as missionaries. Airfields could be cut for short-takeoff-and-landing aircraft, radio training could be introduced, and a Christian press could be established if funds and personnel were available. But Christians are not hopeful at the present.

The bulk of Sikkim's people is still largely unevangelized. Though Sikkim has the strongest church among the Himalayan nations, it flickers like a dim candle in the shadow of the towering mountains. Sikkim's relatively progressive political leadership might someday open the door to missionary evangelism, though it is doubtful at this time. Bible translation, publication, and distribution from nearby India could be a major contribution to evangelism temporarily. But a renewed church with a vision of evangelism is the greatest hope to reach Sikkim's small but unreached population in this generation. Pioneer Missionary MacFarlane's dream of using Sikkim as a steppingstone to Tibet, Bhutan, and Nepal has never been realized. But this too is not impossible if revival should touch the tiny church here.

Nation and People

Of the four Himalayan sisters—Nepal, Tibet, Sikkim, and Bhutan—none is considered more geostrategic than Sikkim. Mount Kanchenjunga, the world's third-highest peak at 28,162 feet, is just one of four peaks over 22,000 feet towering within Sikkim borders. The country's 2745 square miles are divided between lofty mountain ridges and deep valleys. Heavy rains fructify the entire land, whose climate ranges from subtropical to arctic. Sikkim's rains, high winds, and breathtaking mountains combine to produce some of the wildest beauty God has created.

Sikkim borders all the Himalayan kingdoms and India, so for centuries she lay astride the narrow "silk route" linking India with China. Today contact with the outside world depends mainly on a recently-opened highway which was built over the old Kalimpong-to-Lhasa mule track from India to Tibet. So far the mountains have delayed construction of an airport. And the cold war tensions in the 1950's suddenly cut the centuries-old movement of caravans through Sikkim and made her the hub of an Indian defense network protecting the approaches to the Natu La pass.

Since vast areas of northern Sikkim are snowbound year-round, most of the two hundred thousand people† live on the lower slopes of central, southern, and western Sikkim, where they farm small plots of maize, rice, potatoes, and 90 percent of the world's cardamom. A few living in the lower valleys herd sheep and yak. Population density is only seventy per square mile; 60 percent of the people own their own land.

Three major population groups make up the Sikkimese nation: Lepchas, Bhutias, and Nepalese, of which only the Lepchas are considered indigenous. Like the Bhutias, who came from Tibet in the thirteenth century, the Lepchas are Buddhist-animists and speak a Tibeto-Burman language. The Nepalese came in a wave of migration during the nineteenth century and now number over 70 percent of the population. These aggressive

†1971 estimate. The population growth rate is estimated to be 1.9 percent per year (*World Population Data Sheet,* June 1971).

Nepalese Hindus, bringing with them a powerful new pantheon of deities, profoundly upset the balance of political power and the economy in Sikkim. In recent years much of internal politics has been involved in balancing power between the culturally dominant Lepcha-Bhutia group and the economically and numerically superior Nepalese tribespeople.

Ruled by a *Chogyal*—a "god-king" who combines temporal and spiritual power—Sikkim is technically an absolute monarchy. Her independent political history is relatively short for Asia. An eastern Tibetan prince invaded and overcame the scattered indigenous Lepchas in 1641 and established an independent Sikkim dynasty which continues to today. A Nepalese war brought British intervention to retain sovereignty for the Maharajah of Sikkim in 1816. But later tension with the British, then ruling India, built up during the nineteenth century, until in 1890 the British made Sikkim a protectorate in a treaty recognized by India and China.

During the next half-century the British fostered local government, establishing a *Durbar* or council of civil officers, which exercised limited power under the ruling Chogyal or maharajah. When Britain relinquished her colonial rule over India after the war, she ceded sovereignty to Sikkim also. But internal unrest forced the maharajah to ask for Indian aid in 1949, and 1950 Sikkim became an Indian protectorate.

Today Sikkim still has no written constitution, but only proclamations issued from the state council. These are supposed to be the basis of constitutionality, but they are extremely vague in many respects, with all authority finally vested in the Chogyal. In practice, however, considerable power is shared with an Indian *dewan* or prime minister and other officials appointed by India. Hopefully the state council, largely elected, will enjoy growing power as various minority groups in the country seek equal representation in governmental decisions.

The present relations between India and Sikkim are similar to those between a newly married couple: the first flush of initial love has subsided, and, fond as they are of each other, their bond is subject to the strains of a husband more concerned with the larger, international perspective and the wife impatient for more domestic necessities. Sikkim feels that it is neglected and that India is not as aware as it should be of its obligations or of the urgency of Sikkim's needs. One example: government officials in Gangtok are aware that they have a tourist gold mine and are anxious to develop tourism as well. But her guardian, India, is reluctant to grant visas, and potential visitors sometimes wait for weeks only to learn that they will not be permitted entry.

His Highness Palden Thondup Namgyal, the present king of Sikkim, seems sincerely dedicated to moving his mountain kingdom into the twentieth century in the shortest time and in the most painless manner possible. He is encouraging the economists who feel that Sikkim's considerable natural resources could, if developed, provide the nation with one of the highest standards of living in all of south Asia. Rich forests, covering 30 percent of the land, could become a valuable source of pulp and paper products. And while there are appreciable quantities of lead and zinc in Sikkim, only copper and graphite are important mineral exports at present. Crisscrossed by mountain torrents of incredible force, Sikkim could also provide great quantities of hydroelectric power to India. Now distilleries and canning factories provide alcoholic beverages and preserves for export, and Sikkim silverware, carpets, and other crafts are sold in India and a number of western capitals. This trade could be expanded.

The rising tide of education in Sikkim adds to the urgent need for quick development. The economy is not yet prepared to employ the young people now in training. Today there are 191 primary schools, 13 middle schools, 7 junior high schools, 5 higher secondary schools, one public school, one basic training school, one monastic school, and four adult education centers. The government of India has also made available 387 scholarships so far to Sikkimese students for studies in schools and colleges in India. "We are gradually having a bigger number of graduates," the Chogyal remarked, "and we have to make sure that we can employ them gainfully right here." Educated Sikkimese have displayed a psychological aversion to being "just teachers." To get around this difficulty, a more prestigious Sikkim Education Service is being organized, and a Sikkim administrative service is also envisaged. Promising candidates would receive a year or two of practical training in Indian services and institutions before being returned to the most suitable positions in Sikkim.‡

National Religions

With Tibetan prayer flags snapping in the breeze, prayer wheels spinning, and monasteries perched precariously on many hillsides, one doesn't have to be in Sikkim long before he realizes the major role which Tibetan-style Buddhism plays outwardly in the religious lives of the people. Even the Nepalese have a syncretistic form of Hinduism which incorporates much of Buddhist teaching. One of the largest Buddhist libraries in the world, the Institute of Tibetology, is located in Gangtok, the capital.

But animism and spirit worship are the everyday religion of the people, and many aspects of Sikkimese religion are pre-Buddhist. The national day, for example, Phunglhapsol, is celebrated with masked religious dancing to honor Khangchendzonga, the traditional deity of Sikkim. Out-

‡P. N. Kurien of the India Every Home Crusade has contributed helpful insights to internal attitudes and conditions here.

side government offices with modern typewriters hang eerie animal skulls on posts. Constructed by wizards, these "demon traps" are designed to keep evil spirits from forcing their way uninvited into the affairs of state. Charms and fetishes are frequently seen, and astrologers or fortune-tellers are relied upon for most major decisions in both personal and national affairs. The Chogyal by the very nature of his religious role is required to be a Buddhist, though Christianity and Islam are both recognized by the government and are granted relative freedom to carry on their religious activities.

Christian History

The first missionary contact with the Sikkimese Lepchas was made by an unidentified German missionary early in the nineteenth century, but all trace of this effort has been lost. A Scottish missionary to India, William MacFarlane, was first challenged by the soaring Himalayas and the unevangelized sister nations when he visited Darjeeling on the border in 1870. (Then part of Sikkim, Darjeeling was fast becoming a favorite spot for British forces; but since it was too far from Gangtok for adequate defence, Sikkim eventually "presented" Darjeeling to the British.) MacFarlane soon returned to set up a school for Nepali boys in Darjeeling, and by 1874 he had baptized his first convert. He viewed tiny Sikkim as a steppingstone to the other Himalayan nations.

With a watchful eye on inland Bhutan and Sikkim, MacFarlane continued work among the large Lepcha population in Darjeeling. In 1885 he was able to make his first visit into Sikkim itself, but the ruling rajah refused to permit him to open a mission in the country. Still determined to pioneer the land, he returned to Darjeeling to set up an institute to train twelve Lepchas to return to their homeland with the Gospel.

"I have no hope," wrote MacFarlane, "of being able to influence the people of Sikkim except through efficient native agents."[1] After moving the institute to Kalimpong in order to be closer to inland Sikkim, MacFarlane died in 1886 and never saw his dream come true. But in 1887 other Scottish misisonaries were able to complete the school, so that when the British gained control of Sikkim in 1890, the mission was ready to begin work within Sikkim itself.

Restrictions seemed endless, and the Scots were not permitted to begin work in Gangtok. By 1900, though, the native workers had begun twelve Christian schools, and 206 Christians had been baptized. Thirty years after MacFarlane began his work, almost 3,000 Lepcha and Nepalese Christians were living on the Sikkim border in Indian Darjeeling and Kalimpong.

In June of 1915 Sadhu Sundar Singh and a youthful Lepcha Christian named Tharchin La trekked through Sikkim trying to get into Tibet; en route they preached in two towns (see chapter 27, "Tibet"). Tharchin La later played a key role in the development of the area, including a brief penetration of Bhutan.

But without doubt the most significant event for the church in Sikkim was yet to come. In 1924 a young and headstrong single Scottish woman missionary, Mary Scott, managed to make friends with Sikkimese royalty and for awhile became the guardian of the young princess. One of the only foreigners in Sikkim at the time, she was permitted to begin an all-girl school with only two pupils. The school has continued until this day and still has a missionary from the Scots mission as its headmistress over nine hundred Sikkimese girls.

Possibly Mary Scott's greatest contribution was employing a promising young Lepcha, converted and educated in Darjeeling, to help her in the early years. This youth, C. T. Pazo, gradually assumed pastoral responsibilities for the believers in Gangtok and went on to lead the emerging national church (then Presbyterian, now covertly affiliated with the Church of North India) until today.

Other missionary work in Sikkim has been very limited. Years after the Scots pioneered, the Finnish Free Mission began a work with a small number of workers. There are now no Finnish missionaries there, but they left behind a tiny group of about forty believers located in Ghoom near Darjeeling. Their work was originally located in Mangen, but their only missionary man was drowned. They apparently never had a national pastor to follow up the work of this one missionary. A Finnish woman married to a Bhutanese works in Assam, it is reported.

NOTES

1. Robert W. Weir, *A History of the Foreign Missions of the Church of Scotland,* pp. 95-99.

BIBLIOGRAPHY

Appasamy, A. J. *Sundar Singh: A Biography.* London: Lutterworth Press, 1968.

Dash, Arthur Jules. *Darjeeling.* [Bengal District Gazetteers]. Alipore, Bengal: Bengal Government Press, 1947.

Hooper, J. S. M., and Culshaw, W. J. *Bible Translation in India, Pakistan, and Ceylon.* Mysore: Oxford University Press, 1963.

Hunter, W. W. *Imperial Gazetteer of India.* Vol. 4. London: Trubner & Co., 1885.

Karen, Pradyumna P., and Jenkins, William M. *The Himalayan Kingdoms: Bhutan, Sikkim, and Nepal.* Princeton, N.J.: D. Van Nostrand Co., 1963.

Rustomji, Nari. *Enchanted Frontiers: Sikkim, Bhutan, and India's Northeastern Borderlands.* Bombay: Oxford University Press, 1971.

Stewart, William. *The Church Is There in North India.* Edinburgh: Church of Scotland Overseas Council, 1966.
Weir, Robert W. *A History of the Foreign Missions of the Church of Scotland.* Edinburgh: R & R Clark, 1900.

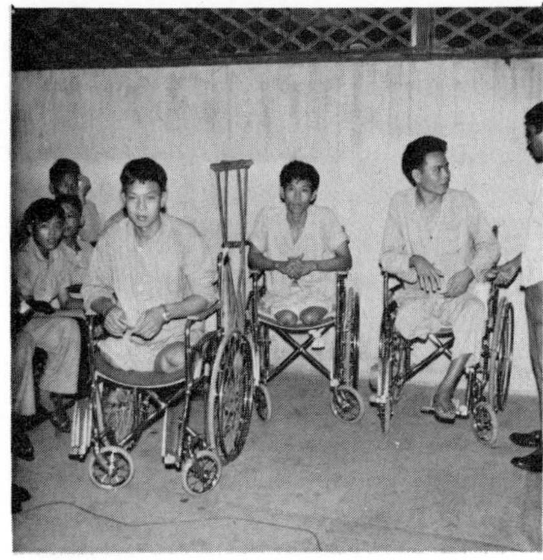

Wounded soldiers in World Vision wheelchairs

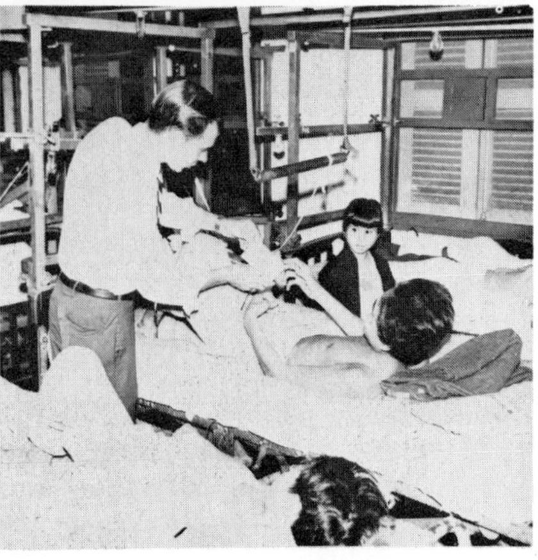

Missionary Richard Drummond visits military hospital

Group of Vietnamese pastors

A typical rural church

CMA Bible school pastors in 1971

26

SOUTH VIETNAM

by Reginald Reimer

The Church Today

VIETNAM was vaulted into the spotlight of world attention during the 1960's, with the acceleration of its civil war. Though the news media flooded the world with information about that once-obscure Asian country, accurate data about the people of Vietnam and their life still remain in short supply. Especially is this true about the Christian movement among the Vietnamese. Even though Christians around the world often took a leading role in meeting human need and in protesting the horrors of war in Vietnam, now that the American involvement is ended there is a tendency to want to forget the whole Vietnam decade. In the process, rightful Christian concern for the people of Vietnam is in danger of becoming a casualty.

REGINALD REIMER has been a missionary under the Christian and Missionary Alliance in South Vietnam since 1966. Furlough studies at the School of World Mission and Institute of Church Growth, Fuller Theological Seminary, equipped him for further in-depth studies of the Vietnamese church upon his return in early 1972. With his wife, he has been involved in evangelistic and humanitarian ministries and in nationwide church growth research.

The chapter on Vietnam was first written in 1968 by Rev. Gordon Cathey, a missionary under the major Christian and Missionary Alliance Mission. Because the entire volume has been delayed five years, during which radical changes have marked the whole Vietnam picture (climaxing with the conclusion of the war in 1973), Rev. Reginald Reimer, also a missionary of the Christian and Missionary Alliance, and who is now engaged in church growth research evangelism, rewrote this entire chapter in the light of recent church and historical developments.

Due to recent happenings in Vietnam, a brief updated report is given on page 589.

Among the seven countries of mainland southeast Asia, South Vietnam has by far the largest Christian community. God is working and giving rapid church growth. Three and one-half centuries of Roman Catholic efforts and some sixty years of Protestant missions have brought more than 2 million persons into the organized churches—11 percent of the population. In all of Asia only India and the island nations of Indonesia and the Philippines can boast larger Christian communities.

The Protestant movement numbers about six hundred churches. Their distribution is so remarkable that not a single one of Vietnam's forty-four provinces is without at least one congregation. Several provinces have more than twenty churches. At the end of 1972 the Protestant community numbered 154,000. Some 53,000 of these were communicant members, which are by definition of their churches baptized adults. About two-thirds of the Protestants in Vietnam are ethnic Vietnamese, while most of the remaining third derive from a dozen or so of the highland tribes collectively called Montagnards.

Because of a unique missionary history, in which one Protestant mission held a virtual monopoly in Vietnam until the mid-1950's, 83 percent of these Protestants in the country belong to one major denomination, the Evangelical Church of Vietnam (ECVN—sometimes referred to as the "Tin Lanh Church," after the Vietnamese word for "gospel"). It has existed as an independent body since 1928, the fruit of the work of the Christian and Missionary Alliance, which dates its beginning in Vietnam to 1911. In the late 1950's, during a period of relative peace following Vietnam's war of independence, the CMA was joined by other evangelical mission boards, which began evangelism (see later section in this chapter titled "Christian History"). Together the newer missions, along with several small independent churches, now have about twenty-five thousand adherents. At this writing all are experiencing slow to moderate growth among the ethnic Vietnamese. Acceptance of Christianity by the tribal minorities, however, continues at a better rate, with at least one significant people's movement among the Stieng tribe currently in progress.

Roman Catholic Christians outnumber Protestants about thirteen to one. Their large church is the fruit of a long and vigorous missionary saga which began 2½ centuries before the French colonial administration of Vietnam. In 1960 Pope John XXIII crowned these 350 years of missionary labor wtih the creation of a full ecclesiastical hierarchy, including eight dioceses and two archdioceses, complete with Vietnamese archbishops. Today some two thousand Vietnamese diocesan priests look after the faithful. Catholic Christians hold prominent positions in government and society. The church has long taken a leading role in education and more recently in providing other badly needed social services in this war-torn country. Roman Catholics have also provided the backbone of anti-communist resistance among the Vietnamese people. Even in North Vietnam, where perhaps an additional million Catholics remain, there are strong indications that the church has not capitulated to pressure. However, the evangelistic fervor of early Vietnamese Catholicism has apparently dissipated. Statistics released by the church indicate that the influx of new converts has been reduced to a trickle.

But what of the church in severed North Vietnam? Reports on Protestant Christianity in North Vietnam are conflicting. Almost no one is optimistic. When the country was divided in 1954 only about a thousand baptized believers and a handful of pastors stayed behind. There are no indications as to their number now. A Christian officer of the International Control Commission reported seeing Protestant churches boarded up and used as granaries. In 1969 reports of a national Protestant meeting came out of North Vietnam. They indicated that nine clergymen and eleven congregations were still active. It was significant that Protestant leaders in South Vietnam recognized all the faces except one in a photograph of the North Vietnam Protestant gathering; only one new face in fifteen years does not testify to growth. A South Vietnamese Christian prisoner who had been taken to the north in 1972 and released in 1973 reported that the government control of remaining Protestant activities was virtually complete. We may gather from our scant sources that the Protestant church in North Vietnam has fared no better under the communists than churches in other Asian countries.

Catholic Christianity, however, has been reported to be alive in North Vietnam. At the end of 1973 observers visited churches and attended mass there, having been granted an interview with the reigning Catholic hierarch in Hanoi. He reported that Christians were faithful in church attendance and interest and that there were "thousands of the faithful."

What has been the overall effect of the bitter Vietnam war on South Vietnamese churches and missionary efforts? This question elicits widely varied answers even from those on the scene. To present a balanced answer to this question, I will begin at 1964, which in a real sense marked the beginning of world attention on Vietnam because of the large-scale intervention of the United States during this year. Calculations based on the records of ethnic Vietnamese congregations of the ECVN showed an average annual growth rate of 6.6 percent in the decade before 1964 and an average of 4.1 percent from 1964 to 1970. In plain language, church growth was slowed by more than one-third. This calls into question the careless statements of some who have said that the war was good for the Christian movement.[1]

REFUGEES AND RESPONSIVENESS

Accurate statistics may never be known, but at least one-fourth of the population of South Vietnam was uprooted at one time or another during the war, probably about 4 or 5 million people! People were dislocated in one of two ways. One was by spontaneous flight in the face of danger or actual battle; an example of this type of dislocation took place during the 1972 Easter invasion, when North Vietnamese forces smashed their way across the seventeenth parallel into South Vietnam. A half-million people in the two provinces of Quang Tri and Thua Thien fled southward, where they were organized into temporary camps in the area around Da Nang. The second type of dislocation was a planned, though usually involuntary, relocation of entire villages or districts for both military and political reasons. In both cases a settled, agrarian people were torn from ancestral lands and familiar surroundings. Such dislocation is much more than physical, and of necessity people in such circumstances are open to innovation, including religious change. Away from ancestral tombs and disillusioned with the host of local spirits who were supposed to take care of them but didn't, refugees looked around for something with which to integrate their lives. Experience in Vietnam revealed that even people from areas formerly resistant to the gospel suddenly became responsive. In central Vietnam, for example, almost any systematic presentation of the gospel met with a welcome response and produced visible results.

However, time and time again the war presented difficulties which prevented solid church growth. Sometimes the same people became refugees several times over, and their continued economic and social uncertainties were not conducive to good church growth. In one case some thirty new groups of Christians, carefully nurtured in a highland resettlement area, were forced to flee. In their dispersion they were lost as countable Christians in identifiable churches. In another case a promising Christward movement among refugees in Quang Ngai province produced eight new congregations in 1966 and 1967, but three years later only two still functioned, both held together by lay leadership. Already shorthanded, the church leaders could not provide trained pastors for new congregations, and regrettably they did not make alternate provision by training local lay leaders. As a result, in case after case promising churchward movements melted away, leaving only the sparest of fruit.

A BRIGHT SPOT—TRIBAL CHRISTIANITY

The most rapidly growing churches in Vietnam today are those in the highland tribes. Collectively called Montagnards, these attractive, bronze-skinned people are divided into four tribes of over a hundred thousand population each, plus twenty-five or so smaller tribes. Their ethnic-linguistic diversity has long presented a challenge to Christian missions. However, though Protestant missionary efforts were begun only about forty years ago, there is now a total Protestant community of forty-five thousand people, including an established, growing church in every major tribe. Most of the evangelism and church-planting has been done by missionaries of the CMA, with assistance by Vietnamese missionaries of the ECVN. CMA linguists have completed the New Testament in two tribal languages and are well along in two others. Wycliffe Bible Translators, who began working in Vietnam in 1960, are now producing literacy materials and translating Scriptures in another twenty languages. There are now only six tribes (with a total population of less than fifty thousand) who have no Christian witness.

The work of the church among the tribes has often gone forward in the face of great difficulty. For one thing, the tribes have been treated much like the Indians were in American history. Also, by reason of their location the tribes have often been caught between the opposing sides in the war.[2] In the early 1970's tribal churches were touched by revival fires, with miraculous acts of the Holy Spirit frequently reported.[3] One of the outstanding results of the revival among the tribal churches was confession of the sin of reliance on fetishes by many second-generation Christian young people. A considerable number of spectacular happenings (instant healing, rocks splitting, raising from the dead, appearance of angels, etc.) were reported, often raising the eyebrows of sophisticated Western Christians. I have heard these things reported with such simple sincerity by reliable believers that I have frequently been convinced of their authenticity.

The rapid conversion of many tribesmen is continuing. Because of their closely knit social structure, the tribesmen often make their decisions together. When many people of one particular tribe make the decision to become Christian, within a short space of time a people's movement occurs. Such a phenomenon is now going on in the Stieng tribe. Three years ago there were only a hundred Stieng Christians; now (early 1974) five thousand Stieng have become Christians in spite of the fact that their entire tribe was uprooted twice in two years and was forced to move dozens of miles each time. All this has happened with only one full-time Stieng worker and one missionary, both of whom early saw the need of training lay leaders. These leaders are doing the bulk of day-to-day spiritual teaching. Naturally, the mushrooming infant church among the Stieng is faced with problems, but thankfully they are problems of growth!

The tribes' churches, thanks to movements such as that among the Stieng, are an encouraging development in Vietnam Christianity. If these present trends continue, the Montagnards in spite of their diversity could be on their way to becoming the first fully evangelized group in the country. Calculations based on 1973 statistics of the ECVN are revealing: though Montagnards make up only 6 percent of South Vietnam's population and 33 percent of the membership of the ECVN, they accounted for a whopping 53 percent of the baptisms! The tribes' churches have also formed a "mission" to carry the gospel to unreached sister tribes.

EVANGELIZING THE MILITARY

The war did not greatly restrict opportunities for evangelism, as might be imagined. In fact, the war presented some unique opportunities for Christian witness. Also, the cruel uprooting of peoples from ancestral lands and villages as a result of the war had the effect of making people more responsive to the gospel than they were before. One of the most remarkable evangelistic ministries to develop during the war was among Vietnam's large military establishment. This ministry was pioneered in the 1950's by Mrs. Ruth Jeffrey, veteran Vietnam missionary and daughter of Jonathan Goforth. During the 1960's this ministry gave a Christian witness to hundreds of thousands of Vietnamese soldiers in training camps, military hospitals, military prisons, and even forward battle posts. A team of Vietnamese evangelists led by CMA missionaries Garth Hunt and Jim Livingston preached and distributed gospel literature and gift packets to thousands of Vietnamese servicemen from the Mekong delta to the demilitarized zone. They also distributed hundreds of wheelchairs and crutches supplied by World Vision and the Kathryn Kuhlmann Foundation. This unique ministry continues today under the direction of Glenn Johnson of Overseas Crusades.

Experience in Vietnam has shown that family solidarity has often proven a barrier to giving the gospel a fair hearing. In the military, however, thousands of young men, many of them literally boys plucked against their wills out of their family units, were thrust into battle with only minimal training. Many already lay near-neglected in military hospitals, having escaped close brushes with violent death. Thus those who gave themselves unsparingly to witness to such men often found them eager to receive the gospel. The recorded decisions for Christ and the number who signed up for Bible correspondence courses was in the thousands. Unfortunately, however, the mobile nature of military life made the follow-up of new converts very difficult. The handful of Vietnamese Protestant military chaplains was too thinly spread or too concerned with other affairs to pay much attention to these new believers. Yet I believe that many of these men and their families may become responsible church members in more peaceful times.

WELFARE-EVANGELISM TENSIONS

The Vietnam war brought with it a considerable influx of new missions (see later section in this chapter titled "Christian History"). Of the twenty-five foreign Protestant agencies in Vietnam in 1973, fifteen came after 1963, and for the most part these new agencies were concerned with meeting the intense human needs brought on by the war. Their help was welcomed because the existing evangelistic missions simply did not have enough physical resources, though they, too, contributed to emergency relief. These new organizations represented Christians in at least ten different countries, but the bulk of financial resources came from the United States. This American generosity in alleviating human suffering in Vietnam demonstrated that the consciences of Christians in the United States were concerned about the Vietnamese people. Missionaries carried on the two tasks of evangelizing and ministering to human need in an admirable, selfless fashion. At least eleven missionaries died at the hands of the communists during the 1960's.[4]

Not enough can be said about the multitude of good works done by such Christian agencies as World Vision, Vietnam Christian Service, Mennonite Central Committee, World Relief Commission, and others. By the care of neglected infants, the feeding and clothing of refugees, and the provision of medicine and prosthetic devices for the sick and wounded, they demonstrated the love of Christ. In addition to providing emergency relief in terms of food, clothing, shelter, and medicine, several of these agencies set up more permanent aid programs in the areas of child care, education, medical assistance, vocational training, and community development. And at least in one instance, the generous example of foreign Christians helped inspire the formation of an effective all-Vietnamese organization called Christian Youth for Social Service.

While the positive social contributions of these organizations is well-known, their overall effect on Vietnamese Christianity and the propagation of the gospel has not often been discussed. On the plus side, large-scale Protestant involvement in social welfare gained for the small Protestant minority a new recognition and respect. Yet there were problems. Mismanagement and occasionally outright corruption were not absent. Generally the Protestant organizations with an ecumenical orientation suffered most in this way because of their failure to work with or (at times) even consult the Vietnamese Protestant leaders, who were all evangelicals. The most effective work was usually done when the welfare assistance was channeled through existing churches.

This proved to be no simple matter. Local churches and their pastors had almost no preparation for this added task thrust upon them. The tendency was for the responsibility of relief distributions and the running of schools to fall on pastors, thus robbing them of the time necessary to provide spiritual care for their flocks. Experienced observers, both foreign and Vietnamese, noted with sadness a decline in the spiritual and evangelistic vigor of the churches. Following the cessation of the war, many Vietnamese pastors, having become accustomed to the economic power and independence which came with involvement in social welfare, are now reluctant to give up that role. Until they learn to entrust the "waiting on tables" to others and return to the scriptural priorities of prayer and preaching the Word, the spiritual life of the church may be expected to languish.

The newfound recognition which came with the availability of foreign resources for social welfare raised other questions of priorities in Christian responsibility among Vietnamese church leaders. Some leaders of the forty-five-year-old ECVN asked why their founding CMA mission did not help them get involved in education and welfare activities sooner. The new involvement in social welfare and especially in education, it was sometimes assumed, would attract more new converts than the traditional evangelistic approach. Before this theory was disproved by the facts, some of the more tried and tested methods of evangelism were abandoned. It is perhaps true that the CMA mission could be criticized for underestimating the cultural mandate. But Vietnamese Christians are now in danger of viewing as normal the overbalanced emphasis of foreign missions on welfare and social work during the war emergency. To do so will impart a distorted sense of priorities in mission. While applauding the Christian involvement in helping alleviate the Vietnam tragedy, one must also recognize the fact that the influx of new missions which are largely engaged in social work has not measurably speeded the discipling of the Vietnamese people to Christian faith.

EFFECT OF U.S. INTERVENTION

There were those who were quick to blame this slow acceptance of Christianity directly on the U.S. military involvement.* It was true that the large expeditionary force was soon supporting a huge parasitic community of those who made their living by the vices which accompany war. Having been present in Vietnam during those years, I saw the development of a black market of incredible proportions. And at the height of the war, free world forces, chiefly those of the U.S., were supporting tens of thousands of prostitutes, thereby exposing a seamy side of America to

*One eminent European churchman who is usually knowledgeable about missions speculated that the Vietnamese would turn a deaf ear to the gospel for five generations because of what the U.S. was doing. This opinion has proved as mistaken as that of those who said the war was good for churches and missions.

the Vietnamese. Worse still were the frequent incidents when drafted American soldiers, embittered by having to be in Vietnam, became vindictive toward all Vietnamese.

But, remarkably, the Vietnamese were usually willing to judge each individual on his own merits. While anti-American prejudices did develop, many Vietnamese openly admired many American characteristics. "Every nation has its good and its bad people," I was frequently told. Too, the many selfless deeds of American soldiers in generously assisting orphanages and schools, for example, helped provide a counterbalance to their more publicized vices. Today, only a year after the Americans have officially pulled out of Vietnam, there is a greater and more open interest in the gospel than at any previous time. Even as I was writing these lines I was interrupted by a teenage student from a government school who came to request Bibles; he reports that forty to fifty boys have begun on their own to study the Scriptures.

Opponents of the gospel in Vietnam have often tried to frustrate the advance of Protestant Christianity by calling it the "American religion." In the early years the Roman Catholics coined this epithet. The fact that many of the early missionaries who brought the gospel to Vietnam were Americans, and that these missionaries did not always distinguish between the gospel and their own cultural expression of it, helped reinforce the idea of an "American religion." During the massive American wartime presence there was an upsurge in this type of criticism. A leading Catholic clergyman with influence in Vietnamese intellectual circles published a statement saying that wherever the American military went, Protestant churches sprang up. This connection was exploited most by communist propagandists, with telling effect in the areas they controlled. Just how much the alleged connection between Protestantism and America hindered the acceptance of the gospel in government-controlled areas of Vietnam is debatable.

The U.S. presence did have some interesting side effects on the thinking of the Christian community, which soon found out that all Americans were not the same kind of "Christians" as the missionaries were. The tremendous diversity in life-style and theology of the hundreds of U.S. military chaplains baffled some Vietnamese, whose only previous experience had been with evangelicals. Often Vietnamese churches and pastors became the beneficiaries of the generosity of chaplains or military units who supported church projects with cash and materials to the tune of thousands of dollars. This generosity, coupled with incredible wastefulness in U.S. civilian aid and military programs, had the effect of convincing most Vietnamese, Christians included, that U.S. resources were limitless. Some found it difficult to understand why American missions, too, could not keep up the abundant flow of goods and money.

In summary, I conclude that the U.S. presence has not been nearly as negative for the propagation of the gospel as was expected. Certainly the Vietnam War gave a lot of Americans, including many Christians, the opportunity to see dire physical and spiritual need firsthand. Some of them returned to Vietnam on missions of mercy. And the worldwide attention on Vietnam has helped stimulate the size of the missionary enterprise there to its greatest proportions ever.

A SATURATION EVANGELISM PROGRAM

As mentioned above, the war seems to have had a moderately negative effect on the spiritual life of the church. This included a decrease in evangelistic zeal. Recognizing this, ECVN and CMA leaders combined to draw up a program of saturation evangelism known as "Evangelism Deep and Wide" (EDW). The drafters of the program were influenced and inspired by the evangelistic congresses of the 1960's (Berlin and Wheaton) and by Evangelism-In-Depth (E/D) in Latin America. Thus the program that emerged in Vietnam incorporated several of the principles of Evangelism-In-Depth but differed in some key points. The basic principle of lay mobilization was retained, along with the general cycle of organizing prayer cells, training Christians for evangelism, systematic visitation, etc. However, the E/D requirement that these activities should be carefully programmed within a specific time limit was not kept. Evangelistic campaigns which culminated E/D programs were downplayed. The architects of EDW insisted on a cyclical but time-flexible application of the basic principles. EDW theory also included specific plans for planting new churches. The customary prayer cells were renamed evangelism cells and were viewed from the beginning as nuclei for new churches.

This practice, however, has not been as good as the theory. Though officially launched on Christmas Day of 1969, four years later there is no evidence to show that EDW has successfully mobilized the Christians in evangelism or that it has changed the slow growth pattern of the church. In fact, EDW leaders say that with the exception of a few localities the program has not even been implemented. EDW appears to have been stymied by internal ECVN politics and has been affected somewhat by church-mission tensions. It was especially undermined by one foreign organization which paid lay Christians to do what EDW hoped to inspire them to do as their Christian duty. But perhaps the greatest problem was that EDW attempted too much: it was intended as a total program of church renewal, evangelism, and extension, and to this end all kinds of supportive literature was produced—so much, in fact, that it produced confusion rather than fruit. By the time the proponents of EDW recognized this and moved toward simplification it was too late. The magic had gone out of the catchy name, and fatigue had already set in. Now some other way may have to be found to reintroduce the essentially sound principles of EDW into Vietnamese Christianity.

TRAINING THE MINISTRY

The predominant evangelical church, ECVN, has three main pastor-training institutions: a large school for Vietnamese pastors located at Nha Trang and two smaller ones which train tribal pastors in the highland towns of Da Lat and Banmethuot. The Southern Baptists have a small residence school in Saigon and the United World Mission has one in Da Nang. The Nha Trang school is moving in the direction of self-support, with the mission at present underwriting only one-third of the operating expenses. Probably few theological schools elsewhere in Asia could boast such a record, especially in a war-torn, developing nation. The military draft instituted during the war seriously hampered the recruitment of students, so that in the mid-1960's enrollment dropped from one hundred to fifty students. The school's leaders countered this crisis by lowering age and educational requirements to get pre-draft-age students. Only in this way was it possible for students to get ministerial deferments from military service. While this action solved the recruitment problems in terms of numbers, it did not provide the kind of leaders the church needed; the ECVN was placed in a position where it had to place very young men, some only teenagers, into pastorates. In an age-conscious society this had serious repercussions.

The Theological Education by Extension (TEE) movement has in it a built-in solution for this kind of problem. Since 1970, when a TEE workshop was held in Saigon, church and mission leaders have discussed TEE principles and passed a number of resolutions in favor of implementing them. But it was not until 1973, when the dean of Nhatrang Theological College caught the vision and sold his colleagues on the idea, that anything was actually done. The program was launched in the fall of 1973, with some four hundred students registering to study one to three of the six courses offered. These students were to meet at intervals with their professors in one of five regional centers in order to go over prepared course materials. A dozen new centers and several new courses are to be added in the spring of 1974. While initially there have been problems in the administration of such a far-flung program, it shows great potential for training leaders. As a part-time teacher in the program, I am particularly impressed with the caliber of the students who enroll. They are often capable, experienced adults who are already making significant contributions to their local churches.

The Baptists, who have also experienced great difficulty in recruiting suitable students in their residence program, are now launching into an extension program and are working on the preparation of programmed materials.

Schools for training tribal pastors are having an even harder time in meeting the need for pastors, mainly because tribal churches are growing considerably faster than the Vietnamese. In past years these schools bracketed their semesters into the slack periods of tribal rice cultivation cycles. Pressure on these standards, however, has lengthened semesters and in the process increased recruitment problems. Consideration is now being given to some modified form of extension education for the tribes. Fortunately, tribal churches are more open to lay leadership than the Vietnamese churches.

Nation and People

During the Vietnam war, this lazy, S-shaped country on Indochina's eastern seaboard became a familiar sight to TV viewers and newspaper readers around the world. Both ends of the "S" spread into large river deltas—the Red in the north and the Mekong in the south; these deltas are joined by a long, narrow strip of land. The geographical feature which sets Vietnam aside from the rest of Indochina is the Annamite mountain chain. The seventeenth parallel was set by the 1954 Geneva accords as the political dividing line between North and South Vietnam. Each of the Vietnams today compares roughly to the size of the state of Washington, or about three-fourths the size of Great Britain.

The central feature of North Vietnam is the Red River Valley. Here a gigantic human effort, begun before the Christian era, tames an unpredictable river and makes its delta habitable and productive. Today the Red River Valley in places supports two thousand people per square mile, a world record for agricultural land. The mountains of North Vietnam provide rich mineral resources: coal, manganese, tungsten, antimony, tin, and chromium, to name only the chief ones. The north, like the south, takes advantage of easy access to the sea for food and transport.

The narrow strip of land which runs southward between the deltas is geographically divided into a flat lowland strip adjacent to the sea and the interior mountains. In South Vietnam the country widens, and the mountains spread into a vast plateau called the central highlands, where the temporate climate and fertile soil combine to support productive plantations of coffee, tea, tobacco, and rubber, though vast areas of the plateau are still undeveloped. Along South Vietnam's long coastline the warm, blue-green waters of the South China Sea, friendly except for autumn typhoons, yield a bounty of fish, crustaceans, and salt for the Vietnamese diet.

The southern delta, transversed by the several branches of the Mekong River, is a veritable garden of Eden; it could well serve as the rice bowl of southeast Asia. In the years before the destructions of war three rice crops produced each year provided a large surplus for export. In addition to rice, the bountiful production of fruits and vegetables makes the region coveted real estate. By far the greatest portion of the population lives on the river deltas and on the narrow coastal strip, where tropical climate, flat and fertile land, and an abundance of moisture have made rice cultivation the natural means of livelihood. The highlands have for centuries been the home of the aboriginal tribes; only in the last two decades have the Vietnamese begun permanently settling in that region.

The estimated population of South Vietnam reached 19.1 million in 1973, while the population of North Vietnam was slightly higher, at 22 million. With an annual growth rate in excess of 2 percent, there could be a total of 75 million Vietnamese by the end of this century. Considerable difference of opinion on the precise origin of these Vietnamese people remains. Their forebears appear to have been born in a complex process of racial and cultural mixing between the people of mainland Asia and the people of the Pacific (in the Red River Valley) centuries before the Christian era. Racially the Vietnamese belong to the Mongoloid group. They are a yellow-skinned people with strong racial unity, remarkable vigor, and a well-developed, highly Sinicized civilization. For at least two thousand years the Vietnamese have been an agrarian people whose culture revolved around the rice cycle. Ethnolinguists do not agree which element is the dominant one in the Vietnamese language, and Vietnamese is usually placed in a subclass of its own.

In addition to the Vietnamese who form the dominant majorities, both Vietnams have ethnic minorities. In the south about 15 percent of the population is made up of minorities, of which the largest is the Khmer (Cambodian) population; it is estimated that there are about 1.4 million Khmer concentrated in several regions of the Mekong delta, and in several provinces they make up a majority of the population. These Khmer are the least evangelized people in South Vietnam, and until recently no concerted effort had been made to reach them. In late 1973, however, one missionary couple with long experience in Cambodia began gathering a core of Khmer workers and found the Khmer to be more open to the gospel than ever before.

A million Chinese, mostly Cantonese-speaking, also live in South Vietnam. Each of the major cities and towns of Vietnam has a Chinese business community, but most of the Chinese live in the huge Cholan quarter of Saigon, where through their banks and warehouses they wield tremendous economic power. The total Protestant community among the Chinese is only two thousand Christians, who meet in about a dozen congregations divided among three mini-denominations. Five expatriate missionaries are at work among the Chinese.

The Montagnards number somewhere between eight hundred thousand and a million people. They reside chiefly in the central highlands, where they survive by swidden (slash and burn) agriculture; a few tribes with a wet-rice culture survive in pockets on the lowlands. Linguistically the thirty or so Montagnard tribes are divided into two main classifications: Mon-Khmer and Malayo-Polynesian, but each tribe has a distinct language, and the social structure between tribes also varies considerably. (The Rade are matriarchal and the Jeh are patriarchal.) The Montagnards are quite receptive to the gospel. A dwindling minority of about fifty thousand Cham people is all that is left of the once-proud kingdom of Champa, which once ruled the territory now known as central Vietnam (its culture influenced predominantly by India). The Cham have so far proven very resistant to the gospel, and there is only one Cham Christian worker.

National History

Recorded Vietnamese history begins ironically with the imposition of a thousand years of Chinese domination in the year 111 B.C.[5] In it Vietnamese culture, at first confined to the Red River Valley, was thoroughly Sinicized in both material culture (especially rice-paddy farming) and social institutions. The Chinese language, too, left a lasting imprint on the Vietnamese. The most remarkable feature of this long period, which ended in A.D. 939, was the emergence of the Vietnamese as a separate and distinct people, a true testimony to their unity and amazing vitality. Then followed nine hundred years of Vietnamese independence, interrupted by only one brief Chinese interregnum, in the fifteenth century. In the thirteenth century the Vietnamese were able on three separate occasions to withstand attacks from Kubla Khan's numerically superior hordes through the use of guerrilla warfare. Not only were the Vietnamese able to maintain independence, but they embarked on a course of southward expansion. Their first obstacle was the kingdom of Champa, which stood astride present-day central Vietnam. This once-powerful Indianized civilization was finally crushed in a decisive battle in 1471. Three hundred years later the present borders of Vietnam were achieved when the Vietnamese wrested most of the fertile Mekong delta from their second enemy, the Cambodians of the declining Khmer empire. This growing land area of

Vietnam presented Vietnamese rulers with serious difficulties in maintaining political unity, and as a result a series of divisions prevailed from the sixteenth to the nineteenth centuries.

The sixteenth century witnessed the beginnings of Western mercantile and missionary penetration of Vietnam. First Portuguese, and then, a century later, Dutch, British, and French ships sailed into Vietnam's harbors—all without notable trading success. When the merchants' interest in Vietnam dropped off in the seventeenth century, it was Roman Catholic missionaries who stayed on to play an important role. Early Catholic missions met with remarkable success, due in large part to men like the French Jesuit Alexandre de Rhodes, who laid the foundations of the great Vietnamese Catholic church more than any other single man. He is better known in secular history for the Romanization of the Vietnamese alphabet, a by-product of his missionary work. The church, as we shall see below, made good progress in spite of fierce official opposition. By the time the French established their political hegemony over Vietnam in the nineteenth century, there were nearly a million Vietnamese Catholics.

Just how the French were able to establish their control is a matter of historical controversy. The underlying cause was an overtly expansionist French foreign policy in competition with European neighbors. The man who helped precipitate the first armed intervention, however, was the overzealous Catholic missionary bishop Pigneau de Behaine. He formed an unholy alliance with French gunboats to help him enthrone a deposed Vietnamese prince, whom he had protected and raised in the hope of placing a Christian monarch on the Vietnamese throne. But it was not until 1883, some sixty years later, that the French were actually successful in taking control of Vietnam. It is still not popular to speak of the colonial era in any way but polemically, and because of later events the French control of Vietnam receives particularly bitter criticism. Yet the French period did bring blessings in the form of modern roads, a nationwide rail system, irrigation and reclamation, schools, hospitals, control of epidemic diseases, and other benefits. Some scholars are beginning to challenge the long-held assumption that the only French motivation was economic exploitation, and they are now suggesting that the greatest sin the French committed was their unwilling and disgraceful exit from Vietnam.

French intransigence, along with Allied (particularly British) acquiescence, tragically permitted the French to regain a foothold in Vietnam after World War II, when the Japanese occupation had effectively ended French authority. A long and bitter anachronistic war of independence ensued. During this war America was drawn into supporting the French and "nationalistic" forces when the independence forces of Ho Chi Minh took a communist turn. The war ended, albeit temporarily, with a major French defeat at Dien Bien Phu. The Geneva Accords of 1954 dictated the terms of a tenuous peace agreement by dividing Vietnam at the seventeenth parallel.

But ten years later the struggle in Vietnam had heated up to the point where the U.S. under President Johnson felt that massive intervention was necessary in order to save South Vietnam from communism. After eight years of bitter war, in 1973 the U.S. pulled out the last of her troops under terms of a cease-fire. The outcome of the war was inconclusive. Indeed, it continued scarcely abated for the Vietnamese. The first year of "peace" claimed the lives of another estimated sixty thousand soldiers from both sides, more than the total number of Americans lost in the entire war! Under terms of the cease-fire South Vietnam was now divided, with a large number of areas under de facto communist control. At this writing a political settlement is still not on the horizon. The threat of another North Vietnamese invasion and of economic problems arising out of long, near-total dependence on the U.S. makes precarious (humanly speaking) the continued existence of South Vietnam. A relatively stable government under the leadership of President Nguyen van Thieu for eight continuous years is a rare, good sign.

Men of faith, having witnessed the hand of God restrain the oppressors before, are encouraged that God will do it again. Hadn't pessimists and self-proclaimed "realists" been predicting the closing of Vietnam for twenty-five years? Yet the door still remains open. Unequaled opportunities of gospel witness persist to this very day.

National Religions

The religious picture in Vietnam is complex and widely misunderstood. Though most Americans in Vietnam during the war assumed that most Vietnamese are Buddhist, few Vietnamese can articulate Buddhist beliefs, few ever attend organized Buddhist rituals, and only a minority even claim to be Buddhists. The unwary observer is often deceived because in recent years Buddhism has occasionally become the rallying point for political dissent. In such instances large numbers of Vietnamese became Buddhists for political reasons. It is my conclusion that there are fewer orthodox Buddhists in Vietnam than Roman Catholics!

The underlying web of everyday religious belief and practice is an all-pervasive animism which continues to affect many people who claim adherence to Buddhism, Cao-Daism, or even Christianity. This animism manifests itself in myriad ways: astrology, numerology, palmistry, geomancy (determining directions in relation to the influence of the elements), and zoochiromancy (use of animal parts in divination). Traditionally, unusual rocks, trees, or water formations; as well as countless other things, were believed to be inhabited by spirits. The description and classification of spirits is almost an impossible task. Some spirits are common and are given proper names, such as the "Spirit of the Earth," the "Thunder God," etc. Every power or natural force has a spirit, every craft has a patron genie, every locality has its own spirit. "The true religion of the Annamese is the worship of spirits," wrote Father Leopold Cadiere, the leading authority on Vietnamese religion. Most of the spirits are believed to be intensely active, attaching themselves to a human being at the moment of his conception and continuing with him to death and beyond. They produce life, death, disease, loss of harvests, failure in examinations, and sterility in women. They watch over all the acts of man's life. The spirits are to be appeased, frightened, duped, fed, or flattered, depending on the situation.

The one unified, highly developed cult which has grown out of basic animism is ancestor worship. So developed and universal is this cult that some are tempted to classify it as a separate religion. Anthropologically speaking, however, ancestor worship is animism. Man is believed to have three souls and nine vital spirits. After death the souls of the deceased are honored during funeral rituals and thereafter at the ancestral altar. The souls of those not so honored become feared, malevolent, errant spirits which on certain days demand ritual attention by everyone who would avoid falling victim to them. This Vietnamese animism did not disappear quietly with the coming of Western educational influences and scientific thought. The French colonizers were surprised to find that the Vietnamese created new spirits for the machines they introduced. During the war American military advisors were sometimes horrified to find that horoscopes played an important part in military strategy. Even the new 1967 national constitution is categorized in such a way as to take numerology into account in the belief that perhaps the right combination of numbers will bring success.

The three great Eastern religions of Confucianism, Buddhism, and Taoism came to influence Vietnamese life especially during Vietnam's millennium under Chinese domination. Buddhism and Confucianism enjoyed periods of ascendancy in Vietnam's history but faded again. Modern Vietnamese Buddhism is felt by some to be in a mild state of revival, marked by the joining in 1963 of sixteen Buddhist organizations, including for the first time sects of both the Theravada and the Mahayana branches in what has been loosely translated the "Unified Buddhist Church of Vietnam." The record of this organization, however, would indicate that it is more a testimony to the weakness of the component parts than to their united strength.

Confucianism left its mark on Vietnamese culture more as a social and political philosophy than a religion. But even its social ideals were soon woven into the web of Vietnamese animism. Ancestor worship, for example, was seen as the logical extension of filial piety. Some remnants of the Confucian system of government persisted until the early years of the twentieth century. Taoism, which originated in China as a speculative philosophy, was known in Vietnam primarily as a system of magic, divination, and sorcery based on animism. Syncretized and interwoven with animism, the great traditions have left their mark.

Two significant religious movements sprang out of the Mekong delta in the last forty-five years. The Vietnamese tendency toward syncretism is seen in the rapid rise of the Cao Dai religion. In 1926 its founder, influenced by Taoist mediumship and European spiritism, professed to have been divinely led to attempt deliberate syncretism. Hence Confucianism, Taoism, Buddhism, Christianity, animistic worship, and other beliefs were incorporated. The deliberate syncretism is seen in Cao Dai buildings, which incorporate the cathedral, the mosque, and the pagoda. The Cao Dai religion, starting from zero, gained a million followers in its first generation and today claims 2 million adherents. A second religious movement, which could be classified as a Buddhist revitalization movement, was spawned by the prophet Huynh Phu So in 1939. He gained wide popularity by his mysterious ability to heal the sick and his appeal for a simplified Buddhism which was not burdensome to the poor and oppressed. His Hoa Hao movement also gained a million followers within a generation. Doubtless both the Cao Dai and Hoa Hao movements owed some of their popularity to an anti-French political stance, for each maintained a powerful militia for that purpose.

Animism also plays a predominant role in religious beliefs of the ethnic minorities. The Montagnards were animists to the exclusion of everything else before Christianity came. The Chinese religious practices are every bit as animistic as the Vietnamese. The Khmer people are Theravada Buddhists. Though their Buddhism is considered more "pure" than the Mayahana variety, it too is riddled with animism. Many Khmer monks in fact are animistic practitioners who are sought out by the Vietnamese for their spiritist powers.

Christian History

CATHOLIC MISSIONS AND CHURCH

Roman Catholic missions began a full three centuries before Protestant efforts, and, though this volume's perspective is evangelical Protestant, I feel compelled to give the Catholics equal time because, as I have discovered, they have a remarkable but little-known history in Vietnam. The size and strength of the Catholic church today is the more remarkable when one is aware of the great odds against which early missionaries labored. In contrast to Latin America or the Philippines, where the Christianization of relatively weak and fragmented cultures was easily achieved, the conversion of the Vietnamese was an uphill struggle. Missionaries encountered a well-developed, reasonably united culture of long standing.

In 1615 a band of Jesuits (including five Japanese!) established the first permanent Roman Catholic mission in central Vietnam, and in 1627 another mission (which proved unusually fruitful) was established in Tonkin, or present-day North Vietnam. By 1660 the lowest estimate places the number of Vietnamese Catholics at three hundred thousand; in 1680 one estimate, probably exaggerated, claimed eight hundred thousand. Whatever the precise figure, it is clear that there was phenomenal growth.

Some insights into the evangelizing process can be gained by following the remarkable career of a French Jesuit named Alexandre de Rhodes. Within three years of establishing the Tonkin Mission, Rhodes recorded the baptism of sixty-seven hundred converts, including members of the royal household and a number of "idolatrous priests." Rhodes himself attributed much of this success to "the constant miracles taking place in the birth of the church." Both his writings and those of his contemporaries reveal that they firmly believed that they and their catechists had been invested with divine power to perform miracles of exorcism, healing, restoring of sight, and even raising the dead. Their superior power apparently convinced not a few animistic priests to become Christians. Evangelicals today will not be surprised that this confrontation, power-encounter approach resulted in conversions. One cannot help but notice the sharp contrast of this approach to modern missionary ideals, which often tend toward tolerance and dialogue.

The long-term success of Rhodes' ministry was due to two farsighted policies. First, his converts were prepared for baptism by the study of the rigorous Eight-Day Catechism, which emphasized the radical error of their previous non-Christian beliefs and grounded them in doctrine. Second, Rhodes started from the very beginning to train a functional indigenous clergy—a "celibate lay brotherhood," he called them—though complications of church law prevented their ordination until 1660. Rhodes' catechists and these brotherhood members were the vanguard of the early Catholic movement.

It is not surprising that such success in converting the Vietnamese soon raised the suspicions of the temporal authorities. Before long the converting and teaching missionaries had to carry on their work underground. Rhodes himself was expelled from the kingdom on several occasions. Finally, in 1645, he was permanently banned from returning on penalty of death. Though his total career among the Vietnamese spanned less than twenty years, Rhodes was called the "apostle of Vietnam"—and he was not yet through, for on his return to Europe he made three more important accomplishments on the behalf of missions in Indochina!

First, Rhodes successfully agitated for the creation of a special missionary office in the church, called an "apostolic vicar," which paved the way for the formation of a duly recognized national clergy in Vietnam and other Asian countries. Second, he generated a tremendous amount of popular and missionary interest in Vietnam by his tireless speaking and prolific writing. Finally, he helped inspire the formation of the Societe des Missions Etrangeres de Paris (MEP), which was the first Catholic order founded specifically to train and send missionaries (many of whom came to Indochina).

In the later years of the seventeenth century the Catholic movements in Vietnam entered a new and difficult period. The spontaneous expansion stopped. No net gains were recorded for over a century, and at times the movement even dwindled. Why, after such a good beginning, did this reversal occur? The reason most commonly given is simply political opposition. The ruling Confucianist mandarins feared, not without reason, that the new religion would upset the status quo, and they reacted accordingly by burning churches and even taking Christians' lives. Missionaries and priests had to innovate all kinds of ingenious ways of carrying on. But this kind of opposition could not have been the sole reason for interrupted growth, because in the nineteenth century growth resumed and continued in spite of even more severe anti-Christian persecution. The "perverse religion of the Europeans" was now officially proscribed. Christians were systematically dispossessed of their property, and the villages and churches were put to the torch. Thousands were imprisoned and forced to wear a twenty- or thirty-pound square wooden yoke. Those who recanted their faith were branded on the cheek, while those who refused were submitted to a hundred different tortures and cruel kinds of death. Christians were strangled, sawed apart, hacked limb from limb, and for sport tossed to be trampled by wild elephants. Estimates on the number who were martyred range from 80,000 to 130,000 people! How does one account for such a persevering faith and growing church in spite of such repression? A serious student of Christianity in Vietnam must come to terms with this question.

How different the picture today! Though the Vietnamese Catholic church is now large, powerful, and wealthy, playing a significant role in Vietnamese society, the early dynamic is gone. One looks in vain for that ancient evangelistic zeal of Rhodes' catechists. Where is the power that once cast out demons, healed the sick, and even raised the dead? The gospel is half-hidden. In her attempt to be culturally relevant the church has been ambushed by creeping syncretism. Virtually the only Vietnamese who are becoming Catholics today are the children of Catholic parents, and even some of these are lost to the church. Can these bones, being dead, live again? Let us pray that they might.

PROTESTANT MISSIONS AND CHURCH

The first Protestant witness in Vietnam was launched in the late 1820's by the British and Foreign Bible Society. Because of hostility from both the Vietnamese and the French, the Society operated from Shanghai. In 1890 Monsieur Bonet, a professor at the Paris School of Oriental languages who had undoubtedly spent some time in Vietnam (though this cannot be confirmed), translated the gospel of Luke into Annamese (the Vietnamese spoken in central Vietnam), basing his work on an earlier French version. In 1898 two Britishers, James and Lawrence, sailed from Shanghai to central Vietnam to explore missionary possibilities. They purchased a boat and sailed along the coast and up the rivers, distributing gospel portions in Vietnamese. Less than a year later they were expelled from the country for "illegal religious practices," but not before James had translated the gospel of Mark into Vietnamese.

In 1903 Charles Bonnet, another Frenchman, met with more favorable acceptance. Shortly after he entered the country he gathered around him a number of Vietnamese, whom he trained as colporteurs, and began distributing the Word of God, assisted by two French Protestant clergymen, Pastor Pannier of Hanoi and Pastor Richemond from the Hue area. While these latter two men probably ministered exclusively in the French language, one may assume that their lives and ministry made an impact upon the Vietnamese as well. When Bonnet's failing health forced him to return to France in 1911, he was replaced by Monsieur Gidoin, a French merchant in the city of Da Nang. Before Bonnet left, the two men had made a decision to sell the Bible Society residence in Da Nang and relocate in Haiphong. In the providence of God the first missionaries of the Christian and Missionary Alliance arrived in Da Nang before Bonnet left, were encouraged by these men, and purchased his residence and the adjoining property.†

The oldest and largest of the Protestant churches in Vietnam today is the Evangelical Church of Vietnam, born of the work of the Christian and

†The Bible Society published the entire New Testament in Vietnamese in 1923, a joint effort of CMA misisonaries John D. Olson and W. C. Cadman, assisted by a committee of nationals and other missionaries. In 1925 the Old Testament was completed. There was a revision of the text in 1954, and currently another revision is nearing completion, based on the text of the *New English Bible*. This will be a church translation, updating the text in the vocabulary understood by the average Christian. A simpler, common-language version for the man on the street will also be completed soon.

Missionary Alliance. A three-man team from south China arrived in Da Nang in 1911 (just before Charles Bonnet returned to France on health leave), headed by Robert A. Jaffray. Jaffray, representing the relatively young North American Missionary Society, had already established a reputation for daring faith by pioneering in the Kwangsi province of China. Years later he was to spearhead the work of the Alliance in Indonesia, Borneo, and West Irian. Convinced that God had at last opened the door to Indochina, Jaffray almost immediately purchased the Bible Society property in Da Nang. Two missionary couples soon took up residence there, and in 1913 a tiny thatched chapel was built in the city.

The first decade of CMA missions in Indochina (1911-21) may be called the exploratory period. The first missionaries experimented with a number of approaches. They suffered an early setback when French colonial authorities severely restricted their activities during World War I. From the very beginning, the missionaries felt that the training of national workers and the wide use of literature would be necessary to evangelize Indochina. Accordingly, at the end of the first decade the missionaries were operating a productive printing press in Hanoi and had opened a Bible school in Tourane. Sensing a great opportunity, the CMA sent a total of twenty-two missionaries to their new field. By this time more than half of the New Testament was already in circulation. The three major centers of Vietnam—Hanoi, Tourane, and Saigon—had been occupied by missionaries who had baptized a core of believers in each place.

The second major period of CMA missions spanned the two decades from 1922 to 1940, which have been called "the remarkable years." They were characterized by an amazing response among the Vietnamese, particularly in the Mekong delta and central Vietnam—a response which came in spite of the fact that French authorities for a time officially proscribed Protestant Christianity in large sections of Indochina. Nearly twenty thousand Vietnamese were baptized during these years. In 1928 the Vietnamese congregations were organized into a church body, today called the Evangelical Church of Vietnam (ECVN). By 1940 there were 123 churches, of which 86 were fully self-supporting. The early missionaries deemed their efforts at evangelizing the Vietnamese so successful that they began to direct their attention to the other peoples of Indochina as well. A mission to the Khmer in Cambodia was begun in 1923, and in 1929 CMA missionaries began to work among the highland tribes in Vietnam, Laos, and Thailand.

The year 1941 marked a definite turning point in Vietnam's political and missionary history. In that year began a series of wars which have continued nearly unabated for three decades. The first was the Japanese occupation (1941-45), the second was the war of independence (1946-54), and the third is the present Vietnam war, which began gradually in the early 1960's and continues to this day. These three wars have affected the work of propagating the gospel in Vietnam in quite different ways. The young Vietnamese church rose to meet the challenge presented by the Japanese occupation of Indochina. When in 1941 mission financial support was virtually cut off and in 1943 those missionaries who remained were interned by the Japanese, the church nevertheless continued to grow both in membership and in self-reliant status, until in 1945 it was larger and stronger than it had been in 1940.

The August Revolution in 1945 signaled the start of a bloody, eight-year struggle by the Vietnamese to rid themselves of their longtime colonial masters. This war of independence had drastic consequences for the church, and despite the return of missionaries the church suffered its first major setback. In 1954 fewer Christians could be counted than in 1944. The dispersion of congregations and the tremendous destruction of property shattered the self-support principle. For a number of years both church and mission concerned themselves with recouping losses rather than with making new gains. The Geneva Accords of 1954, though they tragically divided Vietnam at the seventeenth parallel, at least brought a brief period of peace to the South. The church soon recovered its strength, and the CMA mission in the late 1950's responded by bringing in the largest influx of new missionaries ever, placing them in the major unevangelized areas of the country. In keeping with the new political divisions being shaped in Indochina at this time, the CMA Indochina mission divided into separate organizations in Thailand, Laos, Cambodia, and Vietnam. In 1953 it also seemed wise to form two missions in Vietnam, one to the Vietnamese and one to the Montagnards or tribes. Separate tribal and Vietnamese mission organizations existed until 1959, when new political developments encouraged a merger.

OTHER MISSIONS AND CHURCHES

The brief interlude of peace after 1954 was marked by the coming of several other evangelical missions, ending the virtual monopoly of the CMA.‡ The new arrivals have met with varying success. The Worldwide

‡Chinese colporteurs representing the Seventh-Day Adventists of South China had visited central Vietnam in 1920, but governmental authorities would not permit them to stay. Almost a decade later Elder and Mrs. R. H. Wentland officially opened the Adventist work in Vietnam, but returned to the United States shortly afterward because of poor health. In 1936 he returned to establish a church in Hanoi (1938) and a church and clinic in Djiring (1940). A spiritual foothold which the Adventists had gained among the Montagnards in the central highlands and the Vietnamese in Tra Vinh, My Tho, and Soc Trang prior to 1942 was dissipated during the difficult years of Japanese occupation. In that same period, however, a strong Chinese congregation was established in Cholon under the leadership of four Chinese, the guiding hand being a layman by the name of Tran Canh Huy, who was a Swatow Adventist weaver

Evangelization Crusade (WEC) mission, which began in 1956, set as its goal the evangelization of the Montagnards in northern South Vietnam. But since unstable conditions often confined their missionaries to the cities, they also had opportunity to establish churches among the Vietnamese. In 1968 sponsorship of the WEC churches, called "Vietnam Christian Mission" churches in Vietnamese, changed to the United World Mission which now continues (under the leadership of Gordon Smith) with national churches, two orphanages, and a leprosy rehabilitation center. In 1973 these churches numbered thirty-seven, with an estimated total community of fifteen thousand Christians.

Mennonite missionaries of the Eastern Mennonite Board arrived in 1957. Concentrating largely on social concern ministries and maintaining a peace witness during the war, their efforts have so far given rise to only one Vietnamese congregation.

The Wycliffe Bible Translators arrived in 1957 and are now carrying on a vigorous and fruitful translation work among more than twenty tribal languages, of which more than half now have portions of the Scriptures. Their wide influence has strengthened the evangelical church, created favorable government contacts, and opened wide doors of service. The Overseas Crusade began work in 1956, largely in the Da Lat area of the highlands, where they have a school for tribal children. The Pocket Testament League has distributed over a million New Testaments among Vietnamese and American military men.

Mention should also be made of the numerous organizations carrying on a ministry of Christian social concern in the country. The Christian Children's Fund entered Vietnam in 1952 and is now giving financial assistance to thousands of children. The World Relief Commission of the National Association of Evangelicals has been carrying on relief work, vocational training, and model farm work since 1956. The Mennonite Central Committee sent workers in 1954. In 1964 World Vision began a ministry of relief, orphanages, and educational assistance, working closely with all protestant missions. In 1965 the Asian Christian Service began emergency relief work. The Church World Service and Lutheran World Relief joined with the Mennonites in establishing the Vietnam Christian Service Organization in 1966. Today they have a large staff of workers, including doctors, nurses, social workers, home economists, agriculturalists, and community development workers. More recently, and on a more limited basis, Quakers, the Salvation Army, and others have also joined the organization.

who had come to Vietnam in 1937. After World II missionaries and nationals alike found a much better attitude toward the gospel. Membership within the church increased, and the French government gave permission for the establishing of a medical hospital in Saigon to be directed by American missionary physicians; it was officially opened in 1955.

The Challenge of the Future

Serious problems face the expansion of the gospel and the establishment of a strong and united Christian witness in Vietnam as the nation rebuilds for the future. Foremost among these is the problem of integrating the small churches of the newer mission organizations with the established, nationwide evangelical church. This would provide a desirable witness toward the total community, but such unity will be difficult to achieve because of the diversity of church government and theological expressions within even the evangelical camp. Liberal theology is also present in Vietnam, and along with some early liberal teaching has come the heavy infusion of cultist groups: Christian Science, Jehovah's Witnesses, Mormons, and Unitarians, who have established beachheads largely through the American military and U.S. AID workers.

A critical problem within the church has been the long-standing tendency of the clergy to completely dominate the churches. Even though some of the church's social institutions and business affairs might better be handled by lay Christians with expertise in these areas, potential lay leaders often complain of being stifled. However, the new depth-evangelism program is beginning to alter pastoral attitudes, and Inter-Varsity Christian Fellowship and other youth efforts are strengthening the voices of young people in the churches. Another continuing problem will be that of maintaining balance between social concern and evangelism. Already involvement in social activities has sapped the strength of many evangelicals. Wise leadership is imperative in order to prevent very real social needs and the influx of large foreign funds from swamping the church in social welfare administration and thereby cutting the nerve of aggressive evangelism.

Conclusion

In Vietnam today God is giving beauty for ashes and the joy of gladness for mourning. The gates of hell throughout the war did not prevail against the church of Christ. Vietnam is a receptive area that must be exploited for the glory of God and the evangelization of its people today. What has been achieved must be considered as merely the firstfruits of a much greater harvest ahead. Although growing increasingly strong, the existing churches are still a tiny minority who actively seek the help of sister churches around the world in their task of evangelizing this nation. The Christian mission in Vietnam stands at the beginning of the age of maximum blessing and growth.

As the inevitable defeat of South Vietnam became imminent in March and April of 1975, fear for the safety of Christians mounted. Because of their association with the international Christian church and American missionaries, pastors and lay leaders were feared to be marked for persecution and martyrdom. Evangelist Billy Graham tried desperately, up to the last minute, to charter a special airplane to evacuate several hundred Christians, who were praying and waiting in the International Church in Saigon. His efforts failed.

By the time Saigon fell, the frantic evacuation efforts of the American government were estimated to have included 800-1200 Vietnamese Christians. Later reports indicated that scores of Christian farmers probably escaped in small boats and were later picked up by American ships. Thus, the Rev. Grady Mangham, director of southeast Asia for the Christian and Missionary Alliance, estimates that 1,600 Christians (one percent of the total of the Evangelical Church of Vietnam) may have escaped. In late spring these refugees were being processed in four camps in Guam, California, Arkansas, and Florida for relocation throughout the United States. Nightly evangelistic meetings by Christian and Missionary Alliance missionaries and pastors saw hundreds of refugees confess Christ. Mangham estimated that thirty-seven pastors were among the Christians who escaped. President Mieng of the denomination chose to stay with his flock.

The fate of nine American missionaries who were seized in the Danang area in April is still unknown at this writing. Official United States government appeals have been made for the release of Mr. and Mrs. John D. Miller and their five-year-old daughter; three Christian and Missionary Alliance missionaries, Betty J. Mitchell and Mr. and Mrs. Richard Phillips; and three government-related Americans. In addition to these American citizens, a Canadian couple associated with the Christian and Missionary Alliance, Mr. and Mrs. Norman Johnson, are believed to be with the group; they were last reported to be prisoners in a camp in Pleiku province.

Late reports (June 1975) indicate that Christians in Saigon have been relatively unmolested, since the city is a Vietcong showcase, with many Western reporters. It was reported that in Ban Me Thuot, however, a pastor was subjected to a mass trial and buried alive. Persecutions and martyrdoms are probably inevitable. But God is there, and the revival movements among the tribespeoples of recent years and the courageous witness of Christians may well cause the church to grow.

Another recent report indicated the presence of possibly 10,000 Protestant Christians in North Vietnam who are meeting quietly with supposedly little repression.

DONALD E. HOKE
June 23, 1975

NOTES

1. This is statistically documented in Reimer's thesis, "The Protestant Movement in Japan," p. 136.
2. The highland tribes' heroism in the face of danger has been popularized for the Christian public in Homer E. Dowdy's *The Bamboo Cross*.
3. Aspects of this revival have recently been published in a small book titled *The Holy Spirit in Vietnam*, by Orrel Steinkamp (Carol Stream, Ill.: Creation House, 1973).
4. See James C. Hefly's *By Life or By Death*.
5. An excellent recent history is Dennis J. Duncanson's *Government and Revolution in Vietnam*.

BIBLIOGRAPHY

Christianity

Dowdy, H. E. *The Bamboo Cross*. New York: Harper and Row, 1964.

Gheddo, Piero. *The Cross and the Bo-Tree*. New York: Sheed and Ward, 1970.

Hefley, James C. *By Life or By Death*. Grand Rapids: Zondervan, 1969.

Hunter, J. H. *Beside All Waters*. Harrisburg: Christian Publications, 1964.

Irwin, E. Franklin. *With Christ in Indo-China*. Harrisburg: Christian Publications, 1937.

Phu, Le Hoang. "A Short History of the Evangelical Church of Vietnam." Unpublished dissertation presented to New York University, 1972.

Reimer, Reginald E. "The Protestant Movement in Vietnam." Unpublished thesis submitted to the School of World Mission at Fuller Theological Seminary, 1972.

General

Buttinger, Joseph. *The Smaller Dragon: A Political History of Vietnam*. New York: Praeger, 1968.

Duncanson, Dennis J. *Government and Revolution in Vietnam*. New York: Oxford University Press, 1968.

Fitzgerald, Frances. *Fire in the Lake*. Boston: Little, Brown, and Co., 1972.

Hammer, Ellen. *Vietnam: Yesterday and Today*. Boston: Hold, Rinehart and Winston, 1966.

Hickey, Gerald C. *Village in Vietnam*. New Haven: Yale University Press, 1964.

———. *Major Ethnic Groups of the South Vietnamese Highlands*. Santa Monica, Calif.: The Rand Corp.

Mole, Robert L. *Montagnards of South Vietnam: A Study of Nine Tribes*. Tokyo: Tuttle, 1970.

Scigliano, Robert. *South Vietnam: Nation Under Stress*. Boston: Houghton Mifflin Co., 1964.

Smith, Harvey H. *Area Handbook For South Vietnam*. Washington: Government Printing Office, 1967.

Center elephant carries the sacred tooth of Buddha in Sri Lanka's greatest annual "Kandy Perahera" festival.

Photo by Don Rubesh

27

SRI LANKA

(CEYLON)

by B. E. Fernando

Introduction

Lovely Sri Lanka, Asia's "Emerald Isle," is immortalized in Christian hymnody by Reginald Heber's colorful lines, ". . . the spicy breezes blow soft o'er Ceylon's isle, where every prospect pleases. . . ." Yet Ceylon has been a tense area of political and economic upheaval throughout the postwar years. The Protestant church, though more than three hundred years old, has suffered and stood still.

What has happened in recent Ceylonese history and what have been the effects on the church?

From the time that Ceylon gained independence from Great Britain in 1948, her government has become increasingly socialistic. In the process of seeking to discover her national identity after over 450 years of colonial rule, there has been a strong emphasis on the resurgence of the national languages (Sinhala and Tamil*), on Sinhala nationalism, and on the

---

B. E. Fernando is an active Methodist layman who serves as the senior national deputy commissioner of inland revenue in Sri Lanka. Widely traveled in both government service and Christian activities, Mr. Fernando holds the following posts: president of the national council of the YMCA, member of the executive committee of the World Alliance of YMCA's, and member of the world executive committee of the World Methodist Council. He has also been a member of the executive committee of the World Evangelical Fellowship and president of the local Evangelical Alliance.

*Ed. note. Tamil is actually a language of south India. The Tamil-speaking people of north Ceylon originally came from India.

Buddhist religion. At the same time political power has passed gradually from the elite to the workers and peasants. Economically, Ceylon has had severe difficulties with the fall in price of her major export commodities and with her inability to grow the food she needs for a rapidly expanding population.

Ceylon's population is two-thirds Buddhist, and the government, though holding to freedom of religion, actually promotes Buddhism. So the majority of the people look on Christianity with some disfavor for the following reasons.

1) Christianity was introduced into Ceylon by the colonial western powers. Now that Ceylon is independent, all vestiges of foreign domination (including Christianity) should be eliminated.
2) The language and culture of Ceylon prior to the foreign invasions were not encouraged by the "Christian" conquerors but were preserved only under great difficulties by the Buddhist priesthood. It is thus felt that to be a true Ceylonese one must be a Buddhist.
3) There is almost an obsession that Ceylon is the place where Buddhism is to be preserved in its glory and purity. In view of these attitudes it is not surprising that the following developments have resulted:
    a) The Education Code provides that every child shall be instructed in the religion of his father, even if both parents wish otherwise.
    b) Foreign missionaries are restricted, and replacements are allowed only if made within a year.
    c) On all state occasions Buddhist religious ceremonies are held.

In 1960 church schools were vested in the state and a comprehensive system of state education was introduced. The church now runs only a very few private schools, which are compelled to charge high fees and to cater only to those who are able to meet them. As a consequence the church has largely lost a valued opportunity of service to the nation and of contact with those who are not Christians.

Under these conditions the progress of the established church has slowed to an almost complete standstill in many areas, and the spirit of evangelism has now been quenched. The need for revival in the church is great. The non-conservative theological colleges and modernistic literature are not producing committed Christians or successful evangelists. But the lay membership of the churches is still largely conservative, and the impact of evangelical Christianity is slowly being felt.

The Church Today

The church today in a total population of thirteen million numbers about one million. The 1971 government census report did not publish denominational details, but the distribution would appear to be as follows:

Roman Catholics	883,111
Anglicans	54,500
Methodists	26,000
Pentecostalists	7,000
Church of South India	6,000
Baptists	5,000
Salvation Army	3,000
Presbyterians	2,000
	986,611

The Roman Catholic church has one Ceylonese cardinal and five bishops. The Anglican church with its two bishops obtained autonomy in 1930, and since then it has been called the Church of Ceylon. The Methodist church became autonomous in its 150th year, in 1964.

Some church leaders feel that ecumenism is the answer to the churches' stagnation, so church union discussions began with the Methodists in 1940 and a joint committee was appointed, with representatives from the Anglican, Methodist, Baptist, SIUC (Congregationalist) and Presbyterian denominations. The Dutch Reformed church, one of the churches in the presbytery of Ceylon, withdrew in 1952 from the negotiating committee. The final plan for union was issued in 1964, and all but the Methodists voted approval. Subsequently, though all the negotiating churches (including the Methodist) have voted in favor of the Union, the inauguration of the United church has been delayed due to legal action taken by three Anglican laymen.

Some evangelical leaders doubt that such a union will solve the churches' problems. The problem of lack of growth is, as one senior denominational leader has said, that "the church's main concern is pastoral, not missionary."

But this same man, Bishop Cyril Abeynayake of the Anglican church, takes an optimistic view of the future:

> The past 25 years have been exciting and eventful years in church and state. Many Christians feared the developments as likely to be unfavorable to the Christian churches. But it must be remembered that Christianity came to Ceylon in the wake of Portuguese, Dutch, and British conquests. Consequently, Christians were generally regarded as exponents of a western counterculture, aliens in their own country. So the loss of foreign imperial patronage was in retrospect a good thing.
>
> Now it is no longer profitable to be a Christian; rather, it spells not only loss of privilege and position but difficulties in the way of education and employment. To be a Christian today is a challenge to commitment. Christians have been thrown back on their strength and stay, God Himself.
>
> The events of our day are also a challenge to indigenization—the adoption of the art and architecture, the national languages, and the rich cultural inheritance of the country. In all this God has moved wonderfully,

so much so that all Christians are no longer regarded as strangers in the life of the community.

The Sunday weekend was for a time replaced by the Poya weekend (1969-71), which helped to heal the religious hurt of the Buddhist majority. It also helped Christians to realize that all days are to be hallowed and sanctified. The restoration after a few years of the Sunday weekend, doubtless for economic and severely pragmatic reasons, is a fresh call to Christians to observe Sunday aright as a day of worship and witness, but giving life and meaning to every day of the year.

A third deprivation which in turn has proved a mixed blessing was the nationalization of all Christian grant-in-aid schools (1960). This has led to the dispersal of Christian teachers, hitherto concentrated in towns and church schools, into the villages and outlying districts. For the first time the church is present through the life and witness of a Christian teacher in areas hitherto closed to all Christians. We have gained a new sense of perspective and fresh insights into education despite the considerable difficulties that confront us in relation to the religious education of Christian children in state schools.

Thus today there are signs of a reawakening at hand in the Ashram movement, the use of national art and architecture in the erection and adornment of churches, the setting of the liturgy to national music, and the outreach to workers in the city and to peasants in the rural districts. . . . There is a deeper awareness of the problems, more openness to one another, and a realization that unity is essential for mission. (From a personal letter to the editor dated July 1972)

There are also encouraging signs that the older churches are seeking to communicate more meaningfully. Groups of Christians have banded themselves together to witness in the sphere of trade unions, political parties, and the working class movements. The Sinhala and Tamil languages and oriental music are being used increasingly in worship. Centers have also recently been established for vocational training and lay Bible teaching. There seems to be among the people an increasing awareness of the contribution that Christianity can make to the development of a modern state. Some interest is displayed in the central teachings of Christianity. But this interest can be developed only if the activity, worship, and life of the church bear an attractive witness to those teachings.

Despite the recent years of turmoil, there have been great opportunities for aggressive evangelism, and there have never been any real barriers to preaching the gospel, reports Don Rubesh, Evangelical Alliance missionary engaged in radio and Bible correspondence work. "Today people are more open to the gospel than ever before," he reports. Of the books and periodicals published in Ceylon in 1968, religious books were second in popularity. Of pamphlets published, the largest number was religious. A survey recently carried out by the Ceylon Broadcasting Corporation showed that the most popular program is religious. The Back-to-the-Bible Broadcast is preparing regular programs in the local languages, which are being beamed to Ceylon from FEBC, Manila, and FEBA, Seychelles. In October 1971 the government reconsidered the matter of gospel broadcasting after several years of prohibition. Now they are again allowing English and Indian vernacular-language gospel broadcasts over the Ceylon "All Asia" channel, though not the local beam.

The Hindi program over Radio Ceylon planned by the Back-to-the-Bible India office a few months ago has received an average of four thousand letters of inquiry per month. "There are many enquirers and many new decisions, and thousands write to say that the messages have made a great change in their lives, it was reported in mid-1973.

Established in Ceylon in 1955 under Rubesh, the U.S. Back-to-the-Bible work has grown steadily. In 1972 a board of directors was appointed, and incorporation was received by an act of parliament. Back-to-the-Bible has a twofold outreach in radio and Bible correspondence courses. Rubesh reports unprecedented responses to the offer of free courses through the years. Over seven hundred thousand initial lessons and gospels have been sent to every major village in the island. Offered in three languages—English, Tamil, and Sinhala—the greatest response has been for the courses in Sinhala, the national (Buddhist) language. Additonal courses have been added to the original "Light of Life" course, until seven are now offered, and a thousand students have completed all of these. Buddhist youths comprise 80 percent of those who enroll in the classes.

Many hopeful signs may be seen in the evangelical groups, both inside and outside the mainline denominations, which are distributing Scriptures and tracts, doing follow-up work, and bearing effective witness. The interdenominational Youth for Christ movement is well supported by many young people, whereas individual church youth movements are not.

Bishop Chando Ray in an August '71 report records:

> The biggest gospel crusade in the history of Colombo north . . . at Ungodawatte, Maligawatte, was held recently. These are areas where pickpockets, hoodlums, and thugs reside. . . . A good many raise their underfed and sparingly clothed children in the midst of filth and dirt. . . . Alcohol and dope sap the vitality of many young men. Circumstances and environment lead young women into prostitution. But Frank Williams of New Life Center and his helpers from Colombo went out to meet them. Four thousand people came the first day in an open air meeting. Night after night they came, and every meeting was more glorious than the previous one. . . . Hundreds were responding to the invitation, and the prayer tent was packed to capacity. . . . The sick were being healed and the wounded hearts were being soothed; sinners were saved and there was

> great joy in the area. One day the failure of electricity almost wrecked the meetings, but the people stayed. Another day torrential rain dispersed the people and the equipment almost was lost, but the people covered the P.A. system under plastic sheets. A team of helpers have visited almost all those who came for prayer . . . about a thousand people. . . . Bible classes have been formed, Scriptures have been distributed.[1]

Evangelism like this seems to be done largely by Pentecostals and independents. Small but solid work is being established, and the future is as proverbially bright as the promises of God.

Challenges and Opportunities

For future evangelism and church growth in Ceylon today certain emphases seem needed. Among a people whose standards of health are not high, the biblical teaching that the gospel makes for wholeness is essential, and the healing ministry is effective. To persons bound by astrology, horoscopes, and magical charms, the liberating power of the Holy Spirit when manifested in human lives is irresistible. An interesting survey revealed the main reasons why Ceylonese become Christians. These were: forgiveness can be found only in Christianity; the life of Jesus Christ is so fascinating; the example of a Christian's life is so different. It is these essential differences in the Christian message that need to be stressed in Ceylon today, and not the similarities with other religions which some try to show.

The great religions in Ceylon are each centered around a book—Buddhism around the *Tripitaka,* Hinduism around the *Bhagavad Gita,* and Islam around the *Koran.* Christianity has relevance and hope in Ceylon only as it is firmly rooted in the Bible. And the Word of God has been translated into all the languages of Ceylon. A complete revision of the Sinhala Bible, whose first New Testament translation dates back three hundred years, is now underway. The gospels are already out. There is also the prospect of a common Catholic-Protestant version in the future.

Bishop Abeynayake feels that Ceylon's best days for evangelism may be just ahead:

> It is evident that we are at the beginning of a period of evangelism at depth. There is an awakening interest in what Christianity has to say and how the gospel is to be related to the life of eastern people in a socialist community. The resurgence of Buddhism and Hinduism has in turn provided a religious climate in the country which is not inimical to the proclamation of salvation through Jesus Christ. The response to Bible broadcasts, Bible correspondence courses, leaflet evangelism, and revival meetings has been encouraging. We live at a time basically of "sowing" and not of "reaping." The "soil" has changed, the "times and seasons" have

changed. But the seed is the "Word of God" and the field is the "world," now as always. One notes today a troubling of the waters as betokens the quickening power of the Spirit: a rustling on the treetops, such as David was given as a sign that the Lord had passed before him, beckoning him to move on. (From a letter to the editor dated July 1972)

Nation and People

GEOGRAPHY

"Pearl of the Indian Ocean" . . . Taprobane . . . Lanka. . . . Ceylon has been known by many names. This lush, pear-shaped, tiny tropical island (only 270 by 140 miles, with 25,000 square miles) lies just south of India and just above the equator, with no other land surface lying between it and the South Pole. Its splendid beaches and warm seas, it varied climate, its cool hills covered with tea bushes, its gems, its exotic ruined cities, its game sanctuaries, and its historic colorful pageants make it an almost undiscovered tourist paradise.

POPULATION

The population of over thirteen million consists racially of 71.9 percent Sinhalese, 20.5 percent Tamils, 7 percent Moors and Malays, and 0.6 percent others. The two main languages are now Sinhala and Tamil, both well-developed. While Buddhists are usually Sinhalese-speaking and Hindus are Tamil-speaking, Christians are found among both Sinhalese and Tamils. Thus the Christians, though few, are in a unique position to promote the unity of the nation.

The rate of increase of population was as high as 2.8 percent in 1960, but it declined to 2.4 percent in 1971.[2] In 1965 the state adopted a population control policy in cooperation with the Family Planning Association and the Swedish government, which provides material aid. As a result, in addition to the religious objections some of the leaders are raising the absurd cry that this will reduce the influence politically (and otherwise) of the majority community by decreasing their numbers. Without slowing this population growth, however, government plans for increasing the economic growth and raising the living standard may be defeated.

ECONOMY

Ceylon's economy is agricultural and depends heavily on exports of three primary agricultural products: in 1968 (a representative year) the percentage distribution of these exports was: tea, 50 percent; rubber, 17 percent; coconut, 17 percent; all others, 7 percent. Ceylon is the second-largest tea producer in the world, producing almost one-fourth of the total world output; she also produces about 5 percent of world production of natural rubber, with 572,000 acres under production. When the world rubber price falls by one U.S. cent, Ceylon's annual loss is over two million U.S. dollars! Ceylon is also the world's fourth-largest producer of coconuts, with 1,152,000 acres under cultivation. Thus the recent continued decline in world prices for all three of these products, plus the rise in prices for imported industrial goods, has severely strained the economy and forced a more than 20 percent unfavorable balance of trade.

Rice paddy production has recently increased phenomenally due to increased utilization of fertilizer and of high quality seed. But the government provides every person with a measure of rice free of charge weekly, and since rice is the staple diet of the people, this subsidy is very large and costly. Thus today Ceylon's economic plight is grave. With a population growth rate still relatively high (2.4 percent in 1971) and an economic growth rate of only 4 percent, average income is a meager $150 per year. Despite a devaluation of the rupee in 1967, runaway inflation is reducing its real value. Unemployment in early 1972 stood at 15 percent.

Foreign aid until now has taken the forms of program or community aid, project aid, and technical assistance of three kinds: experts, equipment, and scholarships. A new Five-Year Plan has been launched, in part financed by the World Bank, with the aim of providing 150,000 new jobs a year. But massive foreign aid is needed to tide the country over the immediate future. Ceylon, being a non-aligned nation, has been getting aid from both capitalist and communist countries, with the government looking increasingly to the latter in recent years despite the fact that the bulk of the aid in the last twenty years has been from the U.S.

Ceylon is tending toward a welfare state. During the last five years about 25 percent of the total government expenditure has been for social services. Education has claimed a lion's share of this.

EDUCATION

Christians first initiated popular education early in the nineteenth century. But at the turn of the century Buddhists and Hindus showed increasing interest. Later the state gradually took over more and more responsibility for education, until in 1941 it assumed full responsibility for the pay of all teachers' salaries, even in the schools run by religious bodies.

Today all education is free, from kindergarten to university. Every effort is being made to increase literacy, which now averages 72 percent (80 percent for males and 64 percent for females). But, regrettably, over 60 percent of the schoolteachers are unqualified, and nearly half a million children in the compulsory-education age group (five to fourteen years) are not in school. The most acute shortages in the economy are for technicians, foremen, draftsmen, supervisors, etc., and thus technical education is an urgent need. Four universities, with fifteen thousand students, are serving the needs of higher education.

When the government began to subsidize all education, ten Christian schools wisely rejected this assistance, for a few years later, in 1960, the government decided to take over the complete management of all schools run by religious bodies which were receiving government subsidies. But some protests forced the government to permit six to stay open under unique conditions: they must meet their expenses not from school fees or government grants, but through voluntary donations, by funds raised by special efforts, and by some help received from abroad. They have managed to survive so far only with the greatest difficulty.

National History

Primitive Veddahs inhabited this jungle isle in prehistoric days until the Sinhalese invaders from northern India subjugated and assimilated them in the sixth century B.C. With the coming of Buddhism three hundred years later this civilization flowered with elaborate irrigation works and a magnificent capital at Anuradhapura. Then followed two millennia of political and economic invasions: the Chola conquest of the eleventh century only temporarily brought the island under India; the Tamils imported Hinduism; and the Muslim Moors from the Persian Gulf settled there to promote trading.

The Portuguese, attracted by the pungent odor of cinnamon (which at that time Ceylon alone produced) gradually conquered the western maritime provinces in the early sixteenth century. For 150 years they ruled coastal Ceylon and introduced Catholic Christianity. The Dutch, also motivated by the cinnamon profits, finally succeeded in supplanting the Portuguese in the mid-seventeenth century with the aid of the king of Kandy, a hill state. Then the British sent a military expedition in 1796 and finally succeeded in subduing the whole island with Kandyian aid in 1815. Thus ended 2537 years of Sinhalese independence. British rule continued until Ceylon finaly became an independent member of the British Commonwealth in 1948.

The subsequent years have seen a steady swing from the moderate United National party's control in the first parliament (modeled after Great Britain's) to a sweeping majority control by the Sri Lanka Freedom party, a former center party which has formed a united front government together with the left-wing Lanka Sama Samai party and the pro-Moscow Communists. Mrs. Sirimavo Bandaranaike, widow of the first SLFP prime minister (who was assassinated in 1959), in 1960 became the world's first woman prime minister. Her government is taking steady and speedy steps toward "democratic socialism" and socialization of the economy.

In June 1972 a new constitution was formally adopted and Ceylon was proclaimed the Republic of Sri Lanka, though it continues to remain within the British Commonwealth. The constitutional head of state is now the president appointed by the prime minister, who in turn heads the cabinet and the government. Thus for twenty-five years Ceylon has been going through radical political and economic changes marked by two severe riots which at times gravely threatened her security—one by Buddhists and Hindus in 1958 and another by radical leftist youths in 1971. But the government has survived these crises, and the prime minister's united front government now has over 80 percent majority in the National Assembly.† The government has now closed the British naval and air bases and nationalized both the foreign oil companies and its own extensive bus transportation system.

National Religions

The census of 1971 (latest available) recorded the following distribution of religious loyalties:

Buddhists	67.4%
Hindus	17.6
Christians	7.7
Muslims	7.1
Other	0.1

BUDDHISM

The *Mahavansa*, an ancient chronicle, avers that on the day of his passing away the Buddha addressed Sakra, the king of the gods, thus: "My doctrine, O Sakra, will eventually be established in the island of Lanka." This was in the sixth century before Christ and over two centuries prior to any Buddhism coming to Ceylon. An Indian emperor, Asoka, became a Buddhist, and his son, Mahinda, brought Buddhism to the country of Ceylon at a time when the only religion in Ceylon was a crude form of animism.

Of the two major schools of Buddhism, Mahayana and Hinayana, the latter (claiming to be purer) prevails in Ceylon. (See chapter 28, "Important Religions of Asia.") A Buddhist priest in Ceylon takes vows of celibacy and poverty; he does not eat after mid-day; he possesses only 2 sets of robes, a begging bowl, a razor, a needle, and thread. Spending his

†Ed. note. Many in the West have written off the government as a communist state because of its increasing closeness with China in foreign affairs. Others say, however, that Mrs. Bandaranaike stands between democracy and Communism. The leader of the opposition party, J. R. Javewardene, a strong anti-Communist, said in the National Assembly in early '72, "I believe Mrs. B. is the only leader capable of saving our country from communism" (reported in Japan's *Mainichi News*, Feb. 20, 1972).

time in study and meditation, the recitation of sacred texts, preaching and teaching when necessary, he lives in a typical temple where there is a shrine room containing one or more statues of the Buddha, a stupa containing some relics of the Buddha, and a Bodhi-tree like that under which the Buddha himself attained enlightenment. Their worship consists of offering flowers at the stupa and the Bodhi-tree, with clay lamps lit and incense burning near the shrine.

Community worship is also led by the priest in which the people respond with certain formulas and end up by taking vows known as the "Five Precepts" and by abstaining from intoxicants. It is claimed that the offering of flowers is a symbolic gesture of honor and gratitude and also stimulates in the devotee's mind a desire to cultivate the qualities of the Buddha. However the influence of Hinduism is gradually infusing Buddhism. Hindu images are appearing in Buddhist shrine rooms, and vows are being made to these gods also.

In 1954 the Buddha Jayanthi celebrations (twenty-five hundred years of Buddhism) were observed with great enthusiasm by the people and with government support.

HINDUISM

A main characteristic of Hinduism is its catholicity—it is comprehensive and elastic, embracing many varieties of religious beliefs, though all professing to go back to the old Brahamic scriptures. One of these, the *Bhagavad-Gita,* records Lord Krishna as saying, "They who worship other gods with devotion, full of faith—they also worship me. Thus Hinduism has had no difficulty adjusting to Ceylonese Buddhism.

Siva and Krishna are the best known Hindu gods, and their worshippers are all known as Saivites and Vaishnavites, respectively. The majority of Hindus in Ceylon are Saivites who distinguish themselves by ash on their foreheads. The Ramakrishna mission is active in social and educational work among the Tamils. The Hindus are largely Tamils, including both Ceylon Tamils and Indian Tamils in about equal proportions. The Indian Tamils, mainly plantation laborers who have no vote, are being sent back to India under a 1964 agreement between the two countries, which may account for the decrease in the percentage of Hindus recently.

Christian History

The earliest reference to Christianity in Ceylon is in the *Topographia Christiana* of one *Cosmas Indicopleustes,* who recorded that in the sixth century a group of Nestorian Christians had come from Persia (see chapter 7, "Christianity Comes to Asia"). There is also a tradition that the Apostle Thomas himself visited Ceylon and preached at a spot where the present

Saint Thomas Church Gintupitiva stands, overlooking the Colombo harbor. But after the sixth century there is no clear record of any Christians until the arrival of the Portuguese in 1505. During their occupation of the maritime provinces (until 1658) the Portuguese promoted Catholicism in every possible way, not always commendably. Accurate numbers are not recorded, but in 1663 Baldaeus writes that the Christians of the Jaffna district alone amounted to 65,145.

The Dutch colonizers, who were Presbyterians, took over from the Portuguese in 1658. They not only persecuted those who had become Catholics under the Portuguese regime but also made it quite obvious that there would be no jobs available in the government except for Presbyterians. The number of Presbyterians increased phenomenally. When the Dutch had to give way to the British in 1796, the number of Protestants was listed as more than one-third of a million.

With the British conquest of the maritime provinces, Anglican missionaries came out to Ceylon. The diocese of Colombo was formed in 1845 and became an autonomous church in 1885. Today it has two bishops and an almost wholly native ministry. The Anglican church owes a great debt to the pioneer missionaries sent out in those early days by the Church Missionary Society, the Zenana Mission, and the Society for the Propagation of the Gospel.

In the early years the British rulers were liberal, and in 1806 the restrictions in worship imposed on the Catholics by the Dutch were removed. So it was no surprise that large numbers of those Catholics who had become Protestants for the sake of employment under the Dutch went back to Roman Catholicism, while many others reverted to Buddhism and Hinduism. Thus the number of Protestants in 1810 was reported to be half the number of 1801, and the decline continued. The Dutch had not provided or promoted local church leadership, which also contributed to this quick decrease. Thus at the present time the Presbyterian church, which had such large numbers under the Dutch occupation, is now one of the smallest Protestant bodies, with only a few thousand members. The Roman Catholic church apparently rebuilt on firmer foundations, for it continued to increase in numbers, as shown in the following tabulation:

1873–184,399; 1901–285,018; 1911–339,300.

The Catholic priests concentrated on pastoral care of their own adherents rather than on making conversions from other religions, and general population increase did the rest.

The early nineteenth century's great wave of world missions reached Ceylon also. The Ceylon auxiliary of the British and Foreign Bible Society was formed on August 1, 1812, and was the second-oldest auxiliary of the worldwide Bible Society (which was officially inaugurated only eight years earlier). The first British Baptist missionaries arrived also in 1812, while the first British Methodist missionaries came in 1814. The American Board Mission (Congregational) followed two years later.

Work by these societies continued with intermittent success until World War II. After the war apparently few new missionaries came, and even fewer new mission groups. But in recent years Pentecostal churches have been organized and have shown great fervor, resulting in rapid increase. The Ceylon Pentecost Mission has even established some branches in India, Malaysia, France, Sweden, and England. Through lack of adequate leadership there have been some splits, but the Pentecostal teaching is quietly gaining ground.

An Evangelical Alliance for fellowship was also organized for the first time in the postwar period.

Although foreign missionary activity appears to be limited in Sri Lanka for the future, there is still a need for a few able missionaries to pioneer specialized and new ministries within the church and to evangelize wisely on the outside. But the great need is for well-equipped, committed Ceylonese ministers and laymen, steeped in local culture and grounded in the Bible, men who fear no man because they know God. For workers such as these the future is full of promise. But apart from a quickening of the present churches and provision for training such leaders, hope for this is slim. Ceylon needs much prayer and revival within its churches if it is to see nationwide evangelism and church growth.

NOTES

1. *COFAE Newsletter*, Oct. 1971.
2. *World Population Data Sheet* (Washington: Pop. Ref. Bureau, 1971).

BIBLIOGRAPHY

Background Notes: Ceylon. Washington: US Department of State, July 1970.

Central Bank Annual Report, 1971.

Ceylon—Today and Yesterday. Lake House Press.

The Church of Ceylon: Her Faith and Mission. Ceylon: Centenary Volume Times, 1946.

Government Census Report, 1963.

History of the Catholic Church in Ceylon. Colombo: Prakasa, 1924.

History of the Diocese of Colombo. Centenary Volume Times of Ceylon, 1946.

History of Methodism in Ceylon.

Kulandran, S. *Grace in Christianity and Hinduism*. London: Lutter-work, 1964.

Rahola, V. W. *History of Buddhism in Ceylon*. Colombo: M. D. Gunaseka and Co., 1956.

——. *What the Buddha Taught*. Gordon Fraser Galling, 1959.

The Scheme of Church Union in Ceylon. Rev. ed. Christian Literature Society, 1963.

The Story of Ceylon. Ludowyke, Faber and Fato, 1962.

World Population Data Sheet, 1971. Washington: Population Reference Bureau, June 1971.

Revival has accompanied mountain tribe evangelism. Typical mountain women display beautifully made adornments.

In the cities churches are growing, too. A Christian teaches Bible to neighborhood children.

Tribal pastors enjoy lunch.

28

TAIWAN

by David Woodward

Introduction

"No island in the world has become so well known in so brief a time as Taiwan," observed Dr. Hollington Tong, former Chinese ambassador to the U.S. The small island has been a microcosm of shifting Asian tensions during the last thirty years. After fifty years of Japanese occupation, Taiwan was liberated by the Chinese, only to resist the harsh rule of the first Nationalist military government. In 1949 the fleeing Chinese nationalists brought the civil government of the Republic of China to the island. The following twenty years of rapid growth and significant leadership in Asia was then clouded by Taiwan's dismissal from the U.N. when Red China was admitted in 1971.

Possibly largely because of these changes and uncertainties, Taiwan has seen one of the greatest postwar phenomena of church growth. At the end of World War II Christians numbered approximately thirty thousand. Today there are over six hundred thousand, including both Catholics and Protestants. In twenty-seven years the church has multiplied twenty times and now comprises over 4 percent of the total population.[1]

This growth has followed an interesting pattern. The period of maximum

---

David Woodward was born of missionary parents in the Philippines and has served under the Evangelical Alliance Mission in India, Chinese Tibet, Hong Kong, Taiwan, and Korea. He holds the degrees of B.A. from Davidson College, M.Div. from Princeton Seminary, and M.A. from Seattle Pacific College. His missionary ministry has included pioneer evangelism, literature propagation, and Christian education.

growth took place in the decade from 1948 to 1958. One significant factor was doubtless the immigration from the mainland of possibly as many as fifty thousand Christians. But probably even more significant was the receptivity of both displaced mainlanders and islanders, occasioned by the uncertainty, danger, and change forced by political circumstances. Also important was the quality of mainland Christian workers who came—seasoned, experienced pastors and missionaries from many missions and churches descending on the island in large numbers. Significant too was the fact that these workers, perhaps inadvertently, settled in the most receptive urban areas, especially the capital city of Taipei. There the displaced persons were clustered together in poverty. But a Lutheran missionary observer, Allen Swanson, stresses that "lay involvement was the key factor in the rapid growth of the Taiwan church in the 1950's. Lay involvement is still the key factor in the continued growth of the independent churches."[2]

A study of which churches grew during that time is revealing. Overall, the rate and number of both Protestants and Catholics was roughly equal. Among the Protestants the traditional, mainline denomination which had been evangelizing in the country for over a century was the Presbyterian church, led largely by English and Canadian missionaries. This church grew from approximately 15,000 in 1942 to 170,000 in 1960 (total Christian constituency). Growth in the plains churches since then has leveled off, but rapid growth has still been taking place in the mountain churches, which in 1960 made up less than half the total. Also steadily growing during this entire period have been two major indigenous denominations, the True Jesus church, an indigenous pentecostal group, and the Church Assembly, better known as the "Little Flock," which was born under the mainland leadership of Wang Ming Tao. Though both Catholic and Protestant growth leveled off in the decade of the sixties, these groups continue to grow steadily. Swanson states, "they grow because they practice the priesthood of all believers. . . ."[3] Familiar on the streets of Taipei since the war have been the aggressive street meetings of the Little Flock, with each person who participates wearing a similar pillowcase-like shirt over his other clothing with Scripture verses emblazoned on it. Both of these groups have no mission connections and are totally indigenous to the Chinese culture. Among some of the many newer groups which came in during the postwar period, the Southern Baptist Mission experienced rapid growth in the fifties, after a static period between 1962 and 1966. It recovered to see a growth of 841 between 1967 and 1969, and from 1970 to 1972 an increase of 1,337. Their leaders are optimistic that this growth rate will continue.[4]

The growth slump in the sixties was experienced by both Catholics and

Protestants. The increased security of the people and the burgeoning economy are doubtless major reasons. But Swanson also observes that "A rapidly urbanized, industrial society has left most churches in a state of disarray. We do not know how to plant churches in a mobile society, for the structures we have developed do not allow for mobility. Organizational obfuscation effectively prevents any attempt to break away from the worship of ancestral patterns."[5]

A Presbyterian document talking about the rapid urbanization of society comments that "More and more we see city churches turned into upper-middle-class 'worship clubs' by their inability to reach out into the lives of working-class people in a meaningful way." Their closeness to the life of the working people and their total identification with both mainland and local Taiwan culture under lay leadership has doubtless enabled the True Jesus and Little Flock groups to keep growing despite these factors.

In the 1970's there has been some pickup in church growth in some areas, but overall the picture has not been good for either Catholics or Protestants. From 1954 to 1968 the Catholics went from 32,000 to 302,000.[6] Presbyterian growth started well but slacked off early in the sixties. The total Protestant growth rate has been kept up by the many new churches that were started by refugee mainland pastors and missionaries. Over forty groups now compete for Protestant Christian loyalties in Japan. But 81 percent of Taiwan's forty-two denominations have less than twelve hundred members each, and half of the mission-related churches have less than six hundred members each.

The greatest encouragement during the postwar period has been the growth of the tribal churches. There were some four thousand Christians in these remote, primitive areas at the outbreak of World War II. They suffered great persecution under the Japanese during that period. At the close of the war, veteran Canadian Presbyterian missionary Dr. James Dickson and his wife "Lil" pioneered new thrusts into these remote regions. By 1949 they reported thirty thousand Christians; by 1958, fifty-two thousand; and by 1968 seventy thousand. An outbreak of revival among the tribal Tawal Presbyterian churches in 1972 and 1973 reports quickened spiritual life (along with some excesses) and great church growth. "The sales of Bibles, Christian literature, and Sunday school materials have skyrocketed," reports missionary William Junkin.[7] As is true in other Asian settings, a major factor in growth has been the weakness of tribal animism, but even more importantly a definite movement of the Holy Spirit in revival power following faithfulness in persecution. Sadly, this mountain church revival has not been widespread through the island, and its growth has been exceptional, particularly during the sixties and early seventies, when many plains churches have stagnated.

The Church Today

Now, in the decade of the seventies, there are many encouraging features on the Taiwan church scene despite recent political upheavals. Modest though it may be, Taiwan churches are beginning to grow again after having been on a plateau of non-growth. (The latest statistics show a total Protestant registration of 246,000.*[8]) The Taiwanese churches are growing in new ways, too. There has been interchurch cooperation in evangelism, study conferences, pastors' prayer retreats, and Christian service agencies.† Liberal-conservative differences are not accentuated in Taiwan for liberalism has not been strong in the major Presbyterian denomination. The Taiwan Evangelical Fellowship sponsors many of the interchurch conferences, and the Chinese Christian Churches Union helps churches with legal and other problems. Both organizations receive wide support from the Christian community.

There is an increasingly close relationship of the churches with overseas Christians in southeast Asia and North America, helped by the ease of modern transportation, for the Chinese have a sense of common identity which transcends their provincial, linguistic, and cultural differences. Cooperation and fellowship between evangelical Chinese around the world, and particularly in Asia, is being evidenced in many practical ways. A Taiwanese pastor, Chung Chi-an, became the general secretary of the Malaysian Christian Council in 1958. Another well-known Presbyterian pastor, Tai Pei-fu, was called to Singapore in 1973 to work in factory evangelism. When the China Sunday School Association held Christian education conferences in eleven cities around the island in 1973, the main speaker on the team of six was a guest from Hong Kong, Calvin Wong of Christian Communications, Ltd. Fifty churches joined together to sponsor the first Taipei Bible Conference in June 1973, with speakers from New York City and Hong Kong. The widely scattered Chinese are very welcome in Taiwan and usually feel much at home when they get there. A Chinese radio team of the Evangelical Alliance Mission made a tour of southeast Asia in 1973, speaking to 34,000 people and noting 561 conversions. The Chinese churches they visited contributed $7,000 for their gospel broadcasting program to the China mainland.[9] Two-thirds of the China Evangelical Seminary budget in 1972-73 came as contributions from overseas

*But other statistical studies in 1973 almost double this figure. See charts in appendixes.

†A breach in this generally good cooperation emerged at the 1965 Centennial of the Presbyterian church, when only twenty-two churches and organizations were in attendance. The Presbyterian church had joined the World Council of Churches in 1951, and this relationship possibly kept many denominations from participating in the Centennial. This issue was resolved when the Presbyterian church withdrew from the WCC in 1970. Government pressure was alleged, but it is likely that church leaders were motivated in the main by a desire to keep Presbyterians united.

Chinese in Asia and America, showing the stake these Chinese Christians have in Christian work in Taiwan.[10]

Another example of interchange is the flow of missionaries from Malaysia to Taiwan. The Overseas Missionary Fellowship has had ten of these transfers, who are unable to continue work in Malaysia due to a ten-year residency limit but find scope for their experience in Chinese churches by moving to Taiwan.[11]

Missionary activities are shifting in the seventies. With increasingly experienced national church leadership, missionaries are withdrawing from church administration. This has freed some for direct evangelism. Southern Baptists have been involved in "Reconciliation through Christ" campaigns, Mennonites in a new program for factory workers, TEAM missionaries in village evangelism, and Oriental Missionary Society workers in student evangelism. The Protestant missionary force continues at a high level, with 760 resident missionaries in 1972.[12] Although Presbyterian missionaries have dropped from a high of 90 down to 60 and the Methodist Mission has withdrawn, other missions have had increases in workers. More short-term missionaries are serving on Taiwan. The missionary community is well represented by the Taiwan Missionary Fellowship and is blessed by an excellent school system for missionary children, Morrison Academy, with a central school and five satellite elementary schools.

Finally, national church leaders are taking a mature and responsible attitude toward Christian organizations, programs, and activities. Unhappy over the closing down of a mission-sponsored evangelistic magazine, Dengta, in 1971, a board of interested Chinese started publishing a new magazine, Yu-chou Kuang, in Taipei in 1973. Evangelist Wu Yung, a Mandarin church pastor, is chairman of this board. The China Evangelical Seminary, almost exclusively Chinese-led, with Wu Yung as board chairman, had its first graduating class of seven in 1973.[13] The Mandarin churches of Taipei assumed management of the Door of Hope Children's Refuge (a former TEAM mission institution) in 1972. Scripture Union in Taiwan became self-supporting in 1973. The Chinese Christian Mission, a literature agency backed by overseas Chinese, has developed a unique publishing program—it mails out free of charge a monthly paper and occasional printings of evangelistic and devotional books to a mailing list of fifty-five thousand Chinese. The costs of the program are covered by voluntary contributions, mostly from the readers, who are scattered throughout Taiwan, Hong Kong, Indonesia (where there is a famine of literature in the Chinese language), and other Chinese enclaves throughout Asia.

Wilfred Su, business manager of the China Evangelical Seminary, reflects the vision of a rising group of young church leaders here:

> I am convinced that if every Chinese Christian at home (e.g., Taiwan) and overseas really understands the tremendous responsibility which God is entrusting to us, and works to produce the strength of united action, then we will see the Gospel preached to every creature in this generation.[14]

An evidence of this are the seven tribal couples from Taiwan who are evangelizing among the tribes of Sarawak in Borneo in a program first visualized by Dr. and Mrs. James Dickson, Presbyterian missionaries, and furthered by dynamic "Lil" Dickson after her husband's death. Eighteen Taiwanese Presbyterian pastors from the board of what is called the Burning Bush Mission and are responsible for operating this mission. The first of these missionaries has already come back on furlough.

Nation and People

Situated off the southeastern coast of the China mainland, Taiwan is separated from the province of Fukien on the mainland by the Straits of Taiwan, which is only 90 to 120 miles wide. The island's shape has been likened to a large leaf with a rib of mountains down its length, but the main north-south range actually runs closer to the east coast, leaving wide, fertile plains on the west. The central range protects the rich farmlands of the western plains from the worst of typhoon weather, and irrigation systems provide a constant supply of water. Two crops a year are commonplace, and food is plentiful.[15] With an area of 13,808 square miles, Taiwan is slightly larger than Massachusetts and Connecticut combined and slightly smaller than Holland.[16] The Portuguese named the island "Formosa" or "Beautiful," and the name is appropriate: the vegetation is lush and the mountain gorges and peaks are spectacular. Since 1612 the Chinese have had another name for the island: "Taiwan" or "Terraced Bay," named for the rice terraces on its slopes, which are similar to those in the northern Philippines.

Population has increased 2½ times since the end of World War II, and in 1973 it stood at 15 million.[17] The Amoy-speaking Taiwanese comprise almost three-quarters of the population, and the Hakka-speaking Taiwanese make up another 13 percent. Taiwan had an estimated influx of 750,000 civilians and 600,000 soldiers from the mainland of China in 1949, fleeing from the Communists. These refugees have settled down, found employment, and raised families, so that the mainland-oriented part of the population is now well over two million.

From the standpoint of the Christian church a small but significant enclave are the aborigines of the hills. Of Malayan stock, they were the original inhabitants of the island, but were gradually pushed back into the mountains by waves of Chinese immigrants. The largest tribe, the Amis, were sufficiently isolated on the east coast to hold their land in the valleys. Though the tribes have been socially and economically depressed, they have been the group most ready to accept Jesus Christ. Pioneer work among them after the war found amazing openness. A people's movement began, and as a result about 80 percent of the aborigines are now affiliated with tribal churches.[18] About half of these tribal people live on reservations in the mountain areas, and special permits are required in order to visit them. Plains people of Chinese descent keep pressing into the hills, and some ex-servicemen have been given small land holdings in the interior. Meanwhile, many young tribal people are moving to the cities for jobs.

The rising standard of living in Taiwan is perhaps best illustrated by comparison with other parts of east Asia. While 70 percent of Tokyo residents own their own homes, 51 percent do in Taipei. Bangkok follows with 49 percent, and then Manila, Singapore, Seoul, and Hong Kong. In bank accounts Tokyo and Taipei residents lead again, followed by residents of other large cities of Asia.

C. H. Hwang, former principal of Taiwan Theological College, a Presbyterian training school, said, "We are living in an Asia which has been radically changed and is still changing. . . . The new is erupting all around us, and while it speaks with many and conflicting voices, the keynote everywhere is change, and everyone is caught up in it."[19] These changes have been drastic in Taiwan: tribal people in remote villages are now watching television programs and are among the million homes in Taiwan which have TV sets. The government has extended free education (in 1968) from the primary level through junior high school. Life expectancy in Taiwan has jumped upward by twenty years. In 1952 a million people on Taiwan were suffering wtih malaria, and now the disease has been practically eradicated.[20] The island is bursting with growth. Within less than twenty-five years the cities of Taichung and Kaohsiung have grown four times; during the same period the capital city of Taipei tripled in size, approaching the two-million mark in 1973; Kaohsiung was close to a million.[21] At the same time export trade passed the three-billion U. S. dollar mark in an economic success story which begins to rival the other Chinese emporiums of Hong Kong and Singapore.[22] Education, too, is booming. Primary education is compulsory and nationwide. In 1973 there were 9,417 overseas Chinese students enrolled in the universities and colleges of Taiwan.[23] In the rapidly upgrading graduate schools of Taiwan are 3,000 students from Taiwan and overseas who are pursuing master's and doctoral programs,[24] some studying for arts degrees and many preparing in modern sciences.

Some fear that the rapid industrialization and technological progress of recent years will erode away the beauty of ancient Chinese culture in Taiwan. But not if the government can help it. The Chinese would like both improved living standards and the maintenance of their culture. The Palace Museum in Taipei houses 250,000 art treasures brought over from mainland China.[25] The College of Chinese Culture, with twelve thousand students, specializes in Chinese philosophy, literature, and arts and seeks to pass on a love of history to their generation. Dr. Chou Lien-hwa, Baptist seminary professor and pastor, has said, "We are trying our best to preserve the culture of China. We are preserving it, studying it, and hoping to make a contribution through it to the whole world."[26]

The nationalist government has made strenuous efforts to guard its ancient and beautiful cultural heritage, meanwhile trying to build a strong, defensible, viable society on the island. It has come in for much criticism, particularly from western liberals and even a few evangelicals. Their view is that the refugee mainlanders have imposed an alien culture and government on unwilling islanders. But sinologist Maurice Freedman points out:

> Two phases of modern history may tempt us to think of Taiwan as a separate country. From 1895 to 1945 it was governed by the Japanese; since 1949 it has been cut off by civil war from the mainland of China. But it is part of China, and nobody familiar with Chinese patterns of social organization and behavior will have any difficulty in recognizing (the Taiwanese) as good Chinese.[27]

Many have also alleged that Taiwan is a harsh police state. But it is important to avoid the stereotypes formed twenty years ago. The government is in firm control, but this is true in ten other Asian nations. The military men are not aging but are young, well-trained, and well-armed. The majority of the people are now conversant in the national language, Mandarin Chinese, but major public addresses are still translated into Taiwanese. The government and civil service have a steadily increasing number of Taiwanese participating, particularly at the local level but in the national assembly as well. Though the government is still basically "mainland," it is cultivating support from all elements of the population. It is important to remember that it is the Taiwanese who have the money and property; they have had the capital to go into industry. The result is that Taiwanese industrialists and landowners are inextricably bound up in the "establishment" of today's Taiwan in both business and government.

President Chiang Kai-shek, who has been the head of the Chinese state since 1927, is now physically enfeebled by age and has been forced from public appearances, though Madame Chiang is still active in entertaining foreign guests. Government leadership has devolved on the president's elder son, Chiang Ching-kuo, who was officially named premier in 1972. Premier Chiang is as expansive and friendly as his father has been dignified and remote. A relaxed, jovial public figure, he can also be a hard-nosed efficiency expert. His administration is producing many surprises. He has closed the mainland research departments in various bureaus of government. The handling of exit visas has been transferred from military to civilian hands. Government officials have been warned not to live high, and they have heeded his warning, for Chiang Ching-kuo was so efficient at closing down vice while mayor of Shanghai that the city fathers sought to remove him.

Premier Chiang has been going out of his way to win over the Taiwanese. It is a sign of the progress in the strained relations that have existed between native Taiwanese and mainlanders in Taiwan that government publications can discuss the problem,[28] for previously it was seldom mentioned.[29] Possibly nationalist China's expulsion from the United Nations and its decrease in diplomatic recognition will draw the population of Taiwan together for mutual protection.

Dr. Tong lists the Premier and his wife as Christians in his book *Christianity in Taiwan.*[30] It is known that Chiang Kai-shek was so impressed by the devotional book *Streams in the Desert* that he helped arrange for its wide distribution among the military. He frequently quotes from the Bible in his public addresses, but little more is known about his personal faith.

National History

The Chinese were aware of Taiwan as early as 135 B.C., and Chinese migration began as early as the sixth century. They found a land which was rich in natural resources and inhabited by aboriginal peoples related to certain tribal groups in the Philippines. Over the years these aboriginals were pushed off the fertile plains and into the mountains. After a brief fifteen-year Spanish rule over northern Taiwan early in the century, the major influx of Chinese took place during and after the seventeenth century, when the Dutch gave the island political stability and made it attractive to Chinese refugees fleeing the turmoil of the closing decades of the Ming dynasty. The subsequent Manchu conquest of the mainland accelerated this migration. During this period China made no claim on Taiwan, although it was a Chinese pirate-rebel (Koxinga or Cheng Cheng-tung) who ended thirty-seven years of Dutch rule (1661) when he sought to make the island his base from which to restore the Ming dynasty on the mainland. His efforts were short-lived. The Manchus captured Taiwan in 1683 and from then on exercised a somewhat irresponsible rule over its restless people. During the nineteenth century the island was torn by more than thirty costly revolts.

As late as 1887 Peking suddenly came to realize its political and economic potential. An excellent administrator, Liu Ming-chuan, was appointed, and reforms were instituted. Too little, too late! By 1895, as a result of her defeat in the Sino-Japanese War, the Manchus were forced to cede the island "in perpetuity" to the Japanese. During the fifty years of Japanese control from 1895 to 1945 the population increased from 2½ to 6 million. Unfortunately, the island was developed as a colony, not as an integral part of the Japanese nation. Nevertheless, crime decreased, sanitation improved, trains ran on time, sugar and paper mills were built, and there was work for everyone. But the Taiwanese were second-class citizens, denied the right to go to school with the Japanese and barred from all professions but medicine.

When World War II arrived, the Taiwanese were caught up in the mighty struggle; they were forced to serve in the Japanese armies and suffered from Allied bombing. Thus they welcomed the Chinese armies of liberation. It is tragic that the Nationalists did not grant to this relatively highly developed province more equal status with the mainland. Instead, they imposed military rule under the leadership of Chen Yi, the infamous governor of Fukien province. Exploitation and oppression followed. On February 28, 1947, the Taiwanese revolted and presented "Thirty-two Demands" for reform. In response Chen Yi's henchmen launched a reign of terror that took the lives of more than ten thousand people.[31] American pressure forced Chiang Kai-shek to replace Chen Yi (who was then appointed the governor of Chekiang!). Eventually, the former mayor of Shanghai, Dr. K. C. Wu, was appointed governor of Taiwan, and he began to give the Taiwanese the government they needed and deserved.

In 1949 Taiwan became the nationalist government of China's refuge from the Communists, and the island's future looked even more uncertain. Then the Korean War intervened, and on June 27, 1950, President Truman ordered the U.S. Seventh Fleet to protect Taiwan by patrolling the straits. Security from mainland communist attack and infusions of American foreign aid spurred a rapid national recovery.

The land reform program of 1949 broke up the large landed estates and made landowners of tenant farmers, a major step forward.[32] Though American economic aid ended in 1965, by 1973 Taiwan was paying over 95 percent of its own defense costs.[33] Industries have multiplied and agriculture has boomed. The current industrial boom in Taiwan has been helped by special tax-free enclaves called "export processing zones," which have proved inviting to foreign capital.[34] Farm demonstration teams have traveled from Taiwan to other countries in Africa, the Middle East, southeast Asia, and Latin America, and Taiwan has trained eight thousand technicians from more than fifty countries.[35]

With Taiwan's expulsion from the U.N. in 1971, the resulting breakoff of diplomatic relations with Japan, and her precarious military position just off the mainland of red China, the nation seems dangerously insecure to an outsider. Yet internal morale has been high. The economy continues to boom. Japan has contrived covert ways to continue the mutually profitable trade. Tiny Taiwan may well continue to preserve her national integrity and remain an important factor in the Far East for years to come.

National Religions

Traditionally, the main folk religion of the majority of Taiwanese has been Taoism, though primitive animism dominated the aboriginal highlanders. The various migrations and governmental changes brought with them elements of Buddhism and Confucianism through the years. Thus today the native religion is a mixture. Buddhist and Taoist priests may both be called in to chant their prayers side by side at a funeral service.[36] While Taoist temples number two thousand and Buddhist temples six hundred, there are innumerable small shrines, including family altars in homes and shops. The worship of millions in Taiwan is basically polytheistic, with shrines to at least 250 gods.[37] Today, despite the fact that secularization is growing in Taiwan, it is being accompanied by a remarkable revival of traditional religious practices. New temples and shrines are being constructed, and they are crowded by the faithful.[38]

Thus contemporary Taiwanese society is in a state of religious and ethical flux. Dr. Song states:

> In our society here in Taiwan the traditional family ethical codes, closely bound up with Confucianism, are being secularized; they are no longer as sacred as before. The concepts such as authority, obedience, and filial piety, which subsisted on the strength of a feudal structure of society, and the reality these concepts used to carry with them, have been going through a process of disintegration.[39]

Christian History

The Dutch first established Protestant churches in the seventeenth century, and Christians once numbered close to six thousand. With the fall of the Dutch, Chinese Christians were killed along with their Dutch pastors, a number of them being crucified,[40] and the church was apparently totally eradicated. Both Protestant and Catholic missions began again in the mid-nineteenth century and developed as extensions of work already established in Fukien province, since many of the Taiwanese spoke that dialect.[41]

Catholic work actually began in 1859. Protestants sent their first missionary in 1865, Dr. James Maxwell, an English Presbyterian. Together with three Chinese Christian helpers he opened work in southern Taiwan. One Taiwanese, Cheng-hung, was so eager to hear the gospel that he walked the length of the island to meet the Christians. He accepted Christ, but within a short time he was attacked and murdered by a mob.[42]

The Canadian Presbyterian Mission sent Dr. George Mackay to the north of Taiwan in 1872. He and other early pioneers faced much initial opposition, but they also won friends. Church work progressed healthily at both ends of the island up to the turn of the century, when work in the north slackened through lack of evangelists. It did not pick up until the 1930's, when John Sung, famed Chinese evangelist, visited Taiwan with tremendous results. Work in the south had continued with steady growth under a succession of missionary evangelists until World War II, when all missionaries were expelled. The war years were full of difficulty. Christian leaders were under constant suspicion and pressure by the Japanese. Nevertheless, the early years of Christian missions left indelible marks on the island. Presbyterian missions gave the island its first good schools and its first hospitals. Missionaries promoted literacy and Christian literature, producing Taiwan's first magazine.[43]

With the end of Japanese occupation and Taiwan's reception of fleeing mainlanders in 1949, the opportunities were so great that the big-hearted Presbyterian missionary, Dr. James Dickson, urged the many missions who were leaving mainland China to relocate in Taiwan. They came in great numbers, and non-Presbyterian churches grew from almost nothing at the end of the war to over a hundred thousand by 1965. Roman Catholics also increased ten times in a decade, helped by a strong force of missionaries transferred from mainland China. The Presbyterian church itself carried out a successful "Double-the-Church Movement" between 1955 and 1965.

The proliferation of new denominations included the Assemblies of God, Christian and Missionary Alliance, various Baptist and Lutheran groups, Methodists, Free Methodists, Nazarenes, Mission Covenant churches, Friends, Episcopalians, TEAM-organized churches, and others. The Oriental Missionary Society came to help the Taiwan Holiness church. The Overseas Missionary Fellowship and Overseas Crusades came to help established churches. Mrs. Lillian Dickson's "Mustard Seed,"‡ Taiwan Christian Service, and the Fellowship Deaconry Mission ministered to crying cases of human need.[44] Dr. Andrew Loo of the Pocket Testament

‡This amazing ministry has grown steadily, beginning orphanages, leper homes, self-help projects, schools, and other valuable works. Her evangelists were among the first to open mountain evangelism among the aborigines.

League pioneered Christian radio in 1951, a field in which Lutherans, Baptists, TEAM, and Overseas Radio and Television are also now active. Expansion of medical work has ringed the island with Christian hospitals and clinics. The proliferation of Bible schools has been criticized, perhaps rightly,[45] but each denomination has wanted to prepare its own church workers.

Denominational and interdenominational student work has been very productive. Summer Bible camps have touched thousands of young lives. Student centers and hostels have drawn inquirers and strengthened new believers. Campus Evangelical Fellowship, affiliated with International Fellowship of Evangelical Students, has built up a dedicated corps of twenty student workers. Campus Crusades has also begun an active evangelistic ministry to students. Student work has specialized in what is probably the greatest need of the Taiwan Church—the practice of personal Bible study. Youth with this training are setting a stronger pace, a marching pace, for the seventies.

Thus an independent Taiwan with growing vital churches and a reservoir of Christian youth faces the future with hope.

NOTES

1. David C. E. Liao, *The Unresponsive: Resistant or Neglected,* p. 9.
2. Allen J. Swanson, *Taiwan: Mainline versus Independent Church Growth,* pp. 218, 235.
3. Ibid., p. 235.
4. Statistics from Baptist headquarters in Taiwan.
5. Swanson, p. 225.
6. Ibid., p. 8.
7. Clare McGill, "Some Acts of the Holy Spirit in the Tayal Mountain Churches in Taiwan," p. 14.
8. *Taiwan Missionary Fellowship Directory, 1972.*
9. Report to TEAM Radio Board, Aug. 1973.
10. *China Evangelical Seminary News Bulletin,* Aug. 1973, p. 4.
11. Letter from Rev. Henry W. Guiness, June 5, 1973.
12. *Taiwan Missionary Directory,* Oct. 1972.
13. *CES News Bulletin,* Aug. 1973, p. 1.
14. *CES News Bulletin,* Oct. 1972, p. 4.
15. Gordon T. Dunn, Formosa, p. 4.
16. *141 Questions and Answers About the Republic of China,* pp. 1, 3.
17. *World Population Data Sheet* (Washington: Pop. Ref. Bureau), 1973.
18. George Vicedom, *Faith that Moves Mountains,* p. 140.
19. C. H. Hwang, "Report on East Asia."
20. *Into a New Era Together.*
21. *141 Questions and Answers,* p. 39.
22. Ibid., p. 42.
23. Ibid., p. 30.
24. Ibid.
25. Ibid., p. 39.
26. *The Unity of the Church: A Message to All Christians,* p. 11.
27. Margery Wolf, *The House of Lin,* p. 12.
28. *141 Questions and Answers,* p. 9.
29. Hollington Tong, *Christianity in Taiwan: A History,* p. 248.
30. Ibid., p. 132.

31. Ibid., p. 1-10.
32. *China Handbook, 1972-73,* p. 30.
33. *141 Questions and Answers,* p. 41.
34. Ibid., p. 44.
35. *China Handbook, 1972-73,* p. 38.
36. *141 Questions and Answers,* p. 18.
37. Gerald P. Kramer and George Wu, *An Introduction to Taiwanese Folk Religions,* p. 23.
38. Ibid., p. 2.
39. C. S. Song, *The New Century Mission Movement,* p. 8.
40. Dunn, p. 15.
41. Tong, p. 22.
42. Ibid., pp. 24-25.
43. James Davidson, *The Island of Formosa,* p. 604.
44. Tong, p. 86.
45. Jonathan Chao, *Foreign Mission Theological Education,* pp. 1-16.

BIBLIOGRAPHY

Chao, Jonathan. "Foreign Mission Theological Education: Taiwan, a Case Study." *Evangelical Missions Quarterly,* Fall 1972.

China Handbook, 1972-73. Taipei: China Publishing Co., 1973.

Davidson, James W. *The Island of Formosa.* Taipei: Book World Co., 1903.

Dunn, Gordon T. *Formosa.* London: Overseas Missionary Fellowship, 1954.

Gates, Alan F. "The Church in Growth." Mimeographed. Taipei: Taiwan Missionary Fellowship, 1967.

Hwang, C. H. "Report on East Asia." Bangkok: Christian Conference of Asia, 1964.

Into a New Era Together: The Christian Community within the Total Community in Taiwan. Mimeographed. Tainan: Tainan Theological College, 1965.

Kramer, Gerald P., and Wu, George. *An Introduction to Taiwanese Folk Religions.* Private printing. Raipei, 1970.

Liao, David C. E. *The Unresponsive: Resistant or Neglected.* Chicago: Moody Press, 1972.

McGill, Clare. "Some Acts of the Holy Spirit in the Tayal Mountain Churches in Taiwan." Mimeographed. 1973.

News Bulletin. Taipei: China Evangelical Seminary, Oct. 1972; Fall 1972; Aug. 1973.

141 Questions and Answers About the Republic of China. Taipei: Chung Hwa Information Service, 1973.

Song, C. S. "The New Century Mission Movement. Mimeographed. Tainan: Tainan Theological College, 1967.

Swanson, Allen J. *Taiwan: Mainline Versus Independent Church Growth.* South Pasadena: William Carey Library, 1970.

Taiwan Christian Yearbook. Taipei: Overseas Crusades, 1968.

Taiwan Missionary Fellowship Directory. Taipei: Overseas Crusades, 1972.

Tong, Hollington. *Christianity in Taiwan: A History.* Taipei: China Post Publishing Co., 1961.

"The Unity of the Church: A Message to All Christians. Mimeographed. Taipei: Presbyterian General Assembly Office, 1965.

Vicedom, George. *Faith That Moves Mountains.* Taipei: Presbyterian General Assembly Office, 1967.

Wolf, Margery. *The House of Lin.* New York: Appleton-Century-Crofts, 1968.

Yin Ying. *Christian Literature Work.* Taipei: Taiwan Lutheran Church, 1970.

Bangkok's floating market teems with activity.

Indigenous music enlivens a Baptist evangelistic rally.

The Congress on Evangelism brought new unity and impetus to evangelism there in 1970.

Traditional temple marks the old way of life.

Photos by Pacific Stars and Stripes

29

THAILAND

by Leon B. Gold

Introduction

WITH ONE OF THE SMALLEST Christian communities in all of Asia after 450 years of Christian missions (less than 0.5 percent total Christian population and 0.1 percent Protestant population), strategic Thailand finally began to see encouraging signs of spiritual growth in the early seventies. Prophetically, the first Thai Congress on Evangelism in January 1970 chose as its motto "The Hour Has Come." And God began to work.

The Congress was called the nearest thing to revival in the 140-year history of the Protestant church. Deeply stirred by the Asia-South Pacific Congress on Evangelism in Singapore in 1968, a tiny group of predominantly national leaders met to plan and pray for a Thailand Congress. With faith and fear they sent out invitations, not knowing who would attend. But from almost every denomination and Christian organization in Thailand 250 came. An amazing new spirit of unity was born. A new air of expectancy arose. And in the months immediately following at least 125 prayer cells for revival sprang up.

LEON B. GOLD, Australian, began his missionary career in the highlands of northern Thailand in 1954 with the Overseas Missionary Fellowship. Later switching to the Christian and Missionary Alliance, he continued tribal evangelism for several years and then launched a ministry of gospel broadcasts recorded for transmission over radio station FEBC in Manila. In 1968 Mr. Gold was loaned by the Alliance to FEBC to establish a recording studio and follow-up ministry in Bangkok which would serve Thailand, Laos, Cambodia, and Burma. This ministry, called SouthEast Asia Continental, coordinates gospel broadcasts and assists film evangelism by dubbing sound tracks of gospel films into the languages of the four previously-mentioned countries.

Then in the northern hinterland God began to work sovereignly among the Thai youth around "The Farm," a community development center with a nearby Christian high school. Early in 1971, at some special meetings, revival began among nominal, second-generation Christian youth. Night after night there were confessions, conversions, singing, and prayer till after midnight. A wise pastor advised the converts to form prayer and Bible study groups and witness bands. These went to churches in nearby communities, and the revival continued with scores (possibly hundreds) of conversions among the nominal believers. Healings and miracles in these meetings have been reported.

In mid-1971 at a conference on prayer cell evangelism at Bethlehem Church in Chieng Mai province backsliders were restored, the church revived, and eight evangelistic prayer cells begun in surrounding villages. The movement spread to the McCormick (Presbyterian) Hospital, where thirty to forty cells met for many months. Then in December 1971, at the annual conference for churches at the Phaya Bible School in that area, the witness teams came and the revival continued. Though some of the elders originally opposed the revival meetings, later many people were restored or converted. One man confessed murder, sale of country girls to Bangkok for prostitution, and embezzlement.

At the opening worship service of the WCC "Commission on World Mission and Evangelism" in Bangkok on December 31, 1972, the executive secretary of the Church of Christ in Thailand (largely Presbyterian) exulted that in that year the conversion rate had doubled, and that a new day of evangelism was opening in Thailand.

Following the 1970 Congress on Evangelism, an interdenominational "Revival Committee" was formed. One fruit of this was a citywide evangelistic campaign in Bangkok in late 1972 with twelve hundred in attendance the last night and one hundred decisions. In the last two or three years new leaders have also been amazingly raised up in the churches, especially in the capital city. Led to Christ through Campus Crusade while studying in the U.S., one professor at the agricultural university has reportedly led over a hundred students to Christ. Holding a Christmas party for students at the university in December 1972, he had twelve hundred attend and six hundred request gospel literature.

To a 1971 conference on church growth came over two hundred pastors and missionaries; a smaller conference was held in 1972, with more nationals in attendance. Theological education by extension is being planned by Presbyterian, CMA, OMF, and other missionaries. And a swing to a more conservative position is noted by several in the United Church of Christ. Currently the chairman and executive secretary are evangelistic conservatives.

The Church Today

The expectancy of a new breakthrough for God has been heightened by remarkably increased response to mass communication efforts in the last two years. The "Good News" radio broadcast of the Far East Broadcasting Company, the oldest broadcast in the country, now has eighty different broadcasts each week over fourteen stations. In 1969 mail responses jumped to five thousand, and in 1970 over ten thousand letters came. Now evangelical broadcasts total two hundred weekly over thirty-four stations, covering the entire country in tribal and national languages.

An upsurge has also marked Christian literature sales and reading, as evidenced by larger printings. Letter response to tracts has also jumped. Despite a nominal 70 percent adult literacy rate throughout the country, the real figure is probably much lower. Therefore cartoon-type literature has become more popular. The Overseas Missionary Fellowship, Christian and Missionary Alliance, Southern Baptist, and other smaller groups are concentrating on literature, along with the Bible Society publications, now totaling over seventeen million Scriptures in five languages.[1] Thai authors have been raised up to write many tracts and other publications. Bible correspondence course enrollments have also increased. In 1970 in the CMA course alone, five thousand students enrolled, 84 percent of whom completed their courses.

"The Thai people are ready to listen to Christianity," a twenty-year missionary veteran stated in early 1973. "There is the greatest opportunity ever for evangelical missions and missionaries to relate to the church and influence it for evangelism," he said.

The groundwork for this recent encouraging movement in Thailand came at the end of World War II. For 118 years up until 1946, missionary work had penetrated only twenty of Thailand's seventy-one provinces. After the interned missionaries had recuperated in their homelands and returned after 1946, work in these twenty provinces was gradually reopened. And heightened missionary interest in the western nations saw new recruits coming to the field.

But Thailand's greatest evangelistic impetus came through the closing of China to foreign missionary work in 1949. At that time there were only one hundred Protestant missionaries in Thailand, centered mainly in two missions. In the twenty years since then, however, this has increased to over seven hundred missionaries laboring in twenty-five different groups. Most of this increase was a redirection of interest to other fields after the door to China closed. The Overseas Missionary Fellowship has the largest single group of missionaries in Thailand, about two hundred.[2]

The great majority of the postwar, newer Protestant mission groups and missionaries in Thailand are of evangelical, non-ecumenical persuasion. Most are grouped together under the banner of the Evangelical Fellowship of Thailand, which has now been officially recognized by the Thai government as a second Protestant grouping. The emphasis of those associated with the EFT is on direct evangelism and church-planting, with some medical work in certain areas. Unfortunately, these are not equally spread over the country's population.* Missionaries related to the Church of Christ in Thailand have been largely Presbyterian, but unfortunately their members have shrunk to one-half in the last few years through recall. Other missions traditionally associated with the Church of Christ in Thailand have been the German Marburger Mission, the U.S. Disciples of Christ, and American Baptists. In addition to those already mentioned, newer postwar mission groups include Southern Baptists, the Churches of Christ, Christian Brethren, Worldwide Evangelization Crusade, New Tribes Mission, Finnish Free Mission, Assemblies of God, Pentecostal Assemblies of Canada, Scandinavian Pentecostal Mission, and several smaller groups and independents, including Asian Missionaries from Japan, Korea, and the Philippines.

With the large influx of these new missionaries after World War II, church growth accelerated, and by 1969 the prewar Protestant membership had trebled to a total of 32,000. This growth has been almost evenly divided between the Church of Christ and all other denominations. But statistics have never been accurately kept, so in 1972 Dr. Ronald Hill (Southern Baptist) endeavored to make an accurate assessment of Protestant Christians. He recorded 36,316 in nine denominations (22,000 in the 156 congregations of the Church of Christ) and estimates up to two thousand more among independents, Pentecostals, and other groups. It is possible that the northern revival movement may have swelled these numbers by hundreds or even a thousand. At least the rate of conversions to Christ was greatly accelerating in 1971 and 1972. Meanwhile, in the ten Catholic dioceses steady postwar growth has resulted in a 1972 total of 167,194, up from 116,000 in 1963. (These figures include children and

*This chart indicates the missionary concentration in proportion to population, as of 1970:

Area	*Population Percentage*	*Missionary Percentage*	*Number of Missionaries*	*Index*[a]
Bangkok	7	31	224	4.4
Central	30	25	173	0.8
South	13	13	96	1.0
Northeast	35	8	57	0.2
North	15	22	154	1.4
	100%	100%	704	

[a]Index of 1.0 = Average Distribution

nominal adherents.) This growth has apparently been largely the fruit of the widespread Catholic educational system throughout the country.

Thailand has always been a difficult field for missions. Thus today only 0.1 percent of the population is Protestant Christian after over 140 years of missionary activity. Virutally every possible method of evangelism has been tried, but no one method stands out as more successful than another. Only seven of the fifteen church-planting missions in Thailand have over 500 members related to them. Every area is one of evangelistic need, and almost every area offers open opportunities. One strategic field is the vast bureaucracy of government officials. Required to take part in official Buddhist functions, they have appeared formidable and have therefore been neglected in favor of rural work.

In addition to the opposition of deeply entrenched Buddhism and animism, the inroads of false cults are cutting deeply into even the professing church in Thailand today. Because of the tragic lack of mature national leadership in most of the local churches, and also because of the illiterate or semi-literate believers, who have little knowledge of the Scriptures, the aggressive persuasive appeals of the cults deceive many. Their proselyting tactics have probably robbed more Christians from the churches than won new converts from the people. Thus a strategic need is leadership training for the many small, struggling church groups for whom there are not pastors. Laymen's training may be the answer.

Though there has never been a great awakening or spiritual harvest in Thailand, experienced observers feel that the hour has come for a harvest to begin. Opportunities for evangelism in Thailand today have never been greater. The seed of the gospel is being sown more widely than ever before. Most of the provinces have resident missionaries. The door to many new missionaries was opened in mid-1973, when the country's prime minister, Thanon Kittikachorn, told a meeting of religious leaders that he wanted their cooperation in solving some of the nation's problems. He urged them to try to win the hearts of those who were committed to no faith, particularly the young people. "Regardless of what religion you choose, I only ask that you follow your religion wholeheartedly," he said. As a result, missionaries to Thailand will in the future get first priority for residence visas under the country's new Alien Occupation Law. An official of the government department of religious affairs says that just as the government welcomes investments in the economy, it also considers investments of time and money in the spiritual realm to be profitable to the Thai people and government. Thus God has opened the door for the world church to take advantage of Thailand's current spiritual openness. Millions of pieces of Christian literature are flooding the land. Local radio stations are for the most part open to gospel broadcasts, and 60 percent of all homes in Thailand have their own radios, with an average listening audience of twenty-eight million daily.

Thailand today is a lake of comparative calm in the midst of the Indochina peninsula, buffeted by the monsoons of war. Though rimmed by the strife-torn lands of Vietnam, Laos, and Cambodia, Thailand is wide open as never before to the preaching of the gospel. How long this opportunity will last, no one knows. But today the opportunity is there. God is working. In this, God's hour for Thailand, the call to the world church for prayer, recruits, and resources is more urgent than ever before.

Nation and People

Throngs of tourists, pouring in ever-increasing numbers through Bangkok's international airport, are often dazzled by the modernity of Thailand. They see smiling people, wide boulevards, magnificently architectured Buddhist temples, and modern, air-conditioned hotels, theaters, and multistoried office buildings—all framed in a jewel-like setting of lush, green rice fields. Lovely Thai girls in "mod" clothes, color television programs, and FM stereo-multiplex radio stations advertise Thailand's progress, for many government development programs are rapidly thrusting the nation toward modernization.

But behind the glittering facade of modern Bangkok much of Thailand slumbers unchanged. The great mass of wealth is in Bangkok, and outside of Bangkok's three million people there are no other cities with more than 100,000 people. New industry is concentrated almost entirely around the capital.

And behind the smiles lies a hand-to-mouth struggle for survival among the great mass of people. Many millions have virtually no cash income at all (1970's per capita income was only $130). The country people suffer from floods one year and drought the next. Large portions of the country are inaccessible except to four-wheel-drive vehicles, and then only in the dry season. Approximately 90 percent of the population still lives beyond the reach of electricity. Many larger cities have chronic water shortages; in most rural areas one small well serves the whole community as the sole source of water.

But the "Free Land" (*Thai* means "free," and *Thailand* is pronounced "tie-land") is proud of her heritage. Alone among the countries of southeast Asia, Thailand has never been colonized by Europeans. A nation the size of France, she has acted as a buffer between Malaya, Burma, and French Indochina for years. Thus westerners in Thailand encounter little of the resentment so often experienced in other Asian countries.

Since World War II Thailand has allied herself firmly with the United States in opposing communist aggression in Asia. When the SEATO defense alliance was formed in 1954, Bangkok became its headquarters. Thai troops fought alongside the U.S. in Korea and Vietnam, and large air bases in Thailand harbored U.S. bombers flying against the North Vietnamese.

But communist insurgency has become a very real threat within many parts of Thailand; thirty-six of Thailand's seventy-one provinces have been declared areas of communist infiltration, with those bordering on Laos and Malaysia the most heavily affected. Nearly every day Thai police and communist insurgents clash in the rural areas. Assassinations of key government leaders on the village level are common. It is generally felt that the ultimate political security of the nation depends upon peace in Vietnam.

Tropical Thailand's geography has been likened to an elephant's head, with its long trunk extending southward along the Gulf of Siam. A thousand miles long and larger than California, Thailand has four major geographical regions: the northern mountainous region, the Korat plateau in northeastern Thailand, the central plain, and the southern peninsula. All are hot and humid. North Thailand is an extension of the vast mountainous range of Tibet and Yunnan in south China, and here are found Thailand's highest mountain, Doi Inthanon, (8,452 feet), and Thailand's second-largest city, Chiengmai, situated in a beautiful valley. Rapidly becoming a popular tourist center, Chiengmai is located in the middle of many different, colorful tribal groups, which provide an added attraction.

These northern people are largely rice farmers, with a few connected with the teak industry. Here in the great teak forests trained elephants, never outmoded by modern bulldozers, butt and pull huge teak logs to the riverbanks, where they begin the long journey downstream to Bangkok, a voyage that sometimes takes several months or even years.

The tribal peoples of north Thailand number over two hundred thousand, the principal tribes being the Karen, Meo, Yao, Lisu, and Lahu. The people wear distinctive tribal costumes and live in flimsy shacks on the mountainside. The Karens live in the lower areas and the Meo and others in the highlands. For income they have long raised opium poppies.

South of the northern highlands and stretching down to Bangkok is the central plain, heartland of historic Siam. Flowing through its entire length is the famous Chao Phraya River and its tributaries, around which life revolves in central Thailand. The lushest of Thailand's rice fields are to be found here. Almost two-thirds of all Thai farmland is given over to rice fields, for rice is the staple food and the leading export of the country. Tin and rubber are next.

To the northeast of central Thailand lies the Korat plateau, a tableland embracing one-third of Thailand's 40 million population[3] and one-third of the country's two hundred thousand-square-mile area. This northeast section is an infertile region where some rice and cattle are raised; in this area are most of Thailand's 7 million water buffalo and 5.5 million oxen.[4] Here the people are poor and have thus provided a ripe area for communist infiltrators from Laos and Cambodia in recent years.

South Thailand, the "elephant's trunk," extends five hundred miles south from Bangkok and forms the eastern half of the narrow Malay peninsula. The five southernmost provinces in this strip are populated with people of Malay origin (over a million),[5] the country's second-largest minority. They speak predominantly Malay and 90 percent are Muslim in religion. Huge reserves of tin (a big money-earner for Thailand for many years), large rubber plantations, extensive fishing, and the traditional rice fields make this area one of the nation's richest economically.

The biggest ethnic minority in Thailand are the Chinese, who number more than three million. Nearly half the population of Bangkok is Chinese, and Chinese businessmen loom large in commercial life in all the main cities. The Thai government's policies have helped bring about a peaceful assimilation of the Chinese population, most of whom are now Thai citizens.

The favorable government climate and the leadership of aggressive businessmen like these have made the Thai economy fast-developing (5 percent average annual growth rate since 1960) and stable. The country thus has large foreign exchange reserves, a stable currency, and increasing foreign investment. Yet despite this the wealth is not filtered down to the average man. And the large increase in gross national product each year has been offset in part by Thailand's large population increase.

Thailand's forty-million population is increasing by more than a million a year, showing one of the highest population growth rates of any country in the world, 3.3 percent in 1970.[6] Thus the population has doubled in the past seventeen years. Yet by Asian standards the country is still underpopulated and could support even more people.

The official language is Thai, which is spoken and understood by almost everyone, though minority dialects are often preferred in the homes: Malay in the south, Lao in the north and northeast, Chinese in all the main cities, and tribal dialects in the north. Some say that the original Thai language is Lao and that Thai is a perversion of Lao by the influence of many other languages, especially the Indian languages of Pali and Sanskrit. However, this assertion has not been completely verified. Literacy is climbing in the country and is now listed at over 70 percent,[7] though official government surveys reveal that a large percentage of these "literate" people cannot comprehend even first-grade reading materials because of the poor caliber of teaching in most rural primary schools.

National History

The precise historical origins of the Thai people are not clear. It is likely that the earliest inhabitants were of Indian origin who lived in the central valley around the Chao Phraya River. But the Thai culture as such was apparently born in the northern Chinese province of Shansi over two thousand years ago. Possibly internal feuds and physical circumstances forced this people to move further south to Yunnan province around the year A.D. 650, where they established the kingdom of Nanchao. They had probably already begun migrating further south into present-day Thailand when the invading hordes of the Mongol Kublai Khan overran Nanchao. Fleeing in great numbers to Thailand, they established their first capital at Sukhothai. Here they contacted the Buddhist and Hindu cultures of the earlier Indian settlers.[8]

Near the end of the eighteenth century Burmese armies overran the kingdom, but a dynamic king named Rama I arose, eventually driving out the Burmese; his dynasty continues till today. His most famous descendants were Rama IV and Rama V, known in the west as Kings Mongkut and Chulalongkorn. They were immortalized by the book *Anna and the King of Siam.* These kings dramatically modernized the country and skillfully engineered diplomatic treaties with both their neighbors and the West, thereby insuring the safety of their country from European colonization.

At that time Thailand was one of the world's most absolute monarchies. The king was considered so sacred that whenever he left the palace, all commoners along the route were required to close their doors and windows to keep from committing the unforgivable crime of looking on the royal presence. But the modernization under Mongkut and his son removed these superstitions and prepared the way for the transition to a constitutional monarchy, which occurred in 1932.

Thus Thailand was still struggling toward democratic establishment in the early forties when the Japanese swept in. Though the two nations were never technically at war, the Japanese de facto occupied the nation till their defeat in 1945, when Thailand returned to nation-building.

According to several Thai constitutions formulated since 1932, the king is still sacred. He is chief of state, head of the armed forces, and defender of the Buddhist faith (and of the minority faiths as well). In actual practice, however, his position is not much different from that of European monarchs today, though he is still highly revered by all his subjects.

"In the 30 years following its first constitution, in 1932, Thailand had seven different constitutions and 30 cabinets. Changes of government come with bewildering rapidity, usually as the result of a coup d'etat. In 1957, however, Field Marshal Sarit Thanarat suspended the constitution and ruled the country with an iron hand until his death in 1963."[9] The premiership then passed to his deputy, Field Marshal Thanom Kittikachorn, who promulgated a new constitution, followed by free elections, in 1968.

But on November 17, 1971, Kittakachorn called another surprise coup which bloodlessly abrogated the constitution, dissolved the cabinet and parliament, and imposed martial law throughout the kingdom. He declared the coup necessary to keep Thailand independent, pointing out that if the three million Chinese in Thailand favor Communism and back the rising communist insurgency in the country, the internal situation might be seriously complicated. But Kittakachorn was forced to resign following a large student revolt on October 14, 1973. The king immediately appointed a civilian premier, Sanya Thammosak, a lawyer and educator. The student uprising brought the nation's martial rule to an end, and the new premier promised a new constitution within six months. Whether stability can be achieved is still doubtful.

Though Thailand has made great economic gains in recent years, it is generally felt that progress has slowed since the death of the ironfisted Sarit. Extremely corrupt (he kept a hundred wives on a salary of $500 per month and amassed a vast personal fortune), Sarit was nevertheless a benevolent dictator who guided Thailand in the right direction politically and economically. The recent trend toward more democracy has fostered political bickering that tends to hinder the overall prosperity of the country rather than help it.

Among southeast Asian nations Thailand as a whole is admirably stable, solidly anti-communist, and heartily pro-western. Its economy is relatively free of controls and rests largely on private enterprise, but control of most of the businesses is in the hands of a relatively few wealthy men. Even after the coup the government continues to maintain solidarity with the other free-world countries.†

Although 92 percent of the children in the compulsory school age group are in school, this figure is misleading, for this only covers the first four grades. Though the government desires to extend this to the full seven years of primary school, it is struggling to maintain even the first four grades because of the needed increase in buildings and teachers demanded by Thailand's burgeoning population. Only city-dwellers have an opportunity for a high school education, and only a small proportion of these are able to enter one of the eight universities in the country.

†"The relative stability and tranquility enjoyed in Thailand stem from a number of factors: a strong sense of national identity among the Thai people; respect for the institution of the monarchy and for the king and queen; absence of large, disaffected ethnic minorities; relatively good economic conditions; and a long history of independence" (*Background Notes, Kingdom of Thailand,* p. 4).

National Religions

Buddhism is the dominant religion of Thailand, claiming 99 percent of the indigenous Thais. Beautiful Buddhist temples dot the skyline of Bangkok. There are over twenty-four thousand Buddhist temples throughout the nation—over half as many temples as Christians![10]

From the mighty historic temples of Bangkok to the flimsy shacks used for worship in the more remote areas, these temples are the hub around which the life of the communities revolve. In the drab rural areas especially, the entire social life of the community is built around the temple: it is the village hall, the worship center, the fairgrounds, and, formerly, the schoolhouse. The greatest event of the year is the annual temple fair, and people from miles around flock to see the attractions imported for the occasion.

Each morning at dawn anywhere in Thailand one can see saffron-robed Buddhist priests going from house to house "collecting" their food for the day. No word of thanks is ever given. Rather, the Buddhist priest believes he is doing the people a favor in allowing them to gain merit by giving him food. The conservative school of Buddhism (Theravada or Hinayana) which rules Thailand teaches that only good deeds and merit can enable one to achieve higher status in his next reincarnation and thereby eventually reach nirvana.

Gifts to priests and temples are considered highly meritorious, and temple festivities, ceremonials, cremations, and maintenance of temples may claim as much as 10 percent of a man's yearly cash income.[11] But dedicating a son to priesthood, especially the eldest, is an act of highest merit for a mother, so many boys are pledged to the priesthood for at least three months, and all are expected to spend at least a part of their lifetime in the priesthood. Thus in 1972 there were more than 243,000 novices and monks in the more than twenty-four thousand monasteries and temples in the country.[12]

But after the family sacrifices are made, to the common man Buddhism becomes more of a passive philosophy than a religion. Few attend the regular temple meetings, and the ceremonial holidays bring out large numbers to participate in the gaiety more than the devotion. Thus despite the ever-present saffron robes on the streets, there are many signs that the traditional influence of Buddhism is weakening. A newspaper article in 1969 decried the increasing idolatry to Buddhist images and the sale of good-luck badges, coins, and votive tablets, contrary to the pure teachings of the Buddha.[13] There has also been a marked increase in thefts of Buddhist images for sale to tourists.

There is also concern in the country today that Buddhism is slipping in its influence on the morals of the young. Public officials decry the immorality of the young, saying they have taken on the evil western culture and should return to their own culture and traditions. Unfortunately, it seems that to many Thais "culture" and "traditions" are synonymous with Buddhism, so Christianity gets the brunt of the attack, even if indirectly. Yet some priests have been taking Bible correspondence courses and have placed Christian literature and Bibles in the temple libraries. Many have written to Christian radio programs and have visited missionaries in search of more information about the Christian message.

Thus in spite of its many outward trappings Buddhism is not the controlling factor in the religious life of most Thai people. Rather, animism, a fearful belief in evil spirits, dominates the daily life of millions in Thailand: fear of reprisal if offerings are not made daily at the family spirit house; fear of being alone at night because of evil spirits; fear of doing anything that will displease them. Thus practically every home and many public buildings have colorful spirit houses in the yard, where offerings are made to appease the spirits.

> Popular opinion has it that human beings in Thailand are greatly outnumbered by the evil spirit population, who are believed to spend their time generally messing up human activities. These evil spirits, or *phees,* are said to be resident in heaven, on earth, and in hell. The earthly variety reside in homes, gardens, orchards, rice-fields, trees, rivers, mountains, and in the bodies of people; some do not have homes and wander endlessly across the countryside. Since they can be bribed, coerced, and deceived, these evil spirits must be propitiated with suitable gifts, because their help in an emergency can be invaluable, and their hostility can be ruinous.[14]

Perhaps the greatest lack in the preaching of the gospel in Thailand so far has been the failure to proclaim the power of Christ to release men from this bondage of evil spirits.

Among the minority groups in Thailand many religions are observed. The Malays in the south are Muslim. The quarter-million tribal peoples are pure animists. And several traditional religions are observed by the three million Chinese located largely in the urban areas.[15]

Christian History

CATHOLIC MISSIONS

The earliest Christian incursions to Thailand were by Catholic priests accompanying an embassy of Alfonso De Albuquerque in 1511, but the first resident missionary apparently arrived in 1555. These were followed in 1662 by Bishop de la Motte, who arrived with two other French priests and set up his headquarters in then-capital of Avuthva. They were the first missionaries of the newly-established "Paris Foreign Missionary Society," and this mission has continued working in Thailand uninterruptedly for three hundred years.

The earliest statistical estimates placed the number of Catholics at 2,500 in the year 1802, 3,000 in the year 1881; 116,000 in 1963, and approximately 167,000 in 1972. Thus the conversion rate has been increasing recently.

Catholics have traditionally placed great emphasis on schools and convents, largely centering around Bangkok. In 1922 the church listed twenty-two schools and convents throughout the country and ten major churches in Bangkok.[16] Encouraged by the steady growth of the church, the pope divided the country into two church provinces in 1965 and appointed its first archbishop. Today Thailand has two archbishops, eight bishops, thirty religious orders, and an apostolic delegate headquartered in Bangkok.[17]

PROTESTANT MISSIONS

Although two Protestant missions were instrumental in opening the land to the gospel initially, they were later compelled to abandon their work in Siam (as Thailand was previously named). From the very start those who worked in Siam (largely among Chinese) saw nothing but discouragement, with many deaths from diseases that were rampant throughout the land. Thus much of the early work was among the Chinese, and the first-fruits of evangelism in Thailand were Chinese believers.

The first known record in Protestant annals of anyone's concern for the Siamese is that of Ann Judson, wife of the famous pioneer to Burma. In 1819 she studied Siamese for eighteen months and translated a catechism and the gospel of Matthew into Siamese, though only the former was actually published. These were initially used among the Siamese people who were contacted in Burma.

The first Protestant missionaries to actually set foot in Thailand were Carl Gützlaff, a German who came at his own expense, and Jacob Tomlin, an Englishman of the London Missionary Society. They reached Siam on August 23, 1828. Within six months of their arrival they had translated the four gospels and Romans into Siamese and had proceeded with an English-Siamese dictionary as far as the letter "R". A year later, in December 1829, Gützlaff went to Singapore to have printed (on the very press that Ann Judson had used) some of his translations. There he married Maria Newell of the London Missionary Society, and together they returned to Bangkok in February 1830. Within one year they finished translating the entire Bible into imperfect Siamese and also translated portions of the Bible into the Lao and Cambodian languages. But tragically the tropical climate and diseases claimed the life of Mrs. Gützlaff, and Carl Gützlaff was also forced to leave because of ill health within four years. Tomlin also left Siam for the last time in January 1832 to rejoin his family.

But the need of Siam continued to burden these two pioneers, and they sent a strong appeal to the London Missionary Society to open work there. The Congregationalists in England could not see their way clear to pioneer another territory at this time, so the appeal was sent to the Congregationalists in America. The American Board of Commissioners for Foreign Missions took up the challenge, sending their first missionary, David Abeel, M.D., in 1831. But after eighteen years the work had to be abandoned because of the death of some of the missionaries and the continued ill health of others. But one of their workers, Dr. Dan Beach Bradley, resigned from the mission after the death of his first wife in 1845 and returned to Bangkok under the American Missionary Association. After purchasing presses and property for the mission, Dr. Bradley accepted no further financial help from it, but supported his family by instituting Bangkok's first newspaper in 1844. However, "he continued to preach, to heal the sick, to write, and to translate and print the Scriptures."[18] Dr. Bradley died in 1873, and his second wife died in 1893, after spending forty-three years in Siam without a furlough.

The American Baptist Mission (Northern) was the next to enter Thailand. Their first workers, Mr. and Mrs. John T. Jones, arrived in 1833, and their first church was established in 1837. (This Chinese Maitri Chit Baptist church was the first Protestant church established anywhere in the Far East and is still flourishing.) The Joneses had come from Burma, to which a call had been sent by Gützlaff and Tomlin. Their Siamese work was never prosperous and was given up in 1893. The American Baptist Mission has taken a new interest in Thailand in recent years, however, with their most fruitful work being among the Karen tribespeople in the north.

Heroic as these first pioneer works were, they were short-lived. It was the American Presbyterians who first established a lasting work among the Siamese. The first Presbyterian missionaries, the William Buells, landed in 1840, though the work cannot be looked upon as having officially commenced until 1847, with the arrival of the Stephen Mattoons and Dr. Samuel House. Known as "the man with the gentle heart," Dr. House was the first surgeon in Siam (and possibly in all of Asia) to use ether as an anesthetic.

The first thirty-three years of Presbyterian missionary work in Siam was concentrated in Bangkok, followed by a gradual reaching out into other areas as a result of the burden borne by such pioneers as Drs. Daniel McGilvary and W. C. Dodd. The period of the expansion of missions in Thailand and the early days of the Presbyterian work are identical.

In 1867 the Presbyterians penetrated the far north and began evangelism in Chiengmai. There a deep work of the Holy Spirit gave birth to churches in the Chiengmai and Chiengrai provinces, which are now the heart of the Presbyterian work in the land. In the area today are a large leprosarium, a theological seminary, a nurses' training school, primary and high schools, and a hospital.

Out of the Presbyterian mission work has grown the Church of Christ in Thailand. Today several smaller mission groups have also introduced their churches into this denomination, which embraces approximately 60 percent of all Protestants in the land.

Missionaries of all groups in Thailand can be grateful to God for the farsighted, pioneer work of the Presbyterian Mission. In the early days of missionary work in this land, their influence with the government went a long way toward keeping the land open to the preaching of the gospel. Their work was marked with a spirit of pioneering and soul-winning evangelism that gave strong impetus to the whole work of Christ in Thailand. They also introduced modern medicine into Thailand, and several modern hospitals still continue their early work.

In 1928 some members of the Christian and Missionary Alliance in Cambodia felt impelled of the Lord to enter Thailand. The whole of the eastern section of the land was still without a witness to the gospel, though missionary work had already been carried on in Thailand for a hundred years. (The Alliance later accepted the entire nineteen eastern provinces as their responsibility.) So on January 1, 1929, their first station was opened at Ubon, in the largest province outside of Bangkok, which today encompasses over a million people. During the next twelve years five other stations were opened as workers arrived, but response was slow, and only eighty-five converts were baptized.

Then came the tidal wave of Japanese over Asia. In a self-protective effort, the Thai government sought to eliminate all western influence in the land, and the church fell under pressure. In the providence of God Dr. John Sung, the dynamic Chinese evangelist, toured the churches of Thailand just before the outbreak of the war, and God visited many of them with spiritual quickening and revival. One senior missionary credits this visit with strengthening the church to withstand the ensuing five years of Japanese oppression, for once the Japanese entered Thailand the work of all missions was brought to an abrupt close, and many of the missionaries went into a concentration camp.‡ Though technically Thailand remained

‡According to Rev. Asher Case (CMA), who was himself interned, there were 26 missionary adults and 10 children in the Thailand concentration camp, among 325 people altogether:

CMA (7 adults and 3 children)	10
Churches of Christ	2
Presbyterian Mission (9 adults, 7 children)	16
Seventh-Day Adventist (2 doctors, 2 single people, possibly another couple)	6
American Bible Society	2
	36

independent, it was actually an occupied nation, and the heel of Japanese oppression ground heavily on the tiny church.

But the end of the war brought freedom again, and with it new interest in Thailand among churches in the West. The first great new missionary advance began in 1946, and the second in 1949, with the missionary refugees from China. God's Spirit began to work. The church began to grow. So now today suffering Thailand is open to the gospel and to its emissaries as never before. And the opportunities both with regard to population and receptivity in Thailand are probably as great as or even greater than those of any other nation on the war-torn southeast Asian peninsula. To the world church, Thailand is issuing an urgent Macedonian call for spiritual help.

NOTES

1. *Thailand Yearbook, 1969-70,* p. C-5.
2. Statistics taken from *Missionary Directory,* Christian Information Service, Bangkok Bureau, 1970.
3. *World Population Data Sheet* (Washington: Pop. Ref. Bureau, Apr. 1971).
4. Valentin Chu, *Thailand Today,* pp. 19-22.
5. *Thailand Yearbook, 1969-70,* p. A-17.
6. *Background Notes: Kingdom of Thailand,* p. 3.
7. *Thailand Yearbook, 1969-70,* p. 17.
8. Ibid., pp. A-4, 5.
9. Chu, pp. 180, 181.
10. *Thailand Yearbook, 1969-70,* p. C-6.
11. Ibid., p. C-6.
12. *Guide to Christian Work in Thailand* (Bangkok: Vision Press, 1972), p. 28.
13. *Bangkok Post,* June 27, 1967.
14. Chu, pp. 56-57.
15. *Background Notes,* pp. 3, 4.
16. *Thailand Yearbook, 1969-70,* pp. C-12, 15.
17. Ibid., p. 15.
18. Kenneth E. Wells, *History of Protestant Work in Thailand,* p. 14. See also historical summary on pp. 5-22.

BIBLIOGRAPHY

Background Notes, Kingdom of Thailand. Washington: U.S. Dept. of State, Nov. 1970.

Brown, Russell E. *Doing the Gospel in Southeast Asia.* Valley Forge: Judson Press, 1968.

Busch, Noel. *Thailand: An Introduction to Modern Siam.* Princeton: D. Van Nostrand Co., 1959.

Chu, Valentin. *Thailand Today.* New York: Thomas Y. Crowell Co., 1968.

Cressy, Earl H. *A Program of Advance for the Christian Movement in Thailand.* Bangkok: Church of Christ in Thailand, 1959.

Eakin, Paul. *Buddhism and the Christian Approach to Buddhists in Thailand.* Bangkok: Christian Literature Dept., Church of Christ in Thailand, 1960.

Gordon, Ernest. *Miracle on the River Kwai.* London, 1963.

Khantipalo, Bhikkhu. *Buddhism Explained.* Bangkok: Thai Watana Panich Press, 1970.

Kuhn, Isobel. *Ascent to the Tribes.* Chicago: Moody Press, 1956.

Maddox, Catherine. *Healing Hands in Thailand.* Westchester, Ill.: Good News Publishers, 1964.

———. *Paddy Field Hospital.* London: Lutterworth Press, 1962.

Nuechterlein, Donald E. *Thailand and the Struggle for Southeast Asia.* Ithaca, N.Y.: Cornell University Press, 1965.

Rajadhon, Phya Anuman. "The Cultures of Thailand." *Thailand Culture Series,* no. 1. Bangkok: National Culture Institute, 1956.

———. "Chao Thi and Some Traditions of Thai." *Thailand Culture Series,* no. 6. Bangkok: National Culture Institute, 1956.

Sarasas, Phra. *My Country Thailand.* Bangkok: Golden Service Co., 1956.

Swearer, Donald K. *Buddhism in Transition.* Philadelphia: Westminster Press, 1970.

Suriyabongs, Luang, M.D. *Buddhism in Thailand.* Bangkok: Prae Pittaya Co., 1955.

Tarling, Nicholas. *A Concise History of Southeast Asia.* Singapore: Donald Moore Press, 1966.

Thailand Desk Diary, 1971. Bangkok: Temple Publishing Service, 1971.

Thailand Yearbook, 1969-70. Bangkok: Temple Publicity Service, 1970.

Townsend, Ann, M.D. *Once Bitten.* London: Scripture Union, 1970.

Wells, Kenneth E. *History of Protestant Work in Thailand.* Bangkok: Church of Christ in Thailand, 1958.

———. *Thailand and the Christian Faith.* Bangkok: Church of Christ in Thailand, 1968.

———. *Thai Buddhism.* Bangkok, 1960.

World Population Data Sheet, 1971. Washington: Population Reference Bureau, Apr. 1971.

Wulff, Robert M. *Village of the Outcasts.* Garden City, N.Y.: Doubleday and Co., 1966.

Tibetan refugee congregation

Tibetan pastor and wife

Young Christian couple

Drums accompany children's service in a refugee camp

Photos by C. Warren

30

TIBET

by G. Tharchin and David Woodward

Introduction

Remote Tibet, sitting like a great, mountain-walled city astride the northern plateau of the Himalayas, the "roof of the world," has long conjured visions of mysterious, skin-robed nomads with strange customs and a stranger religion. Traditionally ruled by a living god-king and virtually forbidden to foreigners long before the communist Chinese takeover in 1959, Tibet has been relatively impenetrable to the gospel. But suddenly tragedy struck Shangri-la. The red Chinese army surged across the mountain borders and seized control of the hermit kingdom. And the few gospel excursions into its border cities since World War II were abruptly stopped.

What has happened since then? Is there no witness to this ancient nation now that the red bamboo curtain has sealed off the narrow passes into its lofty towns and villages and incorporated Tibet into red China?

Though geographic Tibet is more closed to the gospel than ever before, God has brought over 120,000 of its citizens and national leaders out from their national seclusion into India, and thousands more to Nepal. There waiting national Christians and missionaries are ministering to them. "The Tibetans are more accessible to the gospel than ever before," says Marion Griebenow, retired veteran of 28 years of missionary work among them.[1] "This is not to say they are responding easily," Griebenow continues, "but we prayed for years for the opening of Tibet to gospel missionaries. In answer to prayer God opened the door at least halfway . . . then the door slammed shut more tightly than ever. When Communism moved into

Ed. note. Valuable, original source material for this chapter was contributed by Rev. G. Tharchin, the oldest living Tibetan Christian and currently the pastor of the Tibetan church in Kalimpong, India. Additional valuable material by Rev. David Woodward, missionary of The Evangelical Alliance Mission, who has visited extensively in the Tibetan refugee areas, was compiled with pastor Tharchin's material for this chapter.

Tibet with its ruthless extermination of the Buddhist regime, God opened the door again to let the Tibetans out. They are literally on our doorstep."[2] Now for the first time these isolated people are exposed to a culture other than their own. Change is inevitable. And relative openness is being experienced, as the Christian nationals and missionaries laboring among them are happily finding.

Missionaries accustomed to working with small numbers of Tibetans first realized their opportunity when numbers of Tibetans fled to the hill cities of north India in the late fifties. But they were electrified by the flood of refugees which accompanied the Dalai Lama's flight in 1959. The most immediate help that Christians could give was medical. The Texpur Mission Hospital in Assam became one reception camp for refugees. Munshi Chekub, an Evangelical Alliance Mission evangelist, worked there for three years, acting as an interpreter for Tibetan patients. The Christian clinic of the World Mission Prayer League in Kalimpong opened to the Tibetans and now has about three thousand Tibetan outpatients a year.[3] The Finnish Mission in Buxa Duars on the Bhutan border[4] and the Landour Mission Hospital in the Mussoorie area above New Delhi now both have many Tibetan patients, while a clinic operated especially for Tibetans by the Christian Service Council is conducted in Rajpur, India. Here one of the medical technicians is the son of a former CMA evangelist. Further to the west the Anglican hospital at Manali has an extensive ministry to Tibetans. From Rajpur as a home base, Chekub has served as an interpreter and witness in many of these places.

Nurseries and schools became an immediate imperative for Tibetan children, especially because parents were often given difficult road work in the mountains by the Indian government and could not keep their families together. The Dalai Lama promised to take care of any children turned over to him, and the Tibetan government in exile opened a number of nurseries for preschool children. But from the start of this emergency, Christian churches and missions responded to the needs of these children also. Missionaries have raised scholarships for Tibetan children in existing Christian schools, and as a result several hundred Tibetans are receiving their education in a dozen different Christian institutions in north India.[5] At least three Christian schools for Tibetans, two in Kalimpong and one in Rajpur, were opened: Rev. G. Tharchin, the Tibetan pastor, editor, and oldest living Tibetan Christian, founded one of the fifty schools in Kalimpong, and a Moravian pastor, the late Elijah T. Phuntsok, developed another school in Rajpur, with his brother-in-law, S. S. Gergan, son of the major translator of the Tibetan Bible, serving as principal. TEAM missionaries also opened tutorial schools for young men and women who were over-age and debarred from Indian schools. And two Christian orphanages for the refugee children were opened in Kalimpong, one by pastor Tharchin.

When the Tibetans began to flee into north India, missionaries from several missions who had long evangelized around the nation converged on the refugee communities. They were joined by missionaries from newer groups: the World-Wide Evangelization Crusade, the World Mission Prayer League, and others. These evangelicals sought to coordinate their work and witness with Tibetans through the Christian Service Council and with an annual conference and the interchange of information for prayer. As many as thirty-two Christian workers gathered together to discuss Tibetan radio programs, the revision of the Tibetan New Testament, the provision of evangelistic literature, the precautions necessary in overt evangelism due to Indian government restrictions, and all issues related to Tibetan evangelism.[6] Phuntsok was elected as the first executive secretary of this council until ill health forced him to turn it over to Gergan, who today, along with this work and his home for refugee children, is also laboring on the Bible revision.

The United Church of North India and various missions related to it have concerned themselves more with job training for Tibetans and the provision of basic equipment for light industry. The emphasis has been on social service divorced from any presentation of the claims of Christ; thus they have even given support to a Sakya monastery school for the training of young priests.

In all these efforts the number of Tibetan conversions, though small, is on the increase. Each such work of grace is quickly noted and contested by the Tibetan priesthood. Frequently students who make a profession of faith in Christ are recalled to Dharmsala; their Bibles are taken from them and they are forced to engage in Buddhist worship, even though the Dalai Lama has said that there is nothing in the new Tibetan constitution to prevent a Tibetan from becoming a Christian.[7] Opposition to the gospel has not been open, but the hierarchy is not going to encourage any movement toward Christianity.

The Church Today

It is not easy to know just how to correctly assess the condition of Tibetan churches today. There are five congregations: in Leh (Kashmir); in Rajpur and Kalimpong (India), where Pastor Tharchin, now 84, still ministers to his congregation of eighty-six (in 1971); in Mangan (Sikkim); and in Buxa Duars (India). All of these are small. There are no doubt also isolated Christians in various places, perhaps from fifty to one hundred, but it is difficult to secure any accurate information about them. True to their nomadic traits, Tibetans can be found today all over India as well as in Nepal, Bhutan, and some foreign countries, where there are a number of settlements for Tibetans, particularly in Switzerland. But all of these camps are well guarded, and it is not easy for anyone, even national Christians, to reach them. Thus, ironically, even when they are within reach of the gospel, the Tibetans are still isolated from Christian influence. However, many of them at some time during their journey have had Christian witness, especially in Kalimpong and Darjeeling, and many have had contact with Christians in schools and hospitals on the border.

Tibetan Christians are eager to prove to their fellow Tibetans that, if anything, their faith in Christ has made them more ready to serve their countrymen. Tharchin has consulted with the Dalai Lama on educational matters. Chekub has received the commendation of the Dalai Lama for his labors with the sick. Phuntsok has the wide respect of many Tibetans for his help to the colonies of Amdo refugees in Rajpur and Clementown. Thus increasingly the witness to Tibetans is coming from fellow Asians and from among their own people. And there is strong hope that the tiny church, now meeting in quiet Bible study and prayer groups along the border, will grow steadily.

Missionaries working with the Tibetans in educational and medical projects are still useful. Literature is also a prime factor in Tibetan evangelism, as Phuntsok reminded missionaries in a recent conference. More and better literature could be a stimulus to increased evangelistic results. Missionary help in this area would also be advantageous.

Thus the prospect for Tibetan evangelism today is the brightest in history. The accessibility in settled communities and the relative openness of the refugee Tibetans, particularly in India, are resulting in conversions and the birth of tiny churches. And with possibly relaxed tensions between East and West, the future may see some of these new Christians able to send in Christian literature or even to return to their homeland to witness openly for Christ.

Nation and People

Tibet, so tradition says, was once covered by an ocean. Today it is the highest mountain mass on earth, with Mount Everest peaking up to almost thirty thousand feet near the southern border. Its northern high plateau averages fifteen thousand feet, though the land is lower in the central and west, with valleys transversing it like furrows. Though fabled as a snowy, bitter-cold land, Tibet's total precipitation averages only ten inches per year. But the variation of temperature is probably the greatest on earth—in some areas it may be below zero at night and one hundred degrees in the day.

Modern Tibet covers an area of about 470,000 square miles, and the latest Chinese census gives the population at 1.3 million. This probably includes only the area around the capital, Lhasa, and the west. The exiled Dalai Lama ambitiously overestimates the population at between 7 and 8 million, while the Communists have probably grossly underestimated the population for political reasons. The realistic figure is probably between 3 and 4 million.

Ethnically Mongoloid (though different from the Chinese), the Tibetans are actually divided into two distinct groups. In the valleys of the central and western areas are the descendants of the earliest inhabitants, shorter and more clearly Mongoloid in appearance. In the east and northeast live the taller, thinner nobles and nomads, who are possibly a racial mixture with the Turko-Mongols who invaded the land centuries ago. The nomads consider themselves superior to the more settled central tribespeople, though both groups share a common written language and religious system.

For centuries the simple life of these people has been unchanged. They live in sun-dried brick houses with clay roofs and floors. Their food is mainly barley, yak and mutton meat, cheese, and tea. Tibetan tea is a distinctive brick tea, boiled in sodawater and then churned with butter and salt. The average Tibetan drinks thirty to fifty cups of this brew daily.

Though the mountain nation is rich in minerals (iron, copper, lead, oil, shale, gold, coal, radium, etc.) and forest lands, the economy was primitive until the mid-twentieth century, with the major trade being in tea, wool, rice, and some gold. Through the generations the only wealth in the country was built up by the Dalai Lama, whose private treasury of gold and silver was said to be of incalculable value. Doubtless he was able to take some of this wealth with him, but the bulk fell to the Communists. Banking was begun in the nation only in 1951.

Following their capture of the country, the Chinese began exploiting the tremendous hydroelectric power potential, building iron and woodworking factories, and constructing the first network of roads and a railway from the Chinese border into the Tibetan interior.

The communist invasion in 1959 toppled the world's last theocracy. In the fifteenth century the idea of reincarnation of the lamas developed. According to this theory, at the very hour of the death of the reigning lama, a child was born in whom the lama's spirit was reincarnated. The third reincarnation of the lama was called the Dalai Lama, a title which stuck. Political leagues and intrigues kept this system enforced until the communist invasion.

After the Dalai Lama and thousands of his followers fled to India following the invasion, they proclaimed a Tibetan government in exile. In 1963 they adopted a unique constitution, which called for a democratic theocracy in which all of the officers of the government were elected except the Dalai Lama himself.

National History

According to an ancient myth of Bon, the pre-Buddhist religion of Tibet, in prehistoric days a bright, pure light congealed into a cosmic egg, out of which came the first Tibetan to rule the world. Prior to recorded history (which began in 629, when the Tibetan script was first devised), there had been at least thirty-two successive kings ruling the mountain kingdom, which was then much larger than it is now. In the seventh century King Srong-Btsan extended the kingdom into present-day Nepal and India. The wives he took from both Nepal and China brought Buddhist images into the country, but Buddhism as a religion didn't actually flourish until the last half of the eighth century. In the late ninth century two successive kings were murdered, the kingdom was divided, and Tibet was finished as a great power in central Asia for four centuries.

Later Tibet became a colony of the Mongol empire until the death of Kublai Khan, in 1294. One of the local Tibetan rulers then seized control and conquered much of central Tibet, and the kingdom began to grow in extent and influence. By the time of the fifth Dalai Lama, who was a scholar and an astute politician, Tibet ruled over much of central Asia with Mongol military backing. In succeeding generations Mongols and Manchus fought over Tibet until the mid-eighteenth century, when the Mongol influence waned. A brief Nepalese invasion in 1788 was repulsed with Manchu military aid, and Tibet was then closed to foreign influence.

With the rise of British power in China in the nineteenth century, Tibet exercised a brief suzerainty over Tibetans. When the Chinese revolted in 1911, the Tibetans saw their chance to throw off the Manchu yoke in their land as well. Thus in modern history the Tibetans enjoyed only thirty-eight years of true independence before the communist invasion in 1950.

During its brief independence the isolated Tibetan government had failed to take the trouble to get diplomatic recognition by foreign states, so when Tibet appealed to the United Nations following the Chinese invasion its request was shelved. In the following year the Tibetans signed an agreement with the Chinese which purported to allow the Dalai Lama to retain autonomy in his religious state, though his rival Panchen Lama was restored to equal power by the Chinese. Sweeping reforms were also promised by the Chinese. Two years later the Tibetans rebelled against this disguised Chinese rule, and the bitter Chinese retaliation forced the Dalai Lama to flee to India in March 1959. Further rebellion by the Tibetans brought about the death of a hundred thousand people, while thousands of others followed the lama across the border into India. Despite a weak resolution of protest by the United Nations late in 1959, the Chinese consolidated political and military control over the entire country and began harassment of India along the Tibetan border. In 1965 Tibet was proclaimed an autonomous region of the People's Republic of China.

Since then the Chinese have opened up the interior to progress. By 1966 over ten thousand miles of highways had been built. Two great bridges have been constructed over the Tsangpo and Lhasa rivers. Over sixteen hundred primary schools and seven middle schools have been erected. And at least 15 modern hospitals and as many as 140 clinics in rural villages and remote pastoral areas have been set up. It is probable that both the highways and the medical facilities were erected as much for military purposes as for the good of the Tibetan people.[9]

Meanwhile, the Tibetans in exile, largely along the northern borders of India, have been treated well. Many Christian missions have started schools among them. The Dalai Lama has done everything possible to promote the advance of literacy and education among his people. The probational government in exile has been winked at by the Indian government, since it forms no political threat but is mostly an emotional rallying point for the displaced peoples.[10]

National Religions

Prior to the arrival of Buddhism in Tibet in the eighth century, the people had a primitive religion known as Bon, a mixture of spiritism and shamanism. Since two schools of Buddhism were brought into the country by an early king's wives, the conflict between them was finally resolved in a royal debate in 1792. Only Indian doctrine was permitted by royal decree from that time, though for many years Bon shamanism opposed it. A strong Buddhist renaissance took place through an Indian guru in 1042. But the most significant reforms did not take place until late in the fourteenth century. Then the reformers took to wearing yellow hats, versus the red hats of the older Buddhist group. The yellow hats gained political supremacy early in the fifteenth century, and the Dalai Lama became Tibet's temporal as well as spiritual ruler.

The word *lama,* meaning "superior one," was early used to translate the Sanskrit word *guru* or "teacher." The idea of the reincarnation of the lamas began in the fourteenth century and gave birth to the idea of the true lama, who was a physical manifestation of the absolute Buddha, in contrast to the common monk. Every monastery had one such lama, among whom were the Dalai Lama and the Panchen Lama, the former of whom eventually rose to political and religious power. Prior to the communist invasion, 20 percent of the entire population was in some clerical order. Customarily a family sent its first son to the monastery, considering it an honor. These were educated and soon came to serve as medics, clerks, athletes, and teachers. Political and economic power came to be centered in the monasteries, and many of the peasants became virtual serfs. At the time of the Chinese invasion there were over 170 noble families in the country. They held most of Tibet's political power and economic wealth and were all either relatives of or knighted by the Dalai Lama.

Christian History

CATHOLIC MISSIONS

Early Roman Catholic attempts to enter Tibet from India began with the Franciscans in the fourteenth century. Jesuits and Capuchins followed in the early seventeenth century. A Catholic mission was maintained in Lhasa for almost forty years (1719-60) but was then forced out permanently. In later years the Catholics established extensive work on all borders where it was possible to reach Tibetans. On the Chinese border at Khanting they had schools and a hospital prior to 1949.

Today in the Indian Darjeeling-Kalimpong area the Catholics have large institutions which minister to Tibetans, along with others. Catholic mission efforts among Tibetans have been rewarded by few (if any) converts, either then or now.[11]

PROTESTANT MISSIONS

For over a hundred years Protestant evangelists have laid siege to the forbidding Tibetan stronghold from three sides—from Kashmir on the west, from India on the south, and from China on the east. The first attempt was from Kashmir in 1854, when two Moravian missionaries, A. W. Hyde and E. Pegell, arrived in Ladakh, hoping to traverse Tibet to Mongolia. Stopped there, they began intensive work. H. A. Jaschke joined them two years later and began Bible translation, a Tibetan-English dictionary, and a grammar. Two lamas (indigenous Buddhist priests), Gergan (grandfather of the present pastor) and Gyaltsen, assisted him. Though Gergan never became a Christian, Gyaltsen was the first lama ever to receive Christian baptism.

Books soon began to flow from Jaschke's tiny hand press. A medical dispensary was begun. Ultimately there were three or four tiny congregations scattered along the Kashmir-Tibetan border, of which one, the original at Leh, remains today.

A second attack on Tibet for the gospel was from China, when Dr. James Cameron made a thrust into Batang, eastern Tibet, in 1877. In the years that followed, the China Inland Mission, the Christian and Missionary Alliance, the Christian Missionary Society (Disciples), and the Assemblies of God established themselves at stations along the borders as well as inland. The CIM had work in both the northeast and the southeast. Some of these missionaries laid down their lives, and all lived and traveled under circumstances of great danger. The pioneers on the China side were active in touring the districts of Amdo and Kham in eastern Tibet, and some of them became well acquainted with and wrote about Tibetan life and culture.[12] The CIM established work largely around Khangting or Dhatsedo in the northern part. Their work there continued till World War II and was resumed soon after until the communist shutdown. Still farther north the CMA, including the Griebenows and their co-workers, evangelized the people in the Amdo province. Actually, one of the original purposes of the founding of the Christian and Missionary Alliance by A. B. Simpson was to evangelize Tibet. William Christie and W. W. Simpson established the very first work at Chow on the borders there, and many died in valiant efforts to penetrate the mountain interior.

Orphanages and medical work were attempted for the relatively primitive peoples. An early missionary wrote, "During all these years of labor our work was mostly preaching, Scripture and tract distribution, and some social and medical work. We had the joy to see several accept the Lord Jesus, but only ten to fifteen were baptized. Interruptions, opposition, indifference, and difficult living in the cold, remote borders hindered the work and produced little fruit in those early, pioneer years."

Later, English and American missionaries from the previously mentioned well-known missions were joined by representatives of the Finnish Mission, the English Pentecostals, the Swedish Free Mission, and others—all united at heart to reach Tibet.

But by the onset of World War II only scattered, tiny groups were meeting, and only a few had been baptized in any given place. No strong, settled congregations had been established.

The last and most successful beachhead from which the gospel was launched into Tibet was from the south, from India. There pioneer work developed in two areas: the hills and valleys northeast of New Delhi and west of Nepal, and the Kalimpong-Darjeeling district north of Calcutta on the east. Dr. Martha Sheldon, a Methodist, pioneered medical evangelism in the central area. E. B. Steiner of The Evangelical Alliance Mission revived this work in 1921 with Dharchula as a center and developed a strong core of convert evangelists, both Tibetan and Indian. On the strategic southeast corner, in a tiny neck of land jutting up from India and surrounded by Sikkim, Tibet, and Bhutan, Evan McKenzie of the Church of Scotland initiated work at Kalimpong in 1894 after he was unable to get permission to enter Tibet itself. He organized the first Christian congregation there, which continues till today under the leadership of G. Tharchin.

Born in west Tibet in 1890, Tharchin was educated and converted in the first school of the Moravian Mission in Tibet. In 1907 he met Sadhu Sundar Singh, the fabled Indian saint. After Tharchin had moved to Ghoom (near Darjeeling) to teach in the Christian school started by the Scandinavian Alliance Mission (presently The Evangelical Alliance Mission), Singh came there in 1914, attempting to enter Nepal. Briefly imprisoned, he came back to Ghoom and planned with Tharchin to enter Tibet with the gospel. They started out, applying at Gangtok in Sikkim for a permit to enter. Long delayed there, they were finally refused.

Singh finally gave his life to bring the gospel to the Tibetans. He made several other brief trips into the country, his last in 1929, from which he never returned. His dramatic and well-publicized death has been symbolic of the death of scores of other missionaries who have laid down their lives trying to penetrate Tibet's vastness for Christ.

Tharchin was finally admitted into Tibet several years later through the instrumentality of David McDonald, another unsung hero of Tibetan evangelism. British-born and fluent in the Tibetan language, McDonald was led to Christ at Darjeeling in 1903 by Frederick Franson, intrepid founder of The Evangelical Alliance Mission. McDonald immediately went to work for the mission, serving with them until 1909 and assisting with the revision of the New Testament. Following that he was guided of God to accept a post as British political officer and trade agent at Gyantse, with Tibet itself, where he and his wife gathered large groups of Christians and non-Christians in their home each week for Sunday services. Preaching at these services was actually done by McDonald's head clerk, Y. Isaac, a national Christian from the TEAM mission work at Ghoom.

Early in his work there, McDonald saved the life of the former Dalai Lama, who was fleeing from the Siamese in 1909. Despite this, McDonald was criticized by the British for proselyting the Tibetans and was asked to stop. But the meeting of Christians continued. Tharchin, who went to Gyantse to start a school for the children of the British staff and some Tibetans, remarks about the colonial attitude: "The chief opposition to Bible teaching and witnessing came not from the Tibetans but from the British, who were afraid of giving any offense."

Through this contact with McDonald, Tharchin's life was changed. He subsequently went to work for the Scots Mission in Kalimpong and began work there, which has continued almost fifty years. In 1925 Tharchin started the first Tibetan newspaper on an old mimeograph machine, sending a copy to the thirteenth Dalai Lama who sent a letter of appreciation.

In 1927 Tharchin met the Lama on his first of three trips into the capital city, Lhasa. On the last of these visits he attended the installation of the fourteenth Dalai Lama, who as a small boy in northeast Tibet had been given a gospel portion by a missionary and had had his picture taken holding it. Tharchin found copies of this picture pasted on the altar in the great temple in Lhasa.

When the Tibetan Bible was reprinted in 1950, Tharchin advertised it in his newspaper. The Dalai Lama ordered a copy and sent money to pay for it. When the Lama visited India in 1958, a year prior to his expulsion, Tharchin presented him with an English Bible. Tharchin relates, "The Dalai Lama has been witnessed to by many people and presented with many Bibles. It is said that he reads them from time to time. May God give him understanding and opening of heart with the reading!"

Ordained in 1952 by the Scots Mission, Tharchin is the oldest living Christian worker in India and is still the active pastor of the small community in Kalimpong.

It is in this little neck of India near the southeast corner of Tibet that Christian activity has been centered for the last several decades. At Ghoom at the turn of the century the Scandinavian Alliance and Finnish Mission pioneered with early fruit. However, over the years the ministry there has become almost totally among the Nepali refugees. Finnish Mission work there and in Sikkim and other border towns has experienced slight touches of revival in recent years, particularly among the Bhutanese. Faithful in the face of oppositon and almost total unfruitfulness, a number of outstanding men and women have laid down their lives for Christ there during the last hundred years. In Ghoom, Miss Treschbuck served fifty-six years and Miss Guriva of Finland served forty. The Kellys were long remembered for their influential ministry in Darjeeling, as was a Miss Kemp.

On the China border, the names of William Christie, William Simpson, James Edgar, Theodore Sorenson, Dr. Albert Shelton, the Petrus Rijnharts, Miss Anne Taylor, the Cecil Polhills, and others were among many stalwarts who had the devotion and determination of those unnamed heroes in Hebrews 11. Many missionaries prayerfully and sacrificially sought to penetrate Tibet's cold physical and spiritual barrier for almost a century until World War II. Converts were few and churches were even fewer. Many missionaries died after living heroic lives with little encouragement.

By the opening of World War II there were twenty-seven missionaries still listed on the Indo-Tibetan border and forty-five missionaries on the China border,[13] but only a small proportion of these missionaries devoted themselves exclusively to Tibetan work and were fluent in the language. The majority worked among Tibetans with the use of Hindi, Nepali, or

Chinese, as well as working with other border peoples. Their work included medical evangelism, orphanages, schools, and caravansaries to passing Tibetan traders. A stone mason was even commissioned to carve Scripture verses on rocks in the Tibetan style.

In addition to the missionaries, the converts in those early days also paid a high price for their nonconformity to traditional religion. Since they faced severe persecution, many tended to ally themselves with missions, forming small Christian communities around mission headquarters. And on the China side there were signs that such groups of believers did not collapse all through the 1950's, even after the communist takeover, for orders for Tibetan Bibles continued to arrive at Bible depots at Shanghai and Hong Kong.

Following the war there was an immediate increase in missionaries and missionary societies on the Tibetan borders. All the older societies returned, plus new ones. Of particular interest was the arrival of a number of Chinese missionaries with a call to evangelize in central Asia. They began language study and acclimatization in both the northeast and southeast, sponsored by the Back to Jerusalem Band and other indigenous Chinese societies.

But the arrival of Chinese communist armies bent on the occupation of Tibet abruptly checked this freedom for Christian witness. Foreign missionaries were expelled and Chinese missionaries were restricted. Strange to say, some Chinese Christians drafted into the armed forces went as foot soldiers all the way to Lhasa, the capital city, and beyond. There is hope they gave some witness.

The place of major opportunity for witness to Tibetans has in the last twenty years reversed itself from the China side to the India side. During the first half of this century eastern Tibet, which was under nominal Chinese control, offered Christian workers considerable territory peopled by Tibetans. Not without difficulty, they were able to move and live among Tibetan towns, lamaseries, and encampments. During this period missionaries in India had to be satisfied with a relatively small number of Tibetan traders and pilgrims who crossed into India, while those on the China side could settle among communities of ten and twenty thousand Tibetans.

But all this changed with the communist Chinese takeover in 1949. Then all missionary work stopped on the Chinese border, and some workers shifted to the Darjeeling-Kalimpong area, on the Indian border. Here and in nearby Rajpur the major evangelistic and social work continues today with greater encouragement than ever before.

Why has there been so little response among the Tibetans? Veteran pastor Tharchin cites several reasons.

Tibetans fall naturally into three main classes: the nobility and priesthood, who have been steeped in and are relatively satisfied with lama Buddhism; the trader-middle class, who have been so busy making money that they have had no time for religion; and the poor, who, though sensing a need of help and having a desire to learn, have been held back by fear, superstition, and bondage to a primitive system imposed upon them by their nationality and culture.

In a special way Tibetans are bound by culture, by their religion, and by a willful stubbornness which tenaciously clings to old forms and beliefs even when these are shown to be impotent. Their culture is supremely one of bondage; all of life is proscribed for them, and they cannot even name a child without consulting an oracle or lama.

The Tibetans have been traditionally nomadic, moving so frequently that little prolonged contact with the gospel has been possible.

Strong nationalism binds Tibetans to Buddhism. They are told that if they become Christians they are no longer true Tibetans. Community pressure further seeks to bar them from the gospel. A strong spirit of delusion binds them, and they are not able to see things in the proper perspective.

But God's hand is undoubtedly involved in the Tibetan's flight to India. Culture shock and radical change is forcing a change in attitude. Some adults are coming to Christ. Children are being educated by Christians. God is at work among the Tibetans as never before in Tibet's two thousand years of Christian history.

NOTES

1. Marion Griebenow, *Allliance Witness,* Aug. 1959, pp. 15-16.
2. Ibid., p. 60.
3. *Report of 1968 Tibetan Workers' Conference.*
4. Ibid.
5. Ibid.
6. Ibid.
7. Ken Anderson, *Himalayan Heartbeat,* p. 13.
8. Rate Deshapriya Senanayake, *The Inside Story of Tibet* (Colombo: Afro-Asian Writers' Bureau, 1967), p. 39.
9. Ibid., pp. 60-76.
10. *Encyclopaedia Britannica* (Chicago: 1973), 21:1106 ff.
11. *Moody Monthly,* Mar. 1949, p. 473.
12. A. G. Castleton, *Rough, Tough, and Far Away,* p. 15.
13. W. T. T. Millham, ed. *Central Asia: The Challenge of Closed Doors,* p. 23.

BIBLIOGRAPHY

Anderson, Ken. *Himalayan Heartbeat.* Waco, Tex.: Word Books, 1965.

Bell, Sir Charles. *Tibet, Past and Present.* Oxford: Clarendon Press, 1928.

Bull, Geoffrey, *Tibetan Tales.* Chicago: Moody Press.

———. *When Iron Gates Yield.* Chicago: Moody Press, 1955.

Castleton, A. G. *Rough, Tough, and Far Away: James Edgar of Tibet.* New York: Friendship Press, 1924.

Dalai Lama. *My Land and My People.* New York: McGraw-Hill, 1962.

Davey, Cyril J. *The Story of Sadhu Sundar Singh.* Chicago: Moody Press.

David-Neel, A. *My Journey to Lhasa.* New York: Harper, 1927.

Desideri, I. *An Account of Tibet, 1717-27.* London: G. Routledge & Sons, 1937.

Edgar, J. H. *The Marches of the Mantse.* Morgan & Scott, 1908.

Ekvall, Robert B. *Fields on the Hoof: Nexus of Tibetan Nomadic Pastoralism.* New York: Holt, Rinehart & Winston, 1968.

———. *Gateway to Tibet.* Harrisburg: Christian Publications, 1938.

———. *Religious Observances in Tibet: Patterns and Function.* Chicago: University of Chicago Press, 1964.

———. *Tents Against the Sky.* New York and London: Farrar, Straus & Young-Gollancz, 1954.

———. *Tibetan Voices.* Wheaton: Tyndale House Publishers, 1959.

Evans-Wentz, W. Y. *The Tibetan Book of the Dead.* London: Oxford University Press, 1927.

Harrer, Heinrich. *Seven Years in Tibet.* London: Pan Books, 1953.

Hoffman, Helmut. *The Religions of Tibet.* London: Geo. Allen & Unwin., 1961.

Huc, M. *Travels in Tartary, Thibet, and China.* London: National Illus. Library, 1879.

Johnson, Elaine. "Tibet: Land of Mystery and Sorrow." *Moody Monthly,* Mar. 1949.

Learner, L. *Rusty Hinges.* London: China Inland Mission.

Millham, W. T. T., ed. *Central Asia: The Challenge of Closed Doors.* London: Mildmay Movement (World Dominion).

Moules, Leonard. *Three Miles High.* London: Christian Literature Crusade, 1948.

Murphy, Dervla. *Tibetan Foothold.* London: Pan Books, 1966.

Norbu, T. J. *Tibet Is My Country.* London: Rupert Hart-Davis, 1960.

Norbu-Turnbull, C. M. *Tibet.* New York: Simon & Schuster, 1969.

Patterson, George N. *God's Fool.* London: Faber & Faber.

———. *Tibet in Revolt.* London: Faber & Faber, 1954.

———. *Tibetan Journey.* London.

Playmire, David. *High Adventure ni Tibet.* Springfield, Mo.: Gospel Publishing House, 1959.

Ray, Chandu. *The Story of the Tibetan Bible.* London: Central Asian Mission.

Richardson, H. E. *A Short History of Tibet.* New York: E. P. Dutton & Co., 1962.

Rijnhart, Susie. *With the Tibetans in Tent and Temple.* New York: Fleming Revell & Co., 1901.

Shakabpa, Tsepon W. D. *Tibet: A Political History.* New Haven: Yale University Press, 1967.

Shelton, Flora B. *Shelton of Tibet.* New York: George H. Doran Co., 1923.

Snellgrove, D. Richardson. *A Cultural History of Tibet.* New York: Praeger, 1968.

Stein, R. A. *La Civilisation Tibétaine.* Paris: Dunod, 1962.
Tucci, G. *Tibet: Land of Snows.* New York: Stein and Day, 1967.
Van Dyck, Howard. *William Christie: Apostle to Tibet.* Harrisburg: Christian Publications.

31

IMPORTANT RELIGIONS OF ASIA

by Gordon H. Chapman

Introduction

WHY IS CHRISTIANITY still a rather small minority movement in most of the Asiatic nations? A part of the answer, at least, is that Asia is the cradle of great ethnic religions which in most cases were already fully indigenous before the gospel had its first proclamation in the Far East.

The world's important living faiths naturally fall into two well-defined groups: the Semitic or Occidental, which produced Judaism, Christianity, and Islam; and the Indo-Iranian or Oriental. The two greatest of this latter group, Hinduism and Buddhism, arose in India, with important offshoots in southeast Asia, China, Tibet, and Japan. The Chinese indigenous faiths of Confucianism and Taoism were primarily ways of life or philosophies rather than religions, with filial piety as the supreme virtue. Zoroastrianism (or Mazdaism) arose in the Indo-Iranian milieu as a prophetic system of ethical monotheism and was the state religion of both the first (559-331 B.C.) and second (A.D. 226-331) Persian empires. Together with Manichaeism it exercised a powerful conditioning influence on the early expansion of Christianity, though neither is influential today. In this chapter the Mideastern faiths of Zoroastrianism, Manichaeism, and Islam will be considered first, and then Indian, Chinese, and Japanese religions.

The primitive church originated and developed in the midst of a multifarious religious and philosophical world which was inevitably hostile to the Christian faith, since Christianity proclaimed the world under the judgment of God and called for sole dedication to Jesus Christ, the only

Ed. note. The major author of this chapter is Rev. Gordon H. Chapman (see biographical note in chapter 8, "Christianity Comes to Asia."). However, valuable information on Indian religions was contributed by Mr. Theodore Williams, author of chapter 10, "India, A Seething Subcontinent."

Saviour. Today, though little-known in the West, these religions still flourish in Asian lands and constitute deep-rooted religious, cultural, and psychological resistance to the growth of the Christian church. In these pages, brief summaries of the nature and teachings of these religions put into perspective the problems of evangelism in Asia.

Zoroastrianism

This national Persian faith was founded by Zoroaster or Zarathustra (c. 570-500 B.C.), a native Iranian and a contemporary not only of important Hebrew prophets but also of Gautama (Buddha), Confucius, and possibly Lao Tze. As an heir of the Vedic polytheism of early Hinduism, Zoroaster claimed to have received a divine revelation which led him to protest the cruel and false features of his ancestral faith, saying "if the gods do aught shameful, they are not gods." Thus as the first magus (wise man), Zoroaster exalted the one god, Ahura Mazda, as the all-wise creator of the world and the source of all that is good and beautiful.

In his theology Zoroaster regarded this wise god as being in agelong conflict with Angra Mainyu, the primeval spirit of evil, who is responsible for darkness, filth, evil, disease, and death. This dualism is not permanent, for Ahura Mazda will ultimately win the victory over the spirit of evil. Nevertheless, it is essential that man, possessed of a free will, cooperate by good thoughts, good words, and good deeds, to be enforced by the strict observance of prescribed ritual and various duties. In other words, by living a righteous life man strengthens the power of good and weakens that of evil, with his ultimate fate determined by his faithfulness. This religion was simply a form of moral idealism, an attempt to grapple with the problem of good and evil within the context of ethical monotheism. Like post-exilic Judaism, it became increasingly legalistic, wherein the virtues of the pious save mankind. At best the Zoroastrian ethic was humanistic and utilitarian, a religion of salvation by works which ignored the need of the new birth or the grace of God in offering forgiveness for human sin.

Zoroastrian influences have been detected in the Qumran literature of the Dead Sea scrolls, not to mention some of the Jewish apocalyptic literature. And it is possible that Zoroastrian eschatology was later influenced by Christianity. Members of the Zoroastrian priesthood (magi) had great influence in the Persian court and precipitated much of the persecution of Christians, especially during the last two hundred years of the Persian rule. Zoroastrians were in turn persecuted by Muslims in the seventh and eighth centuries and fled eastward. A number of refugees settled in the Bombay district of India, where they are known as Parsis or Parsees and still practice a form of Zoroastrianism. They are noted for their industry, prosperity, and high educational standards. Small, isolated groups also still survive in Iran and other areas.

Manichaeism

For hundreds of years the early church regarded Manichaeism as one of its most insidious enemies. Denying the unique Hebrew-Christian revelation, it was one of, if not the first, syncretistic attempt to embrace many religions within its gnostic theosophy and framework of ethical practices.

The founder, Mani (c. A.D. 216-76), was born and reared in the neighborhood of Seleucia-Ctesiphon (on the Tigris River), then the chief city of Mesopotamia and a great East-West trade center. About the year 242, on the basis of an alleged divine revelation Mani declared himself a prophet, and at first he had some success. However, his preaching aroused the antagonism of the Zoroastrian magi, and he was obliged to leave the Persian domain. Possessed of a very aggressive missionary spirit, Mani visited north India, central Asia, and even west China. This resulted in Manichaeism becoming the state religion of the Uigur Turks. Mani returned home about A.D. 270 and made some converts in the Persian court. His success again aroused the antagonism of the magi priests, and he was finally executed by order of the Persian king, Bahram I, about A.D. 276.

Mani and his successors were very successful in developing a unique synthesis of religions in which Zoroastrianism, Buddhism, and Christianity were, as he asserted, restored to their pristine purity, with the terminology of each adapted to Mani's purpose. In the Mani system there are the usual opposing or dualistic principles of good and evil, with the redemptive process involving the liberation of the good elements from the domination of the bad, which was associated with matter. According to Mani's teaching, Buddha, Jesus, the prophets, and Mani had been sent to help with this liberation. However, his view of Christ was strongly docetic, with the Marcion denial of the true incarnation and resurrection.

The followers of Mani were divided between the "elect" or "perfect," who led celibate and ascetic lives, and the "hearers," who supported the elect but lived normal lives. Manichaeism had wide appeal and even attracted Augustine for a period of years prior to his conversion. It gained many adherents in Persia and central Asia, not to mention the western world, and it persisted in China into the seventeenth century.

Islam

No religion has been more bitter in its opposition to Christianity than Islam, meaning "submission" (to God's will). Frequently called Muhammadanism because it was founded by Muhammad in the latter part of the sixth and early part of the seventh centuries, Islam swept rapidly around the Fertile Crescent of the Middle East in the first century of its history, and within its second hundred years it had penetrated deep into northern India and central Asia as far as China. Sweeping all before it, the Muslim holy war threatened all of Europe until the Muslims were decisively stopped by Charles Martel at the Battle of Tours in 732.

Following Muhammad's death in A.D. 632, a series of "caliphs" ("successors" or "vice regents" of Muhammad) exercised autocratic political and religious power. Moving swiftly through north Africa, they soon conquered Jacobite Syria, Mesopotamia, and Persia in 650, when Baghdad became their ancient, fabled capital. At first Islamic rule did not extinguish the Christian communities totally, and many survived for hundreds of years under pressure and persecution, though steadily losing ground. Even in committedly Muhammadan Arabia, Christians were allowed to remain, though they were heavily taxed. The apostasy of Muslims to Christianity was effectively curbed by threat of death, and evangelism was stopped, with the result that the Christian movement in Arabia practically died out by the tenth century.

In the Persian-ruled areas Christians were somewhat freer, but there were extensive defections to Islam on the part of nominal Christians, while true Christians were obliged to dress distinctively and were strongly discriminated against. That the churches in those nations under Muslim rule survived at all is a miracle.

In their first two centuries the Islamic governments controlled all of the great trade routes, both land and sea, and this fact alone created a notable shift in the religious balance of power. As a result Christianity was increasingly driven back to Europe until the age of discovery and the great advance in Christian missions which accompanied the development of western colonialism. Thus from late in the first millennium of the Christian era the lands controlled by Islam have been virtually closed to the proclamation of the gospel until modern times.

At the age of forty Muhammad claimed to have a series of visions and revelations from God through an angel who called him to be the last of the great prophets. He recorded these visions in the Koran ("recitations"), which along with his sayings became the sacred Scriptures of the new faith. Threatened with death in his hometown, Mecca, Muhammad fled to Medina, where he established a theocratic state in A.D. 622. Thus the Muslims reckoned their era from that year of Muhammad's flight and establishment, and Mecca and Medina became the two most sacred places for pilgrimage.

Muhammad's genius lay in uniting the idolatrous, divisive, and warlike

Bedouin tribes on the basis of his newly-revealed monotheistic faith. He gave them a sense of mission which inspired their subsequent conquests.

The Muslim faith as laid down by the prophet Muhammad and his successors is a relatively simple one, with only a few clearly defined obligatory practices. The teachings as set forth in the Koran and Sunna (the customs and sayings of the prophet and his immediate successors) are quite eclectic in nature and include not only Arabian but Christian and Jewish elements, with great dependence on the Old Testament. The Koran stresses the the absolute unity of God, or Allah, who has predestined all things, and his righteousness and omnipotence. Idolatry is condemned, and instructions concerning morality and the maintenance of Islamic customs and institutions are included. The descriptions of both heaven and hell are vivid and sensuous, and the warnings of the approaching end of the world are fearsome, with extraordinary stress on the day of judgment.

Though Allah at certain specific times in history has sent prophets, one of whom was Jesus, Muhammad is the last and greatest of them. The deity of Jesus Christ as the Son of God is denied, along with the historicity of His redemptive death and resurrection. Thus Christianity's unique claims are bitterly opposed. Traditional Islam holds that there are four bases for religious authority: the *Koran*; the *Sunnah*, a record of the customs and practices of Muhammad; the *Ijma*, a compilation of Muhammad's and his successors' legal decisions; and the *Kivas*, a commentary of inferences on the above three, much like the Jewish Talmud. The five principal religious practices are: confession of faith in Allah and Muhammad his prophet; ritual prayer facing Mecca five times daily; required charity to provide for all needy Muslims; fasting from dawn to sunset during Ramadan, the ninth month of the Muslim year; and a pilgrimage to Mecca at least once in one's lifetime.

Modern Islam is divided into various sects originating from the messianic claims and new teachings of various other prophets which have arisen in succeeding centuries. The major sects include the Shiah and Sunnah groups. Soon after Muhammad's death the Shi'ites argued for more freedom in speculation, and they politically insisted that authority lay in the inherent right of the semi-divine caliph, or political ruler. This ultimately led to forms of pantheism, mysticism, and rationalism. The Sunnites were driven into existence to oppose the Shi'ites by insisting that all authority lay only in the four bases mentioned above and not in the caliph. Both of these groups through the centuries in different countries subdivided further, but today Sunnites comprise about 90 percent of all Muslims. Their anti-Christian bitterness seems not to have subsided, though in some countries Muslims are beginning to respond to Christian evangelism.

Indian Religions

INTRODUCTION

The pattern of Indian religion and culture is quite different from that of other major religions of the world. Indeed, this subcontinent has developed a pattern of life and religious faiths and a combination of emphases and orientations that has a unique type of self-identity. A prolific mother of religions, India at times has also been hospitable to various faiths imported from abroad. However, certain indigenous religious concepts have been tenaciously retained, and the basic societal pattern which finds its sanction in religion has remained until modern times.

Hinduism, the greatest of Hindu religions, was already a thousand years old when in the sixth century B.C. two major reform movements were born, Jainism and Buddhism. Both represented reactions against the gross polytheistic tendencies in popular Hinduism, especially the ritualistic sacrifices and complicated rites monopolized by the Brahmins. In their original, pure, atheistic form, these religions had no concept of a world beyond and were without god(s) or faith in god(s). Indeed, Indian religions, at least in their highest forms, are all essentially gigantic systems for self-release by self-realization, looking on the present life as ephemeral—a kind of imprisonment in what is unreal. From a western viewpoint this conception is pessimistic, and it demands a kind of spirituality which sets the highest value on a sublime serenity and the contemplative life as the best way to attain release.

Thus the first- and second-century missionaries to India found themselves in the presence of three major religious systems which were waxing rather than waning in their influence on the life of the people! Buddhism was at the zenith of its influence then, but was destined to later almost disappear in the land of its birth. Early Jainism, too, was strong, but it also gradually shrank to become one of a number of smaller sects. But Hinduism, with seemingly unlimited survival qualities, has continued to be the dominant faith of the Indian peoples until today.

HINDUISM

Long the dominant, indigenous faith of India, Hinduism is one of the world's oldest and largest religions. Its name is derived from the Persian word *Hind*, which was given to the Indus River in northern India. But Hinduism is also often called Brahmanism for its central teaching, a word which is now also applied to its priests.

Hinduism teaches that Brahman is the supreme world-soul or spirit, the one absolute, infinite, eternal, indescribable, neuter being, the inmost essence of everything. But while emphasizing the oneness of Brahman, it allows the worship of hundreds of gods as stepping-stones to understanding Brahman. Foremost among the gods are three personifications of Brahman: Brahma, the creator who is unknowable; Siva, the destroyer; and Vishnu, the preserver or renewer. Among these only Siva and Vishnu are usually worshipped. Vishnu, a god of love, has come to earth in different incarnations or avators, two of the greatest of which are Rama and Krishna.

Every living creature has a soul which comes from Brahman, and therefore even animals must be revered. The cow is considered sacred because it is a symbol of man's identity with all life, particularly animals. Thus many Hindus are vegetarians.

The goal of every man is the union of his soul with Brahman, but this cannot be reached in a single lifetime. Thus transmigration or reincarnation of the soul is central in the religion. The soul does not die, but passes on until it is pure enough to be united with Brahman. The law of Karma regulates the soul's progress. According to this teaching, a person's deeds in this life will determine his form in the next reincarnation. There are three ways one can reach Brahman, according to one of the Hindu Scriptures: 1) the way of works or good deeds; 2) the way of thought or philosophy and meditation (sometimes associated with Yoga, the discipline of the mind and body); 3) the way of faith and devotion to one god. This latter method is considered the best.

Practically, however, Hinduism includes a vast accumulation of contradictory beliefs and practices, ranging all the way from a rather lofty metaphysics to primitive animistic spirit worship. In fact, pantheism, polytheism, theism, atheism, and agnosticism have all been accepted and tolerated under the umbrella of Hinduism. There is no carefully formulated system of doctrine which must be accepted, although Hindus do believe in an individual soul which is reincarnated for ages until the burden and responsibility of Karma (the law of causality and retribution) has been satisfied and absorption in the absolute (Nirvana) has been attained. Indeed, the Hindu is more concerned with what he himself does or with his observance of the dharma (obedience to the laws of conduct, which are obligatory within his particular societal group) than he is with any system of dogma.

Though it probably originated with the lighter-skinned Aryan invaders who conquered India between 1500 and 1200 B.C., the caste system became a binding religious teaching of the Hindus, with the law of Karma and the idea of reincarnation serving as its philosophical justification. The system became the basis of the whole social and religious structure which undergirded Hinduism and permanently froze individuals at the various levels of the hierarchical structure of society. The system was based on three assumptions: first, that society is a composite of mutually dependent castes; second, that each caste is an autonomous social entity which has the right and the power to regulate the beliefs and customs of its individual members; third, that the cosmic, moral, and ritual order both sanctions and derives its support from such a hierarchical society.

Traditionally the castes were derived from the four great classes of early Indo-Aryan society: Brahman (priests and teachers), Kshattriya (rulers and warriors), Vaisya (traders, artisans, and farmers), and Sudra (servants). All of these claimed to have originated respectively from Brahma's head, arms, belly, thighs, and feet. But these took no account of numerous additional castes and sub-castes or of the great mass of "outcastes" or "untouchables."

It was the first duty of every good Hindu to observe the rules of the caste into which he was born and in which he must remain throughout life with the hope that, if he remains faithful, he may be reincarnated into a superior caste. From the beginning of the Indo-Aryan cult the Brahmins, or priests, maintained a monopoly on the service of the gods and on the preparation, preservation, and communication of the sacred traditions, not to mention the regulation in every detail of the social and individual lives of the people. Since the vast majority of Hindus were illiterate, they were not expected to partake of the higher knowledge, which was thus restricted to the Brahmin class. For the simple people of the lower castes a great variety of popular devotions, colorful festivals, pilgrimages, and elaborate rites in connection with the important events of life were provided, and participation in these was the only religious duty required.

Hinduism's origins are shrouded in the second millennium before Christ. Though certain elements doubtless go back to the prehistoric past, most date from the historical period of India which was ushered in by the invasion of Aryan people from the northwest, possibly from the area east and west of the Caspian Sea between 1500 and 1200 B.C. During the next few hundred years there was an interpenetration of the Aryan and Indian cultures and religions which ushered in the millennium of Hindu literature. The Vedas (holy books of prayers and praise addressed to nature) were purported to have been given to the rishis, or holy men, about 1000 B.C. Other leaders propounded these and contributed other holy books, including the Upanishads (about 600-300 B.C.), which embody the philosophy of Hinduism, and the Bhagavad-Gita (about the time of Christ, which portrays devotional Hinduism.

Though Hinduism has given birth to other religions which arose in reaction to it (Buddhism, Jainism, and Sikhism), because of its elastic eclecticism, Hinduism has nevertheless been able to absorb some of the values of each of these and remain the largest and most influential of India's faiths.

JAINISM

An indigenous, monastic religion which dates back to the 500's B.C., Jainism is probably an outgrowth of Hinduism, though Jainism denies Hinduism's sacred Scriptures, the Vedas. Although Jainism's early followers claimed it to be the original, true religion, dating back to prehistoric times, and that their great prophet Mahavira ("Great Soul") was the last in a series of twenty-four prophets, most scholars believe that Jainism arose as a protest against corrupted Hinduism. Mahavira was an elderly contemporary of Buddha who claimed that enlightenment came to him after spending twelve years meditating on the miseries of existence and the way of final emancipation, all the while sitting in a squatting position. Following this, Mahavira gave himself to thirty years of preaching before entering Nirvana.

Jainistic teaching holds that self-realization, or the perfection of man's original pure nature, is achieved by following the principles of right faith, knowledge, and conduct. The paramount principle, however, is known as ahinsa, or non-violence: the essence of goodness is never to kill anything, for even the life of the lowliest insect is as sacred and precious as that of a human being. For this reason the principal service activity of Jains is to provide rest houses for old and infirm animals. Women, however, were downgraded and held to be unworthy of emancipation as long as they remained women. Because of the principle of ahinsa, Jains are reduced to a strict vegetarian diet.

One of the largest and most ascetic of the early Jain sects emphasized fasting and nudity, for a true saint should own nothing, not even a rag of clothing. So Jain sadhus (teachers) often dispensed with all clothing except as they were obliged to conform to ideas of decency, especially in Muslim areas in later times. Furthermore, to get rid of Karma as the connecting link that binds the soul to the material body, strict rules of conduct, some very admirable, were imposed.

Jainism shares in the pessimism of Sankhya, Yoga, and Buddhism: life in the world, perpetuated by the transmigration of the soul, is essentially bad and painful, and therefore it must be our aim to put an end to the "cycle of births." This will be accomplished when we come into possession of right knowledge. In these general principles Jainism agrees with Sankhya, Yoga, and Buddhism, though it differs in the methods of realizing it. Today the Jain church consists of celibate priests and a lay community. The twenty-four prophets are now regarded as gods, and their idols are worshipped in temples constructed to their memories. For this reason and for rejection of the Vedas, Jainism is regarded as heresy by the Hindus.

Jainism has never been a proselytizing religion, and there has always been a steady drift back to Hinduism, especially on the part of those who could not bear the strict regime of this ascetic faith. As a result the number of believers has never exceeded two million.

BUDDHISM

In contrast to Jainism, Buddhism is one of the most significant of the world's religions and is probably the most influential of the non-Christian faiths in Asia. Wherever Buddhism has prevailed the gospel cause has languished. Buddhism originally represented a kind of intellectual revolt against Hinduism and was mostly a philosophy of life or system of ethics. It promised emancipation from the bane of ignorance and presented a system of moral conquest as the solution to the problem of human desire. Thus the original Buddhist gospel was escape for the ego-soul into the nothingness of Nirvana. Buddhism became practically extinct in its homeland, India, from the time of the Muslim invasions in the twelfth century A.D.

Yet Buddhism thrived in other east Asian lands, where its teachings were found to be superior to those of the more primitive animistic faiths. Hinayana ("little vehicle" or "lesser career"), the oldest of the two main divisions of Buddhism and frequently known as southern Buddhism, prevails in Ceylon, Burma, Thailand, and Indochina. Mahayana ("greater vehicle" or "greater career") is the more eclectic form of Buddhism and is sometimes known as northern Buddhism; it came to prevail in Tibet, China, Korea, and Japan.

The founder of Buddhism, Gautama (563-483 B.C.) (the son of a rajah of the Sakyas and therefore a member of the ruler-military caste) was born and reared in southern Nepal. Having become convinced that all earthly things were impermanent and worthless, Gautama renounced his life of luxury and indolence at age 29 and became a wandering ascetic, seeking to unravel the mystery of human existence. After six years of living in extreme austerity he realized that this way of life was useless, and he returned to the more normal life of a mendicant. Finally, in 528 B.C., he seated himself on a platform of grass under a pipal or sacred fig tree, and resolved to remain there until he became enlightened regarding the mystery of existence. After being tempted all day with various fleshly seductions and winning the victory, Gautama became Buddha, "the enlightened one," or Siddharta, "he who has accomplished his aim," or Tathagata, "he who has arrived at the truth." He remained under the Bodhi-tree ("tree of enlightenment") for seven weeks, wrapped in meditation and enjoyment of his emancipated state.

The essence of his discovery was that the cause of all human misery is desire, arising out of the will to live and the will to possess. Progress toward the peace of Nirvana (the state of perfect absence of all desire—absorption into the infinite nothing) depends on the recognition of this basic fact of human existence. From the time of his enlightenment to his death, some forty-five years later, Gautama gave himself to a preaching ministry and the gathering of his followers into the Sangha or monastic order, in which differences of caste were eliminated. The monks were itinerant mendicants with monasteries provided for their use in the rainy season. All members of the order were expected to live lives of simplicity, chastity, and poverty. However, from the beginning of his preaching Buddha proclaimed the virtues of the "middle way" that lies between the two extremes of sensual indulgence and asceticism.

The essence of Buddhist teaching as revealed under the Bodhi-tree is embodied in the "Four Noble Truths": the truth of suffering, or the fact of pain; the truth that pain has a cause in intense desire; the truth that pain can be relieved by eliminating self-desires; and the truth that suffering can be relieved by following the "Noble Eightfold Path." This path includes rightness in views, intention, speech, action, livelihood, effort, mindfulness, and concentration. Actually, the "four Noble Truths" and the "Eightfold Path" were little more than a "middle way" between the Hindu quest of emancipation by knowledge and works and the strict asceticism of the Jains.

Buddhism abolished the caste system of Hinduism, the Brahmanic ritual order, the monism of the Upanishads (the most spiritual and esoteric section of the Hindu sacred book), the Hindu conceptions of deity, and the idea of self as an individualized permanent ego or soul. However, the doctrine of Karma and the belief in reincarnation and transmigration of Hinduism were retained. But according to the Buddha it was Karma collected in this life and not the individual self or soul that survived death, an idea that is difficult to reconcile with reincarnation or a trans-eternal being, or Brahma as an absolute without permanent personality, either human or divine. The special appeal of original Buddhism was probably the comparative moderation of its demands and discipline, the elimination of the philosophical subtleties of mystical Hinduism and Brahmanic rituals, and the abolishment of caste segregation.

The two most important divisions of Buddhism came to be identified with the countries of the south and north which embraced this faith. Traditional Buddhism received its initial missionary impetus in the third century B.C. during the reign of the Emperor Asoka, who sent his son to preach the faith in Ceylon. It was later introduced to Burma, Thailand, Cambodia, and Laos. This southern type of Buddhism was originally called Theravada, the orthodox "way of the elders," but it was later dubbed by the followers of the more progressive Mahayana group as Hinayana, or the "little vehicle." It was more conservative and claimed to base its teachings on the Tripitika or Pali Canon, supposedly the closest to the original teachings of the Buddha. In it the ideal saint leaves the world and dedicates himself to attaining enlightenment and Nirvana.

The Mahayana school of Buddhism, which goes back to the first century B.C., was less individualistic and more social than Hinayana and served as a protestant revolt against Theravada strictness. It was known as the "great vehicle" or "career," for in this system the individual aims not at attaining Nirvana only for himself, but he also believes that he should prepare himself for Buddhahood in order to save a great host of others along the path. He first becomes a Bodhisattva, or one "destined for or on the way to enlightenment," one who has deferred his entry into Buddhahood in order to help others attain through his accumulation of merit. His career may extend through many lives, practicing the virtues of almsgiving, moral conduct, patience, heroism, meditation, and wisdom, as he goes through ten stages of training toward Nirvana. This more liberal or progressive school has been popular in Tibet, China, and Japan.

Just before the dawn of the Christian era, resurgent Hinduism challenged Buddhism, along with a number of outside influences from Christian, Greek, Persian, and other central Asian faiths. As a result the monastic order was reformed and consolidated, many heretofore oral doctrines and traditions were codified, and the Buddha's deification was popularized. Since Gautama had been regarded as "the actuality of the basic doctrine, the one who has lived it and reached the goal," it was only natural for the Indians, steeped in polytheistic traditions, to readily accept this apotheosis.

The followers of Buddha from the first were divided into two groups: the sangha, or brotherhood of monks, and the laymen. The former originally lived monastic lives, becoming novices between the ages of ten and twenty-one and then spending twenty years to achieve monkhood. The latter were to live diligent lives and earn merit for rebirth by supporting the monks and monasteries.

SIKHISM

A striking later creed of India, another which protested against her dominant Hinduism, is the Sikh religion. Its founder, Nanak, the first "guru," was born in A.D. 1469, fourteen years before Luther. The traditions of his early career pictured him leading a life meditatively careless of the things of this world until he received a definite call to a divine mission as the expounder of a new doctrine.

Nanak was intensely monotheistic and tried to unite Hindus and Muslims into one great brotherhood, preaching that they were essentially the same. His idea of God was pantheistic rather than theistic, and thus he did not explicitly deny the existence of the countless gods in the Hindu pantheon. He claimed to respect every religion's real essence but inveighed against mechanical worship, ritualism, and Brahman priestcraft.

On a series of pilgrimages which may have reached as far as Ceylon, Kashmir, Russia, and even Mecca, Nanak spread his doctrines and composed his hymns, which became the nucleus of the Sikh holy book, the Granth. Though the Sikhs retain the Hindu reverence for the cow, they are meat-eaters and reject most of the Hindu food laws.

Sikhism flowered in western Pakistan and northwestern India, where a political state was founded in the late seventeenth century. The Muslims conquered them in the early eighteenth century, only to be overturned a few years later by the returning Sikhs, who recaptured Lahore. From there Ranjit Singh united the Sikh communities and extended their rule to most of India north of the Sutlej River by 1824. But succeeding waves of British invaders subdued them by 1850. Then, fearing the return of Muslim power, the Sikhs sided with the British until independence.

Marked by stern features, heavy beards, and turbans, the Sikhs are now solely a religious community, chiefly farmers and soldiers. Over two-thirds live in the United Provinces and Kashmir area of north India, and their total number in 1972 approximated ten million.

Chinese Religions

INTRODUCTION

Though it is often said that the religions of China are Confucianism, Buddhism, and Taoism, aside from the professional religionists the average Chinese did not regard himself as an exclusive adherent of any one of the three. He rather regarded himself as the follower of a general Chinese religion which included both animistic and polytheistic features, including worship of the spirits of heaven, of earth, and of human beings (especially ancestors), not to mention those of both animate and inanimate objects. Though many local gods were somewhat ephemeral, Shangti (the lord of heaven), the gods of land and crops, the dragon god, the god of wealth, the god of medicine, the kitchen god, and the gods of the various clans and professions survived throughout history.

Basic to Chinese religion was the persistent conviction that "as the foundation of all things is heaven (shangti), so the foundation of man is the ancestors," who were regarded as still alive, with human qualities and human needs. As an extension of filial piety, ancestor worship involved making offerings before ancestral tablets, building ancestral temples, an elaborate system of burial and mourning, periodic visiting of graves, and continued respect for both ancestors and living parents.

In popular Chinese religion there is a strong element of superstition, with divination, witchcraft, and magical practices aimed to influence and control all factors in a situation on behalf of good fortune. Thus there is the belief in lucky and unlucky days and in wholesome and unwholesome sites, in which the configuration of land in relation to bodies of water determines peace and prosperity. Though such superstition was dominated by fear, it was also true that worship was often the expression of gratitude, which was thus ethically motivated. The law of retribution expressed in the Confucian saying that "good deeds bring good fortune and evil deeds bring ill fortune" is a reflection of the Taoist concept of response and retribution and the Hinayana Buddhist doctrines of cause and effect and of reincarnation and transmigration. From all this it is clear that Chinese religion was very much this-worldly and basically practical, moral, and humanistic—in other words, rationalistic rather than theological. The eclecticism which has largely determined the development of Chinese religion enabled the Chinese to think of the gods of all religions as members of one general pantheon.

CONFUCIANISM

Closely intertwined with early Chinese religious ideas was the moral or ethical system known as Confucianism, which as originally conceived was not actually a religion at all. Confucius (c. 551-479 B.C.) was a scholar who became a public official in a period of warfare, corruption, and tyranny. He advocated a new system of statecraft based on an ethical code which encouraged peace, justice, and good order in society. He created a pattern of government which emphasized the middle way and the avoidance of extremes, stressing that the secret to success was choosing honest and educated officials. To promote sympathy and understanding among men, Confucius proposed a hierarchical structure of society which would keep men in right relationships.

Confucius' teaching was recorded in the *Five Classics*, which became the bible of Confucianism. In them he expounded the duties and responsibilities of the five basic relationships which were the heart of his essentially political-ethical teachings: the relations of ruler and subject, father and son, husband and wife, elder and younger brother, and friend and friend. In practice, the Confucian "Golden Rule" was to "treat those who are subordinate to you as you would be treated by those in positions superior to yours.*

Originally atheistic, Confucianism was gradually influenced by the basic Chinese religious concepts, especially that of Shangti, the lord of heaven, who dominated earthly rulers. In time Confucius was himself deified; as

*The actual wording of his golden rule was negative: "What you do not like done to yourself, do not unto others." This is vastly different from the positive expression of Jesus.

ancestor worship is the extension of filial piety, so the worship of Confucius became the extension of respect for a teacher. State worship of Confucius began in 195 B.C., when the first Han emperor presented offerings before his tomb and continued with the adoption of his classics as the basis of all civil service examinations; sacrifices in his honor were later decreed in all schools where images or portraits of Confucius were placed. He was further honored in time as the "Foremost Teacher," "King," and "Perfect Sage." In a sense the worship of Confucius was a state cult in that it had imperial or official sanction from the beginning, though it was never an exclusive faith.

TAOISM

More or less contemporary with early Confucianism, Taoism was said to have been founded in the sixth century B.C. by Lao Tzu, to whom was attributed the chief writing of this faith, *Tao Te Ching* or *The Canon of the Way and Virtues.* Tao, or "the way," is "the power that lies in and behind nature and has transformed chaos into the cosmos and may therefore turn it back again. . . . By the power of this Eternal Way the orderly sequence of events is maintained, and, when unhindered by human activity, harmony and perfection prevailed." Thus the basic principle was to refrain from resisting the fundamental laws of the universe by an attitude of quietude, to be maintained by suitable breathing, blankness of mind, and various visionary experiences—doing nothing to achieve everything. Accordingly, the ideal life was one of contemplation in order to become one with the ultimate impersonal reality, and in this respect Taoism resembled the Buddhistic quest of Nirvana.

In actual fact Taoism rapidly degenerated into shamanism and developed a magical system of alchemy and wizardry. When it received imperial support and patronage, it was largely because its principle of inaction made for more submissive subjects. Superstitions grew in the search for magical means for attaining oneness with the ultimate reality, or Tao. Potent medicines and foods were concocted in which the power and virtue of the cosmos were alleged to reside. One celebrated alchemist invented a potion which he claimed would "kill demons, chase off hobgoblins, protect the kingdom, and bring peace to the people." The preoccupation of most Taoist alchemists was to discover edible gold as the elixir of immortality. All these rather bizarre developments were a far cry from the original mystical quietism.

Early in the T'ang era Taoism was given official recognition as a religion, with a pantheon of gods which outrivaled other Chinese faiths. Over all these deities and the influences which they personified the Taoist priests claimed to exercise shamanistic control; they alone could endow devotees with Tao to make them immortal and capable of supernatural powers. Because of the opposition of neo-Confucianism in the Sung era (960-1279), Taoism lost imperial patronage and its influence waned. However, Taoist occultism, alchemy, divination, and exorcism continued to commend it to the unlettered masses. Taoism and its practices have also been heavily involved with the various eclectic sects and the secret societies which have thrived in China, and in community life it sanctioned lcoseness and immoral practices.

CHINESE BUDDHISM

Though the traditional date of the introduction of Buddhism to China is A.D. 67, by the beginning of the Christian era it had already spread from the Honan area to both the south and eastern regions of the Middle Kingdom, and Buddhist sutras were in circulation. While at least three schools of Hinayana were represented, these did not really take hold, and Chinese Buddhism became essentially that of the Mahayana school, with a number of Chinese innovations emphasizing the more practical and moderate aspects of the system. Its characteristics were: a belief in Bodhisattvas and the ability of men to become such; a system of altruistic ethics which emphasized the responsibility to do good in order to accmumulate surplus merit on behalf of all mankind; polytheistic identification of Chinese gods with Buddhas; the worship of images in a colorful and elaborate ritualistic system; and salvation by faith in a Buddha, usually Amitabhator, the "Buddha of infinite Light," who welcomes all the faithful to the "pure or happy land," where they will eventually become Buddhas themselves. Chinese Buddhism is chiefly characterized by a shift in outlook from the other-worldliness and concern for individual salvation of Hinayana to occupation with the needs of this life and universal salvation.

It is not without significance that Buddhism was introduced to China through central Asia by the more or less nomadic peoples who roamed the vast area between the eastern border of the Byzantine empire and China. Thus Buddhism apparently entered from the northwest, and by the end of the fourth century the vast majority of the people in this region of China were Buddhists. This is witnessed to by the famous artificial caverns and Buddhist images carved in the sandstone cliffs of northern Shansi province by the Toba Tartars, who migrated from the region of Lake Baikal and established the northern Wei dynasty A.D. 385-532.

The L'ang dynastic period (A.D. 618-907) has been regarded as the golden age of Buddhism in China, although other religions, including Islam and Christianity, were likewise tolerated and even protected by the government during that period. It was in this period that Buddhism had a profound influence on the art and culture of China, and this was perhaps the principal factor in securing its introduction to Japan. It was not always well with Buddhism, however, for in the ninth century, instigated by Confucianists, efforts were made to suppress this faith; some 4,600 monasteries and 40,000 other Buddhist edifices were destroyed, and the majority of the priests and nuns were forced to resume lay life. The "luminous religion" (Christianity) also suffered severely at this time, but along with Buddhism it was to experience a resurgence in a later period.

Japanese Religions

INTRODUCTION

Japan has been called "the department store of religions," for here numerous sects, well-tailored to meet the emotional and practical needs of the natural man, are available in great abundance. Furthermore, this apparent religiosity has been characterized by a broad tolerance or even indifference to alien faiths, except as these seem to violate accepted social customs or are deemed inimical to the state. Thus violent persecution of a religion has been rather rare. In the absence of strong metaphysical and philosophical concepts, both religious response and expression tend to be pragmatic, and thus the varied needs of an individual may be met by adherence to several faiths at the same time. It is doubtless for this reason that the grand totals listed in Japanese religious statistical tables are usually in excess of the total population. (For example most Japanese traditionally regarded themselves as adherents of both Buddhism and Shintoism.) Even when the eclectic process results in a syncretism of conflicting elements, there is often little or no effort to reconcile them, nor does conflict necessarily inhibit the Japanese tendency to retain outworn traditions.

Buddhism first commended itself to the Japanese people mainly as an attractive vehicle of Chinese culture and an aid to political consolidation, rather than for its mysticism and ascetic practices. Confucianism was attractive because of its ethical system and provision for a well-structured society rather than for its philosophy. The Roman Catholic religion was tolerated in the latter half of the sixteenth century because of Japan's desire for trade with certain Catholic nations, but it was later suppressed because these nations' colonial expansion seemed to be closely associated with the missionary effort of several church orders. Moreover, the introduction of alien religions has usually involved the demand for some degree of accommodation to the native cult of state Shinto. This the Buddhists early did by declaring the members of the Shinto pantheon to be "Bodhisattvas" or "Buddhas-to-be."

Japanese religious history has been characterized by the rise of new faiths from time to time, especially in periods of unrest or rapid social change and revolution, or else when the traditional faiths have been found wanting and in need of reform. The post-World War II period found the Japanese in a state of prostration, anxiety, and insecurity, and the stage was set for another surge of religious faiths. The Religious Bodies Law of 1939, which aimed to make all sects completely subservient to the militaristic government as instruments of wartime propaganda and service, was abrogated. The postwar constitution of Japan provided for unqualified religious freedom, and the way was open for any number of cults to enter the partial vacuum, not to mention the opportunity for Christian groups to redouble their efforts. Within a few years, there were about seven hundred religious bodies officially incorporated at the national level, with many other at the prefectural level. But the Religious Juridical Persons Law of 1951 curbed this proliferation of sects, and the number dropped to about four hundred.[1]

Most of the so-called new religions which appeared in this period were simply new sects with Buddhist or Shinto antecedents, and even borrowings from Christianity. The vast majority are not exclusive faiths, and one may become an adherent without altering his traditional shrine and temple affiliation. Even the most exclusive of the new sects, Soka Gakkai, regards itself as a laymen's movement of the Nichiren Shōshū sect of Buddhism and appears under this heading in official statistics. It is exceedingly difficult to measure the strength, membership-wise, of these new Japanese religious bodies, for even official statistics are based on estimates without any uniform standards as to what constitutes a member, especially when a large percentage of Japanese people have multiple affiliations. However, without question Jinja Honkyō of shrine Shinto, Tenrikyō of sect Shinto, and the Buddhist sects of Tendai, Shingon, and Nichiren have enjoyed substantial growth since the war, with Soka Gakkai claiming an increase of over 4,000 percent in ten years![2]

The more successful of these recent Japanese religious groups share certain common characteristics which are significant and explain their rapid growth: the founder or leader is usually a person of charismatic gifts and dynamic personality and may be regarded as superhuman or a kami in his or her own right; the sect is usually well-organized in hierarchical fashion, with strong, centralized control extending to the local level; headquarters buildings are very imposing and are arranged to excite the wonder and admiration of the adherents, whose sacrificial gifts have made these structures possible; visits to these are encouraged, especially on festive occasions, when the adherents may be encouraged or required to participate in the upkeep and improvement of the premises; the branch churches or group meetingplaces are arranged for easy entrance and are open virtually at all hours, day and night, seven days a week, with someone always on duty to welcome and counsel needy persons.

Most importantly, these religious movements are essentially lay rather than clerical, with a strong emphasis on fellowship and group dynamics by which faith is shared, and the homes of believers are the principal bases for local evangelism. Cooperative activities for various ages and sexes are provided in the fields of education, welfare service, recreation, and the arts, all at convenient times. The basic doctrines and ceremonies and the various activities represent a skillfully devised combination of traditional and modern elements. The central teachings are characterized by simplicity, authority, and relevance to human needs, and worship consists mainly of repetition of sacred formulas and ritual observances. There is very little sense of the ultimate involved, but rather emphasis on immediate benefits which will come to the faithful: good health, success in marriage, a happy home, a prosperous career, and solutions to all the problems of the age of science and technology. Finally, it is quite evident that the new faiths have offered opportunities for emotive response and self-expression which are in accord with the natural disposition of the Japanese people.

SHINTOISM

Claimed by some to be the only pure indigenous religion in the world, Shintoism (literally "the way of the gods") has no universally recognized Scriptures, no one founder, and no clear code of ethics or theology. Yet its influence in Japan in this century has been tragically great.

Evolving from primitive animism and nature-worship in early Japan (whose actual historical origins are shrouded in antiquity but are believed to date from approximately the sixth or seventh century B.C.), Shintoism postulates an ambiguous deity, or pantheon of deities, called Kami. Since the literal meaning of the word is simply "above," it was originally used simply to imply spiritual superiority, and as such it evoked in the Japanese people reverence rather than worship in the western sense. Thus men approached the Kami on a basis of comfortable intimacy, without fear. There were only a few philosophical elements, coupled with a clouding of distinctions between soul and body and no ancestor worship in Shintoism's early stages. The worship of fertility was prominent, and phallicism did not disappear until indirect, early missionary influences caused its removal from prominent display along public roads. Thus there was no sense of sin in Shinto, but only ceremonial defilement, which was simply cleansed by acts of devotion or sacrifice.

Origins of the early Shinto mythology are obscure, since the first records, the *Kojiki* (*Chronicle of Ancient Events*) and the *Nihongi* (*Chronicles of Japan*) date from the seventh and eighth centuries A.D. Already Chinese influences had inculcated a sense of ancestor worship and other elements of Taoism, Confucianism, and Buddhism. Thus when exalted to prominence in the latter part of the nineteenth century, the early myths became simplified into the worship of the sun goddess (believed to be the progenitrix of the Japanese race) and of the emperor Jimmu, ruler of the early Yamato clan.

Shinto was usually divided into state and sect Shinto. In the later nineteenth century the jingoistic-militarist clique seized upon this mythology to exalt the position of the emperor and to obtain religious sanction for his political and military goals. They exalted the emperor as a living incarnation of the sun goddess, who not only ruled Japan but was by divine authority destined to rule the universe. Declaring state Shinto to be national loyalty rather than a religion, they demanded daily worship of the emperor on the part of all citizens as war-clouds gathered in the late thirties. This form of Shinto was officially outlawed by the American occupation forces at the end of the war.

Sect Shinto, on the other hand, has historically comprised a number of heterogeneous sects of ancient origin. Since the war these too have relatively declined in power. Many sects exist within this general category, worshipping many of the deities from the past as well as new ones of the present. Tenri-kyo is probably the most influential of these groups. At present their strongholds are in the rural areas; they emphasize nature worship, unity of man with his environment, and the bringing to expression of the inherently divine nature of the Japanese people. Thus these sects are at the roots still basically nationalistic.

In the late sixties various conservative government officials tried to reestablish, in effect, certain portions of state Shinto by introducing legislation declaring that the Yasukuni Shrine and the Great Shrine at Ise, headquarters of Shintoism, are simply objects of natural reverence. But the history of these sacred spots makes this logically impossible, and this movement has been fought by both Christians and the strong minority Socialist party out of fear that it would lead to a revival of World War II nationalistic militarism.

Traditionally in Japan the three religious systems of Shintoism, Buddhism, and Confucianism have been so intermingled as to all be considered part of Japan's common cultural heritage. Deities of both Buddhism and Shintoism were formally worshipped at the family god-shelf in the home. Custom dictated that a man was married by a Shinto priest and buried by a Buddhist. Though with very little spiritual understanding, these customs are followed by a majority even today.

JAPANESE BUDDHISM

Japanese Buddhism through the centuries has absorbed so many foreign philosophies and has been subdivided into so many sects—that today it enjoys little recognized uniformity of belief or common pattern of worship. Japanese Buddhists originally agreed that Gautama is the founder of Buddhism and that his teachings are the essence of truth: salvation is the attainment of Buddhahood and thereby Nirvana; the three precious things are Buddha, his law, and the church he founded; and the three basic paths are morality, meditation, and intuition or enlightenment. But among the most popular and vigorous sects today Gautama is almost totally overshadowed by their worship of the "Buddha-for-this-day," the thirteenth-century Buddhist saint, Nichiren.

Buddhism originally began as an import from China and became the state religion of Japan in A.D. 594, when the prince regent, Shotoku, was converted. Thus Mahayana Buddhism, along with Chinese culture of the T'ang era, were given imperial sanction early in Japanese history.

But though Buddhism was born in India, it came to flower in Japan. The original Mahayana Buddhism was modified in typical Japanese fashion, and many new Japanese sects came into being through the centuries. Notable among these are Zen Buddhism (with great cultural impact) and Amida or "pure land" Buddhism, which emphasized rebirth in the "pure land" through faith and the mere recitation of a phrase of adoration to Amida Buddha. Popular aspects of this sect were the right of clergy to marry and the idea that even women can obtain Buddhahood.

The most influential of the Buddhist sects in recent years has been that founded by the rebel priest Nichiren in the thirteenth century. His teachings have had a dramatic revival in the postwar period and probably now claim the largest and certainly the most enthusiastic following, which is divided among the several widely differing groups described in this chapter.

NOTES

1. W. P. Woodward, "Japan New Religions," *World Vision Magazine,* Feb. 1965, p. 11.
2. C. B. Offner, "Resurgence of Non-Christian Religions," *Japan Christian Yearbook, 1966,* pp. 37-44.

BIBLIOGRAPHY

General Works

Bouquet, A. C. *The Christian Faith and Non-Christian Religions.* New York: Harper Bros., 1958.

Ferm, V. *An Encyclopedia of Religion.* Paterson, N.J.: Littlefield, Adams & Co., 1959.

James, E. O. *History of Religions.* New York: Harper Bros., 1957.

———. *Christianity and Other Religions.* New York: J. B. Lippincott Co., 1968.

Jurji, E. J., ed. *The Great Religions of the Modern World.* Princeton: University Press, 1947.

Kitagawa, J. M. *Religions of the East.* Philadelphia: Westminster Press, 1960.

Kraemer, H. *Religion and the Christian Faith.* Philadelphia: Westminster Press, 1956.

———. *World Cultures and World Religions.* London: Lutterworth Press, 1960.

Neill, S. *Christian Faith and Other Faiths.* New York: Oxford University Press, 1961.

Pike, E. R. *Encyclopedia of Religion and Religions.* New York: Meridian Books, 1958.

Buddhism

Ch'en, K. *Buddhism in China.* Princeton: University Press, 1964.

Conze, E. *Buddhism, Its Essence and Development.* New York: Philosophical Library, 1951.

Eliot, C. E. *Hinduism and Buddhism.* 3 vols. New York: Barnes & Noble, 1954.

Thomas, E. J. *The Life of Buddha as Legend and History.* New York: Barnes & Noble, 1927.

———. *The History of Buddhist Thought.* New York: Barnes & Noble, 1927.

Confucianism and Chinese Thought

Fairbank, J. K. *Chinese Thought and Institutions.* Chicago: University of Chicago Press, 1957.

Fung Yu-lan. *A Short History of Chinese Philosophy.* Edited by D. Bodde. New York: Macmillan Co., 1950.

Latourette, K. S. *The Chinese: Their History and Culture.* New York: Macmillan Co., 1934.

Hinduism

Hutton, J. H. *Caste in India.* Cambridge University Press, 1961.

Mahahevan, T. M. P. *Outlines of Hinduism.* Bombay: Chetana, 1956.

Morgan, K. W. *The Religion of the Hindus.* The Ronald Press Co., 1953.

Islam

Bell, R. *The Origin of Islam in Its Christian Environment.* London: Macmillan Co., 1926.

Browne, L. E. *The Eclipse of Christianity in Asia from the Time of Mohammed Till the 14th Century.* Cambridge Union Press, 1933.

Gibb, H. A. R. *Mohammedanism: An Historical Survey.* London: Oxford University Press, 1953.

Jainism

Stevenson, M. *The Heart of Jainism.* Oxford University Press, 1915.

Taoism

Waley, A. *The Way and Its Power, A Study of the Tao Te Ching.* London, 1934.

Yang, Y. C. *China's Religious Heritage.* New York: Cokesbury Press, 1943.

Zoroastrianism

Avesta [Gathas translated into English]. London and Brooklyn: G. Bell & Sons, Comparative Literature Press, 1914.

Hanish, Otoman Zar-Adusht. *The Philosophy of Mazdaznan.* Los Angeles: Mazdaznan Press, 1960.

Moulton, J. H. *The Treasure of the Magi.* London, 1917.

Taraporawala, Irach J. S. "Zoroastrianism." *Religion in the Twentieth Century,* 1948, pp. 17-44.

Zaehner, R. C. *The Dawn and the Twilight of Zoroastrianism.* London, 1961.

Zoroastrianism. Washington: U.S. Library of Congress.

INTRODUCTION TO APPENDIXES

FROM THE OUTSET I hoped to have this volume reveal church growth in each nation as accurately as possible. Chapter authors were asked to submit statistics showing the growth of the church from the days of pioneer evangelism to the present. But the deeper one delves into the problem of statistics in these nations, the more complex and difficult they are revealed to be. Therefore, I must say that despite intense efforts by the authors, Dr. Edward Pentecost, the compilers of the *Unreached Peoples Survey* for the International Congress on World Evangelism, etc., these statistics must be viewed as only approximate and suggestive. It has been impossible to make them definitive.

In a few countries the church is too new and too small to have assessed their members. In many other countries statistics were not kept by the early churches, or have never been kept to date. Another problem is the lack of standardization with regard to the basis of computation, i.e., are "Christians" baptized church members only? Are they the total communicant body? Are they adult believers only, or are children numbered among them? A final tragic factor which has become apparent as the last lines to this book are being written is the fact that Christians are being assassinated by the scores, if not the hundreds, on the Indochinese peninsula with the victorious conquest, by the communists there. It may be months or even years until the numbers of those martyred for their Christion commitment are known.

These statistics were finally compiled in 1974 by Dr. Edward C. Pentecost, then a doctoral candidate at the School of World Mission and Church Growth at Fuller Theological Seminary. Along with completing his studies there and collating the statistics compiled for the *Unreached Peoples Survey* (1974), he completed these charts at great personal sacrifice of time. I am deeply indebted to him.

Please note also that the population figures given at the top of each chart are for 1975, but the percentages in the charts are based on population figures recorded from two to five years earlier. Here again, this fact makes the present-day percentage of Christians in each nation approximate though the growth trend indicated by the chart may enable one to extrapolate with some accuracy the percentage of Christians in 1975.

Additional charts showing Christian population by percentages of major ethnic groups have been included for some countries.

Wherever possible, sources for the statistics are listed at the bottom of each chart. Thus, though neither Dr. Pentecost nor I can guarantee the final accuracy of these statistics, we feel that they are a contribution to the knowledge of the size and growth of the church in Asia today.

THE EDITOR

APPENDIX A

CHRISTIAN POPULATION BY PERCENTAGE OF TOTAL POPULATION

BANGLADESH

(1975 Population: 73,700,000)

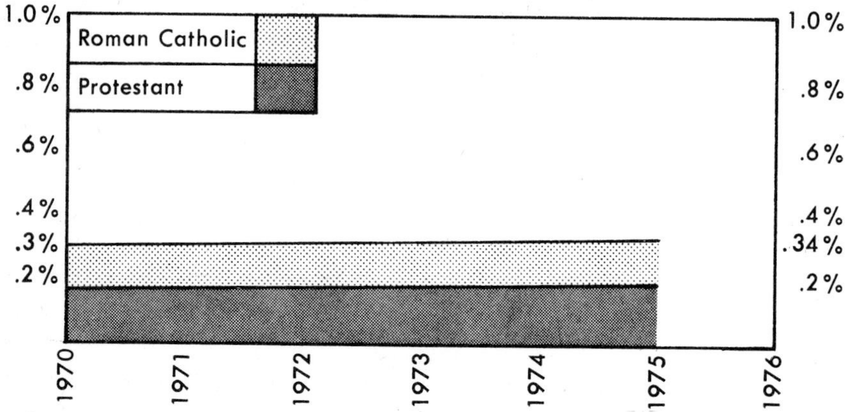

SOURCE: Statistics estimated from reports and personal investigation of Warren Webster.

BURMA

(1975 Population: 31,200,000)

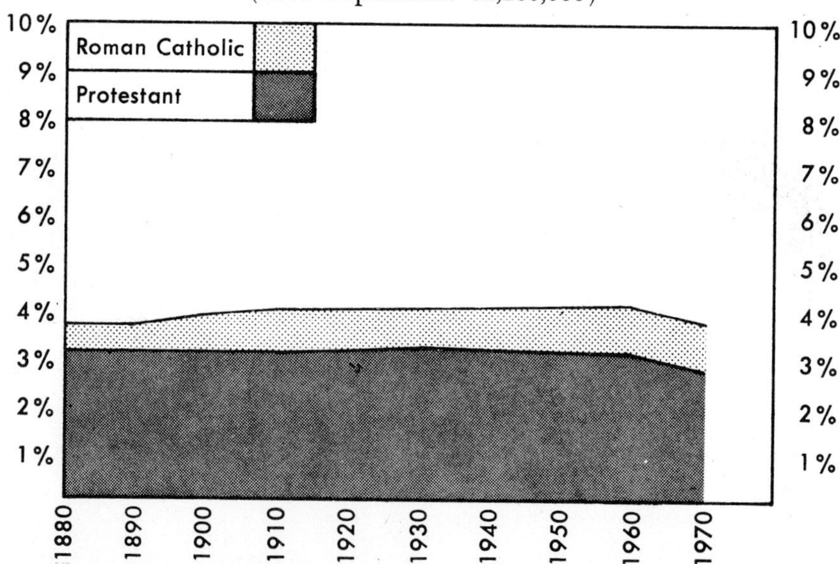

SOURCES: Letters and information to Donald Hoke from Billy Bray, November 9, 1971. H. Wakelin Coxill and Kenneth Grubb, eds., *World Christian Handbook* (Nashville: Abingdon, 1968). *New Catholic Encyclopedia* (New York: McGraw, 1967). Reginald E. Reimer, "The Peoples of Mainland Southeast Asia: A Profile of the Progress of Christianity" (Pasadena, Calif.: Fuller Theological Seminary, 1972). Herman G. Tegefeldt, "An Accurate Picture of My Church: The Kachin Baptist Churches of Burma" (Pasadena, Calif.: Fuller Theological Seminary, 1972).

THE PEOPLE'S REPUBLIC OF CHINA

(1975 Population: 822,800,000)

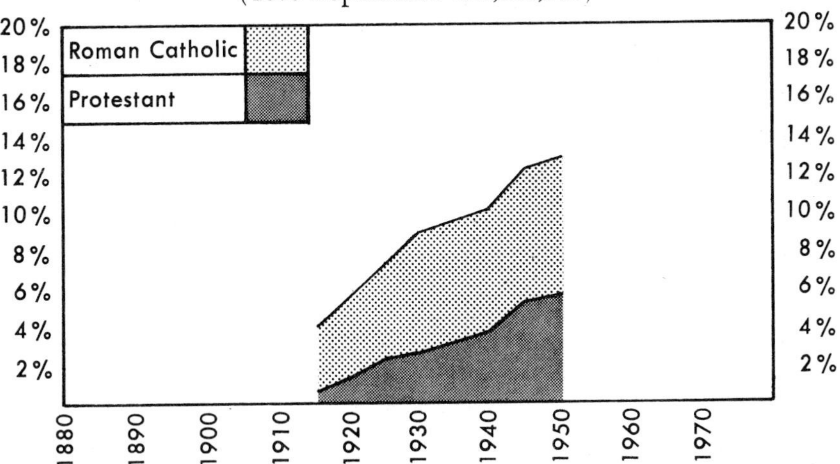

SOURCES: Ernest J. Baehr, "History of Christianity in China" (Pasadena, Calif.: Fuller Theological Seminary, 1971). Dorothy Raber, "The Chinese Revolution of 1911 and Its Relation to the Expansion of Christianity" (Pasadena, Calif.: Fuller Theological Seminary, 1971). Lists Protestant and Roman Catholic figures. R. C. Willman, "A Summary of Changes in Mainland China from 1949 to 1971 Which Have Affected the Church in China" (Pasadena, Calif.: Fuller Theological Seminary, 1971).

HONG KONG

(1975 Population: 4,200,000)

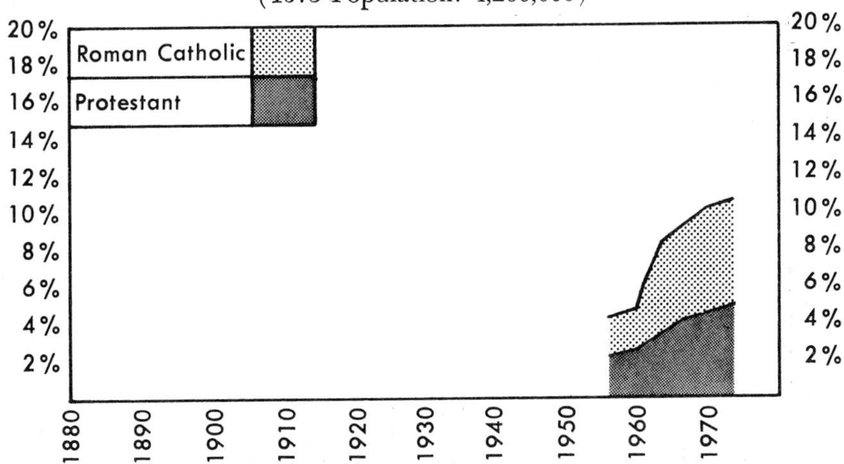

SOURCES: John Branner, "The History of the Church in China" (Pasadena, Calif.: Fuller Theological Seminary, 1970). *New Catholic Encyclopedia* (New York: McGraw, 1967). Bob Phillips, Interview conducted in Hong Kong by Roger E. Hedlund, Fuller Theological Seminary, December 8, 1972. Wayland Wong, Interview conducted in Hong Kong by Roger E. Hedlund, December 8, 1972.

INDIA

(1975 Population: 613,200,000)

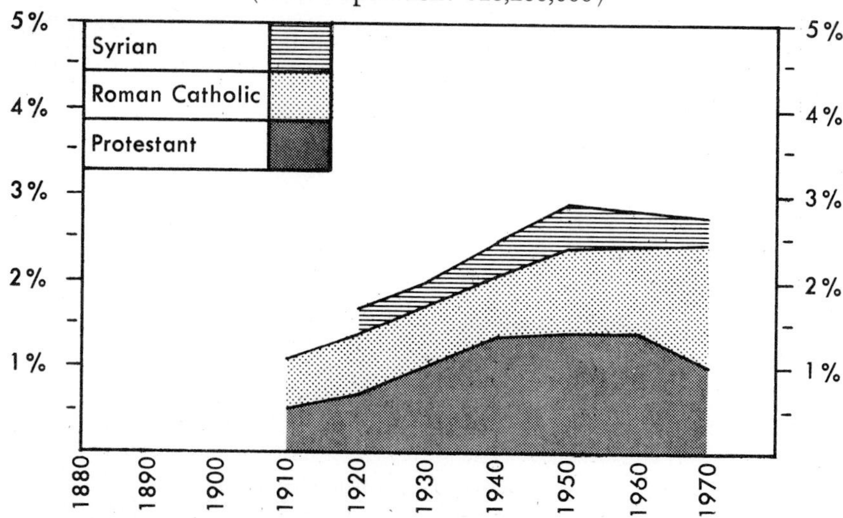

SOURCES: A series of unpublished papers and theses on file at School of World Missions, Fuller Theological Seminary, detailing figures and growth in various linguistic and church areas.

INDONESIA

(1975 Population: 136,000,000)

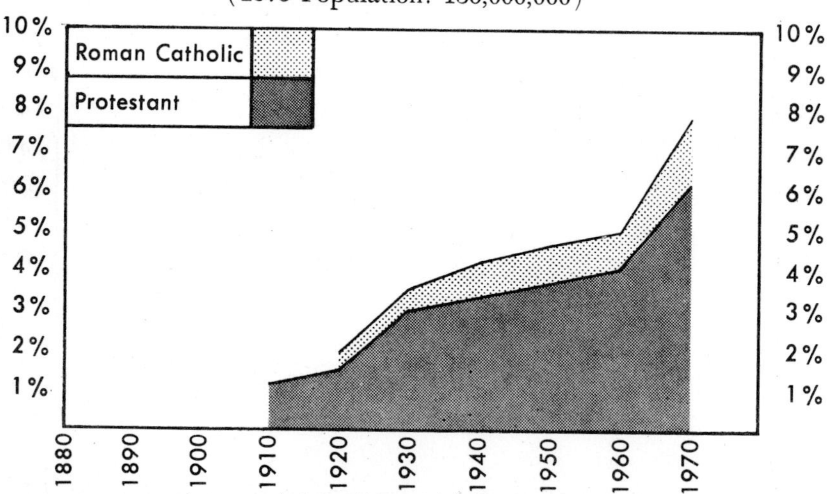

SOURCES: A series of unpublished papers and theses on file at School of World Missions, Fuller Theological Seminary, detailing figures and growth in various linguistic and church areas.

See also "Facts of a Field," *World Vision* 16 (September 1972):7.

JAPAN

(1975 Population: 111,100,000)

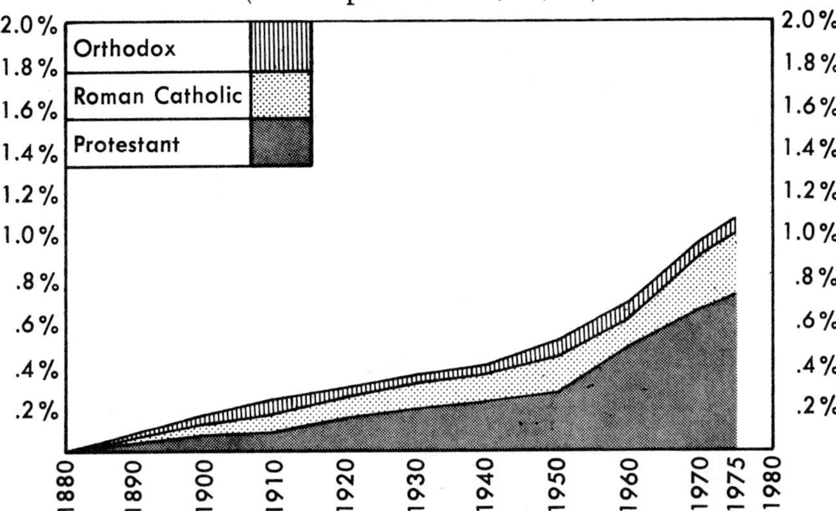

SOURCE: Data compiled from yearly editions of the *Japan Christian Yearbook,* the *Japan Harvest* surveys, and the research of Paul Ariga, director of Japan's Total Mobilization Evangelism program.

KHMER REPUBLIC (CAMBODIA)

(1975 Population: 8,100,000)

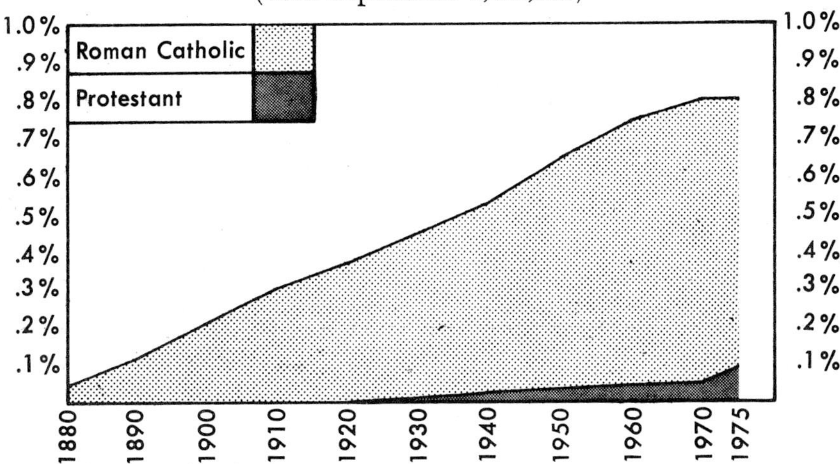

SOURCES: Letter from Merle E. Graven of the Christian and Missionary Alliance, Cambodia, January 9, 1973 to Donald Hoke. W. Stanley Mooneyham, "My Intensely Personal Encounter with the Cambodian People," *World Vision* 16 (April 1975): 4-8. *New Catholic Encyclopedia* (New York: McGraw, 1967). Reginald E. Reimer, "Peoples of Southeast Asia: A Profile of the Progress of Christianity" (Pasadena, Calif.: Fuller Theological Seminary, 1970). Letter from Miss Ruth E. Schenk of the Christian and Missionary Alliance, February 24, 1972, to Donald Hoke.

KOREA

(1975 Population: 33,900,000)

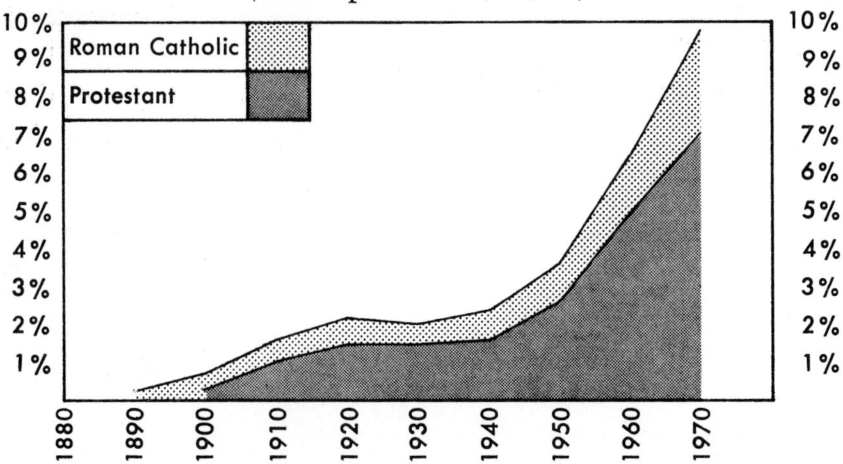

SOURCES: A series of unpublished papers and theses on file at School of World Missions, Fuller Theological Seminary, detailing figures and growth in various linguistic and church areas.

Also extensive statistics were compiled in Korea by Dr. Samuel Moffett, author of chapter 15.

LAOS

(1975 Population: 3,300,000)

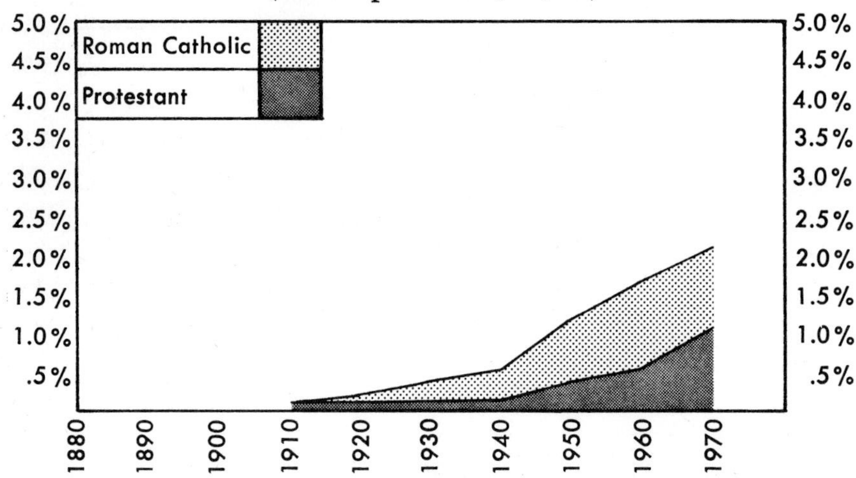

SOURCES: F.E.B.C. Gold, statistics and graphs, 1967; on file at Fuller Theological Seminary. Armand Heiniger, personal letter to E. C. Pentecost, 1974. Samuel C. Kau, "Overseas Chinese in Southeast Asia" (Pasadena, Calif.: Fuller Theological Seminary, 1970). Reginald E. Reimer, "Peoples of Southeast Asia: A Profile of the Progress of Christianity" (Pasadena, Calif.: Fuller Theological Seminary, 1970). Letter from Miss Ruth E. Schenk, of the Christian and Missionary Alliance, February 24, 1972, to Donald Hoke.

MALAYSIA

(1975 Population: 12,100,000)

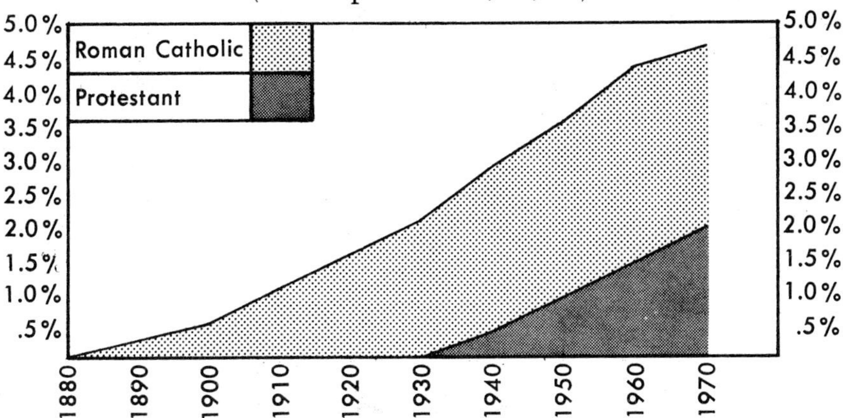

SOURCES: Reginald E. Reimer, "Peoples of Southeast Asia: A Profile of the Progress of Christianity" (Pasadena, Calif.: Fuller Theological Seminary, 1970). U.S. Department of State, "Malaysia Background Notes" (U.S. Government Printing Office, 1968). James Wong, "Charts and Graphs on Singapore and Malaysia" (Pasadena, Calif.: Fuller Theological Seminary, 1972).

PAKISTAN

(1975 Population: 70,600,000)

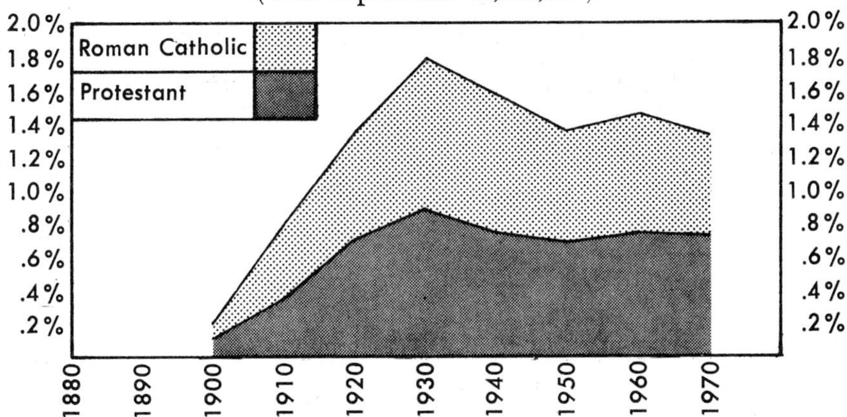

SOURCES: H. Wakelin Coxill and Kenneth Grubb, eds., *World Christian Handbook* (Nashville: Abingdon, 1968). Felician A. Foy, ed., *Catholic Almanac 1969* (Huntington, Ind.: Our Sunday Visitor, 1969). Donald Hoke, Questionnaire sent to church and mission bodies, n.d. Barbara A. Lewis, "The United Presbyterian Church of West Pakistan: American Missionary Involvement" (Pasadena, Calif.: Fuller Theological Seminary, 1972). George W. McBane, "An Accurate Picture of the Church in Pakistan" (Pasadena, Calif.: Fuller Theological Seminary, 1971). *New Catholic Encyclopedia* (New York: McGraw, 1967). Government of Pakistan, Census of Population, 1961. Frederick E. Stock, "Church Growth in West Pakistan" (M.A. thesis, Fuller Theological Seminary, 1968).

PAPUA NEW GUINEA

(1975 Population: 2,700,000)

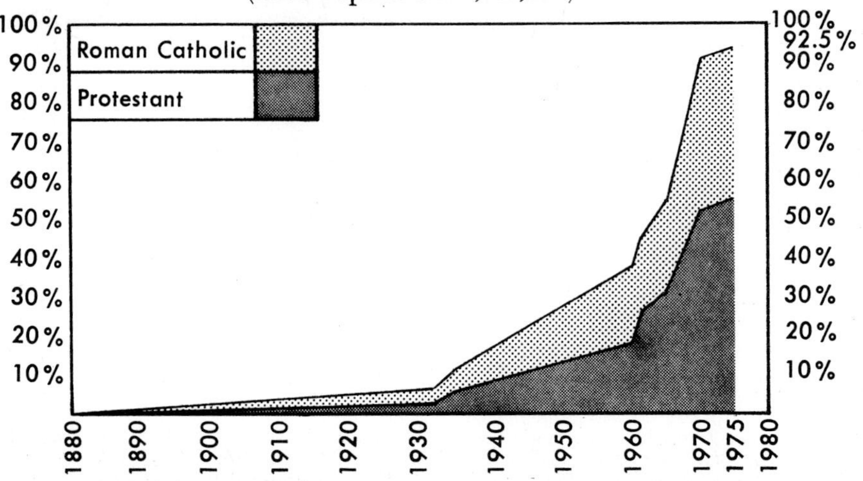

SOURCES: Figures for 1898-1940 are taken from *Encyclopedia of Papua and New Guinea* (Melbourne: Melbourne U., 1972); and for 1959-1971 from Australian government annual reports on Papua New Guinea. Different missions use different methods of determining "adherents" and thus these figures are only a rough guide.

THE PHILIPPINES

(1975 Population: 44,400,000).

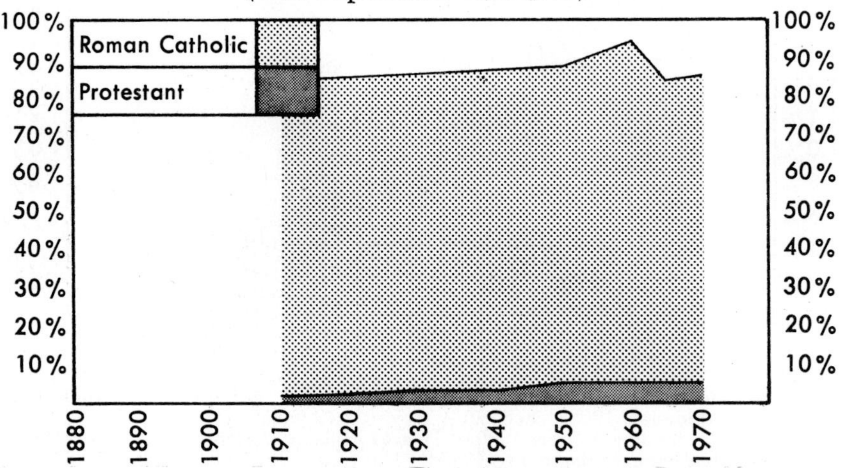

SOURCES: Ron Beech, "The Church of the Nazarene in the Philippines" (Pasadena, Calif.: Fuller Theological Seminary, 1972). Contains graphs of denominational statistics. Dennis, Beach, Parker, Grubb, and Coxill, Miscellaneous graphs, charts, and information so labelled; on file at Fuller Theological Seminary. Samuel C. Kau, "Overseas Chinese in Southeast Asia" (Pasadena, Calif.: Fuller Theological Seminary, 1970). *New Catholic Encyclopedia* (New York: McGraw, 1967).

SOUTH VIETNAM

(1975 Population: 19,700,000)

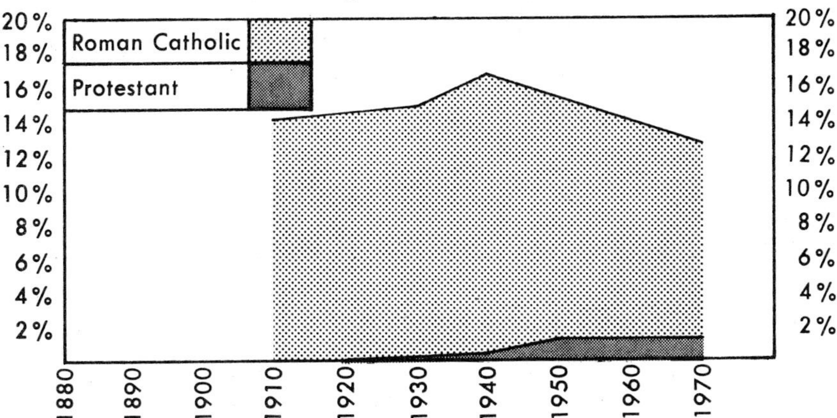

SOURCES: J. Clancy, "The Catholic Church in Vietnam," *China Notes* 7 (Winter 1970-71). Reginald E. Reimer, "Peoples of Southeast Asia: A Profile of the Progress of Christianity" (Pasadena, Calif.: Fuller Theological Seminary, 1970); idem, "The Protestant Movement in Vietnam" (M.A. thesis, Fuller Theological Seminary, 1972). Cyrus Wayne Stephens, "The Unevangelized Peoples of South Vietnam" (Pasadena, Calif.: Fuller Theological Seminary, n.d.). U.S. Department of State, "Republic of Viet-Nam Background Notes" (U.S. Government Printing Office, 1970).

SRI LANKA

(1975 Population: 14,000,000)

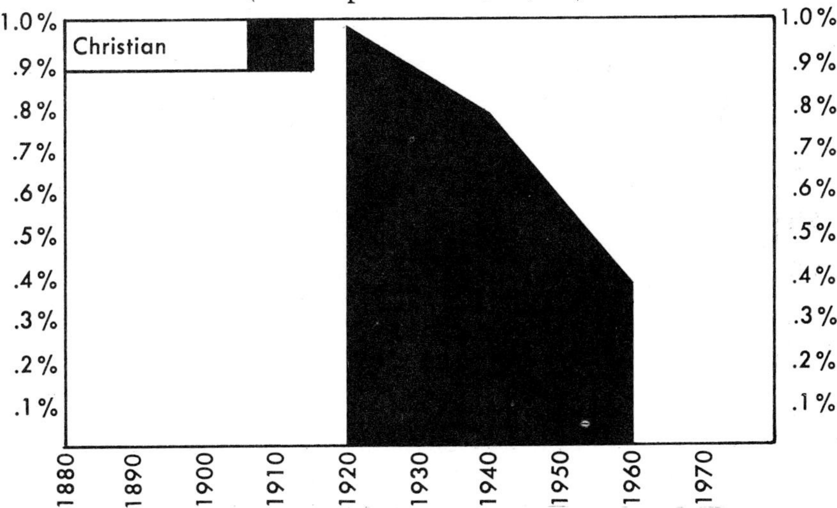

SOURCES: U.S. Department of State, "Ceylon Background Notes" (U.S. Government Printing Office, 1970). Miscellaneous maps and graphs prepared for Donald Hoke, on file at Fuller Theological Seminary.

TAIWAN (FORMOSA)

(1975 Population: 16,000,000)

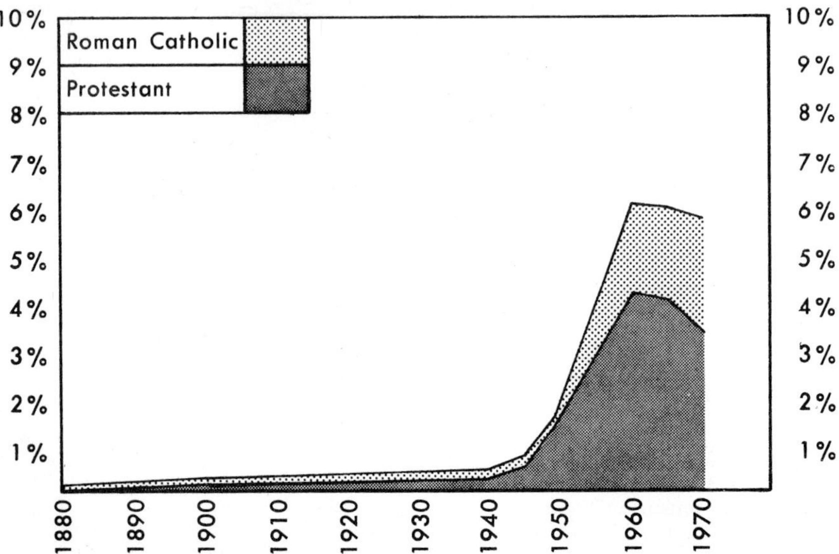

SOURCES: A series of unpublished papers and theses on file at School of World Missions, Fuller Theological Seminary, detailing figures and growth in various linguistic and church areas.

THAILAND

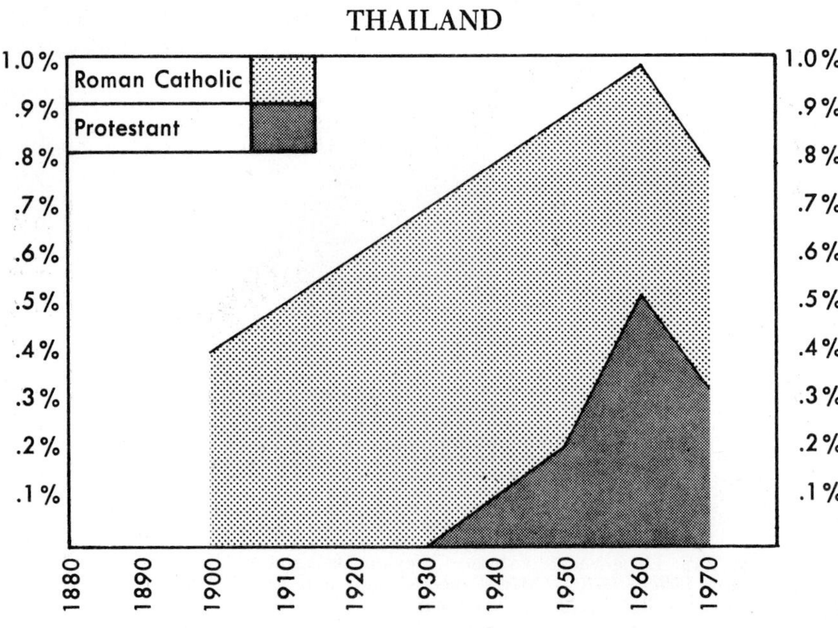

APPENDIX B

CHRISTIAN POPULATION BY PERCENTAGE OF MAJOR ETHNIC GROUPS

BURMA

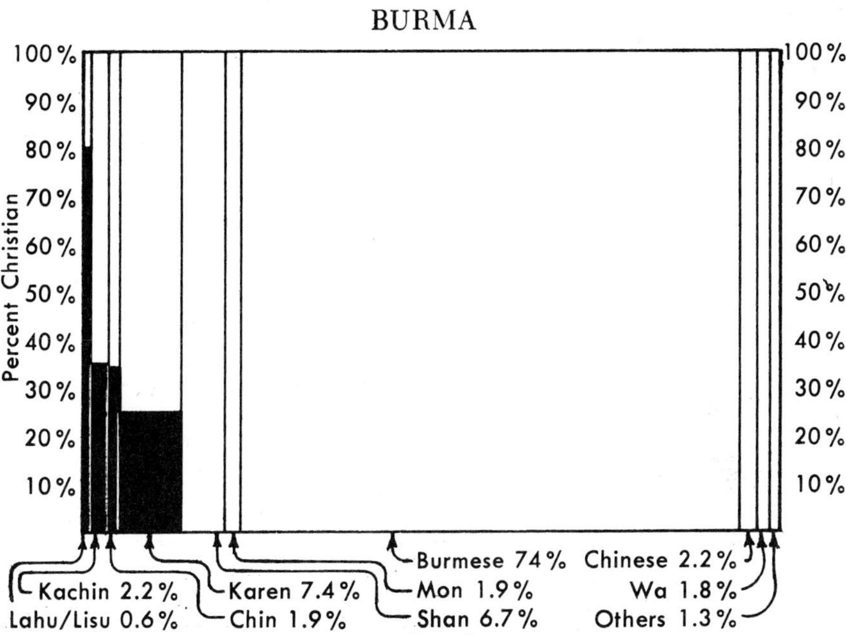

MINORITY PEOPLES OF PEOPLE'S REPUBLIC OF CHINA

(1965 Population: 48,000,000)

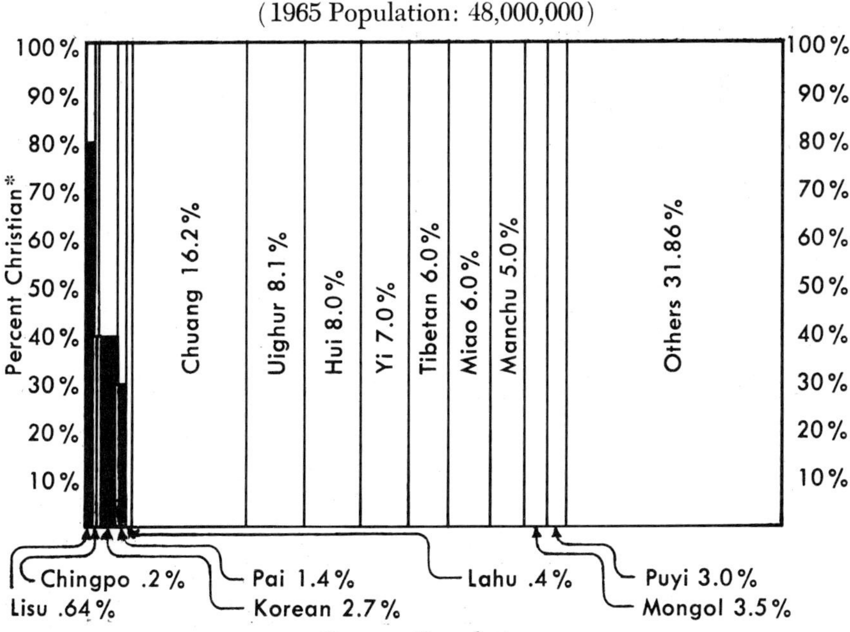

*At last report in the 1940s.

INDIA

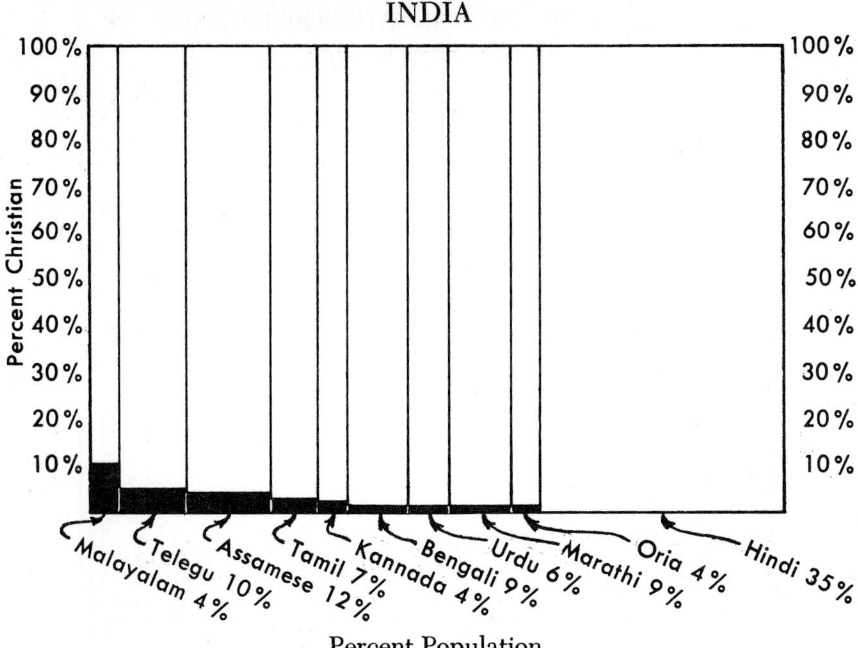

Percent Population

INDONESIA

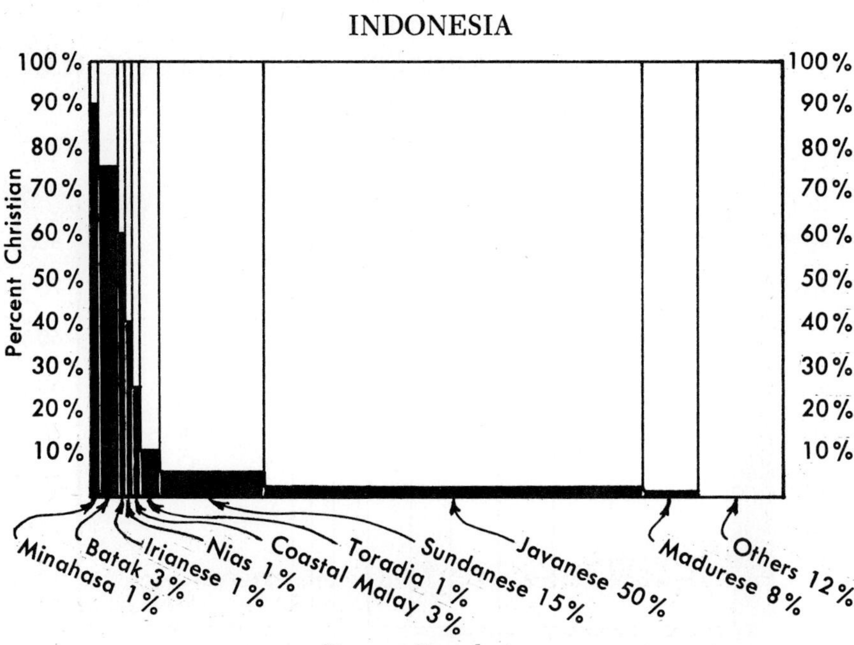

Percent Population

KHMER REPUBLIC

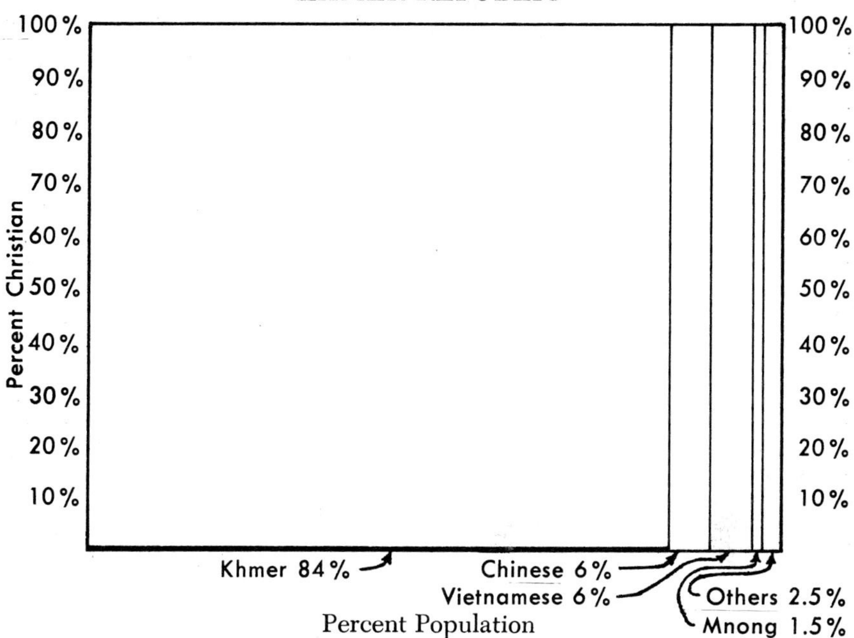

LAOS

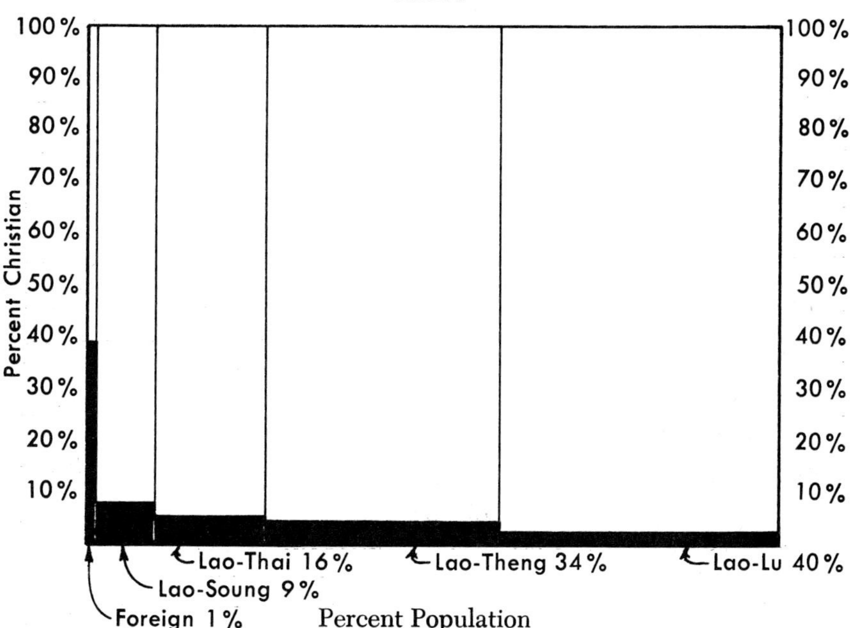

MALAYSIA

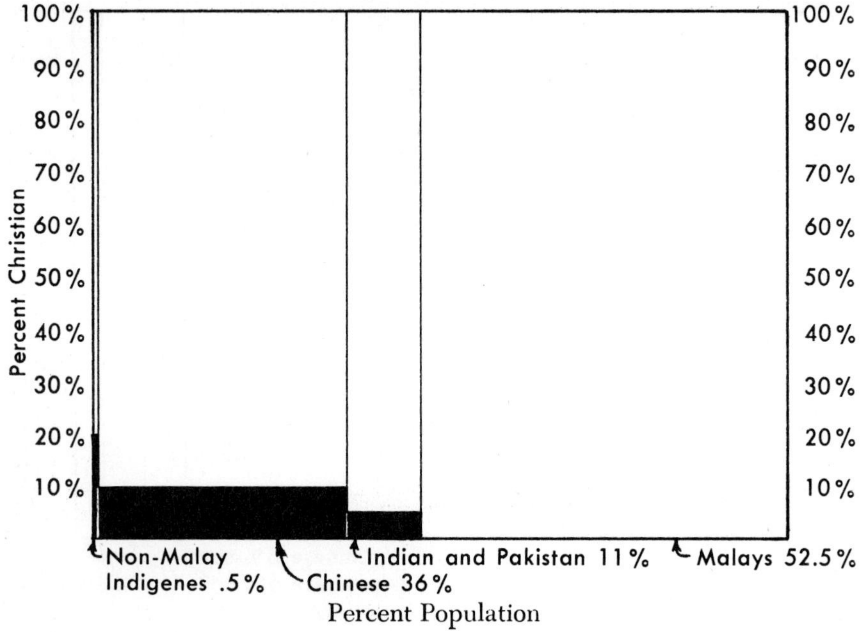

SOUTH VIETNAM

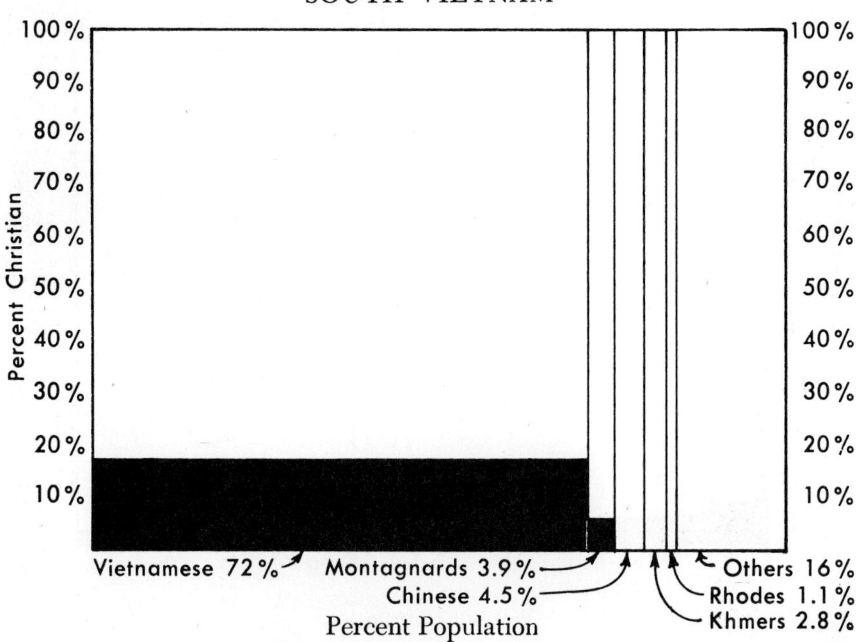

TAIWAN

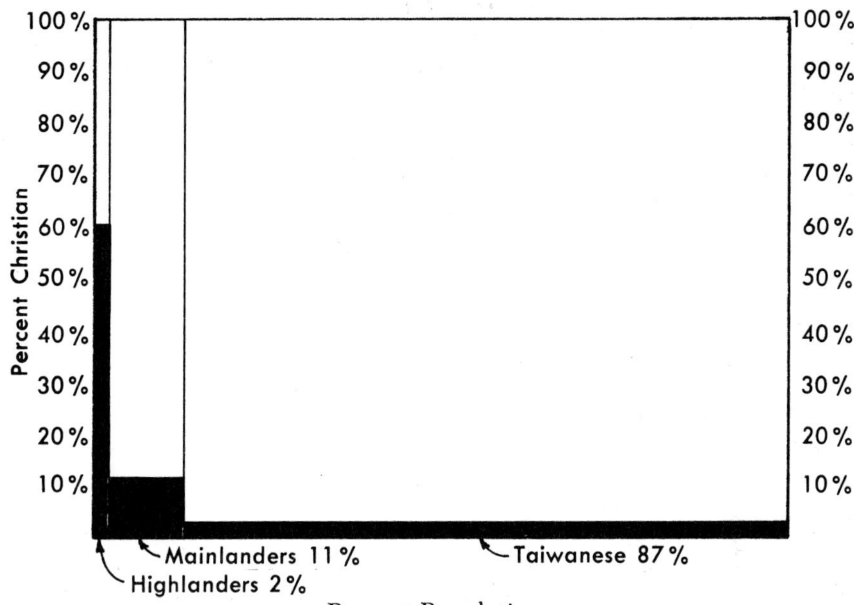

THAILAND

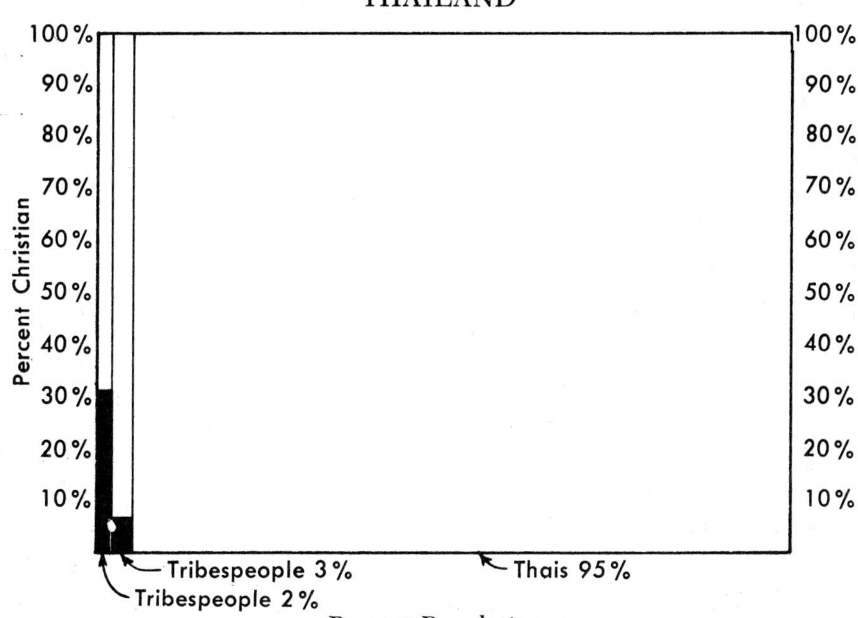

APPENDIX C

CHRISTIAN POPULATIONS OF ASIA

	*Total Population in Millions**	*Annual Rate of Population Growth*	*No. of Protestants†*	*No. of Catholics*	*Christian Percentage of Total Population*
ASIA (excluding SW Asia)	2,167	2.1	22,633,472	56,861,316	.0367
MIDDLE SOUTH ASIA					
1. Afghanistan	19.3	2.5	Possibly less than ten		
2. Bangladesh	73.7	1.7	135,000	110,000	.003
3. Bhutan	1.2	2.3	200(?)		
4. India	613.12	2.4	5,100,000 +1,400,000 Syrian Christians	7,700,000	.026 (1971)
5. Maldive Islands	0.1	2.0	Possibly less than fifty		
6. Nepal	12.6	2.2	450(?) 1973		
7. Pakistan	70.6	3.1	533,500	360,000	.013+ (1973)
8. Sikkim	0.2	2.0	1,500		.0075 (1970)
9. Sri Lanka (Ceylon)	14.0	2.2	103,500	883,111	.076 (1971)
SOUTHEAST ASIA	324	2.7			
10. Burma	29.8	2.3	671,000	252,000	.03
11. Brunei	.145		860	3,440	
12. Indonesia	136	2.6	8,104,000	2,575,474	.09 (1971)
13. Khmer Republic (Cambodia)	8.1	3.0	5,000 (1975)	20,000(?)	.003 (1975)
14. Laos	3.3	2.2	10,000	32,000	.014 (1970)
15. Malaysia	12.1	2.9	247,000	359,000	.05 (1972)
East Malaysia			197,000	171,000	.195
West Malaysia			50,000	188,000	.019
16. Philippines	44.4	3.3	1,443,000	40,000,000(?)	.033 Protestant (1970)‡
17. Singapore	2.2	1.6	160,000	80,000+	.078 (1973)
18. Thailand	42.1	3.3	38,000	167,194	.005 (1972)
19. Vietnam, North (Dem. Rep. of)	23.8	2.4	10,000 (est.)	1,000,000 (1975)	
20. Vietnam, South	19.7	1.8	154,000	1,900,000	.108 (1972)
East Asia	1,006	1.6	?	?	
21. China (People's Rep. of)	799.3	1.7	?	?	
Tibet			50-100 on the outside borders (1970)		
22. Hong Kong	4.5	2.4	179,434	252,937	.95 (1972)
23. Japan	107.3	1.2	722,742 (24,000 Orthodox)	345,000	.01 (1972)
24. Korea, North (Dem. People's Rep. of)	15.9	2.6	?	?	
25. Korea, South (Rep. of)	33.9	2.0	3,214,454	839,711	.123 (incl. sects, 1970-71)
26. Mongolia	1.4	3.0	Perhaps not one family (?)		
27. Taiwan (Rep. of China)	16.0	1.9	490,000	310,000	.057 (1973?)
OTHER					
28. Papua New Guinea	2.7	2.4	1,312,752	671,449	.932 (1966)
29. Overseas Chinese (Scattered in Asia, excl. China, Taiwan)	15		500,000	400,000	.06 (1971, est.)

*Statistics from the 1975 *World Population Data Sheet* (Washington, D.C.: Population Reference Bureau).

†These totals were compiled from the studies and statistical surveys made for this volume and are probably more accurate than the usual generalities.—Ed.

‡Aglipayan Christians, a split from the Roman Catholic Church, possibly number between one and two million.

INDEX

Abeel, David, 638
Adriani, N., 288
Afghanistan, 57-64
  Christian history, 64
  dilaram, 61
  nation and people, 62-63
  national religions, 63-64
Aglipay, Gregoreo, 532
Aglipayan Church, 532
Allen, Horace N., 376-77
Anderson, Clara, 447
Anderson, Hilda, 447
Anglicans
  Bangladesh, 80
  Brunei, 97-98
  Burma, 106, 127
  India, 246
  Malaysia, 414, 430
  Sri Lanka, 604
Animism. *See the* national religions *sections of the appropriate country articles.*
Arabian Peninsula, 186-87
Asia, 17-54
  Christian history, 50-53, 181-202
  communism, 26-27, 49-50
  culture and people, 46-48
  evangelistic objectives, 44-46
  evangelistic priorities, 34-35
  evangelistic strategy, 35-44
  future of evangelism, 30-46
  Nestorians, 183
  religions of, (graph) 48, 659-79
  spiritual facts, 19-30
  statistics, 17-21
Audetat, Fritz, 407

Ballagh, J. H., 309
Bangladesh, 67-82
  Christian history, 78-81
  nation and people, 73-74
  national history, 74-78
  See also Pakistan.
Baptists
  Burma, 104, 106-7, 109, 123-26
  India, 253
  Papua New Guinea, 504
  Philippines, 530-32, 546
  Thailand, 638
Basel Mission
  India, 251
  Malaysia, 414, 431
Bhutan, 85-93
  Christian history, 87-88
  nation and people, 88-92
  national religions, 92
Bible
  Asia, 25
  Bangladesh, 70
  Bhutan, 88
  Brunei, 98-100
  Burma, 105, 109, 124
  China, 143
  India, 233, 249-50
  Indonesia, 285
  Japan, 335
  Khmer Republic, 353-55, 363
  Laos, 395, 398, 407
  Mongolia, 446
  Nepal, 455
  Singapore, 423
  South Vietnam, 588
  Sri Lanka, 598
  Thailand, 637
Bible and Medical Missionary Fellowship, 252
Bonnet, Charles, 585
Borneo Evangelical Mission, 412-15
Bradley, Dan Beach, 638
Brunei, 97-100
  Christian history, 100
  nation and people, 99
  national history, 99-100
Buddhism, 461, 668-70, 674-75, 679-80. *See also the* national religions *sections of the appropriate country articles.*
Burma, 103-28
  Christian history, 123-28
  Christian statistics (table), 127-28
  communism, 105, 118-19
  history and people, 112-19
  national religions, 119-23

Cambodia. *See the* Khmer Republic.
Carey, Felix, 124
Carson, Arthur, 125
Case, Brayton, 126
Catholicism, 53, 376
  Bangladesh, 78
  Bhutan, 88
  Burma, 107, 116, 123, 126-27
  China, 136-42, 144
  Hong Kong, 213
  India, 219, 246-48
  Indonesia, 269, 283-84
  Japan, 305-7, 322-23, 339-40
  Khmer Republic, 362-63
  Korea, 381
  Laos, 405-6
  Malaysia, 429-30
  Nepal, 462

Pakistan, 493
Papua New Guinea, 506-7, 515
Philippines, 534-35, 541-42
Singapore, 429-30
South Vietnam, 566-67, 579, 582-85
Sri Lanka, 604
Thailand, 636-37
Tibet, 650
Ceylon. *See* Sri Lanka.
China, 49-50, 131-75
"Christian Manifesto," 171-72
communism, 161-62, 165-75
introduction of Christianity, 195-200
national religions, 671-75
Nestorians, 134-38
Taiping Rebellion, 144-47
Three-Self Movement, 172-74
China Inland Mission, 149, 152, 158-59, 161, 164
Burma, 127
Indonesia, 270
Tibet, 650-51
Chinese, Overseas, 469-73
Protestant communities (table), 472-73
Chinese Christian Churches Union, 206, 213
Chinese Evangelization Society, 148
Chinese Inter-Varsity Christian Fellowship, 169
Ching Tien-ying, 167, 173
Christian and Missionary Alliance
China, 159, 161
Laos, 392-400, 407-8
Philippines, 536
South Vietnam, 585-87
Thailand, 639
Tibet, 650-51
Church of Christ
Burma, 127
Japan, 309-10, 321, 338
Church of North India, 220
Church of Scotland
India, 250
Nepal, 462-63
Sikkim, 555
Church of South India, 220
Clark, Sidney J. W., 161
Clark, W. S., 310-11
Community Christian Church, 58
Confucianism, 672-73. *See also the* national religions *sections of the appropriate country articles.*
Congregationalist
Burma, 123
India, 251
Thailand, 638
Conn, Harvie M., 383-85
Contesse, Gabriel, 395, 406-7
Cook, J. A., 430
Cooley, Frank C., 263-68, 293-99
Cope, J. Herbert, 125
COW, 162-63
Craig, Albert, 87
Cushing, Josiah Nelson, 125

De Silva, Lennie, 435-38
Dickson, James, 620
Drysdale, Albert, 503
Duff, Alexander, 250-51
Dukpa, Norbu, 87

Ecumenism, 28-30
India, 226-27
Japan, 338, 340
Philippines, 528
Ellison, David, 363
Episcopalians
Philippines, 536
Evangelical Alliance
Japan, 316
Papua New Guinea, 506-8
Evangelical Church of Laos, 394
Evangelical Fellowship of India, 227-28
Evangelical Fellowship of Pakistan, 477

Finnish Free Mission, 562
Fiske, Asbjorg, 87
Fitzgerald, C. P., 147
Fleming, Bethel, 465
Fleming, Robert L., 465
Formosa. *See* Taiwan.
Fraser, MacKenzie, 430
Friederichsen, Paul, 531
Friedstrom, N. J., 447

Gilmore, James, 446-47
Gossner Evangelical Lutheran Mission, 253
Graham, A. K., 93
Grobb, Frank, 407-8
Gutzlaff, Carl, 377, 637

Hammond, A. L., 363
Hatori, Akira, 336-37
Henderson, A. C., 126
Hinduism, 664-66. *See also the* national religions *sections of the appropriate country articles.*
Hodne, Olav, 88
Hong Kong, 205-14
Christian history, 212-14
communism, 209-10
nation and people, 208-10
national history, 211-12
national religions, 210-11
Hong Kong Christian Council, 206-7, 213
Hunt, Garth, 570

Iglesia ni Cristo, 549
Ikeda, Daisaku, 344
India, 35, 187-94, 217-58
nation and people, 233-45

national history, 233-34
national religions, 238-45, 664-71
Indonesia, 261-99
Christian history, 283-92
Christian statistics, (tables) 266, 293-94
nation and people, 275-77
national history, 277-80
national religions, 280-83
Indonesian Gospel Institute, 270
Islam, 34, 186-87, 661-63
See also the national religions *sections of the appropriate country articles.*

Jaffray, Robert A., 586
Jainism, 243, 667-68
James, G. D., 423
Janes, L. L., 310
Japan, 48-49, 303-46
Christian history, 303-23
Christian social work, 332-33
nation and people, 341-45
national religions, 675-79
Japan Evangelical Missionary Association, 336
Jaschke, H. A., 650
Jeffrey, D. I., 407
Jeffrey, Ruth, 570
Jehovah's Witnesses
India, 226
Laos, 396
Jesus Family, 167, 173
Jesus Saves Mission, 423
John, Griffith, 150
John of Monte Corvino, 137
Johnson, Glenn, 570
Jones, E. Stanley, 225
Jonson, Jonas, 170
Judson, Adoniram, 123-24
Judson, Ann, 123-24, 637

Kam, Joseph, 286-87
Kanamori, Tsurin, 317
Keasberry, Benjamin, 430
Keysser, Christian, 416
Khmer Republic, 349-65
Christian history, 362-65
communism, 358-59
nation and people, 351-61
national religions, 361-62
Korea, 21, 369-87
Christian history, 375-83
Christian statistics, (tables) 380, 386-87
national history, 373-74
national religions, 374-75, (table) 375
Kruyt, Albert C., 288
Kuhn, John, 395
Kyodan, 321, 330-32, 334-35

Lamaism, 90, 444-45, 649-50
See also the national religions *sections of the appropriate country articles.*
Laos, 391-409
Christian history, 405-8
communism, 401
nation and people, 400-4
national religions, 404-5
Laymen's Foreign Missions Inquiry, 163
Legaspi, Miguel Lopez de, 541
Little Flock, 167, 173
Livingston, Jim, 570
London Missionary Society
China, 143
India, 250
Indonesia, 285
Malaysia, 430
Mongolia, 446-47
Papua New Guinea, 515
Lowrie, John C., 493
Lund, Hannah, 447
Lutherans
Bangladesh, 80
Bhutan, 87-88
China, 170
India, 248-49, 251
Malaysia, 414, 418, 431
Papua New Guinea, 503, 515-16

McDonald, David, 652
MacFarlane, William, 561
MacGilvary, Daniel, 406
McIntyre, John, 377
Mackay, George, 620
Malaysia, 411-19, 425-32
Christian history, 429-32
East Malaysia, 412-16
Christian statistics, (table) 413
nation and people, 425-26
national history, 426-28
national religions, 428-29
West Malaysia, 416-19
Christian statistics, (table) 417
Maldives, Republic of, 435-38
nation and people, 437-38
national history and religion, 435-37
Malomum, N. T., 87
Malpan, Abraham, 246
Manichaeism, 661
Mar Thoma Church, 50, 189-94, 218-19, 245-46
Marshman, Joshua, 250
Martin, W. A. P., 145, 146, 150, 158
Martyn, Henry, 50
Maubant, Pierre, 376
Maxwell, James, 620
Melanesian Council of Churches, 406-8
Methodists
Burma, 106, 127
Korea, 377-78
Malaysia, 415

Nepal, 465
Pakistan, 495
Papua New Guinea, 515
Philippines, 530, 545-46
Milne, William, 430
Missionary Aviation Fellowship, 60, 394-95
Mongolian People's Republic, 441-48
Christian history, 445-48
nation and people, 442-43
national history, 443-44
national religions, 444-45
Mooneyham, Stanley, 352-53
Morrison, Robert, 50, 143
Mott, John R., 159-60

Nakada, Jyuji, 319
National Christian Council
China, 159, 161
Japan, 316, 332
Pakistan, 476-77
National Council of Churches
Indonesia, 268
Korea, 381
Nepal, 451-65
Christian history, 462-65
nation and people, 456-59
national history, 459-60
national religions, 460-61
Ng, Peter, 423
Ni To-sheng, 167, 173
Nobili, Robert de, 247-48
Nommensen, Ludwig Ingwer, 287-88

O'Hanlon, Lilly, 464
Operation Mobilization
Bangladesh, 70
India, 223
Overseas Missionary Fellowship
Indonesia, 270
Laos, 395
Malaysia, 431-32

Pakistan, 475-98
Christian history, 492-96
Christian statistics, (table) 498
nation and people, 482-85
national history, 485-90
national religions, 490-92
Papua New Guinea, 20, 501-20
Christian history, 515-16
Christian statistics, (tables) 517-20
nation and people, 510-13
national history, 510-11
national religions, 513-15
Paul, Pema, 87
Pazo, C. T., 555-56, 562
Pegell, A. W., 650
Pegell, E., 650
Pfander, Karl G., 493-94
Philippines, The, 525-50
Christian history, 541-50
nation and people, 537-39
national history, 539-41
Plutschau, Henry, 248-49
Presbyterians
Bangladesh, 80
Bhutan, 87
Burma, 127
India, 251
Japan, 308-10
Korea, 370-71, 377-78, 382-85
Malaysia, 417-18, 430
Pakistan, 493-95
Philippines, 543-45
Sikkim, 555-56
Sri Lanka, 604
Taiwan, 620
Thailand, 638-39

Rahm, Kornelius, 446
Reformed Churches
Japan, 308-10
Rhenius, Charles, 250
Rhodes, Alexandre de, 579, 583-84
Ricci, Matteo, 139-41
Richard, Timothy, 150
Rizal, Jose, 539
Roberts, William Henry, 125
Rodgers, James B., 543, 544
Roffe, G. Edward, 391-409
Ross, John, 377
Ruggieri, Michele, 139-40

Saly, Pastor, 393-94
Schwartz, Christian, 249
Scott, Mary, 562
Scudder, Ida, 251
Scudder, John, 251
Seventh-Day Adventists
Bangladesh, 69
India, 226
Laos, 396
Philippines, 328-30, 346-47
Shintoism, 304-5, 677-78
Sikhism, 243, 670-71
Sikkim, 555-62
Christian history, 561-62
nation and people, 558-60
national religions, 560-61
Singapore, 411-12, 419-32
Christian history, 429, 432
Christian statistics, (table) 421
nation and people, 425-26
national history, 426-28
national religions, 428-29
Singh, Bakht, 226
Singh, Sadu Sundar, 561-62, 652
Smith, Ebbie, 261-63
So Sang Yun, 377
South Vietnam, 565-89
Christian history, 582-88
nation and people, 576-78

national history, 578-80
national religions, 580-82
Spottswood, C. L., 530
Sri Lanka, 593-605
Christian history, 603-5
Christian statistics, (table) 594-95
nation and people, 599-601
national history, 601-2
national religions, 602-3
Stallybrass, E., 446
Stenberg, David, 447
Suber, Carl, 447
Sung, John, 421, 620
Swedish Mongol Mission, 447-48

T'ai Tsung, 197
Taiwan, 20, 50-51, 609-21
Christian history, 619-21
nation and people, 614-17
national history, 617-19
national religions, 619
Taoism, 673-74
Taylor, Hugh, 406
Taylor, J. Hudson, 148-49
Teng, Philip, 206
Thailand, 625-40
Christian history, 636-40
nation and people, 630-32
national history, 632-34
national religions, 634-36
Tharchin, G., 643-55
Thomas, Robert J., 377
Tibet, 195, 643-55
Christian history, 650-55
communism, 648-49
nation and people, 646-48
national history, 648-49
national religions, 649-50
Tingbo, M. S., 87
Tingbo, P. S., 85-87
Tingson, Greg, 531
Tomlin, Jacob, 637
True Jesus Church, 167, 173-74
Tsui Hsien-hsiang, 171
Tung, Barnabas, 167
Twyman, Len, 503

Uchimura, Kanzo, 311
United Mission to Nepal, 453-54, 465
Urdaneta, Andres de, 541-42

Vietnam. *See* South Vietnam.

Wang Ming-tao, 173, 175
Ward, William, 250
Wei, Isaac, 173
Wilson, J. Christy, Jr., 58
Wilson, John, 251
World Evangelization Crusade
Indonesia, 270
South Vietnam, 587-88
Wu, George, 171
Wu Yao-Tsung, 171, 172-73
Wycliffe Bible Translators, 223, 588

Yong-nak Presbyterian Church, 379

Ziegenbalg, Bartholomew, 248-49
Zoroastrianism, 660-61
See also the national religions *sections of the appropriate country articles.*